Leadership
Handbooks

OF

Practical
Theology

*Leadership Handbooks
of Practical Theology*

Volume One: *Word & Worship*
Volume Two: *Outreach & Care*
Volume Three: *Leadership & Administration*

Leadership Handbooks

O F

Practical Theology

VOLUME THREE

Leadership & Administration

GENERAL EDITOR

James D. Berkley

Baker Books
A Division of Baker Book House Co
Grand Rapids, Michigan 49516

To my daughter,
Mary Milam Berkley,
who loves to organize things.

Leadership Handbooks of Practical Theology, Volume 3: Leadership & Administration

© 1994 Christianity Today, Inc.

Chapter 7, "Time Management," is adapted with the author's permission from a talk he gave at Claremont, California. Originally published in LEADERSHIP, spring 1982.
The section "Communicating the Vision" in chapter 13 is adapted from *Developing a Vision for Ministry in the 21st Century* by Aubrey Malphurs, with permission from Baker Book House. © 1992 Baker Book House Company.
The section "Leading Versus Enabling" in chapter 13 is adapted from *Leading Your Church to Growth* by C. Peter Wagner, with permission from Regal Books, Ventura, California. © 1984 C. Peter Wagner.
The section "Gifts and Abilities" in chapter 22 is adapted from *Your Spiritual Gifts Can Help Your Church Grow* by C. Peter Wagner, with permission by the author. © 1979 C. Peter Wagner.
The section "Insurance" in chapter 30 is adapted, with permission, from *Business Management in the Local Church* (Moody) by David Pollock. © 1992 by David R. Pollock.
Chapter 35, "Receiving and Recording Money," is adapted from *Church Finances for People Who Count* by Mack Tennyson, with permission from Zondervan Publishing House. © 1990 Zondervan Publishing House.
The section "Nonprofit Status and Reporting" in chapter 38 is adapted, with permission, from *Church Administration.* © 1990 The Sunday School Board of the Southern Baptist Convention.

Copublished by Christianity Today, Inc., and Baker Book House Company. Distributed by Baker Book House Company.

Printed in the United States of America
01 00 99 98 97 96 95 94 5 4 3 2 1

Library of Congress Cataloging-in-Publication Data
(Revised for vol. 3)

Leadership handbooks of practical theology.
    Includes bibliographical references and index.
    Contents: v. 1. Word & worship—v. 2. Outreach & care—v. 3. Leadership & administration.
    1. Theology, Practical—Handbooks, manuals, etc. I. Berkley, James D., 1950–   .
BV3.L33   1992   253   92–21971
    ISBN 0-8010-1033-0 (v. 1)
    ISBN 0-8010-1079-9 (v. 2)
    ISBN 0-8010-1098-5 (v. 3)

Contents

Contents   ix

Introduction

This third volume completes the *Leadership Handbooks of Practical Theology*, a comprehensive reference for those doing the work of ministry. This three-book series, conceived and compiled by the editors of LEADERSHIP journal and copublished by Christianity Today, Inc., and Baker Book House Company, covers the full spectrum of ministry practice. The first volume, *Word & Worship*, deals with the priestly, prophetic, and sacramental responsibilities of a parish minister: preaching, worship, music, the Sacraments, weddings, and funerals. *Outreach & Care*, volume two, provides timely counsel on evangelism, missions, pastoral care and counseling, Christian education, and chaplaincies. And now this third volume, *Leadership & Administration*, handles the pastor's personal management, ministry transitions, leadership, supervision of paid staff and volunteers, church management, and finances.

How to Use This Book

While many will read this series from cover to cover to augment their systematic understanding of the practice of Christian ministry, others may reach for this specific volume seeking reference information on a subject of interest. The index at the end of this volume comprehensively covers all three volumes of the series and will be an invaluable reference aid. The table of contents, however, may prove as valuable a guide to the contents of each volume. Articles are arranged topically, both by volume and by section within each volume. Thus, the following features will help you find what you seek:

- *Table of contents.* Look here for a complete listing of the topics covered in each volume. Articles are titled for clarity rather than artistry in order to give you a clear understanding of the subject matter. Authors' names accompany article titles.
- *Main subject headings.* This volume is divided into seven main subject areas, denoted by Parts I through VII. Here you find sets of articles on Personal Management, Transitions, Leadership, Paid-Staff Supervision, Volunteer-Staff Supervision, Management, and Finances. Each of these main sections is divided into several chapters by subject.
- *Chapter essays.* Each of the 38 chapters is anchored by a main essay that covers the central issues of the topic. Look for the title to indicate the chapter's specific subject matter.
- *Brief sidebar articles.* Most chapters contain a number of concise articles that cover a specific aspect of the subject at hand. If a chapter essay doesn't appear to address your needs, a sidebar probably will fit the bill. The sidebars also provide background and insights in addition to those found in the chapter essays.

Knowing the book's logic, you can take a trial run at finding a topic. Suppose you're planning to call an associate pastor and want to research how to do it well. Looking among the, seven main subjects, you find "Paid-Staff Supervision," and in that section there's a chapter on "Calling Ministerial and Program Staff." Bingo! Further examination finds several sidebars in that chapter that will also prove useful. A look in the index would also turn up the articles by topic.

More Than Information

Authors' names can be found at the end of the articles and in the index, and information about the authors fills the "Contributors" section that follows this introduction. At the end of most of the chapter essays, you will find "Resources," a combination of footnotes and bibliography for further study.

In *Leadership & Administration* and throughout the other two volumes of the *Leadership Handbooks of Practical Theology,* you will find nearly fifteen hundred pages of counsel directed toward those of us who *do* the work of pastoral ministry. Combining insights from biblical theology, scholarly pursuits, and years of practical experience, the writers have one purpose: to help pastors and other Christian workers more effectively serve our Lord Jesus Christ through leading his people into abiding faith and fulfilling ministry. May the Lord bless us and keep us in this sacred trust.

Contributors

General Editor
James D. Berkley

Executive Editor
Marshall B. Shelley

Associate Editor
Kevin Dale Miller

Consulting Editor
Paul E. Engle

Senior Copy Editor
Gary Wilde

Editorial Administrator
Bonnie Rice

Associate Copy Editors
Richard Doebler
David Goetz

Editorial Assistant
Cynthia Thomas

Writers

Leith Anderson, D.Min., Fuller Theological Seminary. Pastor, Wooddale Church, Eden Prairie, Minnesota.

Ann Rauvola Bailey, B.A., University of Minnesota. President, Kairos and Associates, Inc., Leesburg, Virginia.

Greg E. Asimakoupoulos, M.Div., North Park Seminary. Senior Pastor, Crossroads Covenant Church, Concord, California.

Nancy D. Becker, M.Div., Union Theological Seminary (New York). Pastor, Ogden Dunes Presbyterian Church, Ogden Dunes, Indiana.

James D. Berkley, D.Min., Fuller Theological Seminary. Senior Associate Pastor, First Presbyterian Church, Bellevue, Washington.

Warren Bird, M.Div., Alliance Theological Seminary. Senior Editor, Charles E. Fuller Institute of Evangelism & Church Growth, Pasadena, California.

Julie L. Bloss, J.D., Southern Methodist University. Attorney, Annuity Board of the Southern Baptist Convention, Dallas, Texas.

Paul Borthwick, M.Div., Gordon-Conwell Theological Seminary. Minister of Missions, Grace Chapel, Lexington, Massachusetts.

Ray Bowman, M.Arch., Kansas State University. President, Ray Bowman Consulting, Inc., Larkspur, Colorado.

Edward B. Bratcher, Ph.D., Louisville Southern Baptist Theological Seminary. Lecturer and Consultant on the Ministry, Durham, North Carolina.

Stuart Briscoe, D.D., Trinity Evangelical Divinity School. Senior Pastor, Elmbrook Church, Brookfield, Wisconsin.

Douglas J. Brouwer, D.Min., Princeton Theological Seminary. Pastor, First Presbyterian Church, Wheaton, Illinois.

Donald L. Bubna, B.S.S.E., John Brown University. Minister-at-Large, The Christian & Missionary Alliance Church, Colorado Springs, Colorado.

Daniel D. Busby, M.S., Emporia State University. General Treasurer, The Wesleyan Church, Indianapolis, Indiana.

Paul A. Cedar, D.Min., American Baptist Seminary of the West. President, Evangelical Free Church of America, Minneapolis, Minnesota.

Don Cousins, B.A., Trinity College. President, Team Development, Inc., Barrington, Illinois.

Richard B. Cunningham, Ph.D., Southern Baptist Theological Seminary. Professor of Christian Philosophy, Southern Baptist Theological Seminary, Louisville, Kentucky.

James A. Davey, Th.B., Nyack Missionary College. Vice-President, Division of General Services, The Christian & Missionary Alliance Church, Colorado Springs, Colorado.

K. Wayne Day, M.Div., Chicago Theological Seminary at University of Chicago. Senior Pastor, St. Paul's United Methodist Church, Houston, Texas.

Joseph De Buglio. Audio and Acoustical Consultant, Toronto, Ontario, Canada.

Peter F. Drucker, Ph.D., Frankfort University. Professor of Social Science and Management, Claremont College, Claremont, California.

Roger Razzari Elrod, M.A., California State University, Chico. Regional Coordinator, InterVarsity Christian Fellowship, San Jose, California.

Gary Fenton, D.Min., Midwestern Baptist Theological Seminary. Senior Pastor, Dawson Memorial Baptist Church, Birmingham, Alabama.

Kenneth O. Gangel, Ph.D., University of Missouri. Vice-President for Academic Affairs, Academic Dean, Dallas Theological Seminary, Dallas, Texas.

Gary Gulbranson, Ph.D., Loyola University. Senior Minister, Westminster Chapel, Bellevue, Washington.

Eddy Hall, B.A., Southern Nazarene University. Freelance Writer/Editor, Goessel, Kansas.

Richard R. Hammar, LL.M., Harvard Law School. Editor, *Church Law & Tax Report* and *Church Treasurers Alert!* Matthews, North Carolina.

Archibald D. Hart, Ph.D., University of Natal, South Africa. Dean, Graduate School of Psychology, Fuller Theological Seminary, Pasadena, California.

Jack W. Hayford, D.D., Oral Roberts University. Senior Pastor, The Church on the Way, Van Nuys, California.

Steve Hewitt, B.S., Costa Mesa College. Editor, *Christian Computing,* Raymore, Missouri.

Bill Hybels, B.B.S., Trinity College. Senior Pastor, Willow Creek Community Church, South Barrington, Illinois.

Wayne Jacobsen, B.A., Oral Roberts University. Co-pastor, The Savior's Community, Visalia, California.

Darrell W. Johnson, M.Div., Fuller Theological Seminary. Senior Pastor, Glendale Presbyterian Church, Glendale, California.

Sharon G. Johnson, D.B.A., Florida State University. Chairman, Department of Business Administration, Cedarville College, Cedarville, Ohio.

Robert G. Kemper, M.Div., University of Chicago. Senior Minister, First Congregational Church of Western Springs, Western Springs, Illinois.

Wayne Kiser, M.A., Wheaton College. President, Graphic & Editorial Services, Glen Ellyn, Illinois.

Melissa S. Labberton, B.A. University of Washington. Freelance Writer, Yakima, Washington.

Craig Brian Larson, B.S., Illinois State University. Contributing Editor, *Leadership*, Christianity Today, Inc., Carol Stream, Illinois.

Knute Larson, M.Div., Trinity Evangelical Divinity School. Senior Pastor, The Chapel, Akron, Ohio.

E. LeRoy Lawson, Ph.D., Vanderbilt University. Senior Pastor, Central Christian Church, Mesa, Arizona.

Aubrey Malphurs, Ph.D., Dallas Theological Seminary. Chairman, Department of Field Education, Dallas Theological Seminary, Dallas, Texas.

James Earl Massey, D.Div., Asbury Theological Seminary. Dean, Department of Preaching and Biblical Studies, Anderson University School of Theology, Anderson, Indiana.

Louis McBurney, M.D., Baylor College of Medicine. Medical Director, Marble Retreat, Marble, Colorado.

Stephen W. Mead, M.B.A., Northern Illinois University. Business Manager, Wheaton College, Wheaton, Illinois.

James E. Means, Ph.D., University of Denver. Professor of Pastoral Ministries, Denver Seminary, Denver, Colorado.

Jan Mellema, Ph.D., LaSalle University. Mall Manager, Intershop Real Estate Services, Augusta, Michigan.

Kevin A. Miller, B.A., Wheaton College. Editor, *Leadership,* Christianity Today, Inc., Carol Stream, Illinois.

John M. W. Moorlach, B.S., California State University at Long Beach. C.P.A., Senior Partner, Balser, Horowitz, Frank & Wakeling, Costa Mesa, California.

Terry C. Muck, Ph.D., Northwestern University. Professor of Comparative Religions, Austin Theological Seminary, Austin, Texas.

Sylvia Nash, Graduate, California Lutheran Bible School. Chief Executive Officer, Christian Healthcare Network, La Mirada, California.

Grace S. Nicholaou, C.P.A. Controller, Ministry Business Services, Inc., Huntington Beach, California.

Nick B. Nicholaou, B.S., California State University. President, Ministry Business Services, Inc., Huntington Beach, California.

R. Leslie Nichols, B.Arch., University of Texas at Austin. President, Church Building Associates, Marietta, Georgia.

Greg Ogden, M.Div., Fuller Theological Seminary. Senior Pastor, Saratoga Federated Church, Saratoga, California.

John C. Ortberg, Jr. Ph.D., Fuller Theological Seminary. Pastor, Horizons Community Church, Diamond Bar, California.

Larry W. Osborne, D.Min., Talbot Theological Seminary. Pastor, North Coast Church, Vista, California.

Earl F. Palmer, B.D., Princeton Theological Seminary. Minister, University Presbyterian Church, Seattle, Washington.

Ben Patterson, M.Div., American Baptist Seminary of the West. Dean of the Chapel, Hope College, Holland, Michigan.

Victor D. Pentz, D.Min., Fuller Theological Seminary. Pastor, First Presbyterian Church, Houston, Texas.

Wayne A. Pohl, M.Div., Concordia Theological Seminary. Administrative Pastor, St. Paul Lutheran Church, Trenton, Michigan.

David R. Pollock, M.B.A., California Coast University. Business Manager, First Congregational Church of Los Angeles, Los Angeles, California.

Kenneth Quick, D.Min., Dallas Theological Seminary. Senior Pastor, Parkway Bible Church, Scarborough, Ontario, Canada.

Calvin C. Ratz, M.A., Syracuse University. Senior Pastor, Brightmoor Tabernacle, Southfield, Michigan.

Andrew Rudin, M.A.T., University of Vermont. Project Coordinator, Interfaith Coalition on Energy, Philadelphia, Pennsylvania.

Eugene H. Rudnicki, B.B.A., University of Wisconsin. Senior Vice-President, B. C. Ziegler & Company, West Bend, Wisconsin.

Douglas J. Rumford, D.Min., Fuller Theological Seminary. Senior Pastor, First Presbyterian Church, Fresno, California.

Douglas G. Scott, S.T.M., General Theological Seminary. Rector, St. Martin's Episcopal Church, Radnor, Pennsylvania.

Mark H. Senter III, Ph.D., Loyola University of Chicago. Dean, Extension and Continuing Education, Trinity Evangelical Divinity School, Deerfield, Illinois.

Ruth Senter, M.A., Wheaton College. Senior Editor, *Campus Life*, Christianity Today, Inc., Carol Stream, Illinois.

Bruce L. Shelley, Ph.D., University of Iowa. Senior Professor of Church History, Denver Seminary, Denver, Colorado.

Marshall Shelley, M.Div., Denver Seminary. Vice-President, Editorial, Christianity Today, Inc., Carol Stream, Illinois.

Richard Showalter, M.Div., Goshen Biblical Seminary. President, Rosedale Bible Institute, Irwin, Ohio.

Bryan E. Siverly, M.Div., Garrett Evangelical Theological Seminary. Pastor, Waverly First United Methodist Church, Waverly, Illinois.

Julie L. Sloan, M.S., Columbia University. President, McKernan Satterlee Associates, Inc., Brewster, New York.

Fred Smith, Sr. Retired Executive, Speaker, and Author, Dallas, Texas.

Joseph M. Stowell, D.D., The Master's College. President, Moody Bible Institute, Chicago, Illinois.

Charles R. Swindoll, D.D., Talbot Theological Seminary. President, Dallas Theological Seminary, Dallas, Texas.

Mack Tennyson, Ph.D., University of South Carolina. Associate Professor, University of Charleston, Charleston, South Carolina.

Roger Thompson, M.Div., Denver Seminary. Senior Pastor, Berean Baptist Church, Burnsville, Minnesota.

John R. Throop, M.Div., School of Theology, University of the South. Vicar, St. Francis Episcopal Church, Chillicothe, Illinois.

Diccy P. Thurman, B.S., Jackson State University. Partner, Owens & Thurman, P.C., Dallas, Texas.

Philip M. Van Auken, Ph.D., Texas Tech University. Professor of Management, Baylor Center for Church Management, Waco, Texas.

C. Peter Wagner, Ph.D., University of Southern California. Professor of Church Growth, Fuller Theological Seminary, Pasadena, California.

Douglas D. Webster, Ph.D., Toronto School of Theology. Pastor, First Presbyterian Church of San Diego, San Diego, California.

H. Gordon Weekley, M.Div., Southern Baptist Theological Seminary. Executive Director, Rebound Christian Rehabilitation Center, Inc., Charlotte, North Carolina.

Robert H. Welch, Ed.D., Southwestern Baptist Theological Seminary. Assistant Professor of Administration, Southwestern Baptist Theological Seminary, Fort Worth, Texas.

Dave Wilkinson, M.Div., Fuller Theological Seminary. Pastor, Moorpark Presbyterian Church, Moorpark, California.

William H. Willimon, S.T.D., Emory University. Dean of Chapel/Professor of Christian Ministry, Duke University, Durham, North Carolina.

Todd Zastrow, M.S., DePaul University. Registered Investment Advisor, Oakbrook, Illinois.

Chip Zimmer, D.J., University of Puget Sound. Foreign Service Officer, U.S. Department of State, Guatemala City, Guatemala.

Part I:

Personal Management

I'm just managing to get by"—isn't that what we say when times are tough and we don't know if we'll make it? It means we're not doing fabulously, but neither are we failing big time; for the moment, we're surviving—barely.

How about "I'm managing to get ahead"? Better. A little like "I'm managing to keep my head above water." It sounds like progress.

Personal management for pastors, however, isn't so much about career progress or outward success. It's more like "I'm managing to keep my act together." Or even better, "God is managing me to keep his act together in me." God has something to accomplish through our ministries, but we need to exercise the personal management to transform bright potential into enduring reality.

We all know why. We've seen the clergy casualties. Some fell out before the battle through lack of concentrated discipline. Others fell in with the wrong company, wooed and wasted by a siren song. Some fell down under the weight of care and responsibilities. And still others fell back under the withering fire of criticism. This ministry business isn't for the faint. So how can we ever begin to manage?

We certainly don't begin by managing others or managing budgets or managing workloads. We start by subjecting ourselves to management by the Master. Here—exploring personal management—is where we begin.

1

The Purpose of
Personal Management

Have you ever gone through a season when, at the end of a long day, you've said, "I just can't go on any longer?" Or have you ever said, while preparing for Sunday's sermon, "I can't do this much longer. I have nothing left inside to give"? Have you ever had a week in which you could not focus, when you could not concentrate or seem to connect with the living God? Have there been periods in your ministry when you dreaded the next appointment and your stomach flinched at the sound of the phone?

Such symptoms may be due to ineffective personal management. A vacation would help — for a while. But if we're honest with ourselves, we'll see that the problem lies deeper. We need a better system of personal management.

Bobby Clinton, a mentor of leaders, has observed, "Few leaders finish well." Many ministers start well but end up spent, empty, and discouraged. That's why personal management is so needed. A good system of personal management includes a number of things to help us enjoy our life in Christ more and enable us to serve in ministry week in and week out with vitality, clear heads, and warm hearts. Personal management can help us develop the attitudes and exercise the behaviors that enable us to finish well.

The apostle Paul exhorted Timothy, his colleague in ministry, to "watch your life and doctrine closely." Why? "Persevere in them, because if you do, you will save both yourself and your hearers" (1 Tim. 4:16). Keeping a close watch on life and doctrine is the very thing to which Paul consistently called himself. "Do you not know that in a race all the runners run, but only one gets the prize? Run in such a way as to get the prize. Everyone who competes in the games goes into strict training. They do it to get a crown that will not last; but we do it to get a crown that will last forever. Therefore I do not run like a man running aimlessly; I do not fight like a man beating the air. No, I beat my body and make it my slave so that after I have preached to others, I myself will not be disqualified for the prize" (1 Cor. 9:24–27).

Charles H. Spurgeon, in his *Lectures to My Students,* expresses the point well: "We are, in a certain sense, our own tools, and therefore must keep ourselves in order … it will be in vain for me to stock my library, or organize societies, or project schemes, if I neglect the culture of myself; for books, and agencies, and systems are not remotely the instruments of my holy calling; my own spirit, soul, and body, and my nearest machinery for sacred service; my spiritual faculties, and my inner life, are my battle axe and weapons of war."

The Need for Accountable Leaders

Personal management means being well (alive in Christ), serving well (alive in Christ), and finishing well (alive in Christ). Our call to ministry is a noble calling—a glorious life and work that can both thrill and terrify us. We are stewards of the mysteries of God (1 Cor. 4:1), handlers of sacred revelation. And the one thing required of stewards is trustworthiness. As the salt of the earth and light of the world (Matt. 5:13–16), we must guard against losing our saltiness. At the same time we must fan the flame within us.

The Great Shepherd has called us to serve as undershepherds: bringing back the scattered, binding up the broken, and strengthening the sick (Ezek. 34:1–16). We are to feed the flock (John 21:15–16), guiding them to God's pastures. We are to walk with them through the valley of the shadow of death (Ps. 23:4), guarding them from the Enemy of our souls (Acts 20:28).

Though we are, along with the whole church, members of the royal priesthood (1 Pet. 2:5, 9), as ministers we are responsible for helping all the priests (that is, the people of God) do their priestly work: to worship and bless God, offering acceptable sacrifices to him through Jesus Christ. We are to ensure the proper administration of the sacraments and ordinances. We are to enable the other priests to serve as instruments of grace and truth in their homes and businesses. We are teachers who are also students, responsible to unfold the whole counsel of God (Acts 20:27), being diligent to present ourselves to God as workers who accurately handle the Word of Truth (2 Tim. 1:15).

A noble work indeed!

We are proclaimers, announcers, "good-news-izers," sounding the essence of Jesus' gospel: "The time has come … the kingdom of God is near" (Mark 1:15).

We are prophets, responsible to stand in the council of the Lord (Jer. 23:18, 22). We are to wait, listen, and then speak with compassion and boldness what we have heard and seen.

We are soldiers in the Lord's army, enlisted to stand firm against the schemes of the Enemy (2 Cor. 2:11). At the same time we are to help the other soldiers in our unit put on the full armor of God so they too can stand firm (Eph. 6:10–20).

We are managers of God's household (1 Tim. 3:4–5), assigned with the task of seeing that everything is done "in a fitting and orderly way" (1 Cor. 14:40), for the greater glory of God (1 Pet. 4:11).

We are equippers of the saints (Eph. 4:12). Like those who mend fishing nets, we are to restore and build up Christ's body for effective service and fruitful exercise of the gifts of the Spirit (Eph. 4:12–16).

We are, along with the whole church, living stones (1 Pet. 2:4), built up into the living temple of the living God (1 Cor. 3:16), the *naos* of God, the very Holy of Holies. We are responsible to seek that holiness without which no one sees God (Heb. 12:14), doing everything we can to make sure the Holy Spirit is not grieved (Eph. 4:30) or quenched (1 Thess. 5:19).

We are responsible to see that the bride of Christ (Rev. 19:7–8) remains loyal to her first love, not straying from a simple and pure devotion to him (2 Cor. 11:2).

As part of the family of God, we ministers are to help our sisters and brothers live out all the "one anothers" of God's Word (welcome one another, love one another, forgive one another, and so on).

We are spiritual midwives (Gal. 4:19), helping others grow more sensitive to the stirrings of the Spirit in their lives. We are to encourage them to take the next steps of trust and obedience.

We are disciples, called to make disciples (Matt. 28:19) who in turn can make disciples who can make disciples (2 Tim. 2:2).

What a calling! What an honor! And what a responsibility! This explains why personal management is so crucial. To better measure up to the assignment, we continually need to evaluate how we are doing (or better, being) with regard to each of these images. Are we growing as disciples? Are we functioning as priests? Are we being reconciled to members of the family? Are we alive to the message of the Kingdom? Are we growing in grace and in love with Jesus?

What to Manage

How can we do it? How can we manage ourselves to be well, serve well, and finish well?

Those who have gone before us have put their fingers on a number of crucial areas to which we must give constant attention. Notice that nothing in the following list involves technique. Certainly technique has its place (voice control, gestures, appropriate dress, and so on). But many have come to realize that what makes or breaks ministers and ministries is not techniques but what goes on within our souls. "Watch your life ... closely," says Paul.

Personal management, then, involves at least being attentive to how we are doing in each of the following areas:

● *Our relationship with the living God.* Are we abiding in Christ? Do we remain yoked, growing in intimacy with the Father? Are we still in love with Jesus? Are we responsive to the stirrings of the Holy Spirit?

● *Our relationships with spouse and children.* Are we moving in the direction of greater closeness and trust? Do we view spouse and chil-

A Private and a Public Person

As pastors, our relationships and roles overlap and, at times, overwhelm us. We may acknowledge the boundaries that *should* exist, but we are constantly tempted to ignore them—those relational and vocational borders that separate our pastoral responsibilities from our personal needs.

Navigating Rough Waters

Our familiar territories of commitment usually include marriage, parenting, administration, community involvement, denominational responsibilities, preaching, counseling, hobbies, ecumenical relationships, personal exercise, the care of aging parents, and more. A kind of continental divide separates these roles and activities into public ministries and private pursuits. Mental, emotional, and spiritual health demands that the boundaries be recognized and respected.

We pastors and Christian leaders are like everyone else in that we want to have a sense of joy, productivity, recognition, and financial reward through our work. But we, too, would like to be able to enjoy family, friends, and activities apart from our role as pastors, and we need mental vacations from the pressing, incessant responsibilities. The failure to separate the two can lead to problems such as career restlessness, passive or active resentment, and even ministry-damaging behavior.

Daily Decisions

In light of our need for a crucial public-private boundary, we need to make wise decisions about the competing demands that come our way every day. Here are four points of the compass that can help us successfully navigate the sometimes rough waters between our public worlds and our private lives:

● *Go west, young pastor!* We must head in a predetermined direction. When at work, we should

dren as the first recipients of our Christlike love? Or do they always get whatever we have left over?

● *Our grasp of God's Word.* Are we increasingly at home in the Bible? Are we continually learning more, submitting all our thinking, feeling, and experience to the gracious scrutiny of the Lord?

● *Our level of prayer.* Are we more mature in our prayers? Do we have the conviction that prayer is a major task? Does prayer have an increasingly deeper hold on us? Are we making prayer our first priority? Are we able to help others move into the various aspects of prayer?

● *Our walk in the Spirit.* Are we learning to yield to the Spirit in our everyday situations? Are we learning to trust him more? Have we grown in our ability to discern where and how he is leading? Are we learning to operate in his power?

---

work—work hard, focusing on the task at hand and keeping our shoulder to the plow and our fingers to the computer keyboard. That requires having a long-range ministry plan, a weekly work rhythm, and a daily "to do" list.

● *Realize the sun will rise in the east tomorrow.* Ted Engstrom, of World Vision, used to say, "Put off to tomorrow what you do not need to do today."

There comes a time at the end of every day to say, "That's it!" Tomorrow is a gift from God to be used and appreciated. Besides, we have other responsibilities every bit as important as the ones at church, and we need to save some energy for them. It is not fair to our families—or ourselves—to retain only the dregs of our physical and mental energies to give.

● *Head south for the border.* In other words, we must take time to play. If we have worked hard, we should have no misgivings about playing hard. A change of clothes on days off and after work helps remind our bodies that we've crossed a boundary. Our congrega-tion needs to see us in casual attire at the grocery store, shopping mall, or football game. So do members of the community. The temptation to "pedestalize" a pastor won't be so strong when people recognize that pastors are people with private lives, too. When at home, we need to be at home. One way is to use an answering machine.

● *Remember the arrow always points north.* We look first to our calling for a sense of direction. Although we take off our work clothes when we arrive home, our true "collar"—our submission to God's will—always stays on. In many people's eyes, we represent God wherever we go.

Obviously, as much as we may attempt to honor the boundaries between public and private commitments, the nature of the ministry requires flexibility. Our calling to serve the Lord takes priority over everything else. The volunteer firefighter in a rural community remains a firefighter whether on duty or not. The same is true of the committed church leader.

—*Greg E. Asimakoupoulos*

● *Our confrontation of sin.* Have we come to terms with its reality? Do we see how pervasive it is? Do we understand how serious sin is? Are we becoming more resolved and better equipped to resist its lure?

● *Our recognition of spiritual opposition.* Can we discern the Enemy's presence and practice? Can we spot his tricks? Are we learning in Christ to stand against the Devil?

● *Our dealings with past wounds.* Do past events sometimes rise up and wreak havoc, or have we been able to forgive those who have hurt us? Have we presented yesterday's hurts and fears to the healing of Jesus? Are we allowing the Father to fill us so we no longer have to be motivated by our own sense of deprivation?

● *Our sexuality.* Are we experiencing greater freedom from the sexual deviance to which we are all prone? Are our relationships with the

---

Forms of Accountability

Accountability is essential for pastors, yet a pastor's accountability can be difficult to structure. At the worst, it can turn into a method to control pastors or complain about them. But at best, properly structured accountability does much more good than harm.

Sometimes we chafe under another's accountability simply because we're prideful. Other times, though, we chafe because we sense something other than loving guidance is being offered. Here are four questions to help determine the legitimacy of the accountability being offered: Are people holding me accountable for their personal expectations? Are they trying to control me? Are they nit-picking? Do they have a critical spirit? All these types of illegitimate accountability have one thing in common: people assume the pastor's ministry revolves around their concerns. That is an oppressive assumption to live under.

Legitimate Accountability

It's helpful to remember we are actually accountable in a number of areas:

● *To God.* It is to the Lord that we owe ultimate allegiance. We faithfully answer to others only because we are trying to please him. If we aim to please the Lord, we are on the right track in terms of accountability.

● *To the members of the body.* We are accountable to the church for a number of things: leadership, pastoral care, administration, and modeling the Christian life, to name a few. But above all, we have a responsibility to feed God's flock and nurture his people.

● *To church leaders.* Our elders and deacons need our leadership, vision, and spiritual guidance.

● *To one's family.* Accountability with our families begins with taking a weekly Sabbath. It's also helpful to ask family members to hold

opposite sex directed by the Holy One? Has our central drive for human intimacy been reshaped by the renewal of our minds?

● *Our intellect.* Are we growing intellectually? Are we increasingly making every thought captive to Christ? Are we able to resist the pressure to conform to the world?

● *Our integrity.* Do we mean what we say and say what we mean? Do we resist the temptation to rely on the ways of the flesh to accomplish a spiritual work? Do we fulfill our promises?

● *Our motivation.* Have we sorted out our inner drives? Do we know whose reputation we are seeking to enhance? Is it clear whose kingdom we are seeking to advance? Can we see to whom we desire to attract people?

● *Our basis for authority.* Do we continually submit to the lordship

---

us accountable for our ministry. Their support and feedback can be encouraging.

● *To the larger church.* One of the major challenges we face is the Lone Ranger syndrome, where we begin to think we're accountable to no one but ourselves and act as if we are in charge of our ministries. That attitude invariably leads to conflict and division. We need to consider giving time and energy to promoting cooperation among churches.

● *To the community.* The command to all Christians is to render to Caesar the things that are Caesar's. Pastors, as leaders of local churches, need to be accountable to the local authorities, too—as long as it doesn't compromise the integrity of the gospel.

Fostering Accountability

We need to take positive action to encourage helpful and healthy accountability. Here are four ways to proceed:

● *Welcome it.* We can work to avoid being defensive when people offer suggestions, maintaining an open ear for feedback. When we protect ourselves with defense mechanisms, we become hard, which is too steep a price to pay.

● *Model it.* Holding others accountable requires a willingness to confront others with some difficult truths, and with love. At the same time, it models to others how they can hold us accountable as leaders.

● *Use opportunities to teach about accountability.* We can talk about what we are doing and why—what principles are guiding the confrontation. Jesus used conflict and misunderstandings as a well-lit stage for instruction.

● *Never question people's motives.* Accusations are like chemical weapons: they poison the atmosphere. When we wonder what's driving others, we can say, "I may be wrong, but it looks to me that so-and-so happened. Tell me how you're feeling about it." When we refuse to question others' motives, they are less likely to question ours.

—Paul A. Cedar

of Christ? Are we exercising the authority he gives in his way through the way of servanthood?

● *Our identity.* Do we know who we are in Christ? Have we embraced our new identity? Are we close to others who are?

● *Our emotions.* Have we learned to monitor our anger? Have we faced up to our underlying fears? Have we come to terms with inner pain, jealousy, grief, and so on? Have we learned to be honest about our feelings without destabilizing our roles as leaders or undermining our relationships with others?

● *Our perspective.* Have we developed a grateful heart, that which many say is a key indicator of health? What flavors our speech and spirit most: complaining and grumbling, or thoughtful praise?

● *Our stewardship.* Have we surrendered control of our time, money, and spiritual gifts to the Lord? Are we seeing God's call on our lives expand into new areas?

● *Our Sabbath rest.* Are we following "the manufacturer's specifications"—that we operate on a rhythm: six days of creative work followed by one day of worshipful rest and re-creation? Or are we letting the busyness of the unredeemed world set our agenda?

● *Our character.* Are we becoming more like Jesus? Is the fruit of the Spirit becoming more evident in us? Are we treating people the way he does? Are we developing more humility and compassion?

How to Manage

There's more than enough to manage! So how do we do it? Not on our own, that's for certain. We have the living God in this with us. Clearly Christ wants our well-being even more than we do. We also have members of the body of Christ to help us manage ourselves. Jesus never sent workers out alone; at the minimum it was in teams of two. Experienced Christian leaders know the value of a support team—a group of people who want to see us growing in all of the areas listed above. Such a support team can pray for us and hold us accountable.

There are several models of support that could be followed. Three classical models especially commend themselves to us (articulated more fully by Foster 1992, 59–63).

The first is the way developed by Ignatius of Loyola in his *Spiritual Exercises.* Ignatius designed what best works in a retreat setting, but which also can serve us well in ordinary situations. This model is based on four themes: (1) sin under the power of grace; (2) the life of Christ; (3) the suffering and death of Christ; (4) the resurrection of Christ. In each of these sections, Ignatius provides reflections and exercises that build the truths into our lives. As Foster summarizes it, "We all need a deeper musing upon our perennial knack for disobedience and God's unbounded habit of forgiving. We all need a richer contemplation upon that life, which shows us the way so we may follow in his steps. We all need a fuller meditation upon that death, which sets us free. We all need a more profound experience of that resurrection, which empowers us to obey Christ in all things."

The second model is the way developed by Saint Benedict. Benedict builds on the image of Jacob's ladder, a twelve-step ascent to humility. He offers activities that involve mind, body, and spirit and help us face our deeply rooted desire to be our own lords. This model helps especially with control of the tongue and cultivation of simple silence.

The third model, called the Little Way, was developed by Therese of Lisieux. She calls us to disciplines that help us gain victory over self-centeredness and selfishness. She challenges us to choose intentionally the menial tasks (put away the chairs after a meeting), to welcome unjust criticism (we know about that, don't we?) to befriend folks who give us grief (now we're talking depth of character!), and to keep serving those who are ungrateful.

Other models are also available. One is to gather together a group of six to twelve people who freely enter into a covenant with each other—for example, something like "The Evangelical Order of the Easy Yoke." Built on Jesus' image of taking his yoke upon us (Matt. 11:28–30), this covenant includes working together to identify the essential features of Christ's yoke. It also grants the group the right to hold each member accountable to the others in the group. Its other essential features include: (1) "Our major task in life is to stay connected to the living God"; (2) "Our major responsibility toward Christ is to trust him in everything"; and (3) "Our major responsibility to others is to love them the way he loves them."

Its members agree to be held accountable in several ways: (1) to practice spiritual disciplines that foster openness with one another (so I can ask another, "How is the fasting going?" or "How has the control of the tongue gone?"), (2) to trust Christ (so I can ask, "Are you trusting him for your financial needs?" or "Are you surrendering your need for control?"); (3) to love (so I can ask and be asked, "How is it between you and your spouse?"). The driving force behind the Order of the Easy Yoke is the conviction that we are weary from wearing the wrong yoke, and that vitality and joy will come when we switch yokes by wearing Christ's.

Personal management means choosing to do whatever it takes to be well, to serve well, and to finish well. It's our choice. May God grant us the wisdom to live in such a way that when we come home after a long day (or after a long week of days), we can say, "I am beat, but I can think of nothing else I'd rather be doing. This is life!"

—Darrell W. Johnson

2

The Call to Ministry

I was kneeling on the steps of the chancel with several hands laid on my shoulder. The occasion was my ordination into the ministry, and the pastor was praying a seemingly interminable prayer for God's blessing and power to be upon me. My legs had started to cramp. Sweat was soaking through my black robe, a garment whose origins were in Northern Europe and whose wearer was in Southern California on a balmy May evening. And my knees felt as though they were piercing the scarlet carpet.

Does he think I need more prayer than usual? I thought. Then, as if in answer to my question, he prayed, "Lord, as Ben feels the weight of these hands upon his shoulders, may he feel the weight of what he has been called to do."

Amen.

"But may he feel also the strength of your everlasting arms bearing him up."

Amen and amen!

That is how many of us experience ministry: an impossible, unbearable job accompanied by an improbable, inexplicable strength.

The apostle Paul took inventory of his vocation and asked, "Who is equal to such a task?" My version of that question comes several times a year as I step into the pulpit: *Just what do you think you are doing here? Who are you, of all people, to tell these people what God thinks?*

The question strikes most ministers now and then. They spend countless hours with people crushed by life's weight. They have tried to convey something of the mercy and hope of Jesus. And they wonder: *Verily, just what do you think you are doing here?*

We would have no right, no reason, no hope in ministry were it not for one thing: Almighty God, in his inscrutable wisdom, has *called* us to it. That is all. He has willed it, not us. The Spirit blows where he wants, and he has blown some into the ordained ministry. Like the new birth, we were born into this thing not by the will of a person or an institution, but by the will of our Father in heaven. Yet we still puzzle over this thing we designate a "call." What is it? How does it come? How do we know when it does?

Hearing the Call

There is much we may not understand about the call to ministry, but one thing must be clear in our minds: a call is not a career. The pivotal distinction between the two may be the most important thing we ever understand about the call of God, especially in these times. The words themselves immediately suggest one difference. Our English word "career" comes from the French *carriere*, meaning "a road," or "a highway." The image suggests a course one sets out on, road map in hand, goal in sight, with stops marked along the way for food, lodging, and fuel. With hindsight, we can speak of one's career as the road one took in life. But more often we speak of it as we look forward, as the path we choose and plan to travel professionally, an itinerary charted and scheduled. The destination is primary. The roads are well-marked. The rest is up to the traveler.

A call, on the other hand, has no maps, no itinerary to follow, no destination to envision. Rather, a call depends upon hearing a Voice. The organ of faith is the ear, not the eye. First and last, it is something one listens for. Everything depends upon the relationship of the listener to the One who calls.

Careers lend themselves to formulas and blueprints; a call, only to a relationship. A career can be pursued with a certain amount of personal detachment; a call, never. When Moses heard God call him to free the slaves in Egypt, he first responded as though he were presented with a career decision. Was he qualified? Did he have the proper experience and unique skills required by such an undertaking? He talked to God as though he were in a job interview: Who am I to do such a thing? What if the people don't follow? Doesn't God know that I am a poor public speaker?

All of this was irrelevant to God. All that mattered was that Moses believe God could be trusted when he said, "I will be with you." In short, all that mattered was the call, and that Moses bind himself to the One who issued the call. There was no road map, only the Voice.

The essential nature of the call shines through in a folk tale about a father and a son. They were traveling together to a distant city. There were no maps. The journey was to be long and rough, fraught with dangers. The roads were unmarked and mostly nonexistent. Only the wisdom and experience of the father would get him and his son to their destination.

Along the way, the boy grew curious. He wanted to know what was on the other side of the forest, beyond that distant ridge. Could he run over and look? His father said yes.

"But Father, how will I know whether I have wandered too far from you? What will keep me from getting lost?"

"Every few minutes," the father said, "I will call your name and wait for you to answer. Listen for my voice, my son. When you can no longer hear me, you will know that you have gone too far."

Ministry is not an occupation but a vocation. It primarily demands not professional credentials but the ability to hear and heed the call of God. Therefore, we must stay quiet enough and close enough to hear his voice and be held firm in our impossible task by his everlasting arms.

Discerning the Right Voice

How do we know we are hearing God's voice and not merely the voice of our own aspirations, desires that themselves contain godly ambition and selfishness commingled? How do we sort God's voice out of the clamor of so many messages?

In *Wishful Thinking*, Frederick Buechner writes, "There are all different kinds of voices calling to you, all different kinds of work. And the problem is finding out which is the voice of God, rather than of society, say, or the superego or self-interest. By and large a good rule for finding out is this: The kind of work God usually calls you to is the kind of work, (a) that you need most to do, and (b) that the world most needs to have done. If you really get a kick out of your work, you've presumably met requirement (a), but if your work is writing TV deodorant commercials, the chances are you've missed requirement (b). On the other hand, if your work is being a doctor in a leper colony, you have probably met requirement (b), but if most of the time you're bored and depressed by it, the chances are you've not only bypassed (a) but probably aren't helping your patients much either. Neither the hair shirt nor the soft berth will do."

I like the way Buechner concludes: "The place God calls you to is the place where your deep gladness and the world's deep hunger meet." Without both, we fail.

Too many people in the church are doing things that "ought to be done," but they don't like it. It's just wearing them down, and there's a joylessness about the whole thing. We are failing when we are doing something that "needs to be done" but doing it with no gladness.

Gladness isn't necessarily emotional bubbles as much as it is a sense of significance, meaning, purpose, seeing the work as worthwhile. We can suffer and sacrifice and still be glad about it.

It's just as wrong to do something that needs doing and hate it as it is to just do something that we like but that doesn't really need to be done. So a working theology of a call needs to include this sense of gladness, trying to find the common ground between our deep gladness and the needs we see around us.

Recognizing the Professional Realities

Only with this understanding of the call in mind can we rightly consider the "career" elements of ministry. For only when we clearly see our work as a call can we handle these other matters faithfully.

For instance, there are the educational and denominational require-

---

Biblical Requirements of Leaders

Can you think of any greater privilege than to be called to be a leader in the church of Jesus Christ? The church is his Body, his Bride, the Temple of his Spirit, his Flock, his Army, his Family.

Can you think of any greater responsibility than leading his church?

This is why God's Word has laid before us such challenging requirements for Christian leadership. The standards are rightly high, not only for the sake of the church's vitality but also for the sake of the leader's vitality.

Four Qualifications

The chief biblical texts that develop the requirements of leaders are 1 Timothy 3:1–13, 2 Timothy 2:1–13, Titus 1:5–9, Acts 6:1–6, and Exodus 18:21–22. The qualifications spelled out in these passages can be summarized in four words:

● *Commitment.* Are the would-be leaders clearly committed to Jesus Christ as Savior and Lord? Is there a passion to know him in all his fullness? While passion is expressed differently by different personality types, there must be evidence of a fire to know and obey the Crucified and Risen One.

● *Conviction.* Do the would-be leaders have biblically informed convictions—about who God is, who humans are, the meaning of history, the nature of the church, and especially the meaning of Jesus' death and resurrection? Are they learning what it means to be transformed by the renewal of the mind (Rom. 12:2), to "think Christianly" about every dimension of their lives—money, time, sex, family, recreation? For this reason, Paul warns against being too quick to call recent converts to leadership; commitment and conviction take time to deepen.

ments that precede ordination. Hebrew, Greek, preaching proficiency, all the tests and ordination exams—each becomes a major rite of passage. In other words, the call doesn't take place in a vacuum. There are churches and individuals and requirements that God uses to prepare us for ministry. These things must be attended to with a seriousness that befits one who is called.

Once a person becomes ordained, other professional elements enter the picture. For example, when I was head of a pastoral staff, I had to enter the fray of personnel issues, performance evaluations, salary levels, and housing allowances. These issues don't go away just because they are not central to the call. Again, for those called to ministry, these issues must be attended to responsibly.

In fact, we might think of professional requirements and duties as household chores. Taking out the trash is not the most important part of family life, but things get messy if it's not done. If we do take out

---

● *Competency.* Do the would-be leaders know how to make their way through the Scriptures? Can they help others find their way around the sacred pages (2 Tim. 2:15)?

Have the would-be leaders been entrusted with appropriate gifts of the Holy Spirit (Eph. 4:11–12, 1 Cor. 12:12–31, Rom. 12:3–8)? Do they have a working understanding of the gifts, and can they help others discern and deploy those entrusted to them? Do they have the necessary relational skills for this position? Do their relationships manifest the integrity and love of Jesus, especially in their marriage and with their children (2 Tim. 3:5)? The Kingdom of God, after all, is about righteousness, that is, right relationship.

● *Character.* Are the would-be leaders taking on the character of Jesus? Someone has astutely observed, "It's not a matter of perfection, but direction." Are we moving toward greater and greater Christlikeness? The lists of leadership requirements are finally about char-

acter. Is there self-control, hospitality, gentleness (control of anger), quest for holiness, temperance? Is there evidence of dying to the love of money, to manipulation, to always having it one's own way? Are they faithful to their spouse ("husband of one wife")?

It should be noted that the injunction in 1 Timothy 3:4 that requires a leader to "see that his children obey him with proper respect" is not a demand for perfection. Children can choose to disobey even the best parents (see Luke 15). Paul's concern is that leadership give their best energies and time to training their children.

And "above reproach"? The point is that we should seek to be all the Master calls us to be. It means being above condemnation as we confess and repent of our sins and failures and seek, by grace, to grow.

The biblical qualifications of a leader are commitment, conviction, competency, and character. The greatest of these is character.

—*Darrell W. Johnson*

the trash and do the dishes, home life won't necessarily become great. But if we don't do these things, the house will surely start to stink!

In a similar vein, J. I. Packer likens the theologian to a water treatment plant that eliminates sewage from water. The plant doesn't necessarily make water taste good, but it keeps things from getting too bad. In ministry, things like education and salaries and study leave can never guarantee a fruitful ministry. If pastors don't take care of these chores, however, things start to stink. The best thing that education and professional standards can do is prevent disaster.

These aspects of the call aren't unspiritual, but neither are they the essence of the call. They are simply some of the unavoidable things

Ordination

The picture that immediately comes to our minds when we think of *ordination* probably cannot be sustained by the New Testament. It is a picture of a formal ceremony in which one receives some kind of certification by a duly constituted religious institution. In fact, the New Testament does not use the words *ordination* or *ordain*. Rather, the words are *choose* (Mark 3:14, Luke 6:13), *appoint* (Acts 14:23, 1 Cor. 12:28, Titus 1:5), *number* (Acts 1:26), God *gave* (Eph. 4:11).

Some sort of rite was involved in calling people to ministry, as is evidenced by Paul's words to Timothy: "Fan into flame the gift of God, which is in you through the laying on of my hands" (2 Tim. 1:6); "Do not neglect your gift, which was given you through a prophetic message when the body of elders laid their hands on you" (1 Tim. 4:14).

Four Meanings

Through the centuries, various traditions employing differing languages and symbols have been used in the ordination of ministers. What does ordination in its various traditions commonly entail? At least four things:

● *Recognition.* We are acknowledging and affirming that, yes, this person has been entrusted (by God's sovereign grace) with appropriate gifts of the Spirit for leadership in Christ's Body (1 Cor. 12:28–31). We are acknowledging that, yes, "the Holy Spirit is calling you to this particular work because we see evidence of particular workings of the Spirit of Jesus in your life."

● *Setting apart.* We are then saying that this appropriately gifted person is to be set apart from "normal" responsibilities in order to take

pastors do because of the call. Still, for all that, the far more common danger among pastors is to let such matters dominate their ministry, to think of ministry primarily as a career.

Confronting the Perils of Professionalism

If we view our calling only as a career, we reduce the servant of Christ to a vapid creature called "the professional." Well-dressed and well-spoken, armed with degrees, leadership savvy, management manuals, and marketing studies—all to be used for the good of the Kingdom, of course—we intend to make a mark on the world, gain a

---

up the mantle of leadership in the church. We affirm that all believers are "set apart by God for God" (the meaning of the word *saint* in 1 Corinthians 1:2, for instance). But we also affirm that some are called to be set apart by God for God in a different way, in order to give undivided attention to the preaching of the Word and the equipping of the saints (Eph. 4:11–12). We are saying, "The Holy Spirit is calling you to this particular work, and we, in agreement with him, are setting you apart for it." Usually this also means, "We will do everything we can to take care of your financial and temporal needs so that you, and we, can obey God's call."

● *Empowerment.* We are then empowering the gifted person, usually by the laying on of hands. That is, our hands in that act become the hands of Christ, conveying to the person Christ's divine energy (1 Cor. 12:4–6). And our hands are granting the person authority to function in a leadership role in our lives. We are saying, "The Holy Spirit is calling you to this particular work, and we claim Christ's power for you, and we give you the right to lead us into his will." It is a solemn moment, therefore, not only for the

ordained but also for the church. Is that not why Paul tells Timothy, "Do not be hasty with laying on of hands" (1 Tim. 5:22)?

● *Accountability.* Finally, we are calling those ordained to accountability. We are asking of them fidelity to Jesus Christ as head of the church, to the Scriptures as the final authority in all matters of faith and practice, to our unique theological emphases, and to our special way of doing things. Thus we extract a vow from the person: "Do you promise to uphold our standards?" "Will you abide by our form of disciplines?" "Will you be a faithful minister, ordering your personal life by the Word and Spirit of Jesus Christ?"

In many cultural settings, we are also confirming other special privileges, such as the authority to officiate at weddings and exercise certain tax exemptions. But, essentially we are recognizing gifts, setting apart for special functions, empowering, and entering into sacred accountability.

Is it any wonder that those who are ordained experience both great joy and fear?

—*Darrell W. Johnson*

little respect for the profession, and shed forever the pastor's Rodney Dangerfield image.

Sensible and realistic, professionals expect the church to treat them like professionals and negotiate salary and benefits to match. It is terrifying to realize that professional clergy can apply the skills and sophistication of their trade to build large, exciting, growing churches, and do it all without having to believe anything!

"God deliver us from the professionalizers," says pastor John Piper. Echoing Saint Paul, he asks, "Hasn't God made pastors the last in all the world? We are fools for Christ's sake; professionals are wise. We are weak; professionals are held in honor.... Professionalism has nothing to do with the essence and heart of the Christian ministry.... For there is no professional childlikeness, no professional tenderheartedness, no professional panting after God.... How do you carry a cross professionally?... What is professional faith?"

Worst of all, careerism drives a wedge between the God who calls and the person who answers. It leads us to believe that our performance is more important than our person, that how we do in the ecclesiastical marketplace is more important than how we stand before God.

Careerism tries to give us confidence in ourselves, where we ought to tremble and cry out for mercy. There is no place in the professional syllabus for a Paul who came to Corinth in weakness and foolishness, or for a Jeremiah who ate the Word of God only to get a terrible case of indigestion, or for a Jesus who ended his public life on a cross.

Heeding the Untamed Call

Inherent in God's call is something fierce and unmanageable. He summons, but he will not be summoned. He does the calling; we do the answering.

Jesus told his disciples, "You did not choose me, but I chose you" (John 15:16). There is always a sense of compulsion, at times even a sense of violence, about God's call. Struck blind on the road to Damascus, Paul said later, "Woe to me if I do not preach the gospel" (1 Cor. 9:16). Jeremiah complained that God had seduced him into his vocation and wouldn't let him out, no matter how much it hurt: "If I say, 'I will not mention him or speak any more in his name,' his word is in my heart like a burning fire shut up in my bones. I am weary of holding it in; indeed, I cannot" (Jer. 20:9). Spurgeon saw the divine constraint as such a sure sign of a call that he advised young men considering the ministry *not* to do it if, in any way, they could see themselves doing something else.

At times we try to tame the call by equating a staff position in a church or religious organization with the call itself. But the call always transcends the things we do to earn money, even if those things are done in the church. The same distinction we urge our people to recognize applies to us: Our vocation in Christ is one thing; our occupations, quite another.

Our vocation is our calling to serve Christ; our occupations are the jobs we do to earn our way in the world. While it is our calling to press our occupations into the service of our vocation, it is idolatrous to equate the two. Happy is the man or woman whose vocation and occupation come close. But it is no disaster if they do not.

If tomorrow I am fired and am forced to find employment in the gas station down the street, my vocation would remain intact. I still would be called to preach. Nothing would have changed my call substantially, just the situation in which I obey it. As Ralph Turnbull points out, I may preach as the paid pastor of a church, but I am not being paid to preach. I am given an allowance so that I can be more free to preach.

At times we try to tame the call by "clericalizing" it. Seminary education does not qualify a person for the ordained ministry, nor does additional psychological testing and field experience. Naturally, these may be valuable and even necessary for the ministry, but none of them alone or in combination is sufficient.

No office or position can be equated with the call. No credential, degree, or test should be confused with it. No professional jargon or psychobabble can tame it. No training or experience or ecclesiastical success can replace it. Only the call suffices. Everything else is footnote and commentary.

—*Ben Patterson*

Resources

Cedar, P., K. Hughes, and B. Patterson. 1991. Mastering the pastoral role. Portland, Ore.: Multnomah.

Hughes, K., and B. Hughes. 1987. Liberating ministry from the success syndrome. Wheaton, Ill.: Tyndale.

Peterson, E. 1987. Working the angles: The shape of pastoral integrity. Grand Rapids: Eerdmans.

Professional Development and Career Tracks

After reflecting on several conversations at a recent pastors' conference, you realize that you answered the same set of questions from several pastors. Each wanted to know what position you held and the number of people in your church.

Most questions, of course, are part of the healthy give-and-take of church professionals. But sometimes such questions camouflage another agenda: "Can you advance my career?" Or perhaps, "Where do you stand in relation to me?"

Getting Ahead

Some church leaders feel uncomfortable talking about career tracks for ministry. Servants who aspire to washing feet, the reasoning goes, are not supposed to climb ladders. But is wanting to get ahead inherently wrong?

No, says Robert Schnase, pastor and author of *Ambition in Ministry* (Abingdon 1993). A person can be ambitious for the good, driven to excellence by a desire to improve their gifts. But this desire to achieve can easily degenerate into competition.

"When James and John decided to move closer to Jesus," writes Schnase, "it was commendable and inspired ambition. But when they decided to sit closest to Jesus, their focus changed. Rather than looking to Jesus, they furtively glanced over their shoulders at the other disciples, anticipating that their own spiritual accomplishments had markedly overshadowed everyone else's. Pride redirects ambition."

If our measure of worth is based on arriving at the top position, we will be emotional slaves to a goal contrary to God's values. And we will continually come up short of our own impossible standards; someone will always be perched on a higher rung than ours.

A Higher Trajectory

In Romans 12:3, the apostle Paul writes, "Do not think of yourself more highly than you ought, but rather think of yourself with sober judgment...." Paul refocuses the career question from "How can I reach the top?" to "How can my life have its God-intended optimal impact?" Here are two avenues to maximize our impact:

● *Our spiritual gifts.* There probably have been times when each of us felt stuck in what we considered the backwaters of God's wilderness and watched as other colleagues landed positions that we drooled over. In jealousy, we may have railed against God, "I am as capable as they! What about me?"

By urging us to not to think "more highly than we ought," however, Paul suggests we look honestly at who we are, not who we think we are. We ought not to spend our life living out some fantasy self-perception that has little to do with reality.

For God's optimally intended impact, we must, as Paul commands, soberly assess our gifts. We should ask, "What is the truth about what I have to offer?" We are in touch with our gifts when we can answer the question, "When we serve the body of Christ, where is joyful energy released?"

We can also ask our fellow believers to answer honestly, "What spiritual gifts do you benefit from in my life?"

● *Our call.* Our call is the sphere in which our gifts best function. Is our life's energy being spent addressing the concern that God has planted in our hearts? When our gifts operate in our sphere of call, God's people intuitively recognize the innate authority of our lives and give us room to operate.

The answer to the question "What have you done with the gifts and call the Lord has entrusted to you?" should undergird our career ambitions, wherever they may lead.

—Greg Ogden

Ambition and Contentment

No minister wants to be perceived as self-centeredly ambitious. Yet what church would want a complacent pastor with no discernible ambition? We wrestle with ambition: How much is necessary? And will we ever quit worrying about having as many in worship as the church across the street?

Good, holy ambition drives the mills of excellent ministry, helps us accomplish tasks the unambitious might deem impossible, transforms churches, maximizes gifts. Raw ambition, on the other hand—the desire to claw our way to the top—pours sand in the ministry gears and forces the machinery to produce an unholy product: human pride.

Problem Circumstances

Predictable occasions awaken questions of ambition and force the issue:

● *Decisions.* Should our gifts be used in as large an arena as possible? Or is that just raw ambition wanting to make a bigger splash? Any decision to launch something significant in ministry carries with it questions of personal ambition.

● *Comparisons.* The call of a seminary classmate to a prestigious ministry triggers self-questioning for many of us: *Why him and not me? Have I done as well?* Or we may compare our status and salary with other professionals, such as physicians.

● *Expectations.* We struggle with expectations placed on us by ourselves, our parents, our parishioners. Is ministry for us a frightening sprint toward acceptability through accomplishment?

An Ambition Check

Our ambition may surprise us. Uninhibited, naked ambition seems ready at any moment to bare itself to our shame. It does so in a number of ways:

● *Jealousy and competition.* If "burying the competition"—the other churches in town—becomes our quest, ambition has streaked our souls.

● *Discontent and fruitlessness.* Satisfaction cannot be found in direct pursuit; ambitious striving often produces the opposite effect from the one desired.

● *Self-promotion and divine displacement.* Ambition is out of bounds when *we* become brighter lights than God.

Holy ambition, on the other hand, is Joshua conquering the land, Nehemiah restoring his people, Paul going on to Derbe after being stoned in Lystra. It appears as a desire to do all for Christ, to elevate *him,* to deny self and enjoy the freedom and fulfillment of doing God's will. Holy ambition is willing even to fail if it will further God's purposes.

Training Our Ambition

So how do we tame the ravenous beast of selfish ambition and yet feed the workhorse of holy ambition?

● *Reflectively.* We must allow ourselves time to think with God about how we are investing our life. Stepping back often gives us a fuller picture.

● *Devotionally.* Prayer and Scripture reading remain powerful correctives for vaulting ambition.

Stepping into the pulpit, the Welsh evangelist Peter Joshua would pray, "Lord, I want them to think well of me, but more than that, I want them to think well of you."

● *Strategically.* Our strategies are discipline and accountability. The disciplines of taking a Sabbath for rest helps us keep from feeling too important to take time off, and practicing servanthood can keep us humble. But probably the best strategy is to become openly accountable to friends willing to help us deal with hard issues.

● *Gracefully.* All this soul searching can get heavy, so we need to be as merciful with ourselves as we would be with another. Being tempted and even struggling with ambition are givens; what we do in that battle of mixed motives is up to us and God.

—*James D. Berkley*

3

Our Responsibility to God

Two basic influences mark our way as spiritual leaders: nature and grace. The influence of nature is seen in our intellect, temperament, and gifts. The influence of grace is seen in the touch of God harnessing and enhancing these natural factors so that we are readied for focused service.

When our natural side rightly surrenders to spiritual conditioning, our humanity is disciplined. This allows others to experience us as guides, as a blessing, as the mediated presence of God. As leaders responsible to handle "spiritual things," we are relevant only when God is present and active in what we do, since God is the One who makes our presence and service effective. Thus, it is imperative that we cultivate a committed relationship with God.

The New Testament word that describes a person marked by God is *anointed*. There are at least four features reflected in the concept of anointed service, each of which must be understood in relation to God's gracious choice of us for service: (1) There is a sense of assertiveness, from which we act; (2) there is a gripping knowledge that we are identified with God's will in that acting; (3) there is an intensity to what we do, because our actions are related to the highest frame of reference; and (4) there is an instinctiveness for what we do.

Anointing elevates ministry into the moral and spiritual order. It generates respect and encourages relationships; it endows us with

25

courage, aggressiveness, and authority. Our labor is given a meaning beyond mere human activity. We are protected from becoming "professionally religious." Instead, we become guided and girded servants.

Anointing and Leadership

The theme of anointing is readily apparent in the writings of Luke. He speaks of Jesus as one "anointed" by God (Luke 4:18; Acts 10:38), and his accounts always link Jesus' service to the fact that he was appointed by God. In Luke 4:18 we are given Jesus' own description of his purpose and authority for ministry: "The Spirit of the Lord is upon me, because he has anointed me...."

This use of Isaiah 61:1–2 by Jesus to refer to himself is more than a statement about his messianic uniqueness. It also sets forth a requisite for every spiritual leader: Those who serve in holy things must be accredited for that service by the Spirit of God. Luke highlights this by recounting stories of how the early Christian leaders were used by God to foster growth in the early Church. The basis for their compelling effectiveness is expressed through the use of the words *charisma* and *chrisma*, that is, spiritual giftedness and anointing. These terms point decisively to God's grace, showing that it was God, and not human integrity or power, that sustained the early church. Anointing is God's honoring of those who honor his gracious choice of them.

Beyond Ritual

If anointing does not come by personal achievement but is a gracious gift from God, we will experience it through responsible selfhood and not through prescribed ritual. To be sure, the pastor or spiritual leader is connected with a considerable body of rituals. Many of our actions are "authorized," since we serve, preach, or lead as ordained persons, officially endorsed by some church community. We also carry titles—Reverend, for example—and these titles project certain expectations. Many wear clerical garments and clerical collars. All of these are sign-values that distinguish us in our roles.

Given the fact of our sign-values as spiritual leaders and the meanings associated with our functions, it is all the more important that we take care to view our *work* as honorable and to view *ourselves* in the spirit of humility. Our services are best rendered when there is a disciplined commitment to the God who calls, conditions, and sends us. We are called to deal directly and intimately with people in moral and spiritual matters, which includes cultural and social concerns. With such a calling, we must not only know what ought to be done, but we must do it as committed people. The issue here has to do with living with spiritual realities beyond ritual. It means having a Godward intention, integrity of role, and humility of spirit.

Humility in the Presence of the Holy

Most will agree that Jesus calls his followers to serve with humility. Why is this characteristic so central to Christian leadership?

● Humility is essential because the graciousness of God is behind all our work and witness. As Paul put it, the Lord "considered me faithful, appointing me to his service" (1 Tim. 1:12). It is always sobering to understand that we are called not because of our greatness but because God is gracious.

● Humility is essential because our gifts are limited. Not one of us has all of the gifts necessary to make the church or the world perfect. We are part of a larger whole. Paul stated it this way: "There are different kinds of gifts, but the same Spirit. There are different kinds of service, but the same Lord. There are different kinds of working, but the same God works all of them in all men" (1 Cor. 12:4–6).

● Humility is essential because our individual effectiveness is limited. Leaders tend to have arenas of effectiveness, but no one can draw everyone by his or her handling of the gospel. What appeals to one person may be received indifferently by another. We are limited humans and so must depend on God as he ministers through his Body with all its members.

● Humility is essential because our knowledge is limited. In the presence of the Holy, we, like Paul, are wise to admit that "we know in part and we prophesy in part" (1 Cor. 13:9). While we do "see," ours is a diminished view. However much we may study and inquire, probe and think, we all know far too little to boast.

● Humility is essential because our time to live and serve is limited. Our days are numbered. Despite the greatness of our work—and no work is greater than the service of God—the time must come when we will be forced to let it all go and die. It is no small thing to face this fact. Psychologist Erik Erikson talked of the "ego-chill" we experience when we talk frankly about the fact of our own deaths. One day we will move beyond talking about death and actually die. That reality serves to humble even the most exalted among us.

Commitment, carefulness, and humility mark the life of all who truly honor God's call upon them to ministry. Who else bears such a trust? Who else is sent to affirm creation, proclaim redemption, and lead others in celebrating the Creator? Who else is sent to probe, measure, and exalt life as God's gift to us all? Who else is authorized to "name the Name," speaking about God, as it were, from an inside post?

To sense the depth of such a privilege is to be stirred to gratitude and surrender, praise and prayer, faith and devotion, trust and obedience, humility and morality. Our responsibility to God is openness and obedience—a grateful openness and a love-inspired obedience.

Attuned to Two Worlds

The responsible spiritual leader must know two realms of being and must move between them at all times. One is our humanness; the other is our spiritual side. The first is often all too evident in our lives; the second is mystery laden and is an order that our secular culture professes not to recognize or need. Since we are spiritual leaders, both realities must feed our experience and ministry. We must be able to receive from both the human and the holy as well as serve in relation to both.

In his later years, Andrew Watterson Blackwood wrote a book on *The Growing Minister*. When the book was published, Blackwood con-

---

Personal Devotions

It's easy to feel discontented and guilty about our lack of spiritual development. Some days we wonder: *Am I making any real progress in spirituality? Am I really any more like Christ today than I was five years ago? How do I even pursue that?*

If Jesus practiced solitude, silence, prayer, simple living, submission, and worship on a regular basis, the only way for us to become more like him is to arrange our lives as he arranged his.

Our Disciplines

Here are several disciplines to help us rearrange our lives.

● *Solitude.* Thomas Merton calls solitude the most basic of the disciplines, saying, "True solitude cleanses the soul." In solitude we discover the purpose of life is not simply to find techniques to be suc-

cessful, but to laugh, to weep, to pray, to know God. Being saved means to *live.*

Some pastors come to the office an hour or two before others arrive to take advantage of the stillness. Others schedule a whole day away from the church for solitude.

● *Silence.* One way to practice silence is to schedule a "quiet day" once a week, a fast from noise, in which we try to talk as little as possible. Pastors can take advantage of "quiet opportunities" by not listening to tapes or the radio while driving. During these days many of us realize how addicted to noise we've become.

● *Reading Scripture "uselessly."* It's tempting to try to save time by using the same texts for personal reflection that we later will use for sermons. But in doing so, we often end up focusing on how we can use

fessed, "Among all the books I have written for ministers this one cost me most" (Blackwood 1960, 7). Blackwood wrote that book looking back and forth between those who would read it and his own life. As an older leader, he was acutely aware of the two realms of being as he discussed the minister's work as the highest, the hardest, the holiest, and the happiest in the world. Blackwood wrote after having nurtured his spirit on the truth that ministry is what it is because Jesus Christ is who he is.

Karl Barth, during a lecture trip in America, commented, "Christ is that infinitely wondrous event which compels a person, so far as he experiences and comprehends this event, to be necessarily, profoundly, wholly, and irrevocably astonished" (Barth 1963, 71).

Paul the Apostle was thinking about this when he wrote about the "surpassing greatness (*huperechon*) of knowing Christ Jesus my Lord" (Phil. 3:8).

---

the text in a message. As a result, we may relate it to every soul but ours.

One practice is to read books that give specific exercises for meditating on Scripture. *Spiritual Exercises,* by Ignatius Loyola, can help us contemplate the consequences of sin and examine our consciences for the sin most destructive to us.

● *Confession.* We need someone with whom we can be honest—someone whose spirituality we respect, who can keep things confidential, offer unconditional acceptance, and be utterly truthful.

Dietrich Bonhoeffer wrote, "Confession is the God-given remedy for self-deception and self-indulgence. When we confess our sins before a brother-Christian, we are mortifying the pride of the flesh and delivering it up to shame and death through Christ. Then through the word of absolution we rise as new men.... Confession is thus a genuine part of the life of the saints, and one of the gifts of grace."

● *Service.* One of the best places to practice this discipline is at home. We could begin by scheduling times when we take care of our children or do extra things around the house—and make an internal commitment *not* to keep track.

● *Fasting.* The activity of fasting is foreign to some pastors, but once started, fasting becomes progressively easier. Among other benefits, it can make us much more aware of how hurried we are. There seems to be a link between fasting and the ability to resist cravings for things besides food.

A Disciplined Pastor?

Thomas Merton wrote, "We do not want to be beginners. But let us be convinced of the fact that we will never be anything else but beginners all our life!"

Perhaps the main thing the disciplines teach us is hope—that the effort to become more like Christ has a definite shape. Given a lifetime, change is possible.

—*John C. Ortberg, Jr.*

Christ can be known in our experience, and a union with Christ gives content to our selfhood and our service. James S. Stewart believed this. In his book *A Faith to Proclaim,* he urged: "In particular, let the Christian preacher, the herald of the good news of God, think of his own life being interpenetrated with the very life of Jesus." Stewart further stated:

> We are apt in these days to be besieged by life's unbearable enigmas and battered by its frightening responsibilities.... We tell ourselves it is absurd that we should even attempt to be Christ's witnesses in a world like this and with a nature like our own: for "who is sufficient for these things?" And then across our hectic fever falls the voice of calm: "Lo, I am with you alway, even unto the end"; and we know that, whatever happens, He is quite certain to be there. This is the way to peace, and to the consciousness of adequate resources (Stewart 1953, 157–158).

Personal Prayer

Like the marriage relationship, our relationship with God needs constant care. Though prayer is the communication vehicle through which a relationship with God develops, many pastors struggle to maintain a consistent prayer life. Yet, prayerlessness saps the power of ministry.

Combating Prayerlessness

Weakness of the flesh attacks all of us, especially when it comes to sustaining an unfailing prayer life. And as Paul notes in Romans 8, there is no way to overcome our lower natures but by the power of the Holy Spirit. Utilizing the Comforter's power can be aided by three common techniques:

● *Set up a system of accountability for prayer.* Many Christian leaders hold themselves accountable to others for regular prayer. For example, a denominational district superintendent phones one layman each day of the month as a prayer partner for that day. Another pastor has a designated person call him at a time he has set aside for prayer. He then must face this person about whether indeed he is praying or not. Another pastor has covenanted to meet twice a day with two separate groups in her parish. Meeting with others keeps our prayer lives consistent and keeps us honest.

● *Provide positive and negative reinforcements for prayer.* What forms of reinforcement work? One California pastor sets aside a time each morning for prayer and "will not eat a meal of physical food until I first have some spiritual food and prayer time. Food really motivates me, so I make sure I get

Living Obediently and Trustfully

As leaders, our work cannot rise higher than the quality of our lives or our faith, so we must always serve under the terms of trust. The church, in ordaining pastors to the ministry, recognizes this steward-ship-trust relationship. We pastors are commissioned people whose selfhood and service will be either continually renewed and relevant when we serve in faith, or inadequate and restricted when we serve casually or in selfish competitiveness. God honors those who respond diligently to his call, who take Jesus seriously as Savior and Lord, who remember, as Martin Luther put it, that "it is not we who can sustain the Church, nor was it our forefathers, nor will it be our descendants. It was and is and will be the One who says, 'I am with you alway, even unto the end of the world' " (Plass 1959, vol. 1, 283).

---

my prayer in every morning through this means." An Arizona pastor uses stoplights as times to pray. He gains an additional bene-fit: He used to be frustrated at being slowed down by stoplights. Now they are a positive motivation to pray.

● *Turn prayer into a physical act.* The advantages of physical exercise are obvious and currently popular. Many Christian leaders pray while jogging, swimming, walking, or rid-ing bicycles. The obvious goal of all these practices is to associate prayer with something beneficial to help overcome the lethargy that can strike us all.

Other physical aids prove useful. A Michigan pastor says he prays out loud because it keeps his mind from wandering. Another pastor prays while standing up and walk-ing around: "I have my prayer items written on three-by-five cards, and I flip through them as I'm walking. I haven't fallen asleep even once doing this." Our body language can help us remember that we are talking to a living, active God who is present, power-ful, and listening.

Finding the Right Fit

Obviously, there is no shortage of techniques. Indeed, we are more often paralyzed by having to choose one idea out of so many options. The method used must solve the particular problem each of us has with prayer. If inconsistency is the problem and we are people who relate well to friends helping us, prayer partners may be the answer. On the other hand, others may not relate well to having someone checking up on them, or such a per-son may not be available. For them, a specific period of time in prayer may be a stimulating goal.

In any case, the method should be chosen based on what feels com-fortable and what we will chafe under the least. The goal is to find a method that works, so that prayer becomes a common and vital part of our day.

—*Terry C. Muck*

Spiritual leadership requires a deep, personal concern for living responsibly before God, for cooperating with the urgent guidance of God's Spirit, and for accepting the discipline needed for growth in godliness. Those concerned about godliness will naturally seek methods for creating and sustaining openness to God. They will give themselves to planned times of prayer, corporate worship, open dialogue with other believers, the devotional study of Scripture, and moments of meditation. These methods of openness are really creative responses to the initiative God has shown in sharing his gracious Presence with us. Each of these methods helps us to sense the Holy and stimulates us to receive the vitality that is available to us by the grace of God.

Once when speaking on the subject of arrogance, Howard Thurman told about a time he went to the doctor for a physical examination. The doctor gave Thurman an initial exam and then sent him to five other physicians, who checked him out in their areas of specialty. A week later Thurman returned to his doctor for a report on the examination results.

Sitting behind his desk, the doctor fingered several sheets of reports, lingering over a few pages. Finally he closed the manila folder and reported, "You are in fine shape—your heart, your lungs, all those things are in good order. But, you are too heavy." He then gave Thurman his expert counsel about the damage the extra pounds he was carrying could do to his heart and lungs and blood vessels.

Thurman began to feel somewhat apprehensive. "Then," Thurman remembered, "I looked at him and realized that he wasn't as tall as I was and weighed about 225 pounds!"

As Thurman reflected on the encounter, he realized the dilemma of the trained mind: His doctor was providing accurate and needed counsel, while unaware that he himself needed to address the problem of his own weight. "He thought that his body knew that he was a doctor," says Thurman. "His body did not know that he was a doctor; his body knew precisely what my body knew" (Thurman 1962, 29–30). Being a doctor gave the overweight man no immunity. Until the doctor applied his medical knowledge to his personal lifestyle, he too was in physical jeopardy.

The point is that we, with our specialized knowledge of God and leadership positions and spiritual skills, can fall victim to a false sense of security. We must remember that in teaching others about God, we must know God ourselves; that in calling others to faith, we must be believers too; that in feeding others, we must eat of the food that will nourish our souls as well. Like everyone else, we too need help to grow spiritually.

Holy things can become ordinary to us, so customary and familiar to us that we become casual about them. As "professionals" who work regularly with the contents of the Bible, we must guard against subconsciously viewing the Scriptures as only a literary treasure out of which we teach and preach great things that we falsely assume we have mastered. We must search ourselves, asking: As we routinely shepherd souls, do those who experience our leadership perceive a genuine caring for them? Do they perceive alongside responsible scholarship an evident faith? Do they sense both a love for truth and a heart for God? Do they perceive within our prayers the accent of our personal reverence?

Lawyer and churchman George Wharton Pepper, one of the few nonclerics ever to give the Lyman Beecher Lectures at the Yale Divinity School, talked about the ways preachers are perceived from the pew by laity during worship. He concluded that what people want to see in pastors as they lead in worship or read from the Scriptures is reverence. Pepper explained what he meant by reverence: "It is not a manner or tone or a posture. It is something the effect of which is confined to the man himself ... I am inclined to describe it as the atmosphere exhaled by a man who is aware of the Presence of God" (Pepper 1915, 10).

Our responsibility to God begins and ends in our living and ministering in that Presence.

—*James Earl Massey*

Resources

Barth, K. 1963. Evangelical theology. New York: Holt, Rinehart and Winston.
Blackwood, A. 1960. The growing minister. Nashville: Abingdon.
Forbes, J. 1989. The Holy Spirit and preaching. Nashville: Abingdon.
George, W. 1915. A voice from the crowd. New Haven: Yale.
Massey, J. 1976. The sermon in perspective. Grand Rapids: Baker.
Massey, J. 1985. Spiritual disciplines. Grand Rapids: Zondervan.
McKenna, D. 1986. Renewing our ministry. Waco, Tex.: Word.
Plass, E., ed. 1959. What Luther says, vol. 1. St. Louis: Concordia.
Stewart, J. 1953. A faith to proclaim. New York: Charles Scribner's Sons.
Thurman, H. 1962. The temptations of Jesus. San Francisco: Lawton Kennedy Productions.
Thurman, H. 1963. Disciplines of the Spirit. New York: Harper & Row.
Wells, D. 1993. No place for truth. Grand Rapids: Eerdmans.

Personal Morality

"Personal morality" is a neutral phrase that refers to patterns of conduct—whether good, bad, or just ordinary. But in popular usage, a "moral person" is a good person, and the pastor is expected to be the very model of a good person. There is, in fact, an innate sense in all humanity that the "high God" is holy and just, and that those who speak for God should somehow be like him.

Is this, however, a legitimate expectation?

The hearts of many pastors cry, *No! We are people like any others. Our feet are clay; our inmost selves are as potentially wayward, as vulnerable, as others.*

Leaders in Process

This pastoral heart-cry of identification with common humanity is at once powerfully affirmed and decisively modified by Scripture. The apostle Paul writes that the purpose of church leadership is to build up God's people so we all can attain "to the whole measure of the fullness of Christ" (Eph. 4:13). That, of course, includes pastors. But what a goal—the very fullness of Christ, the Sinless One!

Of course, it is a goal for the road, neither an ascribed status nor an unattainable ideal. Paul uses the future tense again and again: "Then we will no longer be infants ..." and "We will in all things grow up ..." (Eph. 4:14 –15).

Yet in 1 Timothy 3:2, Paul demands that leaders be "above reproach." Church folks rightly expect their leaders to model morality. Here is the foundation for such a morality:

● *A life like Christ's.* Our standard is not a code, a status within the community, or an impossible ideal. It is, rather, Jesus in the midst of us by his Spirit (Rom. 8:9–11).

● *A spirit of openness.* A lifestyle pleasing to Christ will not maintain the appearance of righteousness by carefully guarding our reputation at all costs—even creating a cadre of faithful followers to which blame

is shifted when failure happens. It is rather the eager embrace of the truth about ourselves, especially when there is sin, for in that embrace lies the next step toward "the fullness of Christ."

● *The power of the Holy Spirit.* This is not the independent power of self-discipline or of rational mastery, but rather that which comes from turning to God. The power to live outwardly as Christ would have lived has been given to us through God's Spirit.

● *An unmovable standard.* No contemporary code of ethics or standard of morality can replace that which comes from God's Word (2 Tim. 3:16 –17).

Two Keys

Yet, if we have such resources for patterns of personal morality grounded in God himself, why the breakdown? Why the frequent breaches of trust in financial, sexual, and family responsibilities—and that by Christian leaders?

The answers are complex and multiple, but the safe-deposit box of God's healing and empowering resources is opened by two well-known (but too-little-used) keys: humility and accountability. When both are present, no leader need be defeated.

Allow me a personal example: My father served as a pastor for many years. One day his oldest son (of seven children) heard him speak harshly to a colleague. In passing, the son shared his disappointment with his mother and then forgot it.

But the next morning, his father came to him with tears. "Mother told me what you said last evening," he said, "and I didn't sleep much last night. I feel that I've failed you as a father. This morning I went to ask forgiveness of the man with whom I was speaking, and now I want to ask yours, too. Will you forgive me?"

Humility and accountability—they are the keys to living and modeling the life of Christ.

—Richard Showalter

nature of the pastor's responsibilities are difficult to define, let alone practice. So let's review the biblical image of the pastor, contrasting the distinguishing characteristics of *minister* versus those of *professional executive*.

● *Ministry originates with a divine call, not a human contract.* Vocational ministry has its roots in the call of God. The solution to the modern pastor's identity crisis will not be found in managing people's expectations, keeping a better Daytimer, or buying a cellular phone. The issue is far deeper than scheduling or hiring support staff. The shape of pastoral ministry depends on the Word and the Spirit of Christ. It begins with a response, a vowed commitment before God, not a contractual agreement with employers, to lead people in worship; teach and obey the Word of God; guide people in what it means to follow the Lord Jesus; and pray for people and love them in Christ. Professionals are interested in the latest findings and techniques, but authentic pastors devote themselves to ancient truths and spiritual disciplines. Herein lies the difference between a calling and a career. The call originates with God and is guided by God's grace, God's gifts, and God's glory. Careers are shaped by market forces: supply and demand, competition, financial rewards, and quantitative success.

In lieu of job descriptions and professional profiles, the Bible offers mentors who embody the meaning of pastoral ministry. The apostle John, the pastor, identified himself with this description: "I, John, your brother and companion in the suffering and kingdom and patient endurance that are ours in Jesus" (Rev. 1:9). John expressed how pastors should feel toward those they serve in Christ. Pastoral ministry thrives in the context of this shared identity, a sense of mutual responsibility, and a common goal. Empathy draws pastors and people together. Professional expertise and ego distorts this mutual ministry by fostering both dependency and superiority. The words of Jesus are important for today: "You are not to be called 'Rabbi,' for you have only one Master and you are all brothers.... The greatest among you will be your servant. For whoever exalts himself will be humbled, and whoever humbles himself will be exalted" (Matt. 23:8, 11–12). This kind of humility is essential to true spiritual authority.

● *Ministry uses spiritual gifts, not just human talents.* Pastoral leadership is distinguished by a person's spiritual gifts, character, training, and support. The body of believers is integrally involved in the recognition and development of each of these areas. The apostle Paul wrote, "It was he [Christ] who gave some to be apostles, some to be prophets, some to be evangelists, and some to be pastors and teachers, to prepare God's people for works of service, so that the body of Christ may be built up" (Eph. 4:11–12). The pastor does not have all the spiritual gifts necessary for leading the church. Members of the body have different gifts, all of them necessary.

When the church relies too heavily on one person or lets that person assume too much responsibility, it hinders its own growth toward spiritual maturity. Focusing only on human talents, we burn out pastors by piling too many responsibilities on them because they are often deemed "so capable." This problem intensifies when the pastors are too quick to assume ministry responsibilities that could be better handled by others in the congregation (or by hiring new ministry staff persons).

The church sets apart the person gifted by the Spirit of Christ, not to do the ministry for the church but to prepare the church to minister. This recognition often involves providing the pastor with a salary, a study, support staff, and so on. The apostle Paul believed in a full-time, paid ministry. When he wrote to Timothy, he apparently assumed Timothy's salary and advised that other members of the pastoral team receive salaries. "The elders who direct the affairs of the church well are worthy of double honor, especially those whose work is preaching and teaching" (1 Tim. 5:17). Even though Paul chose not to receive a salary from the church at Corinth, he laid down the spiritual principle for financial remuneration. "If we have sown spiritual seed among you, is it too much if we reap a material harvest from you?" He concludes, "The Lord has commanded that those who preach the gospel should receive their living from the gospel" (1 Cor. 9:11, 14).

There is a compatibility and consistency between being gifted for pastoral ministry and demonstrating the character of pastoral ministry. The pastor sets an example "for the believers in speech, in life, in love, in faith and in purity" (1 Tim. 4:12). Seminary training is important for developing both the gifts and character essential for ministry. A good seminary does not distract from this focus or distort this emphasis by catering to the consumer demand for the modern pastor. If a congregation wants a public-relations expert, a therapist, or a marketer, it should look elsewhere than the seminary for their professional. But if they want a pastor who is fanning "into flame the gift of God" (2 Tim. 1:6), they should look for one who is diligently studying the Word of God, who is prepared to preach the Word "in season and out of season ... with great patience and careful instruction" (2 Tim. 4:2). They should look for a person who has been mentored by mature spiritual directors. As Paul said to Timothy, "You ... know all about my teaching, my way of life, my purpose, faith, patience, love, endurance, persecutions, sufferings" (2 Tim. 3:10 –11).

● *Ministry integrates the personal and private selves, rather than compartmentalize them.* Professional competence distinguishes between the public self and the private self. It compartmentalizes personal time and work time and draws a line between family life and church work. Pastoral maturity, by contrast, integrates personal life and pastoral ministry, family life and the household of faith. This does not mean the pastor never has time alone, since vocational holiness requires it. Nor does this mean the pastor sacrifices family life for the sake of the ministry.

The character qualities for spiritual leadership described by Paul emphasize this integration. Paul looked for a qualified pastor by looking at a person's marriage and children. Even though he saw his singleness as an advantage for the sake of his ministry, Paul examined a pastor's family in order to understand the person's suitability for ministry. He did not look for an organizational genius, but for a well-ordered life. He looked for wisdom, not the ability to perform before an audience. Did the person have a good reputation? Was he respected? Did the person know how to show hospitality? These are the

Responsibility to the Larger Church

Pastors can be called in two distinct ways: (1) God gives gifts and talents to minister; (2) a congregation can extend a call to a particular place. The fact that pastors move to new locations during the course of their ministry careers implies a significant truth: God has intended our gifts and abilities to be invested in a sphere wider than that of a single congregation.

People in secular jobs are entitled to other pursuits outside their career. Their employers rent their skills; they don't buy their souls. The same is true for someone employed by the church. God's call involves more than a congregational call to worship or calling on the sick of a community. Pastoral ministry includes wider dimensions of service: Some pastors are asked to serve on denominational boards or committees. Community ministerial groups offer opportunities for a pastor's involvement in joint evangelistic outreaches or humanitarian projects. Parachurch ministries

also seek church leaders to serve as consultants or teachers.

A Wider Scope

As pastors we must embrace our congregational tasks conscientiously. But we must not close our eyes to further opportunities of ministry outside the scope of our local churches. If we have met our congregational responsibilities and God has equipped us with certain abilities, then we should feel free to invest ourselves in other activities. Here are four benefits (for ministers *and* their congregations) from accepting assignments beyond the scope of the local church:

● Additional opportunities to use our gifts can replenish us emotionally and energize us to deal better with tasks for which we have less ability. There can be many outlets for ministry: speaking at camps or conferences, coaching soccer or Little League, and so on. For example, I've enjoyed writing, which

kinds of questions Paul asked, because the key to being responsible in ministry is displayed in one's personal life, not excluded from it. Relational and communicative effectiveness are important. Without these gifts people should not pursue pastoral ministry. But these gifts apart from spiritual maturity, personal holiness, and wisdom do not make a pastor.

● *Ministry demands faithful effort, not obsessive workaholism.* The apostle Paul seems to give little comfort to overworked pastors. His example borders on intimidation. Most of us would probably hesitate before going to work for the hard-driving apostle. Who could expect much comfort from one who was in the habit of working two jobs, night and day, and routinely suffering all kinds of privations? When Paul spoke of toil and hardship, he wasn't exaggerating by anyone's

---

began simply as a tool to encourage my congregation and later expanded to Christian publications. Writing has helped improve my preaching, counseling, and pastoral care. When we can change the pace of ministry occasionally and look beyond our parish responsibilities, we are energized.

● When we participate with other ministries in our community, we challenge our congregation's tendency toward provincialism. If we focus only on the horizon of the individual church scene, we can easily succumb to tunnel vision. Our activities and priorities can alienate us from other churches. We can be tempted to parrot the separatist's slogan: "My goals are good goals. Your goals are questionable." Joining with other pastors in a common task reminds us and our people that we share the same goal with them.

● We can raise our church's level of awareness by participating in missionary endeavors. A pastoral visit to a mission field or a pastor's short-term stint with a missionary can expand a congregation's king-

dom perspective. As an example, when I took my family for a six-week missions assignment among the Eskimos, my church didn't realize how much *they* would benefit: their pastor became more sensitive to the needs of their far-flung missionaries. Allowing their pastor a taste of missions fueled his passion for world evangelization—and touched the whole congregation with fresh perspective.

● Ministry beyond the local church can enrich denominational structure and shape its future focus. Mission efforts, publications, and other cooperative denominational ventures need the insights, education, and expertise of pastors. While a denominational structure can be a resource that enables a local church to expand its ministries, pastors remain the greatest resource of the denomination. Churches may not always be in a position to offer substantial financial support to the national church, but they can offer their pastoral staff for specific assignments.

—*Greg E. Asimakoupoulos*

standard. Nevertheless, Paul has a lot to offer the workaholic pastor, whose responsibility to the church has become obsessive. When priorities are set and spiritual disciplines followed, a pastor is saved from "spinning her wheels" in frustration.

Much of what pastors do is not what they were called to do. They are exhausted because they are doing everyone else's job but their own. Paul placed a great deal of emphasis on teaching and preaching the Word of God. He expected a pastor to work hard at effectively and faithfully proclaiming the whole counsel of God. This is what a pastor owes the church. All the people contact in the world does not take the place of offering consistent spiritual direction to people who desperately need God's perspective on life. The pastor has the opportunity to offer this not only in the pulpit, but also in the hospital room, in homes, in offices, and around the meal table.

At the center of pastoral ministry is the salvation-making, life-transforming Word, which is absolutely crucial to the church's experience of forgiveness, deliverance, redemption, and holiness. The world can offer entertainment and excitement, affirmation and motivation, but it is the Word of God preached and practiced that shapes a household of faith.

Community and Civic Responsibilities

More than 250 years ago, John Wesley claimed the world as his parish. In his own generation, John Calvin almost ran the city of Geneva singlehandedly from his study. But our congregations pay our salaries, and they expect (rightfully so) that we will devote our primary attention to the work of their church. Nevertheless, a church's mission includes making inroads into its community.

Will You Get Involved?

When attempting to determine whether or when to accept a civic responsibility or political position, pastors must consider numerous issues. Here are three questions to ask ourselves as we evaluate our place in community involvement:

● *What is my real motive?* For example, if asked to offer the invocation at the mayor's leadership breakfast, we might be tempted to accept for a number of reasons: we may want to rub shoulders with the top brass of our community; we might like some free publicity for our church; we may sincerely wish to raise before God—in public prayer—our concerns for our city's future. Any of these reasons might be legitimate, depending on the results we hope to achieve. If our motives and goals are ultimately focused on building God's kingdom, we can feel free to accept the invitation.

● *Will I offend members of my church?* A pastor was asked to run for the public school board. To do so, however, would mean alienat-

Paul never tired of promoting the hard work of preaching, prayer, and spiritual direction. His rich metaphors of the good soldier, the competitive athlete, and the hard-working farmer do two things (2 Tim. 2:1– 6). First, they stress the effort and diligence involved in pursuing pastoral ministry: "Be diligent in these matters; give yourself wholly to them, so that everyone may see your progress" (1 Tim. 4:15). But, second, they also stress a single-minded devotion to the truth. The good soldier does not get involved in civilian affairs, and the athlete competes according to the rules. So much of today's frustration in ministry stems from inflated expectations of what one person can do in the life of the church. Paul encourages us to resist the distractions and focus on offering clear, solid spiritual direction.

To do that, we have to love people and learn to be a student of human nature. We have to understand our culture, how it thinks, where it hurts, and what it wants out of life. We do this not to echo or copy our culture, but to penetrate our culture with the gospel.

We have an awesome responsibility to "make disciples ... teaching them to obey everything" Jesus commanded (Mt. 28:19–20). "We proclaim him," declared Paul, "admonishing and teaching everyone with all wisdom, so that we may present everyone perfect in Christ. To this

---

ing certain members in his church who were committed to home schooling. Yet this pastor felt that by working on the board he could stand up for the traditional values so fervently embraced by his home-schooling members. He eventually declined the offer because it would require so much time away from the church's educational programs. In a different time and place, he might have accepted.

● *Am I called to provide the Christian perspective?* You read in the newspaper about a vacancy on the Human Rights Commission. Of the five members remaining in office, two are pushing for a quota system related to the hiring of homosexuals in your town. Will you throw your hat in the ring to balance an agenda that might affect church hiring practices, youth programs, and school sex-education instruction? Perhaps. Or if your

plate is already full, you could privately encourage an elder to seek the position. But another pastor might avoid the issue completely, believing ministers should not take public political stands.

There are no easy answers to the question about civic and political involvement. Each opportunity raises unique issues, depending on the context of a ministry. However, before making particular choices, every pastor must arrive at a philosophy of community involvement. He or she must determine, in general, the levels at which it is appropriate to work "within the system" to promote kingdom values. In conversation with their congregations, pastors must set appropriate boundaries in order to walk wisely between the extremes of secular capitulation and civic isolationism.

—*Greg E. Asimakoupoulos*

end I labor, struggling with all his energy, which so powerfully works in me" (Col. 1:28–29). We do this one-on-one and in the pulpit, over coffee and around the Lord's Table, in times of crisis and when we pray. This is what we were meant to do. We were ordained to be pastors, stewards of the mysteries of God (1 Cor. 4:1–2). "Do your best to present yourself to God as one approved, a workman who does not need to be ashamed and who correctly handles the word of truth" (2 Tim. 2:15).

● *Ministry promotes harmony among people, rather than valuing political maneuvering.* Paul also helps the overworked pastor by establishing the priorities of ministry and warning the pastor of things to avoid. Titus was warned to "avoid foolish controversies and genealogies and arguments and quarrels about the law, because these are unprofitable and useless" (Titus 3:9). This did not mean Titus was to overlook sin and tolerate evil. In fact Paul told Titus to silence the rebellious people, who he described as "mere talkers and deceivers" (Titus 1:10). Paul was certainly not a believer in dragging out controversies. "Warn a divisive person once, and then warn him a second time. After that, have nothing to do with him. You may be sure that such a man is warped and sinful; he is self-condemned" (Titus 3:10 –11).

Too much time is spent in pastoral ministry catering to spiritually immature and selfish people, those who frustrate God's work by draining the time and energy of the church leadership. Pastors can be poor at offering tough love, because they want to be perceived as caring and patient. However, love and patience are not incompatible with decisive action with the goal of interpersonal harmony.

Concern for people's spiritual welfare and the peace and unity of the Body will lead inevitably to confrontation with evil. As every parent knows, there is a difference between sensitivity and softness, genuine love and mere tolerance. And as every pastor should know, it is the difference between the fear of God and the fear of man. Paul warned Timothy, "Avoid godless chatter, because those who indulge in it will become more and more ungodly. Their teaching will spread like gangrene" (2 Tim. 2:16 –17).

● *Mentoring involves drawing people—not to self, but to Another.* The pastor's responsibility before God is to draw people to Christ, not to himself or herself. The pastor's job is to help people come to Christ and not get in the way of that coming. Pastors are shepherds tending a flock, modeling their ministry after the Great Shepherd (Heb. 13:20). They are not ranchers driving a herd. They are like farmers, but instead of working in tandem with the soil, seed, and sun, pastors work in tandem with God. We wait for God's timing and watch for God's ways and work to God's ends. We harvest a spiritual crop of God's making, not of our doing. We are not shopping-mall developers changing the landscape according to our will, paving the earth with asphalt. Pastors understand that "unless the Lord builds the house, its builders labor in vain" (Ps. 127:1). They understand that their responsibility to the ministry is shaped by spiritual mentors, pastoral metaphors, and theological meaning found in the Word of God. Without a prayerful dependence upon God, we would not survive, much less succeed. The faithful pastor's service ends, as does the morning service, not with applause but with a hearty amen.

—Douglas D. Webster

Resources

Peterson, E. 1987. Working the angles: The shape of pastoral integrity. Grand Rapids: Eerdmans.

Peterson, E. 1992. Under the unpredictable plant: An exploration in vocational holiness. Grand Rapids: Eerdmans.

Wells, D. 1993. No place for truth. Grand Rapids: Eerdmans.

Continuing Education

Continuing education provokes controversy in some quarters. Some congregations wonder why pastors need it, and some pastors fail to use it productively. Still, the church member who may disapprove of a pastor's two weeks "away at some school" would not accept a physician who uses the cancer cures she learned in medical school in the sixties. In this changing world, practitioners of any sort must have continuing education. That includes pastors.

Do We Need to Study?

Many a pastor has found renewed interest in ministry by sharpening pastoral skills through continuing study. There are at least three reasons to do so.

First, many of us need *remedial* education. We have not learned everything by the time the ink dries on our diplomas. For example, I attended a fine seminary yet learned almost nothing about management. Other pastors gravely feel the effects of missed classes in homiletics, counseling, Christian education, New Testament, or any number of other subjects. Seminary alone cannot adequately equip us for a lifetime of ministry.

Second, we also must *retool* regularly. New ideas—often good ones—come along, and we need to update our technique. New trends in society demand new responses from the church. An example was my need to learn how to minister in a "rurban" town, a sociological setting unheard of ten years earlier. Shifting marriage patterns, changing sociological phenomena, and revised pastoral-care techniques demand pastors who give such things ongoing thought.

Personal *renewal*, spiritual and mental, is a third reason for continuing study. Pastors can run dry.

Challenges become problems, and problems can look insurmountable. Along with the need for continuing spiritual input, we need a fresh flow of ideas. Ministry becomes a dreary prospect when ideas are scarce. Pastors may feel all alone in a quandary, only to discover nearly every pastor has faced it. Others may have already conquered the "unsolvable" problem.

Churches probably won't automatically appreciate the time pastors spend studying. It makes their pastor inaccessible. It doesn't appear people-centered. Congregations, however, can learn that pastors need exactly such time to continue the process of education.

Who Bears the Cost?

If continuing education is both necessary and expensive, who, logically, should foot the bill? Often the expenses come right out of the pastor's pocket, since the pastor orders the journals and buys the books. That pastor does benefit from the reading and stimulation; it is his or her education and career. By default, pastors often stretch their personal budgets to pay the expenses.

Yet this is not the most equitable arrangement. Continuing education is actually a *professional* expense, not a *personal* expense. A church receives the fruits of its pastor's continuing education. The church supplies the pulpit he or she preaches from and such necessary items as the office telephone. Since study is also a necessity, shouldn't the church also provide for continuing education?

Most church budgets are strained, yet even a $50 line item for journal subscriptions or books signals both the pastor and the congregation that continuing education is important. A reasonable request for an initial $100 per pastor can eventually grow to a more realistic $300 or more in a few years. Such financial backing, along with a message from the church that the time away is given willingly, adds tools to the pastor's tool box and competence to his or her practice. The church benefits from a more capable and confident pastor, and pastors are freed to use their time, but not their family resources, to continue their education for everyone's benefit.

—James D. Berkley

Sabbaticals

Sabbaticals are ideal for pastors pursuing an advanced degree, such as a D.Min., but can be a powerful tool for any pastor. Yet the pastoral absence required by a sabbatical asks much of a congregation. Therefore, sabbaticals need to be planned well in advance and handled in a businesslike fashion, with specific, agreed-upon objectives.

Why a Sabbatical?

Sabbaticals are seldom golden eras for the congregation. They are endured in hopes of the benefits to be gained from a renewed, refreshed pastor. Therefore, we should be intentional about accomplishing the sabbatical's threefold purpose.

● *Rest.* The time away should be restful. After a few years, the ministry can make us feel as if someone had drained out of our heads everything seminary once put there. Particularly for one who holds forth from a pulpit forty or more times a year, what a joy to take in again instead of giving out! What a relief to enjoy a respite from the relentless return of Sunday-morning preaching!

What's more, the quality of thinking that is possible on a three-month study leave is quite different from that required for week-to-week preaching and teaching. We are able to think "long thoughts" and engage in "offensive study" instead of defensively preparing for tomorrow's sermon or class.

● *Travel.* Sabbaticals offer the opportunity to experience a new environment in an urban or academic setting, or possibly a foreign country. If one's family is coming along, it is best to select a stimulating setting for them to explore and enjoy. Parents need to check out schools for children, and family members should be cautioned to recognize the difference between a sabbatical for study and a vacation for fun.

● *Research.* Preparing a carefully planned course of proposed study, with an attached bibliography, is a good way to build credibility with the church governing body. Together, pastor and board can explore important issues, such as: How will this time away benefit the ministry and strengthen our church? How will what is researched further our mission and goals? In what ways will the pastor be better equipped?

Part of the research can include attending Sunday worship at a number of leading churches. How instructive to spend three months sitting where our hearers sit every Sunday!

Making It Happen

One of the best ways to secure a sabbatical is to negotiate it with the call to the church. At such a moment, granting three months of study to be taken seven years in the future will not seem as daunting to church leaders as it will six years later.

We need to prepare for a sabbatical that will minimize, as much as possible, the disruption to church life and ministry. In solo pastorates, a temporary preacher can be called, while in multistaff churches, the assignment of the pastor's duties to staff members should be clear and unambiguous. The cost of the sabbatical is usually the pastor's responsibility, with the church continuing full salary during the time away.

It is important upon return to graciously and profusely thank those who kept the church going during our absence. Sabbaticals should always be followed by a debriefing session with the church board. Suppose a major goal was to gain skills in strategic planning. The pastor might come back and lead the church in a two-year planning effort. When debriefing with the board, a savvy pastor might want to hand out an annotated bibliography of the 57 books read and reviewed while away, or a report on progress made on a dissertation, or some other tangible evidence of the work performed while away.

—*Victor D. Pentz*

5

Responsibility to Family Members

Virtually every Christian today would say the priorities in life are God first, family second, and career third. The problem is figuring out how to base our lives on our priorities. What does it *mean* to say God is first?

Perhaps the greatest problem with the "God first, family second, career third" perspective is that real-life situations can't be quite so neatly arranged. In practice, priorities can't be stacked like blocks. To put it another way, we can't watch three shows—no matter how good—at once. So we're constantly forced to ask, *Which channel do I turn to? And for how long?*

Instead of seeing God, church, and family as competing demands, it may be more helpful to imagine church and family as the two seats of a teeter-totter, and God as the fulcrum underneath. We aren't expected to sit in both seats simultaneously. The amount of weight we need to place on either side is determined by our God-measured priorities. But all of our efforts are undergirded by the Lord. He is the pivot point for both family life and church life.

Here are several ways to help fulfill our God-given responsibilities on the family side of the teeter-totter.

Strategies for Quality Control

Pastors know the feeling of "not being all there" even when they're there. No one is happy with a half-attentive zombie. Are there ways to improve the quality of our time with our families?

● *At the end of the day, bring home a healthy attitude.* That can begin before we ever leave the office. One pastor in Canada makes sure to work off some of his tension before he gets home. "Sitting at my desk all day is a sure way to guarantee I'll be edgy when I get home," he said. "So now I make sure I take a brisk walk sometime during the day. Even if I have a full day, I find one of my conferences can become a walking conversation, and we'll walk for an hour. That's a great tension reliever."

● *Make a mental switch on the way home.* Or, if that's not possible, do something once you arrive that signals to yourself and your family that you're home at last.

"We have a standing joke in our house: Dad isn't home until his tie comes off," says a minister in Indiana. "I usually shower, shave, and change my clothes when I get home. It refreshes me and helps me make the transition to family life."

● *Let the family know you've been thinking about them in your absence.* For some, this means recounting conversations during the day in which we were able to say a good word about some family member. Or perhaps it's something we give family members when we arrive home—an interesting story from the day's activity, or something more tangible.

A minister recalls, "When I was in seminary, my children were preschoolers. I stopped at the library every day on my way home and checked out one children's book to read to them. They knew I was thinking about them while I was away, and I was compelled to sit down with them as soon as I came home." This minister adds, "My temptation is to put my family on hold—at least until they 'snatch me back,' sometimes vigorously. But if I am too busy for my family right now, I will be too busy for them ten years from now. And they will learn that being too busy for one's family is acceptable, for I will have taught them that lesson myself."

● *Remember the family deserves at least the same care any other parishioner would get.* Being away from the church doesn't mean all responsibilities are over. Gordon MacDonald, pastor of Grace Chapel in Lexington, Massachusetts, learned this the hard way: "It used to be my habit to 'be comfortable' on Monday mornings and come to the breakfast table unshaved, unwashed, and generally undressed. One day my wife asked me, 'Why are you so carefully dressed and groomed for God and the congregation on Sunday?'

"I said, 'I want to offer them my best.'

" 'Then what are you saying to the family by the way you dress—or don't dress—on Monday?' she asked. Pow! She had me. From then on, whenever we're together as a couple or as a family, I'm careful to be as sharp and alert as possible in my mental attitude, dress, and common courtesies. Whatever I would offer to church members, I want to offer that and more, if possible, to my own family."

● *Control the telephone.* While it's not possible or desirable to eliminate people's access to us via the phone, some pastoral families have
found it beneficial to limit it at certain times.

"At times we turn the phone off when we're home at night so we're
not prisoners in our own house," says one pastor.

Another counsels: "We take the phone off the hook during supper,
or moments of family discussion, or periods when study or meditation are extremely necessary. In twenty years I can hardly recall a
moment when being instantly accessible was necessary. We have
learned not to let the phone become our master."

● *Include the family in aspects of the ministry.* A number of pastoral
families have mentioned that some of their best times were participating in ministry together—church socials, camps, even visitation.

"Last December, a single parent in our congregation who was struggling financially was *given* a Christmas by an anonymous donor," said
one pastor. "I was asked to deliver the food and gifts. I took the kids
along, and they still talk about the thrill of seeing the joy and gratitude of that mother and her girls."

Strategies for Quantity Control

Here's how some pastors approach the quantity question:

● *Long-range plans.* One of the false hopes of family life is that
because next month's calendar is currently fairly open, next month
will actually be less hectic than this month. It's tempting to say,
"Things should lighten up if we can just get through the next two
weeks."

Unfortunately, by the time we get through the next two weeks, the
two weeks after that have filled up, and we find ourselves looking
hopefully at the two weeks after *that.* It's a deadly plague known as
"creeping calendar commitments." This condition has driven many
pastoral families to plan family times at least a month ahead.

"Six to eight weeks in advance, we write in major blocks of various
sorts of private time," says one pastor. "We get these on the calendar
before the events of church life begin to appear."

How much family time realistically can be scheduled? This varies
depending on family and church situations, but several pastors use
the following rules of thumb:

—One night a week completely free of anything but family activities—a time for the family to be together.

—One night a month alone with the spouse—either an overnight
getaway or at least a leisurely dinner date.

—One event a month alone with each child—perhaps an outing to
the zoo or a museum, or even a simple breakfast at McDonald's.

Other families develop their own rhythms, but most affirm the value of planning the times they'll be together. If left to "whenever the calendar is blank," somehow those times mysteriously disappear.

● *The weekly routine.* Here are some examples of weekly routines:

"I try to be home on Monday and Friday evenings and for all meals, and to see the kids before they go to school in the mornings."

"I'm always home from 5:30 to 7:30 P.M. to share the meal with my family. Then I'm almost always home two of the five weekday evenings and on Saturday afternoon and evening. Once a week we go out to eat in a nearby city."

"We have a rule of thumb for our congregation that we try to have no more than three nights a week for church events. And I try to model that for the rest of the congregation. So everything has to fit into Sunday night, Wednesday night, and one other night. That

---

Children of Pastors

There's no guarantee *any* child—whether born into the home of a preacher, professor, plumber, or prince—will decide to live in a way that brings honor to God and joy to parents. Nor can pastoral couples guarantee even that their children will find church a place to enjoy rather than endure. But parents can help prepare children for church life. Here are several ways pastors can help kids have a healthy church experience.

Oriented to Reality

If our children are prepared, they aren't as likely to be jolted by difficult people or situations. We should try to teach our children that the church is not above hurts, criticism, and conflict. Children of ministry benefit from periodically being briefed on what to expect. Then when difficulties arise in church life, we can let them know that other people often see things differently—and that's okay.

The most important principle seems to be: Don't overstate the seriousness of the conflict. If we are to err, we should err on the side of *under*stating the problem. Children don't have the perspective their parents do.

Young Children

Here are several techniques when children are preschoolers or in the early elementary grades to give them a healthy church outlook:

● *Bedtime briefings.* Even preschoolers can benefit from briefings, if they're handled simply and with imagination. One church leader used Saturday night, or any night before a church event, to tell his girls about the good things to expect the next day—the friends they would see, the things they would do.

means we usually do some hospitality on Sunday night after the evening service. Wednesday is spent at church, and any committee meetings are the third night out. Of course, any social commitments would be a fourth night, but they don't count as church business."

While some pastors try to limit the nights of church activities, others work from the other direction; they schedule family time first. One pastor gets the family together once a week at breakfast to plan when they're going to be together that week.

Maximizing the Day Off

Another key strategy is the use of the day or day and a half off to which most pastors are entitled. Virtually every pastor gets a day off, or at least is *supposed* to take a day off. This is the church's conces-

---

● *Second home.* Because they're at the church so often, children will naturally begin to see it as their second home. When his children were young, Kent Hughes, pastor of College Church in Wheaton, Illinois, would give them the run of the church building. He wanted to show them the privileges that go along with the pastorate.

● *Warm associations.* We want to make sure our kids associate church with positive feelings. Part of this comes naturally through friends, caring teachers, and the positive perspective of parents.

Older Children

In the later elementary-school years and beyond, strategies change. Here are just two methods for parents of preteens and adolescents.

● *Involve them in church work.* One way is to pay them for office work. "I'll often bring one of my kids to the church when he or she needs to earn a little money," said John Yates of The Falls Church in

northern Virginia. "There's always some filing or sweeping that needs to be done, and I pay them out of my pocket."

● *Occasionally give them special treatment.* A number of pastors' kids recall their parents doing something especially for them, even amid the busyness of ministry. These leave profound and lasting marks on their attitudes toward ministry.

One man, now a pastor himself, remembers: "When I was about 5, my dad had a portrait taken of just him and me with our arms around each other, and he wrote across that portrait, PALS. He hung it in his study. I used to go in when he wasn't there and just stand and look at that picture. It meant more to me at that age than anything in life."

Perhaps the most important element, then, in helping children have a good experience in the church is not to prepare them for the bad times but to accentuate the good experiences.

—*Marshall Shelley*

sion to "balancing" time at home and time at church. How do pastors go about making the most of that time when that's all they have for personal rest, errands, household chores, and family time?

One question on which pastors differ is which day of the week to take off. Many take Monday, either because that's the day they're most tired or because that's the day decreed by the church. Others, however, say that's *not* the day to take, because the natural letdown after Sunday means they're not giving their families a day when they have normal energy. "If I'm going to be mildly depressive, I'm going to do it on company time," joked one pastor who does paperwork and administration on Mondays.

Many others take Saturday off because that's the day their kids are off from school. But that's not satisfactory for some because so many weddings fall on Saturday, and even when nothing is scheduled, they

Ministry's Effect on Marriage

California was devastated by a severe, early-morning earthquake on January 17, 1994. When an earthquake hits, everything is shaken loose. The same is true for the family life of a pastor who is undergoing stress in a ministry situation. When the stress builds, the whole family feels the tremors. As with an earthquake, the foundation and walls may crumble, bringing the whole house (or marriage) down around us.

Marriage Stressors

We humans like to feel we have control over our lives. Natural disasters like earthquakes and typhoons rudely dispel that illusion, and ministry, too, can do that to marriages. Consider some of the effects of this unique form of stress:

● *Lowered self-esteem* can result from ministry's impossible demands. Likewise, a spouse may experience a growing sense of insecurity, failure, and devaluation.

● *Excessive time demands* of ministry can function like an insatiable paramour. A spouse is left with feelings of abandonment and jealousy, and may demand attention and become critical.

● *A sense of isolation* stems from a lack of support other than from one's mate. The spouse often shares the loneliness and carries the burden of the minister's pain.

● *Increased vulnerability to sexual sin* may send signals to a spouse that bring fear and feelings of inadequacy as a partner.

● *Subtle encouragement toward hypocrisy* stems from a desire to keep a mask up and please every-

find themselves preoccupied with the next day's sermon and activities.

Others take another weekday off and try to take advantage of school holidays. One pastor reports taking occasional family outings even on school days. "Sometimes we'll take the kids out of school for a special family excursion. Last week we took Monday off and went to see a special display at the museum. You can't let school stand in the way of an education," he says with a grin. Nor in the way of a memorable family event.

Veteran pastor Donald Bubna, while at Salem Alliance Church in Oregon, had a policy that staff members would work 5 1/2 days a week. "We recommended they work six days one week and then take two days in a block the next week." That approach allowed for more rest and the opportunity for two-day getaways.

Wise use of the day off is one of the easiest ways to acquire a quan-

---

one. Then the spouse feels trapped in dishonesty and ultimately experiences an erosion of trust and respect for the mate's integrity.

● *Drained spiritual and emotional energy* leads to a spouse's development of fear, doubt, and uncertainty.

● *Failure to provide adequate financial support* can cause a spouse to become angry and bitter, while frequently feeling guilty about being "materialistic."

The most common structural damage in the ministry marriage will be a breakdown in the sense of togetherness. Partners become so overwhelmed by the stress that they can no longer find ways to be mutually supportive. Instead, each individual's natural defense system comes into play for self-protection. Typical defenses include quiet withdrawal, outbursts of anger, physical illness, anxiety attacks, depression, controlling behavior, or sexual acting out. The ministry itself may create barriers to facing the conflict that is tearing at the seams of the marriage fabric.

Hope for Healing

Fortunately, the effects of ministry pressures don't have to remain permanent. Couples can learn to control the stressful factors by developing greater awareness of one another's needs, balancing their lifestyles, and learning conflict-resolution methods.

A friend made an interesting comment after he experienced the California earthquake firsthand: "A lot of buildings in California are on a landfill. During a quake those areas become like quicksand; whole buildings collapse. Across the street, where the earth is solid ground, there may be only minor damage."

So it is with ministry marriages. When built on the solid rock of ongoing communication and intimacy, they can withstand the stress tremors. But when the foundation has been neglected and eroded, the entire structure may crumble.

—Louis McBurney

tity of time sufficient for quality moments. But another element of family life also deserves attention.

Vacations

What are the keys to a good vacation? The favorite places to go and things to see will depend upon the family, but pastors have found some principles important in making vacations a building time for the family.

● *Remember that "working vacation" is a contradiction in terms.* Yes, many pastors take families to conferences and speaking appointments, and these can be enjoyable for the family, but they're not always the best time together.

"I have three weeks of vacation, and I decided a few years ago not to take *any* work with me," says a Colorado Springs pastor. "On earlier vacations, I always felt vaguely guilty that I wasn't getting to the books I'd brought along. I wasn't really on vacation at all. Now I take no work along. I even tell the church, 'Please don't call me. Well, if the church burns down—maybe. Just get my books and illustration file out, and *then* you can give me a call.' "

● *Learn to enjoy strategic recreation.* "I've learned to match my recreational pursuits with family needs," one minister explains. "I saw early in my ministry that I could not pursue a recreational life with friends and still have time to pursue a *second* recreational life with my children. Therefore I chose early in life to do things for recreation that my children could join me in doing: canoeing, camping, hiking, and other activities where our time together could be maximized.

"I fear too many fathers spend time on tennis courts and golf courses, and in health spas, and then wonder why they never have prime time with their children."

● *Learn to enjoy the time you do have.* Pastor's wife Dreama Plybon Love tells about her rude awakening to the demands of ministry. She and her husband decided to get back early and spend their last day of vacation relaxing at home.

"It sounded like such a good idea—sleep late, enjoy breakfast out, go for a leisurely walk," she wrote in *Partnership* magazine. "We were in bed asleep, having returned home at 4 A.M., when the doorbell woke us. My husband put on his robe and stumbled to the door. A member of our church was waiting. He looked quite somber.

" 'Sorry to bother you, but yesterday my wife had surgery for breast cancer. She would like to see you at the hospital.'

"At first I felt genuine compassion, but gradually concern turned to resentment at the intrusion. Couldn't we have this one day just for ourselves? Our vacation had been hectic, crowded with friends and family. We needed this time together. Was I being selfish, even cruel, to want to extend our vacation in light of this man's need?"

She and her husband had been married only six months at the time, and already she was struggling with the questions: *Must we always make choices between marriage and ministry? Can I not love my husband and serve my God at the same time?* What eventually happened on that cherished and curtailed vacation day?

"It wasn't so bad. We stopped at the florist and made a hospital call, but we were still able to take that long, leisurely walk. As we walked, we planned *next* year's vacation, and I think next time we'll give ourselves a full week alone—before we come back home."

Freedom to Choose

Do the demands of ministry force us to overactivity? Not according to one pastor, who reminds us of our ability to determine what path we will choose. "I've heard so many times, 'Because of the demands of ministry, I neglected my family.' It sounds as if pastors were somehow compelled to. For solo pastors and senior pastors especially, I found that an invalid excuse. Ultimately we decide how much we're going to give. The challenge is to fulfill both ministry and family roles, but we have the freedom to find creative ways to do that. Perhaps we'll have to be out every night some weeks. But we can often grab lunch or spend even a full morning with our spouse. We may have to cut out something else, but we have that freedom."

At times, however, this freedom has to be asserted with emotional resolve. William Tully, while rector of St. Columba's Episcopal Church in Washington, D.C., described one such painful incident in an article that appeared in the *Washington Post:*

> Most afternoons I break off work and meet my sons' school bus. This is my key family obligation, since I end up working most evenings and at least half of every weekend. (My wife's job downtown doesn't allow her the afternoon flexibility.)
>
> One recent afternoon, while my son Jonah, 8, took part in an afternoon choir rehearsal, his 12-year-old brother, Adam, and I found time for a long-postponed (by me) game of catch. I had impressed him—and assuaged my guilt—by having ball gloves all ready to go. Just as we got into our game on the church lawn, a regular parish visitor—a down-and-out street alcoholic—showed up and wanted a handout. Many times before and since, St. Columba's has helped this man. But since the other clergy who assist me were away that day and the secretaries in no position to help him, he stood on the sidewalk and demanded I pay attention to him.
>
> "I'm not working now. Can't you see?"
>
> The booze in him made him belligerent. "What kind of priest are you, man? You won't even listen to my story."

I ran up for a pop fly that Adam had expertly launched.

"That's right. Besides, I've heard it before. I'm sorry, you'll have to try somewhere else or come back another time."

He turned to go back to the parish office and unleashed a string of obscenities.

"Get out," I shouted. "If you ever want my help again, you'll just have to move on."

It was then I realized that several passersby, probably fresh off the Metro at Tenleytown, had stopped to watch. A few choir mothers had come to the church steps to behold their rector having a tantrum.

I still haven't sorted out the rush of conflicting feelings I experienced then. I did feel strongly that my family came before my vocation. I was also composing fantasy headlines in my head: BUSY NORTHWEST D.C. PRIEST FORGETS SAMARITAN, SHUNS POOR MAN I imagined parishioners listening skeptically when words like *charity* and *sacrifice* pop up in sermons. Still I shagged my last pop fly that day knowing that ethical choices are always messy, that my strong suit is not social justice, and that the words I treasured most that day were, "Thanks, Dad. Great game."

—*Marshall Shelley*

Resources

Kimmel, T. 1987. The little house on the freeway. Portland, Ore.: Multnomah.

Miller, K. and K. 1994. More than you and me. Colorado Springs: Focus on the Family.

Shelley, M. 1988. The healthy hectic home. Dallas: Word.

Shelley, M. 1990. Keeping your kids Christian. Ann Arbor, Mich.: Servant.

A Spouse's Choice of Role

Few roles are as public as a minister's. Consequently, spouses also live in, or near, the limelight. If a partner works for IBM, one may never see the people he or she works with. However, when one's spouse is employed by the people of the church, it is something quite different.

Fortunately, we've come a long way toward allowing ministers' spouses to write their own role definitions, based on a personal assessment of abilities, skills, personality, energy level, and family needs. Yet there are still at least two critical issues a minister's spouse must face: time and criticism.

Prioritizing Time

Deciding how one will spend the hours of the day is complicated by the fact that, for ministers, work equals service to God. Spouses who choose a more low-profile, less-involved approach to their role often feel a great deal of guilt, almost as though they have said no to God. A wise minister is one who is sensitive to the propensity of his or her spouse to take on guilt.

Ministers' spouses are not unique in the multitude of options available to them for investing their time. Everyone has to make such choices, but not everyone has as many opportunities for meaningful interaction with people. Events in parishioners' lives have ways of bonding them with their minister and his or her family. The minister is there for them in births, deaths, marriages, sicknesses, conversions, and dedications. Consequently, the minister and spouse have the potential for developing strong ties with many people. This means they may also feel the need to be available and answerable to many people.

Ministry couples who avoid burnout are the ones who have learned this important fact: No matter how long your tenure with any one congregation, your relationship with the people in that congregation is temporary, compared to your relationship with your family. Choices regarding how both minister and spouse spend their time should reflect this fact. It is particularly appropriate for spouses to keep this in mind, because they are usually the ones trying to juggle another job along with family and church responsibilities.

Handling Criticism

Everyone has an opinion about how public people should, or should not, conduct themselves. Ministers' spouses may well internalize criticism more readily, because they are watching a loved one being hurt. So ministers' spouses must know what to do with criticism. They must learn how not to internalize all negative critiques, not to immediately draw the conclusion that "it's our fault."

On the other hand, "it's all their problem" is an equally dangerous position. A wise alternative would be to ask these questions regarding the criticism: Is it coming from someone I trust? From someone who knows me and my family well? Is there more than one voice of critique saying the same thing? Have I heard this before?

The challenge of a minister's spouse are many. So are the rewards. A wise spouse chooses to focus not on the negatives of being married to a minister but on the positives. As with anything in life, contentment comes not only from doing what we enjoy, but also in learning to enjoy whatever it is that life calls upon us to do.

—*Ruth Senter*

Clergy Divorce

Divorced pastors often say their greatest pain is the loneliness and abandonment they feel. "I feel like a leper," commented one, "a total outcast from the community." Without encouraging or condoning divorce, we can express Christian love and compassion to a colleague considering divorce or struggling with its aftermath.

Helping Clergy Cope

The Christian community feels most keenly the impact of clergy divorce. Since the minister is looked upon as a model for Christian family life—including marital permanence—divorce causes a sense of betrayal within a church and may polarize the congregation. On the personal level, dealing with clergy divorce is much like dealing with death. Pastors will be angry, hurt, and sad. They need permission to express a wide range of feelings, and a time of mourning should be expected.

Recently divorced pastors (or those considering divorce) can use help to find healing and redirection. Here are some things we can do to help:

● *Take preventative steps when possible.* If we are close enough to our colleague's spiritual life, we'll often see marital trouble brewing. We can help our friend acknowledge his or her need for marriage counseling. Many pastors fear rejection if they admit their marriage isn't perfect. Thus it's good to refrain from judgmental attitudes and simple solutions.

● *Help mediate a period of separation.* Before a divorce, separation may be necessary to achieve relief from stress. But pastor and spouse must maintain contact, probably in the presence of a mediator. As mediators, we can help the couple explore alternatives to destructive confrontation, while discouraging well-meaning colleagues or parishioners from taking sides.

● *Deal with our own anger and anxiety.* We must lay aside our fears and come alongside rather than abandon the distressed pastor. Incredibly, fellow clergy tend to disappear at these times, as though they might be declared guilty by association. Yet the divorced pastor and his or her spouse and children need continued support. Divorce is not the unpardonable sin. Each person involved will have to cope with a severe sense of failure, a drastic change in lifestyle, embarrassment and confusion, probable depression, and tremendous financial stress. Only time, love, and friendship can bring healing to these deep wounds.

● *Be available for career guidance.* The divorced pastor needs to explore, with a trusted friend, his or her future in ministry. Many Christians contend there can be no simple formula for determining whether a divorce disqualifies a person from ministry. Circumstances vary considerably, as do the unique responses of particular churches. In some cases, it would seem impossible to retain effectiveness in service; in other cases, resignation might seem unthinkable to everyone involved.

—*Louis McBurney*

6

Responsibility to Self

Early in ministry, as conscientious pastors, we tend to monitor our lives closely in important areas, continually checking two gauges on the dashboard of our lives. We keep a close eye on the spiritual gauge, asking ourselves, *How am I doing spiritually?* Since we know that apart from Christ, we can do nothing, we don't want our life's efforts to be burned up because they were done merely through human effort, clever tactics, or gimmickry. Ever conscientious, we are gripped by the fact that we must operate in the power of the Holy Spirit.

To keep the spiritual gauges where they need to be, many have committed themselves to the spiritual disciplines: journaling, fasting, solitude, sacrifice, study, and others.

If we're at all aware of reality, we also monitor the physical gauge—*How am I doing physically?* We've been impressed by the fact that if we push our bodies too hard, over time we will experience a physical breakdown or psychosomatic complications associated with high stress.

If we don't exercise, eat properly, and rest, we will offer the Lord far less than the full energy we have the potential of giving. The Holy Spirit tugs at us to be wholly available—mind, soul, and body—for the work to which he has called us.

Consequently, many pastors have rightfully committed themselves to physical disciplines such as running and weight lifting. They carefully watch what they eat and receive regular medical check-ups.

61

There's More to It

Since these spiritual and physical gauges—the only two many monitor—usually signal "go" for healthy, young pastors, they often push themselves as hard and fast as possible. But then a different part of their engines begins to misfire.

That's what happened to me. While preparing for a particularly difficult series of sermons, the message that week wouldn't come together. No matter how hard I tried, no ideas seemed worth saying. Suddenly I found myself sobbing, with my head on my desk.

I've always been more analytic than emotional, so when I stopped crying, I said to myself, *I don't think that was natural.* People more aware of their feelings might have known what was wrong, but I didn't. All I knew was, *Something's not right with me, and I don't even have time now to think about it. I'll have to journal about this tomorrow.*

Most of us have learned to force our thoughts back to the sermon and manage somehow to put something together for the service. But we begin to wonder: *Am I falling apart in some area spiritually?* Our gauges probably say no. We're practicing our disciplines regularly and don't particularly sense spiritual malaise. Physically, we're doing okay. So we conclude that maybe this is a midlife crisis, a phase we simply have to endure. But when four or five similar incidents happen in within a few weeks' time, it begins to signal that the anxiety and frustration cannot be ignored.

The next step might be a feeling of being vulnerable—extremely temptable—in areas in which we haven't felt vulnerable for a long time. Eventually the idea of continuing on in ministry seems nothing but a tremendous burden. Where did the joy go? *Maybe God is calling me to a different kind of work,* we think. *Maybe I need a change of calling.*

What is wrong with this picture? We can put so much stock in the spiritual and physical gauges—neither of which indicate a problem—that we may become blind to one further gauge.

The Overlooked Gauge

Many of us overlook an important gauge essential to healthy ministry—emotional strength. Throughout any given week of ministry, some activities drain our emotional reservoirs. I call these experiences IMAS—Intensive Ministry Activities.

An IMA may be a confrontation, an intense counseling session, an exhausting teaching session, or a board meeting about significant financial decisions. Preparing and delivering a message on a sensitive topic, which requires extensive research and thought, for instance, wears me down. The common denominator of these activities is that they sap our strength, even in only a few hours.

Every leader constantly takes on IMAS. What we must realize, how-ever, is that we can gauge the degree of their impact on us. There is no need to be oblivious to the intense drain IMAS cause.

For example, many times while driving home from church, I used to feel thin in my spirit. Sensing something was wrong, I would exam-ine my two trusted gauges, but they seemed fine. But something indeed was wrong. I needed that third gauge—an emotional moni-tor—to determine my ministry fitness.

Reading the Emotional Gauge

What we pastors need to do is install an emotional gauge in the cen-ter of the dashboard and learn how to read it. Our goal is to monitor our emotional resources so we don't reach that point. What signals do we look for?

● *The desire to escape.* If we drive away from a ministry activity and say, "It would be fine if I never did that again," that's a warning sig-nal. Something is wrong when we look at people as interruptions or see ministry as a chore.

● *Family aversion.* Another indicator: On the way home, do we con-sciously hope our spouse isn't having a problem and our kids don't want anything from us? That's a sign we don't have enough left to give. When we hope that the precious people in our life can exist with-out us, that may be a sign of trouble.

● *Attitude toward the disciplines.* A third check is how we approach the spiritual disciplines. Many pastors journal and write their prayers. Let's say for months we find ourselves saying, day after day, "I don't have the energy to do this." We journal anyway, but more mechani-cally than authentically. Most of us dislike ourselves when our Chris-tianity is on autopilot.

Each person has to find the warning signals for his or her own life. But after an intense ministry activity, it helps to ask ourselves some questions:

—*Am I out of gas emotionally?*

—*Can I not stand the thought of relating to people right now?*

—*Do I feel the urge to take a long walk with no destination in mind?*

—*Am I feeling the need to go home, put on music, and let the Lord recharge my emotional batteries?*

Recharging the Emotional Reserves

When our emotional fuel is low, we can't do an Indy pit stop and refuel quickly. Our emotional reserves can be compared to a car bat-tery. If we sit in a parking lot and run all our car's accessories—radio, headlights, heater, horn, rear defogger, power windows—we can probably sap that battery in about ten minutes. After that massive drain, suppose we then take the battery to a service station and say, "I'd like this battery charged. I'll be back to pick it up in ten minutes."

What would the attendant tell us? "No, we're going to put the battery on our overnight charger. It's going to take seven or eight hours to bring it all the way back up." It has to be recharged slowly or else the battery will be damaged.

A slow, consistent charge is the best way to bring a battery back to full power. Likewise, to recuperate properly from an emotionally draining activity takes time.

That can feel frustrating, especially when we look at our average week and discover that almost every day has an IMA. We likely finish most weeks with an emotional deficit. Then, let's say, our family wants us to plan exciting weekend activities for them. We begin to feel

Stress and Mental Health

A recent study funded by the National Institute of Mental Health reports that 50 percent of people who have had frequent bouts with depression also have enlarged adrenal glands. Thus, there is an important connection in our bodies between stress and mental health. To ignore our stress is to court emotional disaster.

Sources of Stress

People stress us! Pastors don't stress out primarily because computers break down or earthquakes rattle the rafters. The most significant stressors for pastors spring from the conflicts, crises, and connivances of ordinary human beings.

Stress is the body's response to an emergency, and it mobilizes us for action. Under stress, the rate of adrenaline production jumps sky-high, sleep becomes disturbed, and our whole system becomes aroused to action. Normally this is healthy, but prolonged, repeated arousal of this emergency system eventually leads to stress disease—ulcers, high blood pressure, headaches, eventual heart disease, and many emotional disorders, including depression.

What determines whether our stress reactions are normal or not? Several factors affect how our bodies handle stress, such as: the intensity and duration of the stress, the level of coping response, and the level of social support available. But one thing is clear: The more our bodies perceive that we are in control, the less damaging the stress.

To strengthen resistance to stress, we can follow three key guidelines:

as if we're going to overload our circuitry and one day find ourselves in the proverbial fetal position.

So, we need to recharge. Some people recharge by running, others by taking a bath, others by reading, others by listening to music. Usually it means doing something totally unrelated to ministry—golfing, motorcycling, woodcarving. The important thing is to build a ministry schedule that allows adequate time for emotional recharging.

Returning to Our Gift Areas

Here's another principle about maintaining emotional resources for ministry: The use of our major spiritual gift breathes life back into us. When we have identified our spiritual gifts and use them under the direction of Jesus Christ, we make a difference. We feel the affirma-

---

● *Try to anticipate stressful events.* Research shows that if we can predict a stressor, our bodies experience less panic. Being able to predict a stressor also means that we can immediately take steps to control or eliminate it.

● *Resolve stressful situations quickly.* Don't let the sun go down on conflicts or unresolved disputes. This relieves the body's high state of arousal created by anger.

● *Build a strong personal support system.* Every pastor needs a small, trusting group of friends. People with strong social ties reduce stress symptoms and increase their life expectancies. A support group gives us one absolutely essential stress-busting benefit: a listening ear.

Improved Coping

A pastor can improve his or her stress-coping response in several ways. Here are a few suggestions:

● *Respond to stressors with direct action.* This means we must build our assertiveness skills and avoid denial. It's healthy to keep in con-

trol, never surrendering control to anyone—except God.

● *Learn a good relaxation exercise.* Many good relaxation-response books offer such exercises. We can benefit from learning about and practicing daily some form of contemplative prayer.

● *Set up internal boundaries for the work day.* Our bodies are like clocks. We can tell them, by our attitude, when to start and when to finish our work. If we don't regulate ourselves, adrenaline continues to pump and do its physical destruction.

● *Get enough sleep.* Anyone who must use an alarm clock to wake up is not getting enough sleep. Sleep deprivation keeps our minds fuzzy, our tolerance for frustration low, and our susceptibility to headaches high.

● *Enjoy the journey.* By focusing more on the process of ministry and less on achieving personal goals, we can keep stress under control.

—Archibald D. Hart

tion of God, and many times we feel more energized *after* service than before.

Conversely, serving outside our gift areas tends to drain us. If I were asked to sing or assist with accounting, it would be a long hike uphill. I wouldn't feel the affirmation of the Spirit, because I wouldn't be serving as I have been gifted and called. This is why many people bail out of various types of Christian service: they aren't in the right yoke.

The principle is self-evident, but unwittingly we can allow ourselves to be pulled away from using our strongest gifts. For example, about the time Willow Creek Community Church was founded, I analyzed my spiritual gifts. My top gift was leadership. My second gift was evangelism. Down the list were teaching and administration. I asked two people with well-developed teaching gifts to be primary teachers for the new congregation. Both people declined to teach, however,

Vacations and Time Off

Sometimes ministers feel like Linus when he said of his security blanket, "Only one yard of outing flannel stands between me and a nervous breakdown." When that happens, it's time to take a break, do something different—take a vacation.

The Five Getaways

Tim Hansel's thinking about vacations is helpful. In *When I Relax I Feel Guilty* (Cook 1979), he describes not one kind of vacation but five.

● *Supermaxi vacations*—a sabbatical, a vacation coupled with conference time, or some other long-term break from ministry.

● *Maxi vacations* are what most of us think of when we hear the word *vacation*.

● *Mini vacations* are what Hansel calls one Sabbath day per week.

● *Midget vacations* "fall along the same idea, but take even less time,"

Hansel writes. "We're called not only to structure sufficient time into each week for rest, recreation, and worship—but also into each day."

● *Minute vacations* are sixty-second versions of "the pause that refreshes" during the day. Says Hansel, "Minute vacations are the time of quiet miracles."

We're all well-acquainted with the maxi vacation and the mini vacation. The other three, however, at first seem either odd or completely out of reach. But they are possible.

Midget and Minute Vacations

The secret of the midget vacation is that *doing* something, be it ever so small, is critical for refreshment. Most of us, when we're discouraged, want to sit and think about it, to stew in it. "I've found a sure cure for mild depression," says Fred Smith, a Christian business execu-

and we had already set our starting date. I remember thinking, *Okay, God, I'll start as primary teacher, but please bring a teacher and let me lead and evangelize as you have gifted and called me to do.*

Then, when I hit emotional bottom, I did another gift analysis. The results were exactly the same as 18 years before: leadership and evangelism above teaching and administration. But as I thought about my weekly responsibilities, I realized I was using teaching as though it were my top gift. Seldom was I devoting time to leadership or to evangelism activities.

I have talked with well-respected teachers across the country, and I have never had one tell me that it takes more than five to ten hours to prepare a sermon. They have strong teaching gifts, so it comes naturally and quickly to them. If I, on the other hand, don't devote twenty hours to a message, I'm embarrassed by the result.

---

tive, "and a guarantee for its continuation. The guarantee for its continuation is inactivity. The sure cure for its cessation is activity."

Here are ways to keep refreshed and on the move during down times in ministry:

● Shutting up oneself at home and listening to sacred music.

● Working around the home.

● Wearing blue jeans, so we feel like we're having a day off.

● Having a guest preacher so we get a Sunday out of the pulpit.

Rest Without Guilt

For some, the tough hurdle in taking a break or being with family is not so much the external difficulties of making sure things will be taken care of while we're gone, but the internal difficulty of guilt. We think of the desk not cleared, the phone messages yet to return, and the people we really ought to visit, and then we hear in our conscience the words of Charles Spurgeon: "The man who does not make hard work of his ministry will find it very hard

work to answer for his idleness at the last great day."

But great work, fruitful work, comes only through rest and refreshment. It may seem, when we head for the YMCA, the retreat center, the restaurant, that we are wasting time. It's tempting to think how much we could be doing if we weren't sitting at our son's baseball game. But when we've spent time with our God, our family, and our friends simply as a person—and have been loved—we return with an inner vitality that not only fuels our work but is our work.

We may shudder when we think of the tireless output of John Wesley, who during his 52 years of itinerant ministry traveled over 200,000 miles—mostly by foot or horseback—and preached some 40,000 sermons. But Wesley knew a secret: "Though I am always in haste, I am never in a hurry, because I never undertake more work than I can go through with calmness of spirit."

—*Kevin A. Miller*

In order to adequately prepare my messages, I had delegated away almost all leadership responsibilities. And too often in elder or staff meetings, I was mentally preoccupied with my next message. My life became consumed by the use of my teaching gift, which wasn't my most fruitful or fulfilling ministry. Yet people kept saying, "Great message, Bill," and I wrongfully allowed their affirmation to thwart my better judgment.

Once I realized this, we implemented a team-teaching approach at Willow Creek. It was well-received by the congregation and allowed me to provide stronger leadership in several areas. As a result, I felt much more fulfilled.

As a result of freeing up time, we may find new opportunities for our first-level gifts. That happened with me not long after we had reorganized our ministry. I met with three guys at an airport—one a Christian and the other two his best friends, whom he was trying to lead to Christ. As we talked, I could feel the Holy Spirit at work. After our conversation ended, I ran to my gate, and I almost started crying. *I love one-on-one evangelism,* I thought. *This is such a big part of who I am. I've forgotten how thrilling it is to share Christ informally with lost people.*

If we are using a third- or fourth-level gift a lot, we shouldn't be surprised if we don't feel emotional energy for ministry. We operate with more energy when we're able to exercise our primary gifts. God knew what he was doing as he distributed gifts for service.

Balancing the Eternal and the Earthly

Finally, we Christian leaders have to strike a delicate balance between involvement in the eternal and involvement in the mundane. The needs of the church can inexorably squeeze out our earthly pursuits. We can become consumed with the eternal. From early morning until we fall asleep at night, barely one moment of time is not related to something eternal. The mounting pressures keep us from exercising. If we do make time to work out, we read theological journals while we're cycling. When we pump weights, we listen to tapes or think of illustrations for a message. Eventually, the eternal co-opts our daily routines.

In the Bible, after Jesus ministered or delivered an important discourse, usually we find a phrase like this: "Then Jesus and the disciples went from Judea into Galilee." Those small phrases are highly significant. Such journeys were usually many miles long, and most of the time, Jesus and his disciples walked.

What happens on a long walk? Guys tell a few jokes, stop and rest awhile, pick some fruit and drink some water, take a nap in the afternoon, and then keep going. All this time, emotional reserves are being replenished, and the delicate balance between the eternal and the mundane is being restored.

It's a different world today. Put car phones and fax machines and jet airplanes into the system, and suddenly the naturally forced times for the mundane disappear. As a result, we must renew our commitment to integrate into life more activities that are not church related—golfing, water-skiing, making music. If we don't schedule these things—if we wait until our calendar opens up—they won't happen. In Christian ministry the needs of people are endless.

Our goal should be to monitor our spiritual, physical, and emotional resources so we can minister, by God's grace, for a lifetime. God wants us to live so as to finish the race we've started. That's the challenge of every Christian leader. And monitoring all three gauges—spiritual, physical, and emotional—plays an important part in our longevity in the role of pastor.

—Bill Hybels

Resource

O'Neill, J. 1994. The paradox of success. New York: Putnam.

Handling Disappointments

Defeats and disappointments should not surprise us, but they usually do. Most painful are the defeats of rejection, when people leave the church. Or when a major program idea bombs. Or when a spreading rumor is increasingly believed and can't be stopped.

Disappointments can be tough, but they don't have to be terminal. Here are several ways to soften the inevitable blows of defeat.

Anatomy of Defeats

Rather than wallowing in defeats, it's better to try to analyze them. That helps us get up after being down, and feel somewhat in control as we see what went wrong and how to do things differently in the future.

Sometimes defeat is a result of our not leading hard enough. Other times, an early negative vote or thumbs down on a project often points to a dearth of research and development; we haven't done our homework.

We sometimes present ideas that end up defeated because they were sprung on the church, catching many by surprise. People hate surprises. In some cases, though, what seems like a defeat is simply a necessary loss. Sometimes it's a case of personality conflict or an honest difference of opinion.

Graceful Defeats

Sometimes the difference between a professional and a rookie is the grace with which he or she handles defeats. Here are a few lessons to help us do a better job:

● *Get up.* Mike Singletary, former linebacker for the Chicago Bears, was famous for initially getting blocked out of a play but still making the tackle. What happened after he got knocked down on the first block?

He got up.

There's a lot to say for good, old-fashioned grit. It's probably healthy to take five minutes a day to worry and then get up and do something else.

● *Switch to something fun.* The world has not ended with any of the defeats we've endured, so one helpful practice is to go play. For me that usually means basketball or jogging or a walk with my wife; for others it's reading a good book or listening to music. Breaks are a big help and certainly intended by God for our mental health.

● *Find a shoulder to cry on.* It's good to share some of our frustrations with others. Maybe that person will be someone on staff with whom we can laugh as well as share our pain. Or maybe it's a pastor friend of long duration with whom we can talk through the defeat or

vent some of our frustration.

The Prevent Defense

Some disappointments can be avoided. Let me mention two keys to preventing future defeats.

● *Don't expect most people to share the vision.* For example, one of my greatest frustrations has been getting lay leaders to share my vision for the church. I've found myself agitated that I was the one always promoting, pulling, dragging, and educating to bring them up to speed on church vision. But then one day it hit me: Don spent 50 or 60 hours a week farming, David spent 50 or so teaching college and administering, and Robert spent at least 50 running a small computer business. But I spend my waking hours each week thinking about church. No wonder these men can't match my enthusiasm, passion, and vision for ministry.

● *Don't take votes that won't pass.* The wise pastor will avoid unnecessary losses at the board level. "Let's pray about this decision and vote on it next month," a pastor I once worked with would often say about decisions teetering precariously at a board meeting. His wise example is something we all do well to make our common practice.

—Knute Larson

Addictions

Pastors and church leaders are not exempt from addictive diseases, and the denial that exists in many of these individuals is unusually strong. Many attempt to hide their addictions behind a screen of super-spirituality. Others sincerely desire to change but find themselves caught in a deadly cycle of improper behavior, followed by self-disgust and desperate attempts to atone for themselves.

How Ministers Struggle

Here are some of the major addictions with which many pastors and church leaders struggle:

● *Co-dependency.* The co-dependent says, "Let me help *you* because I don't know how to help *me.*" Individuals attempt to obtain inner self-worth through external relationships. This helps them avoid looking at root causes and conditions in themselves that keep them from healthy relationships. Co-dependency is one of the most difficult addictions to confront in church leaders.

● *Chemical addictions.* Substance-abuse problems begin long before the actual chemical use. Chemicals are used to cope with life by numbing emotions that are producing inner pain, such as fear, sadness, or anger. Severity depends on the length of time and amount of chemicals used.

● *Workaholism.* Workaholism, which makes one think, *I'm too busy to deal with my feelings,* is an effective way to avoid handling emotional problems. The "work" is presumably for the benefit of the church. The compulsion to be busy at work makes it impossible to have deep and meaningful relationships, even with God.

● *Sex addictions.* Pastors may use these addictions to validate an irrational core belief that says, *I am basically a bad and unworthy person.* To commit illicit sex acts or to engage in pornography is a sure way to prove the shaming messages that were ingrained into the person's subconscious years earlier. Also, the thrill of rebellious behavior actually creates a chemical change in the brain. However, once the acts are committed, the person is left with feelings of self-disgust.

● *Eating disorders.* Victims of these addictions think, *I will have control over one area of my life.* Anorexia is punishing the body by withholding nourishment. Bulimia is binging on food, then purging through vomiting—satisfying a strong need to be in control. Compulsive overeating is feeding feelings in order to dull their pain.

● *Gambling.* This addiction offers people the chance to say about themselves, *You're a success.* The search for this illusive feeling often drives the individual to personal and spiritual bankruptcy. This addiction acts like chemical addiction: the surge of norepinephrine in the brain (similar to cocaine's "buzz") is a strong driving force.

How to Intervene

Many addicted ministers are not confronted, even though signs and symptoms become increasingly evident: changes in personality, physical appearance, and job performance. As in dysfunctional families, the congregation's fear most often produces mass denial, because, after all, this is our pastor! Fearing confrontation, congregations withhold possible life-saving measures, such as intervention.

Intervention should take place in a carefully rehearsed, well-prepared manner. Church leaders can bring the pastor into a surprise meeting and, with care and tough love, cause him or her to focus on the negative effects of the destructive behavior and offer a set of alternatives as a means of healing.

Everyone involved must realize that recovery takes time. The saying that "it's fifty miles into the woods and fifty miles out" is true. Time, faith, patience, love, understanding, and education are the elements needed when a church leader is offered the journey toward recovery by a loving congregation. Then the recovering minister must be willing to continue the journey through the sanctification process, with support and direction from the Holy Spirit and other victorious children of God.

—H. Gordon Weekley

7

Time Management

Many discussions of the pastor's task start with the advice to plan one's work. This sounds eminently plausible. The only thing wrong with it is that it rarely works. The plans always remain on paper, always remain good intentions. They seldom turn into achievement.

Effective pastors, in my observation, do not start with their tasks. They start with their time. And they do not start out with planning. They start by finding out where their time actually goes. Then they attempt to manage their time and to cut back unproductive demands on their time. Finally they consolidate their discretionary time into the largest possible continuing units. This three-step process of recording time, managing time, and consolidating time is the foundation of effective time management for pastors.

Recording Time

We have realized for the better part of a century that one has to record time before one can know where it goes and before, in turn, one can attempt to manage it. That is, we have known this in respect to manual work, skilled and unskilled, since scientific management around 1900 began to record the time it takes for a specific piece of manual work to be done. Hardly any country today is so far behind in industrial methods as not to time systematically the operations of manual workers.

We have applied this knowledge to the work where time does not greatly matter; that is, where the difference between time-use and time-waste is primarily efficiency and costs. But we have not applied it to the work that matters increasingly and that particularly has to cope with time: the work of the knowledge worker and especially of the pastor. Here the difference between time-use and time-waste is effectiveness and results.

The first step toward pastoral time-management effectiveness is therefore to record actual time-use. The specific method in which the record is put together need not concern us here. There are pastors who keep such a time log themselves. Others have their secretaries do it for them. The important thing is that it gets done and that the record is made in real time, that is, at the time of the event itself, rather than later on from memory.

A good many effective pastors keep such a log continuously and look at it regularly every month. At a minimum, effective pastors have the log run on themselves for three to four weeks at a stretch, twice a year or so on a regular schedule. After each such sample, they rethink and rework their schedule. But six months later, they invariably find they have drifted into wasting their time on trivia. Time-use does improve with practice. But only constant efforts at managing time can prevent drifting.

Managing Time

Systematic time management is therefore the next step. One has to find the nonproductive, time-wasting activities and get rid of them if one possibly can. This requires asking a number of diagnostic questions.

● The first question to ask is: "What would happen if this were *not* done at all?" If the answer is, "Nothing would happen," obviously the conclusion is to stop doing it. It is amazing how many things busy pastors are doing that never will be missed.

● The next question is: "Which of the activities on my time log could be done by somebody else just as well, if not better?" Ministers, as a rule, don't know how to delegate. They think delegation means turning something over to somebody else. That's not delegation; that's abdication. In order to delegate, we decide, "What is the job? What are the objectives? What are the minimal standards? What are the needed results?" Then we seek someone else to do it. That's management.

● The third question is: "Am I wasting the time of my staff members?" A common cause of time-waste is largely under pastors' control and can be eliminated by them: others' time the pastors waste. There is no one symptom for this. But there is still a simple way to find out. That is to ask other people. Effective pastors have learned to ask systematically and without coyness, "What do I do that wastes your time without contributing to your effectiveness?" To ask this question—

without being afraid of the truth—is a mark of an effective pastor.

● The fourth question is: "What time-wasters flow from lack of a system or lack of foresight?" The symptom to look for is the recurrent "crisis," the crisis that comes back year after year. A crisis that recurs a second time is a crisis that must not occur again.

A recurrent crisis should always have been foreseen. It can therefore either be prevented or reduced to a routine that staff members or other church workers can manage. The definition of a "routine" is that it makes unskilled people without judgment capable of doing what it took near-genius to do before; for a routine puts down in systematic, step-by-step form what a very able person learned in surmounting yesterday's crisis. The recurrent crisis is typically a symptom of laziness.

● The fifth question is: "Am I attending an excess of meetings?" Meetings are by definition a concession to deficient organization, for one either meets or one works. One cannot do both at the same time. In an ideally designed structure (which in a changing world is, of course, only a dream) there would be no meetings. Everybody would know what he or she needs to know to do the job. We meet because people holding different jobs have to cooperate to get a specific task done. There will always be more than enough meetings. But if pastors in an organization spend more than a fairly small part of their time in meetings, it is a sure sign of malorganization.

Many pastors know all about these unproductive and unnecessary time demands, yet they hesitate to prune them, fearing they may cut out something important by mistake. But this mistake, if made, can be speedily corrected. If one prunes too harshly, one usually finds out soon enough.

Every new President of the United States accepts too many invitations at first. Then it dawns on him that he has other work to do and that most of these invitations do not add to his effectiveness. Thereupon, he usually cuts back too sharply and becomes inaccessible. A few weeks or months later, however, he is being told by the press and the radio that he is "losing touch." Then he usually finds the right balance between being exploited without effectiveness and using public appearances as his national pulpit.

In fact, there is not much risk that we will cut back too much. We usually tend to overrate rather than underrate our importance and to conclude that far too many things can be done only by ourselves. Even very effective pastors still do a great many unnecessary, unproductive things.

These five diagnostic questions deal with unproductive and time-consuming activities over which every pastor has some control. Every knowledge worker and pastor should ask them. Then they can move on to the task of consolidating time for the most important tasks.

Consolidating Time

Pastors who record and analyze their time and then attempt to manage it can determine how much they have for their important tasks. How much time is there that is discretionary, that is, available for the big tasks that will really make a contribution? It is not going to be a great deal of time, no matter how ruthlessly the pastor prunes time-wasters.

One of the most accomplished time managers I have ever met was the president of a big bank with whom I worked for two years on top-management structure. I saw him once a month for two years. My appointment was always for an hour and a half. The president was always prepared for the sessions—and I soon learned to do my home-

---

Accessibility Versus Productivity

Few areas of ministry can cause more guilt (or frustration) for pastors than their accessibility to their congregations. On the one hand, they know Christian ministry should be people focused. But do church members have the right to demand instant and complete access at all times?

When does accessibility become "excessibility"? The answer may be found by clarifying several misconceptions:

● *My time is my own* or *My time belongs to others.* The truth is that a pastor's time belongs to God. A pastor must be accessible first of all to the Lord.

● *I'm most effective when I've accomplished my goals.* God calls ministry effective when people have been served.

● *I'm most productive when I can stay on schedule.* Actually, schedules can be managed in a flexible way. Furthermore, pastors can increase productivity by making themselves accessible to the right

people—those whom God wants to use to multiply ministry.

● *The more accessible I am to people, the harder it is to be efficient.* The truth is that an efficient ministry will make God more accessible through an accessible pastor.

Two keystone principles of pastoral accessibility emerge as we correct these misconceptions: God is always accessible; a pastor must strive to be accessible always to God. But with people, pastors can't always be accessible. Instead, they can establish priorities that will help them manage how accessible they will be.

Levels of Accessibility

One way to set ministry priorities is to draw a target with rings that represent varying levels of service (that is, accessibility). The outer rings represent those who should have the most accessibility to the minister, with each successive inner ring having less access. For

work, too. There was never more than one item on the agenda. But when I had been there for an hour and twenty minutes, the president would turn to me and say, "Mr. Drucker, I believe you'd better sum up now and outline what we should do next." And an hour and thirty minutes after I had been ushered into his office, he was at the door shaking my hand and saying good-bye.

After this had been going on for about a year, I finally asked him, "Why always an hour and a half?"

He answered, "That's easy. I found out that my attention span is about an hour and a half. If I work on any one topic longer than this, I begin to repeat myself. At the same time, I have learned that nothing of importance can really be tackled in much less time. One does not get to the point where one understands what one is talking about."

---

example, the outermost ring would be those being equipped to serve others. Pastors should lavish their time on these people. Those who are already equipped but may need occasional help will require less time. The innermost ring are those who need ongoing, full-time attention. Pastors should typically avoid such entanglements.

Effective pastors will spend most of their time with people who are learning to serve others. Servanthood—the goal of Christian ministry—provides a basis for evaluating priorities for pastoral accessibility.

Accessible by Degrees

The investment of time and energy into people should have potential for bearing fruit. Appropriate accessibility may not always mean intensive one-on-one contact. Pastors do well to strive to manage a broad and varied repertoire of contact skills, ranked according to the value they have for multiplying ministry. Scheduled meetings with individuals, for example, should be reserved mainly for those whom the pastor is training and equipping. Meeting with several assistants, for example, can multiply the pastor's effectiveness on several broader fronts. Further down the scale would be spontaneous hallway conversations, because they are less effective in extending ministry. The bottom line, however, is that *people* are the purpose of ministry. Better to err on the side of being overly accessible than to be too inaccessible.

Several practices can help pastors remain appropriately accessible, balancing people and productivity. When unscheduled visitors intrude, for example, pastors don't necessarily have to invite them to sit down. Or a pastor can signal the end of a meeting by standing up. In other circumstances, pastors may find it appropriate to state their time "budget" at the beginning of a conversation: "I've got five minutes to deal with this question." If more time is needed, an appointment can be scheduled, with care made to include both the starting and ending times. Often routine needs can be referred to the appropriate staff person or ministry leader.

—*Philip M. Van Auken*

This president accomplished more in this one monthly session than many equally able leaders get done in a month of meetings.

But even this disciplined man had to resign himself to having at least half his time taken up by things of minor importance, things that nonetheless had to be done—the seeing of important customers who just "dropped in," attendance at meetings that could just as well have proceeded without him, specific decisions on daily problems that should not have reached him but invariably did.

Effective pastors therefore know that they have to consolidate their discretionary time. They know they need large chunks of time and that small driblets are no time at all. Even one-quarter of the working day, if consolidated into large time units, is usually enough to get the important things done. But even three-quarters of the working day is useless if it is only available as fifteen minutes here or there.

The final step in time management is therefore to consolidate the time that recordkeeping and analysis show as normally available and under the pastor's control. There are a good many ways of doing this. Some pastors arrange to work at home one day a week; others schedule all the operating work—the meetings, reviews, problem sessions, and so on—for two days a week, for example, Monday and Friday, and set aside the mornings of the remaining days for continuing work on major issues. Another fairly common method is to schedule a daily work period in the morning at home without a telephone.

The method by which we consolidate discretionary time is far less important than the approach. Most people tackle the job by trying to push the secondary, less productive matters together, thus clearing a free space between them. This does not lead very far, however. That still gives priority in our minds and schedules to the less important things, the things that have to be done even though they contribute little. As a result, any new time pressure is likely to be satisfied at the expense of the discretionary time and the work that should be done in it. Within a few days or weeks, the entire discretionary time will be gone again, nibbled away by new crises, new immediacies, new trivia.

Effective pastors start out by estimating how much discretionary time they can realistically call their own. Then they set aside continuous time in the appropriate amount. And if they find later that other matters encroach on this reserve, they scrutinize their record again and get rid of some more time demands from less than fully productive activities.

Managing to Be a Minister

For more than twenty years, a good part of my "charity practice" has been with religious organizations, ranging from an association of Sunday schools to the Jesuit order to small Protestant parishes. They all came to me saying, "We need management and organization, and we don't have it." And they were right. Most of them, like so many of our institutions, were overadministered and undermanaged.

Yet, management was rarely their basic problem. Again and again I had to tell them two basic truths: (1) Mission, purpose, and objectives govern; they come first, long before management and organization; and (2) management and organization are tools, not ends in themselves. The characteristic of a good tool is that it enables the user to do his job without paying attention to the tool. If one spends much time sharpening his or her knife, one is either a poor tool user or in need of another knife.

● *Decide on your unique mission.* Pastors realize the great demands made on their time. If you let these demands manage you, you will not achieve much. There are always more demands than there is time. Therefore, you need to begin with the questions: What is the purpose of all this? What is my *unique* mission?

In my opinion, the central purpose of the minister is the congregation, and the central purpose of the congregation is the person. The *person* is the center of ministry. Only the person can attain faith, hope, and charity. Only the person can attain salvation. And only the person knows despair. Society only knows "problems," which are something quite different. Somebody is needed to look after the person, and the only one who is there for the sake of the person is the minister. Societies need judges and traffic cops and salesmen and legislators and professors and a great many other callings. Only the person needs a minister.

Thus, the purpose, the mission, the objective of the minister is the person. The rest of it is important, perhaps, but it is strictly the side show. Yet the other things are there. They demand your attention. They have to be done.

● *Learn to say no.* This is why you need management. The test of good management is that it enables you to be out of the office doing your real job. Anybody who is preoccupied with management is a toolmaker—and an incompetent manager. There are many around.

Ministers are submerged by demands—demands of organization and running a congregation, demands to take leadership in this or that social cause. You are expected to exercise leadership in a great many community activities, and too often you feel unable to say no. In many cases, however, you should say no. The most important course for anybody who goes into the ministry is an advanced, six-week, intensive course on saying no. Yet it is not offered anywhere.

All demands must be measured against your one unique function—ministry to persons. Say no to the demands that don't fit that role. And say no often, because ministers today are asked to play many other roles.

Management: The Tool We All Need

The minister is not primarily a psychoanalyst. Nor is the pastor a social worker, a community leader, or a teacher. These are secondary roles. The pastor is primarily a person available to other persons. The pastor's job is not healing or reforming or altogether doing. The pastor's job is compassion. For this reason, he or she needs to be able to manage.

Compassion is a time-consuming job. You can't schedule it. You can't say, "My office hours for compassion are nine to twelve." You can't finish it. You can't say, "For this year, our compassion budget has been spent." Yet, it is the one job on which everything else depends.

Pastors need management not because they should manage, but because it is the only way to get the time, thought, and freedom for the real job. It is their tool for making sure all the other things that have to be done get done and yet do not eat them alive in the process.

Management is not the answer to all the problems of ministry. Yet management is a tool all of you need. You must learn to get the other things done by managing yourself, your parish, and your job. You must learn to set objectives for yourself and for the various major tasks you think you should be doing. That's the hardest thing to do: to think through what you are to accomplish.

Learn to set priorities by asking, "What are the two or three things in this parish that, if done well, will really make a difference?" There is no joy in heaven over somebody who tries to do a little bit of everything, because he gets nothing done. Concentrate your time, energies, and human resources on these priorities. Then have the courage—and it takes real courage—to look to the actual events and ask, "Did they produce the results expected?" Drop those that don't.

Whether you like it or not, you are top management in the parish. That means you will have to build responsibility, leadership, and achievement into your congregation and enable them to do the things that need to be done. This is management. But the real test is not how good a manager *you* are. The test is the extent to which managing frees you from being a manager and enables you to be what you want to be—a minister who has compassion for the person.

—Peter F. Drucker

Resources

Asimakoupoulos, G., J. Maxwell, and S. McKinley. 1993. The time crunch. Portland, Ore.: Multnomah.

Dayton, E. 1974. Tools for time management. Grand Rapids: Zondervan.

Engstrom, T., and A. MacKenzie. 1968. Managing your time. Grand Rapids: Zondervan.

Leas, S. 1978. Time management. Nashville: Abingdon.

8

Personal Finances

How we use money tells us much about our trust in God. As Christians—and no less as spiritual leaders—our relationship to money is to be one of stewardship and management, not ownership. Everything we possess—including our money—belongs to the Lord.

We know this truth intellectually, but applying it to our finances is often more complicated. For pastors on modest salaries, just getting the bills paid on time may seem to necessitate a day-by-day approach to money matters. (Wasn't it Jesus himself who said, "Take no thought for the future"?) And even pastors with more substantial incomes find they have little left over to invest as they keep up with their community's standard of living.

But for pastors of every income bracket, there is a place for financial planning, and pastors are obligated to set a sound example of fiscal responsibility for those they lead. Both the Old and New Testaments presume high financial standards for God's people. Paul once put it bluntly: "If anyone does not provide for his relatives, and especially for his immediate family, he has denied the faith and is worse than an unbeliever" (1 Tim. 5:8). Jesus' examples of the need for careful calculations before building a tower or waging war and his parable of the talents illustrate the place for financial stewardship in the kingdom. Even his admonition to give no thought for tomorrow concerns worry, not financial planning as such. In specific and general ways, Scripture teaches us to neither foolhardily disregard possessions nor worrisomely fixate on them. Instead, we are called to wise stewardship, or put in the context of personal finances, we might say pastors are called to worry-free money management.

Money Management Without Worries

Good spending habits are the key to worry-free money management, for both pastors tight on cash and those with more of it. When we learn to control our spending, whether through cash, check, or credit card, our finances can bring glory to God. A good steward or manager will depend on God for income to pay for today's needs and tomorrow's necessities, but paying high interest rates on past spending is not God's plan.

Good spending habits require a long-term view on managing money. Just as small streams converge to form a mighty river, so modest but steady saving and investing over time allow money to grow and compound. If money is placed inside a tax-deferred vehicle like an individual retirement account (IRA) or a 403(b) tax-sheltered annuity (TSA), the power of compounding multiplies, because taxes are not paid until the money is withdrawn from the account.

The long-term view protects us from putting our money into get-rich-quick schemes—those "new investment opportunities" friends clue us in on that promise a 100 percent return within 12 months. It's a proven principle: If the investment is too good to be true, it's probably just that. Or as King Solomon observed millennia ago: "Dishonest money dwindles away, but he who gathers money little by little makes it grow" (Prov. 13:11).

Making It on a Pastor's Pay

Fundamental to wise financial management is understanding one's cash flow—where money is coming from and where it is going. The income of most pastors is simply based on the salary paid by a church. Some pastors receive generous pay, but most get moderate amounts. A few must struggle with below-poverty-level compensation. The question a person should ask is, "Am I handling as efficiently as possible what income I do have?"

This can be answered by figuring one's cash flow. There are four steps:

● Add up income, itemizing where it comes from.

● Figure fixed expenses. Include tithe, rent or house payments, taxes, car payments, insurance, and utilities.

● Determine adjustable expenses. Include groceries, dining out, clothes, travel, entertainments, furniture, credit-card bills, and medical expenses. Put savings at the top of this category rather than leaving it until last.

● Match income and expenses. This shows where money is leaking out.

The fact is that credit is an increasingly important facet of our lives, and building a solid credit rating takes time and effort. Most Christians believe borrowing money is not wrong itself. Financial obligations are taken on every time someone has the electricity connected or telephone service installed. The danger in indebtedness is that it is so easy to become overcommitted without realizing it. Like a hole, debts are easy to slide into, and the hard part is climbing back out. As Jesus said, a wise person will consider whether he has enough funds to meet the obligation he is assuming (Luke 14:28–30).

Pastors must retain a healthy respect for debt. Some will be in a better position to take on larger debts than others. Some may not be able to positively handle *any* debt.

Credit-card debts require special mention. Because of their high interest rates, they should be avoided. Overextended credit-card balances usually cause the greatest heartache for pastors and their families. At the same time, credit cards can be a convenient way to make purchases and record expenses when the balances are paid in full each month.

Getting a Handle on Expenses

One approach to managing cash flow is the budget, but like diets, budgets often don't work. Simple formulas, such as saving ten percent of pretax income or putting aside money for some unspecified future need, lack the human incentive most of us require to be motivated. The better approach is to save to fund specific purchases—a car, furniture, or a vacation.

A key to saving money is realizing that whatever is in the checkbook will likely be spent. To counter this, most people need to channel some money away from the checking account into other accounts that are only tapped into for specially defined purposes. Two such accounts worth opening are:

● *A bank or mutual-fund money-market account.* The best ones let us write checks on the account. This account is for big bills that run up irregularly—like quarterly life insurance premiums, vacations, Christmas presents, and estimated taxes.

A good way to use the account is to look back through our checkbook to see what we've spent annually on "regular irregulars." Then we divide that total by the number of paychecks received each year, and with each paycheck write a personal check for that amount and deposit it in the money market account. When the big bills come in, the cash will be there to cover them.

● *An investment account.* This may be a savings account at a bank or a mutual fund. Every time we get paid, we should write a fixed check to the investment account (and to the money-market account). Or we could have it automatically transferred from the checking account.

Paying into these accounts first serves our cash-management needs better and furthers future financial independence.

Professional Expenses

How should a pastor handle professional expenses and expense reimbursements? Proper handling of professional expenses can make or lose a pastor as much as several thousand dollars per year. Here's what needs to be done to stay on the savings side:

• *Keep good records.* Ministers are notorious for keeping poor records. The point is to not be one of them!

• *Record expenses (and income) in a daily log book.* Keep canceled checks, receipts, or credit-card slips as evidence of expenses. For each expense item, record ministry purpose, ministry relationship (including names of persons present), cost (itemized accounting), time and date, and place.

Pastoral Stewardship

Does it make sense for pastors to support the churches that pay their salaries? After all, it feels strange—receiving with one hand and giving back with the other. What would happen if pastors did *not* support their own churches financially? Would anyone even know, beyond the church treasurer?

Stewardship by Example

One pastor I know says, "They give me so little as it is, what if I just consider as my offering the difference between what they give me and what they *ought* to give me?" Yet there is good reason for a pastor to tithe: the call to lead by example. If we expect the members

of our church to tithe, we ourselves must be willing to do so. In other words, in the area of stewardship, as in other areas, we are called to lead by example.

The apostle Paul discovered that he must lead by example in this area, and so, like Paul, we must give sacrificially of ourselves and then ask the rest of our congregation to consider giving sacrificially as well. Furthermore, we can show that it can be done, even when we may have limited personal resources. We model with our lives the lives we ask others to live.

What makes the leadership argument so compelling is that it answers other questions as well. Tithing pastors, for example, are

Auto expenses are probably the major element of most ministry expenses, and so it's particularly important to record ministry mileage every day. (Driving from home to the church and back is personal commuting miles and doesn't count.)

● *Have expenses reimbursed.* We shouldn't receive an "allowance" for expenses. Ideally, pastors should be reimbursed for 100 percent of their ministry expenses. These include auto expenses (mileage or actual), entertainment, professional books and magazines, supplies, and so on. Many churches reimburse these expenses up to a certain limit.

Why is *reimbursement* for expenses so important? Under current U.S. tax rules, payments for a pastor's expenses that do not qualify under the rules for an "accountable reimbursement plan" are simply considered taxable income. But qualifying reimbursements are not taxable.

Pastors can ask their churches to adopt a formal accountable expense-reimbursement plan if they don't have one. In turn, the pastor then submits expense documentation to the church for a dollar-for-dollar reimbursement.

One note of caution: It is extremely important that personal money

not required to support the church budget singlehandedly with their giving, nor are they required to accept salary cuts or turn down salary increases to help balance tight budgets. (By the same reasoning, pastors certainly should not be expected to make the initial, substantial gifts in a capital campaign, unless they are independently wealthy and can afford to do so!)

A Good Example

Pastoral leadership means setting a personal example of financial stewardship and calling others to live the same way. When a pastor singlehandedly supports a church budget (or leads the way in a capital campaign), that may actually signal a failure of leadership rather than serve as a good example of it. Pastors cannot allow themselves to bear the burden of the bad giving habits of their congregations. Pastors need to be able to speak freely about giving, and to do that, they need to feel comfortable with their own levels of giving.

Giving has much in common with praying, Bible reading, fasting, and the other great spiritual disciplines of Christian faith that we have learned to practice in our ministries. Regular, systematic, and thoughtful giving has the power to deepen our faith and enliven our spirits. No one learns the meaning of trust quite like the person who gives "off the top," what the Bible calls giving the "first fruits." Though the spiritual disciplines of the Christian faith—including consistent giving—are not for pastors alone, all pastors need to practice them.

—Douglas J. Brouwer

be kept separate from church funds. For example, if the church provides a pastor a travel advance, the pastor must account for it promptly and return the leftover money to the church.

● *Save records.* Keep all income and expense records for at least three years after filing the tax return. This is the statute of limitation period during which the IRS can check tax returns.

Insurance and the Minister

It is possible to wrongly trust in insurance rather than trust in God to supply our needs. But a sensible amount of insurance is good stewardship of the resources God lends to us.

Insurance is simply joining with others who share a potential loss. If you are the one in that larger group that has a loss, the funds are available to pay for your loss. This reduces the risk that each person must bear alone. In determining if insurance is needed, the question

---

Gifts and Privileges

Ministers often receive gifts or special privileges from their church or from individual members. Such arrangements not only raise important tax questions, but they also may raise a question of propriety.

Tax Implications

How are ministers who receive special-occasion "gifts" during the course of the year (Christmas, birthday, anniversary) to handle these for federal tax purposes? Consider these guidelines:

● Special-occasion gifts made to a minister by the church out of the general fund should be reported as taxable compensation and included on the minister's Form 1040 and W-2 or 1099.

● Members are free to make personal gifts to ministers, such as a card at Christmas accompanied by a check or cash. Such payments may be tax-free gifts to the minister, but they are not deductible by the donor.

● Special-occasion gifts to a minister that are funded through members' contributions to the church (that is, the contributions are entered or recorded in the church's books as cash received, and the members are given charitable-contribution credit) should be reported as taxable compensation and included on the minister's Form 1040 and W-2 or 1099. The same, of course, applies to any non-minister church worker.

● Members who contribute to special-occasion offerings may be able to deduct their contributions if (1) the contributions are to the church and are entered or recorded in the church's books as cash received, and (2) they are able to itemize deductions on Schedule A (Form 1040).

should be asked whether the potential economic loss could be borne alone. If so, insurance may not be needed.

Here are some important considerations concerning insurance and insurance types:

● *Holding down insurance costs.* The best way to maintain or cut insurance costs is to get the most insurance for the premium dollars. Unless pastors have unlimited finances, they will probably need to prioritize insurance purchases. For example, a broad-based health insurance policy should generally come before a disability policy, and disability coverage should come before travel accident insurance.

It is advisable to buy coverage that is comprehensive and catastrophic. Comprehensive coverage provides a broader umbrella of protection. Catastrophic insurance covers the costs for worst-case scenarios.

Here are basic strategies for saving insurance premium dollars:

—Raise the deductibles to protect from the risk of a *major* loss. The higher the deductible, the less risk the insurance company is exposed

---

● A church can collect an all-cash, special-occasion offering with the express understanding that the entire proceeds will be paid directly to the minister and that no contributions will be tax-deductible. It is possible that in some cases such direct member-to-minister transfers would satisfy the Supreme Court's definition of a gift.

Family Gifts

What are the tax implications when someone, such as a family member, attempts to "supplement" a minister's compensation by making designated "contributions" to that minister through the church? Several things can be said:

● If such contributions are in addition to a minister's stated salary, they ordinarily are not tax-deductible by the donor, since the donor's clear intent is to benefit a particular minister. The church acted simply as an intermediary through which the gift was fun-neled (in many cases, in an attempt to obtain a charitable-contribution deduction).

● If the relatives understand that their contribution will not supplement the minister's salary but rather will be applied to the church's obligation to pay it, then a charitable-contribution deduction may be available (since it is relieving the church of a legal obligation).

No, Thanks

There are times when ministers may wish to decline a gift or privilege in order to maintain professional independence. A prominent church member sometimes offers to confer a valuable benefit or privilege upon a pastor to exert control or influence. For this reason, ministers should carefully evaluate whether or not to accept offered gifts and privileges in order to avoid any appearance of impropriety or undue influence.

—*Richard R. Hammar*

to, and thus the lower a premium will be.

—Buy broad coverage only. We should stay away from narrow policies such as cancer, flight insurance, mortgage and credit-card life, student accident, hospital indemnity, and double-indemnity.

—Find out about discounts. They're offered on all kinds of coverage.

● *Umbrella liability insurance.* Purchasing an umbrella liability policy is a wise investment. These policies provide additional protection beyond the coverage of homeowners and automobile policies, which even at their maximum coverage are inadequate to protect other assets in the event of a major legal judgment. The cost is usually under $150 annually for a $1,000,000 policy.

● *Health insurance.* It is essential that pastors have adequate catastrophic medical insurance coverage, even if it means scrimping elsewhere in their budget. Otherwise, one costly illness can wipe out a person financially.

Health costs can be kept down by avoiding hospital emergency rooms unless it's a real emergency, using family-practice physicians unless a specialist is needed, and buying generic drugs instead of brand names. A pastor's after-tax compensation will be greater if the church pays or reimburses the pastor for health-insurance premiums. Universal health coverage may come eventually. Until then, it is wise to focus on coverage available today.

● *Disability-income insurance.* A person is far more likely to become disabled than to die before retirement, and a family's need for income is usually greater during a breadwinner's disability than after his or her death. When considering disability-income insurance, a pastor should ask: What happens if I cannot continue pastoring after an accident or illness?

Private disability-income insurance is designed to replace income that a person loses if he or she can no longer work. For pastors, benefits from a policy paid by the church are fully taxable (just like the salary that is being replaced). But if the pastor buys a policy himself or herself, the benefits are tax-free.

Like other insurance, the time to buy it is when one doesn't need it—before a disability.

● *Life insurance.* Getting a handle on life insurance today is challenging. The bottom line here is: How would my family be affected if I were no longer there to provide an income?

The key to buying life insurance is determining how much coverage beneficiaries really need. That should be considered before submitting to an insurance agent's sales pitch. Because each family is different, assessing the need—the amount of coverage to buy—is not a simple process. A general rule of thumb is to multiply one's annual earnings by 10. But be careful: Two families may have the same income but a different number of dependents. Their needs will be dramatically different. There are financial-planning computer-software programs available that guide users through a more detailed analysis of potential needs.

Term life insurance is often a good option for younger ministers. However, term insurance rates typically rise annually the older one becomes. There is also no cash value with a term policy. When buying term insurance, it is best to choose a renewable, convertible policy. A renewable policy doesn't require new medical tests to continue coverage in future years. *Convertible* means the policy can be switched any time from a term to a permanent policy.

A person is probably better off choosing term insurance rather than cash-value life insurance if any one of the following statements is true: I need insurance for 10–15 years or less, I can't afford the permanent insurance premium for the amount of coverage needed, or I'm not fully funding other tax-deferred savings options such as a 403(b) tax-sheltered annuity plan or an IRA.

With permanent life insurance—which includes whole life, universal life, and variable life—a portion of the annual premium goes into a tax-deferred savings fund (cash-value account). Unlike with term insurance, permanent premiums generally don't rise after the policy is purchased. The down side is that premiums are four to nine times higher than initial premiums for comparable term contracts (because purchasers are funding the savings account, and the commissions are steeper).

We should buy a permanent policy only with extreme caution—and only with the strong intent to keep it at least 15 years (or until death). People lose thousands of dollars when they drop typical permanent policies after only a few years, because they forfeit hefty sums paid out to agents as sales commissions.

Investments for the Minister

The world of investments can be one of the most confusing and frustrating areas of one's spiritual and financial life—so many choices and so many different levels of risk!

Saving and investing shouldn't be jumbled. A savings plan has a short-term goal (three to five years) to accumulate money for the purchase of an auto or home. An investing plan extends beyond five years.

● *Getting started.* Before beginning an investment program, we should take three important steps:

—Eliminate all credit-card debt. Paying off credit-card debt is one sure way to receive a guaranteed, risk-free rate of return. Each time a credit-card balance is reduced, the return on the investment is equal to the interest charged on that account.

—Build an emergency fund. Fund a money-market savings account equal to (at least) three to six months of after-tax earnings. This is to prevent the forced liquidation of an investment account.

—Establish long-range goals. The first step in beginning an investment program is seeking the Lord's guidance. We need to pray about goals, write them down, and share them with our spouse.

● *Understand risks in investing.* When investing money, it's a mistake to focus entirely on the potential rate of return. Of equal importance is the level of risk. All investments have some degree of risk, and the greater the possible return, the greater the potential risk. Since there is no risk-free saving or investment decision, each person must determine his or her level of risk tolerance and develop a plan within that comfort level.

● *Diversify investments.* Generally there are higher returns with less risk if money is placed into more than one type of investment. For example, a person could place all his or her assets into a savings account, generally considered a low risk. But it does have one risk: the loss of purchasing power. This inflation risk can be reduced by diversifying into other assets, such as common stocks, mutual funds, or bonds.

● *Consider mutual funds.* What do you do if you feel the time has come in your financial situation to venture beyond the bank? Investing directly in stocks and bonds takes time, money, and expertise. Most ministers are reluctant to invest so much energy into such ventures.

The solution for many armchair investors is mutual funds. A mutual fund is simply a large investment company that collects a pool of dollars from many investors. Individual securities are purchased by the fund in the form of stocks, bonds, or money-market instruments.

Mutual funds make it easy to diversify investments (as little as $25 per month can be put into some funds) and allow for dollar-cost averaging. Dollar-cost averaging is investing a fixed dollar amount every period (weekly or monthly, for example) no matter what is happening in the financial market. This technique reduces the risk of putting one's savings in the market at the wrong time.

The choosing of a mutual fund requires asking, "Could I sleep nights owning shares in a fund that might lose a year's gain in a week?" If not, the chanciest fund categories should be avoided.

A second consideration is selecting the basic fund categories, which are growth, total-return, income, and international and global.

A third consideration is which of the two basic kinds of mutual funds to use: load and no-load. A load is a commission paid to a salesperson, financial planner, or broker. The advantage of a load fund is that investors receive professional advice on which funds to choose. A no-load fund means they do not have to pay a commission, but they also don't receive professional advice. Both load and no-load funds have their roles in the marketplace, and people need to determine which fund works best for their situations.

Mom Had It Right

Personal finances often seem like a puzzle that has missing pieces. But when clear-minded thinking is applied, personal finances become quite straightforward. Financial health over the long run depends on those little reminders our mothers use to give us:

● Use a balanced approach.
● Start early.
● Tithe, and then some.
● Put money aside regularly.
● Invest for the long term.
● Trust stocks and stock funds (well, maybe she didn't say it in those words), because over five years or more, they should do better than anything else.

—Daniel D. Busby

Resources

Busby, D., K. Barber, and R. Temple. 1994. A Christian's guide to worry-free money management. Grand Rapids: Zondervan.

Humber, W. 1993. Dollars & sense. Colorado Springs: NavPress.

Moore, G. 1990. The thoughtful Christian's guide to investing. Grand Rapids: Zondervan.

Pryor, A. 1993. Sound mind investing. Chicago: Moody.

Housing Options

Several housing alternatives are available to pastors, each with advantages and drawbacks. Both clergy and churches will benefit when they know the options.

Tax Benefits

Clergy have an excellent tax advantage available through their housing arrangements. The IRS excludes from taxable income the portion of a minister's salary allocated by the church as a housing allowance—provided the allowance does not exceed actual housing expenses or fair rental value of the home, including utilities. This rule applies whether pastors buy a house, rent, or live in a parsonage. Churches who provide a parsonage often forget that they also can allocate a portion of the pastor's salary as a nontaxable "parsonage allowance"—to pay for the expense of running the home.

Private or Parsonage?

Pastors who own their homes have an advantage at retirement unavailable to those who live in parsonages. Pastors in parsonages do not have an opportunity to build up property equity. Pastors who can invest in housing during their earlier working years can build equity and avoid the frustration of searching for affordable housing on retirement income.

Pastors who are provided a parsonage have other kinds of advantages. Some are able to live in homes of much greater value than they otherwise could afford. Avoiding maintenance costs on a home and living almost rent free make it possible for some ministers to build other kinds of savings.

Some churches set up an "equity account" to provide parity for the benefit other pastors gain by investing in their own housing. Church leaders calculate the equity the minister would have acquired by owning a home (one simple method relies on real estate appraisals of the parsonage) and funds are then set aside to give to the pastor when he or she retires or moves. Such an equity account should be set up as a qualified retirement plan—above and beyond other retirement plans. It should not be seen as a part of the regular salary or housing-allowance package; it should be unavailable for current expenses.

Expensive Markets

Providing clergy housing in inflated real estate markets presents unique challenges. Consider the following:

● Have the pastor live in a lower-cost area outside the church community. The downside of this approach is that commuting may become tiresome. Furthermore, living in another community could hinder a pastor's ministry by limiting identity with the members of the congregation.

● Where home values are appreciating, the pastor and church may consider becoming equity partners through a sharing agreement. Both can invest in the purchase of the pastor's housing, sharing at levels comfortable for each. (Fifty-fifty is one option.) The return on such investments could be much higher than passbook interest rates—good stewardship of the church's resources, which benefits both the church and the pastor.

● Churches may also consider providing the pastor with a home loan, although state laws in some states may prohibit this. Even in states where this is allowed, however, this loan should be an "arm's length" transaction—one at a competitive interest rate and with a recorded trust deed. Such precautions will avoid any appearance of inurement and, at the same time, enable a pastor who would not qualify for a bank loan to get into a home. Monthly payments could be deducted from payroll to lower the risk to the church.

Though housing allowances offer pastors tax advantages, long-range benefits may be most evident at retirement. Churches and clergy should work together to evaluate their unique options so they can best meet current and future ministerial housing needs.

—Grace S. Nicholaou

Clergy Taxes

Not every pastor needs professional help with taxes. In fact, attorney and CPA Richard Hammar (author of *Pastor, Church, & Law* and editor of the *Church Law & Tax Report*) suggests that most pastors can prepare their own returns. But since clergy tax issues offer unique problems, pastors need to be well informed, and they may want to seek professional help when they face circumstances such as:

● *Well-above-average pay.* Daniel Busby, (author of *The Zondervan Minister's Tax & Financial Guide* and editor of the *Pastor's Tax & Money*) notes that larger churches and higher-paid ministers more likely will need a tax preparer.

● *The purchase or sale of real estate.* Technical factors such as *capital gains* and the *basis* of property may surpass the amateur's expertise.

● *Income property.* Property depreciation and other details can be complex—and the rules keep changing.

● *Several sources of income.* Income from a church and honoraria is simple enough. But other types of self-employment income may complicate matters considerably.

● *An interstate move.* Tax owed to more than one state may be better figured by professionals.

● *Nonaccountable reimbursement plans.* Unreimbursed business expenses (partially deductible on Schedule C) make for complicated returns. More preferable is an accountable reimbursement plan, in which the pastor is reimbursed by the church for approved and well-documented expenses.

Preparing for the Preparer

Tax-preparation worksheets can cut the time a preparer will need for our returns, meaning lower cost for us. We need to be sure to supply all the information needed, such as W-2 or 1099-MISC forms and other income records, housing expenses (utility costs, mortgage or rent payments, costs of improvements or furnishings, and so on), receipts for unreimbursed business expenses (with date, place, amount, people involved, and purpose for each expense), and tithes and other charitable giving.

When shopping for a clergy-competent tax preparer, we must understand that not all CPA firms will do, even those competent in other areas. Grace and Nick Nicholaou, with Ministry Business Services in Huntington Beach, California, suggest one way to find tax preparers who will do justice to a clergy tax return is to ask if they have taken continuing-education units (required for CPAs) about clergy taxes.

It is the rare general-tax preparer who can handle clergy returns. Most general accounting firms, in fact, may not be best for clergy returns. It would not hurt to ask other pastors about their experience with local preparers to find out who they recommend, or to consult with references given by local firms.

Screening Preparers

It boils down to a personal decision about who to use. Here are some questions to screen potential preparers to find the authentic experts on clergy taxes:

● What percentage of your clientele is clergy?

● How many years have you done clergy returns?

● What is Form 8283 used for? (It's a qualified-appraisal summary used for charitable gifts other than cash.)

● Can Section 107 of the Internal Revenue Code help me? (It deals with parsonages.)

● Are ministers employees or self-employed for social-security purposes? (With respect to church compensation, they're always self-employed.)

● Since I receive a housing allowance, how would you handle my mortgage interest and real estate taxes? (Pastors are entitled to the double benefit of both.)

Once a return is completed by a preparer, we need to examine it for accuracy. Tax preparers may be subject to penalties for shoddy or fraudulent work, but the ultimate responsibility for any tax return belongs to the taxpayer. Since we can be penalized for errors and omissions, we are wise to take time to check it thoroughly.

—*James D. Berkley*

Tentmaking Ministries and Business Ventures

Some ministers hold jobs alongside their ministry duties or have business ventures that bring in income to supplement their church salary. The long tradition of "tentmaking ministers" in the church reflects a variety of circumstances, ranging from financial necessities to church polities that encourage their ministers to identify with the community by holding "common" jobs. Whatever the reasons, three biblical principles should guide the tentmaking minister's approach to money and ministry.

Faith, Focus, and Flexibility

● *The faith principle.* Jesus twice sent his followers on short-term mission projects, telling them to take nothing with them for their personal support (Luke 9:1–6; 10:1–7). It was assumed that those who received ministry would pay for it. The apostle Paul affirmed this principle when he wrote the Corinthians that he had every right to expect financial support for his ministry. He reminded them of Jesus' teaching that those who preach the gospel should live from the gospel (1 Cor. 9:12–14). In general, the framework of ministry should provide for basic financial support.

By faith, tentmakers must strike a balance between the need to care for their family and the need for God's family to care for them. Their work outside the church should not supplant the church members' responsibility to exercise their faith in supporting—as much as possible—God's work in the church.

● *The focus principle.* Jesus made it clear that a servant could serve only one master. His followers could not focus on the acquisition of material things and serve God at the same time. Money was not to be "stored up" here on earth, but instead spent in the service of God (Luke 16:13; Matt. 6:19–20). Regardless of where income originates, outside or inside the ministry, ministers must judge whether its use is consistent with the eternal purposes of God.

With proper focus, tentmakers must fulfill responsibilities both inside and outside the church with an equal sense of dedication and integrity. Ministers who gain a reputation as excellent makers of tents but poor builders of people damage their witness for Christ. The tentmaking minister needs to clearly define his or her expectations at work and at church and be disciplined in applying personal resources to meet those expectations.

● *The flexibility principle.* The apostle Paul personifies this. As a tentmaker (literally), he had abilities and resources that allowed him to choose whether or not he would receive support from his ministry. He chose based on the specific need of his audience. He chose to receive support from the Philippians but not from the Corinthians.

Flexible ministers gauge tentmaking activities by their impact on the needs of those they care for—their congregation and their families. They take care to see that their outside activities do not in some way cripple the church, avoiding, for example, tentmaking activities that use parishioners as business prospects (making for awkwardness in relationships), or business activities that regularly take them away from church responsibilities (placing additional burdens on people who may not have time to handle the extra work).

A Matter of Stewardship

Both tentmaking and outside ventures that bring in additional income become elements of stewardship for any minister. Such opportunities should be seen as an extension of one's overall ministry. A minister, for example, with previous experience in real estate may have natural contacts with business people with whom the gospel can be shared. A minister's personal financial resources can also be used to support personal ministries or to invest in the ministries of others apart from the structure or limits of the church's budget.

—*Gary Gulbranson*

Pension and Retirement Planning

Most of us hope to enjoy our retirement years with financial dignity. Accordingly, we need to set funds aside regularly, determining to build financial reserves in our retirement storehouse. Once we have made this commitment, we must then decide what tax strate-

gies to utilize and which investments to use.

Social security is a mandated
retirement plan for taxpayers,
including most pastors (who pay
self-employment tax). Some pastors
opt out of social security by filing
Form 4361 within two years of
ordination, but this option should
be considered with caution since
financial opposition is not a valid
reason for opting out.

Employer-Provided Options

● *Qualified retirement plans.*
Utilizing a qualified retirement
plan allows us to set funds aside
tax-deferred. As common-law
employees of a nonprofit organization, pastors can avail themselves
of a tax-sheltered annuity (TSA)
under Internal Revenue Code
Section 403(b). These annuities are
portable, have attractive funding
formulas, and can be borrowed
from. Pastors do not pay self-
employment tax on the salary
reduction amounts contributed to a
TSA. (Other employer- or denomina-
tion-provided retirement-plan contributions are also excluded from
self-employment tax.)

● *Deferred compensation agreements.* These arrangements provide
a means for your employer to pay
you later the funds you set aside
now, up to $7,500 per year (I.R.C.
Sec. 457). There are also special
"catch-up" provisions. These funds
are forfeitable, so using a provision
called a "Rabbi Trust" is recommended (Revenue Procedure 92-64).

● *Integrated plans.* If a pastor has
more than one type of retirement
plan with an employer, he or she
must integrate them to determine
maximum contribution limits.

Other Options

● *Personally administered plans.*
Qualified plans that pastors can
personally set up and administer
include an individual retirement
account (IRA), which is funded
based on wages and/or self-employment income (with certain de-
ductibility restrictions). Keogh and
Simplified Employer Pension (SEP)
IRA contributions are based on
Schedule C net income. However,
contributions to these plans do not
reduce self-employment earnings.

● *After-tax opportunities.* Funds
can be accumulated with after-tax
dollars in a pastor's personal port-
folio. An annuity or a whole life
insurance product allows pastors to
defer the income on their principal
until they withdraw funds. Naturally, we must be sure to use
investments we understand and
consider appropriate for the
amount of risk we are willing to
take. Diversity is the key; it's best to
put no more than one-seventh of
available funds into one particular
investment opportunity.

● *A charitable remainder trust.*
Such trusts would serve as supple-
mentary retirement plans. This
instrument and other charitable-
planning options are especially
attractive for those with appreciated assets.

● *Home equity.* Those who own a
home and have equity may find a
"reverse mortgage" an available
alternative at retirement.

At age 59½ we can withdraw
funds from qualified retirement
plans with no penalties. At 70½ we
will be required to make regular,
statutorily determined distributions.

The key to retirement planning is
to start early, be consistent and dili-

gent, diversify with an emphasis on growth and income, and utilize every tax-saving tool at our disposal. Then we can enjoy our golden years with an eye toward proper estate planning.

—John M. W. Moorlach

Part II:

Transitions

What do we have as pastors—a job? How plebeian! An occupation? Better, but so mundane. A career? Closer, but not particularly noble. How about a profession? Closer yet; more altruistic, but still rather secular in feel. Theologically speaking, we name what we experience a *calling*. We get *called* into it. And we receive *calls* to new opportunities.

When we heard the call to ministry, our response, like young Samuel's to Eli, tumbled out to God: "Here am I. You called me." Like Isaiah in the presence of a divine request, we answered: "Here am I. Send me." With training behind us and hands laid upon us, we became pastors, and so we now pursue ministry, both called and commissioned.

But we also get transitioned.

Like Abraham, we are sometimes called to leave our country, our people, and our father's household and go to the land God will show us. Like Philip, so productive in Samaria, we find ourselves on the road to Gaza, and, before we know it, end up in Caesarea. Like young John Wesley, we may miserably fail one charge, only to move on and be surprised by wild success in another. Like most ministers we've ever known, we will probably move.

The goal is to move well. Wisely. At the right time. In the proper way. At God's call. Here is counsel to guide us in our search for all the right moves.

9

The Meaning of Church Vocation

Ministry in the United States today reflects the nation's cultural diversity. The charismatic televangelist, the Catholic parish priest, the Presbyterian local minister, the urban Black preacher, the Fundamentalist political activist, and the female Pentecostal evangelist form a religious rainbow. But they also reflect the light of their common calling. We call it "ministry," because today's ministry, as it did in apostolic times, centers in preaching and pastoral care.

Over the years theology, styles, customs, and ideals of ministry have changed, but the heart for ministry remains strikingly "apostolic." The "call" to ministry is still the burden to mediate the experience and understanding of God as he is revealed in Christ and the Bible. It is still both an inward conviction that God has enlisted one for divine service and an outward call from the Christian community that affirms one's potential for service.

What is different today is the attitude toward ordained ministry. Secular society rushes to expose the failures of prominent clergy. Within the Christian community itself, one can detect a damaging attitude that Thomas Oden has labeled *antinomianism*. This word, used by theologians over the centuries, identifies that undernourished view of God's grace that insists there are no ethical restraints or norms of redemptive behavior present in the gospel. It is, writes Oden, "the weird, wild, impulsive, unpredictable sleeping partner of much contemporary pastoral care. It mistakes the gospel for license, freedom for unchecked self-actualization, and health for native vitalism" (Oden 1983, 8–9). It assumes that God loves us without judgment, that grace opposes obligation, and that "oughts" are dehumanizing, and it forces us to withhold ethical judgments, ape nondirective therapies, and shun any sign of a "preachy" tone.

Historically, the Christian community has held a strikingly different concept of ministry, one where ministry is offered as gift and labor, and, important for our times, one that has form and standards. It is one that called all believers to bear witness, visit the sick, serve the needy, and assist in the building up of the community. In this general sense, ministry is the responsibility of every Christian (Matt. 5:16).

This general ministry, however, does not preclude the authority of those called of God and set apart by the church for the specific tasks of an ordered ministry. Ordained ministry is different from the general ministry of the laity in that the ordained are duly called, prepared, examined, ordained, and authorized to a spiritual service representative of the whole people of God.

The reception of the gift (*charisma*) of ministry and the rite of ordination is essential to this ordained ministry. Ordination combines an internal grace with the external act, in which God's grace is expressed by the laying on of hands and a prayer of intercession. This ordination publicly authorizes the candidate for the ministry of Word, sacrament, and order, and offers the empowerment of that ministry.

Like baptism, ordination is intended to be administered only once, because it is a sign of a lifelong covenant relationship. Just as one is baptized not into the local church alone but into the whole church, so one is ordained not merely by synod, denomination, or conference but for the whole church.

Who is entrusted with the power to ordain? Christians have answered that question differently. Some say bishops, some presbyters (elders), and still others the congregation. Each of these three polities—episcopal, presbyterian, and congregational—claims to find justification in the New Testament documents.

Ordered Ministry in the Bible

The stress on the call to ministry, so common in Christian history, finds little support from the way the word *call* is used in the New Testament. *Call,* in the sense of divine calling, almost universally refers to the process by which God calls those whom he has already elected and appointed, so that he may justify and sanctify them (Rom. 8:29ff). Since the call of God is to salvation, not to ministry, "the called" in the New Testament are the "saints" who make up the churches (Rom. 1:6–7 and 1 Cor. 1:2, 24).

In the New Testament, *call* is only indirectly related to ministerial leadership, in that God's call comes through the message of the gospel

(2 Thes. 2:14) and someone, obviously, must preach the gospel for the church. On rare occasions in the Bible, the apostle can trace his office of apostle to a special call from God (Rom. 1:1 and 1 Cor. 1:1), but these references never suggest how this apostolic call applies to a call to ecclesiastical office.

While the doctrine of ministerial call remains fuzzy, the practice of acknowledging leaders for ministry is present from the beginning. In the Gospel accounts, we see two basic truths: (1) the apostles were "set apart" by Jesus; and (2) the Jewish tradition, from which the Christian churches emerged, had for centuries acknowledged the leadership of elders. Thus, the early churches in Jerusalem and beyond recognized the leadership of elders.

The practice of acknowledging elders is one way the people of the New Covenant maintained continuity with the Old Covenant. As advocates of congregational government point out, early Christian leaders, like synagogue rulers, were known, respected, and called by the people they served. This is the seek-out-among-you principle of Acts 6:3. At the same time, congregationalists insist, the practice of selecting Christian leaders through the congregation is based in the New Testament doctrine of the "priesthood of believers" (1 Pet. 2:9).

By the time the Book of Acts was written in the sixties, a number of the Pauline churches in Asia Minor had adopted a simple form of presbyterian government. The term *prohistemi*, meaning "be at the head of, or rule," in 1 Thessalonians 5:12 refers to those who labor in the church and "are over you in the Lord." Some leaders (apparently "elders" or "bishops") exercised leadership by helping others live rightly and so deserved special esteem and love.

Is this an early reference to office? Perhaps not, but it certainly recognizes the presence and exercise of spiritual leadership. But later in the first century, in the descriptions of church offices in the Pastoral Epistles, *elder* is used to designate those who care for the members and the spiritual life of the gathered church. A few texts even suggest remuneration for these labors (1 Tim. 5:17–18).

In Titus 1:5 and 7, the author seems to use the terms *presbyteros* (elder) and *episcopos* (bishop) interchangeably. These are leaders who have the task of exhorting the saints and refuting the objectors. In other words, they continue the juridical role of elders in the Jewish synagogues and anticipate the ordained Christian office of pastors. In this early period, such authority remained primarily in what the elder taught.

Gradually distinctions between the laity (*laos* means "people") and the ordained clergy developed within the church. Rather clearly by the time of the Pastoral Epistles, the charismatic character of a few of the earlier Pauline churches has given way to an organized system of offices, marked by the titles *bishop* and *deacon* (1 Tim. 3:1, 8).

Some scholars find the first hints of the episcopal view of ministry in the references to Titus and Timothy's work of "appointing" elders in the individual churches in the name of the apostle (Titus 1:5 comparing Acts 14:23). The office of bishop in this sense of oversight or rule is, however, much clearer in the second century.

The Ministry of Pastor

Among the biblical terms pointing to church leadership, the term *pastor* is probably the richest theologically and encompasses all the other functions and expectations of ministry in the Scriptures. It is an image used often in the Bible to describe the Lord. Jesus used it several times to describe his own ministry (John 10:1–30). The pastor is a

---

When to Move

Knowing when to leave a congregation and assume new responsibilities elsewhere can be an agonizing decision. It's a pastor's personal choice, yet a spouse, children, and two congregations typically will be affected. How can we come to grips with these crucial times of transition?

Some pastors explain their moves with clichés: "I just knew this was God's time for me to leave." As important as inner convictions are, the truth is, we pastors don't always have a direct line to heaven. A great many human factors figure into the decision to leave one church for another.

What's at Stake

Some pastors accomplish a great deal by staying in one church a long time. Most larger churches seem to have been built by those who have stayed for decades. On the other hand, some pastors stay too long—long after their ministries have ceased being effective.

Inflated egos can make us think we can do anything—and we hang on too long. Fragile egos can cause us to bail out too soon. So how do we recognize our limitations without despising God's possibilities? How can we see past ourselves to discover God's direction?

There is no simple formula; congregations, personalities, and ministry gifts vary. But there are some factors worth considering:

● *Major problems in the present church.* We can't run from every disagreement, but deep-seated or long-term conflict may mean something more. Regardless of who is at fault, persistent problems may indicate it is time to seek another pastorate. If situations grow beyond my ability to handle, my church

shepherd of souls, and the sheep are his flock—figures suggesting loving, sacrificial leadership. Both Peter and Paul link this shepherding ministry with the oversight of the Christian churches (Acts 20:28 and 1 Pet. 2:25).

Christ himself apparently intended that all ministry embody his own ministry to the church and world, a fact that has sustained and energized Christian ministers through the centuries. The pastor in ministry is a member of the body of Christ who is called by God and the church and is set apart by ordination to preach, administer the gospel ordinances, and guide the Christian community in obedience to the revealed will of God.

The biblical idea of the priesthood of believers persisted, even when later the offices of the church multiplied. In the late second century,

---

needs leadership I can't offer. On the other hand, a lack of problems may not be a good reason to stay. God moved Philip out of Samaria in the middle of a great revival.

● *Ministerial exhaustion.* Every pastorate includes stress. But unusually tough situations can tax our spiritual and emotional strength. To carry on indefinitely and ineffectively can hardly be God's will. Additional training or additional staff may help, but sometimes a move is in order.

● *Financial pressures.* If a pastor struggles to keep bread on the table, God may offer a better opportunity to provide for the family. We need not feel guilty about moving to where we will be better cared for. Though we do not minister for money, God knows our needs and takes note of our faithfulness.

● *Family circumstances.* Ministry location affects our families as much as it does us. A relocation can radically shape the education and social development of our children. So we need to look for some sign of God's will by assessing the impact a move will make upon our family's social, spiritual, and educational needs.

● *Larger opportunity.* The concept of career advancement is a secular notion—foreign to New Testament concepts of ministry. God wants faithful—not grasping—servants. However, as our ministries and abilities mature, God often will place us in positions of greater responsibility. When God opens up new areas of service, we may need to call the moving van.

● *God's voice.* One intangible, all-important factor stands above all the others: We still must discern God's voice. We can hear God in several ways: through the counsel of friends and leaders, through disciplines such as prayer and fasting, through faithful obedience to the opportunities he gives. Pastors often find that if their motives are right and their prayers sincere, God protects them from bad decisions.

One inescapable fact remains: Even when we've carefully followed these principles, doing God's will requires us to take a step of faith.

—*Calvin C. Ratz*

Tertullian could ask rhetorically, "Are we lay people not priests also?" Eventually, however, the gap between laity and clergy widened. In 398, for example, the Council of Carthage formally prohibited laymen from teaching in the presence of clergymen without clergy consent.

The clergy class also diversified. Deacons were selected for service in the apostolic age. Next, deaconesses appeared. Then a special class of readers of the Scriptures in the liturgy, called *lectors*, followed. Later still, additional orders of clergy were organized, including acolytes, exorcists, and subdeacons. By the middle of the third century, according to a letter cited by the historian Eusebius, the church at Rome had 1 bishop, 46 presbyters (or elder/priests), 7 deacons, 7 subdeacons, 42 acolytes, and 52 exorcists, readers, and doorkeepers.

In this historic and cultural development, the churches had left

Retirement

Retirement is a good-news/bad-news story. The good news is that retirement provides time to do many things we have had to put off. The bad news is that much of life as we've known it is lost. As retirement approaches, most pastors find it helpful not only to prepare to leave the full-time ministry but also to live the retired life.

Be Prepared

Saying good-bye properly is one thing. Starting a new life is another. But both are part of preparing for retirement. We can best set out on our new lives by doing some advance preparation in at least six areas.

● *The first month.* The typical inclination is to plan nothing. While the months before retirement may have been unusually happy, they likely were also extremely busy. Many new pastors view the first month of retirement, therefore, as a time to relax at home. Actually, it's probably best to leave town the first day and be gone for at least a month. For both the church and the pastor, there needs to be an immediate, physical separation so the reality of retirement can begin to sink in.

● *Spouse.* A spouse needs preparation. In some ways, retirement can be more traumatic for the spouse than for the retiree. Thus, it's good to spend many hours in deep conversation, sharing feelings, hopes, dreams, and fears about the coming retirement. This is a new challenge in which both parties need each other's support. If the congregation establishes a retirement-celebration committee, a spouse can be included in receiving expressions of thanks and appreciation.

● *Moving.* A pastor typically needs to move away from the church's community upon retirement, since the pastor and congre-

behind the sense of ministry as "ministry of the Word." A threefold ministry prevailed by the middle of the second century: a single bishop in a city, with presbyters and deacons under his leadership. Gradually, the bishop assumed most of the preaching and teaching functions of the church as well as the power to ordain presbyters (or *priests,* as they came to be called). Even then, congregations ratified the choices as they did the selection of new bishops.

These structural developments were paralleled by sacramental ones that held that the priestly power conveyed in ordination included authority to dispense saving grace. The forgiving grace offered in penance was especially significant, being so central to the forgiveness of sins and hope of heaven. The Middle Ages added to these clerical developments the ideals of monasticism by requiring celibacy of the

gation need to make a complete break from each other. Otherwise the next pastor will have to deal both with the memory *and* the physical presence of the former pastor—and one is hard enough.

Sometimes, of course, it's not possible to move, at least immediately. In such cases, pastors must set clear guidelines about their future relationship with the church and its new pastor. Even then, the retired pastor might consider moving after two or three years.

● *Finances.* Financial preparation for retirement is a lifelong endeavor. Most denominations offer their pastors enrollment in a retirement program, in addition to social security. The equity in one's home can also work toward retirement.

Some pastors have to use parsonages and consequently can't build any equity. But even that drawback can be worked with, especially if such pastors recognize the problem early and make wise investments in other areas.

● *Activities.* It's a good practice to plan what we will be doing with ourselves for the first couple of years of retirement. For example, I wanted to research and write on the personal and professional needs of ministers, so needed to be near a good seminary library. Two or three years after retirement, I planned to start supplying pulpits and serving in interim pastorates.

● *Continuing ministry.* Even retired pastors should make plans for continuing their ministry. First, they must set clear guidelines about under what circumstances they would return to a former pastorate for weddings and funerals. Second, they must find a new church home and make every effort to attend not only worship but business meetings, fellowship gatherings, and Sunday school classes. They can express willingness to serve in these areas, but only at the request of the congregation or pastor, and then more as a church member than as a former pastor. It's always prudent to avoid saying or implying, "This is not the way I did it when I was pastor."

—*Edward B. Bratcher*

pastoral clergy, and by subordinating the ministerial offices under the pope.

Reform of the Ministry

When the Protestant reformers challenged the traditional Catholic view of ministry as a special class of mediating priests, they retained the power and authority of the minister as God's spokesperson to lead the people of God. Calvin went so far as to treat acts of contempt of the ministry as serious public offenses that represented a revolt against the divine order.

This divine order, however, was usually bestowed by the congregation. Luther, for example, rejected the Catholic notion that the sacrament of ordination elevated ministers to a new status in the order of priesthood and argued that the ministry made sense only in relation to a local congregation. The belief that no one should be ordained to the ministry unless he had a call from a congregation became a Reformation tenet. Eventually, however, the congregational call became more important than the ordination itself, which was seen as simply a confirmation of the calling and election of a minister.

The particular method of calling and ordaining a Protestant minister differed greatly from place to place, but in general, ordination methods reflected the conviction that ministry is a call, not a man-made order. The teaching and governing ministry begun by Christ continued to the present hour through the inward work of the Holy Spirit and the outward work of his ministers.

In obedience to Christ, then, ministers and teachers had to be called and ordained by legitimate ecclesiastical elections. Candidates for the ministry, accordingly, needed to be examined for their fitness. These examinations were nearly always conducted by neighboring ministers, regional superintendents, and qualified congregational leaders. If the candidate was found qualified, he was elected and commended to the congregation through a ceremony of prayer and the laying on of hands.

Ministry in America

Protestant views of ministry were brought to the colonial denominations in America. None had a more lasting impact than those of the Puritans.

At the heart of Puritan attempts to reform the episcopally governed Church of England was biblical preaching. Clergy in the homeland often were called priests, and these priests considered their primary responsibility to be the altar. Puritans insisted that the Bible knew no such office in the church. The true clergy, they said, are ministers, with preaching and pastoral care as their primary service.

Second only to preaching in a Puritan minister's calling was the responsibility for pastoral care. This included a number of activities, but none more vital than catechizing church members. We are more inclined today to call this Christian nurture or discipleship, but whatever the label, it stood for instructing the people in the essentials of the Christian faith and lifestyle.

Many American Christians gained their essentials of pastoral theology from the Puritans, namely, the personal experience of conversion and call, biblical preaching to the assembled congregation, and pastoral care pointing toward Christian maturity.

Reverence of Revivals

In nineteenth-century America, the frontier was aflame with revival. To this day, *revival* is an enchanting term for evangelicals. It stands for a style of preaching, a method for winning America, a distinctive tradition of Christian worship, and God's alternative to a state church.

The net effect of these waves of revival was an "americanizing" of the views of ordination and ministry. Since divine Providence willed the separation of church and state in the fledgling republic, the churches were left with nothing more than the voluntary response of individual citizens. As a result, preachers thought long and hard about ways to press the claims of Christ upon the lonely soul.

Charles Finney, the converted lawyer and popular evangelist, insisted that it is the task of the preacher and the church to discard "hidebound forms" and adopt "new methods" that would "awaken the unconcerned and reawaken the complacent." The object of the "new measures" used in revivals was to gain the attention of the public. "There are so many exciting subjects constantly brought before the American public," he wrote, "that churches cannot command attention, without very exciting preaching to get the public ear" (Shelley 1992, 101).

In a fledgling democracy where men and women were being emancipated from the dogmas of the past, including church dogmas, and where the future belonged to absolute individuals, not absolute kings or absolute churches, the kingdom of Christ into which the revivalists exhorted men and women was not identified with the visible church. Churches did arise by the thousands, but evangelicals were concerned not with strengthening institutional Christianity but with instilling the rule of God in individual lives. Self-restraint and moral character were primary; church membership was secondary.

The paramount institutions of this evangelical mission were the voluntary societies, forerunners of those ministries today we call "parachurch." They allowed individual Christians, without regard to denominational loyalties or ordination standards, to mobilize their efforts for some specific moral or religious cause.

What of the churches themselves? By focusing on the supreme task of reaching people, evangelicals were in constant danger of making public response the medium for the voice of God, even in their choice of ministers. Faith in the masses often meant that ordination and theology were open to any serious student of Scripture. *Call*, in the terms of a revival experience, became the dominating qualification for Christian leadership.

Thus revivals exchanged the Puritan gathered congregation of visible saints for a new model of the church as a voluntary society. The work of ministry no longer focused so clearly on Richard Baxter's "reformed" image of preaching the Word and pastoral care within the congregation. Now it centered in the conversion of individual souls outside the church and popular or charismatic leaders of the people. Ministers learned quickly that their survival in the pulpit depended upon their ability to meet these expectations. The call to ministry might come through some private struggle of the soul, but it always required the consent of the people. In this sense, pastors had to be popular.

Contemporary Ministry

When the cultural revolution swept over America in the 1960s, ministers responded to the cultural shift by either resisting the changes or by adapting to the changes.

Leaders of the resistance tended to rely upon the traditional ministerial office. In the so-called Christian Right—with its platform against abortion, the Equal Rights Amendment, homosexuality, pornography, and greater government involvement in education and welfare—spokesmen relied on close ties with televangelists. This helped to widen their appeal for support of the conservative moral agenda. Conservative estimates indicate pastors may have succeeded in registering within the churches at least two million voters.

Not all evangelical clergy, however, joined the resistance. Many preferred to think that self-expression could be enlisted for gospel duty. Carol Flake, in her striking portrait of evangelicalism called *Redemptorama*, says that some evangelicals became "image-peddlers." They adopted "the tokens of mass-produced affection, the illusions of community: bumper-sticker smiles, personalized form letters, televised compassion, published advice" (Shelley 1992, 129–130).

In an age of self-expression, individualism threatened to overthrow corporate Christianity. Religion, like nearly everything else, became a matter of personal choice. Traditional values—confession, covenant, vows, ministerial authority, tradition, community—these tend to fade with other memories of the past. The gospel, like the airline attendant's smile, is marketed.

As a result, churches, seminaries, and ordination councils in our time tend to be less concerned about the doctrine and polity of earlier days and more interested in leaders who can communicate feelings. Like families, churches are expected to be places of love and acceptance in a harsh and competitive society. Not surprisingly, today's preachers, churches, and denominations approach their standards for ordination in the light of these expectations.

—Bruce L. Shelley

Resources

Lippy, C., and P. Williams, eds. 1988. Encyclopedia of the American religious experience, 3 vols. New York: Charles Scribner's Sons.

Niebuhr, R., and D. Williams. 1983. Ministry in historical perspective. New York: Harper.

Oden, T. 1983. Pastoral theology. New York: Harper & Row.

Shelley, B., and M. Shelley. 1992. Consumer church. Downers Grove, Ill.: InterVarsity.

Termination

Sometimes a pastor is asked to leave a pastorate. To put it in business terms, sometimes pastors get fired. Like the report of an auto accident, the news is jarring, and the effect on people is devastating and most unwelcome. So what does the pastor do now?

Preparing to Move On

"Shake the dust off your feet" and move on, says Jesus. That is sound advice even in this day. But as we make our way out of town, we will have to traverse some potentially dangerous streets. Here are some basic rules of the road to follow.

● *Be angry but do not sin.* To be rejected is like being struck a blow. It hurts. The natural, visceral instinct is to hit back, to hurt others as we have been hurt. Some pastors, when fired, mount assaults on a congregation, resorting to stealing from the church, destroying records, or telling secrets. Yet, in our better moments, we recognize that we find little help or healing in getting back at people.

● *Negotiate the dismissal.* Even if the dismissal is immediate, the pastor will want to negotiate the maximum severance arrangement and have it put in writing. Although we may not feel as if we're in a strong bargaining position, a body of custom and law is behind us. The church has accomplished its goal— the pastor's dismissal. The price of reaching that goal is subsidized time for that pastor.

A pastor can take advantage of that time to seek health and healing. Use of the parsonage, salary for six months, and benefits for one year (or until the next employment) are not uncommon.

● *Work on family healing.* Dismissed pastors soon realize they aren't the only ones being "fired." The pastor's family also feels the pain. Certainly pastors can expect some support and help from their immediate family, but the care must flow the other way, as well. Family members do not see themselves as vocational counselors; it's not a role they bargained for. So they'll be of limited help in that regard. In addition, they have their own hurts and angers that need attention, some of which must come from the pastor.

● *Confront the shame.* Shame is so powerful because it's directly related to our self-image. We have high expectations of ourselves, of how we should be treated and understood. To lose one's job is to be judged a failure. Yet we can recover from shame in two ways. First, we can develop a realistic perception of what has happened. The fact is, we're never as totally worthless as shame seems to make us. Second, we can allow a sense of grace—God's unconditional acceptance—slowly to grow anew within us.

● *Deal with vocational doubting.* Fired pastors immediately wonder if they were mistaken about their original sense of calling. Not everyone can or should be a minister, of course, and, frankly, sometimes a dismissal is a sign of that. But not necessarily. Certainly deciding such an issue at the time of dismissal is not a wise course. One is too vulnerable then.

Many pastors find it helpful to consult a colleague or trusted member of the congregation to help them work through vocational doubt during a crisis. This often puts the cosmic soul searching about divine vocation into a manageable light.

It's important to remember that being terminated can ultimately become a blessing. It can help pastors finally accept that they are good at some things but not all things. To their amazement and gratitude, they will likely discover that there are churches desperately needing what they do have to offer.

—*Robert G. Kemper*

10

The Search Process

As pastors, our search for a ministry position is much more than a job hunt; it is the search for the place where we can fruitfully exercise our gifts in and through the Christian community. It is a process that touches every dimension of our lives—personal, family, and vocational—as well as the present and future congregations.

The search, accordingly, is an important process that requires our greatest respect, but it need not leave us overwhelmed. It is helpful to recognize that "the search" actually consists of a series of searches. We will consider six such searches here.

Searching the Heart

Because Christian service is rooted in our identity as daughters and sons of God, we need to look within ourselves before we search too far outward. Over the years Christians have done this by writing their thoughts or by sharing with a trusted colleague, counselor, or spiritual adviser. No matter the approach, the time spent searching the heart yields manifold results later.

Three areas for self-examination are:

● *Our relationship with the Lord.* As pastors, we are particularly vulnerable to distraction and deception when we are considering a move. It is especially important during these times that we immerse ourselves in prayer. In prayer, God may free our spirits to answer a more challenging call. If so, we can move forward knowing the decision was made in faithfulness to God and not from personal ambition. On the other hand, God may show us that our hearts are not pure, that our itch to leave is only a desire to run from our problems.

To search our hearts, we can ask God, "Are my confidence and contentment rooted in you, Lord, or am I trying to find them in external places, achievements, and performance?" The quick fix of a move won't give us the sense of validity, affirmation, connectedness, or belonging we truly crave. These qualities spring only from a healthy relationship with the Lord.

● *Ourselves.* Examining our relationship with God naturally leads to searching ourselves. Honestly asking, "What are my motives for seeking a change?" and "What is the Spirit saying to me now?" can protect us from self-delusion and denial.

In our introspection, however, we must remember—and rest in the fact—that God himself has called us and we are in Christ. As we live in this truth, we will become attractive servants of God who can serve with contentment, no matter where that may be.

● *Our family and other relationships.* We must ask, "What time does my family clock show?" Singleness, dual-career marriages, school-age children, aging parents, divorce, and single-family parenting (to name just a few) significantly affect the search process.

The key question is: "What do I and my family require in order to be faithful to each other and to God's call?"

Understanding our needs in areas such as finances, the necessity of time off, and the amount of time we can commit to work, and special areas such as schooling for a child with special learning needs is imperative in a thoughtful search. If overlooked, these issues will come back to trouble us later in the search process or in the early years of the new ministry.

Searching the Past

An intriguing passage to consider in the search process is Psalm 37:4: "Delight yourself in the Lord and he will give you the desires of your heart." The question is, "What is my heart's desire for ministry?"

Career planners often have their clients make lists of their most satisfying accomplishments, the skills they most like to use, and the information and data they most enjoy working with. Pastors can use such exercises to discover themes from their past that exhibit natural strengths, areas of fruitfulness, patterns of giftedness, and signs of affirmation. As pastors, we might ask: "How do I use my discretionary time in ministry? What sparks my interest and awakens my energy? What are the major themes of my life and ministry?" Also asking these questions in the negative will show those activities we least enjoy or that don't fit our gifts.

Another way to search our past is to read old personal journals and schedules, taking note of the patterns, themes, and recurrent activities present in them. Writing on a topic such as "Lessons Learned from Ministry" or completing statements such as "If I could begin again, I would . . ." are other ways we can discern our true interests.

The search of the past does not mean we are locked into repeating what we've already done, but it does provide us with a kind of compass for registering the gravitational pull of our souls.

Searching Current History

There are two areas to contemplate in our present history. First, we must consider what impact a move would have on our current congregation. Perhaps our vision is too different or too large for us to comfortably stay put. At the same time, however, moving could set the congregation back a few steps.

Many pastors have faced—and agonized over—the choice between a new, intriguing ministry opportunity and the welfare of their present congregation. Our decisions need to include a careful weighing of each implication.

Second, we must assess what impact a move would have for ourselves, taking into consideration our present ministry conditions and style of living. A basic question is, "Am I truly ready to move?"

A friend once told me, "You know it's time to move when you stop putting your flag at the top of the pole." Others have found the joy has drained away and they are simply going through the motions. Frederick Buechner writes that in contrast to the hair-shirt mentality that characterizes some pastors, "The kind of work God usually calls you [to] is the kind of work (a) that you most need to do and (b) that the world most needs to have done. . . . The place God calls you to is the place where your deep gladness and the world's deep hunger meet." We should ask, "Where is my 'joy index?'" This can be an important indicator about readiness to move and the direction in which we should move.

One good exercise for assessing a present ministry is to list as many positive characteristics about it as possible. These might include the location of one's home, the quality of the school system, family routines, the pace of life, the working relationships with church boards and committees, and roles in the community. Completing the sentence "I would gladly stay here for . . ." can help highlight positives.

It is also important to consider what is missing in one's current situation. Again, this can be done by completing statements such as: "I would leave here if. . . ," "I would leave in order to. . . ," or "Things I would like to do, but do not feel I can do in this situation are. . . ."

Such exercises give us our first indication of where future issues of grief and joy would likely emerge in the new church community as well as provide us with much of the material needed for our résumé or dossier.

Searching the Ideal Future

The materials generated in the preceding inventory phases now can be pulled together to form a vision for ministry. This is a time for both prayerful reflection and letting the imagination run wild. We can make a wish list, drawing up a description of our ideal pastoring position, or answering questions such as, "If time and resources were no issue, what would I like to do in ministry?"

New concepts may emerge that never were seriously considered before, and if the next ministry is to be a happy one, these ideals should be present in the ministry in good measure. The key in this phase is to unlock the power of vision, since it is so easy to censor ourselves and stifle our dreams as unrealistic. A clear vision unleashes a spiritual energy we may not fully comprehend but that needs to be cultivated.

Preparing a Résumé

The résumé serves both to inform a pastoral search committee of a person's interest in a job and to generate support among committee members for learning more about that person. Recognizing these purposes will help candidates shape the content of their résumés.

Types of Résumés

In general, most résumés ought to include information about our ministry objectives, qualifications, experience, and education. Churches or denominations sometimes require specific résumé formats, but most are based on one of several models.

The first and most typical is the *historical résumé*. This résumé begins with one's most recent position and works backward in chronologi-cal order, summarizing work history and then educational experience.

A *functional résumé* organizes experiences and qualifications around functions, such as preaching, teaching, administration, or evangelism. This is especially appropriate if one has frequently changed positions or has significant gaps in work experience. It is also useful for highlighting a specialization for a particular position.

A third type of résumé, the *achievement résumé*, highlights primary accomplishments but without specifics dates or positions. Since this résumé can come across as boastful, the emphasis needs to be on the results and benefits to others.

Most résumés incorporate all three elements. Many begin with a historical-summary page and follow with an extended narrative sec-

Searching Potential Ministry Opportunities

With the initial inner work completed, we are now equipped to focus on specific ministry opportunities. This part of the search follows three main steps: making contact, exploring, and deciding.

● *Making contact.* The initial contact with a prospective church sets the tone for what follows. If the church or ministry first contacts us, we have greater freedom for initiative and dialogue. In such situations, our prompt response communicates courtesy and energy to the committee. If uninterested in a position, we should communicate this through a polite letter. If somewhat interested, but ambivalent, we should openly share that with the committee, as well, stating both openness to exploring the possibility and any reservations (such as not wanting to relocate too far from family or uneasiness in undertaking significantly different responsibilities).

When a contact looks promising, immediate phone contact should be made to exchange information and to move the process into the exploration phase.

---

tion that addresses issues such as work experience, leadership style, personal beliefs and theological perspectives, and major issues facing the church and how they might be approached.

Putting It Together

The facts that make up a good résumé arise out of reflection on one's vision, qualifications, and experience in ministry. The résumé is usually one page in length, sometimes as long as a page and a half (not including narrative sections).

Résumé writing consists of developing concise, bulleted bits of information, rather than creating complete sentences. Attention to detail goes a long way in capturing a committee's attention, as does the use of vivid images and creative concepts in describing one's ministry. Neatness and precision tell a committee that the person cared enough to offer quality work.

A cover letter is one of the most effective ways to secure a reading, especially if the candidate can mention a mutual friend who might serve as a reference. Of course, the friend needs to know about this and agree to it. A frequently omitted—but important—element in résumés is a clear, concise statement of one's vocational objective.

Sometimes candidates develop tailor-made résumés for specific openings. It is often wise to write different résumés that emphasize certain areas of skill or experience over others, depending on the unique position being sought. An example would be the pastor who is considering either planting a new church or serving an existing congregation as an interim minister. Different skills and strengths would be needed, so it would be appropriate to prepare different résumés.

—*Douglas J. Rumford*

Pastors who initiate contact with a church, perhaps through a denominational or seminary placement system, place themselves in a responsive mode and subject themselves to the pastoral placement system. The best way of getting through the inevitable committee paperwork of such systems is to take advantage of personal connections within the system. If we don't have a personal point of contact, we can stimulate interest by sending a résumé and a cover letter that communicates the reason for the contact and what we believe we could bring to the position.

A variety of protocol questions arise in this mating dance between pastors and churches, such as:

—How aggressive or persistent should a pastor be? There is a fine balance between making a clear and confident presentation and being

---

Candidating and Interviewing

The candidating interview is an effective tool for discerning expectations. At an interview, we can minister to the committee as well as help discern if this invitation is of God.

Upon being invited to interview, one of the first things to make clear is that we will be asking a number of questions ourselves and that we expect our questions to take at least an hour.

We will want to raise three types of questions:

● *Questions of census.* These questions probe the identity of the congregation—their talents, interests, and commitments. The questions also look beyond the congregation to the area it serves.

● *Questions of issue.* Every congregation also has particular issues we will want to know about. Some are low-risk, pleasantly discussed questions of theory; others are powder kegs.

● *Questions of structure.* These attempt to discover both the formal and the hidden networks in the congregation. But they also can probe beyond this particular congregation.

Before the Committee

Both candidate and committee are best served if the committee asks their questions first. That way, we can modify ours to follow up on issues they have raised. Our agenda should include not only our personal concerns but also the task of ministering to their needs.

We can preface our questions with a statement that some of the answers we seek are matters of fact, but others are matters of feeling, specifically their feelings. As a result, we realize there may be different answers to one question, and we welcome that diversity of opinion. Our having a list of prepared questions based on our understanding of the congregation gives a better impression than if we appear to ask questions off the cuff.

too aggressive. Problems arise if we "market ourselves" through too many materials too soon in the process. A related temptation is to rush the committee to a decision. We must realize that there will be dynamics within the committee that slow the process but have nothing to do with us as candidates.

Usually, the wisest approach is to be mildly persistent. For example, we may find it appropriate to follow up on the submission of materials and to check back again after eight to ten weeks. There may be times when it is appropriate to ask the committee where things stand in the decision-making process, whether one is still being considered as a serious candidate, and whether candidates will be informed if their status changes. But more pressure than this might put the committee members in an awkward place—or even antagonize them.

Questions to Ask

Here are a few sample questions to open the discussion at an interview:

● *Why am I of particular interest to you?* This is a good opening question. It is not a case of fishing for compliments, but it helps to know how interested they are, and why.

● *What has been the most significant event in the life of this congregation since you have been a member?* The question serves two purposes: We discover what events are significant to them and we see what ministries this congregation considers significant.

● *Aside from the upheaval of looking for a new pastor, what has been the most upsetting event in the life of this church?* While they may have had plenty of private (and potentially divisive) thoughts and comments before, this question allows them to voice their pain openly. It also allows us the luxury of future vision—knowing what is likely to upset them in the years ahead.

● *What areas of concern need to be addressed by this congregation?*

Delightfully nonspecific, this question may be the perfect invitation for a committee member to open an issue that is unresolved.

● *Has the pastor's family traditionally taken an active role in this church?* In answering this question, committee members may reveal how they felt about the activity of previous pastors' families. Therein lies the key to the criteria by which our families will be judged.

But How Do I Know?

The search for the perfect congregation is futile. Accepting a call is at best a series of tradeoffs. Consequently, before we begin the process, we need to assess our professional needs and our family's social and economic needs.

The interview, stressful and upsetting as it may be, is the best forum for hammering out concerns, commitments, and priorities in an atmosphere of excitement and high expectation. Handled carefully and prayerfully, it can lead to a long and fruitful relationship.

—*Douglas G. Scott*

—Are there ways to read the situation and tailor one's approach, church by church? This may be appropriate, but never at the expense of authenticity. A chameleon pastor may become too camouflaged to recognize.

—Should an applicant ever recontact a committee that has already sent a rejection letter? Rarely. The exception is when the candidate has substantial reason to believe he or she was misrepresented or had not communicated clearly. The best reentry approach may be to have someone known and trusted by the search committee inquire into the committee's openness to reconsidering the applicant.

● *Exploration.* There are two, sometimes three, stages of exploration. The first is with the pastoral search committee. The purpose here is to clarify the church's situation and expectations for their new pastor, and for the pastor to communicate to the committee his or her ministry vision, priorities, skills, and gifts.

Preparation for these interviews should include learning as much as possible about the potential congregation through talking with colleagues, seminary friends, and denomination and association representatives. We should learn about the church's theological orientation, worship style, commitment to evangelism and missions, history of pastoral leadership, relationship with the community, and financial stability, among other issues of personal interest. While we will want to learn about the area's climate, geography, housing, schools, and style of life, it is best to cover these practical issues before the interview, so our interview questions can focus on ministry matters.

The second stage of exploration is with the lay-leadership board, the group pastors work with when they arrive. Most search committees have not considered including the leadership board in the hiring process. This is okay for the initial screening, but a meeting between this board and the finalists is essential, since such meetings provide a reality check for all involved.

Pastors considering larger churches will have a third stage of exploration: meeting with the staff. The pastor should be informed from the start whether staff will continue or change when he or she arrives and how the staff will be expected to relate to the new leadership.

Other questions that arise in the exploration phase include:

—What do we owe the search committee? We owe them an honest presentation of our past ministry as well as the willingness to tell the committee should we decide not to pursue the opportunity further. Before using the committee's money to visit when long distances are involved, it is courteous to participate in thorough telephone interviews first to test whether a visit would be productive.

—What can we expect from the committee in return? As candidates, we have the right to expect and ask for clear communication from the committee. Since both the pastor and the committee are often conducting simultaneous searches, it is appropriate to ask the committee what stage they are in in their process, while communicating to them our situation, especially if there has been a recent change in our status. When this is done in a spirit of humble communication, committees usually are cooperative.

Financially, the pastor can expect the committee to provide the primary expenses for travel and lodging for visits and interviews. In the best of circumstances, this should include the clergy's spouse. The way finances are handled at this stage usually speaks volumes about the way they will be handled in the future.

—What do we say to our current congregation and key leaders? The traditional model is to inform a congregation only when a call is in hand. This keeps the congregation from anxiety during the uncertainties of a search, and it allows the pastor to maintain an active ministry without the complications and confusion of "leaving issues."

On the negative side, since the congregation is told of the decision cold, the congregation will not have had the opportunity to negotiate and otherwise process the decision with the pastor. Sometimes the grief and frustration that follow an abrupt departure disrupt congregational life for months and years to follow.

In another model, especially fitting for those who have had a long pastorate, the pastor informs the congregation early. This allows the congregation to process their grief. It is also the most risky method, since there is no turning back once the people have been informed.

No matter which style is chosen, the issues of loss and grief over pastoral change must be taken seriously and processed intentionally by both the pastor and the people.

—How do we deal with the emotional side of the process? The emotional impact of the search varies greatly among pastors. Some are able to keep a sense of detachment and objectivity, while some answer the phone every day expecting to hear an unknown voice eagerly asking for "The Reverend We-Want."

The wise approach is to not overinvest in any one situation. This is where a spiritual adviser can be helpful to us, supporting us throughout the roller-coaster ride of the entire process. We should also avoid getting ahead of our family members, and we need to find ways of preparing our children for the process and seeking their input.

How do we handle rejection? We need to remember that a rejection is solely for one particular place of ministry at one particular time—a far different perspective than seeing it as rejection of one's self and ministry.

● *Honing in on a decision.* By this point, we should be clear on what we seek: ministry vision, priorities, and staff configuration, along with personal household issues such as finances, time off, housing, relocation expenses, and timing for a move. Matching our criteria with the church's, we are ready to negotiate the specific terms of a call. The decision to accept the call will be marked more by art than mechanics, as tangible facts and observations mingle with intangible feelings and intuitions. Answering the question "What does God need to show me for me to truly accept this as God's call?" can help us clarify the issues.

An important question that must be considered when moving toward a decision is, "Are there danger signals that ought to be addressed before accepting a call?" As with marriage, the illusion that "things can be worked out later" lays a sandy foundation for the future. Common differences include the expected frequency and nature of communication, and the depth to which the congregation is willing or unwilling to go in regard to past conflicts and congregational tensions.

It is important that salary and benefits be thoroughly discussed before the call is accepted. Candor from all parties at this time can help secure fairness for the future and reduce the risk of disillusionment and frustration.

Searching the Heart—Again

Finally, we return to where we started: searching the heart. Testimony is given time and again to the fact that after all the necessary work of human seeking and evaluation, the final decision is made by the heart in a suprarational way. That is, ultimately, the whole search process is rooted in faith.

The story is told of a salty old ship captain who was required to learn all the modern navigational aids. After doing his calculations, he would then go on deck, smell the wind, feel the pitch and roll of the waves, and correct his calculations. Our best calculations will clarify what the issues are that need prayer and dialogue. The final step is one of faith, not of sight, as we trust the Lord of the journey.

—Douglas J. Rumford

Resources

Bolles, R. 1992. The 1992 what color is your parachute? Berkeley, Cal.: Ten Speed Press.

Drain, P. 1992. Hire me! Los Angeles: Price Stern Sloan.

Gerberg, R. 1986. Robert Gerberg's job changing system. Kansas City: Andrews, McMeel & Parker.

Kemper, R. 1978. Beginning a new pastorate. Nashville: Abingdon.

11

Negotiating the Terms of a Call

By the time a search committee makes its selection and the pastoral candidate has agreed—in theory at least—to come to a church, a long process has been concluded. At this point, however, a shorter but equally vital process is about to begin. It's time to talk about the terms of call.

Often the committee initiates this process and goes through the terms of the call as the members understand them. Sometimes, however, we may need to formalize these assumptions ourselves, by saying something like, "For both of our sakes, let's make sure we have this all worked out. I need to know your expectations for this call, and you probably want to know mine. Could we work through some items about the call?" The point is: Make sure the process is begun.

Avoiding the Adversarial

Since we want to begin our relationship with a congregation on a warm, nonadversarial tone, it's a mistake to enter discussions with dogmatic expectations. Rather than declaring my needs, for instance, I like to begin the talks by asking for information. Say I'm talking about continuing-education opportunities. Instead of declaring, "I must have two weeks continuing education and $500 per year," I would ask the committee, "What has been your previous experience with continuing education?"

This is especially important when the church has had a bad experience in the area being discussed. If, in the example above, the previous pastor had used continuing education to sit on a Florida beach, the church would naturally be reticent about study leaves. But when I ask, "What do you think about continuing education?" the committee can relate their bad experience. Then I can remain sensitive to their concerns, saying, for instance, "I certainly can see why a continuing-education leave has left a bad taste in your mouths. But let me say why I consider study leave important *and* what I intend to do with any time you might give me."

This approach isn't aggressive, but it does allow us to get our concerns on the table. If I feel continuing education is crucial for my development as a minister, I'm setting myself up for disappointment and anger if I don't bring it up. It's like marrying and then trying to iron out differences over whether or not to have children. It doesn't work. *After* I become their pastor shouldn't be the first time they hear about my strong desire for continuing education.

In short, we must approach this part of these negotiations neither dogmatically nor passively, but like this: "Here are some of the things important to me, and as we move along in this pastoral relationship, let's continue to talk about them. I trust you to do the right thing." Even if we have to give on some points, we leave open the possibility of further consideration down the road.

A related problem to avoid is entering the discussion with a long and detailed list of expectations. We sometimes hear the counsel, "You're borrowing trouble if you don't make your needs known in a detailed and specific way. You and the church need to know exactly what to expect from each another." That's true to a certain extent, since the working arrangements need to be clear. But when it's taken too far, trust is undermined, and only a binding contract remains.

Some details we do need, of course. While we don't want too detailed or dogmatic a list, we do want to achieve clarity and understanding as we come to terms. What details, other than reimbursement, we want to put into writing depends on our unique concerns. But we should assume nothing about those things that are important to us.

Remuneration Ruminations

Central to the terms of call is remuneration. But before getting into details, we should be aware of the many factors that determine remuneration. For example, the previous pastor's salary often sets limits on how much the church is willing to pay the new minister, at least at the beginning of his or her pastorate.

Then again, what other ministers earn can be a greater factor still. Although one congregation I served had been financially gracious to me, they found that after I left, the salary I'd been given didn't match what pastors candidating for the position were receiving. Finally the committee had to approach the congregation, saying, "Folks, we won't be able to talk seriously with the kind of pastor we want, based on what we paid Ed." The church agreed and raised the salary package.

Churches sometimes set the pastor's salary close to the mean or median salary in the congregation, thinking the pastor should live on the level of the average member. Another rule of thumb is to look at the pay of comparable professionals in the community, such as a high school principal, for example. Naturally, the size and budget of a church also sets limits on what churches, no matter how well intentioned, can realistically afford.

Two factors to be weighed carefully are first, the needs of the pastor (size of family, children in college, etc.), and second, the compensation of other pastors of similar churches in the community. Earnings vary considerably by denomination and by church, but it's helpful for people to become aware of what other local congregations are paying.

Finally, although most congregations have determined more or less what they'll pay a pastor, the search committee and candidate can apportion the dollars within the pay package. Creative and personalized distribution of the gross pay can satisfy both the church's desire to be fair but thrifty and the pastor's need to maximize the utility of the gross pay.

A Package of Many Parts

To see how, in fact, pay can be apportioned, let's look at four major components of a salary package.

● *Salary.* Salary is what we must live on. Therefore, the salary portion of our pay package needs to remain distinct from reimbursements for expenses we accrue by doing ministry: mileage costs for hospital calls, long-distance church calls from home, dinner out with the guest evangelist, and so on. Salary is what we're paid; reimbursements pay us back for costs that ought not come from our pockets.

In most churches, our salary figure is tied closely to our housing figure, because the two categories together constitute what is salary for nonclergy. When a congregation does not provide us a parsonage, it's not uncommon to divide the total salary into portions for salary and housing allowance that best fit our needs. The cost to the church remains the same, but our tax advantages can be significant.

While talking salary, it's a good idea to make clear when and how salary reviews will take place. Will they be yearly? What criteria will be used? Who initiates the review, and who will conduct it? Since living costs continue to rise yearly, some provision for regular salary review is important.

We don't have to pin down a church to specific details about the salary review, such as expected percentages. But we can show we expect people to treat us equitably year by year.

● *Housing.* Two arrangements are common: (a) a house (parsonage) provided free by the congregation, or (b) a housing allowance paid to us to secure housing of our choice. Since the value of the parsonage or the money given in a housing allowance is not taxable for income tax purposes (although it is for self-employment taxes), the provision of housing is in effect an income tax–free segment of our salary. We pastors gain a great benefit from this provision, and we are wise to convert as much as possible of our salary/housing payment into housing, given, of course, the limitations placed by the IRS.

If paid a housing allowance, generally we are wise to make the allowance large enough to cover expenses for buying (or renting) a residence, furnishing it, maintaining it, paying for utilities, and even purchasing cleaning or maintenance supplies for it. If necessary, we're ahead if we give up a little salary to obtain a larger housing allowance, as long as we can justify the housing allowance to the IRS. In fact, when determining the housing allowance (or other tax-related items), it's wise to check with a tax accountant knowledgeable about clergy taxes.

If we are to use a parsonage, we need to make clear with the committee which responsibilities are ours and which the church's. Specifically, can we decorate the parsonage, or do we need permission for any changes? Who pays for redecoration? Who fixes a leaky faucet, and do we need someone's approval to call a plumber? Who pays the utilities? These kinds of agreements are important, because pastors sometimes have found themselves in hot water, so to speak, by not knowing the standard procedure.

One distinct disadvantage of a parsonage, however, is that upon retirement the pastor won't have equity in a home. One way to remedy that situation is for the parsonage-dwelling pastor to request that money be set aside each month for a housing fund that he or she will receive at retirement. For example, one minister established an agreement with her congregation whereby they contributed $125 a month and she added from her pay another $100 a month to a tax-sheltered annuity in her name, so that by retirement she will have built a fund toward purchasing her own home. She has since been called to another congregation, but the annuity went with her and will be available when she retires. She and her new church can continue the annuity, if they so choose.

● *Benefits.* Although not exactly pay, benefits certainly enhance the pay package and often add up to a significant percentage of actual salary and housing. Therefore, it's a good policy to discuss exactly which benefits will be provided by the church. These possibilities are often considered:

—*Retirement plan.* Retirement has a way of sneaking up on a pastor, and it's never too early to get started on retirement planning. The government recently has encouraged personal retirement investment through tax-sheltered annuities, known as 403(b) plans, for employees of nonprofit organizations. In these plans the employer deducts money from salary and deposits it directly into an annuity. It is good to talk with the search committee to see if this plan can be made available.

—*Health insurance.* This is practically a must in today's world. If the church doesn't provide it as a benefit, most of us will find it necessary to pay for it out of pocket. If we can get it included as a benefit (even if we have to give up a little salary to do so), we may be able to save a little on taxes, depending on how exactly we itemize our deductions.

—*Disability insurance.* Disability coverage is tremendously important. Since it often isn't automatically included in a pay package, it's well worth negotiating. I knew of a pastor of a smaller congregation who fell down some stairs at his church and was left paralyzed. He didn't have disability insurance, but the church wanted to be fair with him, so they continued his salary for many months. Finally, however, they needed to call another pastor, and they couldn't afford the salary of two pastors. It became a tragic, no-win situation.

—*Life insurance.* Term life and mortgage insurance don't cost a congregation much and can give a lot of peace of mind as benefits. Regular life insurance, which is more of a personal investment, is something many pastors also pursue personally.

● *Expense accounts.* The cost of doing ministry ought to be borne by the church. Therefore, we need to make clear with the search committee just which expenses will be picked up by the congregation—and how payment will be made. Here are some expenses you may want to discuss with the committee:

—*Transportation costs.* According to the IRS, commuting costs aren't professional expenses, so we can't expect reimbursement for driving to and from church. But as pastors, we use a car to do visitation, make hospital calls, attend meetings, and drive for youth events. That mileage adds up, and most churches are willing to foot the bill.

A car allowance is one way churches can repay us for our expenses, but tax experts recommend against it, since we must pay taxes on a portion of it. Two other systems require a little record keeping yet fully reimburse our expenses. Under the first system, we keep a log of our ministry miles and get reimbursed on a per-mile basis (29 cents a mile in 1994). The second system demands that we keep track of our actual expenses (gas, repairs, depreciation, insurance, etc.) and our ministry and personal mileage; then we submit a request for reimbursement for the ministry proportion of our expenses.

Some congregations supply a car or van for pastors to use for church business. Personal use of the vehicle is considered taxable, so it's wise to understand the ramifications of using a church vehicle.

—*Continuing education.* Many churches want to encourage the professional development of their pastor, so they budget money each year to cover the pastor's costs for attending seminars and meetings. Some churches put aside money yearly to fund a sabbatical for the pastor.

—*Books and periodicals.* Building a good library costs money. Churches may want to help pay these professional costs through a book account from which we can draw to purchase commentaries and other tools of the trade. Again, a vouchered account has the best tax advantages.

—*Other expenses.* Pastors accrue other expenses in the course of ministry. For example, when my wife and I had to take a guest minister and his wife to dinner, it could easily cost forty dollars. Or when I took the church secretaries to lunch for Secretaries' Week, it got expensive to pick up the tab. Other pastors join Rotary Club as a community ministry for the church. If churches are to cover these costs, it needs to be agreed upon in advance.

—*Moving expenses.* The costs of a move are considerable, and although some can be deducted from taxes, that deduction doesn't begin to cover the expense. Churches most often will make arrangements to help substantially with the move, but we can't just assume it.

Also, *how* the move is made is important. Are we expected to move ourselves, with help unloading at our new community? Do we hire professional movers and bill the church? Will the church pick up the costs of a professional move, up to a certain dollar figure? These questions need to be ironed out. And since most movers require a substantial deposit, how that is to be paid must also be decided.

Delineating Other Details

Other questions that have little to do with money need answers. Most of these questions revolve around working arrangements. Consider the following:

● *Job description.* A pastor's job is nearly impossible to put on paper. How do you chart a pastor's vision? Yet a general statement of the responsibilities of the job can help formalize what both parties consider important.

For instance, pastors need to know to whom they are answerable and whom they supervise. That's basic. In one of my pastorates, the minister of music and youth supervised the organist, and the minister of education supervised the custodian. But the church secretary reported directly to me, as did the financial secretary. Knowing these formal relationships in advance helped me as I began pastoring that church; I didn't accidently step on another supervisor's toes.

● *Performance reviews and termination.* Many pastors are suspicious of performance reviews. Sometimes it seems that churches perform reviews only when people are critical of the pastor. Furthermore, pastors feel few people are qualified to review their work. But reviews can be helpful. If we will have an effective ministry, we need to hear how our ministry is being received.

It is useful at least yearly to talk with the board of deacons about (1) what has been most meaningful to them in the church in the last year, and (2) what they would like to see happen in the church. Pastors are wise to work out some system of review in the terms of call.

Forced termination has become more common these days, and that makes it important for us to be acquainted with the church's policy for termination. Some churches have no such policy, and in that case, it may be a good idea eventually to place something in the bylaws.

It is not uncommon for the termination policies to stipulate the notice that should be given by either party wanting to terminate the pastoral agreement. Other matters such as references, salary continuation, and continued use of the parsonage often are covered.

● *Vacation and study leave.* It's best to have a clear understanding about the number of vacation days to be given each year. Since pastors' weeks evolve differently from other professionals, vacation days can become confusing. For instance, what does "four weeks of vacation" mean? Twenty-eight days in a row? Four Sundays plus twenty-four other assorted days away? Can it be taken all at once, or should it be spread out a little? These things can be cleared up in discussion with the search committee.

Likewise, study leave for continuing education needs to be agreed upon. Many churches recognize the validity of time away for concerted study and even encourage it. But not all churches, so we need to know which kind of church we're joining. Also, can we accumulate study leave for a few years and take a major break? Can we accumulate the continuing education allowance, if there is one?

And how about a sabbatical? The beginning of the relationship is often the easiest time to request a sabbatical. After all, it remains six or seven years in the future. It's easy to grant when it is so far away.

—*Edward B. Bratcher*

Resources

Biersdorf, J., ed. 1976. Creating an intentional ministry. Nashville: Abingdon.

Bratcher, E. 1987. The walk-on-water syndrome. Waco, Tex.: Word.

Kemper, R. 1978. Beginning a new pastorate. Nashville: Abingdon.

Kemper, R. 1985. What every church member should know about clergy. New York: Pilgrim.

Neuhaus, R. 1992. Freedom for ministry. Grand Rapids: Eerdmans.

Oswald, R. 1989. New beginnings: A pastorate start-up workbook. New York: Alban Institute.

12

Making the Move

Moving from one pastorate to another can be a ministry in itself—ministering to the pain and grief of a former congregation, teaching a new one to welcome us well. However, the most important aspect of a move is our attitudinal choice. That is, we must determine at the outset that we are responsible for the happiness of our family and the quality of the transition we are facing. Further, we must assume that none of the people who have called us to a new pastorate have experience in moving other families, and that in setting clear expectations for ourselves and our congregations (past and future), we are helping them minister to us and to each other.

Our commitment to our family's well-being and comfort before, during, and after the move is more than a tactical necessity; it demonstrates to the church that the family is the primary site of our ministry. With this in mind, we can survey the issues and concerns related to the mechanics of a move from one church to another. These concerns fall into four categories, roughly corresponding to the four stages of the move itself: early concerns to be addressed during the interview process, issues emerging during negotiation and acceptance of a contract, things to do before the movers come, and forming a new home when the move is complete.

When Interviewing

Aside from the obvious issue of whether going to a particular church is appropriate, some portion of the interview process should be devoted to discovering what provisions have been made by the congregation for the actual transition. Here are some questions to explore with the committee or its representatives:

● What provision has been made for housing? If the church maintains a parsonage or rectory, is it adequate for your family's requirements? Is it in good repair? Has the committee made provision for you and your family to tour the house? If the church provides a housing allowance, is it adequate to cover mortgage and utility costs in the area? Is there a real estate agent in the parish who will assist with discovery of an appropriate house—perhaps without fee?

● Is the congregation able to assume the cost of the move, including extraordinary costs for moving pianos, pool tables, or other heavy items requiring special care? Will they accept the cost of insuring objects of art, jewelry, or other valuables during the move?

● Is the congregation able to provide salary and benefits (particularly health coverage) *during* the move itself? While many moves are close enough to be accomplished overnight, a move of more than 300 miles may take longer to accomplish. While the former congregation may provide a generous purse upon departure, the new congregation's willingness to begin salary on the day of the move itself will demonstrate their care for the pastor.

During Final Negotiations

They really like us, but the well-being of our family may not be their highest priority. The call committee is faced with an anxious congregation, budget limitations, and a mandate to get us there as cheaply and efficiently as possible. It helps to make it clear that, while we share their concerns, we must also help them understand what we will face in this transition. This is not an act of selfishness but of self-care, and inviting them into that care makes them responsible stewards of one of their most important resources. Here are subjects to consider:

● Having determined that the receiving church will assume the costs of moving, will they allow you to contract with the mover of your choice? If they suggest that a group of church volunteers rent a truck to move you themselves, will they assume the cost of insurance for damages incurred in the move?

● When you are negotiating a departure from a congregation, is the former church willing to provide time and compensation designated as termination leave? Will health and death benefits be carried through that leave?

● What unrealized vacation time should be included in the termination agreement? If a pastor has not had sabbatical time during her tenure, is the former congregation willing to extend a compensated portion of time beyond the last day of work for unrealized sabbatical time? Many judicatories grant as much as two weeks to one month per year of service as a sabbatical leave.

● If the church provides a rectory, what repairs and improvements will be performed before you move? Who will select paint, paper, and carpet samples (the best answer is you and your spouse)? How much money is set aside in the annual budget for repair and improvement? How often will the church redecorate? Who is expected to care for the grounds around the parsonage? Does the budget contain a line item for landscaping, shrubs, and tree care? What provisions are made for capital improvements?

Those expected to live in a rectory can also ask: Is the church prepared to provide an equity allowance over and above annual salary increases that will allow you to build equity this other way? Will that equity allowance increase year by year, using the same formula as salary increases? Another formula? Which one? By agreeing to live in the church's house, a pastor loses valuable equity that other home-owners build through their houses. The pastor also loses the considerable tax advantages that come with owning a house.

Since pastors are required to pay substantial SECA taxes on the fair rental value of the rectory in which they live, is the church prepared to pay that portion of their self-employment tax? Will that amount be provided in addition to any annual compensation increases?

● If the church provides a housing allowance, will that allowance be adjusted annually to reflect changes in the regional consumer price index? If not, what other schedule or method will be utilized? Will the church assist with the cost of life insurance on the mortgage to provide protection for your family in the event of your death?

One of the keys to success at this stage is to get everything in writing. This is not a matter of trust, but of memory. More often than not, the membership of governing boards rotates, which means the pastor's is the longest memory among the church leadership corporately. A great deal of pain and debate can be averted if our contract with the church has the details of our original agreement spelled out.

Before the Movers Come

This is a time of great anticipation for both a receiving congregation and a clergy family. It is also a time of high anxiety. By directing the events during this time, we, as arriving pastors, accomplish two objectives. First, we take good care of our family's needs, and, second, we also teach the receiving congregation how to care well for their arriving pastor. Having established an attitude of compassionate expectation, we create the benevolent atmosphere of welcome in the congregation.

● In negotiating a departure from a current congregation, we should solicit church members' ideas about how to make their transition easier. But we can likewise suggest that we will need time in our weekly schedule to prepare for our family's transition, as well. It is not unreasonable to devote about a work day per week to transition activities.

● If the new parish is within driving distance, we can plan a few day trips to arrange for new connections. After receiving recommendations from members of the receiving congregation, we can make appointments to visit with new doctors, dentists, and any medical specialists our family will require, taking medical records and x-rays with us. To make transferring funds a simple matter, we can open a checking account in the bank the church uses for its accounts.

We may want to take our children out of school for a half-day visit to the classes they will enter in the new school. It is especially helpful

---

Concluding a Ministry

There's something about closing one chapter of our lives and opening ourselves to a new one that excites us. Along with our joy about the new pastorate, however, there will also be a sense of tension about leaving the present ministry.

The Tasks of Leaving

Most pastors learn by experience, after a few moves, how to handle the tensions and leave properly. Invariably, they point to a few key tasks that have made their times of transition as smooth and as painless as possible:

● *Let emotions have their way.* Many experiences in life cause two contrary emotions to struggle for predominance. Changing churches is one of them. At one moment, the pastor feels terrific—a wonderful church wants me! Then the next

moment his teenage daughter comes to him in tears asking, "Daddy, do we *have* to move?" The ecclesiastical hero has become the family villain.

It's difficult to live back and forth between contrary emotions. But if we try to fight these emotions, we simply complicate an already complex situation. Consequently, it's better to let such emotions weave their way into our lives and let God, in his time, resolve the tensions.

● *Write a good-bye letter.* Moving means having to write a "Dear John" letter. In composing the letter, it's best simply to tell people what's going on with us. In addition, we can remind the congregation of the need for changes, that we cannot do everyone's funeral or confirm or baptize every child. We can celebrate what has been good between us and name high accom-

if children can make appointments to meet their prospective teachers, including teachers of elective subjects such as music, computers, and art. We can also plan to visit places that provide private lessons for such activities as music, dance, or karate, to help children feel their needs in the move are as important as the adults'. Children involved in sports might want to see practices and playing fields, and meet the coaches.

If a spouse will seek employment in the new location, we can ask church board members to arrange for introductions to employers, personnel departments, or employment agencies.

● Pastors moving into church-owned housing can ask the church secretary to notify the local Welcome Wagon of the date of their move. Usually such services are activated only by housing sales in the area, meaning families moving into a parsonage are often overlooked.

---

plishments worked on jointly. Finally, we must assure them that the church goes on.

Lyle Schaller suggests that we include in this letter a variety of reasons for leaving: theological (It's God's will), professional (The new church will use many of my gifts), and personal (We'll be within an hour of my wife's parents), and the like. If we offer multiple reasons, members will surely understand at least one of the reasons and so better accept the decision to move.

● *Minister until the last.* Until the resignation takes effect, we still have continuing duties to perform with professional competence and integrity. For example, people will want us to baptize a child, marry a daughter, or whatever before we leave. Also, elected lay leaders are feeling a new sense of responsibility for the church, knowing we will soon no longer be there to counsel them. So they ask many questions about procedure and propriety, sometimes in desperation. They have heard what to do, but faced with the prospect of having to do it

themselves, they are in a bit of a panic.

Some people need to meet with us personally and privately. No matter how well we communicate our reasons for leaving, a few people may feel betrayed. We need to communicate that the decision is not a personal rejection of them.

There are also those people we've managed to alienate from the church during our tenure. Sometimes one last stab at reconciliation is in order.

● *Graciously accept parting gifts and tributes.* People want and need to bid us farewell, and giving gifts and saying words of appreciation is a way they do that. One caveat: When leaving a parish, we ought to try not to believe all the nice things said about us. In other words, we should receive tributes graciously but also with a grain of salt. If we don't, we may begin to wonder why we're leaving these wonderful people, and we may convince ourselves that the new sense of call was nothing but indigestion.

—Robert G. Kemper

● We may want to ask the congregation to provide some "anticipation." Most families feel some anxiety about the move to their new home and would appreciate something to look forward to. One parish I served distributed slips of paper to each person attending worship for two weeks and asked them to write down something they particularly enjoyed about their community. Some people offered recommendations for restaurants; others shared the location of a favorite picnic spot. Some very thoughtful people included their telephone numbers with offers of baby-sitting. Others promised a quiet afternoon's visit for coffee or tea. Still others offered to pick up our children to play with theirs while we unpacked. My wife and I wrote to each person who responded, and those notes provided me with plenty of reward. Years later, folks would still comment about the time I took to write during such a busy period in our lives.

One congregation provided a "care package" for their new pastor

---

Beginning a New Ministry

In pastoral work, most mistakes can be corrected. Not so with beginnings. We cannot begin at a congregation twice, so we must use this unique opportunity well. If thoughtfully and imaginatively done, the events of the first year set a tone and approach that a pastor and congregation can enjoy for years to come.

Getting Acquainted

Most pastoral search committees want their minister primarily to preach effectively. But preaching, in which people see us only in our "game uniform," is only one part of getting acquainted. We must get to know each other at a deeper level. Four methods help accomplish that end:

● *Declare a moratorium on change.* It's usually best to make practically no changes in the church for a year. Instead, we can

use the first year to be present at everything, to wait, to listen, and to learn. In particular, we can investigate: How are children treated here? How is money handled? Is the stranger made welcome? Are families interrelated? Is the building something of an icon to this congregation? We can take private notes, both appreciative and critical, on what we observe.

In exchange for not making changes for a year, we can ask the congregation to agree to receive a series of recommendations about their church after that first year. Because our recommendations are based on careful observation and a year's worth of trust, they stand a good chance of being warmly received.

● *Write a booklet.* Becoming acquainted involves teaching a congregation how to relate to a minister in general and to us in particular. So even before arriving, we can

and his family. Included in this beautifully packed box was a copy of the local newspaper, a map of the town and surrounding communities, T-shirts for the children with their new schools' names and logos, coupons for a local car wash, names and phone numbers of area clergy families, some passes to a nearby movie theater, and a bundle of gift certificates, including one for a restaurant in their current community to provide a "last night out." A parish pictorial directory and a flurry of welcome notes from members rounded out the package.

● Details abound when planning a move, so it's wise to keep a to-do list on the refrigerator door, adding items as we think of them, such as:

—Contact the post office and arrange to forward your mail.

—Collect labels from magazines and tape them to change-of-address post cards.

—Find out how much time you are allowed before changing dri-

---

send the new congregation a small booklet about ourselves and our concept of ministry. In such a booklet, I can tell them how honored I am to have been invited to become their pastor, how I became a minister, people and experiences that have influenced me, and my credentials. I can also help them understand what I like to do best and what I am good at, and such information as the day of the week I will be off.

I can also help educate the people about my wife's role, explaining that she is not responsible for my schedule, so if they want me to know something, they should tell me, not her. I can gently suggest I'd prefer they call me at the church office to discuss church matters, not at home.

● *Invite people over.* Assuming the willing cooperation of a spouse, a new pastor may want to invite the entire congregation into his or her home in groups of twenty or so for an "Evening with the Pastor." This type of gathering can be kept infor-

mal. People may first want to mingle over dessert and coffee before being invited to assemble. In the group setting, we may want to ask each person to offer his or her personal story, suggesting an outline to follow. We can ask people to conclude by telling their fondest hope for the church. When I have done this, I was continually surprised at what I learned. And it was guaranteed that next Sunday I would see them in church!

● *See parishioners at work.* It is surprisingly worthwhile to visit parishioners at their places of employment—after first asking them to invite us, of course. Although some won't take us up on the invitation, many will. We will spend wonderful afternoons in factories, schools, offices, and institutions, often learning more about our parishioners in one visit to their work places than we could by seeing them in church for a year. In this way we begin identifying with them and their concerns.

—*Robert G. Kemper*

ver's license and auto registrations, if moving out of state.

—Notify your judicatory's pension program of your impending move and arrange to have premiums billed to your new congregation, effective the date of the move.

—Notify life and health insurance companies of the date of your impending move.

—Notify the Social Security Administration of your move (and Immigration and Naturalization, if appropriate). At the same time, request a summary of your payment status for review. Make sure to include your change of address with your next quarterly IRS payment.

● When contacting moving companies for estimates, here are some tips:

—Ask if they have a Clergy Relocation Program. Many movers have special packages for clergy planning church moves; for example: Armstrong Transfer and Storage (800/749-9333), Cord NorthAmerican (800/873-2673), and The Relocation Center (800/733-0930).

—Decide beforehand what items should be moved by hand rather than by the movers, remembering that while we may try to take special care of precious objects, if they break while we are moving them, they will not be covered by the mover's insurance.

—Negotiate a balance between items you pack and items the movers will pack. For example, I have always packed books and other nonbreakables but asked the church moving me to allow movers to pack fragile or delicate items.

● We need to remember to take with us a couple of things we won't find in the new location—a telephone book from the former community and directories from the old parish and clergy groups.

● Before leaving a parish, it's good to take an afternoon to copy from the church records the names and dates of all weddings, baptisms, and funerals we performed there. We will want to keep these people in our prayers as well as have a record of our ministry.

● We must resist the temptation to leave a long letter for our successor, outlining observations of parish dynamics and hot spots. We may choose instead to list the companies who hold service contracts on office equipment, the furnace, and the hot water heater.

Upon Arriving

New pastors are usually overwhelmed by the warmth of welcome and the goodwill greeting them when they arrive. However, the excitement of the new congregation is rarely matched by expertise in integrating the pastor and family into the church or community. Congregations don't resettle clergy often and may not know what to do to make our transition from newcomer to pastor smooth. The simple suggestions we make can actually help them grow in hospitality to others, as well. Ideas such as the following have helped pastors ease their way into church life gracefully:

● Ask people to help arrange a series of neighborhood welcome parties to meet and get to know church members on an informal basis. These welcome parties should be small (15–20 people), and each member of the congregation—and even recent newcomers and visitors—should be included. Name tags can be used in a game of sorts: As you greet people and talk to them, take their name tag. Later in the party, you match the name tags with the people you have met. It is helpful to keep these evenings light, free of any church agenda. We may, however, want to devote a few minutes to sharing a little of our background in a more formal way.

● A later set of house meetings can be used to let people know we want to hear about their story, both as families and as a congregation. We can ask each person to share a little of their journey to this church, including what factors keep them there and what strengths they have discovered in the church's life. We can encourage people to relate such personal favorites as what gifts they have enjoyed in their former pastors, what sermons they remember with fondness, which special services stay with them, what weddings were the most moving, which funerals or baptisms were the most powerful. In sharing these stories, the congregational bond is strengthened and our initiation into the community is reinforced.

● Pastors with small children may want to arrange a party or social event where they can meet other children their age in the congregation. While adolescents may find such a forced gathering uncomfortable, younger children are delightfully free of the inhibitions of their older brothers and sisters.

● It's fun to mark the beginning of a ministry with a tangible sign of some kind. For example, in each church I have served, my wife and I have planted a flowering tree on the church grounds in a ceremony following the service of worship, as a sign of our beginning. I have enjoyed years of comments from young people and adults about how the tree is still flourishing in their church yard.

—Douglas G. Scott

Resources

Alban Institute, Suite 433 North, 4550 Montgomery Avenue, Bethesda, Maryland 20814-3341.

Bratcher, E., R. Kemper, and D. Scott. 1990. Mastering transitions. Portland, Ore.: Multnomah.

Oswald, R. 1978. Running through the thistles. Bethesda, Md.: Alban Institute.

Oswald, R. 1989. New Beginnings: A pastorate start-up workbook. Bethesda, Md.: Alban Institute.

Adapting to a New Congregation

Differences between pastors and churches are sometimes due more to *culture* than *personality*. Even in their native land, pastors sometimes can be "foreigners," but when moving to a congregation that lives in a culture different from the one with which we're familiar, we need the flexible mindset of a missionary.

"To the Jews," Paul writes, "I became like a Jew, to win the Jews.... I have become all things to all men so that by all possible means I might save some" (1 Cor. 9:20, 22). This is good strategy for pastoral ministry, not just foreign missions.

Differing Cultures

Here are three cultural hot spots:
● *Different tastes.* Clothing styles and other preferences can cause contention. Even worship styles involve personal tastes. Things that have lifted us to God may not necessarily touch the hearts of the people we are to serve. Classical music does not impress people who prefer banjo pickers.
● *Different value systems.* Our priorities, habits, and life goals send strong signals to a congregation. It was not wise on my part, for example, to buy a foreign car while pastoring auto workers and their families. Greater sensitivity to their values would have helped me avoid the BUY AMERICAN sticker bonded to my windshield one Sunday. When our values differ from the congregation's, innocent actions can create tension—sending our children to public school, for example, or telling a joke in a sermon.

● *Different leadership dynamics.* Cultural differences also affect our leadership. As churches vary in their attitude toward authority, we need to respond accordingly. A church board made up of executives usually will require a different approach than one composed of union members. Some congregations want decisive leadership, and others want consensus.

Fitting In

Here are some ways to adapt to a "foreign" church culture:
● *Make no assumptions.* We need to look for what makes a congregation unique. What music do they listen to for pleasure? How do they spend their free time? What television programs do they like?
● *Adapt to language differences.* Sometimes conspicuous speech won't matter—a British accent can be impressive. But over the long haul, unfamiliar words or idioms can grate on people. If we can't alter our accents, we can avoid offensive phrases that wave our cultural flag in their faces. And if we pick up some of their phrases, so much the better.
● *Learn the work culture.* Work reflects culture and vice versa. We can meet with church leaders for lunch at their workplace. As we talk about what it takes for them to be productive and successful on the job, we'll learn a great deal about their values and customs.
● *Accept that cultural change in the church is limited and traumatic at best.* A leader's ability to change a church's tastes is minimal.

Cultural shifts require either time or trauma. Unless we learn to tolerate cultural differences, we're in for major frustration.

● *Find how the church culture can provide avenues to accomplish ministry goals.* Missionaries pray that God will show them how to overcome cultural obstacles and provide avenues within a given culture for getting things done. It's a good practice for pastors new to a congregation.

When people see us working to adapt to their culture, they appreciate it. Just as the incarnate Jesus became part of his culture, we need to become one with the people we serve so we can win some.

—Kenneth Quick

Relating with a Previous Pastor

In some new pastorates, we may feel as though our predecessor is with us from day one. He may have left physically, but his spirit sits at our desk, stands in our pulpit, and roams our halls. Then again, some predecessors never physically leave the parish—or they return shortly after retirement. How should we deal with these situations?

Handling the Memory

In dealing with the absent but fondly remembered pastor, it's helpful to remember four things:

● *A strong memory may mean a strong future.* Beloved predecessors likely maintained a solid ministry for a long time. A long pastorate usually signals that a congregation is stable and has a strong sense of identity. It also shows that a congregation has the ability to remain faithful over the long run. That bodes well for the successor.

● *Congregational memory is selective.* Churches tend to forget thorns and remember blossoms, so parishioners often revere only part of what was—the good part. The more the months and years pass, the more beneficially selective is the congregation's perception of the predecessor.

● *The predecessor did some good.* We can assume God called our predecessor to the church and used him or her to minister to people. Thus, it is good to honor and speak well of a predecessor. Besides, our criticism of predecessors would reflect poorly on us. If tempted to judge our predecessors, we can remind ourselves that we all have different gifts.

● *I am somebody's predecessor.* This truth can make us more humble about our situations. When we tire of hearing about the greatness of our predecessors, we can remember that the congregation's memory of us will irritate our successors.

Predecessors in Person

Sometimes a predecessor remains in the community and, worse, in the congregation. That fact is likely to cause a measure of panic in the pastor; however, all is not lost if certain practices are followed carefully:

● *Establish clear ground rules.* As an example, one former pastor informed me that he intended to live in the community and be a member of my church. Naturally, I was concerned. But he promised me he would never comment about my ministry to others, never exercise leadership in the congregation unless I first asked him to do it, and take no public stand on any congregational issue. In this case, my predecessor approached me. If he hadn't, I would have soon made a call on him and worked out this or a similar agreement.

● *Make use of the predecessor.* We can ask the predecessor to perform occasional duties that match his or her gifts and experience, such as calling on shut-ins or teaching an adult class. A predecessor so affirmed is less likely to interfere with the present ministry and, instead, will probably support it.

● *Retain control of the situation.* We need to insist that requests to have a former pastor, present or distant, perform a wedding or funeral come through us. No matter how much we may trust the predecessor's judgment, we need to keep clear the lines of accountability. People must recognize who the pastor is.

● *When trouble brews, take decisive action.* First, we must make sure there really is trouble and not just a misinterpretation. What exactly is the predecessor doing? With whom? To what effect? Second, we need to determine how much of this activity we can endure. For some pastors, *one* interference is too many; others excuse an occasional episode and watch for developing patterns. Third, when our tolerance finally runs thin, we should go to the former pastor and ask him or her simply to cease and desist.

—*Robert G. Kemper*

Relating to a Former Parish

A. W. Tozer once remarked that "leaving a church is like dying and going to heaven and looking back to see what kind of a fool your wife married." The real question, however, is not whether my wife's new husband is better than I. Rather, the question is: How have I prepared my wife for life without me? And now that I'm gone, can I trust God to provide for her?

Preparing the Church

When Donald Seibert was chairman of the board and CEO of the J. C. Penney Company, he once said, "The day I took this office, I began to prepare the way for my successor." He understood the company was not his. As a good leader, part of his job was to prepare the corporation for the person who would follow him.

We also have to remember the church is not ours. It belongs to Christ. We pastors are placed where we are for a season. Others will follow us. Even Moses, who led Israel for forty years, understood this and prepared the way for Joshua. Therefore, as we prepare to leave a pastorate, we have a responsibility to help the people understand that our relationship in the future will be different. This congregation will have a new pastor. He or she will be different from us, but the new pastor will be God's gift to the church. And if people really love us, they will honor him or her.

Even under the best circumstances, a lengthy separation is advisable—perhaps two years—and "circumstances" should not cause us to return frequently. When the reasons for leaving are negative, loving preparation for a successor is all the more important, and the time of separation needs to be much longer. It's best not to allow the time of separation to be interrupted by phone calls or correspondence, either. We don't want to keep cutting the dog's tail an inch at a time. To continue contacts for information or channels of advice can be destructive.

Handling Invitations

It's only natural that some of those we have known for years will want us to return to officiate at weddings or funerals. Great wisdom and discretion are needed here, and dealing with such invitations needs to begin before we leave. In most cases it's best that we not return. A bonding needs to take place between the church members and their new pastor. If it seems, however, that an invitation must be accepted, we need to contact the new pastor to ask for his or her permission and joint participation.

If we can't conscientiously affirm publicly the church and its new leadership, we should not return to the church under any circumstances, no matter how long it has been since we left. The law of love and professional ethics demands that we recognize the new leaders, even if we don't agree with them, and not force them into situations in which they'll be uncomfortable.

Should intervention clearly be needed in the church we've left, we are not the ones to do it. A denominational official should be called in. The more difficult the situation, the greater the glory that goes to Christ when we respond in love and do what is ethical.

At all costs, it's important to avoid meeting with people who were our supporters unless our successor is present and participates in the event. If we treat our successor as our pastor when we are in the community, our supporters will follow our example.

—Donald L. Bubna

Part III:

Leadership

Leadership is difficult. After all, where is it that we find genuine Christian leaders? In the fore, taking the flak. On their knees, working at the foot wash. Away from leisurely pursuits, finishing what someone else didn't. Over a barrel, trying valiantly to reconcile differences. Behind the scenes, orchestrating a grand endeavor. Ahead of the pack, dreaming dreams others may follow. Outside the circle, where it gets mighty lonely at times. Nothing easy about that.

Leadership is necessary. So it is written: Without a vision, the people perish. Sheep without a shepherd are scattered. How can people hear without someone preaching to them? Someone needs to guard the good deposit that was entrusted to us by God. Someone must teach what is in accord with sound doctrine. So God supplies leaders—some to be apostles, some to be prophets, some to be evangelists, and some to be pastors and teachers—to build up the body of Christ.

Leadership is ours. For a number of reasons—some impossibly inscrutable—we now wear the mantle. We have been given responsibility for this generation and for leaving something of value for the next. We are called to shepherd the sheep, mediate the disputes, cast and coalesce the vision, proclaim the gospel. We have a trust; leadership has been bestowed. How will we handle that leadership? Surely with greater command as we are led by the leaders who share their counsel in the following chapters.

13

The Meaning of Leadership

Biblical leadership takes place when divinely appointed men and women respond in obedience to God's call. They recognize the importance of preparation time, allowing the Holy Spirit to develop tenderness of heart and skill of hands. They carry out their leadership roles with a deep conviction of God's will and an acute awareness of the contemporary issues they and their followers face. Above all, they exercise leadership as servants and stewards, sharing authority with their followers and affirming that leadership is primarily ministry *to* others, modeling *for* others, and mutual membership *with* others in Christ's body.

Most Christians would subscribe to such statements about the nature of Christian leadership. But are these foundational leadership tenets merely products of tradition and expediency? Or do they indeed flow to us from an inductive examination of the Scriptures?

Leadership in the Old Testament

In this part of the Scriptures, a theology of leadership is best learned by the study of people whom God has used. The early centuries of Israel's life show us how God dealt with individuals called to lead. Finding people whose hearts were right toward him, God developed within those leaders a vertical relationship that affected their horizontal relationships with others.

Of course, the chief leader of the Old Testament, especially in the Pentateuch, is Jehovah himself. He rules the heaven-designed theocracy, but he shares his role with mortals, so that Moses can spell out accountability for "all of you [who] are standing today in the presence of the Lord your God—your leaders and chief men, your elders and officials, and all the other men of Israel" (Deut. 29:10).

● *Abraham and Moses.* Though no Hebrew or English words for "lead" appear in conjunction with Abraham, he certainly demonstrates distinctiveness of call, the unique choosing by God for a specific leadership task. The Lord had said to Abram, "Leave your country, your people and your father's household and go to the land I will show you. I will make you into a great nation and I will bless you; I will make your name great, and you will be a blessing. I will bless those who bless you, and whoever curses you I will curse; and all peoples on earth will be blessed through you" (Gen. 12:1–3).

But the dominant human leader in the Pentateuch is clearly Moses. Indeed, God so often reminds him of his leadership task that he responds, "You have been telling me, 'Lead these people,' but you have not let me know whom you will send with me" (Exod. 33:12). Moses then learns to share that leadership with others under the tutelage of his father-in-law, Jethro. The dynamic eighteenth chapter of Exodus describes the appointment of numerous leaders. "He chose capable men from all Israel and made them leaders of the people, officials over thousands, hundreds, fifties and tens. They served as judges for the people at all times. The difficult cases they brought to Moses, but the simple ones they decided themselves" (Exod. 18:25–26).

● *Joshua, David, and Nehemiah.* As Israel expands into a monarchy, Joshua plays the role of tribal leader, assuming military command; David represents the epitome of the theology of kingship; and Nehemiah shows us the quintessential Old Testament lay leader, who is thrust into service without the kind of training afforded either Joshua or David.

Much has been made of the appearance of the word *success* in the early verses of Joshua, a term obviously connected with prosperity and material things, such as the conquest of the land. Yet the modern concept of success is quite different from the biblical concept, because the Bible rejects mere wealth or power as its only basis. Rather, biblical success means discovering and doing the will of God. Further, even the greatness of a nation's leaders—their ability to conquer and control—does not determine that nation's success. The greatness of the people of God themselves must also be evident. But in the historical books of the Bible, both dimensions stand clearly in view—the physical acquisition and protection of land and the spiritual maintenance of devotion to Jehovah.

Jehovah clearly tells Joshua, "You will lead these people" (Josh. 1:6), and he does so by heading up numerous subordinates referred to variously as "the leaders of Israel" (8:10), "the leaders of the assembly"

(9:18), and "the leaders of the community" (22:30). The intricacy of organization in the latter days of Joshua's control appears in 23:2, where we read about "elders, leaders, judges and officials."

By the time David enters the scene, the people appear quite prepared for the leadership role of a king. Indeed, they had asked Samuel to "appoint a king to lead us" (1 Sam. 8:5), and the old prophet tells the people, "Now you have a king as your leader" (1 Sam. 12:2). Even while he was fleeing from Saul, of David it is said, "All those who were in distress or in debt or discontented gathered around him, and he became their leader" (1 Sam. 22:2).

By 445 B.C. Nehemiah served as special cupbearer to the king, a noble representative of the people who had long since left spiritual leadership behind and had forgotten how God had called them to lead other nations of the world. Nehemiah responds to the call and follows through with a strong sense of mission and accomplishment. Christian leaders today can learn much from the example of Nehemiah. Indeed, we ought to emulate him.

Old Testament Leadership Principles

From Creation to Moses, leadership spread from the embryonic role of Adam supervising Seth to the later military-leadership needs of a nation preparing to invade the territory of other peoples (Deut. 20:5–9). Several lessons seem to stand out:

● *Biblical leadership begins by divine appointment.* Whether we observe Noah, Abraham, Moses, or Aaron, we see Jehovah designating, clearly and directly, those whom he wishes to exercise leadership over others. In every case, the call seems clear both to the intended leader and to those who follow.

● *Leadership moves from single to multiple.* Noah and Abraham appear to stand alone, defying the onslaughts of a pagan world. Once the nation of Israel is formed, however, Moses parcels out leadership responsibilities to others, shares authority, and exercises what we might call today a participatory leadership style. We read about "the leaders of the community" (Exod. 16:22), "leaders of the people" (Exod. 18:25), "leaders of the Israelites" (Num. 13:3), and "the leadership of Moses and Aaron" (Num. 33:1).

● *Leadership requires accountability.* The Law spelled out the greater responsibilities of those called by divine appointment: "When a leader sins unintentionally and does what is forbidden in any of the commands of the Lord his God, he is guilty" (Lev. 4:22). Miriam criticized Moses and became leprous; Moses hit the rock in anger and was forbidden entry into the Promised Land; minor rebellions or major anarchies (like that of Korah) were immediately put down from on high.

These are the lessons from Creation to Moses, but what can we learn from the way God dealt with his people from Moses to the advent of Christ? Perhaps a few principles can at least provide examples of the many, such as:

● *Leadership requires a time of preparation.* We see this principle clearly in the life of Joshua, who served for years as Moses' servant. We see it in David, who trained in obedience and duty at home and then lived the life of an active soldier before his anointing as king. In Nehemiah, too, we see the heart preparation essential to any spiritual leadership.

● *Leadership requires a heart sensitive to spiritual things* (1 Sam. 16:7). David was a skilled fighting man, handy with a sword and bow, but God selected him because of his heart.

● *Leadership requires skill.* To be sure, the terms *leadership* and *administration* are not synonymous. But in God's service, there seems to be dynamic overlap, and Nehemiah provides a wonderful example of one who could organize, plan, delegate, supervise, arbitrate, recruit, train, and evaluate.

Servant Leadership

Servant leadership is not non-leadership. But for many in American culture, the phrase *servant leadership* indicates abdication, that the servant leader abandons leading. Servant leadership is seen as creating a laissez-faire vacuum that merely asks the staff or board, "What do you think needs to be done?" or that simply blesses another's creative program initiative.

On the contrary, servant leaders lead, but with a style not reflective of the popular culture. Jesus instructed his followers to walk away from the prevailing Gentile and Jewish models of prideful leadership, where dominance ("lording it over"), coercion, titles, and public recognition were the goals. "Not so with you," Jesus exclaimed (Matt. 20:26).

Jesus instead spoke of leaders who serve. Servant leaders still do the things leaders do—direct, organize, envision. But with *servant* qualifying *leadership,* the kingdom of God—not one's personal fiefdom—becomes our motivation and shapes our style of leadership.

Recognizing Servants

When servant leadership is incarnate in the church, certain characteristics will be present.

● *Servant leaders are secure, knowing God values us.* Only when we accept our worth before God can we freely attend to the needs of others and empower them to their full potential. In John 13:3–4, we read: "Jesus knew that the Father had put all things under his power, and that he had come from God and was returning to God; so he... poured water into a basin and began to wash his disciples' feet." Jesus

Leadership in the New Testament

Obviously, the key to understanding Christian leadership is learning to lead like the Lord. In the dramatic eleventh chapter of Matthew (vv. 25–30), Jesus describes his leadership as gentle and humble. In the chapter that follows, he quotes from Isaiah 42 to describe the chosen servant as one who "will not quarrel or cry out; no one will hear his voice in the streets. A bruised reed he will not break, and a smoldering wick he will not snuff out" (Matt. 12:19–20a).

Our Lord's work with the disciples provides a pattern of group leadership worthy of the most diligent study, such as is found in A. B. Bruce's *The Training of the Twelve*. As James Hind says, "If there was one modern management trait that carried Jesus Christ from a nobody to a somebody, it was his service to and for the benefit of others—his *servant leadership*" (Hind 1989).

● *James and Barnabas.* Another valuable character study in the New Testament is that of James, moderator of the Jerusalem church.

---

was at liberty to take the basin and towel and wash the grime from the disciples' feet because he knew who he was before the Father. If affirming others somehow diminishes our sense of importance, servant leadership will be seen as a personal threat, and we will not practice it.

● *Servant leaders find joy in encouraging and supporting staff and team members.* They enable others to develop their spiritual gifts in the context of ministry, and they publicly recognize the growth and contribution of others. As a result, the congregation functions as a body where every person is valued, not as an audience that feeds the leader's ego.

● *Servant leaders don't need credit for their ideas or visions.* The old lament applies here: "How much good could be accomplished for the kingdom of God if it mattered not who gets the credit!" Servant leaders glory in the growth of the kingdom of God.

● *Servant leaders are high on relationships and low on control and coercion.* People are motivated by genuine care and "heart connection" rather than by fear and judgment.

● *Servant leaders shun the trappings of authority and status.* Realizing that all are equal before Christ, they avoid titles that support hierarchical pecking orders and opt instead for functional language that describes what a person does. They are also cautious about perks, such as larger-sized offices and specially marked parking spaces.

● *Servant leaders base their authority on character, not the position they occupy.* Moral authority arises from a person's integrity and consistency before Christ. Therefore, true leaders, rather than forcing or coercing people to do their bidding, give followers an attractive model that they will want to emulate.

—*Greg Ogden*

He was Jesus' half brother and the author of the Epistle of James (though not the brother of John and the son of Zebedee). Though not directly trained by the Lord himself, James models a participatory leadership style, able to moderate a public assembly with a broad view to the greatest possible benefit of the body of Christ. He is able to allow all viewpoints to be appropriately aired, summarizing the consensus of the assembly and preserving the unity of the saints.

We can also look at Barnabas, who rises from an apparent layman's role in Jerusalem to become leader of the second New Testament church at Antioch. He affords a brilliant example of unthreatened, secure leadership, being a person who is willing to trust others to exercise the greatest potential of their gifts (with Saul of Tarsus, for example). Barnabas did not defend his own turf nor hold on to position for personal prestige. God moved him out of his first and only "senior pastorate" after one year, and Barnabas started joyously to lead the first missionary journey. Yet leadership soon passed to his

---

Leading Versus Enabling

Many pastors learned from their seminary professors to reject strong, authoritative, directive pastoral leadership. The touted alternative was the model of the pastor as an enabler—a person who acts as a relatively uninvolved ecclesiastical technician who helps others achieve their goals.

Yet, if churches are going to maximize their growth potential, they need pastors who are strong, effective leaders. There may be exceptions, but the rule appears to be this: If a church is not growing, take a close look at the role of the pastor. In some cases you won't have to look much further to discover an enabler model as a major barrier to growth.

The Enabler Model

Certainly overly ego-centered or aggressive leadership is not what we want. Christianity needs no ayatollahs, and so pastors are rightfully warned against ego trips and empire building. It can well be argued that a generation or so ago, churches had become overly clerical. The clergy were the active components of the church system, while the lay people were passive.

From these problems arose the corrective of the pastor as an enabler. Though the enabler ideal probably peaked in the late 1960s, it has not disappeared from the scene. The enabler model is still taught in some seminaries, and few seminary textbooks argue strongly enough for authoritative (not authoritarian) pastoral leadership. Instead, some voices call for pastors to pull back and basically turn the church over to the laity.

David Mains, founding pastor of the innovative Circle Church in Chicago, disagrees. He underwent a

former assistant and, though John Mark seemed somewhat offended by the change, Barnabas never missed a stride.

Though some would fault Barnabas for arguing with Paul at the end of Acts 15, even there the positive note emphasizes his long-term commitment to John Mark. Wonderful results were produced in that young man, who became profitable for ministry under the tutelage and modeling of Barnabas.

● *Paul, Timothy, and the elders.* If the apostles demonstrated the practical outworking of Christ's teachings in the Book of Acts, it was left for Paul and the other epistle writers to formulate New Testament doctrines, including a biblical theology of leadership.

It is impossible, then, to bypass the apostle Paul when considering the nature of biblical leadership. His constant activity of modeling and mentoring, encouraging and exhorting, teaching and training, exemplifies New Testament leadership at its zenith. He describes his own leadership approach in 1 Thessalonians, offering a contrast to

significant transition in his thinking, moving away from the enabler model. Circle Church was founded in the late 1960s at the peak of the enabler concept. Ten years later Mains saw his dreams crumble. The first members of Circle were a part of the anti-authoritarian scene. The body life movement was just beginning. Mains later recalls in LEADERSHIP journal, "In setting up the climate of leadership in the church, I stressed the equality of all believers to the exclusion of the hierarchical gifts of leadership. I discovered the fact too late; I couldn't turn the congregation around." He realized that "if you push servant leadership too far, you can turn the leader into a doormat and destroy him.... Minimizing the pastor's leadership is a disease spreading wildly through evangelical churches."

Leaders and Equippers

The central challenge is to sustain the emphasis on freeing the laity for significant ministry while at the same time maintaining the pastor's role as leader.

This can be done by describing the pastor as both leader and equipper. An equipper is a leader who actively sets goals for a congregation according to the will of God, obtains goal ownership from the people, and sees that each church member is properly motivated and equipped to do his or her part in accomplishing the goals.

The larger the church gets, the more important it is that the pastor be an equipper. The enabler model will work to a degree in churches that have not reached the 200 barrier, but it cannot go much further. If clergy can believe their primary role is that of equipper and if the lay people will give their consent and willingly open the way for their pastor to be such a person, churches can grow both in quantity and in quality.

—*C. Peter Wagner*

first-century pagan understandings. In 1 Thessalonians 2:1–6, he identifies what he did *not* do among the believers there. Then in the next six verses he describes a process of nurture and family care, depicting himself as a nursing mother and a loving father. These metaphors, though uncommon to the modern North American ear, are powerful in the context of leadership.

As we follow Paul's trail, it doesn't take us long to come to Timothy, the quintessential disciple, the end result of modeling and mentoring. How much of what we know about church leadership is linked with this young man because of Paul's two letters! In looking at the life of Timothy, we learn that biblical servants avoid false doctrine, they aim toward godly living, they activate and use their spiritual gifts, and they accept the challenge God has placed before them in whatever leadership role prescribed. From family preparation to pastoral problems, the experience of Timothy provides us a brilliant example of the fact that leadership is learned behavior.

We must note also the group that we commonly call "the Ephesian elders," whose dramatic appearance in Acts 20 demonstrates for us what God expects of lay leaders in local congregations. These elders (v. 17) and overseers (v. 28) were to serve as "shepherds" (*presbyteros, episcopos,* and *poimen,* all appearing in the same context and describing the same people). We link Acts 20 with Ephesians 4:11–16 to see precisely how this kind of leadership creates strength in the unified body of any given congregation.

New Testament Principles of Leadership

Perhaps here we should paraphrase John, suggesting that if every leadership principle available in the Gospels or in Acts were written down, perhaps the whole world would not have room for the books that would be written (John 21:25). But several principles stand out with piercing impact for today's church:

● *Leadership is servanthood.* A servant is a person who submits her own will in order to please her master—and others—without any assurance of reward. Someone once asked Lorne Sanny how it is possible to know whether one functions as a servant. Sanny replied, "By the way you react when people treat you like one."

● *Leadership is stewardship.* We need not do a detailed study of *oikonomos* to emphasize the concept of stewardship. In the dynamic parable of the faithful and wise manager, we can see that the manager is placed in charge of other servants, not to give them their orders but to give them their food allowance. He holds an absolute responsibility for awareness of the master's will and carries out his tasks within the light of the master's return.

● *Leadership is shared power.* Though current secular leadership literature talks a good bit about empowering others, traditionally worldly leadership centers in grasping, retaining, and using power. Such concepts run totally counter to the New Testament.

John Stott correctly reminds us that "Christian leaders serve not their own interests but rather the interests of others" (Phil. 2:4). This simple principle should deliver the leader from excessive individualism, extreme isolation, and self-centered empire building. Leadership teams, therefore, are more healthy than solo leadership for several reasons (Stott 1985, 27).

The proper climate for leadership development emphasizes a decentralized institutional philosophy. Our goal is to push decision making and authority as far down the ranks as possible, so that the people who live with actual implementation have a major voice in the decision.

● *Leadership is ministry.* The emphasis on *diakonia* and the thrust of the gift of leadership in Romans 12:8 show us that if New Testament leadership means anything, it means serving other people. With meekness, the church leader involves himself or herself in concert with other believers to engage in ministry. The smog of selfishness and egoism lifts to make mutual ministry a biblical reality.

● *Leadership is modeling behavior.* We've seen it clearly in the Paul-Timothy relationship (1 Tim. 4:11–16; 2 Tim. 3:10–15). Lawrence Richards and Clyde Hoeldtke (1980, 115) sum it up well: "The spiritual leader who is a servant does not demand. He *serves.* In his service the spiritual leader sets an example for the body—an example that has compelling power to motivate heart change."

● *Leadership is membership in the Body.* The leader must identify with all other members of the congregation. In Romans 12:4–5 Paul writes, "Just as each of us has one body with many members, and these members do not all have the same function, so in Christ we who are many form one body, and each member belongs to all the others." Belonging to the others, the Christian leader serves them in meekness.

How Then Shall We Lead?

Leadership principles do flow from the pages of Scripture, but what shall we do in light of these biblical principles? Perhaps the first step is simply to work at creating an environment—a climate—in our churches in which biblical leadership styles can blossom and thrive. This would be a climate of:

● *Respect,* focusing on individual worth and dignity, and encouraging people to contribute their ideas.

● *Trust,* in which people learn to trust their own abilities and those of others, unthreatened by constant changes in policy and program.

● *Acceptance,* where, within appropriate boundaries, people have room to think and move, to consider changes in their own belief systems and—more important—in methods of ministry.

● *Discovery*, which recognizes that new leaders will make mistakes, that alternative solutions need to be explored without the pressures of immediate answers but with tolerance for ambiguity in the midst of tough problems.

● *Depth*, a depth of spiritual dimensions in individual and corporate leaders and also depth "on the bench" (Gangel 1989a, 169).

—*Kenneth O. Gangel*

Resources

Bickimer, D. Leadership in religious education. Birmingham, Ala.: Religious Education Press.

Bruce, A. 1979. The training of the Twelve. Grand Rapids: Kregel.

Clinton, R. 1988. The making of a leader. Colorado Springs: NavPress.

Gangel, K. 1989. Developing new leaders for the global task. *Evangelical Missions Quarterly*, April.

Gangel, K. 1989. Feeding and leading. Wheaton, Ill.: Victor.

Habecker, E. 1987. The other side of leadership. Wheaton, Ill.: Victor.

Hind, J. 1989. The heart and soul of effective management. Wheaton, Ill.: Victor.

Means, J. 1989. Leadership in Christian ministry. Grand Rapids: Baker.

Richards, L. and C. Hoeldtke. 1980. A theology of church leadership. Grand Rapids: Zondervan.

Stott, J. 1985. What makes leadership Christian? *Christianity Today*, August 9.

The Role of an Associate Pastor

On the average, associate pastors change positions every three to four years. This turnover indicates an underlying dissatisfaction in the role of associate. Two primary reasons for this are: (1) in the church culture, it is assumed that associates worth their salt will move toward a senior position, and (2) within some church staffs, there is considerable dissension between associate and senior pastors.

Building Satisfaction

To nurture longevity and satisfaction in the ministries of associate pastors, the following five principles are important:

● *Associate pastors should defer to the senior pastor.* This is especially fitting advice for the young and zealous associate pastor. Newly ordained associates tend to be passionate and purist in their philosophy of ministry. They also tend to see their senior mentor as compromising and placating. But often when an associate pushes for his or her "better" way (of course, the associate has in mind only "the health of the church"), contention and personal unhappiness follow.

In both attitude and action, associates must be loyal to the senior pastor. Their relationship should be one of public unity and private disagreement, since congregations are infected by the spirit they see modeled in staff relationships. It is more than coincidence that unified staffs generally mean unified churches. In situations where an associate cannot accept the fundamental direction set by the senior pastor, it is time for the associate to move on, both for the health of the staff and for that of the church.

● *Longevity and satisfaction are the by-products of a clearly defined role.* This role recognizes an associate's spiritual gifts and passion for ministry. Associates need to be honored for their unique call and individual identity in ministry. They are not the alter ego of the senior person. Their call is from God, and they are gifted to make a particular contribution. When the congregation and the senior pastor recognize the uniqueness of the call and the role, as well as the associate's particular abilities, the associate will be satisfied in his or her work.

● *An associate's ability to flourish depends on the inner security of the head of staff.* A senior pastor's spirit creates the climate for growth. If the senior pastor attempts to make up for a deficit of worth by stealing the limelight, exercising control, refusing to relinquish power, and so on, associates will find it difficult to establish their own identities and to express leadership in their areas of expertise.

● *Senior pastors serve associates by being committed to their ministry success.* If we follow Jesus' model of servant leadership, the "greater" will serve the "lesser." The pyramid is inverted when senior pastors die to self by encouraging the full potential of the associate. One of the finest compliments a senior pastor can receive is to hear a parishioner say, "I have seen such growth in our associates since you have been working with them."

● *An associate's value is rooted in the call of God, not in the ascribed worth of the position.* A desire to be a lifelong associate pastor is an honorable ambition. The question for anyone in ministry should be, "What shape should my ministry take at this time, based on my gifts for ministry and the call of God?" The assumption that an associate pastor should aspire to be a senior pastor may derive from a worldly, rather than a Christlike, view of success.

—*Greg Ogden*

Setting the Vision

Most people are not visionaries. In a church of hundreds or even thousands of members, a leader might find only a few. Thus many pastors who serve a tradition-entrenched congregation wonder how it can ever move forward: *There aren't enough people with vision; no one sees how things could* be. Yet setting the vision is primarily a pastoral task.

Time to Dream

A few years ago a magazine ad pictured a man standing in his office, looking out the window. The caption read: "Why would a company pay this man $100,000 a year to look out the window?" The ad went on to make the point that every organization needs someone who looks out the window—outside the organization—to the world and to the future. A pastor helps the congregation by looking out the window. But how much time ought a pastor devote to dreaming of the future, especially with a multitude of immediate concerns?

The answer varies with each situation, obviously, but much of the answer is determined by how long a pastor has been with the current congregation. Strangely, natural tendencies work against effective vision.

Typically, when pastors come to a church, they are not vested in the programs. Therefore, they can be objective: "We shouldn't be having this many services," or "We shouldn't be doing vacation Bible school this way." Most pastors start with a burst of energy in envisioning how things could be. In addition, few members call or immediately trust a newly arrived pastor for in-depth counseling. This frees time to look ahead. But new ministers' ideas often are not readily accepted by the people. Even a good vision can die because people haven't learned to trust the pastor.

But after pastors have been in a church five or ten years, most programs reflect their ideas or bear their imprimatur. Their schedules are jammed, so they have little time to dream about the future. Momentum shifts to maintaining the programs they have built.

Trust Building

We need to reverse the process. When we start in a congregation, most of our time should be devoted to current program, not looking ahead. Then, gradually, we need to slide the scale until we spend more time on future projects. Why? Because a congregation won't follow a pastor in looking forward unless it trusts that pastor, and building trust takes time.

Most pastors enter situations in which people remember the past and in which problems exist that need attention. These pastors have to build credibility. The best way is to concentrate on existing programs. As a pastor works hard inside the given structures, the congregation develops the trust that later allows the pastor to lead people forward.

It takes years to reach a point of both trust and time, but the pastor who works toward that sweet spot begins to spend more time on future possibilities than on current programs. Time is found to dream about such activities as starting a daughter church, providing a Saturday-night service, expanding staff, or spearheading new missions projects. At a mature stage of a pastorate, these are fitting tasks, but they typically remain unreachable in a pastor's early days at a church. Pastors need to look out the window, but in the early years particularly, they are better off preparing for that responsibility by spending plenty of time at the desk

—Leith Anderson

Communicating the Vision

The effective communication of vision to a congregation relies on the credibility of a pastor's vision: Do the people believe in it? *Can they believe it?* Any mission vision must have credibility if people are to commit themselves to it.

The Credibility Factor

Three elements can contribute to a credible, acceptable vision message:

● *The content of the vision.* At issue is whether or not the vision is based on Scripture. When visionaries are able to point to a particular biblical principle in support of their dream, they catch the attention of those in the Christian community who have a high view of Scripture. A church is best able to do this when the church's vision is founded on the Great Commission.

Content credibility, however, also depends on a solid relationship between the vision and some untapped opportunity. A vision that is highly sensitive to some obvious spiritual opportunity elicits believability. An example is the current focus on reaching America's nonchurched people. Many churches in America are declining, while the number of nonchurched Americans is increasing. Surveys tell us these nonchurched people are very interested in spiritual things. Some visionaries have woven these factors into a vision to plant churches that target the unchurched.

● *The visionary leader's performance.* People want to know the track record of the visionary leader. This consists of such characteristics as God's evident blessing on a person's life and ministry, prior success, active gifts and abilities, strong communication skills, personal dedication, and a commitment to biblical values. Does the leader show extraordinary ability in any or most of these factors?

When it becomes evident God is uniquely blessing leaders' lives and ministries, they gain extraordinary credibility in the eyes of their followers and even the general public. Sometimes God grants special favor in that person's ministry in such a way that former obstacles are removed and doors that normally are closed are opened.

Prior ministry experience powerfully communicates credibility in Christian circles, as does the presence of strong gifts or abilities, especially in the area of Christian leadership. There is a great need today for men and women with leadership expertise who can direct ministries with sustained excellence, especially through skill in preaching. People are generally impressed by a good communicator, that is, an "up front" ministry that has exposure to more people than other ministries such as counseling.

Of course, the leader's personal dedication to the cause is an absolute must in creating trustworthiness for the vision. Generally, the perception is the greater the self-sacrifice or personal risk of the leader, the greater the trustworthiness of the cause.

● *The visionary leader's integrity.* Leaders who display integrity and trustworthiness are given high credibility by those within and outside the ministry community. Actually, the Christian community is directed to assign credibility on the basis of character. This is clearly spelled out in various passages such as 1 Timothy 3:1–13 and Titus 1:5–9, which detail the character qualifications for church leadership.

Character is the foundation of Christian leadership. A person's entire ministry and leadership rest on his or her character. If the character is flawed in some way, the ministry will be flawed proportionately. This is demonstrated in generation after generation as leaders fall and take their ministries with them. As might be expected, the reaction from both the Christian community and the secular community is to question the credibility of Christian organizations in general. Where integrity weakens, vision is a hard sell, and rightfully so.

—*Aubrey Malphurs*

Maintaining the Vision

Once people have caught a ministry vision, how do leaders help them keep that vision alive? How do they keep it before their people over the long haul of a ministry? Leaders can take three steps that will maintain the impact of the ministry vision: constantly communicate the vision, maintain the vision's credibility, and deal directly with its detractors.

Communicating the Vision

Wise leaders regularly articulate their ministry visions to their followers in numerous ways. The most obvious method is through verbal communication, such as preaching, teaching, networking, and talking with people. Another involves the use of visual images, such as a video or slide-tape presentation, or a well-designed vision logo. A third method is to use an occasional short skit or even a drama that communicates the vision.

Perhaps the greatest way to communicate and maintain the vision is through the lives of the ministry's leaders. In fact, the only limit to the effective communication of the vision is the creative and innovative abilities of the leadership.

Maintaining Credibility

If people in ministry are to embrace and follow the vision over the long haul, it must have long-term credibility. When people were asked to define credibility in behavioral terms, the most frequent response was "They do what they say they will do." Consequently, the articulation and preservation of a vision is a serious matter. If the leadership is not solidly behind the ministry's vision, they should consider another ministry or get involved in some other work.

To maintain credibility, leaders must monitor their ministry culture. Every ministry has a unique culture, consisting of its core values, traditions, heroes, symbols, rituals, and communication patterns. It is critical to the preservation of the ministry that its culture support the vision. For example, a church may claim the Great Commission as the essence of its vision. But the Great Commission involves pursuing and evangelizing lost people and then discipling those who are saved. If the church does not consider evangelism one of its core values and does not hold up those who practice evangelism as heroes, a vision statement that pushes evangelism will not hold its credibility.

Dealing with Detractors

The third step in maintaining the ministry vision is dealing with those who oppose it. Opposition from the outside can anger and catalyze people to accomplish the vision. But unreasonable, misguided opposition from within often causes the most damage emotionally and spiritually to the visionary leader and the ministry. Such individuals might be called "vision vampires" and "vision vultures."

Vision vampires are people in the ministry who either intentionally or unintentionally attempt to suck the lifeblood from the vision. Often they are well-intentioned Christians who sincerely oppose the vision on what they believe are biblical grounds.

On the other hand are the vision vultures, who are, in effect, vision "nitpickers." They do not oppose the vision theologically. Rather, they simply find the idea of change extremely intimidating. They have grown used to sitting in the same pew, hearing the same kinds of messages, and following a prescribed ritual. They do not believe the vision is wrong for every church; it is only wrong for *this* church.

We must deal directly with these vision detractors. In Matthew 5:23–24 and 18:15, Jesus instructs us to go and confront them in love. If they do not respond, the next step may involve a process of congregational discipline (Matt. 18:16–17). Above all, we must not give up. The great visionary Nehemiah was not quick to quit (Neh. 4:14), and we, too, must hang tough.

—*Aubrey Malphurs*

14

The Responsibilities of Leadership

D o you ever wonder what we would look like if our mental, emotional, and spiritual aspects were as visible as our physical bodies? I suspect many of us would be distorted, misshapen, even grotesque. Some people develop their minds to the neglect of their social and emotional health. Others spend so much time studying the Bible that the rest of their lives are stunted.

Mature leadership involves balanced growth. Maturity is obviously difficult to measure, but here are several disciplines necessary for healthy growth and responsible leadership. They can serve as a checklist to make sure we're maturing in all areas of life.

The Discipline of Freedom

Some pastors feel trapped—*I'm called by God to do this, but I don't like certain aspects of the job, and I don't feel free to change them.* This depresses them regularly. They feel like slaves to the church, and slaves have few options. They have emotional options, of course. They can be dedicated, enthusiastic, willing to use their best talents, or they can drag their feet and be insolent and difficult to get along with. But internal control is about the only control slaves have.

When feeling trapped, the key is to recognize we're serving the wrong master. Pastors are to be slaves of Christ, not slaves of the church. This freedom to serve Christ alone, however, requires discipline. It comes with a price. All freedom does.

The price of freedom to serve Christ alone is often our willingness to be disliked. It may cost us our job. It may cost us our relationships. We may be ostracized by our peers.

For example, I was once approached by an active Christian about serving on the board of his organization. I said, "You don't want me, because I would consider my responsibility to the organization and not to you. You couldn't count automatically on my vote." I was insisting on my freedom to discharge my responsibility. In this case, he agreed.

This desire for total freedom has to be tempered, however. Freedom is not irresponsibility. Freedom is an environment in which we discharge our responsibility. One reason for America's productivity is that for the first time in history, responsible people have lived in an environment of freedom. The Puritan conscience was responsible— you have a talent, you're responsible for it, and one day you'll stand before God and be judged. When that was placed into an environment of freedom, it became tremendously productive.

We've seen this more recently with the boat people from Southeast Asia. They came into freedom with a sense of responsibility and the desire to get ahead, and many have succeeded.

One way to remain responsible is by retaining our first love for Christ. For example, an executive friend and I were going on a business trip to Italy. He was a rock climber, very macho and profane. I said to myself, *This is going to be bad. He's not a believer. He's going to chase every skirt he can see.* But by the end of the trip, he had never ogled a woman or made a single suggestive comment. As we were seeing the sights, he kept saying, "I wish my wife could see this." Every day he wrote her. I realized he was totally in love with his wife, and it protected him from any other woman. He wasn't even tempted. By being a slave, totally committed to one person, he was totally free. I realized that only in total slavery do we have total freedom. I believe Paul experienced this as a "bond slave of Christ."

The more total we can make our commitment to Christ, the freer we are. We discipline our desires. We discipline our natural inclination for freedom without responsibility, since freedom carries certain restraints.

The Discipline of Emotions

Emotions can be hazardous to our leadership and productivity. I call certain feelings "blocking emotions" because they hinder performance. Lust and greed, for instance, are blocking emotions; they block our relationship with God. Another common blocking emotion, however, is a "blue funk"—when we find ourselves dragging mentally and emotionally. We can't lead effectively when we're depressed, and yet these moods are a recurring part of life.

For example, the other night I came home tired. After dinner I sat down and went to sleep in the chair. I woke up two hours later feeling good for nothing. In situations like this, I go through a series of temptations: to go immediately to bed, to eat something out of the refrigerator, to start a silly argument with my wife. I realize that other people can't bring me out of a blue funk; it takes self-discipline. Unless I find a way to interrupt the blue mood, I'll fritter away the evening waiting until I can justify going to bed, but I'll wake up the next morning feeling slightly guilty and unrefreshed, and the new day will be off to a bad start.

I have found ways to break that cycle. Blue funks generally happen when I do not have anything exciting to do after dinner. One of my disciplines is to try to have something planned for immediately after dinner. To get me going during these down times, I save little tasks I want to do or articles I want to read.

Another tool that works for me is the telephone. Two things I appreciate about the phone: (1) you don't have to answer it when it rings, and (2) you can call friends when you need help.

I have friends to whom all I have to say when I call is "What's exciting today?" and they're off and running. Just by listening to them, I get motivated. I've tried to develop a list of such people just for the down times.

If all else fails, however, and I'm still in a blue funk, I leave the house, go to a busy restaurant, have a cup of coffee, and watch the people. That puts me among the living. I see some kids who make me very proud of mine. I see people with problems I don't have. I begin to regain a sense of gratitude. I get a couple of thoughts about something I'm working on, and soon I'm moving back toward normal.

The Discipline of Things

Leaders also have to come to terms, in a mature way, with possessions. We live in a material world. That's the way God created it. There's nothing in the Christian faith that is antimaterial. The Garden of Eden was lush. God gave wealth to Job. Joseph ended up in pretty comfortable circumstances. In fact, the early Christians opposed the Gnostic heresy, which claimed that material possessions were ungodly.

But if Christianity allows a place for the material, it is still *antimaterialistic*. When material things become a top priority, they become a stumbling block. Christians know material things are to be used for God's glory. When they become a measurement of success or value, they've become something God never intended.

What is our relation to things? Here are some questions to check if we're growing toward maturity in this area.

● *Am I using my possessions and not just accumulating them?* In most families, heirlooms lend tradition and give us roots. I'm proud of two pictures that hung on the living room wall when I was a small child. When I look at those pictures today, I become again a member of my family. Though those pictures are material things, they're not materialistic things. They serve a healthy purpose.

● *Am I able to share them?* I was traveling in Mexico one time and was offended to see in a dusty, poverty-stricken town a beautiful cathedral. I asked the priest how such a structure could be built amid such misery.

"Mr. Smith," he said, "the only thing of beauty these people can afford is what they have corporately. None of them alone can have anything beautiful, but together they can have this cathedral."

That changed my attitude. By cooperation, they had created a treasure for all.

● *Am I able to give?* Any time we are less than generous with the

---

Setting Up Safeguards

To function with optimum effectiveness, pastors must set up strategies for safeguarding themselves against such pitfalls as wasting time, abusing their authority, satisfying their hungry egos, giving in morally, or even becoming a workaholic. This calls for developing a personal code of behavior or ministry ethic.

An Essential Ethic

Paul says it well in Ephesians 5:15: "So be careful how you act; these are difficult days" (*The Living Bible*). The best of us face temptation regularly, and we should not expect to determine our proper responses anew each time we deal with another potential pitfall. We need some guidelines that go with us as we work with people daily.

Every pastor can benefit from taking into consideration three important principles as he or she develops this professional code of behavior:

● *Accountability.* We must all be accountable to someone. Those who fall have almost invariably developed an attitude of arrogance and isolation; they've unwisely chosen to go it alone. Accountability demands that every leader have a regular meeting with a board or group of peers—for the sole purpose of honestly sharing feelings, revealing temptations, and identifying significant problem areas in personal and spiritual growth. Such practical accountability forces us to see how vulnerable we are and how easily we can be deluded into thinking we are above temptation.

● *Responsibility.* While all pastors should maintain the highest standards of professional behavior, the truly healthy leader is able to balance this quest for professional excellence with a broader sense of

things we have, we are less than Christian. Giving is the only true antidote I know for greed. When we give things away—freely, without expecting anything in return—we help prevent ourselves from becoming possessed by possessions.

The Discipline of Recognition

It's important to get strokes, to be recognized for what we do well. The apostle Paul was constantly recognizing people for what they did. I'm always leery of an executive who says, "Don't brag on your employees; they'll want a raise." There's something mean about that attitude. Recognition is important.

But we need discipline in deciding what kind of recognition we're going after. What kinds of strokes do we appreciate?

Woodrow Wilson said, "Many men are seduced by secondary suc-

---

responsibility that encompasses personal roles and relationships, as well. The pastor must learn to balance the demands of church leadership with the demands of family and personal life. A lack of this broader sense of responsibility leads to an unbalanced life.

● *Integrity.* Foremost is the issue of how we use our power. Do we share the power? Do we use it with compassion? Is our use of power merely ego motivated? Second to power is the issue of honesty. True integrity requires not just uprightness with regard to finances, but also justice in the application of authority, graciousness in what we take credit for, and compassion in how we gain and use privileged information.

Ethics in Action

How do these principles translate into daily action? Here is a Leader's Safeguard Checklist that can help any pastor do a daily ethics evaluation. Test yourself on it at the end of each day and then make what-

ever changes your answers suggest.

● Have I been totally honest in all my dealings with people this day?

● Have I acted appropriately toward members of the opposite sex?

● Have I indulged any unsavory thoughts or sexual images, or fostered any uncharitable feelings toward others?

● Have I been totally above reproach in all my financial dealings?

● Have I fulfilled all my obligations without compromise and with a willing spirit?

● Have I worked too long or too hard without evaluating my true motives?

● Have I spent sufficient time with my family today?

● Have I taken care of my family's spiritual needs?

● Have I attended to my own emotional and spiritual needs and integrated them into my daily walk with God?

● Have I harbored any unconfessed sin or unforgiven hurts?

—*Archibald D. Hart*

cess." Small successes prevent them from achieving big success. They're satisfied too easily.

I knew a runner in high school who set a national record, but he never followed through. He could have qualified for the Olympics, but he didn't want to pay the price. He had already succeeded.

Promotion is a form of recognition. But it takes more than a title to truly say, "I fill this position." Effective leaders are not satisfied once they've gained the title.

Some people who are considered smart may want to develop wisdom. As people start commenting on their wisdom in handling life situations, they will know they're making progress.

A helpful exercise is to write down three words by which our friends describe us, and then write down three words we would most like to describe us. Then we can work on making those traits so prominent in our lives that people cannot keep from recognizing

---

Handling Success

No matter where we are, during some seasons of ministry, programs work, finances are healthy, and people are helped. Though we may not be able to equate this outward success with God's ultimate standards, it is a reality most of us will experience. And it feels good.

No matter how it feels, though, successes, like wealth, are resources of which we need to be good stewards.

Uneasy Achievement

Success in ministry feels great, but it does have a downside. Here are some precarious aspects of success we can experience:

● *Lonely decisions.* We work hard to make leadership a team effort. But we know the more successes we have, the more people look to us for leadership. That, at times, can feel lonely.

● *Fear of failure.* Most leaders of successful churches experience doubts: *Am I doing the right thing?* and *Will it work tomorrow?* Such fear, while healthy in most cases, isn't paralyzing. But it is a pressure.

● *Insecurity.* Even the fame of a superstar like Michael Jordan can't last forever; a fresher, younger face soon comes along and captures the media's attention. That volatility in a church can make the successful pastor feel threatened; what worked last year may not work this year.

● *Work begetting work.* In many areas of ministry, when things go well, it means more opportunities for ministry. Success breeds success—but that breeds work.

Living with Success

Successes, like all of God's gifts, are meant to be enjoyed in freedom. It's proper to enjoy outward pastoral successes. Still we are wise to remember that success brings

them. Leaders need to know what kind of recognition they're after and can't be too easily satisfied.

The Discipline of Accomplishment

Closely related to recognition is accomplishment. Productivity— contributing to the community—seems essential for mental and spiritual health. It is certainly true for leaders.

I was talking with one couple about their 22-year-old son. They said, "He's not doing anything right now; he's waiting to find the will of God."

"Is he working?" I asked.

"No."

"Is he eating?"

"Yes."

---

with it numerous temptations— pride, sloth, and ingratitude, to name three. Here are several strategies to maintain our character.

● *Be generous with praise.* This can be hard when we're striving to work ever harder at being faithful to our calling. But at both church and home, stopping and saying, "Thank you," both to God and the people who have done so much to make something a success, is so important.

● *Stay patient.* When things go well, the natural tendency is to expect more of the same, and the sooner the better. When the next success doesn't happen as quickly or shine as brightly, we're tempted to get angry at the church or move on to greener pastures.

● *Keep focused.* In ministry, we don't want to spend a lot of time thinking about what we've achieved. Instead, we should concentrate on what's next: to finish a sermon, to prepare for a board meeting, to listen to a secretary. If we concentrate on doing the next thing well, we'll

better our chances that things will continue to go well.

● *Remember the past.* This is perhaps the quickest way to regain a sense of humility, a sense that God has given us any success we're enjoying. It's good to reflect on how God uses our background, painful though some of it may be, to give us gifts and opportunities to minister.

● *Pray regularly.* Martin Luther once said that normally he spent an hour in morning prayer. But when he had an especially busy day ahead, he would spend two. The specific numbers may not apply, but the more successful we are, the more we need to be on our knees.

Corrie ten Boom was once asked how she handled all the accolades of people. She said, "Well, I take the flowers, and I thank the people, and I enjoy the flowers a little bit. Then each evening, I put them in a bunch and give them back to the Lord where they belong."

That's how I ultimately want to handle my successes.

—*Knute Larson*

I said, "Tell him he's violating the will of God right now. Scripture says if you don't work you don't eat."

I doubt he accepted that theological position, but work is scriptural; it connects us with the community. Exercising our gifts—contributing them to the body of Christ—is the primary source of our identity. Productivity is the rent we pay for our space on earth.

Obviously, there are different kinds of productivity. One can contribute to temporal things or eternal things. Christians should be involved with both.

Accomplishments come in two kinds: external and internal. Most of us concentrate on externals—our jobs, our acquisitions. But internal accomplishments are equally important. Developing emotional stability, for instance, is a tremendous accomplishment. We don't do that overnight. People who learn to control their tongue, Scripture says, are "greater than he that taketh a city," indicating how God compares internal accomplishment to external accomplishment.

Other people fight melancholia. Dr. Samuel Johnson said that when he was 15, he found he had a disease of the spirit. And yet he did so much, working around that handicap. When we see people like Joni Eareckson-Tada living so productively despite their handicaps, or Ken Medema singing and writing music despite his blindness, we recognize that the internal accomplishments are as great as the external. Leaders are aware of many different kinds of accomplishments and encourage them in themselves and in their followers.

The Discipline of Experiences

Life, like a river, is more easily navigated if it has numerous tributaries. The more sources, the deeper and broader it becomes.

People who are mentally healthy, according to a Menninger Clinic study, get their stimulation from a variety of sources, not just one or two. Sometimes Christians are tempted to be narrow—spending all their time talking only to Christian friends.

Frank Gaebelein, however, was an example of vigorous mental health. He was a Christian, a scholar, a mountain climber, a musician. He drew from varied experiences. To me, he's a great illustration of a mature Christian leader.

But in addition, it's helpful to write down experiences, lest we forget them and lose their benefit. Leaders find that having and recording a wide variety of experiences is immensely helpful to their vitality.

The Discipline of Ideas

Small minds talk about things; average minds talk about people; great minds talk about ideas.

Minds grow as they grapple with ideas, and leaders monitor the kinds of ideas they are handling. Are we interested in ideas? Are we fascinated by what we read in the paper beyond the crime stories and comics? When Stephen Hawking talks about the black holes of space, or when Einstein writes about gravity as the distortion between time and space, does our horizon broaden with fascination?

It's exciting to meet people of unusual mental attainment, if only to measure ourselves alongside them: *Can I understand him? Can I keep up?* We needn't get envious or wonder, *Why didn't God give me that talent?* We can just be happy to know that people like that exist and we can know them. One of the measures of maturity is whether our ideas are growing, whether we're able to handle larger concepts, whether we're comfortable with people who think.

The Discipline of Relationships

Relationships are obviously both the personal and professional concern of the leader.

First, there's our relationship to ourselves. Jean-Paul Sartre was once quoted as saying, "If you're lonely when you're alone, you're in poor company." I once visited a magnificent home built in a remote part of the Colorado Rockies. It was so quiet, you could hear the paint drying on the wall. I thought to myself, *Only a person at peace with himself could own a home like this.* In that kind of magnificent quiet, a person has time to be alone with himself. And one would have to be able to enjoy the company. One of the tests of maturity is the ability to be alone and at peace with ourselves.

A second test deals with relationships with other people: *Am I increasingly able to spend time profitably with people who are different?* Immature individuals, preferring people just like themselves, can't enjoy people who are different. Maturity is being comfortable with diversity.

Finally, we must evaluate the growth of our relationship with God: *Is my walk with God more comfortable? More intimate? More real?*

I had a friend who lost contact with God. The problem? Instead of confessing, he was explaining. God is not very interested in our explanations. He knows why we do what we do. He doesn't need our rationalizing. But God is a marvelous listener to our confessions.

We can explain things to God for years, but only when we get around to saying, "*Mea culpa*—I'm guilty," does our relationship with God begin to grow again. Relation grows out of confession.

Unless we can lead ourselves through these essential disciplines, we will have difficulty leading others. One major responsibility we bear as leaders is to be responsible persons.

—Fred Smith, Sr.

Resources

Drucker, P. 1993. Management: Tasks, responsibilities, practices. New York: Harper Business.

Drucker, P. 1992. Managing the non-profit organization. New York: HarperCollins.

Schaller, L. 1993. Strategies for change. Nashville: Abingdon.

Handling Mistakes

Slip-ups haunt every pastor. Some are minor; others trigger long-term problems. But not all mistakes need to be final or fatal. Here are ways to prevent them from becoming terminal.

Mistake Reflexes

Mistakes can cause our hearts to churn with painful emotions and impulses. Identifying our emotions is important so as not to compound our problems and to put us on the track of recovery. Here are several emotions common to failure:

● *Regret.* Second-guessing ourselves is easy. We think, *I should have been more sensitive with her,* or *I should have guessed what was happening with him.*

● *Frustration.* On paper, our ideas look marvelous. In reality, though, we often find no one wants to have anything to do with our brilliance. When that happens, we do our best to talk people into our idea but only grow more frustrated with them.

● *Self-pity.* We sometimes adopt a victim mentality, feeling sorry for ourselves. That's as natural as holding our hand after burning it on a hot griddle. But if it lasts very long, the wound never heals. The pain never leaves, and eventually we can be crippled.

● *Paralysis.* After a failure, a pastor sometimes can't snap out of it, can't move on with confidence to the next challenge. When we dwell on the past—wishing over and over that we had handled a situation differently, sliding into depression, questioning our abilities—we suffer a paralysis that only compounds our mistakes.

Whose Ears Will Hear?

When we make mistakes, it can be another mistake to tell others about it. Telling eager listeners may backfire. They go home and relate a slightly different version to their friends. Their friends tell other friends a different version still.

Since many can't handle such information, we should admit mistakes on a need-to-know basis. What is the group's role? How would our admission help the hearers? Would the church be hurt if they didn't know?

Yet, at times our mistakes need to be confessed publicly, especially when they involve sin. Spurgeon, in his *Lectures to My Students*, quoted another minister: "When a preacher of righteousness has stood in the way of sinners, he should never again open his lips in the great congregation until his repentance is as notorious as his sin."

Steps to Recovery

David's recovery from his sin with Bathsheba, referred to in Psalm 51, is a model for recovery from any serious mistake. Here are six steps:

● *Admit the failure to yourself.* "I know my transgression, and my sin is always before me" (v. 3).

● *Admit the failure to the Lord.* "Against you, you only, have I sinned and done what is evil in your sight" (v. 4).

● *Claim God's faithfulness and forgiveness.* "Have mercy on me, O God, according to your unfailing love; according to your great compassion blot out my transgressions" (v. 1).

● *Come to terms with your sinful humanity.* "Surely I have been a sinner from birth, sinful from the time my mother conceived me" (v. 5).

● *Ask God to put you together again.* "Create in me a pure heart, O God, and renew a steadfast spirit within me" (v. 10).

● *Turn to the task at hand.* "Then I will teach transgressors your ways" (v. 13).

Our failings don't have to be terminal, though at the time they feel that way. Our God specializes in redeeming our mistakes.

—*Stuart Briscoe*

15

Leading Christians

One Saturday years ago, some stunning, painful news came to me. Through a counseling conversation, I discovered that a pastor in our church had fallen into adultery. Since I trusted the person giving me this information, I knew I had to act—but what should I do exactly? I didn't want to presume his guilt; then again, if he was at fault, I had to deal with him.

The following Tuesday, that same pastor snapped at another staff member, so I decided to call him into my office to talk about that. Meanwhile, I hoped he would acknowledge his immorality in the course of the conversation. Having known this young man for years and even been involved in his training, I could be direct. In fact, I was pretty hard on him about his snapping remark. "We don't treat each other like that," I stressed. Then, spontaneously, I added, "But that's not the only problem here, is it?"

He looked up at me, began to tremble, hung his head, and wept.

I wept with him. He was not an evil man, but he had succumbed to weakness.

In the days that followed, I walked a fine line. I needed to lead, to take a strong stand against sexual sin, both with this man in private and before the entire church. Yet I needed to be pastoral, bringing healing and restoration. Both were essential for this man and his wife, as well as the church.

This is just one example of the tension between leading and feeding. And it is a tension.

When a pastor primarily feeds, people enjoy the church but lack a corporate sense of destiny. They graze comfortably in the valley and never climb to new heights. Sheep don't want to climb mountains. They're happy as long as they have a patch of grass.

If a pastor emphasizes leading, on the other hand, he or she may drive the sheep to exhaustion, pushing them up the mountain without allowing them to stop and eat. If the flock makes it to the top, they're dizzy with weariness, and the burnout quotient increases.

Most of us want to be both the warm, gentle pastor who comforts *and* the visionary leader who challenges. Although difficult at times, it's possible to do both.

The Difficulties

In some ways, leading and feeding can complement one another. But we should be aware of the special problems and difficulties that arise as we try to do both. Here are a few issues that challenge us.

● *Difficult people.* Some people are parasites. Often something terrible happened in their past, and no matter how much attention we give them, they want more—personally, from us alone. When they touch us, we can feel the energy drain right out of us.

In dealing with such people, we become torn between caring for them and attending to the leadership tasks that benefit the entire church. Typically, our job is to show warmth and acceptance, while others with a gift for merciful ministry can give greater, sustained attention to these needy, draining types. As other leaders call the weaker persons to Christian growth and discipline, we can buttress their demands and declared expectations. In that way, we're more than just "nice guys." Our acceptance lays a foundation for the effective ministry of mercy by others—and the tension between leading (calling to growth) and feeding (patient nurturing) is maintained.

● *Misunderstandings.* When dealing with issues such as personal evangelism, faith promises for missions, tithing, or personal devotions, I cringe at the misconceptions people have. Many of their false assumptions can so easily cause misunderstandings. For instance, in any church service, we may have visitors who, when we talk about money, could assume, *That's what I thought. They're after my money.*

So we may need to begin a discussion of money with a few qualifiers: "If you're attending our church for the first time, you need to know that I do not preach about money every week. It is an important subject for every Christian, and Jesus emphasized the impact that money has on our spiritual lives, but it is not the primary subject of the Bible or of my preaching. It just so happens that I'm talking about it today. My goal in preaching about money is to strengthen you, not to fill the church coffers."

We should be as anxious for people to know what we *don't* mean as what we do mean.

● *Challenging without condemning.* About the last thing we want to do is condemn people. But leadership means challenging people, pointing them to a higher plateau in Christ, sustaining a Philippians 3:13–14 "unsatisfied satisfaction." And the more concerned we are with the deeper dimensions of Christian living—commitment, discipleship, purity of life, devotion to Christ, prayer—the easier it is to dump guilt or condemnation on the flock.

In reviewing the manuscript of another writer once, I noticed his style was condescending, calling others to growth with phrases such as "Shouldn't we as Christians do better than that?" and "You wouldn't want to fail the Lord, would you?" The article was negative, invoking a sense of failure rather than hope.

I encouraged him to turn the phrases around, so he wouldn't invoke defeat or guilt but still call people to be responsible. That would sound something like this: "With the Holy Spirit indwelling us, we need never fail our Lord Jesus. In him we can do all things!"

A Way That Feeds

Shepherds lead sheep from pasture to pasture, and so for them, leading is inseparably linked with feeding. I find the same is true for me if I keep the following factors in mind:

● *Time the challenge.* Sometimes our calls to action are better served by a short-term waiting period. The timing isn't right, even though the action is proper, but a strategic wait can spell the difference between successful leading or frustrating ineffectiveness. Most of us can point to valuable endeavors that might never have happened if we had tried to lead the people into something new at an unsuitable time.

● *Pace the challenge.* In a congregation of any size, only a percentage will respond immediately to a challenge. In a church of 150, if a pastor leads strongly on an issue, probably 30 at most will respond immediately and enthusiastically. Most will eventually follow, but it will take time.

People are in various degrees of spiritual health; they differ in their ability to hear, capacity to move, and willingness to follow. We dare not lead at the pace of the fastest sheep in the flock, leaving behind the aged, the weak, or the sick. We're obligated to lead the slower sheep as well.

Church members won't follow if they doubt they can make it. Climbing into unknown territory is frightening. Although some followers can believe in the value of a leader's vision, they may not believe they're good enough or spiritual enough to fulfill it. They doubt themselves more than they doubt their pastor's leadership.

So our leading and feeding will be to no avail unless we believe in our people. We have to believe they would fly if they could, that despite their weaknesses and faults, deep down inside they want to follow Christ. Our people will believe in themselves if we lead at a pace they can handle.

For example, I am sensitive to how many financial appeals we make per year and how often we ask people to find extra time in their schedule for special church activities. When they can handle the schedule and their budget absorbs their sacrificial offerings, it gives them confidence.

A congregation will also believe in themselves if they are being fed.

Understanding Personality Types

Temperament is our unique, God-given behavioral style. We need to understand temperament because ministry involves working with different kinds of people and various behavioral styles. By identifying our own style and the behavioral styles of others, we can increase our ministry effectiveness.

Leadership Styles

As pastors, our leadership styles are important components of our temperaments. Four leadership styles correspond to the traditional four-temperament model of personality types (choleric, sanguine, melancholic, and phlegmatic) developed by Hippocrates 2,000 years ago and recently popularized by Tim LaHaye. In their book *Understanding How Others Misunderstand You* (Moody 1990), Voges and Braund succinctly identify and summarize these styles:

● *Autocratic.* These leaders, like the apostle Paul, are self-starters who love a challenge and expect immediate results. They are quick decision makers who take charge and are good at managing trouble and solving problems. They exhibit a dominant style that is highly task oriented. They make good primary leaders (senior pastors, superintendents, etc.) because they get the job done.

However, due to their high task orientation, autocratic leaders risk offending people in the process. Therefore, they benefit by partnering with those who have good people skills. While people with this style make good leaders, at times they may have trouble being good followers. They can be strong-willed and may respect only those who are strong with them.

● *Democratic.* Peter exhibited this style. Democratic leaders are enthusiastic people who enjoy being around others and motivating them. They make favorable impressions and are usually articulate, preferring to minister in teams. While they listen carefully to others' views, they prefer to make the final decisions.

In combination with an autocratic leader, democratic leaders make some of the best pastors. As primary leaders, they are very people oriented and are good change

A healthy diet builds strength and brings confidence. Hunger brings a sense of defeat. If they feel defeated and hungry where they are, they'll never go farther. Sheep follow if they know the shepherd invariably leads to more food. Feeding shepherds, because they gain people's trust through their servant spirit, just have to give a verbal tug on the heart, and the people follow.

● *Form enclaves for those who respond at a faster pace.* We need to provide settings where we can offer the "Marines" in our churches a stronger challenge. For example, I meet with 100 young men each month to train them for leadership. I'm not gentle with them. I say things like "If you don't believe you're supposed to be serving this con-

---

agents who stimulate and motivate followers to action. They are better leaders than followers. While they have the abilities to follow, they prefer and function best leading various ministries in Christian organizations. They function best when they receive significant amounts of recognition and approval.

● *Participatory.* These leaders, such as Abraham, are patient, good at listening, and able to calm excited people. They are also loyal, focused, and cooperative. This facilitating leader works for peace and smooth operation within an organization.

Participatory leaders serve best on a ministry team in which someone else serves as the primary leader. As primary leaders themselves, participatory leaders prefer stability, resist change, and seek to maintain past traditions. Because they are loyal, patient, and supportive of others, they make outstanding followers and support staff.

● *Bureaucratic.* Bureaucratic leaders, such as Moses, are very analytical, paying close attention to standards and focusing on details. They are critical thinkers who check for accuracy and comply with authority. They serve best on ministry teams in which someone else is the primary leader. They

make good followers because they are logical, thorough, and analytical, preferring that ministry be done well or not at all. Bureaucratic leaders work best with those who are interested in quality. They provide a supportive and predictable environment.

It is possible that a pastor may exemplify one of the leadership styles in a "pure" way. However, it is more likely that he or she will utilize a combination of two of the styles, with one dominating the other. In any case, personal recognition of our leadership style has a direct impact on servanthood. When we understand other Christians' temperaments, we are better able to serve them so that they may better serve others (Phil. 2:3–8).

—Aubrey Malphurs

Resources

Malphurs, A. 1995. Maximizing your effectiveness: How to discover and develop your divine design. Grand Rapids: Baker.

Voges, K. 1985. Biblical personal profile. Minneapolis: Performax Systems International.

Voges, K., and R. Braund. 1990. Understanding how others misunderstand you. Chicago: Moody.

gregation, don't even come. Those who choose to attend here have made up their minds that we are followers of Jesus Christ. We're serious about prayer, we're in the Word, and we're committed to the church. We know that God wants us serving this particular church."

I'll talk in hard-nosed fashion about what kind of TV programs and movies the men watch, whether they laugh at the off-color jokes at work, and how they manage their thought lives, especially their sexual imagination. My leadership in this meeting isn't diplomatic or warm, but it is accepted because of the nature of the group.

If we're going to talk tough with the Marines, we need to be just as tough on ourselves and transparent about our own lives. We shouldn't address subjects solely in terms of scriptural principles; we can tell about our struggles and how we have dealt with them. We needn't act

Motivating People

The average, lifelong church member has been "incentived" to death. Countless attendance thermometers have risen to the top as he invited friends to Sunday school rallies. Pins, Bibles, trips, titles, and strokes have been dangled, and he has pulled like the lead husky. But if the pressure is released or the campaign is less slick, does the performance continue?

The Right Rewards

What is better is a creative environment where guilt-free, confident Christians pursue a few activities wholeheartedly. Reaching this enriching environment does not require groping in shrouded mystery. It has a lot to do with applying genuine biblical motivation.

In Genesis, people were created with something to do. From the beginning, we were given the capacity to "rule over the fish of the sea and the birds of the air," to subdue the earth and fill it, and to work the garden. The *imago Dei* is expressed in dominion and work.

This affects our view of motivation and reward. Work really matters! Our strivings do not have to relate exclusively to the sweet by-and-by. To stay motivated is to find reward in one's work. The Scriptures do not argue this; they assume it. And the greatest reward is seeing progress and achievement in something you perceive as eternally significant. Though we discourage people from asking, "What's in it for me?" we do well, whenever we begin a new program, to ask, "Can my people find legitimate and significant reward in participating?"

The Right Relationships

Without a shared excitement, any discipline can become lifeless plodding. Without a sense of teamwork and support, we risk burnout or latent bitterness. Thus, the Creation account provides us with a second essential quality of humankind. We

as if we have accomplished perfection.

Such transparency cultivates hope among the go-getters, who reason: *Our pastor means business. He's learned a path of fruitfulness with God, yet he also has struggles just as I do. So if he has struggled and overcome, then maybe I can overcome as well.*

● *Accept the inevitable losses.* Any church leader's decisions will result in some people leaving to seek a less demanding environment of commitment. We feel those losses deeply. To be effective leaders, we must overcome impersonal or insensitive ways and find a place of confidence in the Lord, so that if people are committed to leaving, we can "send them with blessing" rather than being pained or declaring them unreliable or disloyal.

● *Keep in step with the calendar.* For many people, the year begins in

---

are uniquely relational. Men and women were created to be in continuing relationships with God and each other.

This duel aspect of human nature helps us understand why we do not live by incentive alone. To simply move from one achievement to another—without intimate personal partnership with God—is meaningless. A world-class achiever, Solomon, concluded that.

The mysterious internal combustion called motivation is sustained, even in the absence of extrinsic rewards, when people know they are sharing the enterprise in a quality relationship. When discernible reinforcements have long since disappeared, this motivation remains.

The Right Purpose

William James said, "Habit is the flywheel of society." Habits carry us through lives that are constantly under change and stress. Good habits, such as giving, serving, teaching, or ushering, often thrive in people who have no elaborate or discernible reward system. Appar-

ently, they find meaning and joy in the enterprise itself. Such behaviors are the bedrock of church programs. We all value this kind of consistency.

However, even among our most faithful people, purpose must be evaluated. The repetition of behavior without purpose can sour even the most faithful. Scripture repeatedly warns us of the dangers of performance without purpose, sacrifice without love. It is the essence of pharisaism. Giving is to be cheerful work "as unto the Lord"; service is to be "in love"; and correction, "in gentleness." Workers can easily lose the connection to the whole enterprise, which not only stalls personal motivation but bottles up others who want to participate.

The longer a behavior is established, the more important is its constant realignment to God's purpose. Means too easily become ends, thereby stifling freshness, growth, and teachability. Constantly renewing our purpose helps us avoid complacency, and it averts demotivating battles over the status quo.

—Roger Thompson

September. They return from vacations and, though busy, are eager for new direction. Our best opportunity to lead them stretches from the second week in September until the middle of November. This is the perfect time to project vision and deliver strength-building exposition.

Holidays consume people's attention from Thanksgiving through the New Year, so we can seek to inspire with truth relevant to the seasons' thrusts. In January people are inclined to think about new goals and ambitions. That's when diet programs and exercise clubs advertise heavily, so it's a good time to focus preaching on discipleship themes, and in February, world missions.

Special opportunities come with the Lenten season, as people focus on what Christ has done for them on the Cross and how they should respond. In that season, we can preach on themes like redemption's perfect work, the promise in following Christ, and the person of Jesus.

There is a post-Easter letdown everywhere, but it can be countered with a strong emphasis in the weeks leading up to Pentecost. Spirit-filled living and resurrection power for service are themes for this time, along with a strong emphasis on family and marriage.

Early June is a time to prepare for summer. Even though people will be going their separate ways, we can lead them into a focus on something together, such as by asking everyone to read the same book, devotionally follow the same Bible readings, or memorize the same Scriptures.

● *Listen for God's direction.* Although we need to be attentive to the calendar cycles, we don't want to become slaves to the church calendar. God sometimes leads us to do things counter to our assumptions. For example, I once held back on a financial appeal, convinced that God was saying to me that our church had a lot of things happening, so it was not the time to add more. That was a difficult decision, but I decided to go with how I felt God leading me. Several weeks later, the Lord guided me to meet our need by writing a simple letter of explanation to the congregation: "We're all busy, and I haven't the heart to put something else on you. I'm simply asking you to pray and give as you feel directed."

We must lead as we feel God directs—but not unless he confirms his direction through our leaders. It's a good policy never to follow unilateral impressions regarding the administrative path of the church.

Balancing the Two

The Sunday after the staff member acknowledged to me his moral failure, I announced to the congregation at the end of our morning services, "For the first time in my 13 years as your pastor, we have had the heartbreaking experience of a moral difficulty with one of our pastoral team. We will address that tonight in our evening service."

That night the building was packed. I taught for 50 minutes on God's perfect design for sexual relationships and why our disobedience to that design hurts him and us. I explained what the Bible teaches about leaders who fall, about what their forgiveness does and doesn't mean.

Then we served Communion. With the bread in my hands, I talked about the brokenness of all our lives but especially how Jesus was broken on behalf of our brokenness. "What we are expecting tonight is wholeness," I said. Then I took the cup in my hand and talked about the cleansing power of the blood of Christ.

Before we drank from the cup, I said, "The staff member who has admitted his moral failure has made clear his intention to turn from his action and seek restoration within the community life of this church." Then I called him by name to come forward.

I could hear people quietly weeping all over the auditorium.

He spoke for a few minutes and concluded with, "I ask you all to forgive me."

After I prayed over the cup, I put my arm around him. I asked everyone to stretch a hand toward him and in unison say, "John, I forgive you." Their voices thundered the response, and we drank from the cup.

No one could have left that service feeling we had swept his failure under the rug or treated it as unoffensive to God. Nor could anyone leave without feeling a holy reverence for God.

Though always in tension, leading and feeding are not in opposition. When best expressed, we lead when we feed, and we feed when we lead. We can't fully do either alone.

—Jack W. Hayford

Resources

Anderson, L., J. Hayford, and B. Patterson. 1993. Who's in charge? Standing up to leadership pressures. Sisters, Ore.: Multnomah.

Chaffee, P. 1993. Accountable leadership: Resources for worshipping communities. San Francisco: ChurchCare.

George, C., and R. Logan. 1987. Leading & managing your church. Old Tappan, N.J.: Revell.

Smith, F. 1986. Learning to lead. Waco, Tex.: Word.

Wagner, C. 1984. Leading your church to growth. Ventura, Cal.: Regal.

Building a Team

In a culture unaccustomed to substantive commitment, leadership is necessary to build effective teams, which in turn advance the kingdom of God. The same components that build a small team can transform a local congregation, a neighborhood, or a workplace.

Obstacles to Teams

Let's begin by talking about two obstacles to building an effective team.

● *Individualism.* Our culture esteems individualism over mutuality, competition over cooperation, and winning over pursuing truth. But individualism only cripples team efficiency and effectiveness.

● *Conflict.* Conflict is inevitable, and leaders strengthen their teams when they accept it as such. Conflict is either resolved (spreading grace) or buried over (feeding bitterness). False niceness can limit our credibility, but resolving conflict by confessing, forgiving, and reconciling transforms us, our teams, and our neighbors.

What Is a Team?

Unfortunately, much that passes as teamwork is simply busy groups demonstrating sincerity but little renewal and considerable burnout. Christian busyness is not ministry. A team is a group where there is intentional, risk-taking effort toward the three components of *task, process,* and *people.*

● *Task:* the purpose or objective of the group. It can mean support-ing adult education, planning worship, drafting a vision statement, studying Scripture, or discipling leaders. Ideally members can clearly state their task in one sentence, make a clear commitment to it and have growing ownership of it, know the planned completion or next evaluation date of it, and understand a clear connection between it and the church's vision statement.

● *Process:* the way the team goes about pursuing its task. Process has two aspects. The first is organizational: When, where, and how often will our meetings be? Who is leading? Will we have outside work to do?

The second aspect is more relational: What is happening to and among the members as they work together on the task? Training for and Spirit-led handling of group dynamics determines whether individuals and teams (and congregations) will be built up or burned out by their service.

● *People:* the final but often annoying component of teams. How much easier team building would be if it did not involve people!

Building Blocks

Team building is supported by attitudes, study, and training. In a team-building situation, leaders model a learning posture (about self, others, and God) and find a place to be followers. Here are several important components to build effective teams:

● *Study and prayer.* Spirit-led teams should emphasize regular corporate study of Scripture and prayer to discern God's priorities.

● *Training in basics.* Leaders should receive training in group dynamics, group life-cycles, conflict resolution, and personality factors. For example, training in basic personality types helps leaders discern and appreciate reasons for their own feelings as well as those of other team members.

● *Assessment.* Knowing the components and context (vision) for team building encourages prayerful assessment. For example, is there a core of key leaders who share Jesus' priorities for developing people and who are committed to grow in their ability to do so? If not, this is the place to start to build a core group. If so, does their shared vision mutually determine what other teams they establish and how they lead them? Is there now a second level of leaders who are being developed in their understanding of Jesus' priorities?

Effective team building is not another program. It is a long-term commitment to Jesus' values and God-designed interdependence.

—Roger Razzari Elrod

Sharing and Delegating Responsibilities

Delegation means more than giving orders or simply assigning tasks. Rather, to delegate means to involve someone in an endeavor by coordinating his or her efforts with one's own goals. Delegation (like other relationships) can be complex, because each individual is unique. That's why, to delegate in the church, we need to rely on God's Spirit to be better able to equip and enable those we lead.

How Delegation Fits

Where does delegating fit into the overall leadership scheme? If we think of a sphere of leadership, vision would be at its core. Vision motivates us as leaders of a congregation to see a unique mission. At the next level, we find key objectives for the church, stemming from the core vision statement. Each of those specific objectives has its own leadership cycle; we need to plan, delegate, supervise, and review each task.

Delegating takes the second position, following *planning*, where the details and timing of the objective are settled. Delegation coordinates people and links them with the specifics of the plan. After delegation comes *supervision*, where people are supported and encouraged and the details of the plan are monitored. Finally comes the *review* (evaluation), which ensures that the objective was completed and celebrates successful joint efforts.

Details of Delegation

When we assign a specific task to someone on the church staff (typing a letter, say, or organizing a potluck dinner), we have delegated work to them only in the broad sense of the word. Two steps can help us delegate more precisely:

● *Write a job description.* We must first agree with a team member about his or her position. What kinds of responsibilities will we hand over to that person? What will that person be prepared to accept? That's where a job description, including the specific tasks we intend to delegate, shines.

Though an unpaid worker will not need a formal position description, some kind of written agreement is still a good idea. In it we can summarize the assignment and establish expectations and accountability. Whether we're delegating to paid staff or volunteer workers, we should attempt to choose assignments appropriate to their gifts and character.

● *Give the authority to handle the responsibility.* The temptation is to guard against giving too much freedom. Yet, if we assign someone the responsibility for a task without granting the authority and providing the resources to accomplish that task, we haven't really delegated.

How Supervision Works

To take our associates seriously, we must support them in two tangible ways: (1) through ongoing affirmation and critique, and (2) through performance reviews, perhaps conducted annually.

We can build confidence in people through positive feedback, and we can improve their performance through constructive criticism. Support needs to be both assertive and sensitive. Sincere, timely words or other signs of appreciation for a staff member can make the difference between that person feeling included or ignored.

Job descriptions will need to grow as the congregation grows. New objectives may be assigned as situations change. When we evaluate what's been done, we have an appropriate opportunity to revise an associate's position.

As we learn more about our leadership style (relations versus tasks, authoritarian or collaborative, and so on), we'll increase our potential for success. And as we come to grips with our own identities—our personal strengths and weaknesses, our cultural and ethnic roles, our motivations and drives—we'll be better able to discern and respond to the needs of those we're called to lead. What's more, we'll be better prepared to delegate effectively so that our work and their work accomplishes the Lord's work.

—Roger Razzari Elrod

16

Crisis and Conflict

Paul says, "I hear that when you come together as a church, there are divisions among you, and to some extent I believe it" (1 Cor. 11:18).

The word "conflict" comes from the Latin *fligere*, meaning literally "to strike together." Whenever two or more people pursue mutually exclusive goals, or whenever one person's needs collide with another's, conflict results. If there were no effort among humans to fulfill ideas, goals, or desires, there would be no conflict.

In their book *Church Fights*, Speed Leas and Paul Kittlaus helpfully distinguish three ways in which conflict is experienced:

● *Intrapersonal conflict:* the contest one has when different parts of the self compete with one another. I want to be a beloved pastor, but I also want to be a preacher who speaks the truth.

● *Interpersonal conflict:* personality differences that are not related primarily to issues. I like to think of myself as a strong, independent person, but my administrative board chairperson treats me like an incompetent who must be told what to do.

● *Substantive conflict:* disputes over facts, values, goals, and beliefs. I think we ought to put a new roof on the church, but the social-concerns committee wants to open a clothes closet for the poor.

A given conflict may be a mixture of these types. A substantive argument over the church budget, for example, may also dredge up intrapersonal doubts about my effectiveness as a pastor. To keep from pretending that a given conflict is substantive when it is really intra-personal, a preacher must act with honesty and self-knowledge.

"Know thyself," then, is the beginning of wisdom, as we prepare to address church conflicts. This does not mean knowing ourselves in order to suppress all personal motives. Because the Christian faith lauds self-denial, whenever my personal feelings and needs are paramount to matters of the true, the right, and the just, something seems wrong. So we tend to say, "I'm not arguing this point because of my own feelings in the matter; this is a matter of principle."

That's often where the trouble begins. In claiming that we are arguing not out of personal feelings but on the basis of Christian principle alone, we idealize and dehumanize the conflict. We tell ourselves a disagreement is not simply differences among people but a clash of false faith and true faith. The issue becomes: Which side are you on? In doing so, we eliminate the human and personal side of a conflict, with all its modifying elements.

I must not delude myself into thinking such abstract, detached, pristine propositions are possible. Rather, I must assert everything with a generous dose of humility, aware, with Paul, of all the ways I preach myself as often as I preach Christ. Leas and Kittlaus identify four kinds of substantive conflict:

● *Conflict over the facts of a situation.* Is there enough money to pay for the new roof?

● *Conflict over methods or means.* How do we achieve a solution to the problem? Should we take up a food collection for the poor in town or lobby the town council to take action on decent housing laws?

● *Conflict over ends or goals.* Should this church be involved in direct political action, or is this a matter of concern for Christian individuals alone?

● *Conflict over values.* Should Christians ever be engaged in confrontation and agitation, or should we always be reconcilers and peacemakers in every situation? Values are the source of our goals and the means by which the church gains direction. Values tell us which goals are worth adopting and what means of achieving them are Christian.

Purposes of Conflict

As surprising as it may seem to peacemaking pastors, conflict has a positive role to play in the congregation. In conflict, a group is energized. As an old pastor once told me, "You can put out a fire easier than you can raise the dead." Where there is absolutely no dissatisfaction, no vision of anything better, and no pain, there is little chance of action. A church with a healthy amount of tension and conflict is a church alive.

While gratuitous and self-serving conflict is an abuse of the pastoral office, it is the preacher's duty to expose people to the demands of

Scripture, to assure people that there is a force for betterment and meaning in our world and that the preacher has a vision of something superior to just the present arrangements.

Congregations that confront conflict constructively learn to be creative. They experience themselves not as hapless, helpless victims of external circumstances but as creative, resourceful people who have been given the skills and insights needed to be the church. Inversely, congregations that suppress conflict find it acts like a pressure cooker: the heat builds and finally explodes. The issues triggering the explosion often seem irrational and petty, but the aftermath is not trivial. An open, active parish allows for a continuous release of pressure, and conflicts are less likely to be destructive.

Churches generally overstate their inability to handle conflict. The real danger is their fear of conflict, as they blindly believe that all conflict is wrong or unchristian. Dealing openly with conflict is an affirmation that the issues are worth fighting over and that we can resolve our differences without destroying one another.

Yet we must admit there are certain parishes unable to bear a high level of conflict. When an individual is confronted with too much threat, his or her ability to receive and process information and perceive alternatives decreases.

Conflict makes all of us draw upon the resources of our faith to handle the matter at hand. Down deep, we may doubt we have such resources, but better that such spiritual emptiness be exposed and ministered to than left to fester. Even in a congregation's darkest hours, the Christian faith provides the resources necessary for making sense out of difficult situations and surviving them.

Assessing Conflict

Every congregation is an ecological system in which conflict will be treated in certain ways. To assess how conflict is handled in a church, we can ask: What has been the congregation's experience with conflict in the past? Has it led to growth or retrenchment? What congregational folklore emerges when conflicts arise? Colloquial expressions such as "Let sleeping dogs lie" or "Don't open up that can of worms" reveal underlying assumptions. What is the group's capacity for making changes? When people have been hurt previously by conflict, they fear and avoid it. The more painful past conflicts have been, the more cautious we must be in handling new conflicts.

When faced with a congregational conflict, we generally have two choices: we can ignore the situation or we can intervene. At times, it is possible to practice creative avoidance of crises. Most of us have learned that we must choose our battles, lest minor hassles turn into major confrontations, resulting in a never-ending series of crises. Our

---

goal in avoiding conflict is to guide and affect potential conflict situations without allowing them to become destructive to parish life. That is a difference between ignoring conflict and avoiding conflict.

Here are several steps to use for assessing potential conflict in the earliest stages:

● Obtain as much information as possible. Many conflicts are the result of misinformation or poor communication. This initial step is a relatively nonthreatening gesture toward the parties of the conflict, whereby one is only seeking better understanding of what is at stake.

● Buy as much time as possible. When people are under pressure to reach a quick decision, there is little time to work out differences and seek alternatives. Delay is a means of creative avoidance whereby time is gained to function wisely.

● Make an assessment of the individuals involved in the potential conflict. How mature are they? Is this the work of isolated, chronic

Change Management

"Churches are a lot like horses," said an old farmer. "They don't like to be startled or surprised. It causes deviant behavior." Our fiercest battles are seldom fought over theology. More often than not, they are fought over change, sometimes even the slightest change.

Smoother Change

Though change without conflict is rarely possible, there is still much we can do to limit conflict and overcome resistance to change. The following steps can help us smooth the way and decrease the instances of "deviant behavior" in the church:

● *Test the waters.* It's wise to try to find out ahead of time how people will react should a particular change actually take place. Who vehemently objects? What points do people attack? Which criticisms are legitimate? And most important, what changes are needed before making the proposal finally official?

Testing the waters provides valuable information. At the least, it lets us know if our dissatisfaction with the status quo is shared by others. If not, it's time to slow down and help people see the need.

One way to start is by asking a small cross section of people—board members, unofficial power brokers, and the average man or woman in the pew—what they think of an idea or possible change. Small social settings work well for this. Larger groups tend to silence introverts and inhibit candidness.

● *Listen and respond to resisters.* People who resist our ideas are sometimes labeled adversaries. That's often a case of mistaken identity, however. Rather than view them as enemies to be overcome,

troublemakers trying to create a congregational crisis where none exists? We need to identify these people in order to offer individual care. However, since it is tempting to label people as troublemakers in order to avoid facing legitimate differences within the congregation, we must examine our motives.

● Take the emotional temperature of the conflict. If the anger level is high, what can we do to initiate a cooling-off period? Humor or distraction into some other activity can be helpful in bringing emotions down to more manageable levels.

Often, committee meetings, conferences, and pastoral counseling sessions can resolve these conflicts quietly. But once a conflict surfaces publicly, we need a different strategy. If we take a passive approach once the issues have surfaced, members will think we have lost control and are either unwilling or unable to intervene in a constructive way.

---

we can see them as advisers. They are, in fact, a necessary link in the process of transforming a good idea into a great idea. Their resistance is not always a nuisance; it can be useful. Like pain in the body, it lets us know something is out of adjustment.

An important factor we learn by listening to resisters is where things are most likely to go wrong once the change is in place. We also discover the hidden psychological barriers to be overcome. Just because a change or innovation is a good idea is no guarantee the average member will buy it. To figure out where those psychological barriers are, we can ask ourselves two questions: (1) Are the resisters objecting to the proposal or the presenter? (2) Are the resisters objecting to the proposal or to the way it was presented?

● *Sell individuals before groups.* Studies show that only about 15 percent will adopt a new idea without first knowing who else is supporting it, so we'll normally need to convince enough individuals to give

an idea credibility before we attempt to sell it to the entire group.

The problem with ignoring this principle is painfully illustrated by a long-range planning committee. After they worked nearly two years, they called a congregational meeting to review their findings and proposals. The presentation was beautifully done; their proposals were excellent. But the congregation rejected their plans outright.

The pastor and committee members were devastated. They had assumed a clear presentation of an excellent idea would result in congregational approval. But they were wrong, and the fatal blow to their program was self-inflicted. By presenting the proposal to the entire church first, they forced people to go public with their *initial* reactions. This practically guaranteed rejection, for two reasons. First, initial responses to change are often negative. Second, public responses are usually permanent.

—Larry W. Osborne

Pastoral Strategies

Our goal in responding to conflict is to move those in conflict toward constructive growth or resolution. Fear, denial, and all-out war are rarely constructive. In their book *Conflict Ministry in the Church,* Larry McSwain and William Treadwell suggest that the first step, once conflict is public, is diffusion. Diffusion is effective particularly when the conflict has taken the congregation as a whole by surprise or when it seems to be concentrated within a small group.

When this happens, the following steps are helpful:

● Be sure everyone in the group knows the facts of the situation. Healthy decision making cannot occur otherwise. One faction must not be allowed to pressure everyone else into a hasty decision.

● Ask someone to explain the history of the conflict. Most conflicts are presented as relatively simple matters that require the taking of a stand. Usually they are not so simple, once the whole history of the crisis is known.

Handling Expectations

As pastors, we face normal expectations from every side—peers, denomination, supervisor, church board, spouse. Expectations become more serious, however, when they contain hidden agendas. This kind usually emerges at awkward, inconvenient, or even embarrassing moments. Examples might include the expectation to be just like a predecessor, or to be the perfect pastor for everyone, or to handle doctrine just as a popular pastor does. When we fail to meet even such unfounded expectations, some people will let their displeasure be known.

Deciding How to Respond

Here are some principles for responding to unrealistic expectations and the problem people who so often plague us with them.

● *Know yourself.* Strip away the accretions of the years—those layers of expectations others have laid upon us and we have willingly assumed—and ask: Who am *I?* What can I do? With what do I struggle? What are my strengths and weaknesses? What spiritual gifts do I have—or lack? We should never underestimate the power of others to make us dishonest with ourselves!

If we are serious about this, we may find it helpful to keep a journal of our findings. Or we may discover we need someone else to confide in, lest we fool ourselves. We are far more effective if we spend more time doing the things we do best and delegating the rest (or treating those things with benign neglect).

● *Be transparent.* We can't do it all and shouldn't let problem people make us pretend we can. If we find a certain area of ministry onerous or difficult, we can say so. We

● Refer the conflict to the proper committee for discussion and rec-ommendation. When conflicts emerge in a large group, they must not be discussed there but should be moved quickly to a smaller forum.

● Enlarge the conflicted group with people who can help move the group to a constructive engagement. Sometimes small committees become deadlocked and dysfunctional. By drawing new life into the group, old alliances can be broken and new insights given.

● Delay action until there has been time to attempt to manage the conflict. Each of the above steps is a means of delaying a decision about the conflict until a proper analysis can occur.

With the conflict diffused, the group is better able to move into what McSwain and Treadwell call problem-solving analysis, the phase whereby the group is moved to a decision. At this stage, we can:

● Consider all the gathered facts, feelings, and opinions about the conflict.

● List options to the problem, considering the potential positive and negative consequences of each.

---

need to develop at least enough competency to "pay the rent"—Lyle Schaller's term for the minimal tasks that come with a pastor's ter-ritory (funerals, some administra-tive work, and so on), but then we can seek other church leaders' help in freeing ourselves to operate in areas of strength.

● *Be inner directed.* The inner-directed person derives values, motivation, and purpose from with-in, not from the feedback of prob-lem people. As pastors we should have a fairly clear idea of what we hope to accomplish. We have not become pastors to please people, but God. It is God who called us, who equips us, who works in us. It is God who directs us and provides for us (regardless of who signs the salary check). Unless we develop this perspective, we will be victim-ized by everyone's expectations— the legitimate as well as the lame.

● *Be purposeful in pursuing your course.* The loudest and most ran-corous voice needn't sway us. Texas businessman Fred Smith says pas-tors must constantly remind people of their commitment to the most important thing. He says, "I don't think they would be offended the least bit if [the pastor] said, 'Folks, Tuesday is my day with God. I have to spend some time with my boss to keep this job, and he has called me into conference on Tuesday. He takes a dim view of me answering the phones and appearing at social occasions on conference day.' "

● *Be prepared to absorb some misunderstanding.* One of the most helpful definitions I know is this: "Leadership is the ability to absorb pain." The sooner a pastor realizes not everyone will love him or her, and some will misunderstand even the purest motives, the better ad-justed that pastor will be. Perhaps the whole question of expectations would become academic if we could constantly monitor our lives by this standard: Does it meet God's expec-tations?

—*James A. Davey with Warren Bird*

● List each option in the order of priority.

● Depersonalize the option, since we are not voting on the personalities of those involved.

● Develop a consensus for the option that most nearly resolves the conflict, even if it involves compromise.

Pastoral Styles in Conflict Management

In addition to assessing the various factors involved in a congregational conflict, taking the emotional temperature of the situation, gathering information, and planning strategies, it is important to assess what style of conflict management is predominant in our approach.

McSwain and Treadwell identify five styles that ministers often utilize as they confront (or avoid) conflict within their parishes.

● *The problem solver.* The problem-solver pastor refuses to deny or to flee the conflict, pressing for conversation and negotiation of the conflict until a satisfactory conclusion is reached. The problem-solver style is most effective with groups that share common goals but whose problems stem from a breakdown in communication. The problem solver is gifted in helping participants verbalize conflict in depersonalized ways. Because the problem solver does not fear conflict, he or she can be most helpful to a conflict-laden congregation.

Where the problem solver is less effective is in handling conflicts that arise from opposing goals. Emotionally explosive situations are sometimes beyond the problem-solving approach, since those involved are simply too angry for the dispassionate deliberation required in this style. There is also a tendency, in the problem solver's intense effort to move everyone along to the solution, to overlook other dynamics in the life of a congregation and to become impatient with the intransigent.

To be balanced, the problem-solver pastor must remember that resolving disputes is only one part of pastoral work. The pastor, like the biblical texts that guide the church, must often instruct, encourage, edify, condemn, and envision. People are more than mere problems to be solved, and many of humanity's most basic conflicts will not be resolved as long as we are on this earth. The gospel does have a word to speak to those conflicts, too, but a word that transcends mere solutions. The balanced problem solver will minister to people, even when solutions are not to be found.

● *The super helper.* The super helper is constantly working to help others and gives little thought to self. This person is the "messiah," often passive in conflicts involving self but quite involved in assisting others as they work through their conflicts.

Since pastors are expected to be long-suffering, compassionate, and always willing to help, many super helpers will be attracted to pastoring. But the super helper is not always a good conflict minister. By being so concerned with others, he or she may ignore his or her own physical, emotional, and spiritual needs. The anger and frustration felt by the super helper goes unacknowledged and unleashed, and the result is often burnout.

In a conflict, the super helper will feel a sense of failure if all parties in the dispute are not happy with the achieved solution. He or she will tend to take on too much responsibility for group problems, feeling personally responsible to set everything right rather than to assist the congregation in setting things right. The super helper must learn that many conflicts do not lend themselves to painless solutions.

● *The power broker.* There are conflicts where substantive differences are so contradictory that mutually inclusive goals are not possible. For instance, a church cannot be racially inclusive and exclusive at the same time. Any resolution of this problem will involve someone feeling like a winner and someone else feeling like a loser. In such situations, the power broker uses whatever power is available to resolve and win the conflict.

For the power broker, solutions are more important than relationships. If someone leaves the church as the result of the solution, this is unfortunate but not devastating, because a solution was achieved. In the eyes of the power broker, it is important to "hang tough" in many situations, to assert that "the buck stops here" and "if you can't stand the heat, get out of the kitchen."

Some congregations seem to thrive under the leadership of a power broker, but only those that are willing to give the pastor or a lay group major decision-making power. Congregations that value participatory democracy in governance will be unhappy with the power-broker style. The major liability of this style is that when the power broker fails to motivate the congregation to do what he or she thinks best, the power broker resorts to manipulation. The power broker wants followers, not colleagues or fellow workers.

● *The facilitator.* The facilitator adapts to a variety of situations and styles in order to achieve a compromise between competing factions. Acts 15 presents James as just such a leader in the controversy over the Gentile mission in Antioch. He moved into a tense situation with a spirit of conciliation and proposed a solution that appealed to both sides in the battle.

This style of compromise is most effective for conflicts in which the differences are attitudinal or emotional. But if there are substantive differences, participants may be angered by the attempts of the facilitator to move everyone to some benign middle ground where they can all agree on everything, and the facilitator may be regarded as a weak-principled peacemaker who is always trying to suppress real ideological differences in order to keep everyone happy.

The facilitator style risks keeping a congregation in a constant spirit of compromise, and even suppressing conflict, rather than allowing conflict to move the congregation to a new level of consensus. The lowest common denominator of agreement is sought rather than a truly creative solution.

● *The fearful loser.* The fearful loser runs from conflict. Quiet and retiring in personal behavior, the fearful loser finds that conflict produces intense personal insecurity. The congregation senses this, and if the members are charitable, they suppress all conflict (or move conflict underground) in order to protect their fragile pastor. When the conflict bubbles up and demands to be acknowledged, the fearful loser is likely to resign and move elsewhere.

Because the fearful loser must suppress not only congregational conflict but also his or her own personal feelings, constant compliance and passivity eventually produce hostility. The pastor blames the congregation for unduly restricting him or her, while the congregation impatiently waits for the pastor finally to stand up and take charge. At the root of the fearful loser's problem is his or her own painfully low self-image and lack of confidence.

Most pastors probably operate out of each of these styles at least some of the time. Undoubtedly, the positive, self-assured, trusting style of the problem solver is the most ideal for most parish conflict. As pastors facing conflict, it is useful for us to ask ourselves: Who am I as I move into conflict? What is my style? How does my congregation perceive me in the pulpit and in the committee meeting? Our goal, our calling, and our assurance, as Paul writes, is that God has given to us "the ministry of reconciliation" (2 Cor. 5:11–19).

—*William H. Willimon*

Resources

Leas, S., and P. Kittlaus. 1973. Church fights: Managing conflict in the local church. Philadelphia: Westminster.

McSwain, L., and W. Treadwell, Jr. 1981. Conflict ministry in the church. Nashville: Broadman.

Mickey, P., and R. Wilson. 1973. Conflict and resolution: A case-study approach to handling parish situations. Nashville: Abingdon.

Willimon, W. 1987. Preaching about conflict in the local church. Philadelphia: Westminster.

Willimon, W. 1979. Worship as pastoral care. Nashville: Abingdon.

Mediation and Arbitration

Increasingly, people are turning to mediation to bring resolution to a variety of disputes. It's generally cheaper, quicker, and less stressful than litigation. For Christians, mediation also can demonstrate love in action.

Mediators don't judge conflicts. They simply try to facilitate negotiation, helping people examine issues from a Christian perspective and work toward a resolution pleasing to God. Mediators must remain neutral and can't be advocates for one side or the other. On biblical matters, however, Christian mediators must be advocates for the truth. They can't be neutral regarding the basic principles of Christian living.

The Process of Mediation

Several steps can help us achieve our goals as mediators:

● *Develop ground rules.* Basic rules may include keeping all matters confidential, not meeting privately with either side as a mediator, and doing nothing to belittle or infuriate the other. Generally, the fewer the rules, the better.

● *Facilitate story telling.* Just being able to tell what has occurred is cathartic. A mediator can ask to hear each side's story in turn, encouraging people to keep focused.

● *Build an agenda.* Listen carefully for the real issues. Part of the mediator's role is to help the parties define the conflict accurately. They must first agree about what's at issue before it can be resolved.

● *Create alternatives.* Discuss ways to meet each side's needs. Creating solutions generally is more difficult than analyzing issues, since people invest a lot of emotional energy in being right.

● *Restructure the conflict.* Encourage people to approach issues from a different, more constructive perspective. Help them see points of agreement they may not have considered. Peer beneath the surface to gain insight into what is motivating them.

● *Understand the interests involved.* Fear, greed, pride, vengeance, and anger can grip people in the midst of disputes. But, in many cases we handle, people also know some Scripture and basic Christian values. We can help people to examine and understand their motives.

● *Separate past from future.* People in mediation often want to resolve past injustices. Mediation, however, focuses largely on the future. We want to help people agree about where they want to go from here. Negotiation can become most productive when people let go of the past. Often that's when they discover forgiveness.

Cautions

In mediation, we must maintain our neutrality, which is threatened when we're asked to state a preference or opinion. Our job as mediators is to help the parties resolve *their* dispute, not to give advice and do the work for them. Another threat to neutrality comes when one side thinks we have sided with the other, usually feeling that we're prying too deeply. We can remind both parties that a Christian perspective requires an honest look at all issues—even those they'd rather ignore.

We also need to guard against rescuing people from their troubles. By the time people come to a mediator, they are usually in difficult shape emotionally and spiritually. If we try to solve their problems for them, though, we lose our effectiveness as mediators.

The mediation process is not foolproof. In most instances it works about as well as the commitment of the participants. It is abused from time to time, particularly when one side tries to postpone resolution or wants a socially acceptable way to get back at the other.

When mediation becomes unproductive, we should withdraw from the dispute, suggesting other options such as arbitration or even legal proceedings. We can urge people to see the proper parties to resolve their dispute.

Though challenging, mediation provides opportunity for those first, tentative steps back into relationship. Few activities bring greater honor to God than resolving conflicts and becoming reconciled to each other.

—Chip Zimmer

Pastor-Centered Conflict

To fight or to flee—most pastors face the decision at times of church conflict and especially when that conflict centers on themselves. A decision simply must be made: *Dare I—can I—stay in this church in this situation, or must I leave?*

Often it's a tough call. Both solutions commend themselves. No one wants to depart a loser, yet to remain amid heartache and a continuous succession of battles is sheer agony, if not futility.

Reasons to Leave

There are several good reasons why we may choose to leave:

● *We're unwanted.* When a congregation no longer desires someone as pastor, that person's ministry there effectively comes to a close. Leaving is the only true option. But sometimes congregations are split, with one group begging us to stay and another demanding our ouster. Then the severity of the split often determines our course of action. If staying means splitting a church, we may choose to leave.

● *We're not trusted.* Once a congregation loses confidence in us—even though they may still love us—ministry becomes nearly impossible. When trust is gone, our working relationship becomes mired to the axles amid dubious parishioners.

● *We run out of fight.* Sometimes amid a pastor-centered controversy, we may be able to marshal troops for a battle. Perhaps our side could prevail. But we simply may not have the will to prosecute the battle plan. Often, after years of smaller struggles, our fight has been drained away.

● *Everyone needs a fresh start.* Not

all battles are worth the toll in suffering and problems. As winners, we might find ourselves the possessors of a crippled church. Or we may simply need to begin anew somewhere where personal history doesn't play such a dominant role. Some battle lines should never be drawn, some battles never fought.

Reasons to Remain

If a crisis always signalled the end of a ministry, staff directories would be written on chalkboards. The reasons for staying—even amid trouble—sometimes overwhelm those for leaving. What signals the desirability of staying rather than leaving?

● *The people want us to stay.* This may appear obvious, but in the throes of controversy, that isn't always the case. Inside, we may be saying, *I'm finished! No one's on my side.* At the same time, a loving congregation might be thinking, *We love our pastor and we can get through this together.* It's easy to underestimate a congregation's power to work through difficulties with enough love and commitment.

● *We want to weather the storm and later leave confidently.* Quick flight may actually work damage. It can compound a problem, allowing conflict to have its way. And besides, leaving during controversy leaves a dark cloud on the whole experience. How much better to work through the problem and then decide about leaving, based on less emotion and more prayer!

● *Remaining brings the possibility of better results.* Simply walking away often appears the easiest option. We're gone. Maybe conflict won't dog us to our next call. But our leaving can set back the ministry of a church and place our future in jeopardy.

As messy and as painful as some church fights can become, sometimes they need to be fought for right to emerge the victor. It's not good for the wrong side to prevail, and a pastor's hasty exit may in addition cripple the church and impoverish the now-unemployed (and perhaps unemployable) pastor's family.

In the end, each pastor must make an intensely personal decision: How will this affect the church, my ministry, my family? Am I the problem, or am I part of the solution? Eventually the decision becomes one of determining God's will.

—*James D. Berkley*

Theological Rifts

Almost every pastor will at some time take a risk because of an issue of theology. The Bible chronicles many instances of spiritual warriors who have gone to battle for the integrity of the gospel (see Gal. 2:11ff.). But because theological disagreements can damage or divide congregations, great caution must be taken in identifying a conflict as theological. Many nontheological disagreements get labeled as theological: whether to use plastic or glass Communion cups, the brand of the Communion bread, the presence of altar flowers. Each can be falsely billed as an intricate and essential point of theology.

Deciding the Issue

Finding a point of theology hidden under every altar-flower discussion can be hazardous both to pastoral and church health. Why are many nontheological matters branded as theological? We may want to use theological discussion to avoid tough institutional or interpersonal conflicts. It's easier to pronounce an issue "answered" by an obscure point of theology than to moderate a turf battle between the Sunday school superintendent and the girls' club director.

Some issues, however, can honestly be classified several ways and have varying degrees of theological impact. In a LEADERSHIP survey, pastors said only one-third of the difficult decisions they make in a year concern theological issues, but identifying that one-third is crucial. The following questions help determine whether a situation is truly theological:

● Does this situation threaten a core belief of our church? Or is it a peripheral issue that allows for some difference of position?

● If we leave it unaddressed, will a theological precedent be established that could lead to long-term weakening of our commitment? Or is it simply a reflection of some spiritual immaturity that time and love will remedy?

● Is the issue purely one of theology? Or is theology camouflage for a nontheological problem?

Right and Wrong

Once identified, core theological issues call for vigorous action, according to the "law of right and wrong." The objective—theological purity—admits no compromise. Resolution need not be blunt or hasty, but the risk to achieve the right must be taken regardless.

Following the law of right and wrong is not a simple matter, however. The decision (the goal) may be clear, but how to achieve that goal with the fewest casualties may not be as obvious.

One pastor recalls: "I made a decision, based on my understanding of 1 Timothy 3, that prospective officers must be men who had not been divorced. Several nominees were disqualified, and they and their families grew hostile. A few could not be reconciled, and hostility hardened against me. Looking back I would not have changed the standards for officers, but I would have handled the disqualifications in a more personal, loving manner."

On many issues we simply don't have direct commands from God to obey and are left to sanctified common sense. Here the great temptation is to obey our human ideas, mistaking them for God's. And where mere obedience is used as the criterion for determining interpersonal relationships, varying levels of inhumanity result. We are called to reprove our brothers and sisters to keep our doctrine and beliefs pure, but we are also called to do so in love and forgiveness. As soon as we begin to see ourselves (rather than God) as the repository of all theological truth, we lose sight of our own fallibility. Arrogance and ruthlessness, in the name of

God's work, can result.

What does this mean in the church? It means that if we intend to decide a question on the basis of obedience to the theological canons

of right and wrong, we need to be sure we're dealing with a theological question.

—Terry C. Muck

Natives Versus Newcomers

Most church members would like their church to become a little bigger and healthier—but definitely not different. That's where the problem of newcomers enters in, because in swelling the ranks, they inevitably produce change. And it's that word *change* that causes most of the problems in native-newcomer struggles.

Different People

Natives are people who have been around church for a while. They "own" the church's history and style and vision. They've manned the boards and the nursery, built the buildings, weathered the storms.

A newcomer, on the other hand, is anyone the natives label *new*. In some churches, people remain newcomers for decades. In other, more transient churches, newcomers are those who have arrived recently.

Other differences include:

● *Expectations about change.* Natives typically want to preserve the status quo, while newcomers are more willing to change it. After all, the natives have stayed put, whereas the newcomers have changed churches and even communities. Newcomers don't share the congregational history of battles, compromises, and solutions that produced the present church

culture. They may—horrors!—propose something that has never been tried before.

● *Orientation toward institutions.* Newcomers often feel less attached to institutions, including the church. Natives tend to support institutions because they seem essential to their way of life. Newcomers, however, may approach institutions like a smorgasbord. They sometimes view the natives with bemused smiles as they hustle between what newcomers consider irrelevant activities.

● *Place within social groupings.* Natives—on the inside—enjoy a network of friends, family, and associates, while newcomers search for a place to belong from the outside. Newcomers typically have a history of more tenuous commitments, while natives may boast a sometimes-smug rootedness.

Positive Factors

Churches do grow, however. Natives and newcomers do learn to get along. Native-newcomer conflicts, while common, need not be inevitable or fatal. So how are problems avoided?

● *Godly natives.* Truly gracious, caring natives can overcome the natural tendency to exclude others from a good thing. Certainly change can be painful. Valued buildings, traditions, and social groupings may be lost by the wayside as change marches on. But *Christian* natives know that evangelism and love demand welcoming the newcomer. Even one or two key natives with a godly rather than territorial bent can turn a congregation's culture toward acceptance.

● *Astute newcomers.* Newcomers need to understand the genuine concerns of natives. A willingness to witness a season or two of church life before proposing changes, respect for those who have carried the church to the present, and patient friendliness can open many doors. Honoring the past is key.

● *Prepared pastors.* Probably the pastor's greatest task in these situations is serving as referee. While often considered more newcomer than native, a pastor does instantly belong in a congregation by virtue of the office. Pastors have three main referee responsibilities: (1) anticipating conflicts the changing situation probably will produce, (2) preparing the church to face them gracefully, and (3) interpreting the needs and frustrations of one side to the other.

Whose Church Is It?

The church doesn't belong to the natives, although they have historically supported it. Nor does it belong to the newcomers, who will probably change it and may eventually inherit it. The church belongs to God, and the congregation that keeps that fact in mind will handle native-newcomer conflicts best.

—James D. Berkley

Part IV:

Paid-Staff Supervision

In Greek the word is *episkopos,* made of the roots for *over* and *view* or *look.* We get *Episcopal* from the word, and it's translated as *bishop.* The Latinate word is *supervisor,* from *super* (over) and *videre* (to see). The plain old English word, similarly, is *overseer.* As you can see, all three words mean basically the same thing: watching over someone.

Supervision is a sacred trust, because people's lives and ministries are in our care. By the way we supervise, we can do them ill or do them well; we can make them more productive or more perplexed; we can further ministry or frustrate it.

M. Scott Peck, physician and popular author of *The Road Less Traveled,* says of the supervision of people: "It's the highest spiritual calling there is...." We might call that hyperbole, but Peck wouldn't. "Managers and leaders affect a great many lives," he explains. "They are responsible for creating the kind of environment in which people can flourish or shrink. They have enormous power. They have to deal with terribly difficult issues." With that, we heartily agree.

Human resources aren't manipulable like financial or physical resources. With a stroke of a pen, we can transfer funds from one bank to another, or reconfigure a floor plan to add an office. But we can't just shuffle people like funds; we can't just reorganize a staff like we rearrange furniture. So much more care is needed, so much more conversation.

There's a world of difference between *oversee* and *overlook.* The following chapters help us do the former better and avoid the latter.

17

The Meaning of Supervision

Pastors minister directly with people, but they also work in an organization that is dedicated to doing the work of the Kingdom as a corporate entity. Thus they usually find themselves supervising in some capacity, from guiding the work of numerous staff people to overseeing volunteers and a part-time secretary.

The people pastors work with possess unique personalities and perform unique jobs. And even though within their areas of responsibility they may have much autonomy, they still look to their pastor for overall goals, general advice, and, at times, specific guidance. So pastors must continually wrestle with the questions: What does it mean to supervise in my unique situation? What would effective, godly supervision look like in my place of ministry?

Historical Perspectives

Historically, several schools of thought have attempted to describe the purpose and process of supervision. One approach is to identify the central question and definition of success that characterize supervision—along with the potental fatal flaw.

● *Supervision as position* defines the central question as: "Where do you stand in the organizational hierarchy?" Success is seen as establishing and enforcing the chain of command. This model focuses attention on maintaining order in working relationships. But with its focus on order comes a tendency to pass the buck, since each person has a specifically prescribed territory of responsibility. In essence, no one person is accountable for the whole result of any complex problem.

• *Supervision as power* asks, "What resources do you control?" and defines success by guarding and granting access to resources. This model recognizes the reality of formal and informal authority and advantage. But it may also lead to the belief that "might makes right" and that good ends may seem to justify morally shaky or interpersonally harmful means.

• *Supervision as personality* sees "How much charisma do you possess?" as central, and gauges success by gaining personal influence. The personality model recognizes the contagious influence of enthusiasm generated by charismatic leadership but tends to pose a greater risk of emotional manipulation. Also, when truly tough decisions must be acted on over an extended period, we need to draw on something more substantive than cheerleading.

• *Supervision as process* examines, "How do you find your way through the procedures?" and tries to sustain conformity to bureaucratic regulations. The need to establish uniform, orderly procedural requirements is highlighted by this model, but it may inadvertently foster rigid responses to what may be unique problems and issues.

• *Supervision as partnership* keys in on "What consensus do we have and/or can we build?" Success, here, is measured by building and sustaining warm, friendly relationships. Collegiality through relationships is encouraged, but the model may also encourage an unwanted uniformity of perspectives called "group think"—the tendency of people in a close-knit group to disregard the need for variety in perspective. Such groups tend to press for an unimaginative consensus.

• *Supervision as problem solving* focuses on "How do we solve the problems we face?" and feels successful when rational decisions are made through analysis of the facts. This problem-solving model encourages analysis of issues through a systematic and logical series of steps. That same logical emphasis, however, may lead us to overlook the human emotions and dynamics present in every complex situation. A pure problem-solving approach can have the effect of depersonalizing an issue, focusing attention only on the more obvious, quantitative variables and leaving qualitative matters unnoticed.

• *Supervision as politics* inquires, "Who do you know who can do something for us?" Success means negotiating agreements through clever deal making. This kind of supervision recognizes the need to encounter the real world of resource limitations, seeking brokered deals among competing interests. But the rush to make a deal may lead us to forsake other important values.

It is apparent that each of these approaches to supervision carries both advantages and disadvantages. Each model expresses a degree of truth, and adherence to each model could lead to both positive and negative results. So there is both promise and peril in developing a historically rooted supervisory approach to church staff.

It certainly is tempting to review models developed in the world of business and simply adopt them to church-staff supervision. The argument might be phrased this way: "The church is an organization not unlike many business and nonprofit organizations. The church has resources it applies to realize certain goals. Even though the church has a unique focus on spiritual goals, it also shares goals in common with many organizations: financial responsibility, growth, service to clients. And even in the light of the church's special spiritual goals, the staff interaction required to obtain those goals is not really different from the interactions in other organizations: staff people are hired, trained, assessed, and supervised. Achieving performance within a church is not really different than achieving performance in a hospital or a financial-services firm."

Problems arise, however, when we merely adopt the historical supervision models to a church setting. First, all the models focus more on "doing" rather than "being." That is, the essence of each model is the presupposition that supervisors succeed because of what they do or how they do it. None of the models (and this is true of almost any secular supervisory model we might investigate) speaks to the issue of who supervisors are, the kind of person they are on the inside. The models assume successful supervision is a function of technique and specific talent. Personal character is either assumed or ignored.

Second, the models do not make clear what their underlying beliefs about people are. A political model assumes people are out to make deals that benefit them personally. Presumably a partnership model assumes people want to seek an agreeable consensus with one another. These fundamental beliefs usually are not clearly articulated, nor are they convincingly demonstrated.

Third, the models flow from a purely human perspective, not God's. None of the models reflects awareness that a Supreme Being might have something to say about what constitutes successful supervision.

Building a Theology of Supervision

Christians need a model of supervision that has its roots in God's divine claim on who supervisors are, what they believe, and how they act. The "ABCD Model of Supervision" fits that description. The biblical foundation for this model is found in a couple of passages.

The first, Philippians 1:9–11, reads: "And this is my prayer: that your love [ACTIONS] may abound more and more in knowledge and depth of insight, so that you may be able to discern what is best [BELIEFS] and may be pure and blameless until the day of Christ, filled with the fruit of righteousness [CHARACTER] that comes through Jesus Christ—to the glory and praise of God [DIVINE CLAIM]."

The second, 2 Peter 1:5–8, says this: "For this very reason, make every effort to add to your faith [DIVINE CLAIM], goodness [CHARACTER]; and to goodness, knowledge [BELIEF]; and to knowledge, self-control [ACTION]; and to self-control, perseverance; and to perseverance, godliness; and to godliness, brotherly kindness; and to brotherly kindness, love. For if you possess these qualities in increasing measure, they will keep you from being ineffective and unproductive in your knowledge of our Lord Jesus Christ."

● *Actions* speak about how and when we respond as supervisors; the focus is on our hands. Actions are at the top of the pyramid because they are the most visible component of supervision. As with the tip of an iceberg, our actions are the most visible part of us, and they have the most obvious impact on people. However, as an iceberg's tip barely reveals the larger ice mass under water, so too our actions are also the smallest part of the pyramid. In other words, our actions rest on a much broader foundation of beliefs, character, and God's divine

Staff Organization

Three qualities make church staff members successful: competence, godliness, and loyalty. Competence is the ability to do the job well. Godliness is a righteous life. Loyalty is what enables staff to relate as team members.

Providing Structure

Good staff organization is designed to free people to succeed as competent, godly, and loyal ministers and employees within the local church. It should not bind people or burden the organization.

Peter Drucker, the father of modern management, says that every soldier has one right: the right to competent command. In other words, if the leader expects competence from staff, the staff has a right to a competent leader. Someone has to be in charge, and whoever that is needs a clear picture of where the church is going and how to enable staff members to help get there.

Almost all church staffs are divided according to program and support people. *Program staff* includes pastors and others who plan and implement church ministries, such as worship services, Christian education, and pastoral care. *Support staff* enable the program staff to get their jobs done by providing secretarial, custodial, and other technical help.

An ongoing debate concerning the organization of program staff is whether to organize by age (children, youth, adults) or by function

claim. Beliefs direct (not determine) our actions, and actions reinforce our beliefs.

The short letter to Titus provides an example of the kinds of specific ways Scripture can guide supervisory actions. Titus was placed by Paul to be a supervisor over the church at Crete. At several points in Paul's letter to Titus, we can identify important action guidelines.

In Titus 1:5, where Paul left Titus in Crete to "straighten out what was left unfinished and appoint elders in every town," the foundation for organizational success is found in the hiring action. The degree to which this action is carried out with thorough attention to both the skill and character of the people we hire will in many significant ways determine how effective every other action we take will be.

In Titus 1:10 and 13, Titus, in handling "rebellious people," is told to "rebuke them sharply, so that they will be sound in the faith...." The supervisor must act to root out ineffective performance and attitudes. Supervisors must deal especially strongly with character flaws that threaten the well-being of the organization.

In Titus 2:1–6 he is told to "teach what is in accord with sound doc-

---

(music, evangelism, pastoral care, discipleship). On paper, it is a stretch to make everyone fit into one category or the other. In real life, it is impossible. The realistic solution is to allow some overlap.

Key Ingredients

Once the basic structure for staff organization is in place, three ingredients go a long way toward making it work:

● *Written job descriptions* for every staff member should include qualifications, responsibilities, and relationships. Relationship descriptions answer: "Who do I work with? Who do I work for? Who works for me?" Good job descriptions take time to write, are best if kept short (no more than a page), and should be acceptable to everyone involved.

● *Clear reporting relationships* that clarify to whom a person is ac-

countable answer the question: "Who is my boss?" While churches are notorious for insisting that staff members have multiple bosses, the fact is it works much better if staff report to just one person, not a committee. The supervisor should be motivated by the success of the employee ("If you succeed, I succeed!").

● *Regular staff meetings and frequent communication* are the lifeblood of healthy staffs. Even with only one pastor and a part-time secretary, there should be weekly meetings at scheduled times—and written agendas distributed in advance. The meetings need to be held regularly and consistently, even when there is nothing pressing to cover. Those at the meeting should be allowed to make agenda requests and to participate in the discussions, though the designated leader should run the meeting.

—*Leith Anderson*

trine." The supervisor must expect and press for the best and accept nothing less from the people they supervise.

Titus 2:15 states that Titus should "not let anyone despise" him when he teaches, encourages, and rebukes. Effective supervisors are willing to assume the power of supervision, even in the face of opposition.

In Titus 3:9, he is advised to "avoid foolish controversies and genealogies and arguments and quarrels about the law, because these are unprofitable and useless." To be effective, supervisors need to minimize the time they spend on low-return activities.

● *Beliefs* speak about what and why we think as we do as supervisors; the focus is on our head. Beliefs are reflected in our attitudes, hypotheses, principles, and perspectives. Beliefs are sustained by our character because our character gives the power of will to our intellects. And, over the long run, our beliefs reflect our character.

The Bible speaks in many places about the attitudes and perspectives that should characterize a godly approach to supervision. The thirteenth chapter of Proverbs is a good example of how the Bible proposes beliefs:

—Verses 2–3: Effective supervisors believe that the words they use have real impact, and should be used carefully and thoughtfully.

Authority and Responsibility

The senior minister has numerous critical responsibilities in addition to preaching, teaching, and enforcing the values of the institution. Hiring, firing, and motivating paid staff members come high on the list. But doing these things requires authority, and unless the minister and lay leaders agree on the scope and boundaries of pastoral authority, trouble is sure to follow.

Pastor-Driven Staffing

The challenge of building a ministry team is no small task, a challenge that falls largely to the senior minister. This is clearly reflected in a conversation the chair of a pastor-parish relations committee had

with a church consultant. "What is the authority of the committee and of the senior minister when it comes to staffing?" he asked.

The answer was clear and direct: "The senior minister should have at least 60 percent of the input, versus 40 percent for the committee. Any senior minister who cannot successfully hire and lead a staff will constantly face administrative problems."

While pastors feel called to preach and teach, many would rather forgo the administrative tasks. Yet it is difficult, if not impossible, to delegate the hiring and motivating of key staff people. Why is this the case? First, because accountability for the work of the staff person ulti-

—Verse 4: Effective supervisors believe diligence or persistence pays off.

—Verses 10, 13, and 20: Effective supervisors believe that decisions should be made in counsel with other people. The interplay among multiple perspectives leads us to better decisions.

—Verse 12: Effective supervisors believe that linking today's actions with tomorrow's results increases motivation.

—Verse 18: Effective supervisors believe that mistakes (both their own and those of the people they are supervising) are opportunities to learn and grow.

—Verses 9, 11, and 21: Effective supervisors believe that high ethical standards are linked to success that endures.

● *Character* speaks about who and whose we are as supervisors; the focus is on our heart. Character is reflected in such things as our soul and our personality. Character is transformed by God's divine claim in our lives. Character reveals our response to God's divine claim and the transforming work God is accomplishing in our lives.

The Scriptures provide many role models who demonstrate character traits desirable in godly supervisors: Joseph's far-sighted vision anticipated and provided for future needs. Moses' persistent obedi-

---

mately falls to the senior minister. When the call comes from the choir retreat that the choir director is drunk, even though a lay committee may have chosen and may be supervising this person, ultimately the senior minister must resolve the problem. Since being responsible for outcomes creates stress, delegating the selection of key staff positions will likely produce many sleepless nights!

Forming a Team

A second reason for the senior minister–driven model of staff development is that staff teamwork is critical to success. Almost everyone who has been responsible for staffing has had the experience of bringing before a lay committee someone they thought was an excellent candidate, but upon seeing the person interact with potential colleagues, realizing the fit wouldn't be a good one. Information is power, and there is some information about the future success of any staff person that only the pastor can fully discern.

Though senior ministers bear the ultimate responsibility and authority for staffing, they must recognize that successful churches are no longer one-person shows. Even the most devoted, talented, and able leaders must depend on the "supporting cast's" ability to work together. A successful church leader brings together a lay-leadership team that has good judgment, an understanding of the church's mission, and a solid feel for who will likely become a successful staff person in the church.

—*K. Wayne Day*

ence led his people through significant change. Joshua's courageous convictions allowed him to see opportunity where others saw only obstacles. David's deep loyalty demonstrated that means were as important as ends, even when some of his closest counselors advised otherwise. Nehemiah's contagious enthusiasm generated the ability to motivate and channel the efforts of others to help accomplish an impossible task—against imposing odds and in record time. Daniel's devout integrity gained him the respect and confidence of superiors (as well as the jealousy and intrigue of some of his peers). Paul's discipleship drive helped build a corps of capable and committed leaders.

● *God's divine claim* forms the foundation of our life pyramid. God has purposes that he wishes to realize through the character, beliefs, and actions of the supervisor. God has a stake in the way we hire, develop, and utilize people in our ministry, seeking to accomplish important purposes through the supervision we exercise. Micah 6:8 captures the essence of God's concerns: "He has showed you, O man, what is good. And what does the Lord require of you? To act justly and to love mercy and to walk humbly with your God."

God wants our actions to exhibit justice, fairness, attention to due process, and adherence to standards of lawfulness. Our attitudes should exhibit the quality of mercy, a fundamental recognition of others' needs for loving kindness. With humility, we acknowledge our dependence on his power and provision.

Supervision as a Call to Service

Supervision is not easy, nor does it come naturally. In fact, effective supervision demands that we do neither the natural nor the obvious. Ultimately we are faced with a biblical mandate to focus on *who we are* before we focus on *what we do*.

Once Christ's disciples were arguing about their supervisory powers. His response to his early followers is instructive to those of us called to be Christ's disciples today: "They began to question among themselves which of them it might be who would do this. Also a dispute arose among them as to which of them was considered to be greatest. Jesus said to them, 'The kings of the Gentiles lord it over them; and those who exercise authority over them call themselves Benefactors. But you are not to be like that. Instead, the greatest among you should be like the youngest, and the one who rules like the one who serves? For who is greater, the one who is at the table or the one who serves? Is it not the one who is at the table? But I am among you as one who serves' " (Luke 22:23–27).

The word for "lord it over" refers to the exercise of power or control over someone. Christ called his disciples to service rather than lordship. To serve others does not mean to be soft or to expect less than excellent effort and effective performance. Rather, it means to see our task as working with people to achieve what is best for God's kingdom and, thus, best for those we supervise.

To serve others as their supervisors, we must be aligned, aware, alert, and attuned: aligned with God's divine claim on our own lives, aware of the mix of strengths and weaknesses that make up our character, alert to the values and perspectives that constitute our beliefs, and attuned to the best fit between our own actions and the nature and needs of the people we supervise.

In his devotional book *Bless This Desk,* Ken Thompson wrote a poem that expresses the tensions faced by godly supervisors. It focuses on the difficult act of reprimanding an employee, but the emotions expressed could as well apply to any of the scores of decisions faced by supervisors every day:

Getting Chewed Out
(The Chewer)
Why me, Lord?
Why do the stinking jobs fall to me?
Somewhere there are persons
who don't have to fuss at others.
Those who punch a clock
draw a check
and do a job
that's not at all like mine.
Teach me to correct more constructively,
reprimand more fairly,
and understand more fully.
Help me, Lord,
to leave room for you
in what I say and do
to yours.

To supervise well is, indeed, to seek to develop skills and to learn new approaches that can enhance our ability to help others achieve their tasks with both greater effectiveness and efficiency, even when doing so means we must admonish and correct as well as encourage.

But beyond being good, we must also seek to be godly. That requires more than skilled hands and smart-headed insight. It requires a heart that seeks God's best, both for the person being supervised and for the organization.

—Sharon G. Johnson

Resources

Ford, L. 1991. Transforming leadership: Jesus' way of creating vision. Downers Grove, Ill.: InterVarsity.

Houtz, E. 1989. Desktop devotions. Colorado Springs: NavPress.

Rush, M. 1983. Management: A biblical approach. Wheaton, Ill.: Victor.

Ulstein, S. 1993. Pastors: Off the record. Downers Grove, Ill.: InterVarsity.

Word in life study Bible: New Testament. 1993. Nashville: Thomas Nelson.

Staff Relationships and Communication

A pastor with a staff is both a manager and a communicator—roles never more challenging than with today's church staff consisting of baby busters, baby boomers, lingering members of the Depression generation, and "boomerang kids" who have returned home to live with their parents. To communicate effectively with such generation-diverse groups often means breaking out of traditional management patterns.

To be effective with such a staff, leaders must possess an attitude that asks, "How can I meet your needs?" Today's work force is no longer content with simply working from nine to five and bringing home a paycheck. In addition to making a living, they feel the need to make a life—a fulfilling one. Today's typical staff members are motivated by the potential for contributing to the church's mission. Our job, accordingly, is to fill their jobs with creativity and challenge. If we are successful in this, staff longevity and ministry stability will increase.

We need to communicate the passion, vision, and expectations of our church mission to staff. At the same time, we must also listen intently to what staff tell us through spoken and unspoken messages. Their hurts and pains become our concern.

Handling Conflict and Failure

Nothing eats away at staff morale like conflict and stress. Unresolved issues that are allowed to fester eventually affect the entire team. The sooner we can resolve conflict and open the lines of communication, the happier and more productive the team will be.

For example, one morning a colleague of mine stormed into the office without his usual greeting and smile. We all knew something was wrong, but no one dared to break the silence, for fear of becoming the recipient of his rage. At last, I tiptoed into his office and asked if I could do anything to relieve his stress. I could sense an immediate change in him as he shared with me the pressure he was feeling under numerous urgent tasks that were pushing him over the edge. My gentle question didn't take care of those pressing demands, but it did let him know someone cared, and it gave him the emotional support needed for tackling those tasks. That was what he needed right then.

The Edsel was one of Ford's biggest failures, but the management at Ford decided to use the Edsel's unpopularity to study the lifestyles of the American people. From the study, the company created the Thunderbird, one of Ford's greatest success stories. When a church team knows that errors will be looked at as opportunities for learning and growth, fear is replaced with trust and creativity. Conversely, a team functioning from fear squelches creative thinking.

Communicating Clearly

Lorissa, all of 6 years old, was flying alone when the flight attendant asked her if she needed to go to the lavatory. She answered no. Asked why she had turned her light on, Lorissa responded, "Because I have to go to the bathroom." Communication is complete only when *both* parties understand what is being said.

Here are some tips for communicating effectively with staff:

● Since we all communicate differently, we need to learn how to communicate at the level of the recipient. As Peter Drucker put it, "Enable performers to perform their way—not your way."

● We're wise to come to the table with the goal of solving the problem, not pointing fingers.

● We should practice affirming loudly but correcting quietly. Praise is public, and reprimand is private.

● We need to give co-workers the benefit of the doubt, even in situations that seem clear to us. One party simply may have misunderstood the other.

—*Sylvia Nash*

Personnel Policies

Consider the bind a church without a sick-leave policy finds itself in when the secretary develops a pattern of Monday and Friday absences, the janitor undergoes heart surgery and no one is sure how much paid time off he should get, and the pregnant bookkeeper is confined to bed three months before her twins are due and the church does not know if it should hold her job open.

Personnel policies set forth and explain the rules that apply to employees at work. In so doing, they protect church leaders from making on-the-spot, emotional decisions that may have serious financial implications for the church, and they protect churches from charges of discrimination for treating employees differently.

Some churches remain without personnel policies simply because no one has taken the time to write them or because it is assumed that personnel issues will be addressed on a case-by-case basis. Legally and financially, these approaches can be big mistakes.

Writing Policies

Personnel policies should address issues such as vacation, sick time, working hours, and benefits. Here are tips for developing legal personnel policies.

● *Formulate policies before you need them.* A well-developed, reasoned policy takes time. The pressure surrounding personnel emergencies may lead to precedents that can be detrimental to the church.

● *Be familiar with employment laws that apply to your church.* The committee charged with drafting personnel policies can become informed by reading articles, attending educational programs on the subject, and consulting an attorney or someone in the church experienced in the field. For example, sick-leave policies involve issues found in the Americans with Disabilities Act (ADA), the Family and Medical Leave Act (FMLA), and the Fair Labor Standard Act (FLSA). Those are just the federal laws; states have their own employment statutes.

● *Issue written policies to employees.* Personnel policies should not be secret, and employees need to know the policies that apply to them. A loose-leaf, employee handbook works well and can be updated easily. Written policies distributed to employees must be current, since out-of-date policies can be a source of irritation and potential lawsuits.

● *Follow your stated policies and apply them fairly.* If the policies do not work, change them. If a church ignores a stated policy, an affected employee could claim employment discrimination. Also, it's important to have an opening statement in an employee handbook that the church reserves the right to change policies at any time. It's wise, however, to avoid making retroactive decisions that decrease employee rights or benefits.

● *Do not make promises you cannot keep.* Some courts have interpreted promises to employees as binding contracts. For example, it's best to refer to an employee's status as "regular" rather than "permanent," since some courts have construed "permanent" to mean the employee has been promised a job for life. A church may have regular full-time employees or regular part-time employees. It may have temporary full-time or temporary part-time employees. But no employee is ever permanent.

—Julie L. Bloss

Male-Female Staff Dynamics

In the church, differences between men and women sometimes clash, hindering their work for God. What seems logical to a woman may seem illogical to a man, and what he sees as effective may appear haphazard to her.

When we learn to appreciate these differences, however, we'll see that men and women can become effective partners in ministry. In spite of their differences, masculine and feminine qualities can complement each other in ministry.

Observed Differences

At the risk of overgeneralization, several observations may be made about the differences between the sexes:

● *Meetings and motions.* A woman

may make decisions in a completely different way than a man. If Susan is prepared to discuss Sunday-school curricula, for example, she may be stunned by Bill's quick motion to select a particular one. While other men on the committee vigorously debate Bill's motion, Susan may feel left out.

In meetings with women, Susan expects discussion that leads to consensus before voting. Pros and cons are discussed and help shape the vote. In such free-flowing discussions, however, a man may feel a lack of focus. Meandering conversations can frustrate his desire to reach resolution.

The point is, neither approach is better than the other. Both can contribute positively to the decision-making process.

● *Conversing and competing.* For men, conversation can become competitive—a chance for each to drive his point home. Though some women have strong opinions, women tend to wait for someone to invite their input. When a female member of a predominantly male group is not drawn into the conversation, she may feel intentionally excluded. Meanwhile the men usually assume that those who want to speak will take the initiative to do so.

A woman frequently in male-dominated conversations might need to step in and say, "I wonder if I might say something here." Men can also be encouraged to invite women into discussions. Making the sexes more sensitive to each other's conversational habits will help them work together better.

● *Organizational differences.* Men and women often organize their work differently. Women are more likely to do work as jigsaw puzzles, solving challenges and dividing up the work as they go. Many men prefer to have a clearly defined set of steps at the outset of a project—to be done in sequence—so that progress can be measured at any point.

● *Diplomacy or disagreement.* Men and women also seem to tolerate conflict differently. Men appear able to put up indefinitely with on-going personality conflicts. Many women, on the other hand, become uncomfortable when people are felt to be at odds. They want to straighten everything out while avoiding confrontation.

Bridging the Gap

I wouldn't want these generalizations, based on my limited experience, to be applied too strictly to any particular individual or situation. But these observations can help us identify gender-linked tendencies in our work with men and women. Here are three important reminders:

● *Our way isn't necessarily wrong.* Then again, we can't assume our way is right. It's just different. Men and women have much to learn from each other—if we accept each other.

● *Keep a sense of humor.* Don't take difficulties and confusion too seriously. Treating the gender differences in a light way can help us recognize and bridge the gaps.

● *Be real.* God has called us to serve with our unique personality and gifts. Women don't need to be like men, and vice versa. Men and women can work together, though in different ways, to do God's will.

—*Nancy D. Becker*

18

Hiring Support Staff

One of the most critical aspects of church management is selecting support staff to serve the church. The decisions made can mean lasting joy or lasting distress for the church, other staff, and those hired.

Making wise selections—and not simply filling a vacant chair—has financial ramifications, as well. For example, in industry the turnover cost for a base-level secretary typing 60 words per minute averages about $12,000. Unfortunately, bad fits are not uncommon. The Marketing and Research Corporation of Princeton, New Jersey, once reported that 50 to 80 percent of Americans were in the wrong jobs.

On the other hand, hiring the right person for a job can boost an entire program. Tom Phillips, president of Phillips Publishing, said the growth of his company from a kitchen-table operation with revenues of $300,000 in 1974 to $40 million for 1989 was based on hiring quality people. "We hire bright, enthusiastic, aggressive and 'growable' people," he said. "And as these people grow, both personally and professionally, our company grows."

In addition, because of the important investment of themselves support staff make in church life, we need to exercise prudence in the hiring process so the results will be win-win relationships. James Patterson and Peter Kim state: "Over their lifespan, the average American worker will spend 76,900 hours on the job. That's a big part of their lives—by far the biggest waking activity" (Patterson and Kim 1991, 154). Support staff, as much as any other leaders, need the satisfaction of fulfillment in their work.

To Hire or Not to Hire

While being understaffed is bad for morale and can pose legal problems, being overstaffed is unhealthy, as well, resulting in lethargy and low productivity among staff. So before hiring staff, it is important to ask, *Do we really need a new staff person at this time?* If uncertainty or limited budgets cause worries, it's best to begin by hiring someone part-time or on a temporary basis.

Once we decide to hire, we can crystallize the particular staff need with a well-defined job description. This is a good time to change anything no longer relevant or not current with today's legalities. This job description will guide how the church publicizes the position and what job qualifications will be required.

Some churches hire support staff from within the church; others hire only from outside. Both approaches have benefits. For example, hiring from within is often perceived by church members as an expression of confidence in members of the congregation. Those who use this approach say they have a better chance of knowing the individual and less opportunity for a mismatch, since they have watched them as volunteers and know their gifts.

On the negative side, terminations can be difficult—to the point of dividing churches—and staff often discover they can't easily worship or participate in other church functions because they are constantly being approached by church members requesting help. The advantages probably equal the disadvantages. The important factor is that a church arrive at a consensus on an approach.

Another major step in the hiring process is deciding who will be involved in the selection process. Should a committee be formed? Should the pastor be a key player, or a senior staff person, such as the business manager, or a key supervisor? Whoever the leadership chooses, more than one person doing the interviewing helps maintain a balanced perspective.

Finding Candidates

Candidates can be found through word of mouth, Sunday bulletins, other churches in the area, denominational headquarters, agencies such as Intercristo (800/426-1343), personnel offices of other Christian ministries, college bulletin boards, local newspapers, and family and friends of current staff (though some churches have a nepotism policy against the hiring of staff relatives).

Because of many changes in employment law, application forms need to be reviewed regularly to remove conflicts with the law. For example, questions on race, age, marital status, height, weight, handicaps, and birthplace should not be listed on the form.

Before candidates are solicited, those who will do the hiring need to reach a clear understanding with the person who will supervise the new employee. They can hash out such questions as: What is needed to make a good fit? What are the negotiables? The nonnegotiables? What attributes would be on a dream list?

Examples of negotiables might be a college degree, ability to lift 50 pounds, being bilingual, or shorthand proficiency.

Nonnegotiables might include the ability to type a certain number of words per minute, computer skills, being a self-starter, being a Christian, or willingness to sign a doctrinal statement. (In some states, if a staff worker such as a custodian is not required to share the gospel, it may be difficult to require the applicant to be a Christian.)

Applications can be reviewed as they come in. Those that do not fit the nonnegotiable criteria can be eliminated immediately. There's no need wasting our time or theirs if they lack certain "must haves." It's important to monitor possible warning signs from an applicant's past. If the applicant has held numerous jobs in a short period of time, he or she may have problems keeping a job. It's often wise to list the salary range in promotional literature. The church offering nine dollars per hour to a candidate who requires twelve dollars per hour can assume the candidate likely is overqualified or may leave soon because of financial dissatisfaction.

Interviewing Candidates

Applicants who look promising can be scheduled for an interview. Good interviews depend on adequate preparation. For example, in scheduling interviews, it's good to keep in mind one's mood patterns. If mornings are generally a good part of the day for your group, schedule appointments then—and do so for each interviewee, so all are treated fairly. In a study of how moods affect people's assessment of others, psychologist Robert Baron asked 71 persons to play the role of personnel managers interviewing someone for a job. He writes:

> Just before the interview, [the interviewers'] moods were influenced by giving them a test and then providing feedback on their performances that was designed to put them in a good, bad, or neutral mood. Unbeknownst to the interviewers, all the job applicants were trained to give the same answers in every interview. The interviewers given positive feedback (in a good mood) rated applicants more favorably than those who had heard negative things about their performance (in a bad mood). In fact, they were more likely to hire the applicants and to rate them as more highly motivated. Interviewers in a good mood after-

wards remembered more of the applicants' positive qualifications, while those in a bad mood recalled more negative information (Baron 1989, 5:10).

It is a good practice to freshly review a person's application form before the interview to become reacquainted with where the interviewee is coming from in his or her responses. However, when interviewing for a specific position, it is important to ask the same set of questions of each interviewee to ensure fairness.

Interviewers need to create an atmosphere that will put the applicant at ease. Methods might include getting out from behind a desk, having coffee or water available, and opening with nonthreatening

---

Job Descriptions

Written job descriptions allow churches to use their human resources wisely by matching skills to jobs. It is important to have a job description for each paid position in the church.

Job descriptions specify the duties and skills needed to perform a job. They are not merely job titles; the duties of a church secretary at one church may differ vastly from those at another church, for example. Neither are they descriptions of a particular person: a particular church business administrator may have a Ph.D., but the job description for business administrator should not list the Ph.D. degree unless the position itself requires it.

Getting It on Paper

When writing job descriptions, we can ask other churches for samples and look for help from church members with experience in personnel services. Other tips worth considering:

● *Develop written descriptions for every job.* It's wise to format job descriptions similarly, using headings such as "skills," "responsibilities," and "internal and external contacts."

● *Seek the input of current employees and supervisors.* When an employee quits is not the time to write job descriptions, since those performing the jobs often can best describe the requisite skills and duties.

● *Focus on quantifiable skills, not on nebulous qualities.* This means detailing the specific skills required. For example, saying the position requires a "good typist" isn't as effective as saying it demands "typing skills of 60 words per minute." It's best to emphasize job-related requirements and behavior, not characteristics like personality and attitude.

● *Understand how the employment laws that apply to your church affect job descriptions.* Churches that do not understand applicable

questions, such as: "I noticed in your resume that you played soccer at college. Why soccer instead of another sport? What did you gain from that experience?"

Much can be learned by observing candidates as they arrive for their interviews. A friend tells how he once was running late for an interview. In his urgent rush, he raced his car into a vacant parking spot, cutting off another person in the process. To his utter embarrassment, the gentleman he had cut off was the one interviewing him for the position—an expensive lesson!

The task of the interviewer is to dig deep. If an applicant says he or she "developed," "produced," or "coordinated" something, the interviewer can ask exactly what is meant by the word. Did "coordinate"

---

employment laws might develop discriminatory job descriptions. For example, requiring excellent health could violate the Americans with Disabilities Act. And job descriptions requiring college degrees, unless the church can demonstrate the degree is job-related, may be seen as discrimination against minorities. (Courts generally do not interfere in the relationship between churches and clergy, so churches may be able to impose requirements on ministers that would be illegal if required for other employees.)

● *When duties change significantly, change the job description, too.* Churches should periodically review job descriptions to see if they remain valid. Changing technology may mean changing job descriptions. For example, if a church gets a computer, the secretary will probably need to use it. The job description should reflect this change.

Many Uses

We can utilize job descriptions as tools for hiring, discipline, and termination. It's hard to determine whether an applicant is the right person for the job without first examining the job in detail to see what it requires. When an applicant fails to meet the minimum job standards found on a job description, an interview simply isn't necessary. Interviewing unqualified applicants "as a courtesy" wastes time for both parties.

Job descriptions help employees understand what is expected of them. When a church uses a probationary period for new hires, supervisors need a standard for measuring performance before making people "regular employees." Job descriptions provide that standard, and employees who cannot perform the minimum standards of the job become subject to corrective actions or termination, if necessary.

The employee's legitimate question—"What is expected of me?"—receives a clear answer through a carefully written job description. Most church employees want to do a good job, and their job descriptions give them the guidance they seek.

—Julie L. Bloss

mean making three phone calls, or did it mean the individual supervised an entire project?

If looking for an applicant with self-initiative, we may want to make such requests as "Give us an example of how you saved an activity from falling apart when it was in jeopardy" or "Provide an example of a time when you did something before anyone required you to do it."

Questions should elicit more than yes or no responses. Consider asking:

- How would your current boss describe you?
- How would your peers describe you?
- What are your strengths?
- Would there be anything that would hinder you from performing the essential tasks according to the job description?
- What are your weaknesses?

Determining Salary Packages

Church staff members can easily become underpaid when churches fail to count the hidden costs of poor salaries. People do not work effectively when money is a constant worry. They become resentful and unproductive, and the ministry suffers. Their families may bear the scars for years to come.

Since our staffs should be as free as possible from money worries so they can concentrate on their ministries, churches should seek to remove money as a preoccupation. Yet this is not to say that arriving at a proper wage is easy.

Who Gets Paid?

A basic question needs to be answered in discussing staff salaries: Who should be paid and who should not? The list of people who normally work without financial compensation is long in most churches: teachers, ushers, kitchen workers, music personnel, and a

host of others. No one, including most church boards, wants to pay for something they can get for free.

But there are situations where a volunteer simply won't do. When should we begin to pay someone for ministry to the church? Here are two guidelines:

- *Determine the level of expertise needed to do the job.* There is a great difference in the time and ability needed to manage a Sunday school of 500 versus 50. As the complexity of the situation grows, so does the need for a paid staff member.
- *Decide if program quality will diminish without a paid staff position.* If a paid staff member isn't overseeing a program, will it be less effective? Sometimes it is wise to "grow your own" staff by hiring key volunteers.

Setting Pay

It is a fair and valid question to ask, "What is an individual worth to

- What would your family say your weaknesses are?
- Describe a situation where you messed up and how you corrected it.
- What was your greatest success this past year?
- Tell me about a time when you had to work under pressure. How did it arise? How was it resolved? What did you do?
- How do you organize yourself for day-to-day activities?
- Why did you leave your last job?
- What types of people do you get along with best? (If the description fits potential co-workers, be encouraged. If not, be cautious.)
- What skills have you perfected in recent years?

As is the case on application forms, there are questions to *avoid* asking for legal reasons. These often include age, physical characteristics (such as weight and height), maiden name (it may indicate an attempt to determine the person's ethnic background), citizenship,

---

our congregation?" Some churches base staff pay on a member's contribution to the ministry. Performance and results play a big part in this decision.

In setting an initial salary, the governing board can first determine top and bottom cost barriers. Once this framework is established, the person's position, experience, and education factor in. Work record plays a significant role in salary decisions. Someone who worked well elsewhere is likely to perform well in the new setting as well, and it's much easier to set salaries for achievers than for those who seem to retire on the job.

Should all staff members be paid the same? Some have argued that every individual, though each might differ in gifts and abilities, is of equal value to the church and should receive equal pay to avoid showing partiality. This is a distortion of biblical thinking and sound business practice. It sets aside the teaching on diligence, rewards for investment of talents, and the idea of fairness. People need to be re-

warded for effort, and a positive evaluation coupled with a monetary reward is a strong motivational tool. Should we pay staff members simply for breathing? Such forced equality is the ultimate unfairness.

Salary Increases

The process of establishing yearly salary increases affects all the staff. In some churches, a committee determines the range of increases the church can afford to offer—say, 3–8 percent. The minimum number should not be below the annual cost-of-living index. Then the staff supervisors need to evaluate employees on their work performance and determine the rate of salary increase on a person-by-person basis. Supervisors talk with each staff member, stating the suggested raise, discussing the employee's response, and perhaps revising the figures. These suggested increases are then given to the board for final approval or amendment.

—Wayne A. Pohl

children's names (also, don't ask if the applicant plans to have children or arrange child care), arrest records (but you can ask if they have been convicted of a crime), smoking (though you can state that your office is smoke free and they will need to abide by the office rules), and AIDS and HIV (violates the Americans with Disabilities Act).

It has been said that 85 percent of our judgments of an individual are made in the first seven seconds of meeting that person. If in the first few minutes of the interview we realize the candidate does not fit our needs, we may want to end the interview quickly, thanking the person for his or her time.

Two cautions are in order:

● We should not become so impressed with the interviewee that we fail to ask critical questions. Some candidates are gifted talkers, and we can be fooled. One administrator admitted he was so impressed with a candidate that he hired the person before objectively looking at potential shortcomings. The match ended just three months later, with hurt feelings on both sides.

● We must avoid the tendency to sell the church rather than learn about the person. A good rule of thumb is that if an interviewer has talked more than 30 percent of the time, he or she has talked too much.

A useful final step—after we have reviewed the job description with the interviewee and have gained enough information about the person to make a good assessment—is to ask several open-ended questions, such as: "Is there anything I should have asked you that you would like to share with me?" "Are there any skeletons in the closet that might eventually be an embarrassment?"

Some churches also give candidates a personality test to identify qualities in the candidate needed for a position. For example, if a church is looking for a receptionist with good people skills but the test indicates a candidate is "very shy," caution is advised. The information gained from the test along with the interview makes a balanced assessment possible. To be both legal and fair, it is important to treat all candidates the same with personality tests; if a test is given to one candidate, it should be given to all.

Obtaining References

A crucial step in the hiring process is checking references. These allow us to know how others feel about candidates. If we trust our intuition and bypass this last step, we forfeit an excellent source of counsel.

When seeking references, we can ask applicants if they are willing to sign a reference waiver that allows us to *confidentially* solicit references from former supervisors and others (the applicants voluntarily give up their right to see completed references). We may want to request further references—prior supervisors, co-workers, colleagues—from some applicants whose applications list only friends.

I once called a reference listed by a candidate, and since that person was not in, the man answering the phone asked if he could help. When I shared what I wanted, he replied, "Oh, I was her supervisor. I'm the one who can give you the information you need." We were looking for a candidate who would be particularly dependable and trustworthy, especially in my absence while traveling. When asked about her dependability, he shared, "One never knows when she comes in or leaves. In addition, she often takes long lunches and leaves us shorthanded, especially if I'm gone." That was exactly the information I needed to know.

The best questions asked of references should elicit more than yes-or-no answers. However, organizations are increasingly reluctant to talk about current or former employees for fear of being sued. Assuring complete confidentiality sometimes helps elicit a response. Another approach, suggested by Patricia Amend, is to "ask the candidate to furnish us with names of references who used to work for the company but are now employed elsewhere. This approach will overcome this limited information many companies supply because they fear lawsuits" (Amend 1990, 9:5). The candidate should call those references to let them know they will be queried. This will help them be more open to cooperating with a reference check.

Questions to ask of references include:
- How long did the candidate work for you?
- How would you compare the candidate to other secretaries (or whatever position you are trying to fill) who have worked for you?
- What counsel would you give to bring out the best in this candidate?
- What was your relationship to the candidate?
- Would you hire this person again if given the chance?

Making a Decision

Once candidates have been interviewed and reference checks completed, the time arrives to rely on both facts and feelings to make a decision. Using our checklists, we can determine how many of the negotiable and nonnegotiable qualifications fit each candidate. How closely does the person match our dream list? Next, we can score the candidates, based on a ten-point scale, on their interview skills. Another consideration is how each candidate would fit with other support staff members. And remembering to pray is important. We know the Lord will direct in a powerful way if we seek his direction.

Once we select a candidate, our next step is to send a letter of confirmation with important data such as starting date, pay period, office hours, benefits, and salary. It's wise practice to list salary by hour, week, or month—never annually. Otherwise, the church may be held responsible to pay the entire amount if a dispute arises and termination is necessary before the year is up.

Letters need to be sent to candidates not selected, and the sooner, the better, so they can seek other avenues for service. The letter can be short, stating simply that "another candidate was selected whose skills more adequately met our needs." If appropriate, we can indicate that we will keep their applications on file for other positions that open up. After all, we already may have completed half the work for the next opening.

Since beginning a new job is stressful, we need to pray for incoming staff members that the Lord will bring them great joy and satisfaction in their new assignments.

—*Sylvia Nash*

Resources

Patterson, J., and P. Kim. 1991. The day America told the truth. New York: Penguin.

Baron, R. 1989. One's mood does affect interviews. *The Pryor Report* 5:10.

Amend, P. 1990. *Communication Briefings* 9:5.

Dingman, R. 1989. The complete search committee guidebook. Ventura, Cal.: Regal.

19

Calling Ministerial and Program Staff

Hiring ministerial and program staff may be one of the most frightening things a senior pastor does. If we choose poorly, our personal stock depreciates and our ministry team is weakened by a staff member who is more trouble than help. Yet, if we choose well, we'll enjoy the rewarding benefits of working with a team of spiritual leaders.

The implications of such choices are many: The spiritual welfare of the church will be affected. Relationships among existing staff will either be strengthened or weakened. And the ministerial development of those called will be significantly affected.

Calling ministerial staff is not like hiring employees. In the church, unlike secular corporations, we cannot ignore the spiritual dimension of knowing God's will. Other challenges to seeking, screening, and selecting staff for the church also exist: Congregational politics and expectations can complicate matters. Mistakes are difficult to undo. Dismissing a wrong choice for assistant pastor can cause misunderstanding and criticism within the congregation.

Nor is the process like calling a senior pastor. The dynamics are different, the protocol more private, the lines of authority more confusing. Generally, the senior pastor, in cooperation with the church board, will play the dominant role in deciding about new ministerial staff. The congregation as a whole is not necessarily involved.

Planning to Add Staff

There are several reasons for seeking additional staff—to spare the strength of an older senior pastor, to serve more people in a more personal way, to offer new or alternative ministries. None of us has all the ministry gifts necessary to meet all the needs of a growing congregation. More staff means a greater variety of styles and personalities to serve people of all ages, interests, and spiritual needs. We may be able to pastor an existing congregation alone but need help to expand into the community. Or we may need to gather our own support staff when beginning a ministry in a multistaff congregation—much as a president selects his own cabinet at the beginning of his term.

● *When to call additional staff.* Church leaders debate this, but there are some general guidelines that can help us make the decision.

The first consideration is the size of the church. One rule of thumb calls for a full-time pastoral staff member for each 150–200 people in the congregation. The catch is this: adding a youth pastor to a congregation of 250 may provide specialized ministry to teens, but the change won't improve care for adults already part of the church family. So this rule of thumb fits primarily the congregation content to serve its existing constituency; congregations desiring growth must think differently. The debate between the two approaches seems to hinge on whether we should call additional staff *before* growth or *in response to* growth. Usually, adding the right staff fosters growth; churches that wait for growth before hiring generally wait a long time.

A second consideration is the church's growth mode. Churches already growing, either as a result of successful ministries or being located in a growing community, probably need to add staff sooner than churches that aren't growing. Adding staff, however, will not guarantee numerical growth. A congregation must be receptive, and new staff must have appropriate gifts and job assignments.

Community conditions represent yet another factor to consider. Congregations located in communities with many outreach possibilities will have more ministry opportunities than congregations in declining areas facing greater challenges. In an expanding community, additional staff can increase a church's ability to respond quickly to the growing needs of the area.

A final consideration before adding staff is the church's financial capabilities. While we should not make hasty or foolhardy staff decisions, the church that waits until it can afford additional staff without any risk undoubtedly will miss opportunities for expanding ministry. Often new staff must be seen as an investment—with some degree of risk involved. If all other indications are that it's time to add new staff even though we may not quite be able to afford it, we should remember that the right person can help the church to grow. The increase should soon pay the salary of the new staff person.

● *Who should call additional staff.* Traditions and practices vary. Some boards are actively involved; others approve the financial expenditure and leave the rest of the decision to the pastor. Typically, the smaller the church, the more everyone wants to get involved.

Church boards unfamiliar with the dynamics of church growth or unaware of the demands of modern pastoral ministry are sometimes unsympathetic to the need for additional ministerial staff or hesitant to add to the church payroll. Church members-at-large may be even less familiar with the need and rationale for additional staff. Clearly, the senior pastor must take the lead in the process.

As pastors, we probably have a good grasp of current programs and pastoral loads, as well as a vision for future ministries to meet the needs of the congregation and community. These are key factors that affect the call of new ministry staff.

One of the most important reasons to be personally involved in decisions about a new staff member is that we will be working closely with him or her. We need to look for a person with a personality compatible with our own, someone whose vision harmonizes with ours. By taking the lead in hiring, we also intensify the link of accountability the new staff person will have with us.

Even though pastors take much of the initiative in seeking new staff, the church should not be left out of the process. It's important that a church board and congregation understand the rationale for additional staff. We need to communicate openly, explaining that new staff is not intended to duplicate anyone's ministry just so more of the same can be done. New staff will provide opportunity for specialization; fresh ministry gifts can begin to do work not being done by the existing staff. For example, there's no point in calling new staff for pastoral care and visitation if the congregation is still going to expect the senior pastor to visit everyone who is sick. New staff is brought on either to release the staff from existing responsibilities or to engage in new ministries.

The congregation needs to understand whether we're looking for new staff to expand our care for the existing congregation or to foster church growth. Communicating our vision and philosophy of ministry is key: If we desire to improve platform ministries, then strong preachers, drama personnel, or musicians will be sought. If we want to emphasize body ministry, we'll want small-group leaders or counselors. A focus on families may lead us to expand through Christian-education staff.

A helpful tool in assessing the church's needs for the next phase of ministry is to solicit the views of the congregation: What jobs need to be done? What ministries do we want to begin? What are priority needs at this time?

No formula fits all churches, so we'll have to evaluate our needs in light of several factors: congregational need, community demographics, and the vision and philosophy of church leaders. Surveying church people may sometimes lead us to volunteers within the congregation that could do the job. Other times we may be alerted to overworked volunteers who need to step aside for hired staff.

Another approach to discussing staff needs is to hold a pastor-board retreat. Still another approach is to work with a church growth consultant—an outside specialist who often can carry more weight with a board than the pastor. The expense is small in comparison with the expenditure for a new staff member.

Seeking New Staff

Once the decision to add staff is made, the next question is: Where do we find the right person?

We need to start on our knees. Jesus said, "Ask the Lord of the harvest ... to send out workers into his harvest field" (Luke 10:2). That applies to church staff members as well as missionaries for Africa.

The Search Committee

The painful argument began when my opponent, a dear friend who was serving on a search committee for our associate pastor, told me a particular man (who I *knew* God wanted for the job) was not the right person. It took more than a week before I began to see that he was right and I was wrong.

Fortunately, God speaks both individually and corporately. To emphasize one at the expense of the other is to lose crucial pieces of the guidance puzzle. Search committees are one practical expression of those spiritual guides God uses to direct the church.

Committees and Roles

A search committee is a group of people selected by the church to discover the person God would have to pastor that church. Given the importance of their task, the members on a search committee should come from among the best and most spiritually sensitive people in the church. It is a mistake to choose them according to a representative grid of the various groups in the church (gender, age, ethnic, theological, and so on); this is foreign to the spirit of the New Testament. Rather than hearing primarily the voice of the people, the search committee is commissioned to hear the voice of God, and rather than giving political guidance, they are called to provide spiritual guidance. Once the committee has been formed, however, it should meet with the various groups of the church to hear their ideas and hopes, needs and concerns.

In many ways the committee is like a miniature church, and as such, it should function as one. In its search for a pastor, it should spend time worshiping, praying, studying, and fellowshiping together, so that members' ears may be opened and their vision sharpened. To paraphrase Matthew 6:33,

Here's where to look for staff members:

● *Ministerial colleagues.* Probably the best source of leads is close friends and ministerial associates. They know us and may know our church. They likely know who would fit. We need to let our friends know we are looking.

● *Denominational officials.* Bishops and superintendents want our churches to succeed and are interested in helping. They likely have a file of available candidates and pastors considering a move. The danger is that denominational leaders, in their eagerness to place someone, may recommend a candidate who is less than suitable.

● *Seminaries and Bible colleges.* Many seminaries and Bible colleges have placement offices or at least a faculty member assigned to help graduates find places of ministry. These resources can recommend promising graduates. The danger is that they may not know us or our churches. Also, some academically oriented colleges may make rec-

---

"Seek first God's kingdom, and all these things, including the right person for the job, will be given to you as well."

On the practical side, every search committee should have strong clerical support, since the amount of paperwork involved in handling résumés and correspondence is enormous.

The pastor should be deeply involved in the selection process, though not made chair of the committee. Ideally, the committee and the pastor should work together to reach a unanimous decision on a candidate, with both the pastor and the committee possessing veto power. While meaningful involvement of the pastor takes time, it is the best way for the committee to know what kind of person would work well with the pastor. What's more debilitating than staff relationships gone sour?

Stages and Jobs

In the earlier stages of the search process, the committee should spend time getting to know each other, learning to pray and worship together, reviewing the policies and procedures pertaining to the task, and determining the job description, if one has not been already written.

The later stages include advertising and canvassing for the position, evaluating candidates' résumés, interviewing, and finally presenting the candidate to the congregation.

Once the right person has been found and brought on staff, the temptation is for the search committee to breathe a sigh of relief and quit. But a key (if often overlooked) responsibility of the search committee is to midwife the birth of the new staff person into the church. The committee knows the new person better than anyone else in the church and so is uniquely qualified to interpret the person to the church and the church to the person, and to explain the church's and the pastor's style, customs, vision, and ethos to each other.

—Ben Patterson

ommendations based on scholastic achievement rather than passion, dedication, and spirituality. Good students don't always make good pastors or leaders. Sometimes it pays to visit a college personally to meet several prospects informally.

● *Large, growing multistaff churches.* Large churches often have capable staff members who long to have a broader area of ministry beyond their current restricted assignments. Some may be open to a move—even to a smaller church—that would offer them more diverse experience.

● *Unsolicited résumés.* Most senior pastors have a steady flow of applicants looking for ministry positions. These applications need to be treated seriously, answered, and filed, even when we are not look-

Interviewing Candidates

Interviewing a candidate for a ministerial position is a lot like dating and courtship: the purpose is to decide if there should be a marriage. As in courtship, there needs to be mutual respect, honesty, and openness.

Ten Commandments

Here are guidelines to make the process successful:

● *Limit the number of interviewers.* Too many interviewers can intimidate the interviewee and make consensus difficult for those conducting the interview. In some situations, the senior pastor takes the lead, with no more than two others present. Once the field has been narrowed to one candidate, that person is presented to a larger board or constituency.

● *Prepare.* Interviews will rarely uncover pertinent information unless good thought goes into their preparation. Prior to the interview, interviewers can prepare by praying for guidance, researching the candidate by checking the résumé and references, listing the questions to ask so nothing will be overlooked, and determining who will ask which questions.

● *Express seriousness.* After opening pleasantries, we should express the seriousness of the meeting by saying something like, "This is an important meeting for both of us. We need God's guidance, and we need to be open and honest with each other."

● *Set the tone of the meeting.* The atmosphere should be serious, yet relaxed and candid. The tone of the meeting should approximate the tone of the working environment of the church. The interview is not a confrontation but an exploratory search for God's will.

● *Ask the interviewee to pray.* This may catch the candidate off guard, but that can be good. It will show how a candidate handles unexpected situations. It also reminds the interviewee that the decision is ulti-

ing for staff. When the need arises at a later time, this file can be a source of applicants.

● *Magazine and newsletter announcements and advertisements.* Several magazines list staff members looking for positions. While not a prime source, they provide options to consider.

● *Members of the congregation.* When the congregation knows we are looking for staff, members sometimes submit names. At times, church members, themselves, may be prime candidates. The drawback is that some may have hidden agendas, perhaps wanting to promote a certain type of program or even a relative. Sometimes members lack the big-picture perspective for assessing strengths and weaknesses of the type of personnel needed.

---

mately a spiritual decision. And the way a person prays says more about the person's walk with God than perhaps anything else. It's hard to fake prayer.

● *Get the interviewee talking.* We aren't going to learn what we need to know if we do all the talking. Our purpose is not to lecture the candidate but to ascertain if the candidate is suitable for the position, so we must get the candidate talking about himself or herself. Most people will gladly do this. If a candidate cannot speak candidly, it may be a sign of insecurity. "Why are you interested in this position in this church?" is a good starting question.

● *Ask open-ended questions.* We should avoid questions that can be answered with a yes or no. Better are questions like "What do you think about X?" or "What's your opinion of Y?"

● *Ask personal questions.* I've found the question "What are your three greatest strengths?" followed by "What do you think are your three biggest weaknesses?" to be especially revealing. The answers not only indicate personal information and ministerial gifts but also

reveal a person's self-image.

● *Read body language.* The interview is not primarily designed to discover educational background or details of past ministerial positions. That information is garnered from résumés and references. The purpose of the interview is to discover character and evaluate personality. Body language will reveal as much as the answers given.

● *Allow time for questions.* The interviewee has a right to ask questions, and questions should be encouraged. A candidate without questions probably doesn't know much about the realities of ministry. The questions a candidate asks also reveal what he or she values.

When a candidate is eventually brought on staff, the interviewing process will continue to bear fruit. People tend to perform at the level at which they were recruited. If the interviewing process is casual and sloppy, that's the approach the staff member may assume on the job. If the interviewing process demonstrates seriousness and elevates the position, the staff member will treat the position accordingly.

—*Calvin C. Ratz*

Screening Candidates

We can use résumés and references to save time while screening the initial list of prospects. It's good to check references carefully but not rely on them alone, since references often are friends of the candidate and hesitant to say anything negative. Eventually, we can develop a short list with no more than three or four names, ranked according to the information we have and prayerful consideration.

If one candidate emerges as the obvious choice, it's not necessary to waste time interviewing several. Interviewing more than one can confuse and divide a selection committee. The pastor sometimes conducts the key interview rather than the church board. If board members are involved, a committee typically operates better than the entire board. The board, however, can protect a senior pastor from a hasty or ill-advised choice.

Three areas stand out as particularly important when screening potential ministry and program staff:

● *Character qualities.* A pastoral staff needs to be a team. The senior pastor may be the quarterback, but everyone has to play together. Does the recruit consider his or her ministry so specialized that he or she cannot respond to other needs? Or is there a sense of responsibility for the whole church, with particular assignments in a certain area? The whole church has to be more important than any one department.

Other personal qualities need scrutiny. A potential leader's home environment can often predict ministry effectiveness. We should spend time with the candidate's spouse and children (if any), and perhaps involve our own spouse in the process. Is the candidate flexible to cultural conditions within a congregation? Someone raised in Michigan may struggle fitting into a Mississippi church, while someone raised in the city may have trouble communicating with folk in rural communities. Financial matters must be above board if the person is to be trusted with spiritual responsibilities (Luke 16:11). Budgeting, indebtedness, and financial lifestyle are all critical factors.

● *Passion.* Does the person give evidence of motivation and passion that indicate a call to ministry? Is there energy and vitality to back up spiritual commitment?

Is the prospect a self-starter, someone who responds to a need without being told? Does he or she exhibit creativity and an openness to try new approaches to ministry?

Are the disciplines of prayer and personal study in place? When we ask a candidate to pray during the interview, the way he or she responds in prayer quickly reveals a warmth or coldness to the discipline of prayer.

How sensitive is the person? Pastors who have overcome hurts, setbacks, and tragedies often have a brokenness of spirit that greatly enhances their ministry among other broken people.

● *Skills and knowledge.* A depth of biblical knowledge serves as a good foundation for ministry. Is there waffling on any basic theological issue? In addition, does the potential staff member have diverse experiences? (There is a difference between having ten years' experience or having one year's experience ten times.) When we can call experienced staff, we gain the advantage of maturity that increases the likelihood the recruit will contribute to the church's ministry. We may call a recent graduate to gain zeal and enthusiasm, but we should be prepared to offer more supervision.

A person's education is the easiest factor to determine. We will want to evaluate it in light of the congregation's demographics.

A bit more abstract is the candidate's philosophy of ministry. We can find it by asking questions that reveal an approach to ministry— those things considered critical for growth and for meeting the needs of the congregation. We'll want a candidate with an approach to ministry that is compatible to ours and the church's.

Ministerial staff need three types of skills: People skills are the ability to work with people, resolve conflicts, and demonstrate empathy. Administrative skills enable a pastor to organize programs and volunteers, and manage finances. Such traits as promptness, the ability to manage time, and attention to details also fit here. Platform skills include the ability to speak publicly, whether to preach or to lead meetings. People skills often are more important in a small church; administrative skills will be more beneficial in larger churches.

Making the Selection

Ultimately, the choice we make about additional staff will be a spiritual one. We must remember the experience of Samuel in the choice of King David: "But the Lord said to Samuel, 'Do not consider his appearance or his height, for I have rejected him. The Lord does not look at the things man looks at. Man looks at the outward appearance, but the Lord looks at the heart' " (1 Sam. 16:7).

We need to discover God's will—who he has chosen to join our leadership team. As we make prayer a key part of the process, the Holy Spirit can give us the inner conviction needed to know who is right to invite on board. I believe if we have right motives and use common sense, God will protect us from making a wrong choice.

While we must take the time to hear from God, it is also important to play fair with all candidates. We must be candid, and we owe them honesty, integrity, understanding, encouragement, and respect. We should keep them informed of the process and when we expect a final decision. We should let candidates know how many are being considered for the position and advise them immediately if they are removed from the list or when someone else has been chosen.

Part of the process of making the selection is to help the candidate see his or her ministry being fulfilled in our church. It is not enough to scrutinize a candidate; a church has to sell itself as well. In the interviewing process, the candidate is interviewing the church as much as the church is interviewing the candidate. During this process, we need to be honest and realistic, while helping the candidate see the potential for ministry and voicing our vision as pastors.

What to Offer

Here are some specific—and some intangible—things to offer a new staff member:

● *Meaningful ministry.* Each recruit needs to find fulfillment in what he or she will be doing. We can't expect to keep staff for long if we pass off all the mundane assignments and hold the most significant jobs for ourselves. At the least, we must offer clear job descriptions outlining our expectations.

● *Protection from congregation or board.* The lines of accountability need to be understood by the whole church. It should be our responsibility to supervise and monitor a staff member's performance. Those who have legitimate complaints may come to us, but our staff members should know that we will protect them from needless hassles.

● *Adequate remuneration and benefits.* What churches can offer their staff in salary and benefits depends on each congregation's financial resources. But we have an obligation to lobby for our staff members' financial needs, being clear about moving costs, salary, housing allowance, business reimbursements, medical and insurance coverage, days off, and additional time off for vacation or outside ministry opportunities.

● *Instruction, counsel, and ongoing training.* Senior pastors owe staff members an opportunity to develop their ministerial gifts. We can do this through personal interaction and assistance with projects, and by providing opportunities for professional in-service training. We should create an atmosphere that says, Let's work and learn together, becoming the best we can be.

● *An understanding congregation.* We should prepare the congregation for the arrival of the new staff member, letting them know about the person, the new ministry assignments, and the lines of accountability. We can take the lead in encouraging the church family to open their hearts to the new minister.   —*Calvin C. Ratz*

Resources

Adams, J. 1976. Pastoral leadership. Grand Rapids: Baker.

Sugden, H., and W. Wiersbe. 1973. Confident pastoral leadership. Chicago: Moody.

Candidating and Voting

Presenting a candidate to a congregation can be as awkward as a blind date or an arranged marriage. A third party has decided these two delightful parties would make a wonderful couple. Now, how do we get them both to see this marvelous possibility?

The difficulty is exacerbated by the fact that a lot of important information must be conveyed in a short time—and often under a bizarre kind of secrecy, without the candidate's current congregation knowing what's going on. How can such a thing be done?

Six Steps

The first two steps are the most fundamental, have the least to do with technique, and must take place before the process begins. Step one is for everyone involved to *realize the impossibility* of the task, humanly speaking. Knowing that, all the participants must throw themselves on the mercy of God, for if God doesn't build the house, the whole thing will collapse. Step two is for the congregation to *trust* the search committee. There is no way everyone in the church will be able to understand all the reasons the committee will do the things it will do. No second guessing is allowed.

With these two understandings in place, there are four more steps. Step three is to *remind* the church what the purpose of the candidating process is: to discern the will of God for the church, not to sell or be sold on a particular candidate. This reminder is especially important for the search committee.

Step four is to *introduce* the candidate to the congregation. A colorful, well-written brochure can be a help. As long as step three is firmly in place, a little gloss and panache can be legitimate in conveying the search committee's excitement to the congregation.

Step five is to *interview* the candidate. Two kinds of interviews are essential: the micro and the macro. The *microinterview* is the intensive and extensive conversations that should take place between the candidate and the ruling body of the church and the staff of the church. Even though the staff usually does not vote on a candidate, its responses to the candidate are an important piece in the guidance puzzle the church is trying to put together. The candidate's theology, temperament, vision for ministry, and proposed goals for the first year of ministry should be carefully scrutinized. It's helpful if these can be put into writing.

The *macrointerview* is another word for the broad kind of socializing we call the reception. It's purpose is to expose the candidate to a wide variety of people in the church. The talk is usually superficial, but so is a lot of talk in the church. That's okay. The warmth and caring a candidate conveys in those "superficial" settings often build the bridge to more significant contacts.

Step six is to *vote* on the candidate. The church's polity will usually prescribe the number of yes votes necessary to call a pastor. From the candidate's standpoint, there is no divinely inspired formula for percentage of yes votes necessary to discern a call. A landslide victory can be as misleading as a narrow margin. Here it is helpful for the candidate to return to step one.

—*Ben Patterson*

Listing the Terms of a Call

When a call is extended, the details of the call may get lost in the excitement. Thus, it's important to place the particulars in writing, so that everybody not only understands them at the beginning but also remembers them in the future.

Following Procedures

The terms of a call typically derive from a combination of tradition, polity, reality, and negotiation.

● *Tradition.* What has the church traditionally given to incoming pastors? Is this a good time to examine the tradition in order to do better?

● *Polity.* Who is given the authority to hammer out and approve the terms of call—the search committee, the church board, the congregation? Some denominations dictate at least part of hiring agreements, and local judicatories may specify minimum salary amounts. Sometimes a higher judicatory must approve the terms.

● *Reality.* A generous committee may want to give a pastor a fabulous salary and a sabbatical every other year, but reality inhibits the possibilities. What can the church afford? What is reasonable, given the budget, existing pay packages, and congregational expectations?

● *Negotiation.* The candidate may enter the discussion, testing the possibility of a larger salary, particular perks, or a redistribution of the elements of a salary package. No church wants to lose a top candidate simply because the package was nonnegotiable. Who does the negotiating for the church, and who approves the final terms?

What to Include

The terms of call—sometimes called an employment agreement— can be written as a letter to the candidate from the party given the calling authority, such as the senior pastor, the search committee chair, or the president of the board. The terms should include at least these elements:

● *Position title and description.* The candidate should know what the position is, such as "Associate Pastor" or "Minister of Music." A brief description clarifies what is meant by the title. What will the person be responsible for doing?

● *Working relationships.* This needs to tell who the person will report to and who will report to him or her (such as a secretary). It may also list the committees or program areas the person will work with.

● *Salary and housing.* What will be the cash salary? Is a parsonage being supplied? What is the amount of the housing allowance? Churches often provide a figure for salary and housing combined and allow the candidate to divide it once housing costs are known. For tax purposes, however, the housing figure (even if supplied by the candidate) must be approved by the church board or congregation prior to the candidate beginning work.

● *Benefits and reimbursements.* What other benefits will be offered, such as medical, dental, liability, and group term life insurance; pension plan; and club memberships; and reimbursements for automobile, entertainment, books, and other professional ministry expenses?

● *Time off.* What day or days can the pastor take off in a typical week? How many days of vacation will be granted yearly, and can they be taken all at once? How many days of study leave will be granted yearly, and can they be accumulated if not taken in a given year? How

much of the cost of a study leave will the church bear? What, if any, are the provisions for a sabbatical?

● *Starting day.* When will employment commence? When will benefits (especially health coverage) begin?

● *Moving arrangements.* What moving expenses will be covered: Professional movers? Travel expenses while moving? Expenses for house-hunting trips?

For clarity's sake, it is wise to note any common benefits *not* included in the terms of call, such as health benefits for grown children or orthodontic insurance.

—*James D. Berkley*

Determining Salary Packages

"What shall we pay our pastor?" It's a good question that concerns fair-minded churches. Unfortunately, the answer isn't always clear—or accurate. Considering pastoral compensation in four distinct blocks—expense reimbursements, benefits, housing, and salary—clarifies the picture greatly.

Expense Reimbursements

Operating expenses belong to the church, the employer. No one expects the pastor to pay the electric bill for the lights in his or her office, for example. And professional reimbursements are just that: reimbursements. These expenses paid by the church merely return to pastors money they have spent for the church out of their own pockets

in the course of their ministry.

Churches that understand this concept often set up "accountable reimbursement programs" for such clergy expenses as books and periodicals, continuing education, travel and entertainment, professional memberships, and clergy liability insurance. This money paid in reimbursements is in no way money earned by a pastor.

Benefits

Benefit packages commonly include such items as health insurance, life insurance, pension plan, disability insurance, and self-employment tax allowance. Many benefits have the added ability to shield portions of compensation from taxation. For instance, if the church pays the pastor's insurance premiums, that money generally isn't considered taxable income. If, however, the church pays the pastor a like sum (so the pastor can purchase insurance), around a third of the payment likely will be lost to taxes, leaving only two-thirds to pay for the insurance.

Although any money paid the pastor to help pay self-employment tax is, itself, considered taxable income, this allowance helps pastors shoulder the hefty self-employment tax burden (15.3 percent in 1994), none of which the church is allowed to pay directly to the government for the pastor.

Housing

The housing allowance can be a pastor's best financial friend. The part of the pastor's remuneration that is officially designated by the church as housing allowance (and can be justified by actual expenses or fair-rental value plus utilities) is not subject to income tax. Even though it *is* subject to self-employment tax, the housing allowance gives a pastor hundreds, if not thousands, of dollars more a year—without costing the church any more. Pastors with any out-of-pocket expenses for housing costs should have a housing allowance set up in advance by an official action of the church board.

Salary

The cash salary is true pay, from which the pastor must support a family, pay taxes, provide a car, buy groceries, put children through school, pay all the bills, and keep the wolves from the door.

Most churches determine one total figure to pay for salary and housing combined. Once the housing amount is declared, it is subtracted from the total. The salary is the remaining portion. It is important, however, that the salary and housing figures remain separate once they are determined at the beginning of the year. The salary is not simply whatever part of the pay package the pastor didn't spend for housing during the year. Figuring salary that way is technically called *recharacterization of income.* It can cause the pastor to lose the benefits of a housing allowance.

Because a portion of a pastor's salary package is designated as housing allowance, the salary itself may appear a little thin when compared to others' pay. That's okay if the housing allowance adequately fills out the total figure. Since the salary portion is most vulnerable to loss of spending power through taxation, it is wise to put as much of the pay package as is legally and morally possible into tax-free benefits and a housing allowance.

—*James D. Berkley*

20

Managing Staff

The key to fruitfulness in ministry is fruitfulness in the lives of the individual workers. Therefore, an effective leader must be committed not only to the organization's goals but also—and especially—to the people making them a reality.

Jesus said, "Whoever wants to become great among you must be your servant" (Mark 10:43), and then he modeled servant-style leadership. What is this kind of leadership? Simply put, a servant-leader is more committed to the fruitfulness and fulfillment—the success—of his staff than to his own.

The rewards of staff-oriented leadership are obvious, but they don't come without effort. Enhancing the fruitfulness and fulfillment of the people who work for us involves three specific steps: communicating clear expectations, providing personalized leadership, and offering accurate and honest evaluation.

Communicating Clear Expectations

Peter Drucker has observed that one of the major problems in business today is that employees often see their primary tasks differently than do their employers. If the worker thinks he's supposed to do one thing and his boss thinks he's to do another, misunderstanding and conflict are inevitable. Therefore, from the start, leaders need to make sure expectations are clear. We can accomplish that with two tools:

● *A job description.* This is a general guideline listing what a worker does, not a detailed job outline. A job description that's too broad, such as "oversees the youth ministry," functions more as a position title than a working description. But a grocery list of specific assignments—"plans games at summer camp" or "buys supplies for Sunday school"—makes the job description unwieldy.

A good job description typically lists four to six major responsibilities. For a small-groups director, it might include: recruits new leaders, trains them, matchs them with small groups, and provides them ongoing support. This draws the rough boundaries of the position. It doesn't answer all the questions of specific tasks, but it tells the worker he won't be responsible for securing curriculum or maintaining group directories.

Individual assignments may change. The youth director may plan a retreat over Presidents' Day weekend, but that shouldn't be put into the job description. It's best to have something like "plans and executes special events to build youth leaders' commitment." The particulars of execution are then left for planning with a supervisor.

● *A monthly listing of priorities.* We must set both "A priorities" (the top-priority tasks of any particular ministry) and "B priorities" (ancillary tasks that support the higher priorities). In order to make expectations absolutely clear, staff members and supervisers can determine together their A and B priorities for the next thirty days.

The amount of input this requires from the pastor depends on the worker's experience and competence. New workers may not know yet what their priorities ought to be, so supervisors can help determine them. Experienced staff members simply submit their lists to keep their supervisors informed. In either case, every month both workers and supervisors see on paper what their essential tasks are for that month. That keeps them on the same wavelength.

Such communication must, of course, take place in a safe, secure environment. We can create this environment through attitude and manner of speaking. We wouldn't want to say to a staff member, "Here's a list of priorities. I expect you to produce, because I need these tasks finished. I'm going to be checking up on you next month to make sure you're not goofing off." That creates a threatening psychological environment.

Instead, we need to say, "Let's work out your priorities for this month. I'm committed to helping you fulfill these tasks, and I have confidence that you can accomplish great things." That tells staff members we are on their side and frees them to trust us enough to say willingly, "Hold me accountable."

Such conferences, over a few months, can point out inconsistent work habits, overloaded job descriptions, or inappropriate placement. They help both the pastor and the worker refine or alter the expectations they mutually agree upon. That not only enhances the person's fulfillment and job satisfaction, but it also makes the church's ministry more fruitful. Workers whose time and abilities reflect their priorities usually accomplish their ministry objectives. Over the course of a year—if we're setting the right A priorities and the workers are well suited for their positions—they should enjoy significant fruitfulness and fulfillment.

Providing Personalized Leadership

Any parent knows you can't handle every child alike. One disobedient child may need to be rebuked sharply or even spanked. Another crumbles at the mere look of disappointment on his mother's face. Treat both children the same, and one will be crushed and the other unswayed. For parents, the challenge is to know what kind of leadership each child needs.

Likewise, different workers need different kinds of leadership. Some people need a tight leash, others space. Some need to be shown clearly, almost harshly, when they blunder, because their characteristic response to mistakes is a mere, "Oh well." Others need only a gentle prod, because they've already died a thousand deaths over their error. Giving individuals the type of direction they need is one of the most important aspects of pastoral management.

An excellent model for individualized leadership comes from Ken Blanchard's *Leadership and the One Minute Manager*. He calls it "situational leadership." I prefer to call it "personalized leadership," because it reminds me that I'm leading people, not just handling situations. Blanchard sees four different leadership styles—direction, coaching, support, and delegation—which should be used according to workers' competence and confidence.

● *Direction.* If we hire an inexperienced youth pastor straight from seminary, we can hardly delegate the ministry to him; he doesn't yet know how to run a ministry. He lacks confidence because he's never done it before. He comes to our planning meetings with a blank slate and says, "What do I do? Where do I go first?" He may have admirable character, a strong spiritual life, and the basic gifts to get the job done, but he needs point-by-point direction until he gains experience. Our job then is to give him detailed instructions and basically lead the ministry through him, probably for at least a year.

● *Coaching.* This is the next level. We can coach workers whose confidence and competence is growing. They come to us with good ideas, and we add some of our own, making the ministry a joint venture. Coaches are involved enough to know exactly what's happening at each step. The key words for coaches are *affirmation* and *redirection*. Coaches are generous with praise and ready to correct when necessary.

● *Support.* Typically, after a year of coaching, a worker is ready for this third leadership style. At this point, the worker sets his own agenda;

he comes into meetings with his A priorities listed and says, "This is what I'm doing." The supervisor's role is to provide emotional support, encouragement, affirmation, and whatever correction and advice is necessary. The worker being supported knows what to do; he primarily needs to know that someone backs him. In short, for the next year, the leader's role is to be a cheerleader.

● *Delegation.* At this point the leader turns the ministry over to the individual, for the most part. Reporting continues, but it becomes less frequent; the leash is long.

Delegation doesn't, however, mean abdication. The delegating leader doesn't hand over the responsibility, walk away, and provide no further leadership. He says, "This is your ministry. You build it. But I want to stay in touch. I'm here to serve you."

Training New Workers

Simply remembering that training takes time goes a long way toward reducing stress for both new employees and trainers. Most management positions, for example, require about six months to cover the basics. During training periods, staff workers need to know it is safe to fail.

For example, less than a month after a new staff person began work, she was in tears over an error she made. Her supervisor listened to her unravel her feelings of guilt and then asked two questions: "Did you know how to do this job when you arrived here?" and "Did anybody train you on this since you arrived?" She answered no to both. "Then how can you possibly be held responsible for something you had never been trained for and for which you had no previous knowledge?" A bright smile emerged. She understood.

The supervisor was at fault for not properly training her; she had been performing remarkably well in the midst of no training.

One common mistake in orienting new staff is to assume (usually unconsciously) that they understand how the church functions. The great football coach Vince Lombardi began football practices each season by holding up a football and announcing, "This is a football." When the new receptionist arrives at the church office, we may need to start with "This is a phone" and explain specifically how the phone should be answered.

The first day on the job is crucial for making new employees feel welcome and positive about their jobs. A supervisor or designated employee can be made responsible for introducing the new employee to each department, telling one or two things about the new employee to help break the ice. Other staff members can be invited to have lunch with the new employee, so social connections can begin early.

Obviously, direction, coaching, and support take more of a leader's time than does delegation. That's why it's so tempting to bring people on staff, direct or coach them for a few months, and then say, "All right, go at it." But too often these workers aren't ready for the delegation stage. What's worse is that often delegation slides into abdication; the leader offers no feedback or communication. When that happens, seeds of discord and disarray grow.

In order to lead each person under our management properly, we have to ask ourselves, *Based on competence and confidence, does this person need direction, coaching, support, or delegation?* We can also take that one step further and "contract" with each person about the kind of leadership we will provide, so each knows which to expect. This contract prevents misunderstanding and frustration.

Training Tips

While each situation will call for different orientation approaches, some activities to consider are:

● Familiarizing new employees with each piece of equipment.

● Showing them where to find important information, such as addresses, phone numbers, fax numbers, and directions.

● Giving them a list of important church meetings scheduled each week. Also, a yearly calendar containing all activities of the church and staff can help new employees pace their work. If the church newsletter goes to the printer each Thursday, it should be listed 52 times, along with the person responsible for making it happen. The calendar is useful for staff planning, and it can serve as a safeguard to keep projects from slipping through the cracks when there is staff turnover.

● Going through the job description, line by line, explaining what each item means and what the expectations are.

● Introducing them to personnel matters, such as making sure all legal papers are filled out and setting them up with the proper benefits.

● Providing them with a list of key people organizationally important to the church, such as board members, chief outside contacts, and key volunteers.

● Compiling and giving to new employees a reference guide with vital information about the church, such as the mission statement, goals, and vision statement. The guide might also cover budgets, information on Sunday services, and an organizational chart listing persons by name, title, and function. Some churches create a "Twenty-five Most Asked Questions" booklet—with answers—to give new employees.

Power of Perseverance

It's good to hold periodic checkups with new staff members to see how they are doing. Such conferences are most effective at the end of the employee's first day, first week, and first month of work. After three months, a formal review can be conducted, and perhaps a small raise can be given.

—*Sylvia Nash*

Once people become familiar with Blanchard's system, a supervisor can sit down with them and discuss their leadership needs. Newer ministry directors often say, "I need direction." So the supervisor might say, "Great! When we meet, I'll do a lot of the talking, and I expect you to ask a lot of the questions."

When a person says, "I'm ready to move on to coaching," the supervisor can tell him, "We'll probably split the conversation in meetings. I'll be there to probe and affirm and make sure you don't get off the track." In a similar manner, the supervisor can tell those in the support or delegation stage what to expect.

This contracting process insures that workers get the kind of leadership they need. Supervisors easily offend people by giving them the

---

Assessing and Improving Effectiveness

One of the church leader's most important tasks is to mentor and monitor a ministry staff. For many of us, the mentoring comes easy; the monitoring not so easy. But even if we'd rather encourage than correct, we'll need to do both in order to have an effective ministry team. Here are some thoughts on three important issues in the assessment—and communication of that assessment—to a staff member.

Communicating

We need to make sure our expectations are clear, understood, and agreed upon by all. A job description filled with spiritual cliches or generalizations serves little purpose. Phrases like "discipling our teenagers" or "developing a Christ-centered music ministry" may sound good, but such descriptions make it hard to pin down the difference between success and failure. We need to spell out exactly, quantitatively what successful discipling will actually look like.

Highlighting priorities is equally important. In the interest of clarity, a job description can become cluttered with details (spelling out every task and minor expectation). When that happens, it's hard for a staff member to filter out what is really important. This results in differing interpretations regarding how well the job is being done.

It's best to list just three to five major and specific goals by which a ministry will be judged. That way, no one is in doubt about what is and is not important. And to gain agreement about and ownership of expectations, we can have staff mebers write their own first drafts of the three to five goals they'd like to be judged by during the coming year. In most cases, the supervisor will need to do only minor editing.

wrong leadership. If people expect support, and we provide direction, they start to wonder, *Why is he running my ministry and trying to tell me what to do?* On the other hand, if people want direction and all we do is stop by every three weeks and say, "Hey, good job. Keep it up," they're going to feel we're not leading them.

The goal is for each individual we manage to become independent enough to reach the delegation stage. Usually it takes around three years—one year in each of the preliminary stages—to reach that point. If a person gets stuck and is unable to progress into delegation, it's either because we placed the person wrongly or we haven't supervised sufficiently. Our responsibility in that case is to make a careful evaluation and take steps to alter the situation.

Evaluating

The job of a supervisor is to sort through the feedback and come up with a fair and accurate assessment of how things are going. To do that, it's helpful to remember that opinions and feedback are best weighed, not counted. Every church has its complainers and encouragers, and both tend to see everything from their own particular slant. A couple of chronic complainers who gripe about the way the Sunday-school classes are administered probably need to be taken lightly. However, an encourager who steps forward to complain should be heeded.

When it comes to evaluating a congregation's response to a staff member, the reviews will almost always be mixed. As supervisors, we must decide which critiques hit the mark and which ones miss. That is hard to do when we focus primarily on what people say rather than who said it.

Timing

If the goal of assessment is not only to tell staff members how they are doing, but also to help them improve, timing is everything. The typical year-end salary review works great for communicating our assessment of someone's ministry, but it's not so great for helping people improve their performance.

A substandard performance review, followed by 24 monthly reminders in the form of a substandard pay raise, can be incredibly discouraging. It is true it lets them know how they are doing, but it gives little chance to show improvement—and no hope of having that improvement quickly rewarded. By separating performance reviews from salary reviews by four to six months, however, we give a staff member who receives a substandard review the time and motivation to get things up to par before next year's salaries are set. Thus, it's often helpful to have two performance reviews: one year-end salary review and one review that functions more like a progress report, allowing time for improvement to be noted and rewarded.

—Larry W. Osborne

A common mistake is to move people through the process too quickly. Generally, staff members tend to slot themselves one step further in the process than they ought to be—a person needing direction, for instance, usually thinks he needs coaching. Too often supervisors, wanting to minimize their output of time, yield to the worker's desire to speed through the process.

We pay a price when we do this. Almost always a worker prematurely moved into coaching will have to be moved back into direction, and that will foster resentment. A horse that has run free in the pasture inevitably chafes when he's brought back to the stable with a bit in its mouth. Better to keep the horse in the stable until we're sure we want it to run free.

Offering Accurate and Honest Evaluation

Good parents openly affirm their children: "We appreciate your good behavior," or, "You're doing a great job in school." They also know when to discipline: "If you jump on your bed again, you will be punished." Thus, children know where they stand and what they need to do.

Staff members need similar feedback. They should not be left wondering, *What does my supervisor think of my work? Am I valuable here? Do I make a difference?* The more secure an employee is, the more freedom with which he or she can operate. That's why leaders need to offer accurate and honest evaluations of those they lead.

The emphasis is on *accurate* and *honest* for good reason. If feedback is inaccurate—all sugar and spice, or clearly out of touch with reality—people lose respect for it. In other words, if I praise efforts for a job poorly done, workers will begin to wonder about my opinion. Similarly, if feedback is dishonest—if I twist the facts or misrepresent a person's performance—the person naturally will lose trust.

It's best for workers to know where they stand—even if they stand on the bubble—than to have them wondering what we think of their work. They won't have to play guessing games if we care enough to say accurately and honestly where they stand. If people are doing well, they can rejoice in that and work with confidence. If their work is unacceptable, they can determine why and make the necessary changes.

We avoid heartache by providing immediate feedback regarding inferior work. If our initial feedback doesn't bring about the desired change, we need to offer more. Eventually we may have to say, "In spite of my repeated expressions of concern, you are making the same mistakes again and again. If this continues, it may lead to the loss of your job." Yes, that creates insecurity, but ultimately honesty is in everyone's best interest.

Leading the Team

Workers who are led well and who enjoy fruitfulness and fulfillment can join together to form a strong, smoothly functioning work team. But just like an individual, the team needs to be led. It needs to be encouraged and motivated; it needs to be informed and educated; it needs to have its vision renewed. The avenue through which this happens is the staff meeting.

The staff meeting is similar to the team meeting a coach schedules prior to an important game. Because the coach knows her players are about to confront the opposition, she prepares her agenda carefully. She determines what her team needs most and lists her primary objectives for the meeting.

A church staff faces a challenge far more important than any athletic event, so it's good for pastors to view staff meetings as opportunities to motivate or equip their team for the battle. It's not effective to make a few announcements, work through a brief agenda, and then wonder why workers come up with so many excuses for missing these weekly meetings.

If staff meetings exist mainly to enable the leader to communicate his or her agenda, staff morale will suffer. But the leader who thinks *What does my staff need? How can this meeting help them grow in their effectiveness?* will find the staff eagerly anticipating the meetings. And when staff members feel served by the leader, they will breathe life into the organization.

A leader who recognizes the various functions of staff gatherings will be able to serve his staff's needs better. First is the business meeting, in which the work of the organization is contemplated and communicated. It's the time for making announcements and comparing calendars. Second is the training meeting, where the staff is educated for greater effectiveness. Third is the relational meeting, which builds unity.

Many organizations spend the bulk of their staff time in business meetings. But leaders devoted to building up their workers know that business is their least important staff objective. If they do have to make announcements, they do so in the context of the vision and purpose of the ministry. For instance, I can say, "Well, folks, we need to fill fifteen slots for small-group leaders. Who can we get?" That's an announcement. But I build our common vision if I say, "Friends, our people need to taste what it is to be used of God. One way we can help them do that is to give them a chance to lead small groups."

Only about 25 percent of staff-meeting time should be spent on business issues. The bulk of staff time—50 percent, ideally—should be devoted to training. Staff meetings can be excellent places for workers to develop skills that lead to increased fruitfulness and fulfillment. We can take our ministry directors through in-house courses on public speaking, lay counseling, and discipleship.

For instance, a staff I lead worked through a book on leadership. We read it individually. Then in regular staff meetings, we broke into small groups to discuss and apply questions I prepared. I worked to use variety in the way skills were taught. Some themes worked best as talks; some were great for discussion groups. Sometimes outside experts, such as a professional lecturer on public speaking, led sessions. Sometimes I asked a staff member who excelled in a particular skill to share his or her insights. Through classes such as these, we can teach our staff how to recruit leaders, build teams, and delegate responsibility. We can discuss confrontation and conflict resolution.

About 25 percent of our staff time can go toward relationship-building activities. Relational meetings can include anything from a volleyball game to pour-your-heart-out sessions of sharing and prayer. Most church staff meetings need to include regular times of sharing and prayer.

Special events also contribute to the emphasis on the relational. A staff can have lunch together on the patio or attend a sporting event. I know of one ministry leader who ran his key lay leaders through a boot-camp-like obstacle course, where they had to work together to make it through. Such activities pay large dividends in team spirit.

Devoting time to nurturing staff members' competence and interpersonal relationships says we value *them,* not just their ministry output. Organizing staff meetings to meet their needs is one of the most important ways we can serve our workers.

Overseeing a staff is hard work. It takes time and energy to communicate clear expectations, provide personalized leadership, and offer accurate and honest evaluation. It takes even more time and energy to forge individual workers into a smoothly functioning work team. Leadership is particularly draining when it involves making tough decisions, but the rewards validate the efforts.

—*Don Cousins*

Resources

Blanchard, K., and Z. Drea. 1985. Leadership and the one-minute manager. New York: Morrow.

Blanchard, K. 1992. One-minute manager. New York: Berkley.

Drucker, P. 1993. The effective executive. New York: Harper Business.

Salary Reviews

Salary reviews can be frustrating, especially when we know ministry workers are overworked and underpaid, and the church isn't overly robust financially. Still, salary reviews can be positive experiences if used for addressing concerns and rewarding performance.

Setting Pay

Salary reviews should be based on objective criteria. For example:

● Salary schedules need to be both realistic and fair, reflecting church size, budget, location, experience, and responsibility levels. It is helpful to know what nearby churches are paying. An administrator can work with neighboring churches to compile salary data, and the results can be shared with all the administrators—each promising to keep the material confidential—for use in setting salaries.

● Grading systems show staff specifically what steps must be taken to reach the next pay level. These criteria should be tied directly to the worker's job description.

During economically tough times, salary increases aren't always possible, but other means can express appreciation and affirmation. Giving extra time off, for example, can ease the pain. One organization initiated a four-day work week (ten-hour days), staggering staff on Mondays and Fridays. This gave workers a long weekend to use as they chose—including freelance work.

Affirming Good Work

The number one complaint of workers is that they don't feel appreciated. Salary reviews are a good time to let them know otherwise.

Generally, staff workers feel more comfortable when reviews are conducted one-on-one rather than by a committee. The ideal person for conducting the review is the supervisor, the person recommending the salary increase.

One valuable approach to salary reviews is to have both staff workers and supervisors complete and return similar evaluation forms prior to the interview. This provides a channel by which workers can comfortably address concerns they have, and supervisors can note areas where praise is appropriate or correction is needed. Comparing the forms highlights communication breakdowns. For example, if the supervisor marks a one on a scale of ten for dependability and the staff person marks a nine, it's time to talk.

Using a standard form for reviews ensures staff members are treated equally. The form might ask workers for their response to categories such as their greatest success during the last year, greatest disappointment, areas of growth, changes they would like to see implemented, challenges they expect to face, goals for the upcoming year, areas where a supervisor could be more helpful, one piece of advice for management, and a new challenge they would like to have. The form can also include a section for workers to rate themselves concerning attitude, attendance, initiative, communication skills, productivity, and responsibility.

Following a salary review, if we have been successful, the staff worker should walk out feeling affirmed and loved, even if correc-tions were offered in some areas. Football coach Bear Bryant prac-ticed giving eight positive state-ments about his football players before he gave a negative one. "By that time," he explained, "you have earned the right to make a correc-tion; you have built a confidence in them."

—Sylvia Nash

Mediating Disputes

In the interface between pastors and staff members, major areas of conflict continue to surface: genera-tional differences, theological dis-agreements, preoccupations with power and control, or hierarchical structures that don't allow for both accountability and freedom to min-ister. Yet foundational to most staff disputes is some form of miscom-munication.

Maintaining Communication

"All conflicts are communication problems" may be a bit overstated, but miscommunication certainly ac-counts for its share of conflict. For example, we all know staff mem-bers who burn with vision as they begin their new vocations, not un-derstanding they were hired simply to perform certain tasks. While the pastor sits in the church office won-dering why staff members can't set-tle into their responsibilities, the staff members are frustrated trying to reconcile cleaning the kitchen with the ministry they envisioned.

Honesty is the critical element here. We probably should worry more about potential staff members understanding what we expect of them than trying to make sure they like it. Perhaps we suffer from homiletic hangover, but it's easy to make a staff position sound greater than it is. It may help in recruit-ment, but it leads to trouble in the long run.

Daily miscommunications—not sending the right information or the same information—create the same potential for conflict. Working together effectively requires lots of talking to one another. We need to ask questions; use memos galore; make sure people understand what is going on, especially when it will affect something in their field of ministry, no matter how distantly.

Miscommunication can also be negated by demonstrating mutual loyalty. One staff pastor, for in-stance, tries to do things his pastor cares about deeply, even though they may matter little to him, such as picking up a gum wrapper on the carpet. He likened it to bringing his wife flowers. Likewise, supervisors need to find ways to visibly demon-strate love and support, such as writing a note of thanks or offering to handle some busywork we weren't asked to handle. It will cover a multitude of miscommunications.

Strengthening Relationships

Key terms in disarming conflict are respect, understanding, freedom, submission, deference, honesty, and openness. These words describe personal relationships, not institutional systems. Management systems don't create destructive conflicts; people do. Where conflict destroys ministry, you can be sure that relationships have deteriorated. Preventing deterioration requires maintenance.

● *Relationships must stay familial.* It is easy to let ministry relationships slip into mere professionalism. Yet, the most productive staff relationships happen where love is expressed in personal friendship. For example, I'll never forget the morning my pastor came by on his way to the office to sit and talk with my wife and me after our apartment had been burglarized.

● *Relationships must remain supportive.* If our goal is to minister to people and extend the kingdom, we must work at encouraging one another. Will a staff member support the pastor, even if the pastor opts for a different action than the staff member suggested? Will the pastor care about helping a disappointed staff member continue on?

● *Relationships must keep maturing.* Being a minister means saying more than just the things others want to hear. Leadership must also have enough maturity to give and receive correction without being hurt or angry. Jesus' closeness with Peter did not keep him from rebuking him when he sought to keep Jesus from the Cross. James and John were blasted for wanting to destroy an entire village. Such relationships do not spring up overnight; they are cultivated. Fear of committing time to personal relationships is the greatest deterrent to a healthy staff environment.

—*Wayne Jacobsen*

Supervising Interns

Churches occasionally hire a college or seminary student to join the staff as an intern for a limited time. For the student, an internship can be an excellent way to test ministry skills. For a congregation, an internship provides an opportunity to participate in a student's development in the work of the church. For the staff, an intern usually brings a fresh perspective to the practice of ministry.

The Demands

Though intern programs can bring many benefits to a church, such programs also make demands on a congregation and its staff members. Therefore, a congregation needs to ask itself—at the beginning—what it hopes an internship program will do, not only for the congregation and staff, but also for the student. Making expectations clear will go a long way toward making the internship experience positive for everyone. Specifically, the congregation needs to recognize three key facts regarding the demands of internships:

● *Interns bring hidden costs.* Having an intern is not simply an economical way to cover unstaffed areas of ministry. Interns may indeed help congregations who are not yet financially able to call another full-time staff member, but they come with hidden costs (not always financial), and those costs need to be acknowledged up front. For example, interns require a high level of commitment from both staff and congregation. Staff members must be willing to invest large amounts of time in training and supervising an intern, and the actual return on investment may not be visible for some time. When staff members work with interns, therefore, it is wise for them to see their investment of time as a gift to the future ministry of the church.

● *Interns need intensive supervision.* Every intern will require a well-defined job description and clear lines of accountability. Changes in either can obviously be negotiated during the internship, but interns need to know exactly what is expected of them and who they can turn to for help. Churches known for their successes with interns often assign a staff member as supervisor. This person isn't necessarily the senior pastor, but he or she is particularly adept at working with seminarians. In some cases, board members have handled the task well. The point is, supervision is required, and the supervisor

needs to be equipped to handle the responsibility.

In many cases, seminaries and even colleges provide opportunities for off-site reflection about the internship experience. Generally speaking, congregations should take advantage of the resources provided by the educational institution and encourage the student to do so, as well. Developing a close working relationship with the educational institution will be one important way to help clarify expectations, set minimum salaries, receive occasional guidance, and avoid common mistakes.

● *Interns require patient understanding as their skills develop.* Congregations must view their involvement with interns as a gift to the future ministry of the church. This may frequently call for a spirit of self-sacrifice. Many congregations who have had successful relationships with interns over the years actually list the salary for the intern on the mission side of the budget rather than on the personnel side! Unorthodox bookkeeping, maybe, but a clear statement about the purpose of the internship program—and the possible return on the investment.

Yet churches with successful internship programs find something to celebrate in the contributions of *every* intern, no matter how rocky the time together may have been. Such celebrations acknowledge not only an intern's on-the-job growth and the congregation's role in shaping a life for future ministry, but also the intern's contribution to the life of the congregation.

—*Douglas J. Brouwer*

21

Terminating Staff

Consider three people in three different situations:

Gary, a seminary student, is a paid part-timer who works with youth. He's an older student, with years of ministry experience prior to entering seminary. He has a healthy, growing marriage, an amiable spirit, and a sincere desire to serve others. But he is mismatched with this particular job. Youth require enthusiasm, sometimes boisterousness; he is docile and retiring. The work needs a lot of initiative to create new ideas; he is a better follower than visionary.

Fran is a volunteer Sunday school teacher. She loves teaching, has a solid grasp of Scripture, and is a capable communicator, but her personal life is in shambles. An uncontrolled lifestyle combined with undisciplined habits has led to financial debt and a poor reputation in the community. Her skills as a teacher are severely impaired by her inconsistent life.

Chuck serves as an associate pastor at a nearby church. He works hard with Christian education, the youth ministry, some visitation, and occasional preaching. He is a zealous worker, but his abrasive personality causes some to criticize his ministry style. Although loved by most, he is maligned by others.

Over the past year, all three of these people were fired or asked to resign. Gary was indeed mismatched to his job in terms of gifts, desire, and ability. Fran was counseled to get some help organizing her life before she returned to teach others. Chuck was fired suddenly without warning.

Having been directly involved in the first two cases as the "firer" and indirectly in the third as a friend, I had to come to grips with some tough questions: Is the church a community of healing or an efficiency-based organization? Do we focus on forgiveness and grace, or stewardship and responsibility? Where does church discipline belong in these scenes? Are church leaders guilty of "shooting their wounded"? Then again, should we put the wounded at key positions in the battle?

In working through such questions, we realize that while dismissal is never easy, it must sometimes occur—in accordance with biblical values. Here is a series of questions that can help church leaders decide whether firing is required, and if so, how to do it.

Tough Questions

The hard thinking ahead of any action should include asking the following questions:

● *Does the person really need to be replaced?* Is he or she unable to fill the position? This was true of my co-worker Gary. He was trying to do something that demanded a personality opposite of his. A variation of this question is: Has the church outgrown this person (or vice versa)? In the case of another associate pastor, Larry, the church simply grew beyond his aspirations. He thrived on personal contact, hands-on ministry. Yet because of the church's numerical growth, Larry's job became increasingly administrative. He could do the desk work, but he was frustrated. When the issue came to a head, both he and the church decided it was time for him to move on and for the church to find a different type of associate minister.

We can sharpen our thinking about the need for termination by carefully considering three key issues. First, how much harm is being done? This question especially applies in the case of volunteers. If they are causing little damage, the decision to remove them may evoke more trouble than it is worth. Even professional staff members are at times "carried" by the church in spite of their ineffectiveness because they seem to be doing no harm, and therefore no one has the heart to take action.

Second, what if the position goes vacant for a while? Would that be better than the current state of affairs? In some situations, the answer is yes because of the financial or personal pressures being generated by the ineffective worker. But in other cases, the answer will be no, because a replacement would be mandatory—and difficult to find.

Third, what standard am I using to measure job effectiveness? Sometimes we think a person needs to be let go simply because we are stacking the person up against an impossible standard. The high turnover rate in youth ministry positions is due—at least in part—to this kind of thinking. We must be careful to distinguish between someone who cannot do a job and someone who *can* but happens to lack the flair, polish, or gifts of someone else we may have in mind. Chuck's dismissal was partly due to a church board that did not care for his style, even though Chuck seemed to be doing the job.

● *Who believes the person needs to be replaced?* If you are the only firmly persuaded person, look out! All sorts of trouble can arise when the issue of firing becomes a skirmish between two people. In the cases of both Gary and Fran, I made sure my decision was based on more than my own subjective opinion.

The counsel of elders, deacons, and personnel committees is essential to keep a leader from engaging in a personality war. Effectively collecting their input means taking caution not to color the picture with comments like, "It seems to me that John is really failing as a teacher; would you sit in on his class and tell me what you think?"

On the other hand, sometimes we find out later that even the person being fired agrees with us! In Gary's case, for example, he had been as frustrated with his job as I had been with him. Why hadn't he said anything? He needed the money, and he knew I had no other paid positions for him. So he hid his frustration, even though he knew he was mismatched.

In many churches we practice the Peter Principle with lay people, promoting them to the level of their incompetence and causing frustration for all. Sometimes we need to step back and say, "Mr. Jones, you are such a gifted teacher that I don't think we are making the best use of you as Sunday school superintendent. Would you be willing to return to teaching?"

● *What will be the basis for dismissal?* There are several options:

—Relational: The person's personality is fundamentally unsuited for the job. (Are we sure?)

—Moral: Sexual transgressions, mishandling of finances, and sinful lifestyles are serious, but have we followed the pattern of Matthew 18 as closely as possible? Should the church offer remedial counseling (assuming the person is not in blatant rebellion or outright denial of wrongdoing)? Would a temporary leave allow the person to get needed help and then return to duty?

—Theological: Sometimes a line must be drawn. When Mrs. Smith had a "vision" that the world would end by December 1978, we did not allow her to broadcast her prediction. Even here, we must ask ourselves: Is this person defiant or just ignorant? Maybe she's just caught in the backwash of a conference where a persuasive speaker overemphasized a certain doctrine. Will a little time and explanation restore equilibrium?

—Inability: The basis for dismissal may simply be that the man or woman could not do the job assigned. If the job expectations were clear and realistic, and if the person gave it his best but could not perform, then perhaps dismissal is the least of the evils. Before acting, however, leaders must evaluate whether the job really was realistic.

For instance, a pastor once sent me the five-page, single-spaced job description of the youth minister his church was seeking. The person would have full responsibility for junior high, senior high, college age, singles, and—whenever possible—young couples. Sunday school, activities, retreats, and occasional preaching were all part of the mix in this church of more than eight hundred members. I wrote back to pose one question: How many people are you seeking to fill this job?

Legal Aspects of Staff Terminations

While courts rarely interfere in the relationship between a church and its *clergy*, churches do face a greater risk of being sued when they terminate nonclergy employees.

The "employment at will" doctrine says an employer may terminate an employee at any time for any reason or for no reason at all. Of course, there are exceptions. Congress and state legislatures have passed laws to prevent employers from firing employees for discriminatory reasons, and employment contracts may restrict employers' rights to terminate.

Some courts have ruled, for example, that employers created implied contracts by promising employees jobs for life or by referring to them as "permanent." Some states recognize public-policy exceptions to the "employment at will" doctrine, so that an employer cannot fire an employee who refuses to commit a crime.

People who file law suits for wrongful termination cannot win unless their state recognizes an exception to the "employment at will" doctrine or unless their employer violated a specific employment law. Nevertheless, churches that treat employees fairly reduce their risk of being sued by terminated employees.

Five Termination Tips

When terminating an employee, we can avoid unnecessary problems with the following actions:

● *Be sure employees know what is expected.* A written job description should be used when hiring employees, and we shouldn't hire anyone without the minimum qualifications. We need to give new employees adequate training and regular feedback; we should document progress and give performance appraisals annually, even if the church cannot give raises.

Also, we can use a 90-day probationary period before the employee becomes a regular employee. Termination can be easier when employees know they have to complete

The pastor never answered, but I watched his answer unfold. They burned out youth pastors at the rate of one about every three years. Were they all unable to perform, or was the job impossible?

● *Should we give a second chance?* Before we terminate an employee, we need to consider the church's role in reconciliation and healing. If the person is unclear about what is expected in the job, we do not fire; we clarify. In the case of moral questions that are borderline, people may just need to be warned they're getting close to the cliff. People not performing up to expectations should first be told their work is being scrutinized.

---

a probationary period successfully. In some cases, it may be appropriate to extend the probationary period. Usually, however, if an employee cannot meet minimum job standards during that time, the employee should not remain on the payroll.

● *Do not violate employment laws.* Knowing the employment laws that apply to one's church is essential. For example, a church with 20 or more employees is subject to the Age Discrimination in Employment Act (ADEA) and cannot terminate an employee or encourage him or her to retire because of age. A church with 50 or more employees becomes subject to the Family and Medical Leave Act (FMLA) and cannot terminate employees who want unpaid time off to care for their sick children.

● *Use a progressive disciplinary system.* Only in extreme emergencies should an employee be fired without warning. It is better to address performance problems first with an oral warning. If that does not work, we should use a written warning. We might then put the employee on probation for at least 60 days, setting goals and meeting with the employee regularly during that time. If performance is still unacceptable, termination is the final step. It's also wise to document each step in writing.

● *Carefully arrange the termination.* It's good to conduct the termination privately, giving the employee an opportunity to resign. We shouldn't let the employee argue (the progressive disciplinary system should have set the stage), and we should ask the employee to return keys and other church property. Interestingly, human-resource professionals recommend avoiding terminations on Friday.

● *Handle references carefully.* Attorneys recommend neutral-reference policies. That means we give only "position held" and "dates worked." This protects supervisors from charges of libel or slander. Church leaders uncomfortable with following a neutral-reference policy should ask for a written release from the employee before giving references. It's important to stick to documentable facts and to avoid innuendo and gossip. If we know a former employee poses a danger to others (for example, a convicted child molester), it may be better to disclose this information, even with a neutral-reference policy.

—Julie L. Bloss

For example, as soon as my superiors confirmed my fears about Gary, I told him he would be watched for a month to see if he could meet the demands of the job, after which we would evaluate his performance and his future with us.

Nothing like this happened with Chuck. Several elders simply decided they did not want to keep him and began lobbying other elders to join their position. They talked about some failures in his work, but those were mostly a pretext; the real sticking point was personal style. Hence, there was no warning, no second chance. In fact, one elder finally told him, "Chuck, we are not going to give you a chance to prove yourself in your work, because we have seen your zeal, and we know you'll pull it off. We've decided you're not the man for this church, and so you have no real recourse."

Second chances are not necessarily easy to provide. Can the church afford to give a staff member a leave of absence to get healed? Will we invest the time and dollars to provide more training?

To be honest, I must say that Gary, although warned, did not get a second chance. I asked him to evaluate what he needed from me to do his job. He replied that he needed more time with me, more training from me, more supervision. I had to admit I could not give him that, and so we dismissed him in order to find someone who could do the ministry with less bolstering. Ruthless? Or realistic? We naturally feel uneasy about such circumstances.

● *What is God directing us to do?* The Scriptures offer scant guidance on letting workers go. Jesus stayed with Judas to the bitter end. Paul seemed to "fire" John Mark but later changed his mind. So how does God direct us?

We naturally expect him to guide us through our prayers, thoughts, and impressions. But the Bible is clear about the need for a cleansed heart. God does not collaborate with impure motives or personal anger. We must make sure a vindictive spirit is brought under control before expecting God's direction in such a sensitive issue. Also, biblical precedent tells us that by the mouth of two or three witnesses everything should be confirmed. We need to hear other leaders before proceeding.

Making the Courageous Decision

Assume we have worked through the tough questions. We have tried to balance mercy with stewardship, forgiveness with accountability. The decision becomes clear: this person must be removed from ministry responsibility. Then what? Here are seven practical approaches that can make the rough road ahead a little smoother.

● *Do it personally.* Sending a letter or memo is just too cruel. That would magnify the feelings of desertion and cultivate bitterness. A personal encounter allows for tears, anger, and other emotions that accompany such a blow. It also gives the person being terminated an opportunity to raise questions. Obviously, the news should be delivered promptly and directly by the leader who is taking the action, before the grapevine has a chance to reach the worker being terminated.

● *Do it gently.* There's no need to write a twelve-page list of the person's shortcomings. Instead, we can spend some moments imagining the pain of the person being fired, feeling the deep confusion ("I *thought* I was doing what God wanted; how could this happen?").

When we finally utter the dismissal, the person may become angry or defensive. That is the time for "a soft answer"; we needn't get into an argument. Gentleness, however, does not require dishonesty. If the person is ill-equipped for ministry or leadership, it is more harmful to pretend otherwise than to tell the truth; "faithful are the wounds of a friend." But how and when these messages are given is all-important. Sometimes the particulars are best discussed in a second meeting, after the emotional grief has dissipated.

● *Do it without bitterness or malice.* James 1:20 reminds us that "man's anger does not bring about the righteous life that God desires." We who deliver the message of dismissal must be under the Spirit's control. Emotional outbursts or attacks on the person's character are counterproductive to the goal of the person's growth and eventual healing.

● *Close off responsibilities quickly.* The last day of work ought to be within a month, if not sooner. The longer people have to drag on, the lower their productivity and the more they depress the zeal of others. A drawn-out firing process opens the door to lobbying for a reversal and excuses for poor performance. We may even begin to lose our objectivity when we start getting pressure, and begin to second-guess our decision to fire.

● *Be consistent.* If one elder says a minister was dismissed for moral reasons, while another mentions inability in preaching, the seeds of gossip have been sown. Leaders must be of one mind about the reason for the termination.

● *Be discriminating.* All the facts do not need to be divulged to those whose interest is slander or gossip. The details of a moral failure may serve to titillate warped appetites for scandal more than promote healing in the body of Christ, and lawsuits can result from inappropriate comments. We must choose our words cautiously and look out for the person's future ministry.

● *Anticipate the problems.* Not every firing comes off without backlash. Churches have been split because pastors were admired by one sector and despised by another. Asking someone to step down from the position of Sunday school superintendent can become issue number one for the next year. We need to think through possible ways to

Part V:

Volunteer-Staff Supervision

The concept of *volunteering* is actually an amazing thing when we step back to examine it: A piece of work needs doing, and no one person is compelled to do it, yet someone steps forward to take it on. Who would expect it? It counters the fundamental selfishness that rules the resolution of so many decisions. It burdens the very one who had the opportunity not to be burdened but chose to be so anyway. It doesn't make sense, humanly speaking.

Yet volunteerism is the primary means by which God's work gets accomplished.

In the best-ordered congregation, volunteers—bless their hearts—*do* the ministry of the church. They *are* the ministers. There is no church task, no ministry, no sacrament that volunteers haven't done somewhere, some time, somehow. And that's how it's supposed to be, according to the One who set up the system, issued the spiritual gifts, and rationed the time. That's how a Body functions.

And when all is going well, God's economy causes a delightful thing to happen to Christian volunteers: those who give, receive. A bedraggled college student volunteers to counsel at church camp "to help out those kids," and returns from camp—having worked hard—joyously affirmed in ministry gifts. A retired stock broker "adopts" a church flower bed for the summer, and in planting and weeding and watering, reaps more satisfaction than in his last ten years in the stock market. God doesn't recruit people only to drain them; he fills his volunteers, overflows them.

That, of course, is when all is going well. And it doesn't always. In many churches, new volunteers are scarce and old volunteers are scattering. Some situations altogether illustrate the wisdom of the old Army advice: Never volunteer. Some volunteers would try the patience of Job.

What, then, makes the difference between all going well with volunteers and all the volunteers, well, going? Answers to that question and many more fill the next four chapters.

22

The Meaning of Volunteerism

The muscled bodies that compete in the Olympics look perfect to us. They're not, of course. They still suffer with sore limbs, torn muscles, bleeding blisters, and even broken bones. But despite their human flaws, Olympic bodies are finely tuned.

The imperfect but high-performing body is a picture of an effective church, made up of imperfect but redeemed people who work together to advance God's kingdom. In reality, however, achieving high performance with a volunteer corps is not easy. In many respects, paying everyone to do the work of the ministry would seem easier than using volunteers. The church would certainly run smoother, but is running smoothly a valid goal for the body of Christ?

From the beginning of the early church, people gave their time and talents freely to spread the Good News of Christ. While Scripture does not speak against professional ministry, it does affirm that most ministry should be carried out by volunteers. Note the address of many New Testament epistles—"to all the saints."

The Bible also lays out a leadership structure of pastors, teachers, elders, and others who assume significant responsibility for the spiritual welfare of believers. But structure doesn't preclude the Bible's emphasis on total involvement of the entire Christian community.

Four Images of Ministry

Let's look at four sections of the New Testament in order to lay the theological base for church volunteers.

● *The servant leader.* The best place to begin is with our Lord, who, shortly before his death, arranged for one last time of fellowship with his beloved disciples. As the meal was served, he rose, removed his outer clothing, wrapped a towel around his waist, and commenced washing his disciples' feet, a task normally allotted to the lowliest of servants. He washed feet that had spent the day walking through dusty, unpaved roads splattered with animal excrement. John the Baptist had described himself as unfit to untie Jesus' sandals; now this same Jesus washed his disciples' feet.

The task completed (over Peter's objections), Jesus rejoined his companions at the table and said, "Now that I, your Lord and Teacher, have washed your feet, you also should wash one another's feet. I have set you an example that you should do as I have done for you. I tell you the truth, no servant is greater than his master, nor is a messenger greater than the one who sent him" (John 13:14–16).

Thus the first step in building our theology of volunteerism lies in recognizing that those who carry leadership positions in the church also carry—first and foremost—the responsibility of serving those volunteers, in whatever lowly manner may be necessary.

● *The holy priesthood.* The apostle Peter, so vocal during the foot-washing scene, wrote, "But you are a chosen people, a royal priesthood, a holy nation, a people belonging to God, that you may declare the praises of him who called you out of darkness into his wonderful light" (1 Pet. 2:9). This verse brings into clear focus the inappropriateness of making a sacred-secular division of work and life. Today all Christians bear the responsibility originally placed on the shoulders of only a few.

There exists no hierarchy of vocation—all function as priests, although clearly not all are involved in "church" work. For Christians, there exists no "secular" vocation. As we build our theology of volunteers, we must respect the sacredness of volunteers' weekday work. Their calling to their jobs carries no less godliness or need for commitment than the pastoral vocation; within those callings the royal priesthood will minister.

● *The body concept.* The third image recognizes that every member plays an essential part in contributing to the health of the whole church. "Just as each of us has one body with many members," Paul writes, "and these members do not all have the same function, so in Christ we who are many form one body, and each member belongs to all the others" (Rom. 12:4–5).

The expansion of this imagery in 1 Corinthians 12 has particular relevance to our theology: "The eye cannot say to the hand, 'I don't need you!' And the head cannot say to the feet, 'I don't need you!' On the contrary, those parts of the body that seem to be weaker are indispensable, and the parts that we think are less honorable we treat with special honor. And the parts that are unpresentable are treated with special modesty, while our presentable parts need no special treatment. But God has combined the members of the body and has given greater honor to the parts that lacked it, so that there should be no division in the body, but that its parts should have equal concern for each other. If one part suffers, every part suffers with it; if one part is honored, every part rejoices with it" (vv. 21–26).

Our theology of volunteers must be built on a foundation of Scripture set within a cultural context. The highly individualistic emphasis of North American society almost guarantees a problem with the practice of this theology; many live unaware of how individual inaction impacts group health. However, God uses the physical body as an image of the church to drive home this point: No one within this holy priesthood may consider himself or herself unessential to the ministry of the whole.

Let's summarize for a moment: Jesus set an example of servanthood for those who function as leaders within his church, essentially a volunteer structure. Each member of the structure holds a position of honor, for each forms part of a holy priesthood. The structure suffers harm and/or inefficiency when parts of it remain inactive and do not contribute to the health and work of the whole. The question of how to avoid that harm and inefficiency leads us to a fourth portion of Scripture, which further builds our foundation.

● *The equipping leader.* The book of Ephesians, and particularly the section in chapter 4:11–16, serves as a standard of volunteerism. As a whole, Paul emphasizes unity throughout this book, and he does so in a rather unique and perhaps a bit oblique fashion. He only uses the word for unity twice (4:3, 13), but the theme comes through more clearly in the Greek text than in translation because of an unusual use of compound verbs. Fourteen times, Paul attaches the prepositional prefix *sun* (meaning "with" or "together") to his verbs, creating several compounds not found elsewhere in the New Testament. The result? An overwhelming sense of leaders working alongside followers, seeing themselves as co-laborers, joining hands and talents for the furtherance of the gospel.

The last part of chapter 4 adds further detail to the concept. God has appointed leaders charged with equipping believers to do the work of service. (Interestingly, commentators of an earlier day, particularly in England where the church operated under a pronounced clerical-lay division, inserted another comma in verse 12. The passage would thus indicate that ordained leaders were to: (1) prepare God's people, (2) do the work of service, and (3) build up the body of Christ. We may disagree in theory, but our practice often betrays us.)

Paul follows his charge that leaders spend their time equipping God's people with a goal statement in verse 13 and then a twofold purpose statement in verses 14–16. His stated goal: that all believers might reach a state of maturity characterized by unity in Christ and knowledge of Christ. The purpose statement follows: First, the knowledge of Christ will keep believers from being distracted and deceived by improper teaching. Second, the unity in Christ will keep us connected first to him, as our source, and then to each other, as each part supplies what the other part needs, all the while speaking the truth to one another in love.

From this passage we learn how servant leadership functions in this army of volunteers: not as a means to force them into service or to heap guilt on them so they reluctantly take their places—counting the days until the sentence of service runs out—but to equip them so they serve with competence.

A true theology of volunteers believes the work of God's kingdom goes on even when the formal or informal programs of the church may seem inadequately staffed. As equippers, we must ensure that God's people have an adequate knowledge of Scripture and an adequate unity in Christ so they can grow to maturity. These goals are

Determining Ministry Needs

It seems no ministry ever has enough volunteers, gifted lay leaders, or professional staff to do all the good things that could be done. So, as pastors, we are forced to determine priorities in light of limited financial and human resources.

Four Considerations

When faced with a limited number of volunteers, a lack of gifted leaders, or inadequate resources to hire enough ministry staff, four questions can help us make the most of what we have:

● *What are we doing well?* Churches, like people, have a unique set of strengths and gifts to offer the kingdom. It is important, as management experts stress, to focus on our strengths as a congregation rather than our weaknesses.

The natural tendency, however,

is to focus on our church's weaknesses, since those are readily drawn to our attention. But a focus on weaknesses, instead of shoring up our shortcomings, may undermine our ability to develop excellence in the areas we already do well. Seldom will such a focus help a church rise above mediocrity in those areas of weakness.

Since no church can do everything well, we are wise to concentrate our limited resources on those things God *has* enabled us to do well.

● *What are our potentially fatal flaws?* If stressing general weaknesses is counterproductive, ignoring certain weakness can be fatal.

A "fatal flaw" is a ministry deficiency that either drives people away from our church or keeps significant numbers from coming in the first place. For example, if a

best accomplished through the teaching and worship ministries of the local church, and the effectiveness of that teaching and worship demands intense volunteer involvement.

An Evaluation

Is it possible that we have talked ourselves into a circle? By freeing God's people to see their work as sacred, are we allowing them to abandon the needs of the church? Or could it be that freeing people to see all work as ministry will help them see their need for further instruction and preparation for that ministry?

When building a theology of volunteerism, many tend to start with a need ("We have a great need for Sunday school teachers or ushers or host homes for visiting missionaries or worship leaders or gardeners or secretarial help") and then move to Scripture to justify that need. How easy to remind church members, "You were saved to serve"! But, when we start with the Scriptures, we learn that leaders

church has no one who can carry a tune, the poor quality of music may make people feel uncomfortable with its worship. Ministry weaknesses that scatter people to the winds require our immediate and full attention.

● *Whom are we reaching?* In marketing, it's called "finding your niche." Every church has a personality that can be seen in the profile of the average attender. While not everyone fits into this profile, the majority do. Whatever the profile, a church will have the most success reaching those closest to their profile. Those who don't fit the profile can still be reached, but, more often than not, they'll end up settling at the church down the street where they can find more people like themselves.

Since our human resources are limited, it's best to focus our efforts on ministries and programs that fit our capabilities, reaching those we are best equipped to disciple over the years. A church full of young

families probably would do well to focus on the nursery and kids programs rather than beginning a senior citizens fellowship.

● *Who else is already doing it?* This is a question churches too seldom ask. If another church has a fantastic Christian school, a thriving midweek children's ministry, or a successful seniors program, why not encourage people with those needs and interests to become involved in those programs? Our competition is found in the world, not in other churches.

This approach can be much more effective—and efficient—than trying to duplicate these ministries. Furthermore, it frees us to do what we do best, and it strengthens, rather than undercuts, the ministry of the other churches. If a ministry is not vital to our own church's health, we have the freedom to leave it to those God has burdened and gifted to do the job well.

—Larry W. Osborne

first must see themselves as servants. These servant-leaders then help
believers grow to maturity as they find their unique niche in the larger
body of believers.

When we focus on individual maturity, not slot-filling for programs,
a theology of volunteerism begins to emerge: All God's people carry
vital roles for the advancement of the gospel, and all need help in
finding those roles and learning to do their work gracefully, compe-
tently, and with maturity. Appointed church leaders hold the responsibility to develop God's people both individually and corporately. In
the process of this development, as believers recognize their own
necessity to the health of the church, church leaders—co-laborers—
can encourage them to take their rightful places of ministry, both
within the programs of the church and in the marketplace.

A theology such as this provides a base of great freedom from

Gifts and Abilities

A spiritual gift is a special attri-
bute given by the Holy Spirit to
every member of the Body of Christ
according to God's grace for use
within the context of the Body.

There are 27 spiritual gifts found
in lists in the Bible: prophecy, service, teaching, exhortation, giving,
leadership, mercy, wisdom, knowledge, faith, healing, miracles, discerning of spirits, tongues, interpretation of tongues, apostle, helps,
administration, evangelist, pastor,
celibacy, voluntary poverty, martyr-
dom, hospitality, missionary, intercession, and exorcism.

The great majority of the spiritual gifts are mentioned in three key
chapters: Romans 12, 1 Corinthians
12, and Ephesians 4. One of the primary spiritual exercises for any
Christian is to discover, develop,
and use his or her spiritual gift or
gift mix.

What Gifts Aren't

● *Natural talents.* Every person
possesses certain natural talents,
but spiritual gifts are reserved exclusively for Christians. In some
cases, God takes a natural talent in
an unbeliever and transforms it into
a spiritual gift when that person
enters the Body of Christ. But even
in such cases, the spiritual gift is
more than just a souped-up natural
talent; it is given by God.

● *Fruit.* The Fruit of the Spirit is
described in Galatians 5:22–23:
love, joy, peace, longsuffering, gentleness, goodness, faith, meekness,
and self-control (temperance). Fruit
is not discovered like the gifts. It is
developed through the believer's
walk with God. While spiritual gifts
help define what a Christian *does*,
the Fruit of the Spirit helps define
what a Christian *is*.

which to minister. With the emphasis on servant leadership and the growth of the individual, all leading to corporate health, leaders may undertake the joyous and fearful responsibility of encouraging spiritual maturity through the proper use of recruitment, training, and motivational techniques.

A Quick Look at History

This theology seems straightforward and easily drawn from the pages of Scripture. Does church history bear out the implementation of such a strategy?

Not always. From the earliest days, we see the church dividing its ranks into spiritual/unspiritual, sacred/secular, clerical/lay, orthodox/heretic. People hastened to rank themselves in some way, as if to

---

● *Roles*. Roles are Christian practices such as having faith or being a witness to the gospel. They are slightly different from the Fruit of the Spirit in that they involve more doing than being. And they are different from spiritual gifts and similar to the Fruit in that they are expected of every Christian.

Faith is a spiritual gift and Fruit of the Spirit that is also a role. Faith is required to become a Christian, but over and above this is the special gift of faith that is given by God to only a few members of the Body. The gift of faith is much more than the fruit of faith and role of faith that we see in an ordinary Christian. Another example is celibacy. Some are gifted with it, but all Christians must be prepared to practice the role of celibacy if single or widowed or even when on a business trip without a spouse.

The Benefits of Gifts

What happens when people discover, develop, and use their spiritual gift or gifts?

● *They become better Christians*

who can do more for God. People who know their gifts have a handle on their "spiritual job description." They find their place in the church with more ease. They tend to develop a healthy self-esteem. This does not mean they "think more highly of themselves than they ought to think." But they learn that no matter what their gift is, they are important to God and to the Body. Crippling inferiority complexes drop by the wayside when people begin to "think soberly of themselves."

● *The church is made healthier*. Ephesians 4 tells us that when spiritual gifts are in operation, the whole Body matures, and when "each separate part works as it should, the whole body grows" (Eph. 4:16 TEV). There is clearly a biblical relationship between spiritual gifts and church growth.

● *God is glorified*. First Peter 4:10–11 advises Christians to use their spiritual gifts and then adds the reason why: "That in all things God may be praised through Jesus Christ." What could be a more worthy goal than glorifying God?

—*C. Peter Wagner*

affirm the spirituality of some and to deny it in others. In time, all the work of the church became done by the clerics. A person seeking spirituality could find it only in a celibate, monastic life. That priesthood carried remarkable similarity to the Old Testament order.

With the Reformation, lay movements sprang up around Europe, movements that profoundly affected the early history of the United States. The Puritans carried a strong sense of the holiness of all life, disdaining the sacred-secular division mentioned earlier.

The church is rarely divorced from the politics of its time. When functioning in a society with a rigid hierarchy, Christ's body will often find itself with a hierarchical bent, using Scripture to justify its structure. A church functioning in a slave-supported economy will point to the Bible to justify its abominable practice. In North America, which has a democratic form of government, we believe our contributing into the decision-making process is an inalienable right, available to all. But the pastor in a tribal area of Burma is expected to make all the decisions and perform all the ministry of the local church. The concept of active lay involvement would remain inconceivable to such a person, although he might hear it taught day after day in seminary. We cannot ask the Burmese pastor to separate himself from his culture, but we can ask him to examine the New Testament: Whom does God expect to do the work of ministry?

Growing the Church

It's plausible to conclude that paid staff—and paid staff only—should do the work of the church. Throughout its history, the church has often practiced that model, and to some extent, it continues to do so. Yet such a decision would grieve the heart of God. Jesus died for all humanity, and those who become believers must grow to maturity.

The responsibility to encourage that growth has been placed on the shoulders of the church's appointed leaders—the pastors, the teachers, the prophets, the evangelists. But how do we help our volunteers grow? How do we encourage their involvement without just "using" them for the sake of corporate growth or greater numbers? How do we love their weaknesses, affirm each one as a necessary part of the body of Christ, put up with the inefficiencies of a volunteer organization, and still carry on God's work? It might just be that these questions actually define the work of ministry.

—Kenneth O. Gangel

Resources

Gonzalez, J. 1984. The story of Christianity. San Francisco: HarperCollins.

Habecker, E. 1990. Leading with a follower's heart. Wheaton, Ill.: Victor.

Hendricks, W. 1993. Exit interviews. Chicago: Moody.

Peterson, E. 1992. Under the unpredictable plant. Grand Rapids: Eerdmans.

Stevens, P. 1985. Liberating the laity. Downers Grove, Ill.: InterVarsity.

23

Volunteer Recruitment

M ost of the work of the local church is done by volunteers. If the volunteers are ministering effectively, the church is ministering effectively. If they're not, the church is not. It would be difficult, therefore, to conceive of a pastoral responsibility more important than helping volunteers be effective in their ministries.

Working with volunteers in the church involves three basic responsibilities: motivating people, guiding them to the right ministry, and supporting and supervising them as they minister.

Motivating People to Minister

Motivation is not a mysterious science. It simply requires an understanding of people and what they need. Here are a few guidelines for motivation within the church.

● *Use gratitude rather than guilt.* Guilt is probably the most powerful motivator in the church. It's quick and effective. When people are desperate to get a job done, they readily employ guilt. Yet guilt also carries a high price tag: resentment. People motivated by guilt develop a subconscious hostility toward the leader and the institution. It is far better to motivate by appealing to gratitude—gratitude to God for all he has done.

I once attended a fundraising banquet for the seminary from which I graduated. Before I walked in, I had my check made out. For me, at the time, the gift was substantial. When the banquet host launched his appeal, he told how seven or eight faculty members were paid less than garbage collectors in New York City. (I remember thinking, *So what? Most people in this room are paid less than garbage collectors in New York City.*) His underlying message was, "You, the supporters of the school, don't pay the faculty enough." He was laying guilt on us.

I felt bad. I had wanted to give cheerfully. By the time he'd finished his speech, I had folded my check and put it in my pocket. I was sitting at the head table, but when the ice-cream bucket came by, I didn't put in my check.

That host could have motivated by gratitude: "This faculty has had a great impact on your life. You're benefiting from them every day. You've got their books; you've got their lectures; you've got their example. God has blessed you through them. In response to the tremendous gift you've been given, you have an opportunity to say thank you." If he would have said that, I probably would have torn up my check and written one for more.

The same principle applies to motivating people to volunteer. We can say, "God has taught us wonderful things. He has richly blessed us. Here is a great opportunity God has given us to say thank you, to pass on his blessings to somebody else." That kind of appeal may not have an immediate effect, but for the long term, it's much more effective.

● *Tap into people's existing dissatisfactions.* A satisfied need never motivates anyone. People who are totally satisfied won't even get up in the morning. Before they can be motivated to do anything, they must be dissatisfied. The wonderful thing about the church is that within it there is always an adequate supply of dissatisfaction.

One person is dissatisfied by the loss of identity in a society that treats him more and more like a number. The church can say, "Here is a chance for you to be a significant person in a ministry." Another person is dissatisfied with the church facilities. That becomes a motivation for her to help plan for new facilities.

Many churches have an abundance of leaders, and some people are dissatisfied because they want more opportunity to lead. We can say, "Do you want to run things? If you have those skills, great! We'll start another church for you to help lead." We need to look for ways to harness people's dissatisfaction for ministry.

● *Give volunteers more than they put in.* This could be terribly misunderstood, but the main thing that keeps volunteers motivated is the sense they are getting more out of their service than they are putting into it. If they reach the point where they perceive they are giving more than they're getting, they will quit.

Teachers often say, "I get more out of the class by teaching it than I could by sitting and listening to the lesson." People volunteer so they can experience personal growth, find the satisfaction of serving God, become part of a significant organization, or enjoy camaraderie with other workers.

For example, Sunday school superintendents hold departmental meetings that people think are designed primarily to plan for the next quarter. But the main purpose of the meeting is to say to teachers, "When you're alone teaching six kids, really you are not alone. You're part of a team. If you become sick or go on vacation, somebody else will take over." The feeling of camaraderie the teachers take from these meetings gives them the motivation to continue.

Even if a task involves pain or frustration, when people feel they are gaining significantly from it, they will continue to serve. This means we can expect a lot from people as long as we "pay" them a lot.

For example, several years ago our church held a seminar with a church growth consultant. As part of it, we scheduled a board meeting for 1:00 on a Friday afternoon. Although all the board members work on Friday afternoon, everyone was there. Afterward, the consultant commented that having everyone attend wasn't typical. I had never considered the possibility that anybody *wouldn't* come. I expected the board members to do whatever they had to do—take vacation, if necessary—to be there.

They are willing to do that, however, because their pay is high. Those board members consider board meetings the highlight of their month. In addition, if an elder calls me he gets through immediately. I might not change my schedule for somebody else's wedding, but when elders' kids get married, I'm there. I build my life around them and give them preferential treatment, and they know that. Volunteers' performance remains high when their pay remains high.

Rules for Recruiting

The church has a long history of using people to meet institutional needs. Not only is this approach disrespectful, but it also destroys motivation. Many churches are now learning to reverse the process, to begin not with the institution's needs but with the individual's gifts. Instead of saying, "We need a nursery worker for the fifth Sunday of the month," congregations are learning to ask, "Where should you be serving Jesus Christ?" With this approach, people become better matched to their responsibilities.

Admittedly, this takes time. For example, our church has established a policy that people cannot be asked to serve until their names have been cleared through the staff. This means most of our staff meeting is spent talking about where people can be deployed in ministry. If no one on staff knows a person, a staff member will meet with the person and discuss his or her spiritual development and interests.

Although this approach consumes everyone's time, it protects people. If, for example, a volunteer is needed urgently in a music program and the pastor who visits the home reports to the staff, "This couple has tensions in their marriage. The commitment to rehearsals wouldn't be good for them right now; they need the time at home," the pastoral staff needs to respect that and determine to find somebody else or shut down that part of the music program.

Frankly, people respond better to an invitation when they discover it comes only after careful consideration by the staff. Suppose, for example, a person is gifted both in music and in working with teens, but because he's starting a new business, he doesn't have time to work in both areas. If we decide the greater need is in youth ministry, the youth pastor would explain to this person that he had been considered for another area but is being asked to take on only one responsibility. Volunteers recognize that as interest in them.

Some churches also offer human-resources programs that consist of a seminar, some tests, and an interview with a leader skilled in personnel management. Such programs can help people identify their interests and gifts and look for ways they can use them in the church.

The Demographics of Volunteerism

Church attenders tend to be either *takers* or *givers*. Effective leaders move people from being takers to givers (Eph. 4:11–12). But how?

Contemporary realities make it increasingly difficult to produce givers. The U.S. Bureau of Labor Statistics estimates that 78 percent of women over 40—traditionally the largest pool for volunteers—are employed. George Barna estimates that 56 percent of *all* women are working outside the home (*The Frog in the Kettle*, Regal 1990).

For single-parent homes, this may mean that the parent (often the mother) is living in a "survival mode." For her, volunteering four or five hours a week is out of the question. For two-parent homes, high expectations and high expenses often require both to work. And stay-at-home Moms may be home schooling their children. Time seems tight for everyone everywhere.

Tapping a Shrinking Pool

As pastors, we can either throw our hands up in despair or find positive ways of responding, such as:

● *Researching local demographics.* Local demographics can help identify both problems and possibilities. We can research our own constituency by answering questions such as: How many single-parent homes are in the church? How many two-career couples? What is the percentage of home-schooling families? How many senior adults are in the area? What other community programs rely on volunteers, and how are they recruiting their teams? How much time are those working outside the home spending in commuting?

If a large number of families are led by single mothers or dual-career couples, the midday shortage of volunteers may mean ministry

Another way to tap talent involves asking a group to identify specific talents among its members. For example, for some reason, people are willing to admit they have almost any gift except evangelism. To determine who has that gift, a leader may want to go to an adult Sunday school class—fifty to ninety people who know each other reasonably well—and ask everyone to write down names of people in the group who have the gift of evangelism. Typically, about ten names are repeated. Then a pastor can approach these ten people and say, "The people who have prayed and studied with you—those who know you best—say you have the gift of evangelism. Would you like to develop that gift and use it more?"

Before a person is approached about a position, a job description needs to be developed that outlines the qualifications, relationships, and responsibilities, including term of service. This again helps people determine if the position is right for them.

Recruiting works better when the invitation comes not from some

---

should be consolidated on weekends.

● *Thinking creatively.* To break out of old paradigms when they don't work, we need to ask creative questions, such as: How can the retired community be brought into action? How do people with weekend or flex-time jobs fit the volunteer scenario? Can a job that takes one person ten hours a week to do be done by ten volunteers doing one hour each?

When researchers James Patterson and Peter Kim asked people if they would volunteer if the work addressed our country's real problems, they discovered "a majority of Americans said that they would volunteer up to three weeks right now. Fifty-eight percent of the American people want to help fix this country, but no one is orchestrating the tremendous energies waiting to be put to work" (*The Day America Told the Truth,* Prentice-Hall 1991). But these volunteers required a clear-cut cause, and their willingness to give up three weeks of vacation

time may indicate their preference for short-term, quick-impact, and self-contained programs.

Trying Fresh Approaches

The key question for all groups is: How can we redesign our volunteer endeavors to attract the people we need, given local demographics? Good approaches include:

● *Consolidate training.* For example, hold Sunday school–teacher meetings for three hours once per month rather than every week for an hour.

● *Rewrite volunteer tasks.* Make them more manageable and realistic, given the time that people have available.

● *Recruit retirees as recruiters.* They will be the most effective in recruiting their peers.

● *Offer quality training.* This communicates the church's devotion to a quality program that demands excellence.

—*Paul Borthwick*

full-time church recruiter but from a person involved in that very ministry. Then the invitation is not "Will you do this job?" but rather "Will you join me in doing this job?"

In addition, it's important to recruit well in advance of the assignment's starting date. Recruiting Sunday-school teachers for the fall shouldn't take place in August; it should happen in April. This shows respect for volunteers and gives them time to think and pray about the commitment. The carefully considered commitment is much stronger than the one made hastily.

Normally, a person's first assignment should be small. We wouldn't want to ask someone to teach a large adult group, for example, if we hadn't first seen the person teach as a substitute. Removing people from a position causes them to lose face and to feel they need to find another congregation.

Motivation Versus Manipulation

It has been said that the difference between motivation and manipulation is the quenching of thirst. If so, the key for leaders is to look for thirsty people and identify their thirst. Effective motivators ask themselves, *What kind of water do I have to satisfy that kind of thirst?*

Walking the Fine Line

Motivation is getting people to do something out of mutual advantage. Manipulation is getting people to do what we want them to do, primarily for *our* advantage. Manipulation carries a hidden agenda. Motivation carries an open agenda, allowing for honesty.

Sometimes only a fine line separates the two. For example, it is possible to *motivate* a person without that person knowing what we are doing. We must guard ourselves against becoming manipulators by doing three things: First, recognizing how close we are to manipulation; second, setting a checkpoint, and if the technique doesn't produce a genuine thirst, discontinuing it; third, refusing to use immoral means, even for righteous ends (if that were possible).

Means of Motivating

What are some motivational means? How can we bring out the best in people without resorting to manipulative tactics?

● *Establish a friendly atmosphere.* When we've genuinely motivated someone, we can look that person in the eye and know we have an honest, friendly relationship between us. For this, we need people on our staffs we can motivate with integrity. Some personalities, however, we naturally tend to manipulate, even though we don't intend to. This should be considered when bringing volunteers on board.

● *Enjoy people's uniqueness.* Being friends is beneficial, but having the same tastes is not necessary. As managers, we need to share in our

Of course, no matter how thoroughly we do these things, some placements won't work. Sometimes a person will say, "I've tried this for six months, but it's not my gift."

When that happens, we need to say, "Fine. Then what would you like your ministry to be?"

Critical Ministries and Critical Support

When there aren't enough volunteers to staff a program, leaders need to ask, "Is this something we shouldn't be doing?" Theologically, we assume God will never expect us to do something for which he will not provide the resources. If the resources aren't there, we need to ask, "Should this be dropped?"

The answer lies, in part, in whether the ministry is essential. At our

---

workers' excitement for their work and appreciate their work for the beauty in it. Workers will sense our appreciation and be motivated by it.

● *Know a person's capabilities.* We should objectively evaluate a volunteer's skills, potential capacities, level of commitment, ability to be motivated, discipline, and intensity. This is necessary if we are to nurture our volunteers in their natural abilities without pushing them beyond their real limitations.

● *Know how much responsibility a person can take.* Good leaders know if their people work best when given assignments that detail what is to be done or when given responsibility that leaves the initiative up to them.

● *Look for mutual benefits.* We should look for individuals who want to develop skills from which the church can also benefit. If a person has potential, a good question to ask is: "You have a lot more talent than you've been able to put to use. How much effort are you willing to exert if we give you the opportunity to develop that talent?"

● *Be honest about your goals.* A young minister once sought advice on how he could build his small church into a big church. When asked why he wanted to see this happen, he had to admit, "Frankly, the size church I've got can't pay me enough to live on." For him to begin an evangelism program, he would have to manipulate people. He wouldn't be able to be honest about it.

● *Give a person a reputation to uphold.* Public recognition as well as knowledgeable compliments motivate volunteers, when done with integrity. For example, I know of a boss who had a way of saying nice —and true—things about his workers that eventually got back to them. The workers appreciated it and worked hard to uphold their good reputation.

● *Enjoy working, and let it show.* When staff see we are truly grateful for the work we are privileged to do, they intuit that they can enjoy their work as well.

As we honestly and openly offer water to parched people, we are not manipulating, but motivating.

—*Fred Smith, Sr.*

church, for example, morning worship, Sunday school, and child care would be seen as essential. People expect these basic programs in a contemporary American church, so we would not allow these areas to go unstaffed. But when we didn't have enough men for the men's choir, we dropped the choir. We organized a ten-kilometer run to increase visibility and outreach in the community, but when we didn't have enough volunteers anymore, we cut the program. These we can live without. Sunday school we cannot.

In addition, some volunteer roles are critical to church life. One is a role that might be called "the introducer." This person instinctively knows how to connect a visitor with another person, and then he or she moves on to find the next visitor. This person tends to wander through the halls, and we forgive him or her for not coming to worship services. It is important to not tie up the congregation's introducer in teaching Sunday school. Growth depends on having one or more introducers free to do their work.

Other people to look for are the "epaulet men." On the eve of the Battle of Saratoga in 1778, Daniel Morgan led his Morgan's Rifles against the British army led by Gentleman Johnny Burgoyne. Morgan compared his troops and ammunition to the strength of the British, and it was obvious his Rifles were going to lose the battle. So the night before the battle, Morgan gathered his men and said, "Don't waste your shot on those who fight for sixpence a day. Aim for the epaulet men"—the officers, those who wore insignia on their shoulders.

The next day, Morgan's Rifles went into battle. When they had a private in their sights, they didn't pull the trigger. They waited until they saw an epaulet man. Following this strategy, Morgan's Rifles won the Battle of Saratoga, and some historians say that was the determining battle of the Revolutionary War.

In the church, we also win or lose by determining who wears the epaulets. If we recognize the leaders and nurture them, the privates will line up behind them.

Supervising Volunteers

In most churches, the pastor cannot possibly monitor every volunteer position. How, then, can a pastor hope to ensure that people are performing well and conscientiously?

The first and most important thing we can do is establish the corporate ethos. We can't manage every person, but we can manage the corporate atmosphere, which in turn will govern those people. We can create an atmosphere that is upbeat, biblically based, rooted in prayer. We can set a climate that includes making proposals before we do things, being accountable, and not operating unilaterally. Those principles come to be understood throughout the organization.

How is this ethos created? By the way a pastor relates to people he or she supervises directly. These people, in turn, treat others the way they have been supervised, and the approach ripples through the organization.

It's good to demonstrate to those we supervise that we're there to serve them. After board meetings, for example, we can stay around to pick up the room. That serves both board members and the custodian. Pretty soon, people will begin to say, "If the pastor will do that for me, I'm going to do that for other people."

Patterns like these eventually duplicate themselves in the organization. I have worked with youth pastors who serve their volunteers so well that they had a waiting list of people to serve.

We never want volunteers to be recruited and then abandoned. We must understand that if someone asks a teacher, "Will you teach next year?" but has not talked with that teacher all year long, the teacher probably won't reenlist. The best way to avoid that is to create a corporate ethos that says ongoing support is essential. We can create that ethos by continually supporting those people we directly supervise.

—Leith Anderson

Resources

Anderson, L. 1990. Dying for change. Minneapolis: Bethany.

Anderson, L. 1992. A church for the 21st century. Minneapolis: Bethany.

Drucker, P. 1990. Managing the nonprofit organization. New York: HarperCollins.

Schaller, L. 1977. Survival tactics in the parish. Nashville: Abingdon.

Schaller, L. 1980. The multiple staff and the larger church. Nashville: Abingdon.

Schaller, L. 1988. The senior minister. Nashville: Abingdon.

Handling a Lack of Volunteers

Even the best churches face times when no one wants a particular job. We may try a variety of recruiting strategies, but when the traditional strategies fail, what then?

Ask Key Questions

Before throwing up their hands in despair, both pastors and church boards need to ask themselves several questions. While the questions may not solve the crisis, they will provide new perspectives on it.

● *Should we drop the program?* From time to time, each ministry should be reexamined. A lack of workers, especially when such a shortage becomes chronic, may indicate the ministry has outlived its usefulness.

When surgery put a released-time teacher on the disabled list, the Christian education board had to ask, "What would be the impact of discontinuing the program?" The conclusion, honestly stated, was that they would have a bruised self-perception and nothing more. The released-time program had been seen as the church's effort to evangelize a changing neighborhood, despite the lack of enthusiastic response by the Hispanic children. To drop the class might even force the church to become more realistic about its relationship to the neighborhood.

● *Is there any harm in maintaining the status quo?* What would be harmed by continuing the existing program without the staff we feel we need? Unfortunately, this question frequently is answered by adults who have not spent an hour in an inadequately staffed Sunday school class! Yet there is a time when the short-term harm is an acceptable risk, when, for example, greater harm may be inflicted by rushing spiritually or socially immature adults into leadership. But the emphasis is on *short-term.*

● *Have we tried other programming approaches?* Could other activities accomplish the same ministry goals? Children's church had become impossible to staff at Greenwood Assembly. For one thing, no one really understood what it was supposed to accomplish. Further, there were too few curriculum materials for the volunteers.

Then one teacher suggested the grade-school children be taught to worship through creating puppet programs for the preschoolers. With his enthusiasm, the sewing ability of one of the elderly women, and some children's Bible story and

music tapes, Churchtime Puppets became part of the educational program. Volunteers were much easier to secure, since most adults had seen Muppets on TV and had enough child in them to be willing to work with the idea. In this case, innovation captured the imagination of people whose abilities had been overlooked in the previous recruitment process.

● *Shall we dramatize the need?* When the previous questions have been asked without a satisfactory solution, we may want to consider dramatizing the need for workers. Caution is advised, however. Drama should not be used primarily to create guilt, but rather vision, and workers obtained in this manner likely will need immediate on-the-job training to be effective.

Obtaining preschool Sunday-school teachers seemed impossible in a major West Coast church. The church had provided a full-time staff member and two part-time helpers, but still the ratio of learners to teacher was about 13:1. So one Sunday, at the invitation of the pastor, the entire 3-year-old department was led, hand in hand, down the center aisle of the church during morning worship. The pastor sat down with children all around him and expressed his deep concern that Christian people were not available to teach the love of Christ to such wonderful children as these. Then he taught a brief lesson, with the children responding. For the immediate future the recruitment problem was solved.

—*Mark H. Senter III*

Guiding Ill-Suited Volunteers

Sometimes volunteers are misplaced or ineffective. As pastors, what should we do when we have problems with volunteers? Let's say I am confronted with a volunteer choir director who is unbending in opposition to the direction the church leadership is taking worship. How should I handle it?

● *Inquire into motives.* I should ask myself, *Do I want him removed just because my predecessor warned me to watch out for him? Or is it because he threatens my leadership? Or my power base?* I need to be certain I'm taking action for the right reasons—not to protect my ego.

● *Determine if I plan to stay or leave.* I need to be certain I'm committed to the church over the long haul if I'm going to disrupt the system and replace a choir director who's been there for years. After all, for better or worse, the system has been operating for many years. My entering a power struggle with a person, removing him or her, and then my leaving the church would seriously damage morale.

● *Think in pastoral, not institutional terms.* The Scriptures teach that each person has a place for ministry in the body. The choir director needs to be honored and given another opportunity to continue his or her service to the Lord. No believer should be deprived of this privilege unless extreme circumstances warrant it.

● *Appoint a study team.* Creating a worship study team of perhaps six people that includes the choir director may provide the right context for aligning vision. I might say

to them, "I'm looking for instruction on the styles of worship that have been acceptable in the past. At the same time, I'd like to have you work with me in examining other styles of worship that have found favor in different parts of the country. Perhaps some could be adapted for our use."

● *Develop a group of dreamers.* It may be a good idea to form a second group that could gather unofficially as an advisory body to pray, dream dreams, and thoughtfully consider the future God would have for us as a congregation.

Both groups can protect me from becoming arbitrary in my judgments or actions toward the choir director. No one involved in leadership can trust his or her own judgment all the time.

If the two teams have done their work, they will eventually move beyond the arena of principles to application. In time, they will conclude that the music selection needs to be addressed. That's why the process needs time. Immediate confrontations, while sometimes necessary, can short-circuit the process the groups are moving through.

● *Don't micromanage.* Is it really necessary that I choose all the hymns? Is no one else competent? The choir director may be incapable of selecting the right worship music. Then again, he might be able to rise to the occasion. If I attempt to micromanage, I'll never discover the truth.

● *Follow up with love.* If I have to remove the volunteer director, and the hammer falls, I should immediately send people to minister to him, reaffirming our love for him. And I need to do everything I can to maintain a relationship with him through personal calls, telephone conversations, and notes of appreciation. The action will still sting, but as little as possible.

● *Leave the light on.* Anger is a common reaction to losing one's job. People storm out the door and promise never to return. But some do return, if given the chance.

—E. LeRoy Lawson

24

Volunteer Training

Kimmie and Allen, newly married, want to find a place of service in their church. Ed, the director of Christian education, needs a teacher for the junior high class. He approaches this young couple and encourages them to take the position. Kimmie and Allen hesitate, since they have no experience with this age group. Ed, however, assures them they will be fine and says, "You were teenagers not too long ago yourselves." So they agree to teach the junior high class. He makes sure they have a copy of the teacher's guide for the Sunday school quarterly, shows them where the class meets, and checks that slot off his list, relieved to have one more position filled.

This scenario takes place often, and we might expect one of three possible outcomes:

• Allen and Kimmie discover they have a passionate love for teenagers. They also discover immense reservoirs of creativity with their teaching skills and spend hours each week coming up with new and innovative ways to explain the Word of God. They begin investigating learning-style theories, invest in a large personal library of teaching aids, and eventually end up writing their own book which describes how they grew a class of 10 uninspired teens into a thriving group of 200.

You will probably find this the most unlikely outcome of all the possibilities.

• Allen and Kimmie resign six weeks later after Kimmie sat on a wad of chewing gum placed on her chair by a high-spirited student. That incident alone is not what caused them to quit, however. It came after six weeks of spit wads, paper airplanes, and deliberate yawns. Class attention waned whenever Allen read aloud from the teacher's manual.

Meanwhile, Ed, busy in the 2-year-old room (which he had not been able to adequately staff), had not checked on them during that time. He knew nothing of their frustrations. Allen and Kimmie, embarrassed by their complete failure to control the class, decided that quitting and leaving the church presented the best solution. They resolved never again to volunteer for church ministry.

Some variation on this theme occurs more often than any of us would like to admit.

● Allen and Kimmie serve faithfully in this position for two years. The class neither grows nor declines, though some young people respond with real gratefulness to their continued efforts. However, they note two disturbing trends. One, they feel cut off from church life because of their Sunday-morning isolation from other adults. Two, they find themselves dreading Sunday mornings, because they don't know how to prepare their lessons with more creativity. Furthermore, they see little spiritual growth among their students.

They come home exhausted from church, and wonder how much longer before they can gracefully bow out. They don't know where to go for creative resources. Ed, the c.e. director, seems so busy plugging holes, they hate to bug him with their puny needs. They don't know if anyone would take their place if they quit, so they feel chained to the class. They feel drained and unenthusiastic, and wonder whether they are helping or hurting their students.

This is the most likely situation—saints quietly doing their work but aching for pastoral care and better training.

Would any well-run business consider putting someone in a responsible post without first giving adequate preparation and training? Not unless it wanted to invite disaster. Before Jesus' disciples were sent out, they had spent a great deal of time with him—observing, learning, doing. To follow this pattern, we could using a three-step approach: preparation, implementation, and evaluation. The acronym PIE makes it easy to remember the order.

Training also works best when we recruit people on the basis of their gifts and interests. It makes no more sense to enlist a choir member who cannot carry a tune than to put someone who dislikes children in the nursery. Volunteers may need to learn new skills, but they should at least be developing an area of interest.

Preparation

Several things can be done to prepare future workers to be more receptive toward a new assignment and ultimately more successful in it.

First, we can set the climate. Many enter new learning experiences with apprehension because of previous bad experiences. We can assure people they won't be asked to undertake ministry for which they are inadequately prepared. It may work best to establish a partnership with learners, actively encouraging their ideas and suggestions. A schoolroom atmosphere or authoritative teacher role may prove counterproductive.

Most trainers hold leadership positions in their particular ministry areas, yet, we may first have to train the trainers. Perhaps a refresher course on communication skills and different learning styles would prove helpful. Although this may seem to delay progress, poorly trained teachers producing poorly trained volunteers would be worse.

Next we define the task. Some skip this step to avoid overwhelming volunteers with details. Others assume volunteers already understand what is expected of them. A thorough job description outlining expectations is one simple safeguard to ensure that the task is adequately defined.

We can flesh out a job description from the following skeleton outline: (1) Position title. (2) Position purpose. How does it fit into the mission of the whole church? (3) Description of function. How could the job be summarized? (4) Qualifications. What characteristics will be required of the worker? (5) Responsibilities. What are the specific assignments and expectations? (6) Accountability. To whom and for whom will the person in this position be accountable? (7) Committees. Does this position involve serving on any committees? (8) Goals for the year. What measurable objectives will be used to evaluate job performance?

Third, we provide some model of the ministry. We may require volunteers to spend time with an effective leader who performs the task well. It may be necessary to pay for the prospective worker to attend training seminars or other churches where the particular ministry already thrives. Depending on their initial skill levels, some may need more time than others to observe.

Fourth, we motivate volunteers. Volunteers should be encouraged to think beyond the current specific task. We should let them see long-range benefits of learning new skills. Here are opportunities to be responsible members of the Body of Christ—a chance to discover their significance within the kingdom. If we can't show that the job has any real significance, we should probably discard it. Here also may be stepping stones to further opportunities for work and ministry.

Implementation

Having set the stage, next we'll need to push volunteers into the spotlight. Some may require more nudging than others, but they all must eventually leave the practice hall. Volunteers need to develop their individual styles, so we'll want to back off a bit. If we stay too close, we may inhibit their creative development and build frustration at the same time.

Still, it's not easy to let go. To do so requires personal maturity and an awareness that the Spirit will continue to work in the life of our volunteers. We also must be willing to give a volunteer room to fail; most of us learn more from failure than from success.

Here we face a difficult balancing act. We want to develop individual ministries without jeopardizing the end product in the life of the church. We cannot ignore the need to strive for the best possible ministries. We want to entice people to Christ, not repel them. This leads us to our tightrope act: giving people room to fail and thereby grow in ministry, while at the same time doing our best to reach an increasingly complicated world.

A business organization seeking to develop a superior product will

---

Mentoring

Pastors don't receive a lot of formal training in mentoring. Leading worship, yes. Preaching and teaching, yes. Administration and pastoral care, yes. But help in mentoring others? Not likely.

Discipling and mentoring is the flip side of the pastor's public roles of teacher, prophet, and priest. The mentor helps the person mentored discover the truth, follow Christ's way, and know God's comfort, but in a one-to-one relationship.

Mentoring Relationships

A mentoring relationship is primarily a friendship. Each mentoring situation is unique, but there are several things that can help us develop meaningful relationships with those we mentor. Consider these four:

● *Create encounters.* We can't mentor unless we have contact with people. In my case, I deliberately become a part of small groups so that I might meet people whom I can mentor. For example, I've offered a special theological study group in the spring and fall. For six weeks I have the chance to get close to certain people. Even though larger groups sometimes come, it still opens doors so I can get to know a few of them.

Retreats we attend, and even Sunday-morning preaching, may also open the door for meeting people. We can watch especially for those who make the effort to make an appointment or come talk to us as a result of those encounters.

● *Fade into the relationship.* Naturally, we can't just announce to a likely candidate, "I'm your mentor. I'm going to shape your life." Instead, we have to send signals that let a person know his or her life will be safe with us molding it,

look for the top available personnel—those with the right qualifications and appropriate skills. The church, however, has a different work force from which to draw. As a result, Dayton and Engstrom (1979, 39) call the church the most sophisticated and the most difficult organization to manage. They explain it this way:

> This organization, by definition, accepts the "walking wounded" along with the skilled and unskilled. Imagine how you would feel if one day there were a knock at the door of the business you were managing. Outside are four men carrying another on a stretcher. Their friend is deaf and dumb and physically incapacitated but "loves the Lord and wants to be a member of your organization." What would you do with such a person? He doesn't fit any job description that you have anywhere. The manager of any organization with the sole purpose of accomplishing a task would only say, "Sorry," and send the person away. Yet that is the dilemma faced by the pastor (manager) of the local church.

---

because in the end, it's the other person who has to trust us to be a mentor. We'll typically have to stop teaching in order to listen and to give encouragement where we see spiritual growth. When those signals are flashed time and again, the people we're interested in mentoring begin to let us see more and more of their life.

● *Offer regular check-ins.* Mentoring is rarely an intense, organized relationship. We won't necessarily have a list of people we contact each week, week in and week out. It's more of a natural interaction with people when we happen to see them. Still, we have to make the effort to stay in touch; we want to give people opportunities to check in, to tell us how they're doing and what they're thinking about.

Sometimes it is beneficial to organize opportunities for people to check in. For instance, I regularly offer writing groups, where writers and poets share their work with each other. But I also want this to be a place where before or after and even during the meeting, individuals will briefly and informally tell me what's going on with them.

● *Fade out of the relationship.* Mentoring is not like a therapeutic relationship. It's not seven weeks of sessions that are then terminated. We can think of it more as an ongoing, highly flexible relationship, checking in with another human being, possibly for the rest of life.

There are different levels of involvement, however, and over time, intense mentoring will give way to less-regular, more-infrequent meetings. For example, if I have a good mentoring relationship, even if I haven't seen the person for months, we can check in with each other in a matter of minutes. I find out quickly what the person is thinking, where he is growing, where he is hurting. Consequently, we don't necessarily become overloaded with mentoring relationships, because, while some are relatively intense for a time, they don't remain that way.

—*Earl F. Palmer*

The church offers an open door to the world. Whoever desires a place in the body of Christ will have some ministry to develop and fulfill. As we seek to set up effective training programs, we may find it helpful to take some hints from W. Edwards Deming. His genius revitalized Japanese industry, directing changes that caused the phrase "made in Japan" to be transformed from a symbol of shoddiness into a sign of quality. Here are some suggestions from his business work which find application in a church setting (Walton 1986, 34–36):

● *Institute training.* Workers frequently learn their jobs from those

---

Resources for Training Volunteers

Recruiting volunteers is tough, but keeping them is tougher. The key for recruiting and keeping volunteers, say the experts, is teamwork and training.

Leith Anderson, in *Dying for Change* (Bethany House 1990), points out that "baby boomers tend to respond well to institutions that have high expectations of them." He adds, however, that "with these high expectations must come the provision of enablement to meet them. Enablement means teaching, training, counseling, support, discipline, role models, classes, books, and other tools."

For pastors, the big question is: Where do we find the time and resources for that intensity of training?

Cooperative Training

One answer is cooperative training events, where churches and parachurch organizations share their training resources. Such efforts are not the perfect answer for every situation, but they offer such benefits as:

● A cost-effective way to bring together high-quality resources, trainers, and learning methods.

● Training from specialists in particular ministry skills.

● Stimulating interaction among trainees as they talk with each other and discover that others face the same types of problems.

Potential Tensions

At their worst, shared training seminars can foster unhealthy competition ("Our program or church is bigger than yours") or haughty ownership ("We're so glad that you could benefit from *our* program!"). Or if volunteers are drawn from one church into another—intentionally or not—the church that loses the people may hesitate to cooperate in the future. But these problems can be forestalled if the leadership team that coordinates the training sessions is aware of them and purposes that the training be a *cooperative* event.

Another area of potential tension is within the home church. The three most common problems are (1) participants returning from training events boasting about some other church's program and

who themselves were never trained properly. Start with the top: Train the trainers first, and then move down.

- *Institute leadership.* A good supervisor does not tell people what to do or punish them for not doing it. A good supervisor leads. Leading consists of helping people do a better job and recognizing who needs individual help.
- *Continually improve.* Constantly look for ways to improve the training of your volunteers as well as your relationships with them. No one system will work for all time and in all circumstances.

---

criticizing their own, (2) participants seeing themselves as superior to those who could not attend, and (3) participants trying to implement the training *exactly* the way they received it, even when the situation calls for flexibility.

A trainee debriefing held within two weeks of the training event can avert many of these problems. The facilitator at the debriefing might ask, "How can we implement the principles we learned into our existing programs, and how can we communicate this to others who could not attend?" The facilitator can also have the group discuss the potential pitfalls and how they might be avoided.

Training Possibilities

The potential drawbacks are generally far outweighed by the advantages. Cooperative endeavors, especially those organized through a neutral umbrella organization, foster a deep sense of local or regional fellowship and provide a higher quality of training for volunteers than could be afforded by a single church. Here are ways cooperative training is happening successfully:

- *Regional Sunday-school associations* often sponsor seminars and conferences for lay leaders. The

Greater Los Angeles Sunday School Convention often draws over 10,000 delegates. The New England Association of Christian Education offers a fall training event that involves leaders from all over the Northeast.

- *Specialized training organizations* often offer programs or seminars that churches can participate in together. These include:

—Bible-study specialists, such as InterVarsity Christian Fellowship, Neighborhood Bible Studies, or the Walk Through the Bible Ministries.

—Evangelism specialists, such as Evangelism Explosion or Campus Crusade for Christ. The International Bible Society sponsors a friendship-evangelism seminar called "Love Your Neighbor to Life."

—Pastoral-care specialists, such as Stephen Ministries.

—Youth-ministry specialists, such as Youth Specialities, *Group* magazine, and Son Life.

Local ministerial associations, the Christian Management Association, denominational headquarters, Christian radio and television stations, bookstores, Christian publications, and Christian schools or seminaries are good starting points for gathering information on these training specialists.

—Paul Borthwick

● *Drive out fear.* Encourage your volunteers to ask questions and freely express their concerns and doubts. Deming notes an appalling economic loss from simple fear. We may assume an even greater loss where questioning is not freely permitted.

● *Break down barriers between staff areas.* Deming seems to have understood the scriptural principle of the body: We need to function as a whole, not as disconnected parts. We need to encourage communication between different departments and among staff and volunteers, letting them learn from one another's mistakes and successes. We should make sure workers understand the main mission of the church, so they don't develop conflicting goals and projects.

● *Remove barriers to "pride" of workmanship.* Make an investment in good equipment and curricular materials. If the ministry carries enough importance to take the valuable time of a volunteer, it also carries enough importance for adequate funding so that the volunteer has the necessary tools for excellence.

● *Institute a vigorous program of education and retraining.* Make this a priority, not a last-ditch effort to save dying programs. Keep up on the latest developments and be prepared to make a financial investment in your volunteers with high-quality training.

● *Take action to accomplish the transformation.* None of this will happen without commitment and leadership from the top. The commitment to good training starts in the pastor's office; volunteers will not do it on their own.

Deming goes on to say that lack of constancy of purpose, an emphasis on short-term results, and management mobility are three means to kill the goal of quality.

Evaluation

Finally, leaders must provide adequate feedback to those serving with them. Volunteers left to work on their own without accountability and evaluation rarely continue to work effectively. The story of Barbara illustrates this graphically and painfully.

Barbara, always enthusiastic and able to serve nearly full-time as a volunteer, had a vision—a women's ministry encompassing all the needs and talents of the women in her church, enabling them to reach far and wide into the community. She listed her goals: Bible studies with highly trained teachers, support groups for those who had been raped and/or sexually abused, structured mentoring of younger women by more mature women, a ministry of care and mercy for those in financial difficulties or facing serious family illness, holiday parties for underprivileged children, and Saturday luncheons for women with full-time jobs who may feel estranged from many women's activities in the church.

The church responded enthusiastically and gave her the green light to go for it. But eight years later, exhausted and burned out, Barbara complained to a friend over a cup of coffee, "If I don't do the work, it never gets done. People say they'll do something, but they don't follow through. I spend so much time running around, setting up programs, propping things up, teaching Bible studies. Even worse, after we've set something up, we'll get bumped by another church activity that needs the same space."

Her friend responded, "Barbara, how much contact do you have with the pastoral staff, particularly the one who allowed all these responsibilities to come to you?"

"Almost none. We meet once a year to go over my budget requests. And every once in a while, he'll ask how things are going. He has indicated he is too busy to worry about my program. He says he has lots of confidence that I can handle this on my own."

Another question from her friend: "Do you meet regularly with the women whom you've asked to carry certain responsibilities? What is your organizational structure?"

"I have an advisory board of elders' wives with whom I meet whenever I feel like calling a meeting—really about four to five times a year. However, none of them actually takes responsibility for any programs for activities. The organizational structure is just me, I guess."

One final question: "Barbara, has anyone ever given you loving supervision over your work or taught you how to supervise others?"

"I'm really not sure what you mean."

What kind of evaluation and help could have encouraged this talented woman and kept her enthusiasm alive and well? This list later emerged from further discussions with Barbara:

- *Staff inclusion.* Barbara led a major ministry division, so even though she was not paid staff, she needed to be a part of the regularly scheduled staff meetings in order to see the significance of her ministry and how it fit within the greater scope of the church's mission.

- *Short accounts.* Barbara wanted to know immediately when she made mistakes or when correction was needed. She wanted to be able to deal with the problem as soon as possible so it would not haunt her needlessly.

- *Sound teaching.* Barbara needed to be taught sound administrative principles. The pastoral staff assumed she knew these things. In this case, it seemed more likely that both the staff and highly responsible lay leaders would have profited from a good seminar on church management and people skills.

- *Model mentoring.* Barbara needed someone to model for her the mentoring that she herself wanted to do for the women with whom she worked. It may have been necessary in her case to go outside her local church to find a woman who could adequately mentor her, but she was never encouraged to do so. Indeed, it was never mentioned as an option. In effect, she placed herself, with the blessing of the staff, in a nearly impossible situation: she was to set up a program that she had neither seen nor experienced. Good supervision would have recognized this lack in her experience and sought to remedy it.

● *Loving confrontation.* Barbara was aware of her own tendency to underdelegate. A high-energy person, she could quickly lose patience with those who did not work as she did. But she found it difficult to abandon this lifelong pattern. Barbara needed someone to care enough about her to confront her lovingly and honestly whenever she could not let go of assignments or took back tasks she had delegated.

● *Pastoral care.* Of most importance, Barbara needed to know the pastor was interested in her for more than her ability to create an effective program. She needed to sense concern for her own development and growth in Christ. Her worst discouragements came when she felt most alone, without a coach pulling for her. She knew the women in her ministry profited from this type of support, but after a while she found herself unable to give it because her own reserves were depleted.

No one is exempt from the need to be pastored. It's possible that ministry leaders need it most because of the enormous drain on their emotional energies. If we want to be effective and caring supervisors, we will recognize and meet this critical need in our volunteer staff.

Those of us who train volunteers know we face a difficult and messy task. We have to move from the theoretical (people "should" respond this way) to the personal and real, where people rarely do respond the way they "should." Our best hope lies in understanding that working with volunteers means building people first and staffing programs second.

Inadequately trained people who are seldom supported or evaluated end up hurting themselves as well as the ongoing ministry of the church. But careful preparation, implementation, and evaluation will yield solid long-term results: mature and effective believers with productive ministries.

—Kenneth O. Gangel

Resources

Dayton, E., and T. Engstrom. 1979. Strategy for leadership. Old Tappan, N.J.: Revell.

Gangel, K. 1989. Feeding and leading. Wheaton, Ill.: Victor.

Walton, M. 1986. The Deming management method. New York: Perigee Books, Putnam.

Williams, D., and K. Gangel. 1993. Volunteers for today's church. Grand Rapids: Baker.

Wilson, M. 1983. How to mobilize church volunteers. Minneapolis: Augsburg.

Retraining Veteran Workers

Volunteers can make ministry happen. But as pastors, we also know some can squelch possibilities with an attitude of "We've always done it this way," and others can begin new ministries with great ambition, only to find themselves overwhelmed.

The perennial question "How can we enable volunteer leaders to be creative, realistic, and relevant in their work?" is answered by churches that retrain their veteran volunteers in leadership and management skills.

As the world in which volunteers minister continues to change rapidly, retraining becomes increasingly important. Researcher George Barna notes in *The Frog in the Kettle* (Regal 1990) that "it is likely that ministry in the year 2000 will be as different from ministry in 1980 as ministry in 1980 was from ministry in 1900."

Ongoing Training

Job retraining involves more than helping the Sunday-school teacher make the quantum leap from flannelgraph to Nintendo, and it is more than a one-time event. Important considerations for establishing a positive retraining mentality in our churches include:

● *Language.* If we use words like *leadership development* and *resourcing* in our vocabulary, it is easier for volunteers to recognize that no one has "arrived" and that everyone's skills can be fine-tuned and updated. We can avoid the Peter Principle (the idea that one is being promoted to his or her level of incompetency) and encourage volunteers to look for opportunities for growth.

● *Example.* We need to talk honestly with our volunteer leaders about the rapidity of change in the world, and we need to demonstrate our own willingness to change and adapt. For example, if we want to inspire teachers to move beyond the traditional written and verbal teaching methods to more interactive ones that incorporate multiple media such as overhead projectors, videos, and slides, the training sessions we give them shouldn't consist of 90-minute, noninteractive lectures on educational strategies. Such a style would only reinforce the old methods (information dumping) and undermine progress.

● *Patience.* Allowing volunteers time to change is only courteous. Ousting the 30-year volunteer by demanding immediate, radical changes is a mistake. Instead, our approach should be to recruit the long-termer and, in the process, give that person the chance to change. For example, we might ask a veteran volunteer for his or her help in training others. In doing so, we will naturally be able to show that person the new techniques.

● *Expectations.* The agreement volunteers sign when first accepting volunteer positions should include expectations for regular training updates and "quality control" checks. This reaffirms leadership as an ongoing growth process.

● *Technology.* The idea here is to manage change and technology without worshipping it. Flannel-graphs may still work if the Sunday school teacher has a wonderful relationship with the students and is a great storyteller. Our retraining of volunteers should emphasize overall goals and values and only secondly introduce technologies that can help volunteers achieve these goals.

● *Fit.* Naturally, people work best when paired with jobs that match their gifts and abilities. Barna observes that burnout often results when people do jobs they are ill-equipped to undertake. Matching a person's gifts and ministry calling with the position to be given produces motivated, happy workers.

—Paul Borthwick

25

Supporting Volunteers

The idea of supporting volunteers for their church work is a relatively recent phenomenon. Prior to the early 1970s, the assumption was that the church (or any community) was supported *by* volunteers. Being part of a community meant serving that community.

In 1973, President Richard Nixon changed the nation's understanding of volunteer service when he redefined volunteerism by paying members of the "all-volunteer army" a wage comparable to the private sector. Military volunteers (usually drafted, oddly enough!) no longer served only out of loyalty to the country, but increasingly for personal gain.

As with most cultural trends, the concept of supporting volunteers soon became a major concern in church. Biblically speaking, however, the idea of leaders serving (supporting) followers is not something new or inappropriate. Jesus himself stated, "The Son of Man did not come to be served, but to serve, and to give his life as a ransom for many" (Matt. 20:28).

Unfortunately, attempts by the church to support volunteers have sometimes resulted in a greater emphasis on what the leaders should do than on what the volunteers needed. Today it is accepted that a "one size fits all" volunteer-support system doesn't work. But what does work? How can we specifically support our volunteers as they support the church?

The Readiness of Volunteers

Our supporting volunteers is dependent upon the readiness of those volunteers to be supported. Some Christian volunteers work with great freedom and productivity without significant contact with their supervisor; others feel frustrated and abandoned without frequent interaction with leaders. The apostle Paul demonstrated little need for support, while Timothy appears to have needed encouragement and affirmation on a regular basis. Their *readiness* for support differed.

Hersey and Blanchard (1988, 174) define readiness as "the extent to which a follower has the ability and willingness to accomplish a specific task." These two factors—a volunteer's *ability* and *willingness*—tell the pastor how much and what type of support unpaid (and paid) workers in a ministry need. Consider the following types of combinations of ability and willingness in volunteers:

● *Unable/unwilling.* Though this group may be a significant portion of the congregation, support activities aimed at them will elicit little volunteer ministry. Their insecurity about ministry skills and their lack of commitment to the work of the church confirms their roles as spectators.

So, Mr. Unable/Unwilling is a prevolunteer. He has not made the decision to invest time and energy in serving others in a structured manner. We can best support him by having those involved in ministries stay in contact with him. Should the time come when he moves beyond his insecurity, supporters will be there to help him get involved.

● *Unable/willing.* For many people, the first step into voluntary service comes when they express a personal commitment to the church and offer to do a job, even though they feel insecure. This insecurity may stem from either lack of training or practice in fulfilling the task.

Ms. Unable/Willing, therefore, needs three types of support. If her skills are undeveloped, she needs formal training (frequently in classes) and the encouragement of a mentor/coach. If her skills are rusty from lack of practice, she needs supervised exercise with the skill or perhaps an apprenticeship that employs the skill. In both the training and the exercise, Ms. Unable/Willing needs to have her willingness reinforced by meaningful relationships with fellow workers and those she looks to for leadership. The focus of the support system through all three means is skill development.

● *Able/unwilling.* Experienced volunteers have an entirely different set of support needs. Skill is not the issue. For Mr. Able/Unwilling, there is a relationship problem associated with the volunteer task. Support for this person comes from three directions. For the person who ministers directly to people (as do teachers, counselors, musicians), affirmation must come from those being served. For volunteers working in a team situation (such as departmental teams, club leaders, visitation groups), a positive spirit must exist. And for every volunteer, the support of related leadership members (such as pastors, department leaders, board members) is extremely important.

Church leaders can best support Mr. Able/Unwilling by preventing relational breakdowns, which cause burnout and an unwillingness to serve. Once, however, a person has become unwilling to serve, even though he possesses the appropriate abilities, the supportive leader will seek to discover the source of interpersonal strain and seek to reestablish a sense of fellowship in those relationships. Like wounds, damaged relationships take time and attention to heal.

At times, Mr. Able/Unwilling may be unable to distinguish between the effects of damaged relationships ("It's no fun anymore") and unsubstantiated feelings of inability ("It's obvious that I can't do the job any longer"). When this happens, church leaders can best support the person by helping him discover new ways of employing his spiritual gifts.

● *Able/Willing.* Some people are bothered when others attempt to support them. They simply want to *do* the job for which they are gifted and perfectly capable. Attempts by others to support and even encourage them are felt more as interruptions than as support. Not surprisingly, the self-confidence of Ms. Able/Willing is sometimes mistaken for pride or cockiness, though in reality she is freeing leaders to focus on volunteers who need their encouragement.

The type of support Ms. Able/Willing does need, typically, is material rather than relational. Suitable supplies, appropriate space, and creative freedom, paired with an occasional word of affirmation, are more than enough support to keep her satisfied.

Ways to Offer Support

Given volunteers' need to be supported, how can leaders meet this need? Four methods or styles of support can be employed effectively with volunteers, although they are most effective when used in conjunction with the readiness of volunteers, as described above.

● *Teach/tell.* Narrative is perhaps the most significant means for supporting volunteers—telling the story of why volunteer service has been essential to the church and how it complies with the dictates of Scripture. Leaders must be storytellers and cheerleaders. Church leaders support volunteers by making heroes out of those who serve.

Telling the volunteer's story in both formal and informal settings creates an environment where volunteer ministries flourish. It reinforces the commitment of those already involved, and it sets the stage for prevolunteers to affirm the ministry vision and to make initial ministry commitments.

● *Encourage/train.* "Catch them while they are good," suggests educator Glenn Heck. The idea is simple: compliment their strengths. Church leaders need to provide emotional support and opportunities for skill development for those who have stepped out and made themselves available to meet ministry needs. Unfortunately these are the people who are most often taken for granted by ministry leaders. To reinforce their responsiveness at this stage of their personal readiness, church leaders must discover the volunteers' fears and visions in order to minimize the former and focus the latter.

To encourage and train usually means giving the volunteer the chance to practice appropriate ministry skills, whether in the classroom or in tutorial or apprenticeship opportunities. While many leaders think first of formal training sessions for supporting volunteers, apprenticeships with gifted mentors may be the stronger approach for leadership development.

Imparting Vision to Volunteers

It is not enough that leaders have a vision for their ministries. Legitimate leaders have followers, and those followers must own the vision, too, or it will never be implemented. But how can pastors impart genuine enthusiasm for and commitment to the church's ministry vision? The process is twofold and includes the development and implementation of the vision.

Involvement in Developing

We can involve our followers in the process of developing the ministry vision. This is the team concept of ministry. Birthing the vision may begin with the visionary leader; however, he or she cannot accomplish it alone. Pastors must involve others in the process. A general rule for churches is the larger the congregation, the more the congregation needs to be involved, especially the congregational leaders.

The amount of involvement may vary. Those who lead on a board level will have more involvement than those who are not as active. But even the latter group should have an opportunity to express their concerns, dreams, and personal hopes for the church's future. The fact that they have had the opportunity to speak and be heard is important enough in itself. The point is that when people feel as though they have been a part of the process, and their thoughts and ideas are accurately understood and represented in the vision, they are more apt to commit strongly to the vision.

Involvement in Implementing

It's wonderful to have everyone involved in developing the vision, but everyone must then take responsibility for its implementation. This requires pastors to do at

How do we provide the emotional support volunteers need? Pastoral leaders can give volunteers encouragement, but the most enduring encouragement is most often supplied in the context of a small group of volunteers who are dedicated to the same task and who come together regularly to support and stimulate one another. Times of prayer are usually an important part of these meetings.

● *Support/discover.* Many times volunteers gain the impression from leaders that they are appreciated only so long as they fulfill a role in the leader's agenda (frequently a role prescribed more by organizational need than by the volunteer's gifts). The wise leader realizes God has provided the local church with all of the spiritual gifts necessary to function in a healthy manner. All the leader needs to do is support the members of the Body, help them discover their areas of giftedness, and strengthen (or rekindle) their passion for ministry.

Supporting experienced workers usually means giving them the free-

least three things that will strengthen a congregation's commitment to the vision.

● *Promote individual direction within the vision.* Each person comes into this world with a unique design and direction from God, depending on his or her spiritual gifts and temperament. It is the responsibility of the visionary leader to help the members of the ministry discover and understand their unique design. Biblically speaking, this involves helping an eye to discover that it is an eye, and a hand that it is a hand (see 1 Cor. 12:14–18). The leadership will use this information to help people determine a place of ministry within the context of accomplishing the overall vision.

● *Encourage volunteers to minister together in teams.* To supplement the benefits of individual direction, we must eventually lead people into the New Testament model of team ministry. Though the Savior could have accomplished his vision alone, he chose to work with and through a team of fallible, often inept disciples (Mark 6:7). The apostle Paul did not attempt to implement his vision by himself, but rather worked with a team (Acts 11:22–30). A team brings together a rich diversity of complementary gifts and abilities. Nothing imparts individual enthusiasm for a vision better than working within a group committed to bringing that vision to pass.

● *Let people do the ministry (Eph. 4:12).* The person most responsible for a ministry should be the person actually doing that ministry. If leaders want their constituents to experience the ministry vision as their own, then leaders must seek to give away ministry power—in appropriate ways, at the right times. For many primary leaders, this is a tough control issue. For example, some pastors are afraid that if they are not in control of all that takes place, the ministry will self-destruct. The key to keeping the vision strong, however, is allowing the people who do a ministry to make the critical decisions affecting the health of that ministry.

—*Aubrey Malphurs*

dom to undertake ministries that are new to the church or to them personally. Failure, of course, is a distinct possibility when people venture into uncharted waters. But without granting volunteers the possibility of discovering new ways God can use them, there is little left for them to do except repeat the tired ventures of the past. If staffing the church's ministries becomes less predictable, the creative energy available for ministry increases many times.

Discovery should be a central focus in supporting volunteers. Sometimes a hidden treasure of ministry giftedness will be discovered by the church leader who finds clues in places the volunteer cannot see because she is too close to her own cache. On other occasions, a volunteer's giftedness will be recognized by the volunteer, and all he needs is the encouragement to unlock the newly found prize. In both situations, a respected ministry leader can serve as the catalyst for supporting the volunteer in his or her work.

● *Affirm/empower.* Not every believer is willing or capable enough to launch into ministries or to bring about innovation in the church without close support and encouragement. But in most churches, there are those few who, when given the freedom, will look at old problems in new ways and move to find solutions. Their greatest enemy is a church leadership that jealously guards its "right" to control what they do. If they are to do God's work to the best of their ability, they need to be affirmed and empowered to do freely what God has called them to do. The only affirmation these people typically need is the vote of confidence granted by a pastor who occasionally asks, "Is there anything I can do to make your ministry easier?" Otherwise, the pastor stays out of the person's way, and ministry happens.

Empowerment here has to do with removing obstacles: eliminating irrelevant policies and procedures, providing financial aid outside of budgeted sources or expediting financial support from approved sources, publicly affirming persons or ideas, networking innovators with other ministry entrepreneurs, and resisting traditionalists and nay sayers.

Specific Suggestions

Having a grasp of the basic concepts of types of volunteers and styles of support, we are ready to consider practical applications.

● *Paying volunteers.* Even though there will never be enough money to reimburse volunteers for their service, each person who donates time or energy to support the ministry of the church deserves to be "paid." The nurturing leader will find ways to provide appropriate remuneration.

For some the only "salary" they need is the inner satisfaction of a job well done. For these people the supportive leader will be careful to get out of the way and remove potential obstacles to the successful completion of the desired tasks.

Most people feel rewarded by the public or private affirmation of leaders they respect. Hand-written notes of appreciation, personal compliments that identify specific actions, pictures of volunteers in action posted in a prominent place, acknowledgement made in worship services of specific volunteer activities, gifts of gratitude, and appreciation dinners all serve as means of "paying" volunteers.

For a few volunteers who provide specialized services or who invest unusually large amounts of time, payment may be made in the form of a nominal stipend. Seldom does the money actually cover the value of the services rendered, but it may provide enough income so that the person does not need to cut back on volunteer efforts in order to seek a modest income elsewhere. At the least, it will tell the volunteer that the congregation values the specific service she or he renders.

● *Observing volunteers in action.* The word *evaluation* strikes fear in the hearts of most workers, salaried and volunteer alike. Unfortunately, the idea of having someone observe what we are doing and then commenting upon it gives us the feeling of being in fourth grade taking those geography tests for which we were never prepared. It means bracing ourselves for criticism.

Against this, supporting volunteers through classroom observation means finding strengths in what volunteers are doing and helping them build on those strengths. After obtaining the permission of the volunteer to visit his or her ministry, the pastor or leader might ask the worker what he should focus on during their time together. A Sunday-school teacher, for example, might request, "Tell me how well I use questions in the lesson."

The observer should always look for *strengths* upon which to build. Negative comments should be offered only when persistently sought by the volunteer. Suggestions on how to build upon strengths, and suggestions on resources that the volunteer might use to complement his or her skills, may be a further means for supporting the volunteer.

● *Helping volunteers develop.* Just as a tulip follows its natural course and blooms early in the spring—not just to be the first or the most colorful flower out of the ground—so volunteers blossom from their genetic code of giftedness, which God has placed within each believer. Pastors are farmers, cultivating the seeds and ripening the fruit of ministry.

Tom Peters suggests five means for helping people develop. In a ministry context, they could be explained as follows:

—Educate: This means orienting newcomers to current ministry expectations, training novices to master ministry skills, and facilitating changes in ministry expectations.

—Sponsor: This means enabling gifted persons to make special contributions to ministry and freeing a person from a task that has been outgrown.

—Coach: This means providing special encouragement before or after a first attempt at ministering and making simple, brief corrections in ministry efforts.

—Counsel: This means providing correction when problems have damaged effective ministry and providing specific training not accomplished through educating or coaching.

—Confront: This means eliminating persistent performance problems and relocating people inappropriately placed in ministry positions. Though confronting and possibly relocating a volunteer to a more appropriate area of ministry may not seem like an act of support, it may be the most compassionate action we can take, if it is done in a spirit of edification and encouragement (1 Cor. 14:12; Gal. 6:1).

● *Creating volunteer communities.* It is impossible for a church leader to provide all the support needed for workers in the church to have a sense of sustenance. She cannot pray with every volunteer, sense the hurt or frustration of each worker, provide individual accountability for ministry-team members. It is not humanly possible.

Leaders need to create teams of workers who provide nurture for each other. Not only do they perform the same tasks, but they can also grow in their ability to care for and support each other as brothers and sisters in Christ. Above everything else, this means the team members feel the freedom to express personal concerns with the full assurance the others will support them in prayer and, when appropriate, in tangible expressions of love.

A supportive community of volunteers can be fostered by pastoral leadership through five distinct actions. Spiritual leaders should (1) use Scripture to teach the importance of loving, caring ministry teams; (2) draw upon church life to illustrate the viability of supportive volunteer groups; (3) feature people who are part of encouragement teams by allowing them to testify in public services; (4) stimulate the development of new teams by putting people with similar passions together in ministry; and (5) demonstrate the importance of mutual support by being part of a small group that provides strength and encouragement for each other.

Making Support Happen

In churches attended by fewer than 200 people, support of volunteers is a spontaneous part of a healthy, witnessing community. Everyone who serves in a leadership position, except the pastor, is a volunteer. Sometimes even he is a volunteer. Most people know who is teaching the 3-year-olds, working in the club program, or ushering in the morning service. The network of relationships is limited, and as a result, volunteers have the luxury of being supported and encouraged by a majority of the congregation.

When the spiritual vitality of the smaller church begins to ebb, support systems tend to falter. People begin to feel isolated, taken for granted, and trapped in their ministries. If the smaller church is to regain its ability to have a significant ministry in the community, church leaders must accept the fact that the spontaneous support of volunteers by the people of the church may not be enough to sustain the spirits of those who serve in the discipleship ministries. Those leaders will need to initiate intentional support activities in order to bring about a revitalized ministry.

The larger a church becomes, the more "spontaneity" must be carefully planned. Church leaders will need to formalize the support activities that seemed so natural when the church was smaller. Though the pastor continues to be responsible to shepherd the flock of God (1 Pet. 5:2–4), he or she will need to discover people within the congregation who are especially gifted for supporting and encouraging volunteer workers and then empowering them to serve the body of believers and to support the volunteers of the church.

—Mark H. Senter III

Resources

Gangel, K. 1989. Feeding and leading. Wheaton, Ill.: Victor.

Hersey, P., and K. Blanchard. 1988. Management of organizational behavior, fifth edition. Englewood Cliffs, N.J.: Prentice Hall.

Ilsley, P. 1990. Enhancing the volunteer experience. San Francisco: Jossey-Bass.

Mager, R., and P. Pipe. 1970. Analyzing performance problems. Belmont, Calif.: Fearon Pittman.

Peters, T., and N. Austin. 1985. A passion for excellence. New York: Random House.

Part VI:

Management

In one sense, management may seem far removed from what is classically considered ministry. It's not much like preaching or leading a Bible study or helping a transient find food and shelter. We probably wouldn't discover many pastors whose call to ministry centered on a burning desire to become a bean counter. In fact, many of us leave seminary considering management basically a necessary evil that devours time we would rather give to "real" ministry.

And then we get into the parish and discover some important realities: That fine-tuned organization is necessary to accomplish almost anything worthwhile. That the lack of management hinders many good intentions, cutting short the benefits that might accrue from our efforts if only they were better conceived and executed. That keeping the bases covered and working within organizational structures can prevent a host of problems from developing. That structuring our preaching schedule or organizing Bible studies or coordinating transient ministries proves as vital to their effectiveness as the hands-on aspects.

Management makes things happen. The well-managed business turns a profit. The well-managed home is a joy to dwell within. And the well-managed church ministers more significantly. Its office runs smoothly. Its computers churn out work rather than error messages. Its roof doesn't leak. Its buildings are functional and well-utilized. Its administrative structures promote ministry rather than chaos. The well-managed church is a place where ministry flows purposefully and freely—efficiently, without hindrances.

Just how to make a church such a place is both an art and a science, and the chapters in this section offer a veritable management arts-and-sciences curriculum.

26

The Purpose of Management

From the earliest periods of church history, serious questions about administration have perplexed religious leaders. Many have mistrusted the concept of management when linked with ministry. *Management* sounds secular, so profoundly unspiritual that many have suspected it represented ideology antithetical to the ministerial role. Furthermore, *management* frequently has been associated with manipulation (the words come from the same root), crass business practices, and autocratic control, adding to the apprehension and skepticism. Prayer, preaching-teaching, the cure of souls, and meeting needs lie at the heart of ministerial service, but what about management?

Management and Ministry

Do management and ministry oppose one another? Or are they inseparable Siamese twins? Neither alternative is quite correct. Many status quo and stagnant religious institutions prove management thrives without much intentional ministry. Efficient—not necessarily effective—managers produce well-oiled corporate machinery, but not always fruitful ministry. However, competent people in ministry invariably manage well and consider management a function of biblical ministry. Few deny the basic reality that effective institutional ministry requires good management—and avoids manipulation. Larger and more complex ministries necessitate more skillful administration, and certainly inefficiency and the wasting of resources can never be a part of fruitful ministry.

In fact, no pastoral duties can wholly be divorced from managerial

311

functions, since the essence of spiritual direction involves the stewardship of the church's human and temporal resources. The basic Greek word for ministry, *diakonia,* has been translated "administration" (1 Cor. 12:5; 2 Cor. 9:12 KJV). The Latin prefix *ad-* adjoined to the word *minister* meant "toward ministry." In the best understanding of Scripture and ministry, management refers to the wise ordering of the believing community so that its mission to individual members and to the world can be fulfilled.

Management and Leadership

Many hundreds of books examine every facet of management, mostly in its relationship with business, and many more scrutinize leadership, frequently relating to politics. Obviously, an enormous number of definitions and abstractions confuse readers of this literature. Despite scholarly pursuits and multiplied research studies, no consensus or proven theory has evolved about leadership or management. Confusion, not clarity, marks much of the research and writing. Many suggest management and leadership fall more into the category of art than science.

Many authors attempt to differentiate leadership from management, though the lines of separation inevitably blur. Some suggest that leadership focuses on doing the right things while management occupies itself with doing things right. Managers successfully climb ladders, and leaders determine whether the ladder is leaning on the right wall. If there is any common agreement in the literature on management, it relates to the process of working constructively with resources to accomplish organizational goals.

Perhaps leadership has more to do with dynamic human relationships, and management relates more closely to the stewardship of material resources, though the distinction does not bear severe scrutiny. Leadership includes diagnosis, vision, change agency, the redefinition of direction and goals, motivation, structural reinvigoration, the enablement and maximization of potential—things not always required of managers. Managers plan budgets, order decision making, and wisely use material resources—things not always required of leaders. Most good managers—perhaps all—have some leadership skills, but not all leaders possess managerial competence. Some notable leaders in history lacked the capacity to manage well at all.

A Biblical Rationale

Not many Hebrew and Greek words are translated "manage." Indeed, as Peter Drucker notes, the English word *manage* has no direct equivalent in any other language. In the NIV the word only occurs three times in the Old Testament (1 Kings 12:18; 2 Chron. 10:18; Jer. 12:5), and each time it has nothing to do with organizational administration. Of the twelve occurrences of the word in the New Testament, six are found in the parable of the shrewd manager in Luke 16, and three are found in 1 Timothy 3, which refers to the necessity of the spiritual overseer managing his own family well.

Though the word rarely occurs in the English Bible, ample scriptural support justifies the concept of effective management, both by precept and example. In the beginning God gave to man dominion or rule over all the earth (Gen. 1:26–30). This delegated authority and the accountability associated with it formed a stewardship. In fact, *stewardship (oikonomos)* is the biblical word closest to our concept of management (see Matt. 25:14–27; Luke 19:11–27; 1 Tim. 3:4–5; and 1 Tim. 5:17). Adam and Eve were given the responsibility of stewards over God's creation, ruling and naming the beasts of the earth and the fish of the sea, and subduing and populating the earth.

Joshua and Jehoshaphat were military commanders and as such carried the responsibility of managers of an army. Nehemiah and Ezra demonstrated excellence in the managerial tasks of reconstruction and supervision of personnel. Some suggest that every major modern management principle can be found in Nehemiah. Kings David and Solomon were primary administrators of the kingdom of Israel, with varying degrees of success.

Joseph (Gen. 39:2–9; 41:49) and Daniel (Dan. 6:1–5) commanded the respect of heathen kings because of their personal integrity and superb managerial ability. Joseph first became the overseer of the whole house of Pharaoh and then was given authority over everything in Egypt. He bore the staggering responsibility of managing a food storage-and-distribution system on a grand scale. Can we comprehend or imagine the logistical nightmare of collecting and transporting food from all the farmers in Egypt, constructing grain-storage bins, protecting the food from spoilage—no small task—and then during the drought distributing the food to the needy?

The classic Old Testament prototype of the modern manager was Moses, whose in-service training was extensive. Moses made the managerial mistake of attempting to carry too much personal responsibility for oversight and decision making. Jethro advised wisely:

> What you are doing is not good. You and these people who come to you will only wear yourselves out. The work is too heavy for you; you cannot handle it alone.... But select capable men from all the people—men who fear God, trustworthy men who hate dishonest gain—and appoint them as officials over thousands, hundreds, fifties, and tens. Have them serve as judges for the people at all times....That will make your load lighter, because they will share it with you. If you do this and

God so commands, you will be able to stand the strain, and all these
people will go home satisfied (Exod. 18:17–23).

Numbers 2 tells us of the appointment of 70 elders to bear some of
the burdens of Moses. In Exodus 35–39, Moses supervises the gathering of materials for the tabernacle and its construction. When Aaron
and Miriam opposed his leadership in Numbers 12, Moses was faced
with serious administration problems. These principles of good management—delegation, accountability, problem solving, gathering and
utilizing resources, and personnel direction—have formed the back-
bone of ministerial administration for more than 3,000 years.

In the New Testament, the concept of stewardship is everywhere
prominent in the parables of Jesus, in the functioning of the early
church, and in the unambiguous teaching of the apostle Paul. In
Matthew 25:14–30, Jesus commended the servants who wisely invested
the money of the master, but condemned the servant who was wicked
and lazy. In Luke 19:11–27, the wise servants were given charge over
ten cities and five cities because they managed well that which was
entrusted to them. In 1 Corinthians 4:1–2, Paul referred to himself as
both the servant of Christ and a man with stewardship responsibilities. Such individuals are "entrusted with the secret things of God,"
and as administrators, they "must prove faithful." The word
oikonomos frequently refers to a household manager as in 1 Timothy
3:4–5, and success in that responsibility stands as a requirement for
assuming the larger responsibility of managing the church of God.

The Greek word *episkopos*, usually translated "overseer" or "bishop,"
suggests a man charged with the responsibility of seeing that things
done by others are done right—a significant part of managerial work.
The bishop must conduct himself as a steward of God (Titus 1:7).

The Church and Management

In 1 Corinthians 12:28, the gift of administration is listed with a
variety of other spiritual gifts. The reference is to those gifts that qualify a Christian to give good direction to the church. Here the Greek
work is *kybernesis*, related to *kybernetes*, meaning steersman or pilot.
As a ship's pilot guides the vessel and keeps it on course to its destination, so those gifted with administrative skills guide the local body of
Christ, precisely the work of spiritual managers. In the Septuagint,
kybernesis occurs three times in Proverbs, each time referring to wise
direction (1:5; 11:14; 24:6). God is sometimes called the *kybernetes*,
the One who manages the world. In the Church Fathers, the church is
frequently pictured as a ship with Christ as the Helmsman or Pilot,
safely steering his church through the storms of life and sin. The
undershepherds of Christ bear similar responsibility.

One of the most noteworthy examples of early church management grew out of a dispute between Grecian Jews and Hebraic Jews over the daily distribution of food to widows. The Twelve called a meeting of all the disciples and made a wise managerial decision. They suggested choosing seven men who were "known to be full of the Spirit and wisdom" (Acts 6:3) to take responsibility for food distribution so that the Twelve could give their attention to other priorities. The seven are generally considered to be the prototype of the diaconate.

Obviously, the governance of the institutional church has been a significant part of ministry from the beginning. However, with the rise of the church in stature and power, managerial tasks assumed towering importance: First, in the conquering of the Roman Empire and in the rise of a strong hierarchy among the clergy in the fourth and fifth centuries; second, in the vast monetary and property resources accumulated throughout the Middle Ages; and third, in the Protestant Reformation, which stimulated the religious pluralism and denominations evident in Western Christianity in our day.

The medieval Western Latin church and the Eastern Orthodox church of the Byzantine Empire trace their roots to the dramatic developments and growth of the institutional church during the fourth century. With the collapse of the once-glorious Roman Empire, the church built upon the structures of Rome and became the dominant institution of the Middle Ages. The church in North Africa died in the eighth century because of the sweeping force of Islam, but a second center of Christianity emerged in Constantinople. Eventually, the Pope rose to become the most powerful religious and political figure of Europe; yet, there were great struggles with temporal rulers who battled to control the institutional church. The church reached its political peak in the twelfth and thirteenth centuries.

Medieval Christianity is invariably associated with vast material wealth, land barons, and political power, all necessitating managerial sophistication. However, church riches and power contrasted with the terrible poverty and servitude of the masses who contributed—not always willingly—to the church and to the construction of massive cathedrals all over Western Europe. These magnificent building operations were organized meticulously, financed shrewdly, and managed professionally. In fact, the extensive, seemingly unlimited resources of the institutional church stimulated an urgency and an expertise in managerial skills unparalleled in church history.

The Protestant Reformation gave redirection to virtually every facet of Christianity. Not only was there rebellion against the Roman Church and the Pope, but there was a powerful new effort to merge secular government with the church. John Calvin, who had a profound influence on Reformation thought, attempted to make Geneva a City of God, a city-state that controlled morals, commerce, education, and politics. These heroic managerial—and autocratic—attempts of Calvin to bring all citizens under the church's discipline ultimately failed, and Calvin was expelled in 1538, though he did return and remained in the city until his death.

Calvinism was exported to most of Europe and stimulated Britain's break with Rome. John Knox brought Calvinism to Scotland and joined the cause against Catholicism, which resulted in the establishment of Protestantism in 1560. Calvin, the Puritans, the Scottish disciples of Knox, and the Wesleyans all had a deep sense of organization and discipline.

In more recent times, many developments have contributed to a managerial renaissance, an emphasis upon careful governance, and an integration of contributions of secular knowledge into our understandings of ministry. Denominational proliferation and expansion, missionary fervor, literary profusion, instant worldwide communication, efficient travel, vast financial resources, expensive property, multiplied laws and regulations, the Church Growth Movement, the rise of megachurches, and too many other factors to list make managerial expertise a requisite of effective ministry. Current institutional ministries cannot thrive, and probably cannot survive, without administrative excellence—or at least adequacy. Yet, managerial distinction does not equal ministerial superiority and must not usurp other critical leadership functions.

Debate continues among spiritual leaders over modern managerial techniques such as MBO (Management by Objectives), MBWA (Management by Wandering Around), PPBS (Program-Planning and Budgeting System), and PERT (Program Evaluation and Review Technique). Yet, most agree that any tools or techniques that work effectively, providing they are ethical, may be carefully and wisely used in the church by its leaders to sustain order and avoid chaos. However, abuse of the prerogatives of managerial power and prestige have always plagued Christian communities, and our day is no exception. The various managerial forms used to exercise autocratic control over people must be rejected. Indeed, excellence in spiritual management does not inhibit or control subordinates, but frees and empowers colleagues.

Responsibilities of Managers

Managers bear the responsibility of oversight for the day-to-day functioning of organizations and their personnel. Effective managers see to it that the long-range corporate mission is fulfilled. In other words, they get the job done. They do this by analyzing past performance, planning for the future, supervising and coordinating the activities of associates, and prudently utilizing material resources.

The words of Jesus disclose the heart of managerial responsibility:

"Suppose one of you wants to build a tower. Will he not first sit down and estimate the cost to see if he has enough money to complete it (Luke 14:28)?" Related managerial concepts include administration, organization, planning, controlling schedules, maintaining systems and structures, selecting and training personnel, maximizing physical and financial resources, implementing action, delegating responsibility and authority, integrating, achieving defined goals, evaluating performance, and doing things efficiently. Such a list intimidates many yet is far from exhaustive.

The purpose of church management is identical with God's declared purpose in Ephesians and Colossians—the building up or edifying of the body of Christ, the perfecting of the saints for the work of the ministry. To that end, apostles, prophets, evangelists, and pastors and teachers share the responsibility of equipping God's people to enable them to serve effectively. Biblical managers help people to discover and utilize their gifts for the welfare of the entire community. Thus, management is never an end in itself, but only a means to achieve the goal of implementing the church's mission.

The Greek *episkopos* is sometimes paired with the word *proistemi*, which means to "stand before," "be at the head of," "have charge over," "preside over," "to lead," but also "to represent," "to care for," and "to sponsor." The concepts of ruling and caring are not opposed in Scripture, but are closely related, as in 1 Timothy 3:4–5. In 1 Timothy 3:12 deacons must be heads of their households but with proper care for individual members.

Managerial responsibilities in ministry can be carried out only through appropriate caring, not through autocratic control. This meshes well with the teaching of Luke 22:26 that spiritual leaders are those who serve, a concept significantly different than that of Gentile rulers. Thus, it is important to add this qualifying ingredient of service to the responsibilities of ministerial managers. They fulfill their duties by serving, and their service is motivated by genuine caring for constituents. Ministerial managers with self-serving motivations (an oxymoron) clearly violate biblical directives.

Managerial styles differ widely, but effective managers invariably focus on getting the God-ordained job done. Managers are task oriented, yet they must possess people skills or face the lack of task fulfillment. The best managers and leaders don't manipulate subordinates, but they invigorate colleagues (fellow laborers, fellow soldiers) to join in the common mission of accomplishing the objectives of the organization. Thus, managers encourage and enable individuals to sublimate or merge their personal agendas into a common passion to achieve the corporate mission. They also conserve, utilize, and optimize material and financial resources for the greater glory of God.

—*James E. Means*

Resources

Cousins, D., L. Anderson, and A. DeKruyter. 1990. Mastering church management. Portland, Ore.: Multnomah.

Drucker, P. 1990. Managing the non-profit organization: Practices and principles. New York: Harper Collins.

Hersey, P., and K. Blanchard. 1988. Management of organizational behavior. Englewood Cliffs, N.J.: Prentice Hall.

Jones, B. 1988. Ministerial leadership in a managerial world. Wheaton, Ill.: Tyndale.

Rush, Myron. 1983. Management: A biblical approach. Wheaton, Ill.: Victor.

Finding a Personal Management Style

What is meant by *management style,* and how can we know what ours is and how to use it? The following exercises identify management styles and the typical behaviors that accompany each. Completing the exercises will help us characterize our personal management styles.

Ministry Style Assessment

Using a five-point assessment scale, describe to what extent the 40 attributes below characterize your ministry style. Choose two or three people who know you well to help you think through your answers as objectively as possible. Use a scale of 1–5, where 1 means "very uncharacteristic of me" and 5 means "very characteristic of me."

____ 1. Decisive	____ 21. Perfectionist
____ 2. People-pleasing	____ 22. Accommodating
____ 3. Organized	____ 23. Planner
____ 4. Change-oriented	____ 24. Questioning
____ 5. Exhorter	____ 25. Confrontational
____ 6. Spontaneous	____ 26. Procrastinating
____ 7. Efficient	____ 27. Formal
____ 8. Innovative	____ 28. Long-run focused
____ 9. Controlling	____ 29. Results-focused
____ 10. Informal	____ 30. Emotional
____ 11. Politically sensitive	____ 31. Detached
____ 12. Persuasive	____ 32. Experimental
____ 13. Competitive	____ 33. Power-conscious
____ 14. Sharing and participative	____ 34. Conflict-avoiding
____ 15. Closure-oriented	____ 35. Information-focused
____ 16. Visionary	____ 36. Activist
____ 17. Demanding	____ 37. Dominating
____ 18. Sensitive	____ 38. Contemplative
____ 19. Concern for routine	____ 39. Detail-intensive
____ 20. Nontraditional	____ 40. Controversial

The 40 style attributes are regrouped into four columns below. Please transfer your numerical responses to the questions and total the four columns.

I	II	III	IV
1. ___	2. ___	3. ___	4. ___
5. ___	6. ___	7. ___	8. ___
9. ___	10. ___	11. ___	12. ___
13. ___	14. ___	15. ___	16. ___
17. ___	18. ___	19. ___	20. ___
21. ___	22. ___	23. ___	24. ___
25. ___	26. ___	27. ___	28. ___
29. ___	30. ___	31. ___	32. ___
33. ___	34. ___	35. ___	36. ___
37. ___	38. ___	39. ___	40. ___
Total: ___	Total: ___	Total: ___	Total: ___

Enter your total score for columns I–IV in the corresponding boxes on the matrix. The ministry style with the highest point total signals your dominant, or preferred, ministry-management style. The higher the score for your preferred style relative to the other three styles, the more that style probably dominates your ministry behavior. More than one high score among the four shows you have a broad managerial-style repertoire—the capacity to utilize more than one ministry style.

Ministry Style Matrix

	Directive	Facilitative
Relational	I Commander	II Shepherd
Independent	III Bureaucrat	IV Entrepreneur

Understanding Styles

Consider the following descriptions of management styles:

● *Commanders* (decisive, exhorter, controlling, competitive, demanding, perfectionist, confrontational, results-focused, power-conscious, dominating) combine the directive interpersonal style with a strong relationships orientation. Commanders like being in the driver's seat and thrive on using legitimate power to achieve ministry results.

● *Shepherds* (people-pleasing, spontaneous, informal, sharing and participative, sensitive, accommodating, procrastinating, emotional, conflict-avoiding, contemplative) are relational like commanders, but they prefer to facilitate (guide, encourage, equip) ministry members rather than to overtly direct them.

● *Bureaucrats* (organized, efficient, politically-sensitive, closure-oriented, concern for routine, planner, formal, detached, information-focused, detail-intensive) use formal, official policies and procedures to efficiently direct ministry activities in a way that permits independent action and decision-making, minimizing the need for group deliberation and participative management. Bureaucrats favor orderly, routine operations run "by the book."

● *Entrepreneurs* (change-oriented, innovative, persuasive, visionary, nontraditional, questioning, long-run focus, experimental, activist, controversial) like to operate independent of organizational bureaucracy with an eye toward facilitating change and innovation. Entrepreneurs yearn to start projects hooked to a tantalizing vision of ministry progress.

Style Effectiveness

Which of the four ministry styles is most effective? That all depends on circumstances. Each style has unique strengths and weaknesses, depending on the needs of the particular ministry.

The table below provides insight into the situational effectiveness of each style for the ten most common managerial challenges.

Management Style Situational Effectiveness

	Commander	Shepherd	Bureaucrat	Entrepreneur
Stimulating productivity	A	D	B	C
Defusing conflict	A	B	C	D
Fostering change	D	B	C	A
Bolstering moral	A	B	C	D
Implementing routine work	B	C	A	D
Implementing new projects	C	D	B	A
Building relationships	D	A	C	B
Managing a crisis	A	D	B	C
Goal setting	B	D	A	C
Keeping in touch with people's feelings	D	A	C	B

A = Style of greatest potential
B = Style of second greatest potential
C = Style of third preference
D = Style with least potential

Management-style flexibility is a cardinal virtue. We need to strive to utilize our preferred style (the one God has especially suited us for) in as many situations as possible that benefit from its strengths. We should also use any strong subordinate styles in a similar fashion.

It's important to know where our style strengths are relatively ineffective and seek out partnership opportunities with other leaders who hold complementary style strengths. Ultimately all Christian ministry is a partnership between interdependent team members empowered by God to do his Kingdom work.

—Philip M. Van Auken

27

Managing Church Government

Every organization has its unique set of rules, policies, and regulations. Ideally, these specifications function like the banks of a river, setting boundaries and helping everything flow in the same direction. They enable a church to more effectively accomplish its goals.

However, these policies sometimes function more like a roadblock than a river bank. We've all experienced the frustration of trying to cut through red tape.

But whether the rules serve as a river bank or a roadblock, one thing can be counted on: the members of the group will expect (and even demand) that those in leadership play by the rules.

For strong and visionary leaders, this can be difficult. With kingdoms to conquer and mountains to move, goals can easily seem more important than rules, especially if those rules are bureaucratic, antiquated, or just plain silly. Yet, any leader who ignores the accepted rules of the game (as defined by a constitution, tradition, denominational polity, or corporate culture) does so at great peril. Disregarding the rules often results in conflict, organizational disarray, and the pastor looking for a new job.

In contrast, successful leaders are those who have learned the art of keeping one eye on organizational goals and the other on the organizational rule book. They know when to push and when to lay low, when to take a chance and when to play by the book.

To do this well, there are three areas in which a leader will exercise a level of expertise: (1) knowledge of the rules, (2) an understanding of how to get around or break through bureaucratic roadblocks, and (3) the ability to establish new policies and procedures that foster rather than thwart the long-range goals of the organization.

Learning the Rules

Every church has two kinds of rules: written and unwritten. A leader must have a firm handle on both.

The written rules can be figured out simply by studying key documents, such as the constitution, policy manual, or denominational handbook. It's important not to limit our review of these documents to only the more recent ones. Older documents often contain a gold mine of decisions and policies that can be of present value. For example, one pastor who was pushing to start a cross-cultural ministry in an ethnically changing neighborhood overcame congregational objections by showing that 60 years earlier the church had opened a cross-cultural ministry in the basement of another church across town. For many people, simply knowing an activity was done in the past adds legitimacy to the idea, which otherwise would be suspect.

Make no mistake: knowledge is power. Any leader who wants to be effective cannot afford to be ignorant of past decisions and actions. Such research also helps churches avoid repeating mistakes.

If understanding the written rules of a church is relatively simple, grasping the unwritten rules is another matter. They can be quite difficult to figure out, and (herein lies the rub) it's the unwritten rules that are usually the most important.

Typically, unwritten rules are made up of a series of traditions and powerful assumptions that members or lay leaders hold about the way things are supposed to be done. Often they involve matters of protocol and organizational taboos. In some cases they're known by everyone, but in others, by only a select few. Occasionally they boldly contradict the written rules and policies. But always, they are powerful and important.

The most accurate way of uncovering an organization's unwritten rules is to hang around and observe what happens for an extended period of time—five years would be nice. Unfortunately, few of us ever have such a luxury. A more expedient approach, given our time limits, is to ask lots of questions. The key is to ask the right people the right questions.

Who are the right people? They are the movers and shakers in the ministry, those whose opinions can influence the entire congregation. They wield the power of being the interpreters of the rules. As with a home-plate umpire in a baseball game, what they say, goes. It doesn't matter that last week's umpire called every pitch at the knees a strike. If this week's ump calls it a ball, it's a ball.

It's important to note that those who establish and interpret the unwritten rules are not always in official leadership positions. In fact, in smaller churches, where relationships hold more sway than titles or positions, they are more likely to be found in the congregation and not on the board.

Unfortunately, many a pastor has discovered this fact the hard way. I've seen cases where a candidate wisely asked all the right questions of the pulpit committee before accepting a call. Once aboard, however, the new pastor was shocked to discover that his or her ideas for change, which had been enthusiastically received by the pulpit committee, were soundly rejected by the congregation.

What happened is simple. The interpreters of the rules were not on the committee. The committee hadn't been deceitful; they simply didn't know the rules of the game—the unwritten rules.

How do we identify the movers and shakers? One effective way is simply to ask a variety of people in the congregation questions such as: "Who are the three to five people you think, by their support, can make virtually any new program or idea successful?" and "Who are the three to five people who you think, by the virtue of their personal opposition, can render a new idea or program dead on arrival?" Those whose names are given often are your organizational umpires. They are the folks who know and interpret the unwritten rules.

The next step is to determine exactly what the unwritten rules are. It would be great if we could just go and ask those rule interpreters we have identified for their list of the rules. But that doesn't work. In most cases, they aren't even aware they have unwritten rules, that is, until someone breaks one.

To tease out these unwritten rules, we need to ask a further set of questions, this time concerning the church's past. As we listen to people's stories about what has happened in the church, we can pick up and zero in on those events our storytellers view as particularly good or bad, probing for the blow-by-blow account. All the while, we are listening to what is being said between the lines to discover the church's history of protocol, taboos, old feuds and alliances, and even situations where the written rules were superseded.

One word of caution should be given: It is a major mistake to depend on the stories of just one or two individuals to guide us to an understanding of the unwritten rules. If they are wrong, we will be wrong too. In one situation, a long-time associate pastor quickly earned the ear of a new senior pastor. The associate pastor, by temperament, was extremely cautious and resistant to change. He viewed new ideas and programs as too risky. Unfortunately, he successfully passed off his own fears of change as insights into the corporate culture and unwritten rules of the church. It was only after this associate had moved on to another ministry that the senior pastor realized that, contrary to what he had been told, the people of the church were quite open to the changes he wanted to make. Relying too heavily on too small of an inner circle to interpret the unwritten rules of the game, the senior pastor had been needlessly hobbled.

Getting Around the Roadblocks

Every leader has to deal with organizational roadblocks, those frustrating rules, traditions, or policies that threaten to block progress or ministry. As leaders, our job often is to find a way around or through those roadblocks, all the while working within the framework of organizational polity.

Working with the Constitution

Like other organizations, churches need rules that address matters of internal administration. These constitutions or bylaws, as they are called, promote order and consistency in the life of a church.

Viewed as Law

Constitutions address a wide range of issues, including the selection and removal of members and officers, the conduct of business meetings, and the purchase and conveyance of property. These rules ordinarily carry the force and effect of law. The United States Supreme Court has observed that all "who unite themselves to [a church] do so with an implied consent to its government, and are bound to submit to it." A church's government generally is defined in its constitution or bylaws.

Understanding Constitutions

Here are some important points to note about church constitutions:

● *Detailed language.* Church bylaws often contain ambiguous language, and this is a major source of church disputes. It is essential for church bylaws to be reviewed periodically by the board or a special committee to identify ambiguities and to propose modifications.

A related question is whether the civil courts could intervene in a church dispute over the meaning of ambiguous bylaw provisions. Most courts are unwilling to do so, particularly if doctrinal issues are involved. This means that the church must resolve the dispute though its own means.

● *Relationship to other documents.* Many churches have a number of organizational documents, including a constitution, bylaws, and a charter. There are two issues that arise when a church has more than one such document.

First, what provisions or content should go in each document? A charter (often called "articles of incorporation") is a document that is filed with the state to incorporate

There are two basic types of organizational roadblocks. One type functions like a stop sign, halting progress or ministry by forbidding a specific action. An example would be a constitution that prohibits hiring any staff pastor who has not been ordained by the denomination.

The second type hinders progress or ministry by demanding a specific action. These don't stop progress so much as they slow it down, bottlenecking a ministry with outdated—but mandated—programs and ministries that leave little time and energy for the new.

When faced with either kind of roadblock, the first question to ask is the "damage question." In other words, how much damage is this roadblock actually causing? If it's merely a nuisance, it's usually best to leave it alone, since we all have a limited amount of time, energy,

---

a church. Church charters typically set forth the name, address, period of duration, and purposes of the corporation; the doctrinal tenets of the church; and the names and addresses of incorporators and directors. A constitution (or the bylaws) is a document that sets forth rules addressing members, officers, and meetings. It ordinarily is much more detailed than the charter.

Second, what is the order of priority among the documents? When a church has a charter, a constitution, bylaws, and various resolutions, there is always the danger of conflicting or inconsistent provisions. If a conflict occurs, which provision controls? In general, the order of priority is as follows: charter, constitution, bylaws, state nonprofit-corporation law, resolutions, and established custom. This listing does not take into account denominational documents, which often will apply to churches affiliated with a denomination.

● *Need for specificity.* Churches incorporated under state law generally are free from control by state nonprofit-corporation law. This means they are free to address issues of internal administration in any manner they choose. However, many state nonprofit-corporation laws are "gap fillers" whose provisions apply to a church *if* the church has not addressed an issue in its own documents. For example, an incorporated church is free to determine how vacancies on its board will be filled, but if it fails to do so, then, in many states, the state nonprofit-corporation law will apply.

The point is this: Churches should specifically address (in their bylaws) all foreseeable issues of internal administration, so that such issues are resolved internally rather than by state law.

● *Periodic review.* The organizational documents of most churches are a grouping of provisions that have accumulated over time and often in response to specific crises or concerns. Some provisions may be more than a century old. These documents should be reviewed periodically to ensure that they remain timely and consistent with legal developments.

—*Richard R. Hammar*

and goodwill at our disposal, and it does little good to dissipate them on these minor issues.

For example, as I write, I've served 14 years at a church with an outdated and—at times—burdensome constitution. Frankly, it's a pain. But changing it would have taken up a lot of time and energy, and probably it would have produced a few enemies along the way. It's been a roadblock not worth removing because it's only a nuisance and not a hindrance to effective ministry and outreach.

The second question to ask when faced with an organizational roadblock is, "Is this really a roadblock?" Sometimes what appears to be a roadblock is really only a weakly held tradition.

It's amazing how many of the things we think we must do can be left undone without anyone noticing. Here's a simple rule of thumb: If a program, tradition, or ministry (one not spelled out in the constitu-

---

The Pastor's Role with the Board

When pastors find lay resistance to their leadership, it may indicate that the lay leaders view ministers as mere hired hands, whose only function is to take care of spiritual chores. No church member who deeply cares about her church is going to hand it over to such an "outsider." Yet, for the sake of an effective ministry, pastors need to be initiating leaders. Before this can happen, the board and pastor need to answer two key questions.

Whose Church Is It?

Obviously, a church is the Lord's alone. But those who have poured significant time, money, and energy into a local congregation rightfully feel a sense of ownership. New pastors usually have an easy time leading these people—as long as they avoid campaigning for significant changes in direction. When advocating change, pastors may quickly learn how little real leadership they have. People start asking, "What's he trying to do to *our* church?"

How important that pronoun is! Until board members are convinced it is as much our church as theirs, they will not let us function as their leaders. To overcome this, we need to show a deep personal commitment to the church. In other words, board members need to see us demonstrate our commitment with our finances, our use of time, and our decision to stay with the church even when opportunities to move came along. Those who want to take the responsibility of strong leadership have to give up the privilege of loose commitment.

Who's Best Qualified?

Why shouldn't the chairman of the board, another lay person, or the entire board working together lead the church? The answer is easy. In most cases, the pastor is best qualified to lead, not necessar-

tion) seems like a meaningless roadblock, assume it is. To find out, ignore it for a while and see if anyone notices.

In one church, a tremendous amount of time and energy went into producing an annual report that included a one-page evaluation of every committee and ministry in the church. During the six weeks of production, it bottlenecked the entire ministry, as everyone focused on writing, editing, copying, and distributing the report prior to the annual meeting. The pastor hated the paperwork and begrudged the time it took away from frontline ministry. But since he saw it as part of the polity, he dutifully complied with it each year.

Then one year, right at the beginning of the process, he was hospitalized for emergency surgery. In the commotion that followed, no one got around to seeing that the reports were done. When the annual meeting was held, there were none to distribute. To the pastor's sur-

---

ily by virtue of age, intelligence, spirituality, or force of personality, for many board members can surpass their pastor in these areas, but by virtue of two key factors: time and training.

Full-time pastors are immersed in the day-to-day ministry of the church. Unlike the board members, pastors are thinking about problems and opportunities full-time. They have the time to plan, pray, consult, and solve problems.

Pastors also have an advantage when it comes to training. Formal education and ongoing studies have specifically equipped us to lead a church. Add to that a network of fellow pastors and church leaders, and we have a wealth of information from which to draw. When a church faces a tough situation or golden opportunity, the pastor is the one most likely to have been exposed to a similar situation.

What's Healthy?

Before being allowed to take a strong leadership role, however, most pastors have to clear one more hurdle: the fear of domination. Here are three key guidelines that will help allay that fear:

● *Present first drafts, not final proposals.* Our first drafts should be carefully thought out and forcefully presented, but we shouldn't confuse them with God's final revealed will. That is something we and our boards can determine together.

● *Keep no secrets from the board.* When we keep something from the board, perhaps because of its sensitive nature, we're putting them at a decided disadvantage. If they make a different decision than they would have made with all the facts, they have been manipulated.

● *Follow the board's advice.* We're wise to commit ourselves to following the board's advice not only because we want to avoid resistance to a domineering leadership style, but also because we want to be wise leaders. Wisdom is found in heeding wise counsel, even when we have different ideas, ourselves.

—Larry W. Osborne

prise, no one seemed to care. After checking the church constitution to ensure that it didn't specifically call for the reports, the pastor decided they need never be seen again.

Another case of a nonroadblock is the story of two pastors of different churches who each wanted to introduce contemporary music to their worship services. One pastor sent the idea to committee and then requested a congregational vote to approve the idea. The result was a heated debate about the relative merits of traditional versus contemporary worship styles. When the congregation finally voted, the request was narrowly defeated.

The other pastor, whose church had an identical polity, noted that nowhere was it mandated in either the written or unwritten laws of the church that every new ministry or service had to be voted on. So instead of trying to convince everyone that adding a contemporary service was a great idea, he simply gathered a core of people who were willing to do the work to pull it off. Once they were lined up, he and the board simply announced the start of a new service to be held early on Sunday mornings. Without a forum for a heated debate over the value of different worship styles, there was no catalyst for the opposition to form and crystallize.

The first pastor experienced a roadblock that prevented a new and needed ministry. The second pastor found a way to get around that roadblock by recognizing that what appeared to be a roadblock (a congregational vote) really wasn't one at all. It just looked like one from a distance.

A final consideration in deciding whether or not to go around or break through a roadblock is one's own quotient of relational equity—in other words, our storehouse of goodwill. Issues like tenure, success, and close and loving relationships all contribute to a leader's relational equity. The greater our equity, the greater our freedom to break through or go around roadblocks. When a leader has built up a certain measure of goodwill, there is a much greater margin for error or miscalculation. People are always quicker to forgive those they love and respect.

In contrast, a leader who is on thin ice or who is too new to have developed much of a backlog of goodwill has little room for error. In such cases, it's usually wisest to proceed cautiously before traversing a well-entrenched organizational roadblock.

Developing New Guidelines and Policies

A third task of leadership within the polity is to make sure all new policies and procedures foster, rather than thwart, the long-range organizational goals. Herein lies a great irony. Leaders that are frustrated by arbitrary and restrictive rules from the past often themselves lay down new regulations that, in time, equally frustrate new generations of leaders.

This probably reflects a problem of trust. Or said more painfully, we as leaders sometimes fail to trust the Holy Spirit. Theologically we know God promises to give wisdom and discernment to each generation of church leaders. But practically, our ministry guidelines and constitutions sometimes read as though those following us won't have either the Spirit or a brain. As a result, guidelines and bylaws are often made so restrictive and detailed that little room is left for adjustment or interpretation.

If our world and ministry were static, such strictures might work. But things change, and they change rapidly. It's wisely been said that the only thing we can know for sure about the future is that it will be radically different than we think it will be. If that is so, it's incumbent upon us as leaders to make sure new policies and regulations leave plenty of room for flexibility and adaptation to a changing ministry environment.

How do we do this? One way is to focus on the functions of ministry rather than the forms of ministry. For instance, an important *function* of the church is prayer, and one *form* of prayer is a weekly prayer meeting. In developing a church constitution or ministry policy, it would be a mistake to focus on the form, such as a Wednesday-night prayer meeting. Much better would be a declaration that prayer is to remain a church priority, stopping short of dictating the exact form it should take.

While this sounds obvious, in real life it can be tricky. The problem is that some forms seem so right for the moment that we institutionalize them, forgetting that things will be different in the future. A detailed process for electing church officers that works well in a church of hundreds, for example, can become an inefficient nightmare if the church becomes thousands. Or a mandated midweek prayer meeting or Sunday-night service can make it difficult later to develop a home-fellowship ministry that might carry out the same ministry functions more effectively.

Several practices can help us distinguish between function and form when developing new guidelines and procedures. One is to differentiate between patterns and rules. A pattern spells out how we choose to do it now. A rule spells out how it must be done forever—or at least until the rules are changed. For example, inserting the phrase "At this time we ..." at the beginning of a policy statement, board decision, or congregational motion makes it clear that what is being spelled out is a current pattern and not a law in the tradition of the Medes and Persians.

Another way to retain flexibility is to include an explanation of the rationale for a new policy within the policy. This way, those who come across it later have a better understanding of why it was put there in the first place. Knowing the purpose makes it easier to justify changes.

In general, it's good to move slowly in laying down written guidelines and policies. Looking back, most of us realize it's fortunate we didn't codify many of the things we thought were important when we first began a ministry. We soon come to realize that some of our most closely held convictions don't hold water when put to the test of real life and ministry. Some were too idealistic, some simply wrong. Many would have hamstrung ministry had they been codified and put into a written constitution or policy manual.

What we aim for when creating, restructuring, or developing new ministry guidelines—be it a constitution, policy manual, or a new tradition—is to make sure today's river banks that give guidance and boundaries don't become tomorrow's roadblocks that thwart the work of the kingdom.

—Larry W. Osborne

Resources

Chaffee, P. 1993. Accountable leadership. San Francisco: ChurchCare Publishing.
Hammar, R. 1991. Pastor, church and law. Matthews, N.C.: Christian Ministry Resources.

The Pastor's Relationship with the Board

Pastors and board members often clash because they approach situations from different perspectives. Basically, pastors possess a theological or biblical perspective, a problem-solving method they probably picked up in seminary. Board members solve problems more pragmatically, a tried-and-true method they learned in business. It's the idealism-realism rub.

In-Depth Discipling

People with different perspectives are a lot like two ships passing on a foggy night, moving in different directions and not able to see the other. Perhaps Jesus' periodic struggles with his "board" of twelve were intensified because of this. Yet he described to them a different perspective—the kingdom of God.

Jesus committed himself to those men *in depth*. Robert Coleman, in *The Master Plan of Evangelism*, sums up the idea well: "Frequently he would take them with him in a retreat to some mountainous area of the country.... He actually spent more time with his disciples than with everybody else in the world put together."

Two problems make us question the possibility of in-depth discipling. First, it's genuinely difficult to be candid, available, and confidential. Psychological studies reveal that we ministers tend to be more studious and introverted than the average leader, and we may attract board members with similar personality bents. A roomful of introverts doesn't make for an easy, breezy, let's-become-better-friends group. Second, the task is risky. Really getting to know each other means phony images must crumble and distance-making formalities must be set aside. We need to encourage a first-name basis and an unguarded, give-and-take style.

Practical Suggestions

How can pastors and boards cultivate better interpersonal relationships? Here are four suggestions:

● *Schedule time together between official meetings.* This can be one-on-one or with a few. It can be in the pastor's or a member's home for an evening (with spouses), or over lunch. Sometimes the gathering may simply be for social purposes. We'll probably have to plan these times well in advance, or they won't happen.

● *Get away for overnight retreats.* One of the best decisions we made at one church I served was to have pastor-elder retreats at least twice a year. These were great times for getting beneath the surface of one another's lives as well as evaluating our ministry. We ate together, enjoyed some needed laughter, and had extended times of prayer with each other. Sharing rooms together overnight also helped us break down barriers. We always came back closer and in better harmony.

Leaders can start doing this, perhaps on a once-a-year basis, shortly after the annual election of new board members. It's good to make sure *every* member can attend.

● *Translate attitudes into actions.* You love your spouse, but it sure does help to say so. You enjoy your kids, but a warm embrace communicates your attitude. Pastors and board members need to tell each other how grateful they are for their time, energy, and commitment. Written notes are appreciated. A sincere, firm handshake and an eyeball-to-eyeball look never fail to encourage. A phone call is another way of translating our attitudes into action.

● *Support each team member.* We all have enough enemies; each of us wrestles with sufficient self-depreciating thoughts. Leaders need to be loyal in support of one another, especially in each other's absence. When we have areas of disagreement, and we will, it's best to work them out face to face, courteously and confidentially. As pastors, we shouldn't use the pulpit as a hammer to settle arguments. Board members need to seal their lips when damage could be done to the ministry by an uncontrolled tongue.

—Charles R. Swindoll

Working with a Nominating Committee

Every church has gatekeepers. They are the folks who have the power to appoint or nominate; most often they are members of a nominating committee. Unfortunately, some churches underestimate their influence. Even churches that carefully choose a governing board can be casual when it comes to deciding who will control the initial selections.

Who Guards the Gate?

Some churches make an announcement that anyone wanting to serve on the nominating committee should show up the next Tuesday night in the fellowship hall. If you come, you serve. Other churches simply figure the best selection committee is a cross section of the congregation.

Selecting church leaders, however, is too important to be treated so casually. It demands the best people we've got. The nominating committee may be the most important committee in our church, because it serves like the headwaters of a river. If there's pollution upstream, it eventually will defile everything downstream. If we could choose just one church group to be vested with the wisdom of Solomon, perhaps it shouldn't be the governing board, as much as they need God's wisdom; it should probably be the nominating committee.

Many leaders feel the one person who should always be involved in the process is the senior pastor. In some polities the pastor isn't allowed to take an official role in the nominating process, but even in those situations, a pastor can exercise plenty of informal influence.

A healthy and effective leadership team demands a good working relationship between pastor and board. It seems foolish knowingly to put someone on the board with whom the pastor is at personal or philosophical odds. Like saddling a coach with assistant coaches who differ in philosophy, it's a ready-made recipe for failure.

This is not to suggest we should handpick board members. We should, however, be given opportunity to speak out against the nomination of someone who will cause conflict. Yet even that opportunity will do us no good if we lack the courage to use it.

We have to guard the gate. It's too late to try to build unity after allowing a contentious or divisive person on the board. The damage will have been done. At that point, the best we could hope for is damage control, not unity.

Why Risk Involvement?

Obviously a pastor's decision to get involved in the process holds some risk. As a friend keeps asking me, "How can you do that without being killed?" Actually, it need not create a problem if the committee members observe strict confidentiality. Nominating-committee members need to be instructed that "What is said here should remain here." And in case they may forget, we can remind them about confidentiality before every meeting!

Yes, choosing to get involved in the selection process can be risky. Secrets are hard to keep, and a pastoral veto has the potential for creating hurt. So we must be careful with what we say and how we say it. We trust things we say won't be repeated, but we make sure we can live with them if they are.

My own decision to become an outspoken member of the nominating committee didn't come easily. It went against the advice of some of my most trusted mentors. But after prayerful and careful consideration, I figured I had little to lose. I'd witnessed the results of silence too many times.

—Larry W. Osborne

28

Managing the Church Office

To say the function of the church office is varied and multipurpose is an understatement. The church office plays a unique role in the life of the local church, since it carries out business functions while often serving as a gathering place for church members to interact socially.

What we want to do is create and manage an office that accomplishes the overall purpose of serving God and his people well. That worthy goal deserves quality time to plan the ministry environment and significant effort to manage it on a daily basis. This planning and managing proceeds from a realization that the business/ministry center of a church has four main needs: a purpose, a place, people, and procedures. The wise pastor will recognize these requirements and work to integrate them into a smooth-running organization.

The Purpose

A church office's purpose should reflect the mission of the organization—to care for the multifaceted needs of people, both inside and outside the church family. At the same time, the office must perform necessary business functions. The people who work in the office thus have dual roles of Christian ministry and sound business practice. Obviously a minister has different duties than a secretary or bookkeeper, but the overall goal is the same.

With that in mind, church employees need to have a "customer orientation" about their work, with a ministry-team concept. Telephone

337

calls and walk-in "interruptions" would then be viewed as part of the job and not as sources of irritation. The attitude is not: "I can't get my ministry work done because I have all these people calling me." Rather, "all these people" *are* the work of the ministry.

The responsibility for keeping the office running smoothly and on schedule often falls to the minister. The office may be staffed with no more than a part-time secretary giving a few hours a week, or even the pastor himself pecking out the church bulletin each week and answering the phones. Or the church may have a large, well-staffed administrative center, equipped with state-of-the-art technology and highly trained personnel. However, whether the office houses a one-person operation or a staff of 50, the mission remains the same—to serve the Lord and his people.

The Place

Church office space needs to be organized for the greatest efficiency and effectiveness. As a minimum, the minister should have a private office or a secluded area to work. This space provides a quiet study environment and also allows for confidential meetings and counseling sessions.

A secretary also needs a specific work area, located as close to the minister's office as possible. A wall or barrier—preferably a counter or chest-high wall—should separate the front entrance and the secretary's work area. This establishes a boundary for greater staff privacy and confidentiality.

In general, the office environment should be planned around functions that are basic to maintaining the communications of the church, including: keeping the books and records, answering phones, corresponding, and publishing materials. Once the required functions are identified, the physical aspects of the environment can be planned, such as:

● *Acoustics*. Noise created by office activities should not be allowed to disturb the staff's studying and counseling activities. If this is a problem, churches should make necessary adjustments, from installing sound-proofing materials to simply relocating office machines. For example, a computer printer next to a telephone isn't a good idea. And while acoustical privacy (a quiet place to work) is desirable, so is visual privacy. Screens or movable partitions can serve both purposes.

● *Lighting*. Because glare on computer screens can be a significant problem, many church offices have begun using "work station" lighting rather than overhead lighting exclusively. Whatever the approach, today's office needs adequate, effective, and energy-saving lighting.

● *Carpeting*. Aside from its aesthetic value and noise-reducing effects, carpeting tends to reduce overall maintenance costs, too. When choosing carpet, determine the office's needs concerning wearability, pile height, and static-electricity avoidance.

● *Air-conditioning*. Aside from the obvious comfort advantages, air-conditioning, if working properly, will maintain an acceptable level of humidity in an office. This actually helps office equipment operate better, particularly photocopiers, since the amount of moisture in the air affects the copier's paper-handling ability.

● *Equipment*. The ideal church office would include:

—A phone system. A system with multiple extensions and features is within the price range of most churches.

—A fax machine. How did we ever get along without faxing? An adequate machine is no longer a high-cost item.

—An answering machine or service. These communicate our concern for keeping in touch with people. Many churches now record outgoing messages that give service times and special announcements, along with a promise to call back.

—A photocopier. Buy a copier that fits actual office needs. For example, though all the bells and whistles look good in the showroom, how often do we actually need an enlargement feature? One approach to need assessment is to count the number of copies a church makes in an average month and then add 25 percent to determine copy demand for the first machine.

—Mailroom equipment. Postage meters are convenient but can be expensive. They need to be maintained and usually require a maintenance contract, but they can be a great time saver for churches with large mailings.

● *Status*. While this may seem an inappropriate requirement for a church office, it still needs to be addressed. In offices with a multiple staff, the rule of thumb should be that privacy in a church should be reserved for confidentiality and protection of funds, not to establish rank. Staff people who interact with the public a great deal should be accessible. Putting secretaries in private offices usually is not a good practice within a church culture. However, putting a bookkeeper behind closed doors is certainly warranted.

The People

The number of staff to be hired for the office obviously depends on the church's needs. When a church grows and new ministries blossom, more staff must be added. Factors such as the expectations of the congregation, the availability of volunteers, and the amount of work generated by the pastoral staff also affect staff size. Though some churches add staff for growth as opposed to increasing the staff in response to growth, the cautious approach is to add positions only as the needs arise. Each potential position needs to be evaluated carefully before adding it to the church's financial commitments.

No matter how large the office staff, a personnel policy handbook is absolutely essential. The need to set policy guidelines and rules (and to be in compliance with federal and state laws) makes a written policy crucial. Employees also tend to work better in organizations that have well-publicized rules and standards. In addition, as a church staff increases, an office-procedures handbook becomes useful. The handbook describes standards for routine procedures; tells where important papers, keys, and supplies will be located; and details who is responsible for which specific tasks in the office.

The Procedures

Some church members feel that the office, its employees, and the equipment are there for their personal use. While to a limited degree

---

The Pastor's Role in Office Management

An efficient church office greatly enhances a church's ministries of pastoral care and outreach, because the office is an important contact point for church members and seekers. So it is essential that the pastor have a clear vision for the church-office ministry and take an active role in shepherding the office staff.

Office Ministry

We begin by assuming that all who work in the church office, paid workers and volunteer members, are engaged in *ministry*. They are not merely employees or hired hands but fellow workers in the kingdom. Therefore, we want to surround ourselves with those who believe that what they do strengthens the congregation's life. With such workers, we'll enjoy develop-

ing performance goals and conducting regular work evaluations.

Since good management means getting things done efficiently through effective people, the pastor must envision the ministry, work with the staff to define the tasks to be accomplished, and see to it that the resources are provided to accomplish the task. This type of planning translates into specific tasks to be accomplished in a certain order.

Nothing is more frustrating to a staff member or volunteer than to have the pastor drop a significant work project onto the desk and say, "I need it yesterday." A plaque hanging on the wall in one church office summed it up for the church secretary: "A failure to plan on your part does not constitute a crisis on my part."

Many crises can be avoided when

the office resources should be made available for general church business, basic guidelines must be clear. For instance, here are three important rules:

• *The minister's work takes precedence.* Others may have work they want done, and the minister can decide what other projects have temporary priority. But the minister's work comes first, unless he or she frees the secretary to work on another activity.

• *An office manager should delegate secretarial work.* When offices employ more than two secretaries, all work should be channeled and prioritized through a manager. The receiving and managing of work flow and assignments through one person helps eliminate the problem of who does what for whom. If a board member or Sunday school teacher asks the office staff to do a certain job, the manager can be the "traffic cop," making the work-flow decisions.

• *Specific assignments should be given to specific people.* For example, filling in the church's master calendar should be handled by

---

the pastor schedules and chairs regular staff meetings that include paid and volunteer staff members. Sometimes the pastor's office role involves making sure staff members and volunteers are planning with one another's projects in mind. The pastor sets the example by communicating the new events or ministries in the coming months and reviewing regularly the annual, quarterly, or monthly events in the congregation's life.

Running an efficient office is a little like being captain of a boat. Some pastors are captains of aircraft carriers, others of frigates, still others of ferries and sailboats. It takes much more time and advance planning to turn the aircraft carrier in another direction than to turn the ferry. To carry off effective programming, large churches require significant amounts of intentional planning and supervision, and careful provision of resources.

Small-church pastors, piloting sailboats, must also anticipate the future. However, they do most of the work trimming the sails, steering the rudder, and watching for obstacles. These pastors usually have a part-time secretary or no help at all, so attention to detail is essential.

If detail is the pastor's weak point, someone must be recruited to "sweat the small stuff." Parishioners feel cared for not only when the pastor is with them in crisis or need but also when the Sunday-school curriculum order is placed, the monthly financial report is mailed out, and the newsletter is completed. Whether the church is large or small, the pastor's office-management role is the same: define direction, set priorities, state tasks, evaluate performance, and see the church office as a focal point for caring.

—*John R. Throop*

one person, ordering supplies should be designated to one person, and so forth. It works best to divide up the regular duties and make assignments.

In addition to establishing these three rules, there are many ways to make an office more efficient and to make better use of the pastor's time. Time is a precious commodity, and the pastor needs to know how to use it more effectively. Here are some suggestions:

● *Keep a time log.* Time-study experts recommend tracking daily activities in half-hour increments and then evaluating efficiency regularly. Daily or weekly calendars are available through most stationery stores.

● *Consolidate activities.* For example, rather than making many trips to the photocopier for single copies, wait until several things need to be copied and then make the trip once. When the minister steps out of his office, it is often "open season" with questions and

The Church Secretary

The church secretary is the crucial, hidden link in the chain of most church projects. Unfortunately her value is often taken for granted—until the chain breaks or she goes on vacation!

Satisfied Secretaries

Here are ten ways we can help keep a secretary motivated:

● *Prepare her for reality.* Secretaries often hear how blessed they must be to work in a church office. In reality, secretaries may be shocked by the level of nit-picking, cattiness, and hypocrisy they see among churchgoers and staff. As pastors, we need to prepare incoming secretaries for the fact that the church is full of very human people.

● *Keep her informed.* To see how well we are communicating with our secretaries, we can ask ourselves: Do I tell my secretary when I leave the office, so she can let

callers know? Do I update her by phone when my schedule changes? Does the secretary know my time preferences for counseling, studying, visitation, and other activities, so she can schedule people accordingly? On new projects, do I communicate our expectations with precision?

One helpful practice is to compare calendars at the beginning of each week to see that they agree.

● *Be aware of* all *her responsibilities.* Secretaries do many tasks the pastoral staff may not notice, such as bookkeeping, reporting to local authorities, financial accounting, and banking. Remembering this can help us regulate the amount of work we give her, and when.

● *Highlight her work as a ministry.* A church secretary performs a vital ministry: she is the servant's servant. We must affirm her in this. Some churches include secretaries in staff meetings. Others have done

requests. Even a simple "out basket" on the pastor's desk (for the secretary to check once an hour) will cut the number of disruptions.

● *Handle routines efficiently.* For example, handling mail is one of the great time wasters that needs to be controlled. It isn't necessary to read every letter thoroughly. Merely scan the letter and route it to the appropriate person.

● *Make to-do lists.* It's best to prepare this list each night before going home. Some experts suggest we start the day with the routine tasks we least like. Getting them done early can be a morale booster, and we can look forward to the more pleasant tasks.

● *Avoid interruptions.* Often just repositioning a desk can cut down on the number of distractions. Does the desk in your office look directly out into the office area? Can people who enter the front door see you directly? Making eye contact is how interruptions often get started. Also, a simple phone system, with more than one station and

---

away with the distinction of "ministry staff" and "clerical staff."

● *Don't put her on the spot.* A secretary's services shouldn't be volunteered to church committees we serve on, at least not without her prior consent. Also, when church members request help, the secretary shouldn't be asked to respond in front of the inquirers.

● *Watch for "internal injuries."* Secretaries hear a lot of complaining from all quarters of the church. A good secretary shields the pastor from much of this—but at an emotional cost. The caring pastor will be sensitive to what she bears and give her opportunity to ventilate.

● *Be a pastor to her.* A good secretary is professional, so it's easy to mistake her professionalism for perfect emotional equilibrium. But secretaries can hurt, too. We must look to the person behind the secretary role to ensure that she is faring well spiritually.

● *Trust her.* A relationship of trust is essential to any secretary's emotional and professional well-being. In one sad case, the board sharply questioned what the secretary did with her time and actually sent men in to monitor her work. She was deeply hurt and soon resigned.

● *Support her publicly.* At a minimum, we should not announce a secretary's blunders in public: "The secretary made a mistake in the bulletin this week," or "My secretary failed to tell me about this appointment." Also, we should be ready to stand by her when she is wrongly accused.

● *Affirm her regularly.* Church secretaries are often noticed only for the mistakes they make. Affirmation and encouragement create the proper kind of atmosphere for a church office. Honoring her on her birthday and Secretaries Day (the fourth Wednesday in April) are important starts.

These ten reminders can make our ministries—the secretary's and the pastor's—more positive and effective.

—*Kenneth Quick*

a hold button, will work wonders in cutting down the number of direct phone calls to the minister. These calls can be intercepted and screened when necessary.

● *Let the computer help.* The computer provides us many shortcuts in dealing with routine functions. For instance, the mail-merge feature of most software programs can save on the time it takes to generate personalized form letters. Many other time-saving features are built into these programs. Wise users periodically read the software manual to pick up new labor-saving tips.

Mailing-list programs can help us easily remind people about meetings on a routine basis. If we keep a separate file for each group, we can simply run labels for those groups as needed. Many of the larger church-software programs have special codes that indicate participation in various groups. A mailing can be produced in just minutes by having the computer select only those people who belong within specified groups.

Whenever possible, the minister should allow the secretary to handle as many of the office or clerical functions as possible. In most cases, church members would prefer to have their pastor pastoring rather than typing.

—David R. Pollock

Resources

Alston-Kline, Inc. 1992. The personnel policy manual and employee handbook. Edmonds, Wash.: Alston-Klein, Inc.

Christian Management Association. 1984. The record retention guide. Diamond Bar, Cal.: Christian Management Association.

Merriam-Webster's secretarial handbook. 1993. Springfield, Mass.: Merriam-Webster.

Nicholaou, N. 1993. The optimal office. *Your Church* July/August 21–23.

Pollock, D. 1994. Managing the staff of the local church. Diamond Bar, Cal.: Christian Management Association.

Schaller, L. 1985. The middle-sized church: Problems and prescriptions. Nashville: Abingdon.

Effective Church Publications

Every church attempts to communicate with its members outside of weekly worship, and one of the most frequent ways is through printed materials. Churches send newsletters, prayer letters, mass mailings, financial appeals, budget envelopes, and a host of similar items to the homes of their members and potential members.

Sending Your Best

Effective churches try to make sure their printed messages are coherent, appealing, and straightforward. Behind that effort is the ability to do three things well:

● *Communicate frequently.* The larger the church, the more frequent the communicating needs to be, according to some consultants. Since one announcement in the weekly bulletin is usually not enough to communicate effectively with everyone in the church, important information needs to find its way to members in several different ways. When dealing with an indispensable bit of information, churches should consider at least three separate ways of getting the message out.

Ever-increasing postal costs are obviously a limiting factor here, but churches that once survived nicely with only a monthly "news and events" newsletter are now increasingly adopting a weekly printing and mailing schedule. A month is a long time in the life of a busy church, and members who, for whatever reasons, are absent from their church for a month may find themselves feeling unconnected.

To meet the need for frequency and variety, some churches send newsletters from various ministries within the church. For example, with computer mailing list–sorting capabilities, it's easy to send out a different newsletter to the women's organization, the youth group, and the various music groups. Churches should create a common look among these mailings, perhaps through the use of a church logo, but desktop-publishing capabilities now make it possible to target smaller groups within the church.

● *Pursue quality.* People in our culture have learned to expect a high degree of quality from all the organizations to which they belong. Churches that skimp on quality in their printed materials risk losing the very people they seek to attract. Desktop-publishing and copying capabilities are within the reach of virtually all churches, and churches can use this technology to produce the highest quality publications.

Since a church generates so much printed material, it is wise to appoint a communications team to coordinate the effort. Churches with effective publications give their printed materials not only a unifying look but also a clear and transcendent theme. A communications team can help translate the church's mission statement into quality graphics and design.

● *Contain costs.* While quality is an essential ingredient in church publications, church members also expect their financial gifts to be used wisely. Spending lavishly on paper, color, printing, or design may send the wrong message to members about the church's priorities. Therefore we need to produce materials that at least have the appearance of frugality (a neat trick, since even modestly produced materials now can have the look of great expense).

Churches, like other volunteer organizations, should probably credit the individuals or businesses who have supplied labor and materials to make the publications possible. Such crediting not only thanks the appropriate people but also sends the message that an effort was made to contain costs.

—Douglas J. Brouwer

Printing

Since the first Gutenberg Bible, the church has aimed for both quality and economy in its printed products. There are a number of ways churches can make sure they get quality and economy today.

Working with the Printer

When choosing and dealing with printshops, several things can be done to ensure quality at a fair price:

● *Hire a printer with the right equipment for the job.* It costs extra money to run a small job on sophisticated equipment designed for high-volume printing, since part of the cost is for the specialized setup. Conversely, if a job contains difficult design features, such as large solid areas, a small press may prove disappointing.

● *Compare prices.* The cost for a job may vary considerably from one printer to another, since the volume of ink and paper purchased, the quality of the presses and folding machines, and the number of current jobs waiting affect each printer's base rate. A good approach is to use a low-cost printer for all-text pieces on standard paper but a higher-end printer for productions with photos on glossy paper.

● *Provide written job specifications.* Before a printer can give a price estimate, the printer needs to know: the number of copies, the dimensions of the publication when opened, the way the publication is to fold, the number of colors of ink (including black), the kind and weight of paper, the number of photographs (if they are not already scanned onto a disk), and the form in which the original will be given (on paper or on a disk).

● *Look for cost cutters.* Most printers are willing to help find ways to cut costs. For example, a small, unhurried job may be able to be run with another job to avoid some of the setup costs. The best way to maintain costs is to not make last-minute changes that require resetting type. Printers will work to keep costs down for customers who pay their bills on time and who give the printer sufficient lead time.

Creating the Original

A printer uses an *original* to make plates for the printing process. The traditional method for producing the original is to give a typesetter (usually a print shop staff member) a manuscript, any drawings and photos, and a layout (a pencil sketch of how the final product should look).

A popular alternative is desktop publishing, which allows for in-house design and typesetting. Design and word-processing programs (typically used on Windows or Macintosh computers) allow the designer to manipulate typefaces, lines, colors, and artwork on the computer. This design then becomes the original either through a computer printer or by a service bureau.

Original Tips

A computer printer (dot-matrix, ink-jet, or laser) can be used to make a paper original. It is a good idea to print on a stable (high bond) paper and keep screen tints at minimum percentages (10 percent or less), since type placed beneath darker tints is difficult to read. When the original is to be printed on an offset press, spend the money for the printer to drop in the screen tints and halftones, since screens and photos are the weakest parts of laser-printed reproductions.

An alternative is to save the desktop design onto a disk and take it to a service bureau that specializes in making film images. The printer then uses the film directly for making the printing plates. The quality increases noticeably, since most laser printouts have a resolution (the fineness of printed lines and letters) of 300–600 dots per inch (DPI), while service bureaus and print-shops use equipment with up to 2,400 DPI.

—Wayne Kiser

Mailing and Correspondence

Enter any church office, and you will see signs of mailing and correspondence. Churches thrive on contact with their members, who are scattered throughout the area. If staff members and volunteers realize the benefits of the automated office, learn to use computer software, and determine to set up mailing schedules, the smallest to the largest church can create an efficient climate for communication.

Computers Increase Efficiency

Even the smallest church can benefit from the efficiencies of the computer in the area of correspondence. Letters, board reports, newsletters, calendars, schedules, and other standard mailing pieces can be revised or changed with just a few keystrokes. Some specialized church software enables the user to combine name and address records with attendance, ministry activity, and even giving history. Almost any version of word-processing software enables the user to create a "shell," or basic outline, of a document and insert variable information as changes or updates are needed. For example, a personalized birthday greeting can be sent to each member by using a shell document and inserting date, name, address, and even specific references to the person's life situation. It's surprising how much repetitive material a church needs to send out. Some time spent creating the format shells pays off in major efficiency on a daily basis.

Address lists can also be maintained accurately with the computer. Software programs with a mail-merge feature enable a user to combine the address list with letters. For example, the mail-merge function will insert addresses and salutations into the yearly stewardship letter shell for mailings to members each year.

The church secretary can create a

master schedule for mailings or reports to ease the work flow, but this works only if the staff—especially the pastor—is willing to be scheduled. Calendar programs can remind the pastor of special family occasions, prompting a brief handwritten note. Pastors can keep a stack of special church note cards handy for this purpose.

Mailings Require Attention

Until the "information highway" links every home electronically, the mail will remain the primary communication tool outside of personal contact on Sunday morning. Preparing mailings requires attention to detail, because postal regulations and rates change periodically.

Generally, bulk-mailing rates require a minimum of 200 pieces in a mailing, and a permit must be purchased that is valid for use only by the purchasing organization. These rates are nearly two-thirds cheaper than first-class postage, but they can be used only with printed matter that has no personalized messages. Patrons can receive additional discounts for bundling and presorting into ZIP codes but only if they mail from a Sectional Center Facility (usually the main post office in a metropolitan area).

There are further discounts for ZIP+4 presorting, carrier-route sorting, and barcoding (which requires special equipment). Dimensions must be no greater than 6.5" × 11.5", and pieces can weigh no more than about 3.3 ounces (about six to eight pages). The exact cost is determined from a mailing statement the sender must complete with each mailing. One's local post office may not be clear on all the regulations, so it may be best to work with a bulk-mail specialist at a Sectional Service Center.

Though postage meters aren't practical for small churches, they become useful when mailing more than 200 pieces of first-class mail per month. The user leases the machine and buys postage from the post office, where the meter is reset each time.

—John R. Throop

Maintaining a Calendar and Records

Record keeping is a vital function of the church office. Maintaining the church calendar and keeping the membership records requires a significant amount of organizational skill and, of course, diplomacy. The question is, when the roll is actually called up yonder, will it match the church's records?

Keeping the Records

Two key words surface when we speak of effective record keeping: continuity and confidentiality. First, to maintain continuity, we must identify each of the different record-keeping functions in the church and group them by similarity. Then we must decide where in the office the records should be kept. For instance, the adult Sunday school rosters may be a part of the church's overall attendance records, which may be listed together in the same set of books or within the same software program.

Another factor to consider is the

confidentiality of recorded information. Generally speaking, the records of contributors should be kept private. Minutes of some board meetings, especially when they are convened in closed or executive session, ought to be kept confidential, as well. Records of this nature should be stored in a locked file cabinet or have a restricted access code if in a software program.

In general, it's best to limit record access to as few people as possible. Ideally, the responsibility for managing these records should be assigned to *one* individual.

One of the most active church files is the membership directory. People come and go, get married, and have children; the directory changes continually to keep the membership list current. Many churches use a registration form on Sunday mornings to track attendance, addresses, and phone numbers. Some churches use a change-of-address form that any staff or church member can fill out and turn in to the office to note changes as they occur. Church staff should also keep an eye on mail returned from the post office with address changes.

Controlling the Calendar

The best scheduling method is to maintain one central church calendar. Once again, only one person should be designated as the calendar keeper. This individual should be a "people person," firm but fair. Many churches reproduce their calendars and have them distributed on a periodic basis—weekly, biweekly, or monthly. It is not uncommon to publish a three-month calendar.

Some computer programs for calendars allow unlimited information to be placed in a specific date, time, and location slot.

A simple room-reservation form can make it easy for people to reserve space for their events. The form need not be complicated, but it should come in at least two parts, providing copies for the church and the member. The staff member handling the calendar needs to communicate often with the custodian. A room in need of repair shouldn't be scheduled for an activity until approved for use.

At the least, churches need basic room-usage guidelines in print. Time, setting, and proximity must be considered before deciding who gets what room and when.

● *Time.* The time of day is important because it may have an effect on other activities. Schedulers must be sure event leaders will not have to fight over time and space.

● *Setting.* The activity needs to be appropriate for the room or setting. We need to be especially aware of members' ideas about what is, indeed, appropriate for the sanctuary or chapel.

● *Proximity.* Having a band performing in a room next to the monthly elders meeting is not an example of good scheduling! We need to check to see who is scheduled where and what the expected noise level will be.

—David R. Pollock

Office Furnishings and Layout

Some church offices are more a collective progression of necessary solutions than a well-executed plan. The result when church offices are carved out of classrooms, basements, and closets is scattered, hard-to-locate staff in inadequate, poorly designed workspaces, rather than an efficient office suite. Good office design keeps staff in office groupings. If the facility requires offices in multiple locations, staff should at least be grouped by function if possible.

Some churches choose to establish their offices off-site. Leased office space often is more flexible and costs considerably less than new construction and maintenance. Also, off-site offices reduce the number of interruptions by well-meaning members who stop by to chat.

A Quieter, Gentler Office

While church offices are to be friendly spaces, the completion of work requires a degree of quiet and privacy, provided by such means as:

● *Traffic control.* Ideally, visitors coming to the office should enter a reception area with seating, a reception counter, and a simple gate to control office access.

● *Office layout.* When many people share an office, visitor and phone conversations become distractions. Modular furniture, while costly, allows for more usable workstations in a room. Modular furniture is a combination of desk space, drawers, cabinets, and upholstered panels.

● *Effective lighting.* Lighting makes a big difference in office morale and productivity. There should be plenty of fluorescent lighting, and lamps should have a minimum *color rendering index* of 92 percent.

Equipped for Effectiveness

● *Phone system.* Churches often purchase systems, but some are returning to leased arrangements with the phone company's centrally located and maintained system. A central system often proves less expensive and less problematic.

● *Facsimile machine.* For many items, this technology provides an instant alternative to the postal service, and many churches find it a wonderful tool for communicating with overseas mission workers at less cost than phone conversations.

● *Answering machine.* Rather than hearing an unanswered ring, callers can hear worship-service times and the church location, and they can leave messages.

● *Photocopier and duplicator.* Copiers are rated by the number of copies they can handle per month. To determine what class of copier you need, calculate the number of copies your office makes in a month. Also, poll the staff about options that will be used frequently.

Some churches rent copiers, liking the ease of upgrading and the vested interest the company has in keeping the equipment reliable. Used equipment, on the other hand, often costs a church more in downtime than was saved in price.

● *Mailing equipment.* Labeling machines or computer programs that add the postal bar code to addresses can save significant dollars in postage. But postage meters, while convenient, can cost $1,000 or more per year. Most churches are better off buying stamps.

Computing Benefits

A computer can automate or simplify many office tasks. Choosing hardware (equipment) and software (programs) can be tricky, but a strategic plan leads toward sound decisions:

● *Identify your needs.* In what ways do you hope a computer will help you? The answers will probably fall into the categories of word processing (letters, sermons), member information (addresses, birth dates, contribution and attendance tracking), accounting (general ledger, check writing, payroll), graphics production (fliers, bulletins, newsletters), and Bible-study helps (word searches, sermon illustrations).

● *Find fitting software.* If a church identifies its highest priority (such as a good fund-accounting package) and finds the best software to meet that need, the question of what kind of computer to buy is basically answered by the recommendations of the software provider.

—Nick B. Nicholaou

Office Supplies and Central Purchasing

Like any other organization, churches need supplies. Church offices consume such things as paper, toner, ink, cleaning materials, and other goods, and purchasing these items should be done with care. If possible, a church should purchase items under the retail price, under the best delivery conditions, and under control.

Affordability

Whether a church is large or small, its purchasers can try to get a local supplier to give them a discount on *all* of their purchases, no matter how small the orders. Purchasers can let chosen merchants know they will be the church's exclusive supplier, and it is common, for example, for stationery stores to offer 10 to 20 percent discounts on purchases. Many will supply a free catalog for telephone orders.

A second option is to wait until supplies are low and then shop at a warehouse store, if one is nearby. Managers can do this by setting a minimum inventory level for supplies and keeping a clipboard near the supply area for people to write down items that need replacing. Or, once the last item at the predetermined level is removed, a reorder form can be filled out. A small slip of paper inserted near the bottom of a stack of supplies might read: PLEASE REORDER WHEN LEVEL REACHES THIS POINT. An assigned person can also inventory the supply area on a regular basis.

In large churches, it's best to

determine the annual usage of products and then solicit bids for resupply with two or more vendors. Many companies will drop their prices when they are competing for a steady customer. When entering any purchase agreement or annual contract, however, managers should determine up front what the terms will be, such as the policies regarding discounts for early payment, the amount of time allowed for payment, penalties for late payment, and minimum-order amounts.

Availability

Multiple shopping trips around town trying to find the absolute best price on items typically aren't a good use of a church worker's time. Also, along with cost, we need to factor in availability and delivery time. A great price for something that takes several days to obtain may not be such a good deal after all. If, on the other hand, we can anticipate our needs well in advance and not run short of supplies, the good price with a longer delivery time may be acceptable.

Delivery costs need to be considered, and it's always worth a try to have merchandise shipped free. Free delivery allows for ordering more often, thus keeping inventory levels down.

Accountability

The key to maintaining accountability is to assign one person to do the ordering. In a multiple-staff church, if several people are ordering from various suppliers, it makes budgeting, paying, and controlling inventory more difficult.

It can be challenging to keep track of who takes what. In a smaller setting, simply having a supply closet may suffice. However, if several people or departments have access to the supplies, it's best to keep supplies locked up and available only through a requisition system, using a simple form available to all concerned. This helps the church maintain a consistent inventory level and cuts down on pilfering. Another advantage of requisitioning is that it allows supplies to be charged back to departments.

Recovering costs can actually have the effect of lowering usage. When people realize the pens and envelopes are not "free," but in fact will be charged back to their departments, they usually respond with greater restraint.

—David R. Pollock

29

Managing the Church Computer System

Perhaps no invention since the Gutenberg press has of-fered so many opportunities for change in ministry methods as the personal computer (PC). Computers that fit on a desktop or in a briefcase would once have been cramped in a two-car garage. Then in 1959 microelectronic innovations produced the integrated circuit (IC); the microprocessor came along in 1971. Suddenly, the computer's CPU (central processing unit) was reduced to the size of a single silicon chip.

In 1979, IBM introduced its own microcomputer model, the IBM PC, a milestone in a burgeoning field that proved the microcomputer was more than a fad and would become an essential tool for small business. The introduction of a powerful 32-bit processor in the mid 1980s made possible advanced, high-speed, multi-user operating systems. Simpler, user-friendly methods of operating PCs became available. A graphical user interface (GUI) offered by Apple Macintosh allowed the user to select icons (graphic symbols of computer functions) from a display screen instead of typing commands. The watchwords of the computer industry seem to be *simpler, smaller, faster,* and *more powerful.*

How Churches Can Use Computers

Like any service or sales business, churches have a need to keep track of their constituents. Computers can help streamline office tasks that once were tedious and required many workers or volunteers.

Large mailings—even with personal greetings and notations—can be created in minutes instead of days. Membership information that once filled file drawers can now be tracked in a convenient database and stored electronically. Updates, information retrieval, and even cross-referencing of membership data can be accomplished with a few keystrokes.

Computer advantages for the church go far beyond the reduction of staff costs and resources. One pastor tells how his computer helps him track thousands of impossible-to-remember ministry details: His calendar program reminds him of church members' birthdays, wedding anniversaries, and anniversaries of a significant death—and prompts him to write pastoral-care letters to these members. "My computer helps me to serve my people better. Not that it increases my level of caring, rather, my computer helps me to express my concern in ways I couldn't without it," he says.

Computers can increase the possibility for creative and effective evangelism. For example, many church-growth experts claim that members who lapse into absence for three weeks or more are in danger of becoming permanently inactive. Most church-management software tells who those nonattending members are and can even assist in making contact by automatically generating a predefined letter or a visitation list. Some software packages can also alert pastoral staff to those who have increased attendance significantly—perhaps indicating a pastoral-care need. Also, many churches have used the mail-merge capabilities of computers to perform nearly effort-free direct-mail canvassing.

Specific Applications for Churches

Each church and pastor will find computers can serve them in different ways. Here are some of the uses to keep in mind:

● *Membership records.* Keeping track of church membership can be a monumental task, even in small churches. Some couples move south in the fall and return home in the spring. Some college students live away from home during the school year. Computers can be used to keep complicated mailing lists up to date.

● *Accounting.* Church budgets and accounts can be tracked in ways that can't be done on paper without countless hours of tedious effort. Enter offerings and pledges once into the church computer, and the information can be added together, processed, and distributed to the various accounts. Church-management software keeps track of individual giving and generates statements of donations for members for tax purposes. Most software packages also handle bills and payroll (including check printing). Some even may generate the appropriate forms for taxes or social security withholding.

● *Correspondence.* Writing, mailing, and filing correspondence is a breeze with the use of a personal computer. Many pastors and administrators find they write many letters that can be used over again in much the same form. Most word processors allow building templates for often-used letter formats. A church database or management software combined with a few keystrokes can prepare personalized letters with identical content for the whole congregation or certain groups of individuals within it. Each letter has inserted into the format the address of the recipient, the salutation, the current date, and so on. Another keystroke or two prints a perfectly formatted envelope, complete with postal bar code.

Filing letters in computer directories of various categories saves office space and allows for quick retrieval. For example, knowing that a letter was written referring to a certain memorial gift might lead to quite a search through the filing cabinet. No more wondering, *Was it filed under "thank-you letters," "memorials," or "committee projects"?* In many offices, the letter is probably in a huge file creatively named, "outgoing correspondence." The computer can search the entire system in a matter of moments for any specific reference in a letter.

● *Publications.* Computers can improve dramatically the quality of church publications and documents, while at the same time saving printing and typesetting costs. A good desktop publishing program and the use of a high-quality computer printer can produce professional-looking documents. Computers that help a church look good in print greatly enhance the image of a congregation.

● *Sermon preparation and Bible study.* Writing and editing sermons is simplified with the word-processing capabilities of computers. Most word-processing software offers outlining functions. Cut-and-paste operations make moving sentences, points, or entire thoughts effortless. In addition, Bible-research software (including the original languages), historical maps, Biblical commentaries, and Bible dictionaries are all available now for use on a PC—some on compact disks with large storage capabilities.

● *Faxes.* A dedicated office fax machine can cost $300–600 and usually prints on curly, hard-to-handle thermal paper. Plain-paper fax machines are available for nearly twice the price.

But any office with a computer and a printer has the capacity to add a fax machine for the minimal cost of purchasing a modem and software. A modem enables a computer to send and receive electronic information—including faxes—over a telephone line. Better yet, faxes received by the computer can be printed on regular paper, making them much easier to handle. Often a fax doesn't need to be printed at all; it can simply be viewed on the computer screen—a helpful option in these days of environmental concern. Faxes received may also be transformed into a text file through optical character recognition, making it possible to insert information from a fax into other documents without retyping.

● *Music ministry.* An inexpensive addition to a computer is the MIDI (Musical Instrument Digital Interface) port, which can expand the musical potential of any church. Most organs, electronic pianos, and keyboards have a MIDI port that allows direct control by a personal computer.

Music played on the keyboard of the controlled instrument can be interpreted by the computer and converted into musical notation. The music may then be printed, edited, transposed, or even played back by the computer. With the use of a scanner, written music may be interpreted and played by a computer. "Optical music recognition"

Computer Buying Tips

The best-value price point for computers hasn't changed much in over a decade of computing. About $2,000 buys a computer adequate for modern office needs.

Of course, tomorrow's technology is always more affordable tomorrow. That means if we buy the most advanced system available at the moment, we'll pay a premium price and won't get as much computer for the dollar.

When purchasing a computer for the church, it's usually wise to work through an ongoing computer committee. The committee should include staff members who will use the computer and volunteers who work as computer professionals. The key jobs are to determine needs and buy hardware that can run (at an adequate speed) the software the church plans to use.

The committee, with the pastor, should meet at least annually to evaluate computer performance and to note problem areas. It's usually cheaper to upgrade than to

struggle with outdated equipment. It makes for a happier staff, too.

Where to Buy?

Do you buy mail order or from an office or computer store? The price shouldn't be the only guiding factor. Computers need servicing when things go wrong, but the service provider need not necessarily be a local store. Many mail-order companies offer on-site service at no additional cost, and some have technical support with long hours (some 24 hours a day) and toll-free numbers.

It is important that the place of purchase be a stable business that will be in operation long enough for the church not to get stuck with an orphan. Buying from a church member's brother-in-law who assembles computers in his basement isn't recommended; the church can lose a member or two if things go bad. And before buying used equipment from a company that is up-

software converts the notes on the page to MIDI format, making it possible to play back the music on any instrument with a MIDI port.

● *Voice mail.* Although some people dislike answering machines and barely tolerate voice mail, it may be a trend that is becoming more accepted. Though churches won't want to implement something that makes ministry sound more impersonal, some churches are effectively using computer voice-mail systems.

For example, one small church uses a voice-mail system to transfer calls from the church—which often has no one there to answer the phone—to a live person. The church computer offers a menu of persons to which the call can be transferred. When the caller makes a selection, the computer dials that person's home number. In case of a

---

grading, we need to make sure the reason for the upgrade wouldn't apply to our situation, as well.

Which Computer?

When it comes time to shop, here are some tips to keep in mind:

● More expensive brand-name computers may use proprietary parts that are specially designed and not interchangeable with other systems. Repairs and upgrades for these machines can be expensive.

● The ability to upgrade the system is an important consideration. Many computers offer components that can be replaced with more advanced models as they are produced. Some promised upgrades, however, never materialize. For example, many computers were manufactured with Pentium "upgrade sockets" for a special chip that may never be produced.

● Laptop and notebook computers (and their smaller companions, sub-notebooks and palmtops) offer the advantage of easy portability. However, in this fast-changing market, the cost of miniaturization often means fewer features for the dollar and a sacrifice in expandabil-

ity. Portables and the smaller personal digital assistants do make an excellent choice for the pastor who prefers to do work away from the office.

● Buy a good printer, and don't sacrifice good-looking output for a low price. Without good output, many of the advantages a computer can bring to an office can be lost.

● A fast modem pays for itself in reduced phone charges.

● Buy the most memory and storage you can afford. Programs continue to require more memory. Only a few years ago experts were predicting that a 20-megabyte hard drive was more than anybody would ever need!

Learning to Compute

Training staff to use the computer can be difficult, but training is often offered through community colleges, vocational schools, computer retailers, and companies that specialize in on-site training. Perhaps the easiest and least expensive training tools are the many videotape courses available.

—Bryan E. Siverly

pastoral-care emergency, another option routes the call to the pastor's pager service. Shut-ins (or others) can choose to listen to a devotion recorded by the pastors. Another option lists church events and worship times.

Such computer voice-mail systems require an inexpensive hardware addition to a computer. Some of these systems run in the background (that is, while the computer is being used for other tasks). Others require an inexpensive additional computer dedicated to the task.

Some voice-mail packages allow for automated calling routines to deliver a taped message. For example, if a pastor wants to let the church board know of a change in meeting time or location, the automated system would call only those on the church database who serve

Purchasing Management Software

Many software programs are designed specifically for churches and church managers. These programs can track attendance, run mail lists, keep contribution records, map prospects, inventory membership talents, and even telephone special groups within the church and deliver voice messages.

Five-Step Selection

With so many church-management software (CMS) packages on the market, finding the best one for your church can seem complicated. Consider these five steps in your selection process:

● *Form a research group.* No one wants *another* committee, but this is a good way to involve qualified people. Obviously, it is important to include people with computer backgrounds, but it is also important to involve those in touch with the needs of the church and its staff.

● *Consider your budget.* The temptation, of course, is to get the cheapest package possible and hope to get by with it. Yet a properly outfitted computer can save time and money over the years through efficiency of use. If cash flow is a problem, churches can consider buying from a company that sells CMS packages in modules. This means they can first purchase the one module they need most (perhaps one for tracking membership) and later add a second one (perhaps a contribution tracking-and-reporting module).

● *Determine your needs.* It's good to list what we want in a CMS package and rate each function for importance. This is helpful in comparing packages.

The aim, of course, is to match the caliber of the software with the size and skills of the church staff. If the church has professional secretaries with computer experience, the features of more-sophisticated

on the board and deliver the message. If no one is home, it would either leave the message on the answering machine (it is smart enough to wait for the beep), or it would call back until it received an answer.

Such automated message systems can even ask for a response to a question. In this particular example, the taped message could ask if the person could make it to the newly scheduled meeting—press "1" for yes, "2" for no. The system would then keep a record of those responses.

● *Access to information.* Computers can be linked via a modem through telephone or cable television lines to a wealth of information and possibilities. Not only do such connections allow for instant com-

---

software will be beneficial. But if it will be used by less-experienced secretaries or volunteers, the software should be less sophisticated and more user friendly.

● *Create a list of potential* CMS *packages.* More than 50 companies provide packages. These can be found in advertisements in Christian publications (many have a special computer issue once a year) and specialized magazines or newsletters (such as *Christian Computing* and *Church Bytes*), in the small advertisements in the back of secular computer magazines, and in Christian direct-mail pieces sent to churches. Churches can send for information on packages that look like they may meet the entries on their needs list.

● *Sort and match.* Once the committee has assembled information and demonstration disks, it is ready to narrow its options. That task involves finding and reading software reviews, calling or writing churches using the programs (CMS companies can provide names), asking the companies to provide an in-church demonstration or finding out if they will be at a nearby exhibit soon, and visiting a church

with the CMS package you are considering to watch the staff use it.

Assessing Quality

When buying a CMS package, a church is purchasing more than the program itself. To discover what kind of service to expect from the company and the software, the committee can ask: How often does the company provide upgrades, and at what cost? What kind of technical support is provided, and is it at an additional cost? Is there a training plan? Is a network version of the software available? How long has the company been in business, and how many churches use this software? How many employees do they have? While a product or company that is new shouldn't be overlooked, a church should proceed more cautiously.

The key is to find the program that will best suit the church's needs and will actually be used. If a program is too complicated or becomes unsupported and outdated, it will not be used. But a computer with the right CMS package can be a vital ministry tool.

—*Steve Hewitt*

munication through electronic mail, computer users gain access to experts and peers in various fields. Those having trouble with a particular brand of software or computer hardware can contact the manufacturer for technical assistance. Pastors can dialogue with other religious professionals about sermon topics, church-growth ideas, prayer concerns, and so on. Networks like Compuserve, Prodigy, America Online, or the vast university network called the Internet have interest areas or forums that stimulate discussions covering a wide range of topics.

Excellent computer programs called shareware, with a policy of "try now, buy later" (if you like it, that is), are usually available to download (transfer to the local computer). Shareware titles are usually transmitted in compressed form to reduce transmission costs, and must be decompressed locally after transmission.

● *Office integration.* Most office equipment is being manufactured with computers in mind. Copiers, folding machines, and perhaps even coffee pots may one day be controlled by the office computer. This kind of office integration will reduce the cost of manufacturing additional controlling equipment, while at the same time it will enhance the products' usability.

Linking Computers in Networks

A computer network joins computers by various kinds of wires (some use widely available phone wire) and inexpensive interface cards. Other networks don't require wires for the connection, working through walls and floors by way of radio transmissions. Although in the early days of computing, networks were complicated and expensive, those obstacles have mostly been removed by today's networking-ready operating systems.

Networking church computers makes sense for a number of reasons. Perhaps the best is the sharing of resources. Data storage is expensive, and workstations through a network can share the storage of a single master computer or *server.* Expensive components like laser printers or high-speed modems can be shared by everyone in the office. In this way, networks save money.

Also, users at different workstations will be able to share the same information and have access the most current data available. For example, the church database could reside on one computer that serves the information to all the others. Any workstation would then be able to view, edit, update, or otherwise manipulate data without having to place it on a diskette, use it, and load it back in the original computer from the diskette.

On a network, personal schedules or calendars can be viewed (or edited) by anyone in the office. A secretary is able with a few key-

strokes to find the pastor's calendar for a certain date and fit a counseling appointment into an open slot (labeled as an appointment to be
confirmed upon the pastor's return). Special meetings can be scheduled by having the computer search every staff member's calendar to
find an open time.

Interoffice communication can be enhanced by using E-mail mes-
saging via the network. Messages can be forwarded to the computer
screen of anyone in the office without the wasteful paper "while you
were out" notes or the footwork involved in delivering them.

Church-Computer Concerns

A number of issues confront churches with computers: Who will
care for the equipment? Who will make it work when it crashes? It is
important that churches develop policies and procedures that make
computer operations work smoothly. Other concerns include:

● *Security issues.* Since the church computer contains confidential
and sometimes sensitive information, security must be an issue. Not
everyone in the church should have access to the equipment. At the
very least, the computer should be kept in a locked office.

It's best to use password protection for certain sections of programs
that contain the most sensitive information. Passwords should be difficult enough to trip up would-be snoops. Some of the most common
passwords are the word *password*, the operator's name, a pet's name,
or family members' names. These all are bad choices. Some (unbeliev-
ably) have their password written down on a scrap of paper kept near
the computer.

It's wise to make sure the computer system is adequately insured by
the church's insurance policy. It may be a good idea to carry computers in a special "all risk" rider on the policy. We should keep an inventory of equipment and serial numbers (including software), and make
sure the insurance company has a copy. If a pastor uses his or her
own computer in the church office, it will not usually be covered in
the pastor's personal homeowner's policy (without a special rider). If
it isn't, it is a good idea to add it to the church policy.

● *Data integrity.* The cardinal rule of computers is: Back up often.
Backups safeguard data stored on the computer from being lost. This
simple procedure, one of the most neglected computer tasks, should
be done at least weekly, and preferably daily. Accidents can happen,
and an unfortunate computer data failure can become a catastrophic
failure without a recent backup.

A tape backup device makes the process much easier, and huge volumes of data can be saved to a single tape. Although the initial cost of
such devices may be higher, the savings will soon be realized in lower
media costs (a single tape is much cheaper than hundreds of disks)

and convenience. For even more security, the backup (tape, disks, or whatever) should be stored away from the church. That way, if something should happen to the building where the computer is stored, the data remain safe.

● *Liabilities.* Prolonged computer use has been cited as the cause of occasional health problems. Some have required surgery to correct pain caused by strain on the wrists or back. Operators who complain of headaches or eye strain may be affected by cheaper *interlaced* monitors, which flicker noticeably at high resolution. There are also fears that the high radiation output of some monitors may cause injury.

For these reasons, we should consider purchasing wrist supports for each keyboard in order to reduce the possibility of wrist and hand injury. We should also enforce breaks for keyboard operators and encourage hand-stretching exercises during those break times. Comfortable chairs with good lower-back support are essential for those who sit for prolonged periods at the computer. Purchasing noninterlaced monitors with a high vertical refresh rate (screen is updated quickly and often) will ease eye strain. Low-radiation monitors are also worth considering.

Computer Temptations

Dangers accompany our computer purchases, such as:

● *Addictions.* Computers can become an obsession, especially for the people who are technology lovers or "gadget freaks." Time savings gained by a computer can be swallowed up in a black hole where a pastor or staff person spends excessive amounts of time with the computer at the expense of many other needed tasks.

● *Ethical decisions.* Because computers can do in a matter of moments what used to take days, there may be a temptation to capitalize on that advantage. Several activities require ethical thought by the pastoral staff and administration.

For instance, when someone calls, I can pull up the name from my database and instantly recall the details I noted about our last conversation. It is tempting to leave the impression that my recall comes from an incredible memory or superhuman level of pastoral concern.

Mass mailings can be produced with personal salutations and even personal data, and there is the temptation to leave the impression that each letter was individually typed.

Sermon services now produce diskette versions of their pulpit helps. After a hectic week with little time for sermon preparation, it can be tempting to pass off someone else's work as our own.

● *Copyright laws.* Whatever a computer reproduces, including clipart drawings or photographs, should be carefully evaluated in light of copyright laws. It can be costly to violate these laws.

Software piracy is epidemic. One pastor was beaming about his church's computer bought for a small price from a local business: "I feel like the Lord delivered us this wonderful tool. It even has Word-Perfect and a whole bunch of other software already installed." Many churches are unaware that all legal copies of software must include manuals, original disks, and licenses. Copies made by friends or those that come with used equipment cannot be used in good conscience.

—Bryan E. Siverly

Resources

Boone, M. 1993. Leadership and the computer. Rocklin, Cal.: Prima.

Carlson, R., and B. Goldman. 1994. Fast forward. New York: HarperCollins.

Levy, S. 1994. Insanely great: The life and times of the Macintosh, the computer that changed everything. New York: Viking.

Smith, B. 1993. Computer hardware and buyer's guide. Indianapolis: Que.

Spencer, D., ed. 1993. Webster's new world dictionary of computer terms. New York: Prentice Hall.

Computer Security

Most experts agree, it not a matter of *if* a computer will crash, but *when*. Thus it's important to protect a computer system from problems that definitely *will* arise.

Electrical Problems

Electrical-current irregularities cause the greatest number of system crashes. Churches can protect their computer systems from impure and unstable electricity in different ways, depending on the setup.

● *Single units.* If the computer is a stand-alone unit or a network workstation, a high-quality surge protector is recommended. Since surge protectors vary widely in effectiveness and cost, it's important that the unit have at least a two-year warranty and carry the following Underwriters Laboratory listings: UL 1449 (high level of surge suppression), UL 1282 (high EMI/RFI noise filtering), and UL 497A (for modem and communication protection, if the computer has those capabilities).

● *Network file servers.* If computers are networked, the file server (the computer that serves all of the connected workstations) should have an uninterruptable power supply (UPS) for maximum electrical protection. The UPS should be online (always operating) as opposed to standby (waiting for a problem before it activates); be rated at 600,000 to 1,200,000 volt-amps; switch on in less than two milliseconds; be able to shut down the system without an operator; include surge protection, brown-out protection, and noise filtering; have a battery life long enough to shut down the server in an orderly manner when the power fails; and have at least a two-year warranty.

Preventing User Error

People can make computer mistakes, too, so it is good to provide security against human error. Three systems are recommended:

● *Limiting access.* Allowing only the right people on the computer in the first place can eliminate many problems. The computer can be kept in a locked room or cabinet, with access only by authorized people. Another good way to add to security is by using passwords to control access to computer functions. Only authorized personnel who know the passwords can manipulate files.

● *Training.* The least-expensive safety measure involves training operators in methods of safe operation. This includes handling floppy disks with care and understanding software commands and standard operating procedure.

● *Backing up data.* It's best to regularly back up a stand-alone computer's data onto one of two sets of floppy diskettes or tape cartridges. Each time you back up your system, use the set other than the one used for the previous backup.

Larger churches with networks need to back up data on a daily basis. This works best on a tape back-up system that can perform its task unattended during off hours. It's easiest and safest to use a separate back-up tape for each day of the week.

When churches follow these guidelines, data ought to be there at the press of a key, and they will have spent little "protection money" for the security.

—*Nick B. Nicholaou*

Desktop Publishing

With bulletins, newsletters, youth fliers, and congregational mailings to print, churches increasingly are using desktop publishing (DTP). Professional-looking graphics make church publications inviting, and today's desktop-publishing capabilities put the power to produce them literally at our fingertips.

What Equipment?

Churches wanting to take up DTP need to be sure their computers are powerful enough to handle the programs most DTP software requires. What to look for:

● *A fast computer.* Most DTP programs require lots of computing muscle, something that slows older or smaller systems to a crawl. Churches using outdated, underpowered equipment will find DTP work an exercise in frustration as they wait a minute or two for a page to be redrawn on the screen.

Most churches choose between the Apple Macintosh line and IBM compatibles, although the differences keep becoming more insignificant. The Macintosh, designed with DTP in mind, started and led the desktop-publishing revolution in its early stages. Among IBM compatibles, systems configured similar to the Macs typically cost 25 to 50 percent less but usually are harder to set up and learn.

● *A large hard drive.* Without a hard drive, a church shouldn't even attempt to try DTP, and the larger the drive, the better. It's not unusual for a DTP program and files to name up many megabytes of hard-drive space. Graphic images can quickly fill a smaller hard drive.

● *Lots of RAM.* Most DTP programs require huge amounts of internal computer memory (RAM) in order to load, and those that produce graphics need even more. Early programs could be run on 4 megabytes of RAM, but 8 or more megabytes make the computer run much faster.

● *A good monitor.* The resolution and size of the monitor are important considerations. Higher resolution monitors allow more of a page to be shown in greater detail on the screen, and a larger screen size reduces eye strain. It's important to find out whether the monitor is interlaced or noninterlaced. At higher resolutions, cheaper monitors update every other line in a screen scan (interlacing), causing noticeable and irritating screen flicker. Larger screens (at least 15 inches diagonal) are highly recommended.

● *A high-resolution printer.* The old dot-matrix printers are inadequate for DTP, which requires either a laser or an ink-jet printer. Laser printers are far less expensive than they used to be, and they are unquestionably the best output devices for DTP. The higher the resolution in dots per inch (DPI), the better, and some printers have 1,200 DPI or greater.

Which Software?

Among the top DTP software programs at this writing are Ventura Publisher, PageMaker, Quark-Xpress, and FrameMaker. All are available on both IBM and Mac platforms, and files can be shared from one platform to the other. When looking into software, it's best to buy from a retailer with a "try before you buy" policy. Many stores allow customers to evaluate a program on an in-store computer. Some have a 30-day, money-back guarantee on software, so people can try the program at home at their leisure.

Before buying a DTP program, make sure the computer's present word processor won't be sufficient, since many word-processing programs have extremely functional DTP capabilities.

Also, several companies provide video and audio training programs for the major DTP programs. Training in desktop publishing is essential for the best results.

—Bryan E. Siverly

30

Managing Buildings and Grounds

For many people in our communities, the "church" is the facility, the building they see on the corner of Main and First Street with the steeple and stained-glass windows. Though church members usually focus on the ministries and programs that happen inside the structure, the nonmember or visitor may view our facility as the most tangible expression of our faith.

Thus, we will benefit from periodically looking at our church facilities through the eyes of a potential member. Does the structure look inviting? Does our sign truly identify the church? Is the lawn well-kept, the parking lot lighted and marked? Can a visitor on Sunday find the worship and Bible-study areas easily? Is the nursery inviting and safe? Are rest rooms clean and free of odors? Asking such questions regularly can help us remove unnecessary hindrances to our proclamation of the gospel.

A well-designed church facility should be functional, attractive, flexible, safe, and economical. Since it is impossible for the pastor alone to assure that these qualities exist, a property committee works well for these purposes. Usually this committee is made up of lay persons of the church who have interest and appropriate skills in construction, building trades, or facility management. The church may want to include people who have a flair for the aesthetic appeal of the property as well as those with a general interest in maintaining a clean, effective worship facility. The pastor or some other staff member should act as an ad hoc committee member.

Along with doing periodic inspection of the facility and arranging repairs as necessary, the duties of a property committee might include establishing guidelines for use and maintenance, ensuring safety and security, overseeing costs and equipment purchases, managing custodial operations, and keeping house indoors and outdoors.

Establishing Use and Maintenance Guidelines

Regulating what goes on inside the walls of the church, and when, is crucial to the wise stewardship of our facility resources. Many churches have found a "space-utilization plan" to be an effective approach to use management. Setting up the plan normally includes these basic steps: finding out when the facility was built and who the designers and contractors were; gathering blueprints and diagrams of the exterior and interior layout, along with heating, mechanical, electrical, and plumbing blueprints; doing a room-by-room analysis of construction, finish, and equipment characteristics; and deciding how and when each space will be used during the week. Based on the overall space plan, the property committee schedules inspections, plans repairs and modifications, and budgets for equipment replacement.

A church must decide whether to restrict the use of the facility to in-house programs or to open its doors regularly to the community at large. Once that decision is made, the members of the property committee can develop guidelines and procedures relating to scheduling, safety, security, and habitability. Written use-policy guidelines should cover at least these issues: who can use the facilities, along with a statement about how to gain access; what security and safety requirements must be met by the users; what equipment is available; what restrictions apply (such as use of alcoholic beverages, types of activities, time limitations); and how fees are established and paid.

The ministry advantages of opening the facilities to the community must be weighed against certain drawbacks. For instance, if outside use is approved, the church probably will need to comply with the access provisions of the Americans with Disabilities Act (especially when the church serves as a polling place). If nonmembers regularly enter the building, the church must have liability insurance—which usually involves higher premiums—and comply with local and state fire safety codes. In addition, if a church routinely charges for events at a rate that exceeds normal reimbursement for utilities, setup, and cleanup, it may forfeit tax exemption for part or all of the facility.

Ensuring Safety and Security

Church leaders have a moral obligation to maintain safe, clean, and secure places of worship and ministry. Though churches have long been exempt from the laws and ordinances that ensure facility safety, this is beginning to change in communities across the nation. Courts and municipal offices are now requiring compliance with safety and building codes, and making churches liable when people are injured.

Fortunately, most church insurance agents are now trained to help their clients reduce the risk of liability and loss. In this regard, each year the church should schedule an insurance review that covers new equipment acquisitions, building modifications, personnel, facility-use policy, and program changes. In addition, every other year the church should arrange through its agent to conduct an inspection of the facility.

Based on the insurance company's suggestions for improving the safety and security of the facility, the church may be able to save significantly on premium costs. For example, one church was able to save over $200 in annual premium costs by simply installing additional fire extinguishers in the kitchen area and smoke detectors in children's meeting rooms. The local fire inspector can uncover such hazards as poor electrical circuitry, unsafe or inadequate plans to evacuate a room, faulty or dangerous mechanical or heating systems, and inadequate or poorly selected fire equipment.

If the church operates a kitchen facility for its various programs, local and state health inspectors enter the safety picture. For example, in some locales, if the church routinely feeds a certain number of people from an on-site kitchen, the facility and personnel must comply with food-safety codes and be licensed to operate. This is especially true when the church operates a day care or school program.

Overseeing Costs and Purchases

A third duty of the property committee is to gather information about budget needs and suggest the most cost-effective approaches to purchases, new projects, and ongoing maintenance. From the facility-administration budget, the committee can expect to spend about 36 percent in personnel costs, 27 percent in utility costs, 17 percent in building-maintenance costs, and about 10 percent in insurance costs. The remaining funds in the budget go to purchasing supplies and equipment.

Efficient operations oversight can reduce costs, and effective facility administrators will constantly ask themselves, *What is it costing me to do this, and is there a more cost-effective alternative?* Churches can save on utility costs simply by conducting an energy audit. Numerous no-cost and low-cost actions may be taken to reduce bills, such as scheduling all meetings on one night, using localized heating and cooling systems, turning off lights when not needed, setting back water heater thermostats or placing timers on them, caulking cracks around windows, or replacing weather stripping.

Other cost savings come with a wise approach to equipment selection. A church may not need a Cadillac to do Chevrolet work, but it shouldn't use a horse cart to do the work of a pickup truck. For example, if the facility has a large amount of tile flooring, a 1,500-rpm burnisher is better than a 300-rpm polisher and can likely cut floor-operations time in half. Since floor maintenance represents nearly 40 percent of the custodian's responsibilities, that is a significant savings.

Renting rather than buying expensive equipment—such as a carpet extraction-cleaning system—can also save money. Renting the equipment once or twice a year has distinct advantages: the use of good equipment, no money tied up in the equipment, and no maintenance costs.

What maintenance equipment does a church need? Here's a basic housekeeping-equipment and consumable-supply shopping list:

Use Policies for Buildings and Equipment

Policies are management decisions that express a church's operating philosophy. Policies answer questions before they are asked and guide people in responding to routine situations before problems occur. Every church should develop policies that convey the desires of its members. The policies should be formulated in concert with those who will implement them, according to stated procedures.

Policies and Procedures

Policies are best communicated in writing. When voted on by the congregation, they become a permanent expression of the church's mission and purpose. They also serve as a manual of training for new staff and committee members, a guide for making future decisions, and a handbook of church operations for the membership.

Procedures are the steps to implementing what a policy calls for. Naturally, procedural processes are best developed by the individuals who will be called upon to carry them out. They should be detailed enough to sufficiently respond to actions required by the policy, be understood by the staff and church members alike, be understood by a nonmember if the policy is applicable, and be carried out effectively by volunteers outside of the policy-making department.

Churches should strive to transmit policies in standard ways, since the reason for policies is to encourage consistent administration. For example, a typical policy and procedure might look like this:

It is the policy of Community Church that church properties and equipment will be used only by church members.

1. Individuals or groups who desire to use church facilities or equipment will complete a Use-Request Form 1010.

a. The form must be completed at least two working

● *Equipment:* Vacuums (commercial upright, backpack, and wet-dry); water-extraction cleaner; wet mops; mop buckets with ringer; dust mops; brooms (standard and push); squeegee (floor and window); johnny mop; sponges; janitor cart; hand dusters; duster on a telescoping pole; whisk broom and pan; buckets; bulk dispensers; hand sprayers; buffer; cleaning and polishing buffer pads; ladder; step stool; and hand tools.

● *Consumable supplies:* Glass cleaner; nonacid toilet bowl cleaner; cleanser (powder and spray); disinfectant; deodorant sprays; germicidal spray; urinal screens and blocks; toilet blocks; tile and grout cleanser; baseboard cleaner; furniture polish; liquid soap; hand towels and wipes; drain opener; carpet shampoo concentrate; carpet spot cleaner; general purpose floor-cleaning concentrate; dust mop treat-

---

days before the day of need.

b. The request must be approved by the pastor.

c. When church facilities are to be used, the request must be placed on the church calendar.

d. The member making the request will also be the person responsible for the security of the facility and will be the only one issued a key.

2. Fees and charges.

a. No fees will be charged for church-related activities.

b. Activities such as weddings and receptions will be charged a one-time fee of $25 to pay for janitor and utility costs.

In this example, the general policy was stated, leaving no room for misinterpretation. The procedures then outlined important rules and guidelines related to implementation. Another type of policy and procedure statement might express a general philosophy and then delegate the responsibility to define actual implementation. For example:

It is the policy of Community Church to maintain the church

facilities in a clean, habitable, and safe condition at all times. It will be the responsibility of the Church Property Committee to recommend and implement actions that will meet this objective.

1. Housekeeping. It will be the responsibility of the senior custodian to create schedules to ensure church facilities are kept clean.

a. All offices will be policed daily.

b. All Area A and B rest rooms will be policed on a daily basis.

c. Hall carpets will be vacuumed on Monday, Wednesday, and Friday.

d. And so on.

This format allows the one implementing it the freedom to modify and alter procedures as he or she sees fit, while making sure that the policy is adhered to. Other subdivisions in this policy might include grounds, equipment, and safety procedures.

—*Robert H. Welch*

ment; floor stripper; floor finish; buffing treatment; plastic bags; and gloves.

Managing Maintenance

Every church needs someone to perform maintenance and custodial functions. Many churches need at least one in-house maintenance custodian. Larger churches may add personnel as the needs increase, or they may employ a contract janitorial service. The average trained custodian cleans about 2,250 to 2,500 square feet per hour. This will vary, depending upon how often the custodian returns to the cleaning closet for more or different equipment and supplies. Also, certain special operations, such as floor stripping, will require additional time. (See

---

Hiring, Contracting, or Using Volunteers?

Good maintenance not only keeps a church in shape, it can also create an environment that attracts new members. However, churches typically operate in a world punctuated by statements such as "Nobody volunteered to clean the rest rooms today" or "The janitor is in the hospital" or "Maintenance Masters charges too much for our budget."

Three Steps

If such laments sound familiar, perhaps it is time to reevaluate your maintenance program. Solving the problem may be relatively uncomplicated using a three-step guide:

● *Determine what needs to be done.* The need inventory should indicate not only what needs to be accomplished but also how often and how professionally. The inventory should include, as a minimum, the church's need for vacuuming, floor waxing, rest room cleaning, window washing, lawn mowing and

trimming, and snow removal in season. A church may also want to include the purchasing of janitorial supplies and regular upkeep of such items as the lawn mower. A "how often" category for each task can sort those that need to be done daily, weekly, monthly, quarterly, and yearly.

● *Investigate the options.* Once needs are determined, maintenance typically is handled in one of three ways, each with distinct advantages and disadvantages: (1) Asking volunteers to do the work has the advantage of being the least expensive option, and volunteers usually enjoy using their gifts to serve God. Disadvantages, however include difficulties with the control and coordination of untrained volunteers, often creating a lack of consistency. (2) Hiring paid employees means consistency in the work and regular hours, but employees may not be talented in all areas of maintenance, and payroll costs add up.

Holcomb or Chandler in the "Resources" section for detailed time standards for custodial operations.)

Only about 80 percent of the work day is usually available for custodial operations—both indoor housekeeping and outdoor maintenance. The remaining time is administrative or errand-running time. The objective is to maximize the 80 percent.

Facility maintenance and housekeeping operations should be scheduled, based on a thorough analysis of what needs to be done to maintain the facility. The schedule will probably develop over time and should also include the input of the supervisory custodian. Depending on the number of custodians available, direct work on housekeeping and maintenance should be assigned to the 80- to 90-percent level to allow for setup and administrative time. Specific

---

(3) Contracting with a professional maintenance company assures insured workers who are specialists and able to provide their own supplies and equipment. The disadvantage is that this is usually the most costly alternative, and contract personnel aren't always available for special needs.

● *Figure the cost.* Costs will depend on the options a church chooses. If the church is not prepared for the financial burden of paid employees, volunteers can be used for projects that members have the talents and availability to perform. The church pays only the cost of insurance, periodic equipment repair, and supplies.

For a church employee, the congregation must pay at least minimum wage and possibly benefits, not to mention social security and other taxes. In 1994, a church could plan on spending about $25,000 per year per employee, with the added cost of purchasing, maintaining, and repairing equipment and buying supplies—a few thousand dollars more annually.

Janitorial service with five cleanings a week for a typical church cost $400 to $600 per week (up to $31,200 per year) in 1994. This figure, however, did not include special services, such as carpet cleaning, pressure washing, window cleaning, or any exterior services. Lawn mowing and trimming ran about $50 to $100 per trim, depending on the size of the lawn. Snow removal cost about $50 to $200 per trip.

Churches deciding on contract services need to ask key questions up front: Is your service hourly, by the trip, or a lump sum or seasonal flat fee? Do you provide your own cleaning supplies and equipment? Are you bonded for nonperformance? For security? What kinds of training do your employees receive? How can we terminate the contract? Will you provide a written guarantee against price increases and overruns (for lump-sum and seasonal work)? The key is to be prepared to shop for price each season, because some services give a low bid just to get business and then bump up the price the next season.

—*Jan Mellema*

cleaning and maintenance responsibilities should be scheduled and assigned to the individual custodian.

Posted schedules help direct the work activity and should include routine daily operations as well as weekly or unique activities. Schedules allow the supervisor to know what is being done, when to inspect the facility, and how to evaluate the work. Routine inspections by assigned church staff or property committee members will ensure the facility is maintained in a clean and safe condition. Inspections, based on inspection forms, spur the repair of items suffering from wear, deterioration, and abuse. The results of monthly, semi-annual, or annual inspections can be inserted into work schedules.

Inspection forms can be derived from the space-utilization plan that describes the characteristics of the facility by area and room. (See Holcomb or Welch for sample forms.) Describing the urgency of needed action is the key to effective inspection: Does it have to happen now, or can it wait until the money is available?

Keeping House Indoors

The offices, major hallways, and rest rooms should be policed daily. Policing involves vacuuming, mopping the floors, emptying wastebaskets, dusting, and straightening up the area. Other housekeeping duties should be scheduled throughout the week, but before any space will be used again. All carpets should be vacuumed weekly to prevent dirt's migration into the base of the fiber. Soiled areas of carpet should be cleaned weekly, using the bonnet or dry-chemical or foam process. Spots, spills, and graffiti should be cleaned up immediately, before soiling agents set up.

The use of a pH-neutral cleanser will avoid problems with water-chemical reaction. Detergents of the citrus base d'Limonene will clean nearly all grease, oil, or gum-soiled areas without emitting the odors of some of the oil-solvent cleaners. QUAT disinfectants are almost odor-free and are now capable of killing nearly all surface germs and bacteria. They make excellent choices for cleaning nurseries, children's areas, and kitchens.

The choice of cleaning products is almost as critical as their proper application. It's usually good to buy all supplies and equipment from one individual, choosing a product supplier that can provide a wide range of products, offer discounts and bonuses for bulk and long-term contract purchases, visit your facility to offer consultation about difficult cleaning problems, and train your personnel in the use of the products. Buying bulk and premeasured-portion products saves money, since you are not paying for packaging and added water. If you do not need the volumes sold by your distributor, consider sharing the costs and products with nearby churches.

Some housekeeping operations require special effort and scheduling. Carpets should be extraction cleaned at least once yearly. Resilient and wood floors should be stripped of old finish and rewaxed annually. Because of the large amount of time required to do these things and the special equipment needed, facility administrators may find it cost-effective to contract these operations with professionals.

Maintaining the Grounds Outdoors

The appearance of the exterior of our facilities is the most basic invitation card we offer our community. We all look at the cover of a card before we read the inscription inside. The cover sets the tone. Here are some ways we can help people *want* to come inside:

● When choosing grass for your region, select varieties that grow well for your soil type and condition, do not require large amounts of water, and grow slowly. It's good to check with a local county agent or nursery vendors for advice.

● Plant slow-growing evergreen shrubs around the facility. They are low-maintenance and provide color all year.

● Highlight your church sign by making it part of the overall landscape. Replace lights when needed, and keep the sign's message current.

● Plant deciduous trees on the south side, for summer shade and winter sun. Plant evergreens on the north side to protect facilities from winter winds. This is a good energy-conservation method.

● Keep parking lots well marked and lighted, and offer handicap access (about 1 for every 25 spaces).

● Repair potholes using a premixed concrete product. Choose a product that attains tensile strength quickly and will set in all types of weather.

Along with our pastoral duties, we must remember that facility management is an ongoing activity, too. Through effective planning and strict attention to the details of the process, we can make our churches clean, safe, and durable places of worship.

—Robert H. Welch

Resources

Chandler, R. 1992. Improving facilities maintenance. Fort Worth: National Association of Church Business Administration.

Holcomb, T. 1990. A maintenance management manual for Southern Baptist churches. Nashville: Convention.

McCormick, G. 1992. Planning and building church facilities. Nashville: Broadman.

Welch, R. 1992. The church organization manual. Fort Worth: National Association of Church Business Administration.

Insurance

Your building is damaged by fire, a visitor is hurt, a church employee is injured on the job, the church is burglarized—insurance is the usual answer to these unfortunate events. But having the right insurance to handle such misfortunes requires careful thought and planning.

Options in Risk Management

There are four ways a church can cope with the possibility of claims arising from injury or other forms of liability:

● *Eliminate the risk.* Some risks can be removed. For example, churches can fix low clearances, slippery surfaces, faulty wiring, broken stairs, and other areas demonstrating clear negligence.

● *Lower the risks.* The next-best solution is to reduce the risks. A critical examination of buildings and grounds can show what precautionary steps might be taken to lessen hazards. While the danger of falling off a ladder cannot be eliminated, safety ladders with guard rails can reduce the risk.

● *Accept the risks.* A *self-insured* church creates a contingency fund to pay for claims instead of paying liability-insurance premiums. This practice, however, is hardly practical, considering the cost of legal fees and the amount of damages awarded by the courts.

Accepting at least part of the risk can be appropriate when the risk cannot be totally eliminated or the cost of insurance is prohibitive. While it is possible to buy insurance for almost every conceivable risk, that simply isn't practical for most churches.

● *Shift the risk.* Purchasing insurance coverage enables the church to transfer its risks. In effect, when a church buys insurance, it agrees to absorb some of the smaller, periodic losses (in the form of premiums and deductibles) in exchange for avoiding the large, uncertain claims.

Many Types of Insurance

Churches that shift the risk to insurance companies have many options available:

● *Fire insurance.* Most standard policies cover the buildings, the property contained within them, and property temporarily removed from them because of fire or lightning. Normally, this coverage does not extend to accounting records, bills, deeds, money, and securities, or to windstorms, hail, smoke, explosions, vandalism, automatic-sprinkler leakage, or malicious mischief. To keep a policy valid, the church must take every reasonable precaution to protect its property both before and after a fire.

● *Liability insurance.* Church leaders are responsible for the safety of church employees as well as those who attend. Most liability policies cover losses stemming from bodily-injury or property-damage claims, medical expenses arising from an accident, investigation expenses, and court costs.

These policies pay claims depending on per-accident and per-person limits. If, for instance, a policy has a per-accident limit of $400,000 and a per-person limit of $100,000, and if one person receives a $300,000 judgment against the church, the insurance company will pay only $100,000 and the church will pay $200,000.

● *Automobile insurance.* Automobile insurance is essential for any church-owned vehicle. Coverage should include bodily-injury claims, property-damage claims, medical payments, uninsured-motorist damage, damage to the church's vehicles, and towing costs. The cost of coverage normally depends on the value of the vehicles and the kinds of driving involved (deliveries, carrying passengers), as well as the church location.

● *Worker's compensation insurance.* Churches must conform to worker's compensation laws, which can be viewed as the government absorbing some of the liability risks relating to employee injuries or disabilities. Under worker's compensation, the carrier pays all claims the employer is legally required to pay a claimant. Basic insurance rates are set by law in most states, but a church can still control its premiums to a certain extent. Since rates vary according to the occupational category, it is important to make sure all church employees are classified correctly.

—David R. Pollock

Safety

Only .001 percent of all accidents occur in church, yet we must remember that our parishioners expect us to provide safe and secure places of worship and ministry. Here are four practices that can help keep a church a place where safety matters.

Plan for Safety

At the least, a church must train its ushers in emergency procedures and post emergency-escape routes in each room. In addition, the church should post near its phones the instructions to be given to fire, police, and EMT personnel when anyone calls for help. Instructions might include giving the name and location of the church, stating where the emergency is, and providing a telephone number for return calls.

Some churches have gone a step further by organizing "emergency reaction teams" made up of qualified staff and lay personnel. The team stands ready to assist in emergencies that might occur during worship and fellowship times. Members who are firefighters, police officers, Red Cross volunteers, or nurses are good candidates for such teams.

Equip for Safety

Along with having a well-equipped first-aid kit, it's essential that every church train its personnel in the safe operation of equipment, especially electrical or motorized equipment. It's also a good idea to have emergency oxygen and equipment available for personnel trained in its use, and to designate an area of the church that will have a cot, blanket, towels, and other supplies ready for emergency use.

Of course, every church must provide adequate fire extinguishers. OSHA recommends placing one in every 2,500 square feet of space. Extinguishers classified as ABC will be able to put out any type of fire.

Build for Safety

Building codes dictate the number of exits per room, based on load limits, but a rule of thumb is that no person should have to move further than 30 to 40 feet to escape the room. Stairwells must be fire protected, able to be closed off from the remainder of the structure, and well-lighted. Well-marked emergency exits must be able to be opened from the inside, opening outward from the interior. Green exit lights that stay illuminated via an alternate power source are also required.

Sound building practices also dictate that furnace and mechanical rooms be fireproofed with masonry or sheetrock walls, ceilings, and floors; that emergency cutoffs be located outside the building for all gas, oil, and electrical supplies; and that heat sensors be installed to detect fires.

Inspect for Safety

Someone should be designated to inspect the facility for safety and deliver periodic reports. Here are some of the tasks this person (or committee) could monitor:

● Arrange for snow removal, as well as the application of deicing and traction products.

● Provide walk-on/walk-off mats at doorways to prevent falls.

● Make sure fire alarms have both an audio component and a flashing strobe light to aid blind or deaf individuals.

● Repair or replace damaged children's toys and equipment.

● Get rid of extension cords and plugs that are brittle, broken, or frayed.

● Inspect areas where flammable materials may be stored, making sure, for instance, that there are no open-bulb lighting fixtures in those areas. Designate authorized storage areas and store all flammable materials only in rooms that have ventilation to the outside.

● Prevent clutter and clear stairwells and escape routes.

● Check all seats for seat belts in the church van or bus, and encourage a policy of seat belt use.

—*Robert H. Welch*

Energy Conservation and Ecology

When a church determines to use less energy, it adds money to the budget (by reducing expenses), lessens environmental damage, helps equipment last longer, and demonstrates good management.

But church members must approach energy management as a continuous process rather than a one-shot event.

We may think a sanctuary that uses relatively little energy must have efficient equipment, automatic controls, and lots of insulation. This is not necessarily true. The key factor in reduced energy use is to elect a single person—an energy warden—who takes responsibility for controlling energy use on an ongoing basis. Property committees are no substitute.

Insulation and storm windows have little effect on energy use when the heating or cooling system is turned off, as it should be when the buildings are not being used. Since worship centers are usually occupied for far fewer hours than most church buildings, the energy warden should be concerned about the conditions of the *unoccupied* building.

The Warden's Duties

An energy warden performs the following tasks:

● *Purchases energy at the lowest cost* by: (1) contacting the utility companies to determine if the church is billed according to the most advantageous electric and gas rates; (2) purchases the lowest-cost fuel by doing competitive pricing; and (3) determines that the facility is not paying unnecessary state sales tax and, in the case of schools and day care centers, federal excise tax.

● *Continually gathers and summarizes energy invoices.* The warden measures the outside dimensions of the facility to determine the number of square feet of heated and/or cooled floor area. Using one year's energy units per square foot, the warden can rate usage in relation to other churches. In a warm climate, the average church uses 5 kilowatthours of electricity per square foot annually, compared to 2.5 for a thrifty church; and .10 therms of natural gas, compared to .05 for a thrifty church. In a cold climate, the average is 2.2 kilowatthours average (compared to .5 for a thrifty church) and .6 therms (.35 for the thrifty).

● *Visits the building at least once annually when it is not occupied* and makes a list of energy uses that can be turned off or reduced.

● *Restricts coincident peak demands* (if the facility is being billed for electric demand) by installing time clocks on electric water heaters and interlocks on cooling compressors.

● *Inspects the building* to identify pathways that allow conditioned air to escape or outdoor air to enter the building. Air pathways can be restricted, unless there is evidence of increased condensation or odors.

● *Purchases only energy-efficient lamps.* Examples: 34- or 32-watt tubes for standard 40-watt tubes; 60-watt tubes for 75-watt tubes; compact fluorescent lamps for incandescent lamps; tungsten-halogen floodlamps for standard floods; and fluorescent exit retrofit kits for incandescent exit signs.

● *Reviews all maintenance contracts on equipment* to assure that contractors are doing what they agreed to do.

● *Adjusts the domestic hot-water thermostat* to heat water no hotter than 110 to 120 degrees F (or what local codes require).

● *Consolidates the contents of partially used refrigerators and freezers* into as few appliances as possible. Empty refrigerators should be cleaned, unplugged, and left to dry with doors ajar in a manner that is safe for children.

● *Cuts vending-machine power usage* by installing timers on nondairy machines and disconnecting the machines' fluorescent lamps.

● *Adjusts pilot-light flames* to their lowest practical height and turns off heating pilots during non- heating months.

● *Changes filters in air handlers regularly.* Inspects all finned-tube radiation, hot-water, and chilled- water coils, convectors, and unit heaters to ensure that dirt is not restricting the transfer of heat.

—*Andrew Rudin*

Handicap Access

Nearly 43 million members of our society have a hard time getting around at church. What can churches do about their accessibility problems?

Legal Expectations

The Americans with Disabilities Act of 1990 (ADA) was a significant piece of civil-rights legislation. One section especially affected churches: Title III—Public Accommodations. It requires buildings to comply with the reasonable-access provisions of the law if owners offer use of their facilities to the general public (and that may include churches). Daycare centers, schools, and voting sites are prime examples. While ADA specifically exempts churches from most provisions, *local* building-regulatory agencies may require churches to comply to the ADA provisions.

Making Buildings Accessible

Perhaps the greatest challenge to the church is meeting ADA guide- lines for assisting people who require mobility aids, such as walk- ers or wheelchairs. To do this, churches can:

● *Modify seating* to accommodate wheelchairs. A cabinet maker can shorten and reinstall pews at reasonable costs. ADA requires a 2" raised bumper rail and a maneuvering space of 5' × 5'. Since pews are usually spaced 30"–32" apart, two pews will have to be shortened to create one space.

● *Build ramps.* Where enough space exists, ramps are one of the best ways to move people up a step or two. ADA requires using inclined ascents for any elevation rise over ½". Also, no more than 1" of rise is allowed for 1' of travel—a 1:12 incline (an inclined ascent of 10", two steps, would require a 10' ramp).

ADA also mandates a 5'-square resting platform every 30' for ramps 30' or longer, handrails between 27" and 34" high that extend 12" beyond the ramp, a minimum rail-to-rail width of 36", and nonslip flooring.

● *Install a stairway seat or chair lifts.* When ramps are not feasible, the seat or chair lift might be the best option. They take up less space than a ramp, can be installed alongside existing stairs, and are cheaper than an elevator or vertical lift. However, they are usually limited to one floor of movement (10 feet in elevation).

ADA requires a mechanism to secure the person or chair, a size sufficient to accommodate the person or chair, platforms of at least 3' × 4', and controls that accompany the occupant.

● *Install vertical chair lifts.* When a stairway cannot be used, the vertical chair lift may be the answer. Usually occupying less than 6' × 6', this hydraulic lift will move a person in a wheelchair up to 12' vertically. ADA requirements include a minimum floor of 54" × 68", controls that can be reached from a wheelchair and travel with the rider, and restraints to keep the chair from rolling off the lift.

● *Install an elevator.* Facilities

with fewer than three floors are not required by code to install an elevator, but many churches choose to do so. Three types of elevators are the hydraulic piston, the hydraulic drawn cable, and the gear-driven cable.

The hydraulic piston and hydraulic drawn-cable systems seem to be the most cost effective for churches, since new technology allows for hydraulic systems to be installed without having to drill a big hole in the base of the elevator shaft. However, piston-holeless systems are limited to two levels (about 25 feet of travel), while the cable-drawn systems can extend six stories.

ADA requirements include a minimum of 54" interior depth, a width of 68" for side-opening doors and 80" for center-opening doors, and a doorway opening of at least 36".

—Robert H. Welch

Parking Lots

A well-planned parking area tells people that yours is a friendly and inviting church, and that you use your resources wisely. An excellent parking area will be convenient (Is your lot conveniently located and easy to use?); functional (Is conflict and confusion between vehicles and pedestrians kept to a minimum?); and well-groomed (Is the area well-maintained, properly lighted, and nicely landscaped?) Effective parking solutions will help a church meet these criteria—and send a positive message to attenders at the same time.

Planning Parking

As a church begins its project, leaders will need to answer questions such as: Where will people walk? Where will parents drop off their children? How will the elderly and handicapped access our facility? Where will deliveries be made? How can our parking design minimize confusion at occasions such as weddings and funerals?

A church will probably want to seek professional help when building a lot to help think through the following factors:

● *Building plans.* It's best to use an updated facility plan that identifies both current usage patterns and future development projects to prevent having to needlessly redo parking lots.

● *Local building codes.* These codes set most of the requirements and help identify what is permitted.

● *Lighting.* If possible, it's sensible to install lights on the outside wall of an adjacent building to avoid extensive conduit and light-pole expenses. It's also wise to consider energy-efficient lighting, directional shields to keep lights from bothering neighbors, and light-sensor controls instead of time clocks.

● *Line of sight.* Landscaping should not block the line of sight of drivers or pedestrians. It's best to landscape only with low bushes or shrubs.

● *Natural aisles.* A church with long drives can add parking on one or both sides of them if possible. It saves the cost of building an aisle between rows of parking places.

● *Parking angle.* When space allows, parking off both sides of the aisles at 90 degrees is the most cost effective.

● *Waste collection.* Place dumpsters and waste-collection points as close to the street as possible. The weight and constant starting and stopping of garbage trucks on an asphalt lot will destroy it.

● *Drainage.* Providing proper drainage can double or triple the cost of a simple parking lot. Thus it's best to position and slope lots so that water runs off onto grassy areas rather than into costly storm drains.

● *Snow removal.* This affects where to position bumpers, light poles, and landscaped islands. We should avoid placing items that will be hard to see and easy to clip with a blade.

Maintaining a Lot

A properly built and cared-for parking lot should last 15 to 20 years. Here are some ways to help a lot live a long and fruitful life:

● *Seal-coat properly.* Allow new asphalt one year to settle and cure, and then seal-coat it to fill in small fissures that sometimes develop as a lot hardens. Sealing also protects against damage from gasoline or oil.

● *Fill new cracks.* It's good to seal cracks as they develop. A paving contractor can demonstrate the procedure and recommend locally available products, and then volunteers can do it for the church. They should determine the cause before attempting a repair, looking for water runoff from a building or dips that may result from sewer or drainage lines sinking or shifting.

● *Resurface as necessary.* We should overlay a new asphalt coating when necessary, but overlaying a badly deteriorated lot with a poor foundation is simply a waste of money. The lot must be in reasonable condition with no foundation problems and with cracks well-maintained. A fiberglass membrane will strengthen the new surface.

—*Stephen W. Mead*

Protecting Stained Glass

Do the dangers of our modern world necessitate special exterior protection for stained-glass windows? Not necessarily. Every window and installation is different.

For example, it is a mistake to install the same type of protective glazing in every situation. In fact, some "protective" coverings can actually damage stained glass. Also, protective glazing is not restoration and will not halt the deterioration of a stained-glass window. It *may* lengthen the life of a window in good condition, but deteriorated windows should be restored first.

What to Protect

Before installing protective panels, thought should be given to each window's situation. Adding protection is recommended if the windows are prone to deliberate damage or theft, or if they have extensive exterior painting or are made of an unusual or fragile glass. In some nineteenth- and early twentieth-century windows with fired vitreous paint, pollution and humidity may cause unprotected windows to become more unstable. Also, in windows by La Farge and modern artists that experimented with fusing or appliqué, the glass is unstable and needs protection.

What to Use

A number of factors go into deciding how to protect windows, such as:

● *Materials.* Glass is commonly used. It looks better than plastic, doesn't scratch or yellow, and will not affect the color or amount of light transmitted. Glass allows greater design flexibility, and it has a variety of textures. Also, tempered or laminated glass is resistant to breakage and can take an impact instead of the stained glass. A disadvantage of glass is that it provides little protection against vandalism or accidental breakage, and the weight of the glass places increased stress on the window frame.

An alternative to glass is polycarbonate plastic (not acrylic). Polycarbonates (such as Lexan) are unbreakable and have greater resistance to abrasion and light degradation. Lexan, however, costs more than plate glass, and appearance is a drawback, since it is installed only in large sheets, and eventually weather will yellow and scratch the surface.

● *Panel size.* Glass can be installed in full sheets, and all plastics and plate glass must be installed this way. While typically a faster and less costly installation than a leaded pattern, full sheets often reflect light, obscuring the stained-glass window from the outside. Also, plastics tend to bow, are highly reflective, and may become abraded by the wind or turn iridescent.

A better approach is clear glass fit into panes (called quarries) held together by lead came. Its drawbacks are a higher price tag and the extra shadows on the window from the lead.

Perhaps the best alternative is fully patterned leaded glazing. This ultimate protective glazing recreates the window design by copying all the lead lines from the stained glass or only the essential ones. However, it too can leave double-shadowed lead lines on the interior, and it is the most costly method.

Spot glazing can be used when only certain pieces need protection. This method is useful on windows restored with epoxy, copper foil, or fragile paint. It adds little to the window weight and doesn't change its appearance.

How to Do It

Before installing protective glazing for energy conservation, an infrared photograph should be taken of the building to locate the greatest heat loss. It is notable that more heat is lost through an uninsulated attic than through stained-glass windows.

The protective glazing should be installed at least 1" from the stained glass, and the cavity should be ventilated at the top and bottom of each protective panel, since moist air from inside that gets trapped between the window and the protective covering can cause damage.

—*Julie L. Sloan*

Church Signs

Church signs communicate an image that affects how members and potential attenders perceive the congregation. Untidy signs say, "We don't care." Worse yet, if bulbs have failed, the paint has faded, or the surface has become overgrown by shrubbery, the sign may not be readable.

A helpful exercise in "sign language" is to look at the sign again as if for the first time: Can the sign be read from the street? Is it modern and attractive? Does it communicate an image suited to the congregation? New insights can also be gained by having several people who do not attend church relate what the sign says to them.

Four Key Considerations

Features to consider when assessing an old sign or planning a new one include:

● *Purpose.* What do we want the sign to do? We can ask this question of key church groups early in the decision-making process. Different committees—finance, evangelism, property—will raise different concerns.

● *Setting.* What is the speed limit where the sign will be posted? The size, style, lighting, and placement of the sign will differ greatly if the speed limit is 30 miles per hour in a residential neighborhood or 45 miles per hour on a major arterial with an array of signs. At 30 miles per hour with a clear view, motorists should be able to absorb the information in about three seconds.

● *Content.* Do we want a sign that only identifies the church name or one that also can display specialized messages? Some churches display a Bible verse or upcoming program information. Including the church logo on the sign is a good idea, since people remember a vivid symbol better than words.

● *Regulations.* What are the zoning regulations regarding signs? Many communities have strict codes on placement, size, height, materials, and style.

Sign Design

While the materials and designs used for church signs are nearly limitless, here is a sampling of approaches:

● *Internally lit signs* use a translucent plastic shell, contrasting lettering, and lighting from inside the sign. This kind of sign is often constructed in two sections: one section permanently displays the name of the church; the rest of the sign provides space for a message using removable lettering on tracks.

● *Top-lit signs* are common along the sidewalk fronts of many city churches. As the sign is traditionally constructed, the church's name appears at the top of the sign, and an enclosed bulletin board (used to clip lettering for sermon titles and service times) appears in the lower, larger section. The bulletin board is illuminated from above, and the church name stands out at night as light shines through its translucent lettering.

The small, traditional top-lit sign is difficult to read from the road, though it can be effective in city neighborhoods where pedestrian traffic is heavy.

● *Raised-lettering wood signs* work well if the information on the sign rarely needs to be changed. Some use a sandblasted background and color finish. Floodlamps are commonly used for lighting, and sometimes top-mounted fluorescent lamps.

● *Painted wood signs* can be an inexpensive alternative. Major church-sign manufacturers offer this service, as do many local sign painters. A drawback is that usually the church is responsible for the design and layout of the sign, and results vary according to the skill of the painter.

● *Computerized message boards* use an electronic panel to display lighted text that can be programed to move, flash, or remain constant. (Banks often use these to display time and temperature). Messages are input by computer and can be changed easily. However, few churches have used them because of cost.

—John R. Throop

31

Managing Construction and Remodeling

A church may initially view its construction project as the purchase of a single, though expensive, solution to the problems that have been created by growth. However, in contrast to purchasing a single item, being involved in construction means participation in a complex, time-consuming, and expensive process. A large network of hundreds of participants must work together to produce, deliver, and guarantee the end result.

Fortunately for the church, construction relationships can be clearly defined and maintained by a written contract, making the actual process and result somewhat predictable. In reality, however, the pastor or the building committee cannot expect to grasp, much less manage, the thousands of technical details involved in a building project. Yet they can help offset this disadvantage by using well-written contracts that clearly establish what is expected of the project's designers, consultants, contractors, and suppliers. Additionally, the church leaders' expertise in managing relationships—especially where results depend more upon persuasion and persistence than coercion—will be invaluable.

The importance of good planning cannot be overemphasized. The needs and potential of the congregation must be identified and prioritized through studies, surveys, and projections. Such an assessment must be carried out, because before a church can make realistic decisions about what to build, when to build, and how best to fund construction, it must establish its long-range growth strategy. The issue should not be what kind of *building* the church leaders want, but what kind of *building program* best supports the church's long-range growth plans.

Establishing a Program and Project Budget

Once the church adopts a growth strategy and establishes its immediate building needs, it must write a program that identifies specific space requirements (by square foot). It is not enough to request a wish list from each department involved, since the total square footage desired will invariably exceed the building budget. Each department must become willing to compromise, submitting minimum acceptable requirements as well as preferences. The total required-space estimates must then be weighed against the other, often inflexible, project requirements.

In new construction or major renovation, add about 15 to 20 percent to the net square footage to allow for wall thicknesses, mechanical rooms, rest rooms, corridors, stairways, and elevators that will be required by building codes. If the project increases the present building-occupancy capacity, the community planning authorities will probably require additional paved parking. Generally, about 350 to 375 square feet of paved area per car provides for a legal parking space and access to it. In addition, along with specifying the amount of landscaping, many planning authorities now require an engineered retention pond to temporarily hold rainwater that runs off of paved surfaces.

The next step is to estimate the construction costs, based on current, comparable projects. This information will be most usable in the form of "square foot costs" and can be obtained from the architects and general contractors that are likely candidates for later interviews.

Finally, to the estimated building and site-development costs should be added the costs of furniture, special equipment, professional fees, and the interim financing needed during construction. If the total estimated project cost exceeds the church's financial capacity, the project will have to be reduced, postponed, or financed differently (through a bond program, for instance).

Selecting the Architect

Traditionally, an architect is hired directly by the owner to represent him or her throughout the entire construction project. Full architectural services include designing the project based on the owner's needs and budget, producing legally binding construction documents (drawings and specifications), supervising bidding, and serving as project administrator during construction. This service is typically provided for a fee ranging from 6 to 12 percent of construction costs, depending on the project size, difficulty, and location. The architect gets paid as the project progresses through standardized phases.

Once the decision has been made to hire an architect, the committee should prepare a list of potential candidates from names obtained through members, other churches, building contractors, or sources such as the local chapter of the American Institute of Architects (AIA). The committee should then send a letter to each candidate, requesting the architect's qualifications. It is important to describe the project type, size, estimated budget, and schedule in order to help the architect give the most appropriate responses. Usually architects will want to meet with representatives of the church and familiarize themselves with the site before submitting qualifications.

After reviewing the qualifications of the various firms, the committee should establish a short list of three to five firms for formal interviews. Since the distinctions among architectural firms may not be apparent to those unfamiliar with the construction industry, the committee will need to create a receptive atmosphere for the candidates and allow sufficient time for them to present themselves. It may take more than one interview with each candidate to determine the best firm for the project.

Finally, the issue of the architect's fee should not overshadow the value of his or her reputation, experience with church projects, or ability to complete the work on schedule. The architect is being hired as the church's advocate, not its adversary. The church should understand that the architect must be fairly compensated in order to do his or her best work.

Choosing the Contractor

The architect normally will assist the church by prequalifying the prospective contractors, creating a list of candidates, and advising the committee on final selection, either through bidding or negotiation. As with the architect, the contractor's ability to promise a low price should not overshadow reputation, experience with similar projects, and proven ability to deliver quality work on schedule. A church will invariably pay more than once for low quality and poor performance.

Require all prospective contractors or design/builders to submit a current Contractor's Qualification Statement, published by the American Institute of Architects. This standard form is, in fact, a sworn statement by the contractor that allows the committee to better compare the history, staff, experience, financial strength, and references of the various candidates.

The final choice of contractor normally is done by bidding or negotiation. If the committee chooses to bid the project, it should understand that a considerable amount of the bidders' time and effort goes into bidding. Thus, if the project is to be honestly and competitively bid, and the list of prequalified bidders has been established, the committee should not expect to open the bids and then negotiate the lowest price with the most preferred contractor. To do so would not only be unethical to the bidders, but would undermine the credibility of the committee as well.

Determining the Delivery System

After defining the church's long-range plans and immediate needs, and resolving the various project priorities, the committee will need to determine the construction delivery system. "Delivery system" is merely a convenient way to describe the contractual arrangement that will carry the project through design, costing, and construction.

The Pastor's Involvement

Pastors regularly get involved in building-and-grounds matters, helping with everything from deciding where to place mirrors in a hallway to establishing architectural guidelines for a multimillion-dollar worship center. Some people wonder why we take part in such decisions. In essence, they're asking: What is the pastor's role in building-and-grounds matters? Should pastors stick to leading worship and preaching, or should they also help manage construction and remodeling projects?

Individual Guidelines

The response to these questions will vary with each unique situation, but the following guidelines can help us establish the nature and level of our involvement.

● *Delegate responsibility but demonstrate interest.* During a major building project, pastors may spend little more than half an hour a

week on it. The building committee includes people who may understand building issues far better than we do. They can supply us information, and we attend building-committee meetings. But for the most part, we can allow the committees and subcommittees to make most of the decisions, such as the kind of pews or the color scheme. Unless a decision involves something critical or affects us personally, we are wise to delegate.

Our role is not to make all the decisions but to support those who are responsible for them. The public statements a pastor makes about a building project establish the congregation's attitude toward it, so we must carefully craft what we say. For example, I work to explain how the building furthers the corporate mission, thank those directly involved, and demonstrate that I know and care about the project.

● *Concentrate energies on areas that relate to pastoral duties.* The

Although the committee should be familiar with the various systems, the actual choice of the most appropriate system will be determined by various factors, such as the project's budget, the committee's willingness to control the development of the project, the committee's authority to negotiate the contract, and the availability of competent professionals to deliver the project. Also, the level of risk protection demanded by the committee (in the form of performance bonds, liability insurance, and extended warranties) will affect the price and the acceptability of potential architects and contractors.

All contractual arrangements fall into one of four delivery systems, each providing a different level of control, risk, and cost. Realistically, it is not possible for the committee to maintain a high degree of control and little or no risk at the lowest possible cost. Likewise, it is unwise to give up significant control and accept high risk for the sake

---

stress characteristics of concrete in a proposed church building don't directly affect pastoral ministry (unless there's an earthquake). But other aspects of the building do intersect ministry, and during decisions about these, we need to communicate specific preferences.

For example, pastors usually use their offices to counsel people, and the office surroundings greatly affect that interaction. Decisions related to sanctuary furnishings, the baptistry, the pulpit, pew arrangement, and educational facilities also call for pastoral involvement. Sometimes staff people notice that the way the building committee designed a room makes it unworkable for a particular program. Because this part of the building affects pastoral duties, it is our responsibility to represent the staff in efforts to get that corrected.

● *Become knowledgeable in the areas of pressing concern.* Pastors don't need to know a lot about church buildings and grounds—until it's time to decide something critical. For example, I never knew much about acoustics until our

church began planning a new sanctuary. If preaching was going to be heard in the new building, the sound system needed to be constructed properly. In order to enter those discussions, I studied about reverberation times and decibel levels. While not attempting to become an expert in every phase of a project, we need to become conversant in the key subjects currently under discussion.

● *Teach people to notice what facilities communicate.* It's our job to emphasize that the building is everyone's responsibility, because of the way it affects visitors' attitudes. When the new pastor of one Baptist church arrived, he told the trustees, "We need to do something about the grass in the parking lot."

"We don't have any grass in the parking lot," they said.

"Come outside," he told them. Once there, they noticed the grass growing through cracks. They had driven over that grass for ten years and hadn't seen it—until they looked at it as a newcomer would.

—Leith Anderson

of a low price. Determining the best delivery system requires a frank assessment of the church's expectations and abilities.

● *Design/bid/build.* This system involves hiring an architect as the church's representative to design the project to meet the church's needs. After reviewing alternate solutions and cost estimates with the committee and obtaining their approval, the architect produces detailed drawings and specifications (construction documents) to be competitively bid among a selected group of prequalified general contractors. The architect also serves as the project administrator by

The Building Committee

Next to the pastor, the members of a building committee have possibly the riskiest job in the church, since they are made responsible for managing hundreds of thousands (if not millions) of dollars of the church's money. Besides having decisions and results scrutinized by the congregation, being on a building committee requires a great personal commitment of time and effort.

Recruiting the Right People

The committee should include people who are spiritually mature and willing to devote a great amount of time to the work, and who demonstrate interest in the church's programs. Serving on a building committee requires patience and perseverance, and is not suited for people who demand quick action or immediate results. The members need to be flexible, since sometimes it becomes apparent that the church should not build as anticipated, or should build less or later or not at all.

Selection of the building commit-tee should not be a popularity contest. Thus, it is better for the church to give the pastor or a council the responsibility of selecting the committee rather than leaving it to a general vote. This helps ensure that people are selected who will work together with an attitude of mutual respect and shared responsibility.

It is a common mistake to select committee members based entirely on their vocation in the fields of finance or construction. Without spiritual maturity or involvement in church life, it is unlikely that these "experts" will appreciate the broader purpose and goals of the church. Such individuals might better serve the committee as consultants.

Organizing for Continuity

Ideally, a steering committee should be formed to provide continuity throughout the many months—even years—of preparation necessary to identify the church's needs and potential, and ultimately to recommend specific actions and solutions. The duplication and miscommunication that

approving the contractor's pay applications and change orders and rejecting work that does not conform to the construction documents. This method results in a design that reflects the church's needs, construction quality that is enforced, and a fixed contract price.

However, to impose such controls invariably increases the project cost. For example, full architectural services add 6 to 12 percent to the cost of construction, depending on the size and complexity of the project. Also, bidding itself does not guarantee the lowest possible price, since the bidders are required to comply exactly with the construction

result from committees acting independently can be avoided by treating specialized areas as subcommittees that report to the building committee.

The committee should include a chairperson, a secretary, and subcommittee chairpersons, with the number of subcommittees determined by the size of the church. For large churches, as many as eight or more subcommittees may be needed, representing promotion, growth, program development, finance, property, furnishings, design, and construction. For small churches, these could be combined into four or five subcommittees, each responsible for two or more concerns.

The subcommittees should include several members of the congregation under the leadership of the subcommittee chairperson. In turn, each subcommittee member would lead an individual "work group" made up of additional members of the congregation. For example, the finance subcommittee might include work groups on fundraising, church income, and loan acquisition, or the property subcommittee might include work groups on property needs and land acquisition.

With such a comprehensive organization, the committee not only gathers valuable information about the church, but also involves the maximum number of people without losing control or direction. This further benefits the church by increasing a sense of ownership, strengthening personal relationships, and laying the groundwork for a later capital-fund drive.

Making It Work

The committee should expect a clear statement from the church as to their responsibilities, authority, and expected results. Likewise, the members of the committee, subcommittees, and work groups must be trained beforehand for their tasks. Clear direction and proper training will give the participants a better sense of their responsibilities, an awareness of the overall picture, and strengthened confidence in undertaking the work.

Finally, the extensive communication network coordinated by the building committee ensures that the committee's periodic reports and final recommendations to the congregation are understood and appreciated by more than just a few.

—*R. Leslie Nichols*

documents, without being encouraged to propose alternate materials or methods that might be less expensive. Finally, the contractor, an invaluable source of realistic pricing and current construction technology, is typically excluded from the process, prior to the actual bidding.

Because this system is centered around the design solution, it is most appropriate for churches that must respond to various internal groups competing for the new facilities, and for denominations with a congregational form of government. However, although this system may give church members the satisfaction of having accepted the lowest price among bidders, it does not necessarily deliver the most cost-effective total project.

● *Design/negotiate/build.* This system also employs an independent architect to design the project, meeting the church's needs. However, a single contractor works with the architect with the intention of negotiating a construction contract for either a guaranteed maximum price (GMP), or at cost plus a management fee (cost plus).

As the architect develops alternative design solutions, the contractor contributes realistic cost estimates. These solutions and estimates are reviewed with the church as the project progresses. Upon the church's acceptance of the final design solution and estimate, the architect develops the final drawings and specifications, relying on the contractor to advise him or her on the most cost-effective construction materials and methods.

After estimating the completed drawings and specifications, the contractor submits a formal proposal. If a GMP proposal is used, the contractor is given a financial incentive to complete the project below the guaranteed maximum price. If a cost-plus proposal is used, the church and architect review and approve the contractor's material and labor bids, while the contractor receives a management fee in the form of a fixed amount or a percentage of the final construction costs. If no agreement can be reached, the contractor should be compensated for work already completed in order to release the church from any obligations. The church may then continue the process with alternate contractors until an agreement is reached.

This system poses the greatest challenges and potential benefits to the church, since it requires trust and integrity from all parties involved. Just as the architect and the contractor must go beyond their traditional tasks, the church must be willing to make difficult choices and compromises early in the process in order to stay within budget. It will not be as easy for the committee to blame the architect or the contractor when the church members are displeased with the result. Yet, with the right team members and a spirit of cooperation, it is entirely possible to produce a project that is well-designed, well-built, and cost-effective.

● *Design/build.* During the past 25 years, this system has become more popular throughout the construction industry. It requires hiring a single company to provide all design and construction work to complete the project. Its appeal is its simplicity, since it involves a single contract and provides a single source of responsibility for the entire project. Additionally, it has the potential to lower the project cost, reduce completion time, and streamline the committee's involvement with the project.

However, in return for expedience and savings, the church loses the checks and balances that are built into hiring an independent architect or construction manager. Since the design/builder employs the architect, the committee should expect less, if any, direct communication with him or her. In fact, without independent architectural representation, the committee undertakes a greater legal responsibility to understand exactly what the design/builder proposes to provide, and to accept the completed project as conforming to the construction contract.

● *Construction management.* This system was originally created for large industrial and heavy-construction projects. It involves hiring a professional construction manager (CM) to coordinate and guide the development of the project, reporting directly to the owner. The CM does not replace the independent architect or contractor, and so the church takes on an additional management fee. This system is typically used on large projects where an additional fee is of less concern.

Construction management is perhaps the most misused term in the construction industry. Many design/build companies offer their supervision as "construction management," using some of the same techniques as a CM, but they don't provide independent representation directly to the owner.

Interestingly, this system can be adapted to small construction or renovation projects the church wants to complete with its own volunteers. The CM should be qualified to act as a field superintendent. Reporting directly to the committee, he or she serves to prevent much of the frustration and loss of time associated with projects that use volunteer crews. Ideally, this person provides a professional presence and serves as a capable liaison with local planning and building-code officials.

Resolving Construction Conflicts

Because of its complex nature, a construction project demands some degree of compromise by all parties involved. Two common conflicts arise in most projects. The ability to resolve them is critical to construction success.

First is the conflict created by the attempt to balance the demands for economy and quality within a particular project size. Simply stated: Increased size increases the cost, unless quality is in some way reduced. Since most church construction projects are driven by functional requirements (size) and limited by the congregation's maximum financial capacity (budget), the issue left to resolve is usually how attractive, durable, or flexible (quality) to make the project— without reducing its functional effectiveness or exceeding the budget. This resolution will help determine the best delivery system for the project, since a project with simple quality requirements may be best suited to a streamlined contractual agreement.

The second common conflict surfaces in the attempt to balance control, risk reduction, and cost. Simply stated: The more specific the design and construction requirements (control), and the more protections offered the owner (risk reduction), the greater the project cost. Most committees begin with the expectation that their project will be designed exactly as they wish and built exactly to specification, with all responsibility and risk carried by the architect and/or the contractor—all for the lowest competitive cost!

This has never been the case in construction. Since the owners, contractors, architects, and construction managers have conflicting priorities, there is always some degree of tension between them. For example, the church wants the best project, for the least effort, at the lowest possible cost; the contractor wants a satisfied client and the highest possible profit, with the least risk; the architect and/or construction manager wants a satisfied client and limited professional liability, at the best fee. In order to prevent adversarial relationships and create a cooperative team, it is essential that each party understand and respect the position of the others. Maintaining an atmosphere of mutual respect is critical to a successful building project.

—*R. Leslie Nichols*

Resources

American Institute of Architects, 1735 New York Avenue, N.W., Washington, D.C. 20006.

Bowman, R. 1992. When not to build: An architect's unconventional wisdom for the growing church. Grand Rapids: Baker.

Callahan, K. 1983. Twelve keys to an effective church. San Francisco: Harper & Row.

McCormick, G. 1992. Planning and building church facilities. Nashville: Broadman.

Zoning and Permits

In most communities the relationships between churches, their neighbors, and the municipality clearly is not the privileged one of decades past. In today's changing environment, church leaders who contemplate building new facilities need a new set of assumptions.

Neighbors and Boards

Here are ways to work with neighbors and zoning boards in today's environment to make positive results more likely:

● *Do your homework.* Neighbors are impressed when a church recognizes and addresses potential problems. The biggest objection neighbors raised to one church's proposed 1,900-seat auditorium was traffic. The church answered by paying for a study that projected what traffic patterns would be with the expansion.

● *Call in the experts.* Having experts on hand to answer unfounded objections can avert unnecessary delays. For example, when neighbors feared that having a church property in their area would lower property values, the church called in an appraiser, who testified on the basis of historical data that property values often increase when a house borders a "casual user" such as a church.

● *Be cooperative.* A zoning board can quickly sense whether a church genuinely respects the work they do in maintaining aesthetic and safety standards in the community. They are freed to be more flexible in addressing problems if the church approaches them with an attitude of "This is what we're thinking. What do you think?" Even with less-than-friendly zoning boards, churches need to use the tack that Daniel took when he worked with Nebuchadnezzar.

Neighbors' objections should also be heard carefully. When they speak in front of city council, they're generally scared—scared of change and of what this means to them.

● *Communicate a community vision.* Leading neighbors to accept change depends on motivating them with a picture of what can be, a vision of the positive role the church will play in the community. Churches can hold a community meeting where their master plan is unveiled and their vision for reaching out to teenagers, instilling moral values in children, and promoting good citizenship is presented. These values, especially as they help protect material possessions, will be attractive to neighbors.

● *Document everything.* Doing this can avert misunderstandings later in the process. One church, for example, failed to write down some important conversations they had with the head of the historic-district commission, who said that their purchase of a house would be no problem. By the time they had purchased the house, however, the commission had a new director who didn't agree with the earlier verbal agreements.

● *Take a look around.* If a church finds it is being held to a zoning requirement that is not being enforced elsewhere, this can be the basis for seeking a zoning variation.

● *Regard litigation as a last option.* Because of the wide influence and power zoning boards and city councils wield, a church doesn't want to make enemies of them. It is to the church's advantage to be a peacemaker.

Some circumstances, however, prevent an amicable solution. When a council in effect says a church cannot grow, a difficult decision has to be made about whether to pursue litigation. If public officials deal with a church in an "arbitrary and capricious" manner, or if a zoning ordinance is discriminatory against religious assemblies or is vague or overly restrictive, there is a legal basis for a suit. Getting a case before a judge provides the forum for the facts to be weighed by an objective third party.

● *Recognize that zoning conflicts can be two dimensional.* In some respects, spiritual warfare is always an underlying factor when the church grows and faces opposition. Churches need to be responsible not to blame things in blanket fashion on spiritual warfare but at the same time to bring the project before the Lord for his protection.

—Craig Brian Larson

Cost Estimation and Control

With the complexities of modern construction, how can a church make sure its dreams don't outstrip its resources? Here are some steps to follow, and a running tally of the costs.

Calculating Costs

● *Define the scope of your project.* What types of space do you need? How many people will each component serve? For example, Calvary Church needs a sanctuary to seat 800 plus 200 in an overflow space, educational space for 600 in one session, fellowship and education space for 300 with a serving kitchen, an administrative suite for nine to thirteen staff, and several spaces for weekday ministries.

● *Translate occupancy into building area.* Calvary's building requires about 50 square feet per person in worship. At Calvary this means about 50,000 square feet, including 20,000 square feet for worship, overflow, and foyer; 5,000 for fellowship hall and kitchen; 17,000 for education, nursery, and weekday ministries; 2,000 for music and drama rehearsal; 3,500 for adminis-

tration, reception, and work areas; and 2,000 for storage, mechanical, and miscellaneous.

● *Convert building area to costs.* Construction costs vary widely by region and design, and sanctuaries cost more than education space. If we assume a cost of $60 per square foot, construction of Calvary's facility will run $3,000,000.

● *Add other construction and furnishing costs.* Some costs often are overlooked, such as: parking, sidewalks and landscaping, utilities, assessments, storm-water control, playground equipment, furniture and equipment, sound and audio-visual systems, fees and permits (8 percent minimum), and construction contingency (3 percent minimum). One guideline is to allow 33 percent for these costs. Such factors might bring Calvary's cost up to $4,000,000, excluding land.

● *Add the first year's increase in operating expenses.* Moving in and getting systems operational involves start-up costs. In addition, utilities will cost more for the larger facility. Figure at least the first year's increase. The estimated cost for Calvary would be $100,000, bringing the running total to $4,100,000.

● *Add the cost of financing.* The estimated costs include 2 percent to obtain a loan or bonds, 10 percent interest for a 1-year construction loan, and 8 percent interest for a 20-year mortgage. Let's assume Calvary has saved half the money for construction, and so it needs to borrow $2,000,000. Thus, the loan would cost $40,000, interest on the construction loan would be $100,000, and interest on the debt for 20 years would run $2,015,000, giving a total cost of $2,155,000. This makes the running total $6,255,000.

● *Allow for inflation.* Three to five years may elapse between the first estimate and actual construction, and interest rates may change. A project contingency wisely covers this. Assuming 2 percent inflation for three years and adding 1 percent a year for project contingency, we might add 9 percent of construction costs ($360,000) to Calvary's estimate, achieving a grand total of $6,615,000.

Revising Costs

This is the time to compare the estimate to the church's resources. If the estimated price is too high, a church must consider revising the project's scope. For instance, instead of a sanctuary, the church could build a multiuse ministry center with movable seating, or design a fellowship foyer to serve as both foyer and fellowship hall. If Calvary chooses this total multiuse option, its costs might be only $2,255,000 (25,000 square feet @ $60 = $1,500,000; add $500,000 for site costs, $70,000 for one-year increased operating cost, and $185,000 for inflation and project contingency; finance costs are $0 since the church can pay cash).

Professional cost estimators should verify costs as construction documents are being prepared and again at the completion of the documents. It is important to keep budget revisions up to date to eliminate surprises.

—*Ray Bowman with Eddy Hall*

Conflicts of Aesthetics and Taste

In the first century B.C., the Roman architect Vitruvius wrote that a balance between durability, utility, and beauty (*firmitus, comoditus,* and *venustus*) was the mark of good architecture. For the next two thousand years, through scores of architectural styles and philosophies, no one has improved upon Vitruvius' fundamental test of a good building design. Beauty is as basic to a person's building needs as is utility, comfort, or durability; it is the element of beauty that distinguishes architecture from mere shelter or enclosure.

Attractive buildings help reinforce the self-confidence of a church's members and convey a sense of stability to visitors. An appropriate amount of aesthetics is not an indulgence but a necessity in creating a positive and lasting impression for the occupants.

Sticking with a Style

With some variations, church architectural styles fall into three main categories: classical, romantic, or modern. If possible, it is best not to mix the styles, although, ironically, it is easier to make a modern building look traditional than it is to add a modern wing to a traditional building. Additionally, if the existing buildings are good architectural examples, the church has the added responsibility of respecting and maintaining the quality of existing design. No one style is better suited for serving God than another, and most denominations have built in every style at one time or another.

Setting Priorities

A building is not a single object, but the organization of possibly tens of thousands of technical and visual details. Each of these details serves specific purposes, addressing needs as varied as exits that meet fire regulations to stained-glass windows that create a sense of reverence. The *fixed*, legal requirements mandated by building codes, zoning ordinances, and other regulations will determine many of these details. Depending on the expectations of the congregation, the committee will have to weigh the relative value of the *flexible* details.

Given limited finances, the value of aesthetics must be weighed against the value of square footage, comfort, flexibility, and durability. The success of the committee in overcoming the value differences of its members will depend on two factors: (1) The ability of the members to state their expectations of the building project in terms of physical and psychological purposes, and (2) the ability of the committee to reach a consensus or acceptable compromise. The committee that cannot overcome such differences will have a difficult time convincing the congregation the project is indeed worthy of their financial sacrifice.

Heading Off Disaster

It is important to structure these discussions of values in such a way as to respect the attitudes, experiences, and feelings of the various committee members. For example, those of a utilitarian mind need to appreciate that a good design that conveys a positive church image can be as valuable as increased classroom space or a better heating system. If the committee is working with an experienced church architect or interior designer, these professionals will help put the church's needs in the proper perspective.

Often, the needs of committee members most adamant about aesthetics can be met through less expensive means. For example, it is possible and practical to project traditional values through traditional furnishings set in a neutral space without extensive architectural moldings. Likewise, if top-quality stained glass is important, it is possible to use less glass but position it more effectively—like a single jewel in a display case.

In the final analysis, durability, utility, and beauty will all need to be present to some degree for the building project to satisfy the pre-sent church members and success-fully attract new ones.

—*R. Leslie Nichols*

Acoustics

Planning for good church acoustics involves selecting room shapes and building materials for the purpose of creating a significant emotional effect on people through sound. Though many banks will approve church construction loans without approval from an acoustical expert, building committees should engage the services of such experts anyway. Good acoustics will save a church money in the long run.

Shapes and Materials

Room shape affects echoes, standing waves, and focused reflections. The best time to plan an acoustical shape for a church is before the building committee even approaches an architect. This step alone can save a church thousands in planning, development, and architectural fees. By making acoustics decisions early, a church can include simple, low-cost acoustical remedies, if needed, rather than pay for expensive fixes after the church is finished. This approach also avoids the financial costs (from fewer members and lower budgets) of enduring a church with poor acoustics.

To save time and money, it's probably best to choose a common shape rather than creating an original. An acoustics expert should check the plans to make practical recommendations that for even minor adjustments can have great impact on the church's sound. For instance, changing the angle of two walls just five degrees in a rectangular church can bring about a substantial improvement.

Room materials determine how a church will ultimately sound. Soft materials tend to make the church sound dull. Hard materials make a church sound bright and lively. By combining both soft and hard materials, acoustics planners can tailor the sound according to the style of worship a church desires.

Sound Ideas

Here are some specific guidelines to help churches design buildings for optimum acoustical performance:

● *Pay attention to room shape and size.* Avoid a church that is square or round or has large, concave walls or domes, parallel walls, or a ceiling over the pulpit higher than the one over the seating. As a rule of thumb, ceilings should be kept higher than 18 feet. Start at 19 feet for the first 200 seats, and add one foot for every 150 additional seating spaces. When in doubt, a higher roof is better.

● *Don't design automatic sound-deadeners.* For example, never build

a six- or eight-sided church in
which all walls are the same length
and height. Avoid putting an arch
in front of the choir that will trap
the sound of the choir and the
organ. Also avoid building a large,
flat rear wall that is square to the
altar or platform area. If the interi-
or design calls for soft materials
such as acoustical tiles or split-face
block or bricks, don't paint over
them. It is better simply to clean
them properly.

● *Place musical instruments
strategically.* A piano should not be
placed in a pit or be boxed off, for
instance. Keep the organ and piano
no farther than 15 feet apart, and
avoid placing the choir in front of
organ pipes or organ speakers—
especially if there are plans to
record the choir.

● *Don't neglect external noise
sources.* To be sure the sound system can provide at least 88 percent
intelligibility, plan a building that
will not allow road noise or aircraft
and train noise into the worship
area. Also pay attention to the
potential distraction that can come
from heating and ventilation systems and ceiling fans. A well-
designed sound system can actually
amplify a defective ceiling fan! The
quieter a church is, the better—and
it shows in congregational support.

—Joseph De Buglio

Resources
Egan, D. 1988. Architectural acoustics.
New York: McGraw Hill.

Evert, F. 1989. The master handbook of
acoustics. Blue Ridge Summit, Pa.:
Tab Books.

De Buglio, J. 1993. Why is church
sound so confusing? Weston, Ont.:
Frontline Technologies.

Davis, D., and C. Davis. 1987. Sound-
system engineering. Carmel, Ind.:
SAMS.

Part VII:

Finances

Now we're talking money—God's money in our hands. God has plenty of it. With the cattle on a thousand hills and the earning power of all Christians, God certainly isn't lacking in resources. Everything is at hand to accomplish anything God sets before us. No, resources aren't wanting.

We do, however, have difficulty at times getting our hands on the financial resources that definitely are there. Some hands in the church hold on rather tightly to what is God's, never releasing it to the church, and some of those cattle on a thousand hills prove a little difficult to round up. Breathes there a pastor who couldn't put to use in an eyeblink multiple thousands of dollars more—for missions, for ministries of compassion, for added staff, for upgraded facilities, for new outreaches and ministries?

We have two major responsibilities: harvesting the resources available to the church and then managing them wisely once they are in our barns. A bountiful harvest that is squandered, wasted, or pilfered is as tragic as a sloppy, inadequate harvest that gathers scant produce. In both cases, the resources never get put to use for their intended purposes. What we aim for is a thorough, productive harvest combined with careful, prayerful management of the crop once it is in our hands. It is also in our best interests to keep a weather eye toward the laws regulating the harvest and its disbursement.

Biblical principles, proven techniques, and wise practices fill the following chapters, written by harvesters and warehousemen who have learned how to handle properly the financial realities of this age so that they can affect positively the spiritual realities of the age to come.

32

The Purpose of Stewardship

C hristian stewardship concerns our responsibility to live wholly for God, managing our resources to give him glory and benefit humanity. Stewardship touches every area of life and involves both individual and corporate commitments. It encompasses far more than giving to the church: Stewardship includes the use and care of our natural resources; it includes what we do with our abilities and talents; it involves the way we manage our time.

Though stewardship has often been applied strictly to finances or is seen to be synonymous with giving or tithing to the church, financial stewardship can be understood best within the broader framework of biblical stewardship.

Though we will primarily focus on financial stewardship here, we should remember that biblical stewardship includes the management of all God's gifts to humanity. We will not grasp the full implications of financial stewardship until we know what it means to surrender every part of our lives to God. With that in mind, let's explore biblical teachings on stewardship and its applications throughout church history. We'll also draw several implications about stewardship for us today.

Stewardship in the Old Testament

The Old Testament view of stewardship grows out of the Hebrew view of life in general. The actual usage of words translated into English as *steward*, however, is limited. The major Hebrew terms corresponding to the New Testament idea of *oikonomos* (steward) focus on the idea of "one who is over a house." Perhaps the closest Hebrew equivalent is *aser al-habbayit* (see, for example, Isa. 36:3, 22; 37:2). Yet the idea of stewardship can be found throughout the Old Testament, wrapped up in an understanding of God, nature, and humanity. On one level, based upon the idea of Creation, the Old Testament applies stewardship to all humanity. On a higher level, stewardship is applied to the elect—the covenant people of God.

Stewardship in the Old Testament begins with God. As Creator he holds the right of ownership to everything. The Psalmist writes, "The earth is the Lord's, and everything in it, the world, and all who live in it; for he founded it ... " (Ps. 24:1–2). God asserts, "For every animal of the forest is mine, and the cattle on a thousand hills ... for the world is mine, and all that is in it" (Ps. 50:10, 12).

The Hebrews enjoyed life in all of its dimensions and exulted in natural and cultural goods "of earthly possessions, many children, long life, friendship and love, as well as wisdom, beauty, honour, and political freedom" (Eichrodt 1951, 33). They knew they had been given authority over God's good creation (Ps. 8:3–6). In Genesis 1–2, people are given dominion over the animals, and God instructs the people to fill the earth—to till the ground and subdue it. But he also gave people the freedom to follow or reject his command, setting up the basic components of our stewardship responsibility.

As the elect, covenant people of God, the Hebrews were obliged to do God's will. They were called to be faithful with everything God had given them. They knew, for example, that God had given them the Promised Land (Deut. 25:19). But they also believed God was the owner and that they, as temporary tenants, did not have unlimited use of the land. Old Testament laws acknowledged God's ownership in such practices as offering the first fruits of the crops and first-born of the animals (Exod. 22:28–30; 23:19; 34:26). The commandments shaped Hebrew views on acquiring and disposing of property. The laws regulated proper land use: Crops were left for the poor (Lev. 19:9–10). Fields were to lie fallow in sabbatical years (Exod. 23:10–11). Additional land laws referred to the Jubilee year (Lev. 25:8–17, 23–55), tithes and sacrifices (Lev. 27:30–32; Num. 18:21–32; Deut. 14:22–27), and inheritances (Num. 26:52–27:11).

The Old Testament does not refer frequently to money, though it condemns the improper use of money. Often seen as a sign of God's blessing in ancient times, money is not valued as highly as wisdom in the Old Testament (Job 28:17; Prov. 20:15). Money has limitations: It can't help in times of trouble or death (Job 36:19; Ps. 49:16–17). Nor does it prove that some are loved by God more than the poor.

Tithing was a major aspect of Old Testament stewardship. However, actual practices are difficult to determine with certainty. Most scholars think the tithing passages represent diverse traditions covering a long period of Hebrew history that included many political and cultural changes. The process of funding political, religious, and social needs sometimes blurred in the Hebrew theocratic state.

At its roots, tithing was intended to honor God as the owner of the land and the giver of its produce. But it also supported the temple, the priesthood, and a variety of charitable causes. There are three different tithes in the Old Testament: a celebration tithe of agricultural products (Deut. 12:6–7; 14:22–26), a charity tithe (Deut. 14:28–29), and a tithe for the Levites (Num. 18:21–24). These were harmonized into three distinct tithes in rabbinic Judaism. A devout Jew during the rabbinic period would have given either 20 or 23.5 percent of his agricultural income. No tithes were imposed upon artisans, tradesmen, fishermen, or those with other types of occupational income. By Jesus' time, there were at least twelve regularly prescribed tithes and offerings, plus the spontaneous giving of alms to people in need (Grant 1926, 92–100).

Stewardship in the New Testament

The New Testament introduces a striking new note into the pattern. Christian stewardship depends upon the will of God as revealed in Jesus Christ. The New Testament teaches that God has claimed as his own those who surrender to him through Christ. As a result, stewardship is concerned with more than the resources God has given; stewardship includes believers themselves because they belong to God (1 Cor. 6:19–20).

● *The stewardship concept.* The New Testament Greek word translated as stewardship is *oikonomia,* a combination of two words: *oikos,* "house," and *nemein,* "to divide, distribute, or apportion" (Michel 1967, 119–159). In classical Greek, the *oikonomos* (steward)—found only 20 times in the New Testament—was responsible for the business affairs of a household. Often *oikonomos* referred to a slave with the oversight of the master's money, property, goods, and other slaves.

Jesus used the term *oikonomos* on only two occasions—in telling the parable of the servants (Luke 12:42–48) and the parable of the shrewd manager (Luke 16:1–13). Nevertheless, the concept of stewardship runs through many other parables: the rich man and Lazarus (Luke 16:19–31); the rich fool (Luke 12:16–21); the servants who kill the master's son (Matt. 21:33–46); the unworthy servant (Luke 17:7–10); the unmerciful servant (Matt. 18:21–35); the workers in the vineyard (Matt. 20:1–16); the two sons (Matt. 21:28–32); the talents (Matt. 25:14–30); and the minas (Luke 19:11–27).

The two key parables of the servants and the shrewd manager illustrate the basic rationale. Each focuses on an owner who entrusts his estate to a steward (or manager in the NIV). The steward's task is to be faithful and accountable to the master, increasing the assets. Several themes stand out: God is Lord over all the earth. We are stewards because God entrusts us with things. Though free to act as we see fit, we're expected to make wise decisions consistent with God's will. Finally, we will one day be held accountable.

Stewardship calls us to manage our lives and God's gifts of creation and redemption in a responsible way. The New Testament portrays believers as partners with God to accomplish his purposes in the world. In fact, God is said to practice *oikonomia* (stewardship) in fulfilling his plan from Creation (Eph. 1:10).

The History of Stewardship in the Church

Throughout the centuries of the Christian church, stewardship practices have included such varied approaches as alms giving, gifts,

---

The Pastor's Stewardship Role

Some pastors claim they don't become involved in the financial procedures of the church—although few say this in the presence of their church members! As much as we sometimes rebel against the idea, most of us have come to realize that because we are a part of the church family, we do need to be interested in the family's finances. To avoid all involvement in church finances would be to abdicate leadership. It takes money to build buildings, pay salaries, supply paper clips, and offer curriculum materials.

Five Fundraising Roles

To be involved with finances, though, doesn't mean we have to master the intricacies of spreadsheets. We can be involved in at least five less tangible but perhaps more crucial ways, such as:

● *Stewardship preacher.* Should a preacher preach about money, or is it best to preach "stewardship"? We live in a materialistic society, and often the first line of spiritual skirmish within believers is at the point of spending. Naturally, stewardship is more than asking for money, but it certainly includes money. That means we've got to get specific from time to time. When we ask people to give money, we need to make it clear that this is what we are asking for. That means not avoiding the word *money* just because we are uncomfortable with the sound of it. Jesus touched on money often in his preaching, and we are wise to do no less.

● *Accidental fundraiser.* Most people want to give to a variety of causes, and we sometimes inadvertently challenge people to give when we address deeper issues in their lives. For example, once after I preached a message on compassion for the outcast, a man gave a

offerings, sacrifices, and tithes (Powell 1960, 76–126; Wischer 1966). Some early Christians renounced all worldly possessions, a practice formalized in some monastic movements. When the Roman Empire under Constantine became Christian, the church and state often mingled lines of financial obligations. In medieval times, there was rarely a clean delineation between state taxation and church gifts or fundraising. In many instances, taxes were imposed to support the church. As the institutional church developed over the centuries, practices such as mass fees, endowments, and gifts of land became a standard, often bringing complaints that the church was more accessible to the rich than to the poor. A corrupt medieval church saw "simony"—the dispensing of divine favors for monetary gifts—including the sale of indulgences to shorten time in purgatory, the sale or viewing of religious relics, and pilgrimages to sacred sites.

Early in the second century A.D., the church fathers appealed to the Old Testament tithe for the support of clergy (typified by the Levites)

---

large amount to our church's benevolence ministry. My message made no reference to money, but this wealthy man nevertheless heard his greed and selfishness challenged.

• *Trusted trustee.* To many members, the pastor is the one person they can talk to without feeling manipulated. We are wise to preserve this trust, especially when it comes to financial matters. For example, a wealthy and generous layman told me that in any given week he receives five to eight requests for charitable contributions. Yet he said that when his pastor indicated a need in the church or the community, he was more than willing to give, because his pastor had never, to his knowledge, abused a gift or tried to manipulate him for selfish purposes.

• *Herald of the vision.* The pastor may not be the only one who reminds the congregation of the church's goals, but he or she is usually the one best trained to put the vision into words and images that a broad spectrum of the congregation can appreciate. People give to causes that flow out of the vision. We don't articulate a vision for the sole purpose of raising money, but if we cast a vision well, we will probably see money raised.

• *Conscience of the church.* The pastor, among others, must insist on integrity in financial matters. The pastor must be aware of how money is raised, given, counted, and spent, and how all this is reported. Sometimes integrity issues can be subtle. In one large church, the budget-promotion committee planned a stewardship campaign that used a catchy slogan and creative publicity methods. Unfortunately, they obliquely appealed to guilt and greed. The pastor intervened and asked the committee to redesign their emphasis, which they did. This role isn't the pastor's easiest, but it eventually leads to a better climate for stewardship with integrity.

—*Gary Fenton*

and for charitable works. Though Jewish practice was to confine the tithe to agricultural products, the church fathers extended the tithe to include all income. Some emphasized that it was to be given freely— not because of Old Testament demands. Yet for some, the tithe became a new law, and Christians were urged to give more than Jews. Some changed the demand for a tithe into a promise: those who gave more than a tithe would receive a reward from God. Others in the early church kept alive Jesus' radical command to renounce material possessions.

Political situations often dictated how stewardship in the medieval church was handled. The financial abuse of many people by the institutional church helped precipitate the Reformation. In Europe, religious motivation primarily fueled the Reformation. But in England it was motivated largely by politics and economics. The Reformers only partially corrected the excesses of church financial policies: Zwingli

Tithing

Tithing is not about fundraising. Neither is it about supporting the work of the church. Rather, for Christians, it is about trust, faithfulness, and discipleship.

Old Testament Background

The Christian tradition of tithing begins with Mount Sinai, where God instructed the Israelites to give the first tenth (in Hebrew, *tithe* means "a tenth part") of their crops and livestock to the Lord, for "it is holy to the Lord." That is, it is set apart by God for God (Lev. 27:30–32).

These tithes were paid to the Levitical priests, who had, themselves, been set apart by God for God from normal livelihoods. They, in turn, were to "present a tenth of the tithe as the Lord's offering" (Num. 18:26).

Later, when the Israelites had returned from their Babylonian exile, tithing became an issue again. They had successfully rebuilt

the Temple and reinstituted the religious ordinances, but hopes for prosperity and peace escaped them. In their disillusionment, God spoke through the prophet Malachi to tell the people that their troubles were the result of their unfaithfulness. Malachi spoke the Word of God to them: "Return to me, and I will return to you" (Mal. 3:7ff). When the Israelites asked, "How shall we return to you?" God replied, "Will a man rob God? Yet you rob me ... in tithes and offerings. You are under a curse—the whole nation of you— because you are robbing me. *Bring the whole tithe....*"

Money Talks

There is truth in the maxim "money talks." What we do with money and possessions reveals our true values and allegiances. Our check stubs are our real "statements of faith." In withholding the tithe, the Israelites, despite their hymns

favored voluntary giving and opposed tithing as a legalistic practice. In England, by contrast, elaborate tithing laws were enacted to provide both for the parsons and the poor.

In early America, two different types of financial stewardship developed (Salstrand 1956). Some colonies supported state churches by public taxes, leaving unofficial churches to depend upon voluntary contributions. Eventually religious dissenters refused to pay state taxes for the church. Other private methods of funding the church included such practices as pew rentals or sales, lotteries, bazaars, church suppers, sales of products, the use of subscriptions, and income from church-held cultivatable land.

The modern stewardship movement began early in the nineteenth century as a corollary of the missionary movement and received great impetus with the beginning of the Laymen's Missionary Movement in the latter part of the century. Tithing began to be emphasized about

---

and creeds, were showing that their *real* security, status, and identity lay in their crops and flocks.

How can we be expected to tithe, especially when times are hard? God gives two responses:

● He says simply, "Test me in this ... and see if I will not throw open the floodgates of heaven and pour out so much blessing that you will not have room enough for it" (Mal. 3:10). God wants his people to throw their whole trust on him. He will be faithful, and we will receive even more than we would have had if we had not given the tithe.

● God also says, "I will prevent the pests from devouring your crops ..." (Mal. 3:11). The fact is, when we do not give the tithe, we do not have 10 percent more at our disposal. Why? A "devouring force," Mammon, eats at our worldly possessions: "Moth and rust destroy, and ... thieves break in and steal" (Matt. 6:19). The promise is that if we give the whole tithe, the remaining 90 percent is protected from "the devourer."

Is tithing the starting place, or is it the goal for faithful stewardship? Malachi 3 shows that the *whole* tithe is where we begin. The more we find our security, status, and identity in God, the more we will be able to place at God's disposal.

New Testament Perspective

The New Testament does not speak about tithing. It does speak of our being free in Christ from the ordinances of the Law. So, are we free from tithing? Two observations can be noted in response. First, the New Testament authors don't address tithing because they assume it. And second, the New Testament call goes beyond "some" to "all." Paul writes, "Offer your bodies as living sacrifices ..." (Rom. 12:1). Everything we are and have is to be employed for the Kingdom, and tithing starts us in that direction. What we give and exactly how we do it (Do I tithe before or after taxes?) needs to be decided in this spirit of complete "givenness" to Christ.

—Darrell W. Johnson

1850. A layman named Thomas Kane published and disseminated millions of tracts on tithing to the American churches beginning in 1870, spreading the view that tithing pays—a theme basic in the Laymen's Missionary Movement. A number of stewardship associations were formed in the later years of the nineteenth century.

Many American churches during the twentieth century have emphasized tithing, including a commitment to the idea that the local church is the "storehouse" where the tithe belongs (Mal. 3:10). In fact, the stewardship movement has been largely an American phenomenon occurring in several denominations. Some may have oversimplified the complexity of biblical teachings on the subject of giving. Legalistic overtones have often downplayed the New Testament emphasis on radical sacrifice and joyful giving. Others have continued to provide strong theological undergirding for a biblical stewardship.

The Applications of Stewardship

A biblical view of stewardship will cover aspects of both our possessions and our contributions:

● *Material things.* The Christian's relationship to material things is a good barometer of his or her priorities in life. How we view things can indicate the vitality of our relationship with God. "Where your treasure is," Jesus said, "there your heart will be also" (Matt. 6:21). Though Jesus recognized legitimate material needs, he warned his followers against gathering earthly treasure instead of seeking the kingdom of God. He warned about the dangers of accumulating (or even desiring to accumulate) possessions, which can cause temptations of anxiety, covetousness, pride, and presumption (Matt. 6:25–34; Col. 3:5–6). Jesus taught that "a man's life does not consist in the abundance of his possessions" (Luke 12:15).

Our earnings ought to flow from lives of integrity invested in honest work (2 Thess. 3:12). Riches should not be gained at the expense of others (James 5:1–4). If a desire for money dominates someone's life, that person will suffer spiritual loss (Mark 8:36; 1 Tim. 6:9–10). God intends that we use our material wealth to care for our family (Matt. 15:3–6; 1 Tim. 5:8, 16), support the government (Matt 22:15–21), care for the needy (Matt. 25:31–46; 1 Tim. 5:5–10; James 1:27), and support gospel workers (1 Cor. 9:14; 1 Tim. 5:17–18).

● *Christian giving.* Giving remains a focal point of our stewardship responsibility. Jesus said, "It is more blessed to give than to receive" (Acts 20:35). A major part of Christian giving should go to the church, God's primary instrument in achieving his purposes on earth. Our gifts to God through the church can symbolize our commitment that all our possessions belong to him.

The New Testament teaches several profound concepts with direct implication to us: (1) Most passages on giving relate to God's gifts to us. (2) Most of the remaining passages on giving are about people giving to the poor—often outside the context of the church. (3) The only time Jesus said how much a person should give, he called for radical sacrifice: "Sell your possessions and give to the poor" (Luke 12:33). (4) The major extended passages on giving concern Gentile offerings for believers in Jerusalem—and are not a direct prescription on giving to the church. (5) There are virtually no references to giving to the church; the emphasis instead is on meeting various needs through the church's ministry and mission. (6) The New Testament affirms individual freedom and responsibility as the basis for stewardship. (7) Sacrificial giving is held out as the measure of resources believers should give.

Second Corinthians 9:13 suggests four purposes for Christian giving: to glorify God; to meet human needs; to discipline ourselves (both to acknowledge the gospel and to love our neighbors); and to support the life, ministry, and mission of the church.

Giving ought to be done out of the right motivation and in the right way: We should offer ourselves to God first (2 Cor. 8:5)—a sign that everything we have and all we can do belongs to God. We should give proportionately (as God prospers us, 2 Cor. 8:11–12), systematically (1 Cor. 16:2), generously (2 Cor. 8:2–3), sacrificially (Luke 21:3–4), and voluntarily and joyfully (2 Cor. 9:7) (Cunningham 1979, 87–94).

Christian giving goes well beyond giving to a single local church. Nevertheless, when we join a congregation, we commit ourselves financially to support the Kingdom as it is expressed through that church. The New Testament church, for example, used donations in several ways: Ministers were supported, needy church members were cared for, Christians in other congregations were helped, and the church's outreach to the world was supported (Cunningham 1979, 100). The ministries of a church (and therefore its budget) may vary from time to time, but they should always reflect the church's basic commitments to the priorities of the kingdom of God.

Tithing

Many assume the tithe is the standard for Christian giving. Others, however, point out that the basis for such opinion comes from the Old Testament. The New Testament does not command Christians to tithe, though it mentions the tithe on three occasions (Matt. 23:23 [and Luke 11:42]; Luke 18:12; and Heb. 7:1–10). In each of these passages the tithe is merely incidental to another point being made.

Because believers are under grace and not law, the New Testament puts giving on a basis stronger than the tithe. But it offers no specifics about what Christians should give. Jesus praised the widow who gave two small copper coins, because she gave everything she had (Mark 12:43–44). Zaccheus repaid those he cheated four times as much as he had taken and gave one-half of his goods to the poor (Luke 19:8). Jesus commanded the rich young ruler to sell all he had and give it to the poor (Matt. 19:21)—something we all are told to do (Luke 12:33). This teaching probably motivated the early church to hold everything in common and sell possessions to care for the needs of the people (Acts 2:44–45).

Americans now live in a rapidly changing church scene. Denominational and congregational loyalties are breaking down. Typical church members exercise more independence than ever before in managing the stewardship of their material things and their levels of giving. Whatever changes continue, churches and ministers have an obligation to teach biblical stewardship—that all of life and all of our resources should support the causes of the Kingdom.

—Richard B. Cunningham

Resources

Callahan, K. 1992. Giving and stewardship in an effective church: A guide for every member. San Francisco: Harper.

Cunningham, R. 1976. Creative stewardship. Nashville: Abingdon.

Eichrodt, W. 1951. Man in the Old Testament. London: SCM.

Grant, F. 1926. The economic background of the Gospels. New York: Oxford University Press.

Kauffman, D. 1990. Managers with God: A way to church renewal. Scottdale, Pa.: Herald.

Michel, O. 1967. Oikos-oikoumene. In Theological dictionary of the New Testament, vol. 5, 119–159. Ed. G. Kittel and G. Friedrich. Trans. G. Bromiley. Grand Rapids: Eerdmans.

Powell, L. 1960. Stewardship in the history of the church. In Stewardship in contemporary theology, 76–131. Ed. T. Thompson. New York: Association.

Reumann, John. 1992. Stewardship and the economy of God. Grand Rapids: Eerdmans.

Salstrand, G. 1956. The story of stewardship in the United States of America. Grand Rapids: Baker.

Werning, W. 1983. Christian stewards: Confronted and committed. Saint Louis: Concordia.

Wischer, L. 1966. Tithing in the early church. Trans. R. Schultz. Philadelphia: Fortress.

Preaching Stewardship

We all wish we could confine our talk about money to general theological statements. But specific financial needs arise in the life of any church, and they need to be addressed. How do we mention these from the pulpit, where the appearance of self-interest can be so magnified?

Talking Money

While stewardship effectiveness starts with good foundational practices, it also demands clear and creative preaching about money. Five preaching principles help us as we try to bring our people into the biblical joy of giving.

● *Preach confidently.* We cannot manufacture this; confidence comes from two realizations. First, the Word of God has much to say about giving. We can be confident that as we simply teach from the Scriptures, God will be at work. Second, we need a love for people that is willing to give them what they need. Do we love them enough to tell them the truth? Since giving is a basic part of Christianity—the way we prove our trustworthiness to God—we should teach them the truth about money, confident in the knowledge they would be spiritually shortchanged without it.

● *Preach carefully.* We must work to keep what we say about money grounded in the text, avoiding such traps as promising prosperity, when God promises only to meet our needs (Phil. 4:19); resorting to crisis appeals, when we need to help people consider giving a part

of a daily walk with God, not just a response to a crisis; advocating budget giving, when we should give to God and his work because we love and worship him, not just to finance an institution; preaching "10 percent for God and 90 percent for me" thinking, when biblical stewardship tells us that everything belongs to God and that we will have to account for what we have done with his money.

● *Preach creatively.* It's best to avoid worn-out words and phrases that raise red flags. The word *stewardship* is overused. *Tithing* evokes images of the 10-percent syndrome. *Pledging* may denote coerced payment of a portion of income required by the church. On the other hand, phrases such as "gifts of gratitude" or "investments in the Kingdom" not only sound unique, but they teach a biblical concept as well.

● *Preach centrally.* At the core, giving is a matter of priorities. As Haddon Robinson says, "You can tell a lot about a person's spirituality by looking at his or her checkbook." Giving demonstrates where one's heart is toward God. Giving says people love God and seek to express it whether or not he ever does anything for them. We need to preach that making him Lord of their money is the key to serving God without distraction. To preach centrally, then, requires prophetic proclamation about the core issues in our culture that work against financial commitment to Christ, such as greed, covetousness, and credit madness.

● *Preach consistently.* As we preach throughout the year, we can draw applications about giving from many texts. A consistent (but not constant) emphasis on the attitudes, principles, and adversaries of giving helps keep people in tune with the priority of biblical investing. It's better not to preach on giving only when we have to do so. Preaching when there is no crisis gives the financial facts of kingdom life greater credibility.

—*Joseph M. Stowell*

To Know Individual Giving or Not?

Should pastors know how much individual members give to the church? Few congregations and pastors have stated policies, but many have deeply held convictions. Many churches clearly distinguish between the pastor as spiritual leader and the lay leaders as managers of the church's temporal business. The result, however, can be an unbiblical dualist position: the belief that our use of money is not a spiritual matter. Thus pastors and lay leaders must wisely analyze the arguments for knowing and not knowing.

Not Knowing

A significant argument for the pastor not knowing individuals' contributions is based on the possibility of pastoral prejudice. If the pastor knew the specific level of giving of each member and how well or poorly members performed on a faith promise or pledge, he or she might give the large donors preferential treatment. Or the pastor might hold back appropriate criticism for fear a large gift might disappear.

It is also feared that the pastor might judge members on their giving, thinking, *Mr. Jones is capable of giving much more than he does; his commitment must not be there.* Sometimes, however, lay leaders don't want the pastor to know *their* level of giving, because, in some way, they believe they could give at a higher level but don't.

A third argument might be based on a practice encouraged in the Bible: giving alms in secret (Matt. 6:2–4). No one should know but the giver and God. Of course, this does not work out in practice, since the stewardship chairperson and the bookkeeper know (and sometimes make judgments). Another theological point sometimes raised is that, for Christians, Jesus serves as the only intermediary with God. Human priests no longer bring the offerings of the people to God.

Knowing

Supporters of the case for knowing can point to the principle Paul suggests in 2 Corinthians 8–9, the so-called Collection Passage. Paul was aware that the church in Corinth was far wealthier than the church in Macedonia, and he knew the Corinthians were capable of a far greater gift; in fact, he *expected* it. While we cannot prove conclusively that Paul knew exact levels of giving, the controlling principle is that the pastor can motivate greater stewardship and spiritual growth if he or she knows giving levels. Financial giving is a strong indicator of spiritual maturity. Further, when giving stops or decreases (or jumps), it signals a change that may require pastoral attention.

Moreover, when a church board considers challenging the members to make a significant increase in their giving, or when a capital-funds drive is being considered, success depends on knowing about past giving *and* the potential for future giving. Since the pastor knows the flock better than anyone, he or she must weigh pastoral insight with knowledge of giving. In developing the giving potential, lay leaders will need to know spiritual matters, and the pastor will need to know financial matters, in order to make good decisions.

Tempering this approach to finances, however, will be the demand for a crucial commitment: that we not enter into judgment about one another's giving.

Whether the pastor knows individual giving or not, it is vital that he or she have all the information possible to be the best pastor possible. That includes, in some form, the finances of the members. Good teaching on stewardship challenges the dualistic error that money is not a spiritual matter. Members' attitudes toward giving can reveal their progress in spiritual growth, which is appropriately the pastor's business.

—John R. Throop

33

Planning Stewardship

L eading in stewardship is one of the most demanding and rewarding dimensions of pastoral leadership. Stewardship enables the church to perform its ministries of worship, evangelism, fellowship, nurture, and service. It provides the church resources to touch lives with the gospel, both inside and outside the church. Most of all, stewardship is a way for Christians to grow in grace.

Today it is hard to succeed as a leader of stewardship without understanding the complex differences among generations, each shaped by unique events, attitudes, and pressures. Today we have not two but three generations to listen to and to touch with any stewardship appeal. We need to know who those generations are.

● *The GI generation.* Today's mature adults, born 1910–1925, were heavily influenced by the Great Depression, which inculcated values of thrift, delayed gratification, and "saving for a rainy day." Even though they later worked in the rapidly expanding economy following the Second World War, when personal income rose at an unprecedented pace, they have devoted more effort to saving than to spending. Their primary values are duty and responsibility. They are the most churchgoing generation in American history. They display strong institutional and denominational loyalties.

● *The Boomer generation.* In contrast, the people born between 1943 and 1964 have the primary values of idealism and compassion. Bold, aggressive, bonded together by Vietnam, rock and roll, and the death of JFK, they were born prosperous and with high expectations.

They tend to be impatient, self-absorbed, idealistic, and obsessed with values and ethics. It has been said that their motto is "Hit me in the gut with it." Boomers are motivated by feelings and experience more than by money. Unlike the GI generation, they are not particularly loyal to institutions.

● *The Busters.* On the heels of the Boomers are the Busters, also known as Generation X, or the Thirteeners. Born between 1961 and 1981, the values of this thirteenth generation since the founding of America are pragmatic and street smart. They deal with a world of harsh realities—AIDS, drugs, family dissolution, and economic uncertainty. Divorce doubled during their lifetime. Unlike the Woodstock generation, they listen to their music through earphones. Their motto is: "Whatever works." Robert Bellah talks of how they suffer from "compassion fatigue."

The differences among these generations pose huge challenges for churches planning and executing stewardship programs. Several megachurch pastors were discussing the fact that while their churches were growing by as much as 16 percent a year in membership, financially they were growing at a maximum of only 6 to 8 percent. After launching a study, they discovered the reason was the divergent giving patterns of the generations.

When those who were 55 and older were asked, "Who taught you to give?" they responded, "My father," or "My mother," or "I learned in the home." Those in the 35–55 age group cited a variety of influences—parents, or a teacher, minister, or spouse. But, according to Ben Gill, President of RSI, those 35 and under did not even understand the question.

"Do what? We buy services," was their response. "When I go to the movies, I pay six dollars for two hours of entertainment. When I go to church I put six dollars in the offering and get two hours of worship and instruction." When asked about the Sundays when they don't go to church, they reply, "What happens when I don't go to the movies? I don't get anything, and I don't pay anything."

Many of our churches are being bankrolled disproportionately by the aging GI generation. In one church, after a generous church statesman died, it was estimated that, according to the giving patterns of new members, it would take 41 new families to make up for the loss of this one mature donor. So how can we begin educating and inspiring the younger generations about the blessings of stewardship?

A Year-Round Stewardship Emphasis

The day of guilt and gimmicks is over. No longer can we expect people to give blindly out of institutional or denominational loyalty. Successful churches are developing stewardship ministries that appeal to the human need to give rather than the institution's need for money. Rather than appealing to a sense of duty, they are meshing their approach with the compassion people feel for others and their need for meaning in life.

The positive side of this new philosophy is that it is much nearer the biblical view that stewardship is a way of growing in Christ. Jesus did not speak of raising budgets or keeping the lights turned on. He said, "Do not store up for yourselves treasures on earth, where moth and rust destroy, and where thieves break in and steal" (Matt. 6:19).

The unified budget, in which people dutifully fill out one pledge card once a year, is becoming less and less effective in today's climate. This approach has been based on three debatable assumptions: (1) that the figures placed on people's pledge cards represent a sacrificial portion or a tithe from their anticipated year's income, (2) that people do not enjoy being asked to give to specific projects, and (3) that people are willing to trust the church board to make the critical decisions about how their annual gift should be used. One denominational study shows that most people are giving to five different charitable causes through the course of the year. If the church asks only once a year for support of a broad, unified budget, the church will receive a disproportionately small slice of a person's annual charitable giving.

Some churches that have had a unified budget in the past are now moving toward a more flexible approach. They keep the traditional October annual pledge drive but specify that all giving to this campaign is for support of the local church only. Then in December they have a separate appeal for global-mission causes, celebrating Christ's work in other lands. In the spring they have still another appeal for local-mission causes. If there is an ongoing capital campaign, this gives a member four major opportunities to give within the life of the local church. These separate appeals may have a shorter-term pledge period of three to six months, and they need to specify precisely where and how the money will be spent. Some families will give more to the special appeals than to the regular budget. However, churches are finding that multiplying options and allowing flexibility increases overall member contributions.

With or without this model, it is important to integrate stewardship into ongoing church life. When all stewardship emphasis is compressed into a single month of the year, members can develop thick callouses to the annual pitch. As one man said, "If I can survive October intact, I'm home free!"

Is it possible to emphasize stewardship year-round without turning people off? Yes, by saying thank you all year long. By spotlighting the impact of the congregation's generosity in people's lives, we can inspire and encourage while we educate for stewardship.

Church consultant Lyle Schaller likens the excitement of giving in a church to the game of bowling. If bowling were set up so that a person surveyed the pins, stepped briskly toward the line, flung the ball down the alley, and then watched as a curtain suddenly dropped from the ceiling, making it impossible to see how many pins she knocked down, how popular would bowling be? Church stewardship campaigns typically promise in glowing terms the wonderful results for the Kingdom if the member "lets fly" a sacrificial gift. But once the money leaves the giver's hand, it's the last they hear of the matter. The feedback loop is lacking.

It is demotivating for potential givers to hear of the need for still more money before they've heard what resulted from their last gift. Through newsletter articles, sermon illustrations, bulletin boards, mission displays, and—best of all—personal testimonies, we need to say, "Here is what is happening. Here is what God is doing through your faithful giving." People like to be told how they're doing.

Unified Versus Separate Budgets

Should the church budget be all-inclusive—a unified budget—or should it be broken down into separate funds? Most churches have leaned toward setting up a single general fund. Other churches, however, set up numerous funds, such as a Ladies Aid Fund, a Memorial Fund, a New Organ Fund, a Send the Youth Group to Africa Fund, and so forth. Contributors then choose whether to designate their gifts to a single fund or divide them up among all the funds.

Menu-Approach Problems

Multiple funds can certainly give people options in their giving choices, but this menu approach can also cause problems. Consider cash flow, for instance. While it may make people feel good to contribute toward the new organ, what good is the organ if the electric bill can't be paid? Another problem with the menu approach is that it has the potential of removing some of the authority from leaders who are called to set church priorities when they prepare the budget. If they present a budget that anticipates income in specific areas, and then members decide to give to other projects, the church's priorities have changed. Programming becomes checkbook controlled rather than leadership driven.

Nevertheless, if churches do decide to use separate budgets, they need to set some guidelines when establishing their multiple funds. For example they can limit designated giving to as few funds as possible; give funds a limited life-span by announcing a date at which they must end; and close down inactive funds, moving the balances into the general fund or some other closely aligned account. Perpetual

Three Stewardship Roles

For a church to be successful in stewardship, three things must occur simultaneously: involvement, information, and inspiration. These responsibilities can be divided among three persons. The stewardship chairperson creates involvement, the business administrator or finance committee chairperson generates information, and the pastor supplies inspiration.

● *The stewardship chairperson: involver.* We are truly fortunate when we find one of those rare gems—an organized "people person"—to put at the hub of the operation. This leader needs to be an enthusiastic cheerleader for the direction of the church and respected and trusted across the membership. Ideally, this should be an insider who has a knack for involving outsiders.

A wise involvement strategy is to include many volunteers from out-

---

funds may continue a tradition, but unless they have an active, useful purpose, they should be eliminated.

Unified Precedents

The discussion of a unified budget versus separate funds has at its core an important theological issue. The biblical concept of church leadership may be threatened by the overuse (or misuse) of a budget with separate funds, especially if it is possible for members to contribute directly to these accounts. New Testament believers were truly committed to meeting the needs of others, but instead of giving gifts directly to certain individuals or special projects, they would lay money at the apostles' feet and "it was distributed to anyone as he had need" (Acts 4:35). If church members give only to their pet projects, the basic needs and priorities of the church might not be met. Someone needs to be in charge of this key aspect of the ministry. Shouldn't it be the elected leaders of the local church?

Someone might argue that designated giving or multifund budgets allow people to respond to the promptings of the Holy Spirit and channel their giving where they feel it should go. While this sounds good, it might be compared to the image of a busload of people, each person taking a turn at the wheel.

A good compromise plan would be to develop a budget that has various departments and ministries as *accounts* but not funds. Contributions would go into one budget but would then be allocated to each ministry area, based on the predetermined budget. The practice of designating contributions to different ministry areas could be encouraged during the budgeting process. Thus people would still have a voice in deciding where the financial resources will be applied.

A unified budget can get everyone on the same bus, going in the same direction. The difference is that all the passengers choose where they want to go *before* the bus leaves the station.

—*David R. Pollock*

side the core membership. Too many stewardship campaigns "preach to the choir." People who teach, serve on boards, and sing in the choir simply talk to others who do the same. People who are givers talk to people who already give. The best stewardship campaigns are labor intensive, with phone trees, prayer-a-thons, all-church banquets, and the like involving persons on the periphery.

Another strategy for involvement includes a plan of rotation. Each year, a different segment of the congregation is targeted to enhance its giving. Given the difference in generational values, one year might aim at the GI generation's proclivity for denominational and institutional causes. Such a campaign might reflect something of the historical experience of the church.

One church that began as a mission in a tent by a railroad track over 100 years ago and later built a sanctuary with a tall tower called

---

Special Offerings

How many special offerings can a church receive in a year? Where is the line between giving people the opportunity to grow in Christian stewardship and making them feel abused?

Two Approaches

Some pastors and lay leaders believe that all special offerings are excessive. Instead, they use a "unified budget" method through which special programs, benevolences, and ministries are funded (or not funded) out of the regular weekly offering. (Some call it "putting all their begs in one ask-it.")

Others take an opposite approach. Church researcher Lyle Schaller, for example, suggests that the right number of special offerings a year is about 52. To him, the question is not how much people give, but how much they give through the local church. He believes that numerous special

offerings give people the opportunity to support those things that excite them in ministry.

This approach to special offerings can be compared to the same way optometrists are rumored to sell glasses. When a customer asks how much a pair of glasses cost, the optometrist says, "One hundred dollars." If the customer doesn't flinch, the optometrist says, "That's for the frames. The lenses are another fifty dollars." If the customer still doesn't flinch, the optometrist adds, "Each." Some pastors provide giving opportunities while keeping a sharp eye on the flinch factor.

Exercising Discernment

In general, lay people are open to special offerings, as long as certain conditions are met, such as:

● *A clear statement of purpose.* People want to know what their contribution will accomplish. If the

its campaign "From Tent to Tower to Tomorrow." The next year, emphasizing Baby Boomers, the same church might focus on the church as a network of relationships, with the theme: "We Are the Family of God." Personal testimonies in worship could feature persons sharing their experience of God's faithfulness through the network of relationships in the church. The next year, reaching out to Thirteeners, the theme might be "Giving Is Living," lifting up the personal benefits of a philanthropic lifestyle. Or, another way to involve younger members might be through a straight-from-the-shoulder emphasis on concrete ways that Christ is transforming the lives of persons with AIDS through ministries supported by the church.

● *The business administrator/finance chairperson: informer.* With today's technology, a skilled person with a computer can make church finances understandable to the rank-and-file member. Software pro-

---

offering is for a youth group work project, what will the young people be doing? And when they return, will they share what they did? The key is communication and a sense of joint participation between giver and receiver.

● *Accountability.* Contributors want to be assured the money will actually go where it is supposed to go. With recent financial scandals and reports of excessive overhead in some large secular charities, people are increasingly willing to give through the church—but only if they know they will not be bilked again.

● *Not being nickeled-and-dimed to death.* Lay people become excited about an offering that takes advantage of a special opportunity at home or abroad. But special offerings to pay the light bill are not regarded as well.

Of course, a church that can't pay the light bill or the pastor's salary has a problem. But the problem is better met through stewardship education aimed at the regular Sunday offering, rather than through endless special appeals

(that bring increasingly diminished returns). This is not to say a church that is seriously behind can't have a "catch-up Sunday," but it needs to be a one-time event where people can see that the rest of the congregation is sharing the load.

● *The chance to give realistically and prayerfully.* This includes advance notice before the offering is received. It means hearing how this special offering fits into the giving scheme of the whole year and what other special offerings are anticipated. For contributors, pacing is important, as is knowing what ministries they will have opportunity to support, so they can give to those closest to their hearts. At the same time, people understand the need for special offerings in the event of natural disasters and are glad to take part on short notice.

Properly handled and communicated, special offerings can be an asset to the ongoing ministry of the church. Rather than draining the reservoir, they can help prime the pump of joyful, regular giving.

—Dave Wilkinson

grams can boil down complex financial data to breathtakingly simple-as-pie-chart clarity. The administrator's role is to make the church's financial picture widely known and easily understood throughout the year.

This person coordinates the nuts and bolts of the entire stewardship program, ordering materials, supervising publicity, dogging the details, worrying about deadlines. He or she keeps accurate records and sends out monthly or quarterly financial records to each member. This person must be brutally honest with the pastor about the financial state of the church, recommending strategies for cash-flow crunches or midyear budget revisions.

● *The pastor: inspirer.* The two prevailing church attitudes toward stewardship—the "old realist" and the "new idealist"—are anything but inspirational.

The old realist, usually a businessperson, says, "Look, you have to pay the bills and keep the minister fed and the lights on. And the building maintained. And missionaries supported. Nobody has ever come up with a better way of getting it done than to call time out after the sermon, have the organist play something pretty while you pass the hat, and let everybody dig down deep and pitch in their fair share." The old realist sees the offering as a necessary evil.

Across the aisle from the old realist is the young idealist. He or she sees stewardship as an *un*necessary evil. "Why don't we live like the lilies of the field in this church and have faith and trust God to make ends meet? Why don't we just pray instead of having all these brochures and pledge cards and fund appeals?"

According to the apostle Paul, young idealists and old realists are both subscriptural. In Paul's eyes, the offering is neither a necessary evil nor a unnecessary evil, but a necessary good. "On the first day of every week, each one of you should set aside a sum of money in keeping with his income" (1 Cor. 16:2).

Giving is at the heart of Christian worship. As believers in the priesthood of all believers, we are priests to God. The most privileged person in all Israel was the Levitical priest. On behalf of his nation, he entered into the Holy of Holies and there offered prayers, songs, and offerings to Almighty God. We are today's Levitical priesthood. We are priests inside the Holy of Holies—not to get a blessing, but to give offerings.

The pastor/inspirer helps the church members see their pledges as more than money or a figure on a card. The pledge is many things—the gift of part of myself to Christ and his work, a contribution to our children's Christian education, an investment in a better city, a gift of gratitude to God, a vote for a Christian world, an outreaching hand to other nations, a service to those in sorrow, help for our youth, an expression of faith in the future, our way of walking in the footsteps of Jesus.

What other strategies can we as inspirers use to promote year-round stewardship? For one thing, we can select a clear, brief, inspiring scriptural phrase to capture people's imaginations, such as "Share the Spirit," "A Heart for God," "My Gift for the King," "Giving Is Living," or "Catch the Vision." We should, however, avoid overly cutesy phrases that might trivialize the effort in people's minds. It is absolutely essential that the stewardship motto, if not selected by the pastor, be at least one that he or she is happy with and looks forward to preaching and interweaving into every aspect of ministry.

We can also work to plan stewardship strategy a year in advance for the coming year, including key verses, themes, sermon ideas, and texts. We can ask church leaders and creative people to think of ways to synchronize their programming and work in a convergence of effort. We want to unify the church around common themes and images, with logos, stationary, music, and dinners all echoing the common theme. This theme is not just important for stewardship; it focuses the church in all of its programs and melds together a wide divergence of programs into Christ's work in this particular church.

Above all, the pastor/inspirer declares victory. Like the referee in the game of football, the pastor—and only the pastor—can declare the game over and announce the official final score. Even if the financial goal was not met, it is absolutely essential for the pastor to announce a victory by celebrating what was achieved. After all, what was accomplished represents the sacrifice and dedication of a portion of the church. That response deserves to be celebrated. If the goal was a million dollars for a new organ and only $700,000 was raised, the pastor can say, "Friends, we are $700,000 further along the way toward realizing our dream of a new organ! Praise the Lord!" Not to do this at the end of a pledge campaign could so deflate enthusiasm that members may wonder what is to be served by honoring their pledge; the organ still can't be purchased, so why bother?

The December Push

Many churches need to receive as much as 15 to 20 percent of their required financial resources during the month of December. This is both complicated and helped by the Christmas season. This time of year people's emotions are nearest the surface. Heavy-handed appeals for cash, or panicky fund appeals, can be most unwelcome at this time. Yet people at this season have a heightened appreciation of the importance of the church in their lives, along with greater empathy with the homeless and the hungry. At this time of year, stewardship programs can be an ideal avenue for expressing the Christmas spirit and worship of the Christ Child. A theme like "My Gift for the King" will provide a much better context for giving than "Over the Top in '94."

In the face of a severe end-of-year financial shortfall, a brief word from the pastor prior to the reading of the Scripture each Sunday of December can be helpful. One pastor introduces these chats in a disarming way: "Do you have a special room in the house where you and your spouse talk? For us it's the kitchen. Becky and I sit down, and we say, 'Okay, let's talk. How can we afford that vacation? How are we going to pay the orthodontist's bill? How are we going to send the kids to college?' Well, I would like to invite you into the church kitchen this morning." After this warm, intimate opening, he shares his heart with the congregation, giving an update on "how we're doing." These pastoral chats are brief and, while very candid, also affirming and upbeat.

In a masterpiece of compression, Christian businessman Max De Pree defines a leader in a way that captures the pastoral role in a stewardship campaign. "The first responsibility of a leader is to define reality. The last is to say thank you. In between the two, the leader must become a servant and a debtor. That sums up the progress of an artful leader." Stewardship is more than an annual fundraising campaign. Every Sunday is stewardship Sunday. It is nothing less than all we do with all that we have. It is the heart of worship, requiring the best of leadership.

—Victor D. Pentz

Resources

Easum, W. 1991. How to reach baby boomers. Nashville: Abingdon.

Resource Services, Inc. 1992. Discover the joy: A stewardship education and development program. Dallas: Resource Services.

Schaller, L. 1987. It's a different world. Nashville: Abingdon.

Forming a Policy for Fundraising Activities

The junior highers have a great fundraising idea: a bike-a-thon. And the youth are planning three car washes for their upcoming trip. Also, there's the handbell committee's pizza drive.

It's the world of church fundraisers, and the church that doesn't want to drown itself in its own soap suds or pizza sauce will look gratefully to its written fundraising-activities policy.

The key to this policy is that it be written and adopted before a crisis or a pressing decision forces the issue. A workable policy will also be drafted so that later revisions, modifications, and exceptions can be made.

Seven Considerations

A written fundraising policy should briefly answer these questions:

● *What is our theology of money?*

If money is a means to fulfill God's purpose for the church, how does the church believe God normally provides the resources to accomplish his purposes? Do we believe in tithing, proportionate giving, or other means of fundraising?

● *How do fundraising projects fulfill the purposes of our church?* Some churches disallow fundraisers, except offerings, to avoid a reputation in the community for soliciting their money. Other churches believe fundraisers help connect members to outsiders and are a means of evangelism and ministry. Whatever fundraising policy is adopted, it should support the overall mission of the church and not conflict with the reputation the church seeks for God and itself in the community.

● *Who can use the church name and facilities?* The key issue here is "insiders" and "outsiders." Many churches choose to limit all fundraising done in or through the church to those who directly support the ministry of the church. Some allow outside organizations to raise money through church membership lists, programs, and facilities.

● *Who approves a fundraising activity?* For most churches, it is the governing board. For some, it is the pastor. For others, it is a combination of the two, where the board approves all new fundraising activities but the pastor okays repetition of those activities.

In one church, the policy allowed for special offerings and fundraisers but imposed a limit on the number of those activities. Each fundraising project for the coming year needed to be submitted for approval in November of the preceding year. This encouraged prioritization and discouraged last-minute requests.

● *How will money be handled?* It is important that policies and people be in place to handle money carefully and legally. Typically, the church treasurer is made responsible to deposit the income in a timely manner and to write a summary report to the church board.

● *Are there legal issues?* Before finalizing any fundraising plans, it is a good idea to have an attorney look over the plans. Some regions require licenses, permits, or collection of sales taxes. Also, there are limits on how much money a church can collect through fundraisers without jeopardizing its tax-exempt status. Normally, revenue from sources other than contributions should be a minor portion of the total receipts of the church.

● *How are exceptions made?* It is unlikely that a policy can anticipate every situation. How, then, can a person or organization request an exception to the written policy? Exceptions should be rare to keep the policy from becoming pointless.

A good way to form a policy is to ask ten churches for copies of their fundraising policies. From these policies and the ideas they provide, a church usually can fashion a policy fitting its purposes.

—Leith Anderson

34

Conducting Special Fund Drives

W hen churches need to generate financial support above and beyond the regular income of tithes, "special fund drive" becomes the operative term. These drives, in one way or another, ask members and friends of the church for a "second giving" of funds that are dedicated to a particular project or cause. If the fund drive is successful, the giving goal is reached by the last day of the drive, and the usual Sunday offerings will have not been noticeably affected.

The golden rule of fund drives is that special giving requires special effort, and there are ways to make every effort count.

Fund drives are of such a delicate nature that just the decision to conduct one can fill a pastor with apprehension. However, special appeals can be rewarding experiences for both pastors and laity if approached positively.

The approach taken to a fund drive should depend in part on the type of cause or project needing the money and in part on the amount of money needed.

There are two basic types of fund drives: external and internal.

External Special Appeals

The revenue raised by external special appeals supports the work of groups outside the congregation. Most often this work is sponsored by a denomination, association, or regional group whose goals correspond to a congregation's principles and values. Or sometimes the recipient may be a community-based group that provides help locally for the needy.

External appeals often aim for either increased general awareness of a need or for a set basis of financial support. When awareness is the main objective, information is distributed to an entire constituency, knowing that those who feel most strongly about the cause will respond financially. If the objective is a set basis of financial support, a few select people or groups with known interests and resources are asked to respond. Normally, special fund drives contain a blend of these two objectives.

In general, the more cordial a church's relationship is with a prospective recipient, the greater the giving. People respond to people, and donors are more likely to give—and give generously—if the money goes to help people rather than to fund administration or program overhead. The closer to the donor's heart an appeal is, the greater the return.

One consideration in deciding whether to support an external appeal is the time elapsed since the church last supported an external appeal. Another is the church's internal giving requirements. A church's decision is usually made in a way similar to how a private party decides to give philanthropically. If an asker's time line does not fit well with the church's (the church may be in the middle of a large internal special appeal), the schedule may need to be adjusted or the request may need to be declined altogether. The time between taking on new external special appeals should at least equal the length of the last appeal's giving period. Responses even to seemingly innocuous requests to stick a giving envelope in the bulletin need to be planned and spaced carefully.

In external special appeals, recipients will want to establish a permanent donor relationship with the givers and so will extend thanks and acknowledge the gifts. Churches also need to thank their people for giving and inform them how the money is making a difference.

Internal Special Appeals

Churches make internal special appeals to generate support for such entities as extraordinary budget items, staff additions, land purchases, building projects, and church foundations. In most cases, however, special appeals should not be used to boost a lagging annual budget or to buy a laundry list of unmet maintenance items, such as a roof repair, parking lot surfacing, steeple repair, or interior painting. In fact, it is good budgetary practice to build a contingency fund into the annual budget that can be used for unanticipated projects or needs, such as when the steeple develops a major, unanticipated structural problem. Big fundraising efforts should be saved for truly big projects.

Congregational special appeals normally address a congregation's capital needs for buildings or land. But not all projects generate equal enthusiasm. The pecking order of enthusiasm for projects, from easiest to generate support for to hardest, usually stacks up in this order:

1. Worship space.
2. Education space and building accessibility.
3. Entries with gathering space and fellowship space.
4. Kitchens and youth space.
5. Parking lots and land acquisition.
6. Administration and debt reduction.

Churches also have options about the *kind* of special appeal to conduct, such as:

● *Short-term appeals.* Funds are donated within three months.

● *Local, long-term appeals.* Funds normally are given over a one- or two-year period, and the appeal is handled by local leadership.

● *Professional, long-term appeals.* Funds normally are received over three years of giving under the guidance of professionals.

The following chart provides a perspective on the most appropriate type of internal special appeal to run, given the magnitude of funds needed and the church's annual budget. For instance, a church with a budget of $150,000 that needs to raise an additional sum of $60,000 (40% of its annual budget) can probably use a local, long-term appeal.

Annual Budget Amount	Target Percent of Annual Budget to Be Raised in the Appeal		
	Short-term	*Local, Long*	*Pro, Long*
Under $200,000	15%–35%	35%–60%	> 60%
$200,000–$500,000	10%–25%	25%–50%	> 50%
$500,000–$1 million	8%–20%	20%–40%	> 40%
$1 million and up	5%–15%	15%–30%	> 30%

Do It Yourself or Hire a Professional?

Once a church has reviewed the initial data and determined it needs a special appeal, the question arises of whether to run the drive by hiring outside professional assistance or by using in-church local talent. Good reasons can be found for doing it either way. The important thing is that the many factors involved in the special-appeals process be understood and analyzed carefully. The one wrong reason to decide against professional assistance is the fee. Fees should be seen as investments that assure the greatest possible return. The better question to ask is, "Do we have the know-how and time necessary to generate enough support to meet our objectives?" The success or failure of one special-fund drive can change the course of a congregation's history.

Here are four points to consider when deciding on an approach:

● *Fundraising is as much a matter of faith as it is of finances.* Special appeals are about people growing in faith, spiritual renewal, and understanding of Christian commitment. Leaders must create the climate for spiritual growth as well as financial gain. Interestingly, the success of a drive almost always depends more on how spiritually alive and committed to a project a congregation is than its members' wealth.

● *Preparation is the greater part of fundraising.* Fundraising is 80 percent preparation and 20 percent asking. Time spent studying possible solutions, choosing and generating a solution, communicating the solution, and involving people is time well spent.

Selecting a Fundraising Consultant

A pastor had high hopes when he hired a fundraising consultant. Local unemployment was high, and the church had finished the year with a $6,000 shortfall. It needed a shot in the arm. But the consultant delivered only "expenses and hard feelings" by miscommunicating his fee and ordering materials without authorization.

Then the church hired a different firm, which did a super job. The church's financial future finally looked bright. Selecting the right fundraiser takes work, but it's well worth the effort. It's not wise for a church to base its decision primarily on the consultant's affability, for virtually all are eminently likable. Nor should the fact the consultant is a pastor be given undue weight, for most fundraisers are clergy. Nor should the level of pledges the fundraiser promises be overemphasized, because what counts is not the amount *pledged,* but the total actually *given.*

Most campaigns promise from two to four times a church's annual income (in pledges for a three-year period). A realistic goal is 1.5–2 times annual income. The percentage of pledges that actually come in may range from 50 to 95 percent, and each percentage point may represent thousands of dollars.

Key Questions

Asking these questions can help a church board select a competent, compatible fundraising firm:

● *What will you actually do?* Most firms use upbeat introductory meetings, evaluations of the church's giving potential, recruiting of leaders, home visits, prayer vigils, information periods, all-church banquets, canvass periods to collect pledges, and "Victory Days" to announce results.

Churches should ask specifically about several key points: What church financial records will you

● *Pastors probably shouldn't be directors.* Pastors have varying interests and abilities when it comes to seeking donations. Some feel almost nauseous at the prospect, while others get an adrenaline rush just thinking about it. Both kinds likely should avoid assuming directorship responsibility. Fundraising is time consuming and requires concentrated effort that would detract from other ministry. Pastors can, however, apply their skill and time to the enlistment of qualified lay leaders and then work with them in a CEO-type relationship.

● *Professional partners nearly always increase the dollars given.* Statistics show that over a three-year period, a church running its own drive can expect to raise from 1.25 to 1.75 times its current annual giving. With professional direction, however, a church can expect to raise from 1.5 to 3 times its current annual giving.

If a church elects to hire professional assistance, it should interview

---

want to see? Will you ask some individuals to state publicly how much they will give? How will you collect pledges?

● *What will you expect of the pastor?* Will the pastor be told (or have strongly suggested) an amount to give? Will that amount be made known to the congregation? Will the pastor be asked to preach on stewardship? How often?

● *What will you charge?* The fee usually will be revealed only during a consultant's first visit; comparison shopping by phone proves difficult. Fees are based on location, size, and income of the church, primarily, so they can vary widely. Recent fees for two churches' campaigns were $25,000 and $40,000—and the larger fee was for a much smaller pledge goal! Some firms charge a flat percentage of the money raised, but that approach may encourage high-pressure tactics. Either way, it's good to be clear on the cost.

● *In what types of churches have you been most successful?* "Consider the consultant a short-term staff member who should meet all

the criteria you apply to anyone else on staff," suggests one fundraiser. Does he or she have a theological perspective in line with that of your church? Is there an affinity with the denominational culture?

● *What churches can we call for reference?* Consultants should provide a list of former clients. It's a good policy to ask of several of these churches: Did the consultant reach the goal? What percentage of pledges came in? Did the firm miscommunicate or cause hard feelings? Did the campaign lead to spiritual renewal? And, what other churches do you know that have used this firm? These additional churches, not listed as references, may give a more complete picture.

No regulatory agency governs fundraisers, but only a minute number could be considered unethical. Provided the consultant is selected carefully and the campaign is supported faithfully, the odds of having a bad experience are slim. Most churches report that a fundraising campaign raised not just dollars, but faith.

—*Kevin A. Miller*

three to five firms. Each firm should be asked to provide references, which should be reviewed to see if the firm provided satisfactory assistance to other churches and was able to deliver on its fundraising projections. Of course, any firm selected should hold a similar philosophy to the church's.

Moving Forward with Leadership

The majority of a congregation must embrace an appeal to make it successful. This means approval of a drive should be arrived at through a congregational vote. The process can be organized so the number of times the congregation votes is limited to three: Vote number one grants authority to an appointed committee to spend a stated amount of money in its efforts to define the need and to outline a solution. Later, vote two approves the committee's recommendations (to conduct or not conduct a special appeal). Vote three approves the

---

Financing Building Projects

Churches today often face enormous costs when they launch into their building programs. For example, one congregation (First Presbyterian Church of Yakima, Washington) saw their $1.5 million renovation project mushroom to closer to $3 million. How can a church raise that kind of money?

Building Strategies

Here are eight strategies applicable to any church, large or small, that wants to launch a successful building program:

● *Hire a fundraising consultant.* Few congregations possess the in-house expertise to carry out a major capital campaign, so most churches will no doubt need a professional fundraiser to guide the board and various committees through the process.

● *Preach theologically.* "Link your building renovation to the many biblical narratives dealing with the same theme," counsels former pastor Vic Pentz. "When was the last time you preached a sermon on Haggai 1:3–11? Or did a series on Nehemiah rebuilding the walls of Jerusalem?"

● *Emphasize sacrificial giving.* A key element in this advice is that campaign leaders must go on record with their own stewardship sacrifices first. Then they will be less hesitant about asking others to join them in the sacrifice.

● *Choose a slogan.* The slogan should capture people's interest and commitment. For example, First Presbyterian's campaign theme— "Catch the Vision"—came from the promise of Acts 2:17, in which "your young men will see visions, your old men will dream dreams."

final form the committee thinks the drive should take, in consideration of the projected financial results.

After the congregation has taken the second vote authorizing a special appeal, three to six people should be chosen as key leaders of the drive. They must be supportive of the project, possess the skills to do the job well, be committed to make a significant commitment of time, and be willing to give a proportionately generous gift of money. They assume the responsibility of enlisting the remaining workers and of supervising the appeal's direction. Each leader should be supported with a thorough but brief description of what his or her responsibilities are as well as a time table of when things need to be done. One note of caution: Special appeals are great for discovering new talent and expanding a church's worker base, but the key leadership positions should be filled with tried and tested men and women.

An essential leadership task is to nurture involvement. As many people as possible should be asked to participate by giving of their

---

This theme pictures old and young alike looking to God's future together under the anointing of the Spirit.

● *Use many overlapping communication methods.* Since any one communication method is inadequate, keep the congregation constantly informed through letters, church bulletins, neighborhood meetings, sermons, brochures, and announcements. The logo can be placed on all church correspondence to keep the theme in the public eye.

● *Highlight endorsements by opinion leaders.* Invite beloved, longtime church members to lend their credibility by endorsing the building campaign. The dreams they express, along with their endorsements, help build broader support. People look to these leaders to demonstrate that the vision and its purposes are truly in line with God's will.

● *Flex when necessary.* Many surprises crop up in the middle of building projects, including cost overruns and altered architectural plans. These unavoidable glitches make a commitment to flexibility all the more important. If something as simple as a carpet sample ignites an unexpected firestorm of criticism, the committee can simply suggest another kind of carpet. Inflexibility in such areas will erode popular support for the larger vision.

● *Never stop communicating.* It's easy to become complacent after the money is raised. But the congregation still needs to know what is happening with their funds as the project takes shape.

One pastor, for example, would don a construction hard hat each Sunday morning and give a progress report from the lectern. His news-and-humor format gave people the information they needed to feel personal ownership in the project and to squelch rumors.

—*Melissa S. Labberton*

time and talent—before being asked to make a financial commitment. Informed and involved people are generous people. Most people will want to help, do a good job, and be recognized for their efforts. The wise pastor remembers this and nurtures, teaches, supports, and generously recognizes their valuable gifts of time. Without generous portions of volunteered time, a drive will not be successful.

Setting a Realistic Goal

An appeal's goals go beyond the financial to include the spiritual renewal of people, a broadened view of being a Christian steward, a more clearly identified and focused corporate mission, an expanded and empowered core of leaders, and a sense of mission. Last—and most often mentioned—is the goal of substantial financial growth.

Setting the financial goal is an art. The determining factor should not be the price tag of the project being funded but the congregation's willingness and ability to participate. The *willingness factor* can be assessed by examining current giving patterns and the type of project or cause being considered. The *ability factor* can be measured by figuring the size of the congregation and its total annual income. Success in fundraising depends as much on accurate goal setting as it does on giving.

Let's work through a goal-setting scenario for a hypothetical Community Church, using the data discussed above. Community Church is a growing congregation and is in urgent need of expanded facilities to make room for the new people. Community Church has identified its primary needs as more education and fellowship space. There are 350 active giving members currently contributing $360,000 annually. The last special appeal was 12 years ago for a new sanctuary, which is now paid off. There is no capital debt, but last year's annual contributions were eight percent short of the planned budget. Total annual income for congregational members has been calculated at $12,000,000. Currently the congregation is giving 3 percent ($360,000 divided by $12,000,000) of its aggregate income to the church.

An architect has estimated that expanding and renovating the present facility will cost approximately $1,300,000. Income from investments and other earnings are limited and so are not a factor. The church is located in a community where the annual average household income is $48,000. There is the potential for some priority gifts in amounts of $25,000 or greater over three years.

How does the committee figure its dollar goal? Because Community Church is seeking education and fellowship space (considered a popular goal), multiply the annual giving of $360,000 by 2 to arrive at a willingness-based goal of $720,000 over three years. Multiplying factors for various types of drives are: 3 for worship space, 2.5 for education and building-accessibility space, 2–2.5 for fellowship space, 2 for kitchens and youth space, 2 for parking lots and land acquisitions, and 1.5 for administration and debt reduction. If a church has considerable current debt, the goal should be lowered, but with considerable unrestricted investment, the goal could be moved higher.

The ability factor looks at total membership income for the giving period. In this case, the congregation's three-year income would be $36,000,000. This figure is multiplied by percentages that represent ½ to ⅔ of Community Church's current annual giving percentage, which is 3 percent. Thus, Community Church's ability base would range from 1.5 percent to 2 percent of $36,000,000 ($540,000 to $720,000). The higher percentage can be used for projects known to generate more money.

Thus Community Church's goal would probably fall between $540,000 and $720,000, based on their expected willingness and ability to give.

Thinking Through Methods

The key to fund-drive methodology is choosing a method the church can do well and in a timely and thorough fashion. There is greatness in simplicity. Whatever specific approach is taken, it needs to bring to the special appeal the following components:

● *An orientation session* that clearly connects the church mission with the objectives of the appeal. It should also introduce key leaders, define objectives, sets goals, and finalize the schedule of events.

● *Spiritual-life events,* such as Bible studies, prayer activity, a devotional theme, and a theme Scripture and song.

● *Promotional materials* that inform people of the objectives of the appeal and its financial goals. The material should motivate each individual to participate as a worker and contributor. Promotional methods often include a case statement, brochures, newsletters, banners, letters, bulletin inserts, videos, bulletin boards, and small-group meetings. Visuals and repetition of the spoken and written word are important. Experts say a small group needs to hear a message three times and a larger group seven times for it to be remembered.

● *Instruction of workers.* Committee leaders and people doing visitation should receive thorough written and spoken instruction prior to beginning their tasks.

● *One-on-one visits* to develop the larger-dollar gift. Gifts of $25,000 to $100,000 are there in many congregations but will become available only when cultivated through visitation.

● *Celebrations* involving food, fellowship, fun, and financial opportunity. These are often very successful.

● *A realistic expected "giving response pattern"* (distribution of gift amounts) that resembles the size of gifts typically given by the congregation but also provides for at least a 10-percent cushion above the stated goal to allow for pledges that will never be received.

● *Direct and personal requests for contributions.* This can be done one-on-one or in larger groups. Those making the requests need to be briefed on what makes people give to churches—particularly through second-mile giving. Mature Christians give because they feel called to personal growth as disciplined stewards of God's varied good gifts entrusted unconditionally to their care. That is the beauty of the gospel; we receive much more than we could possibly return.

In practical terms, many respond out of a sense of duty, for tax reasons, or because of guilt or peer pressure, yet even these givers can experience the reward of giving. A church thus can feel good about asking people to give, because it helps them to grow.

● *Follow-up.* There are two common reasons why a special appeal may fail to produce the money first promised. The first is a lack of significant activity on the intended project during the first six months of the drive. It's usually a mistake to plan to put the money in the bank and wait to build or renovate only when all the commitments have come in. Many of them won't ever come in!

The second reason is inadequate follow-up. Two or three years is a long time for people to give, even when dynamic physical changes are visible. To counter this, a follow-up committee can be appointed by the governing board to oversee: (1) keeping the appeal and project before the people in vivid and graphic ways; (2) developing the appeal to its highest financial potential by offering a variety of giving opportunities, such as memorial or designated giving; (3) incorporating new members into the appeal at key times; and (4) reviewing giving records, monitoring all appeal commitments, and taking action when giving attrition rises above 10 percent.

The Pastor's Role

The number one question asked of professional fundraisers by pastors is "What is my role in this effort?" Pastors need to be involved in a variety of ways.

● Believing the drive will be successful. A pastor's courage and confidence will give the people the support they need.

● Working closely with the group defining the need and the solution.

● Lending public support to the drive from the pulpit, in writing, and through personal involvement.

● Asking people outright for their affirming vote and subsequent support of time, skill, and money.

● Attending key committee meetings as a spiritual leader and resource person.

● Helping identify and enlist top appeal leaders.

● Contributing personal financial support and making it known publicly.

● Assisting lay leaders in generating large-dollar giving by joining individual calls as deemed appropriate.

● Preaching sermons regularly (perhaps one sermon a month) that stress personal stewardship of all types.

The more pastors concentrate on money as the primary motivation in fundraising, the more of a struggle raising that money becomes. On the other hand, concentrating on Scripture, vision, and personal spiritual growth produces more celebration and greater financial success. Generosity can be taught and caught. People can be led by the Spirit and example; they want to be generous.

Pastors need to provide the climate for success. When the preparing is over, the asking should be done boldly and with confidence.

—*Ann Rauvola Bailey*

Resources

Gifford, H. 1993. All that God has given. Minneapolis: Augsburg-Fortress.

Johnson, D. 1987. Finance in your church. Nashville: Abingdon.

Mead, L. 1991. The once and future church. Washington, D.C.: Alban Institute.

Zehring, J. 1989. You can run a capital campaign. Nashville: Abingdon.

Bonds and Notes

Churches financing large projects may consider an alternative to obtaining a bank loan: issuing bonds to investors. With bond financing, a church can raise funds for construction, buy property, or refinance existing debt.

A bond is a promise to pay a debt. With bond financing, a church borrows money from investors, who purchase bonds and become bondholders. The bond is the promise to pay bondholders semiannual interest at a fixed rate for a specified time—until their bonds mature. The net proceeds of the bond issue are used for the project, and at the bonds' maturity date, the principal borrowed is repaid to investors.

Any incorporated church that can demonstrate fiscal responsibility through historical financial statements can issue bonds. Church bonds are often first-mortgage bonds, secured by a first-mortgage lien on the church's property. This type of bond is issued whether bondholders are members of the congregation or outside investors.

Common Questions

● *Why consider bond financing?* Bond financing lets the church lock in a low, fixed rate of interest for a long term, usually 15 years. Budgeting is simplified by knowing the debt payments required for the life of the loan. In return for a long-term fixed rate, the church pays fees to the underwriter that cover the cost of underwriting and selling the bonds. These fees can be paid from the proceeds of the bond issue.

● *Who provides assistance with this method?* Typically, the program comes through a reputable bond-underwriting company or investment-banking firm that specializes in underwriting church debt. Bonds can be marketed to church members or only to outside investors, so as to not interfere with tithing or other fundraising efforts. Some underwriters can also offer the bonds to their retail investment clients. A church may benefit from offering bonds to both the congregation and outside investors.

● *What documentation may be required?* An underwriting firm is responsible to its investors, so it investigates the financial stability of a church before it agrees to finance a project. It gathers and considers all pertinent information about the church's operations and ability to repay the debt. Churches should be prepared to provide a synopsis of the project and financial statements for three years.

Taking the Steps

The bond-financing process usually takes a few months, if all goes well, and follows a course like this:

● Church leaders contact an underwriting firm and present their project. The underwriter reviews the project and the church's financial information.

● If the project looks promising, the underwriter visits the church to present a financing program, answer questions, and extend a letter of intent.

● The underwriter reviews a timetable with the church and helps leaders choose an appropriate financing structure.

● Together, the church and underwriter develop a prospectus (a disclosure document giving information about the project to prospective bondholders). The underwriter obtains clearance to market the bonds from the National Association of Securities Dealers and from each state where the bonds will be marketed.

● Bonds are issued and sold. A few weeks later is the settlement date, when the church receives the proceeds of the bond sale. A trustee bank is appointed to act as the church's paying agent. If the proceeds are for construction, the trustee holds the funds and invests them on the church's behalf until they are disbursed for construction draws. During the term of the loan, the church services the debt with regular payments to the trustee, who then makes semiannual interest payments to the bondholders. When the bonds mature, the trustee repays the remaining principle to bondholders, and the process is complete.

—*Eugene H. Rudnicki*

35

Receiving and Recording Money

A good internal-control system is a central part of proper stewardship over the money God gives to us. *Internal control* is accounting jargon for a checks-and-balances system to prevent stealing. Control of assets is kept apart from the record keeping of assets. In the church setting, the internal-control process has two parts—internal control over cash *receipts* and cash *payments*. We'll focus here on receiving money and keeping track of it.

Internal Control Over Cash Receipts

A church, which often receives cash, needs a good system to handle that money. To set up internal control over cash, the church board needs to appoint a treasurer and a helper. The helper controls the cash, and the treasurer keeps the records. The helper is not the assistant treasurer. That is, if the treasurer is absent from church for a time, the church must find someone other than the helper to take over the treasurer's duties. Likewise, the helper must find someone other than the treasurer to take over the helper's duties. This keeps the duties separate.

A good helper needs to be reliable, the kind of person who is regularly in church or can find a suitable substitute when necessary. The helper must be able to add and subtract accurately and keep a neat checkbook. The helper keeps the church's checkbook, and the treasurer does the bookkeeping.

Suppose a church names Trish as church treasurer and Hank as the helper. They process receipts in the following manner: After the church service, Hank and another person serving as a counter take the offering into a back room. They first count the loose offerings. Then they open the envelopes and compare the amount in the envelopes to the amount written on the envelopes. The counter makes a note of the amount of loose receipts and later gives it to Trish (the treasurer). Hank puts the loose offering in an envelope. Later, from the envelopes, he makes a list of the names of each person who gave and the amount. One name on the list is "loose receipts." He totals the list and makes a deposit slip. Three totals must agree: the list total, the deposit slip total, and the cash and checks total. This process is simple if the helper is careful. Careless counting or incorrectly writing down amounts will cause the totals to differ.

When all three amounts are the same, Hank takes the money to the bank in a sealed bag to deposit it. He gives Trish the donor list and bank receipt, keeping copies for himself. He also gives Trish the offering envelopes, because they tell her which funds to put the money in. Trish checks to make sure the list and the bank receipt agree. She records the receipts, using Hank's list, just as though she had received the money. She compares the loose receipts amount from Hank's list to the amount on the counter's note.

With this system, no one can steal. The counter watches Hank, and Trish never touches any money. Hank is the only one who touches the money. He can, of course, take the money and run, but he cannot secretly steal the money. If Hank steals some money and lies about the loose receipts, the amount for loose receipts on his list will differ from the amount the counter reports to Trish. If Hank steals and lies about what a member gave, the receipt Trish gives to the member will show the lower amount, and the member will question the difference. If Hank tells the truth on the list but does not deposit the full amount, the bank receipt will differ from the list, and Trish will question him when she balances the bank account. A good system covers every angle.

If Trish did each step herself, she could steal the money, falsify the records, and not get caught. With good internal control, the one who holds the money cannot steal without the records showing it, and the record keeper cannot swindle the church, because he or she never touches the money.

The Art of Record Keeping

Church record keeping is easy to understand but sometimes hard to do. Treasurers need to know about the church's basic records and how to keep them. The system shown here is handy for small and medium-sized churches. Simplicity, ease, and cash control are its major features.

● *Funds.* A fund, for our purposes, is money that is ready for a specific use within the church. For example, many churches have a building fund, money set aside for the building. Donors may specify that the money they give is only for the building. Also, the church board may approve transfers into it from the general fund. Specific gifts and transfers increase the building fund; checks written for work done reduce the building fund.

Other funds are handled in the same manner. For example, the youth fund is money set aside to pay for youth activities. It comes from specific gifts or transfers from the church general fund. Funds can be set up for such things as evangelism or telephone expenses.

One fund all churches have is a general fund. It covers the church's routine expenses, such as electric bills and salaries. Using this fund, the church board also provides more money to other funds, such as for the building or for youth work.

Generally a church has only one checking account, but each fund claims some of the money. Suppose the following funds have these balances:

General	$2,000
Building	4,000
Youth	1,000
Homeless	500
Fund total	$7,500

The checking account balance is $7,500. If the board transfers $500 from the general fund to youth work, the general fund will become $1,500 and the youth work fund will become $1,500. The checking account total will still be $7,500. The funds' total must always equal total cash.

A church can have as many funds as it wants. For example, a church that sponsors a refugee family may have a refugee fund. People give directly to the fund, and the church board gives it some general fund money. Then the project leader will know exactly how much to spend.

Each fund is under someone's care, which is a good feature of the fund system. Youth leaders look at the youth fund and know exactly what they have to run their program, church board members know what they can spend from the building fund, and so forth. It's a popular system. The program leaders know exactly how much they have, and the church board can easily move money into a specific fund, freeing them from dealing with continual requests. This system also frees the treasurer from concern over how much money there is for each program. If the youth leaders ask for some money for a teen outing and the fund has the money, they get it. If not, they must go to the board. Keeping track of how much is set aside for the youth is a simple process for the treasurer.

Some funds the church treasurer handles belong to other groups. Suppose a denomination has a foreign-mission thrust named the Hudson Taylor Foreign Mission Offering. Once a year the church promotes this offering, and during the year members also give to it. The church needs a fund that receives the money that comes in and holds it until it can be sent by check to the proper place. Without a fund system, the mission money could easily become mingled with other offerings and perhaps be spent on the electric bill.

● *Journals.* Let us now look at the nuts and bolts of record keeping for treasurers and their helpers (the "you" in what follows). First, you need some tools, such as a desktop adding machine that makes a tape. A handheld calculator is not sufficient since having a tape will help you find errors. You also need a journal, an oversized book with metal pegs binding its hard covers and allowing the user to add or

Financial Reporting

Pastors typically are not number crunchers and don't need to be. But they do need to be able to interpret the financial information given them. Some of these basic financial reports and concepts include the following:

● *Balance sheet.* The balance sheet provides a snapshot of the church's financial picture on any given date. It shows:

—Assets. Current assets are cash and any items that can be converted into cash in a short time. Other assets include the value of the church's land, buildings, and equipment.

—Liabilities. This is money the church owes to others. Current liabilities are those items the church is required to pay for within one year. An important comparison to make is between current assets and current liabilities, to see which is greater.

—Net assets. This section of the balance sheet simply shows the difference between an organization's assets and its debts or liabilities. This is sometimes referred to as the "fund balance."

● *Designated funds report.* Designate or restricted funds are unique to not-for-profit organizations. This report tracks how the church's designated offerings are being spent and what the remaining balance is. For example, if a contributor states that a contribution can be used only for a certain purpose, the church is obligated to use that money for that purpose. It is a good idea for churches to set a policy on what types of designated gifts they will or will not accept.

● *Income statement.* Other names for this are "profit and loss," "support and revenue over expenses," and "statement of activity." This statement shows how much income was received and what the expenses were for a given period.

remove pages. Each page *back* has a two- or three-inch-wide column for writing the reason for each entry. The rest of the page has columns for numbers, as does the reverse, or front, side.

Imagine these pages bound in a book. When you open the book, you see the first page's front. It has nothing but number columns. When you turn the page, things neatly fall together. The first page's back has the column for writing the reason for the entry. To the right of that column are many columns for writing numbers. The columns extend across the facing pages of the open book. This gives you a description column on your far left and many number columns to the right of it.

The first step in using a journal is the most difficult because it depends on the existing records. You must find out exactly how much money the church has, including the balance of each fund. You will

---

The report can be presented monthly, such as at a board meeting, or annually in a year-to-date format. This statement should be looked at with the balance sheet to get a full financial perspective of the church or organization.

● *Budgeted financial statement.* This is an expanded income statement that is used to compare actual income and expenses to their budgets. The difference between the actual and budgeted amounts gives the *variance,* either positive or negative. This is an important management tool and should be studied to determine if adjustments in spending patterns are needed.

Accounting Standards

It is not uncommon for churches, especially new ones, to do their accounting via the church checkbook. This may keep the bills paid, but when financial records are needed for making informed management decisions, or when a church needs a loan and the banker wants to know the church's assets, liabilities, and net assets, the checkbook method will prove inadequate. Such information is much easier to marshal if it has been recorded regularly (rather than pulled together later) in accounting books that use a double-entry format. (Double-entry accounting can be done manually or on computer, but it is important that the software can produce both balance sheets and income statements.)

In accounting parlance, this is called "generally accepted accounting principles." It means employing those standards established by the accounting profession to control the way transactions appear on financial statements. The larger a church becomes, the more important it is for that church to meet these accounting principles. This may mean hiring the counsel of a qualified accountant, if necessary. Churches that conform to accounting principles can know their reports are accurate and can be understood by anyone concerned with the church's financial situation.

—*Grace S. Nicholaou*

also need to know the checking account's reconciled balance, which is last month's ending reconciled balance. After you know your checking account balance, finding each fund's balance involves determining the money each fund can claim and then subtracting that total from the cash balance. This will give you the general fund balance. When you finish, the total of the funds equals the amount of cash.

Once you find your starting balances, open your journal to the first two-page spread. Write at the top your church's name and the month and year you are working with. Next, write a heading at the top of each column. Label the first column "Cash." This is where you record what happens in your checking account. In this column you add deposits and subtract checks written. Label the second column "General Fund" and the other columns with the names of the other funds. Each fund's column tracks what happens in that fund.

Next, write the cash balance on the first line of the cash column and each fund's balance on its respective first line. The fund columns'

Designated Giving

Designated giving has great benefits. It often helps people give their first significant gift, it teaches people the rewards of sacrificial giving, and it enhances nonurgent ministries. But there is a serious potential problem with designated giving: it can entice people to want to control the program or ministry toward which they give. The solution is for church leaders to maintain control of designated giving just as they do with the regular budgeted finances.

Maintaining Control

Yes, donors may try to control the ministry or program to which they have donated. That can undermine the leaders' authority and become divisive to the church. There are ways, however, to check this potential problem:

● *Draw up a policy.* Having a pol-

icy regarding how and when designated giving is received can save a great amount of conflict. The policy can be as simple as: "Our church will seek to spend all designated gifts for the purpose the donor desires, as long as that purpose is in keeping with the purposes, policies, and philosophy of the church. If the gift is designated to purchase products or secure special services, the appropriate committee reserves the right to select the vendor or the provider of the services. The designated monies and any item or service purchased with these monies is the property of the church." A church can simply print this statement on all receipts for donations.

● *Anticipate such gifts.* During the budget process, leaders can try to estimate the amount and nature of designated gifts for the coming year. They can do this in two ways: by observing what causes and

total should always equal the cash column. Check often to make sure this is so.

● *Receipts.* Let us look for a moment at receipts. Have your church print shop provide two copies of each receipt. One copy is yours, and the other is the donor's. Every week record donations on the receipt. Record the total amount and the funds given to. When the month ends, add the total monthly gifts and add the specific funds given to. The receipt's fund totals should equal the member's total gifts.

● *Loose offerings.* Also prepare a separate loose-offerings receipt. Often the loose offerings belong to the general fund, but the board may choose other funds to receive the money. For example, they may decide that on certain days the youth get it. Or other days the building fund may get it. Whatever fund receives it does not matter; simply prepare a receipt as you would for any member. Label this receipt "loose offerings."

The total of all the receipts should equal the week's bank deposit.

---

needs are being publicized and promoted in the community, and by recalling the causes the pastor has mentioned in his sermons. If the church's leaders can discuss the implications of such ministries ahead of actually receiving the gifts, they are in a better position either to turn down the gift or to expedite its use.

● *Give donors some choices.* In one small church, a family sought to give a $40,000 memorial gift to be placed in a trust, with earnings designated to purchase fresh flowers for each Sunday's worship service. Each Monday, the flowers were to be placed on the graves of the deceased family members of the donor. The donating family had specifically named the florist the church was to use and what color of flowers were to be purchased. The memorial committee tactfully declined the offer. After refusing the gift, however, the committee could have offered the family other avenues to remember their loved ones. That would have allowed both giver and church to retain some control over the gifts.

● *Make sure it's deductible.* In one church, a man gave money to the pension fund of a staff person nearing retirement. The staff member had served the church nearly thirty years, and for the first twenty, the church had provided no retirement benefit. Now the minister was edging into his 60s without adequate retirement provision. However, an auditor found this gift violated IRS regulations, and the donor could not be given a receipt for a tax-deductible gift. The donor was shocked at the loss of a significant tax break.

One church prevents such potential embarrassments by having a committee review each designated gift. In addition to determining if donors' gifts are in keeping with the philosophy of the church, they also inform donors if the gift can legally become a tax deduction.

—*Gary Fenton*

Keeping the Journal

At month's end record each receipt into the journal. Write the donor's name in the description column, the total amount the donor gave for the month in the cash column, and the totals for each fund in the respective fund columns. Treat the loose-offering receipt like all the rest.

Add the columns. When you are adding, do not add the balances carried over from the preceding month. All you want is the total deposits for the present month. Add each of the fund-column totals. Make sure the sum of these totals equals the cash-column total. If these are not equal, find your mistake. There are three ways you could have erred: (1) You made out an individual receipt incorrectly, (2) you copied a receipt incorrectly, or (3) you added incorrectly.

After you balance the receipts, add the deposits to the opening balances written on the first line. Again, make sure the column totals for the funds equal the cash column.

The next job is to record payments made by way of the month's checks. Simply drop down a few lines and record the checks written, working from the checkbook. Enter the date of the check in the far left column, the check number and payee in the description column, and the amount in the cash column. Also enter the amount under the specific fund the check was written from.

If a check is written for more than one fund, divide the total among the funds. Suppose that a check for $300 is written to the Bible Bookstore. Of this amount, $100 is for youth work, $50 is for evangelism, and the rest is for general church needs. You would record the check this way: Write "Bible Bookstore" and the check number in the description column. Under the cash column write $300, under youth work write $100, under evangelism write $50, and under church general fund write $150. Keep the funds' amount equal to the cash amount. Now add the amounts of the checks in all columns. This total should equal the check total for all funds.

After you balance, *subtract* the totals for the checks from the last-column totals made after the deposits. Again, make sure all the fund-columns' totals equal the cash-column total.

Now balance the bank statement to your cash column. When balanced, the cash column will equal the checking account balance.

After you have reconciled the cash column to the bank statement, record any interfund transfers. These transfers must be approved by the board. Nothing you do will change the cash column; only the fund totals will change. Suppose the board approves a hundred-dollar transfer from the general fund to the youth fund. You would record this transfer by writing "$100.00" under the general-fund column and putting brackets around it, and "$100.00" under the youth fund without brackets. Bracketing signifies the amount has been subtracted.

Your monthly record keeping is complete: (1) the cash column balances with the bank statement, (2) the funds' totals show what the funds have at month's end, and (3) all the fund columns equal the cash column.

—*Mack Tennyson*

Resources

Busby, D. 1993. The Zondervan church and nonprofit organization tax & financial guide: 1994 edition. Grand Rapids: Zondervan.

Chaffee, P. 1993. Accountable leadership. San Francisco: ChurchCare Publishing.

Hammar, R. 1993. Church and clergy tax guide. Matthews, N.C.: Christian Ministry Resources.

Tennyson, M. 1990. Church finances for people who count. Grand Rapids: Zondervan.

Dealing with Large Gifts

Giving a large gift raises a person's interest in, commitment to, and feelings for the church. Many can be easily offended if they feel the church does not respond or follow through properly. Therefore, nurturing and caring for donors after they give is just as important as motivating them to give in the first place.

Gift Followup

If the entire experience of giving a large gift is positive and donors truly experience what the Scriptures promise—that it is more blessed to give than to receive—people will look forward to giving again. Deep-pocket donors will continue to enjoy giving if we do these three things well:

● *Recognize their gift.* When people use their spiritual gifts in a special way in the church, pastors often mail them thank-you notes. It's no different when people give

special monetary gifts. For example, in a special note I remind givers of what good will result from their gifts, affirm their ultimate motives for giving—to serve Christ and his kingdom—and remind them of the church's gratitude.

We shouldn't, however, recognize such gifts from the pulpit. Generally the larger the gift, the less the donor wants it known. Most often the one condition set by deep-pocket donors is that no one know about their contribution but the pastor. They don't give to impress others, and sometimes they are concerned about attracting a line of people at their door, hats in hand.

● *Inform them of the status of a purchase.* When people invest heavily in a project, they "own" it. It's important to them, and they wonder how it's progressing, imagine how it will look, and perhaps worry about everything being done right. These are natural feelings that we are wise to respect. If significant problems do arise, we should communicate them to the donors immediately and forthrightly. Typically people understand difficulties; they do not, however, understand being ignored or misled.

● *Properly allocate gifts.* No matter the pressure, a pastor can't think for a moment about reallocating designated money. Here's a case in point: With our church in the middle of a building program, we were feeling intense cash-flow pressure. People were shifting their giving to the building, so the general fund was down. Yet one Sunday I mentioned in my sermon the needs of many in our congregation. The next Sunday one man approached me after the service and said, "My wife and I have been praying about what you said last week. I have a check here for $15,000. I want the church to divide it among members with needs."

At that moment my feelings were mixed. Part of me was rejoicing that we could help those who were hurting. Another part of me, feeling the church's financial pressure, was thinking, *Why didn't I preach on something else last Sunday?* I knew, however, that the money must go exactly where it was designated. Misallocating funds is not only immoral and illegal; it's detrimental to good stewardship. If a congregation ever learns that money has been reallocated without congregational or donor approval, trust is destroyed.

—Wayne A. Pohl

Handling Memorial Gifts

Designated giving cannot take the place of a good budget, but no church can afford to ignore this funding source. Since the bulk of funds will remain in a unified budget for years, these donor-directed gifts can be used to enhance the church's ongoing ministry.

Know Your Policies

Because the pastor works so closely with the family and friends of the deceased, he or she plays a vital role when a family wants to give a memorial gift. Therefore it's helpful to know in advance how you will handle the matter. Consider these basic guidelines:

● *Make clear the church's policy on memorial gifts.* When people ask about making a memorial contribution, we can send them a letter explaining the church's policy regarding memorial gifts. This prevents some common misunderstandings up front.

The letter can include a pamphlet with a list of the ministries and items the memorial committee has identified as especially appropriate for gifts. It can explain how the church acknowledges memorial gifts or such policies as why the church does not attach memorial labels or markers on memorials. The pamphlet can also give the name of the staff member to call if people have further questions.

Sometimes the family has asked for suggestions before we've had a chance to talk with them. When that happens, we may want to confer with the memorial committee to find out if the family's ideas are appropriate. We can also list those as options in a follow-up letter.

● *Help the family time their giving.* On occasion, we may need to encourage the family to wait until a later time to make the memorial gift. Here's a case in point: A local pastor ministered to a family who had lost a son in a well-publicized tragedy. Prior to the funeral, the family immediately wanted to establish a memorial fund at the church in memory of the boy. They were willing to make an initial contribution of several thousand dollars and asked the pastor to mention it at the funeral.

The pastor, however, encouraged them to wait. He knew their making such a gift would be economically difficult and would also manipulate the congregation at the funeral. Several months later, the church received a small but more appropriate gift from the family. Although this church could have used the money, it was more important to keep the integrity of the pastor and the church completely free of any question.

● *Continue to encourage memorial giving.* Not all families are tuned into the idea of giving memorial gifts. Maybe they have never had the opportunity, or they are not aware of what a difference it can make. Yet since so much good can come from memorial giving, perhaps we should consider it one of our duties to encourage it.

One way to do this relates to the honorariums we receive for officiating at funerals. We can give them to the church in memory of the deceased. For example, I write the family thanking them for the honorarium and explaining what I have done with it, letting them know what types of things their memorial may end up doing for the church. The financial secretary also sends notification to the family that a memorial gift has been given by the pastor in their loved one's memory. Many people are grateful not only for my gift but also for the idea I've planted in their heads—that the life of their loved one can count for one thing more.

—*Gary Fenton*

Substantiating Charitable Contributions

On January 1, 1994, the federal government placed new restrictions on churches and other nonprofit organizations receiving contributions taxpayers expect to be tax deductible. Since a number of rules apply, it is best to examine contributions by type, understanding that since more than one rule may apply to a particular contribution, it is important to follow each rule that

does apply. All the rules are for *individual* contributions, not several contributions lumped together.

● *Rule 1*, for cash contributions of less than $250. Such donations can be substantiated with any *one* of the following: a canceled check, a receipt or letter from the donee church showing the church's name and the amounts and dates of the contributions, or any other reliable written record showing the church name and the amounts and dates of the contribution.

● *Rule 2*, for cash contributions of $250 or more. Donors will not be allowed a tax deduction unless they receive a written receipt that satisfies several requirements. The receipt must: (1) be in writing, (2) identify the donor by name (no social security number required), (3) list separately each contribution of $250 or more, (4) state whether the church provided any goods or services (other than "intangible religious benefits") in exchange for the contribution (and if so, include a good-faith estimate of the value of those goods or services), and (5) be received by the donor on or before the earlier of either the date the donor files a tax return claiming a deduction for the contribution or the due date for filing the return.

● *Rule 3*, for *quid pro quo* cash contributions of $75 or less (part contribution and part payment for goods or services received in exchange). These contributions are deductible only to the extent they exceed the value of the goods or services provided in exchange.

● *Rule 4*, for *quid pro quo* cash contributions greater than $75. In addition to following rule 2, the church must provide a written statement to the donor that: (1) informs the donor that the amount of the contribution that is tax deductible is limited to the excess of the contribution over the value of any goods or services given in return, and (2) provides the donor with a good-faith estimate of the value of the goods or services furnished. A written statement need not be issued if only token goods or services are provided (generally,

with a value of $64 or 2% of the amount of the contribution, whichever is less) or if the donor receives solely an intangible religious benefit that generally is not sold in a commercial context.

● *Rule 5*, for noncash property valued at less than $250. These gifts can be substantiated with a receipt that lists the donor's name, the church's name, the date and location of the contribution, and a description (but not value) of the property.

● *Rule 6*, for noncash property valued at $250 or more. Donors will not be allowed a tax deduction unless they receive a written receipt from the church that satisfies the requirements of Rule 2 and that describes the property (no value needs to be stated).

● *Rule 7*, for noncash property valued at $500 to $5,000. Income tax regulations require that all donors of noncash property valued at $5,000 or less maintain reliable written records with respect to each item of donated property. The records must include the following (in addition to the requirements of Rule 6): (1) the name and address of the church, (2) the date and location of the contribution, (3) a detailed description of the property, (4) the fair market value of the property at the time of the contribution (including a description of how the value was determined), (5) the cost or other basis of the property, (6) if less than the donor's entire interest in the property is donated during the current year, an explanation of the total amount claimed as a deduction in the current year, (7) the terms of any agreement between the donor and the church relating to the use, sale, or other disposition of the property, (8) an explanation of the manner of acquisition by the donor (purchase, gift, inheritance, or exchange), and (9) the cost or other basis of the property immediately preceding the date on which the contribution was made.

In addition, a donor must complete the front side of Form 8283 and enclose the completed form with the Form 1040 on which the charitable contribution is claimed.

● *Rule 8*, for noncash property valued at more than $5,000. In addition to complying with Rule 6, a donor must obtain an appraisal of the donated property from a quali-fied appraiser, complete the back side of Form 8283 and have it signed by the appraiser and a church representative, and enclose the completed Form 8283 with the Form 1040 on which the charitable contribution deduction is claimed.

● *Rule 9*, for *quid pro quo* contributions of noncash property. Apply Rules 2, 3, and 4.

● *Rule 10*, for everyone. When in doubt, contact a competent tax attorney. Rules change, and the onus is on the church to keep abreast of new developments.

—Richard R. Hammar

36

Managing and Apportioning Money

C hurches typically have budgets, and those who set the budgets exercise much say in a body's ministry. Having a select two or three people determine the budget may be efficient, but it is not healthy. More people need to be involved in something so important.

Yet once we open up the process to the congregation, even through their elected leaders, we must deal with a multitude of questions about how much to give each ministry and line item. Answering such questions is never easy, but it is what good stewardship of the church's resources is about. Here are some principles to use in helping a church settle its budgeting priorities.

Prepare Yourself

The extent to which pastors have input in this process depends on church polity and policy, the tradition of the particular congregation, and pastoral leadership style. In order to be effectively involved in the budget process, we need to answer the following questions:

● *Who really sets the budget?* Most churches use some type of committee structure to formulate the budget, but a "paper-trail" study of these committees' duties does not usually explain who really determines the budget. In many churches a budget committee, or a subcommittee of the board, has each church committee and organization turn in their projected costs for the year. The finance committee then evaluates these requests and puts together a combined budget.

In some churches, the finance committee does little more than total the figures turned in and determine how the budget will then be presented to the church. In other churches, the finance committee looks at each request to evaluate it in terms of churchwide goals and objectives. Many figures get altered in this process.

In either case, in most churches the budget is pretty much set early on by committees or the leaders of those committees. If we want to have input into the budget, we must do it in the right place at the right time.

For example, a pastor friend who moved to a larger church had saved his vision-and-dreams speech for the budget-planning meeting of the finance committee. He was frustrated when his ideas had little impact on the committee as it gathered and tallied figures. It would take another year for his concerns to be reflected in the budget. He not only needed to begin earlier, he also needed to discover who really determined the budget—respected leaders in each of the committees—and talk with them first.

● *What does the budget reveal about the church's ministry priorities?* We have to understand the actual values of a congregation before we can effectively influence the budget process. Often the budget is the best indication of what the leadership values. One church I know of has always said it is a strong missions congregation. A quick glance at the budget seems to confirm this, but a closer look reveals that most items in the mission section of the budget are not really for mission support. It turns out that anything the leadership wanted but thought might be difficult to "sell" to the church was labeled missions.

As a result, the mission section of the budget was bulging with children's and preschool ministries. The new minister of education at the church was at first concerned at what appeared to be a lack of funds for her ministry, only to realize that the actual budget priority and her priority were the same.

● *What are the nonnegotiables?* Ideally, a church should be responsive and resilient enough to base budget expenditures around needs and good stewardship. But churches, because they are composed of people, frequently spend because of feelings, rather than objective reality.

Sacred cows do not begin as golden calves. Generally these nonnegotiables were at one time effective means of ministry. But there is not much to be said for fossilized good ideas and ministries that have outlived their usefulness.

For example, a lay leader from another church once related how a certain bank for a number of years had financed all their church projects. The bank had been good to the church, waiving some fees and never penalizing the church for late payments. The bank also had given the church favorable interest rates.

But when interest rates declined, the pastor was recommending that the church refinance at a lower rate with another financial institution. When the finance committee voted down the pastor's recommendation, he complained that they were not being good stewards of the Lord's money. The committee felt tied by honor to the bank that had seen them through tough times.

As pastors, we must not only discover quickly these nonnegotiables, we will also want to pay tribute to their contribution to the church. If we are to suggest a change, it will have to be after we've gained the respect and trust of the congregation, and it will have to be a change that is based in respect for the past: "In the past, this system has served us extremely well. I'm thankful for the people who put this practice into effect. For the coming decade, however, we may need a new strategy."

● *Is our mission clear?* In other words, do those who are responsible for building the budgets share our interpretation of the church's vision? If the church has a clear mission statement, it makes setting priorities easier, but it does not take away all the difficulties.

Mission statements are subject to interpretation, and often people assume wrongly that because they are on the same page and reading the same words, they have the same pictures on their mind's screen. However, if the leadership does not understand our interpretation of the mission statement, our attempts to influence the budget will likely lead to frustration.

Once the leadership—including ourselves, as pastors—has a common understanding of where we'd like the church to go, we can begin putting the dollars-and-cents issues on the table for discussion. All through the process, though, we must aim to understand the views of the lay leadership. Even at the dollars-and-cents stage of budgeting, although we are now going in the same direction, we sometimes fail to aim at the same specific target. We may agree that evangelism is our highest priority, for instance, but whether we should invest in evangelism training for members or bring in an evangelist for a week is another matter.

Avoiding Traps

How we work out disagreements at the dollars-and-cents stage of finances requires patience, fortitude, and wisdom. Few people are opposed to a particular line item receiving funding in a budget, and as a result, the issues often hinge on *the amount* line items or ministries receive. In the process of determining how much, congregations can become polarized. As the discussion ensues about who receives how much, we can help the church avoid several traps:

● *The line-item trap.* Someone who places a high priority on youth ministry notices in the budget that the line item for youth ministry is only half of that for the music ministry. This person concludes, with some disappointment and anger, that the church thinks more of music than youth. Line items in a budget, however, are usually designed for administrative purposes. Taken in isolation, they don't necessarily communicate what a church's feelings are about a ministry. Sometimes we have to dig deeper into the budget to determine those feelings.

As a case in point, in my early months at one church, a couple of families met with me regarding the lack of funding for the youth ministry. Without fully examining the total dollars available to youth ministry, I hastily agreed with them. I soon found I had spoken too soon.

Fiduciary Responsibilities

Civil law imposes various "fiduciary duties" upon the officers and directors of nonprofit corporations because of the special position of trust they occupy. When church members become members of the church's governing board, they become representatives of the corporation and must act in the church's (and not their own) best interests. Generally, this means officers and directors have fiduciary duties of due care and loyalty to the church. These duties are recognized by statute in some states and by court decisions in others.

Good Faith

Governing board members are under a duty to perform their responsibilities in good faith and in a manner they reasonably believe to be in the best interests of the corporation. They are responsible to give such care as an ordinarily prudent person in a like position would use under similar circumstances. This duty commonly is referred to as the "prudent person rule" or the "fiduciary duty of due care." One court described this duty as follows (in a case involving a religious corporation):

Good faith requires the undivided loyalty of a corporate director or officer to the corporation and such a duty of loyalty prohibits the director or an officer, as a fiduciary, from using this position of trust for his own personal gain to the detriment of the corporation. In this instance, there are no shareholders of the corporation; however, even though there are no shareholders, the officers and directors still hold a fiduciary obligation to manage the corporation in its best interest and not to the detriment of the corporation itself.

Lawsuits against nonprofit directors for breach of their "duty of

After some research I discovered the budget line item for youth ministry showed only about 40 percent of the funds used in the youth program. Many other expenses for youth ministry were scattered throughout the budget, under "administration" and "personnel," for instance. The ministry to youth was more important than the line item showed.

● *The higher-priority-means-more-money trap.* As a pastor and other leaders work through the priorities, they may assume that by giving more money to a ministry, they are giving that ministry a higher priority rating. This works on the mistaken assumptions that (a) giving more money is the only way to raise a ministry's status, and (b) a church has only one budget.

---

care" are rare. Still, directors of churches and religious organizations can reduce the risk of liability even further by (a) attending all of the meetings of the board and of any committees on which they serve; (b) thoroughly reviewing all interim and annual financial statements and reports, and seeking clarification of any irregularities or inconsistencies; (c) affirmatively investigating and rectifying any other problems or improprieties; (d) thoroughly reviewing the corporate charter, constitution, and bylaws; (e) dissenting from any board action with which they have any misgivings and insisting that their objection be recorded in the minutes of the meeting; and (f) resigning from the board if and when they are unable to fulfill these duties. As one court has observed, "The law has no place for dummy directors."

Loyalty

Directors of churches and other nonprofit corporations have a fiduciary duty of loyalty to the corporation. This duty generally requires that any transaction between the board and one of its directors be (a) fully disclosed, (b) approved by the board without the vote of the interested director, and (c) fair and reasonable to the corporation.

In most cases, a director breaches the duty of loyalty only through some secret or undisclosed interest in a transaction with the corporation. To illustrate, directors who own a business (such as insurance, real estate, furnishings) may violate the duty of loyalty by asking the board to enter into a transaction with their business without fully disclosing to the board their personal interest in the transaction. Additionally, such "interested" directors ordinarily should abstain from voting on the transaction, and the transaction should be fair and reasonable to the corporation.

In summary, officers and directors of churches must understand they have been placed in a position of special trust and must rigorously pursue the best interests of the corporation and avoid any action or decision based on self-interest.

—*Richard R. Hammar*

But every congregation has at least three budgets, and only one is the financial budget. A second and equally important budget is the time budget, otherwise known as the church calendar. To make a ministry a priority may not mean more money but instead involve giving a program a better time slot on the church schedule.

Another budget is the pulpit-emphasis budget. Some priorities with good time slots and adequate funding go lacking because they are not emphasized by those who share the pulpit. When properly promoted through the pulpit, however, many ministries can flourish.

For example, once a minister to single adults told me about the turning point in her ministry. A church had called her to build a strong singles ministry. Funding and facilities were provided, but the ministry did not really have the support of the church until the pastor wrote a column about the ministry in the church newsletter and

Cash Flow

Generating income and meeting expenses are two rather difficult beasts to tame in many churches, so how do we do it? Through forecasting. It's a lot easier to go with the flow when we know where it's going.

Making Informed Guesses

Forecasting, to be more than mere guessing, requires a method to provide accuracy. It's best to track giving patterns over the last three years to evaluate the level of revenue and expected changes. We can do this in four steps:

● *Plot income.* We can use graph paper to draw an income graph for three, twelve-month periods, collecting income information from the church checkbook, the income journal, or bank deposit slips. These will show when we received money and how much we took in. First we plot on the graph the income for the first month. For each successive month, we add to the total the income generated that month and plot the point on the graph. Then we can connect the points to form a line rising from lower left to upper right. At the end of the first year, we can repeat the process in other colors for the next two years, starting from zero each time.

● *Plot expenses.* We repeat the graphing process for monthly expenses, using information from the church's checkbook, disbursements journal, or other record of paid bills. We simply add up the expenses for each month and connect another set of points on the graph.

● *Look for variations.* Here's what we should look for: High- and low-income months, seasonal periods of greater spending, points at which income is low and spending is high, and vice versa. We're trying to spot any overall trends. For example, is giving up each year? Plateaued? Falling? How much? Is one year quite different from the others? Why?

asked two single people to lead in prayer during worship. This young minister said the senior pastor's public endorsement was more valuable than a large increase in funds.

● *The easy-compromise trap.* Budget-preparation time is one of the most stressful seasons of the year. Competing priorities bring inevitable conflict. In churches with large staffs, these conflicts can escalate into ego wars, with staff members becoming battalion commanders, and members, the ground troops.

The pastor may try to avoid these conflicts and quickly seek compromises: The missions people and the youth-ministry enthusiasts each want 10 percent increases for their respective ministries, but there is only enough money to give 10 percent to one. Solution? Of course, give a 5 percent increase to each.

Often, however, such compromises, although they reduce tension,

---

● *Project next year's graph.* Using the data from the three-year historical graph, we can hazard estimates of the coming year's income and expenses. While we should expect some variations in the future, just as we find them in the past, this process will help us make reasonable cash-flow projections.

Heading Off Trouble

A cash-flow graph provides important pieces of information: points of negative or positive cash flow, and the break-even points, where income and expense lines cross. At these points we have taken in and spent equal amounts of money. Ideally, both the expense and the income lines would travel identical paths on the graph in a continual break-even mode, but this is hardly ever the case. Most churches hope to keep the lines reasonably close, breaking even over time, if only at a few given points.

Keeping our fingers on the pulse of cash flow is important. We need to understand how and when funds come in and go out, paying careful attention to where the flow is disproportionate in either direction.

What can we do about expected cash-flow problems? Here are two suggestions:

● *Forward-thinking budgeting.* A church can create two or three spending plans, because a single budget doesn't allow for setbacks, unless surpluses are budgeted. With this setup, we can budget at a certain rate but plan to cut expenses by, say, 10 percent at a specific date if income isn't keeping up with outlays. Knowing that cash flow may be a problem, the drafters of such a budget include alternative spending plans to match the income during a given period.

● *Planned saving and spending.* Almost every church experiences dips in income during the summer. A wise cash-flow manager will set aside a cash reserve during the fat months to cover the lean ones. It's also wise to plan discretionary expenditures to take place during high-income months.

—David R. Pollock

fail to construct a budget according to the church's priorities. If the church has previously determined that youth ministry is to be the top priority for the coming five years, the compromise has done the church a disservice. Certainly compromise is necessary in every budget process, but if everything falls into place without healthy confrontation and discussion of church priorities, it may mean the official priorities of the church have been put aside for the comfort of church leaders.

● *The meaningless-motto trap.* One temptation is to have the church's priorities articulated in words and mottoes that have little relationship to reality. For example, last year I received a copy of a church budget that had BALANCED MINISTRY printed across the top of the page. The budget was divided into four areas: evangelism, missions, ministry, and worship, each with line items listed underneath. Each of the areas equaled one-fourth of the budget. It was obvious, however, that someone had spent time tinkering with the figures so that they would be equal. Although every church does have to seek balance, it is wrong to assume balance must be measured in terms of equal funding.

Guidelines for Effective Change

Churches have difficulty changing because their message appears to contradict the call to change. The message of Christ is the same yesterday, today, and forever, but the careless member may hear that the *church* is to be the same yesterday, today, and forever.

A church budget, since it reflects ministry with people, has to be dynamic. It will have to change significantly from time to time. Pressure, political power, and smooth pulpit rhetoric will not encourage change as effectively as education, pastoral care, and a good dose of patience. In particular, in seeking to help a church make significant changes in a budget, the following guidelines will be helpful:

● *Be prepared for passionate resistance.* Any change brings resistance, but change regarding the use of money brings resistance with passion. People and organizations are dealing with values when they spend money. How we spend our money says a lot (although not everything) about what we believe is important.

At the same time, the church attracts people to whom values are important, and it continues to teach them that values are important. Consequently, when values-driven people are encouraged to change how they spend their money, there will be sparks. The old line, "Let's not fight over money," doesn't work in the church precisely because we know money represents something more than dollars. Therefore, we should not see all resistance as evil. We best encourage change when we allow people to disagree but do not question their spirituality.

● *Introduce the change before you request the change.* We pastors may tend to see ourselves as the only ones with real vision, and we sometimes act as if lay people hardly have the courage to do what the Lord wants. The truth is that not only are lay people as courageous as clergy, but we clergy also are less visionary than we sometimes think.

For example, some time ago I was in a meeting concerning charitable giving, and one of the speakers discussed the trend toward designated, or donor-directed, giving. I found myself resisting this idea, as I had been a strong advocate of unified-budget giving.

It took about six weeks and a couple of articles in a periodical for me to see the virtues and the possibilities of designated giving. When I did see its value, I discussed it with our finance chairman. He was opposed to the idea for the very reasons I had been. It became obvious the idea was not ready to be discussed with the entire committee.

I noticed, however, that I was angry that the chairman, as well as the committee, did not immediately share my enthusiasm. When I remembered my journey, I was able to be a little more patient.

● *Go slow with changes in philosophy.* Almost any church can be maneuvered or manipulated into making temporary changes in the funding process. Most members can be persuaded to postpone or delay their favorite ministry projects if they believe these projects will soon be restored to their previous levels of funding. Some changes are not intended to be temporary, however, but indicate a major philosophy shift. To deliberately minimize philosophical changes is not only dishonest but shortsighted. Individuals and constituencies who have accepted a "temporary" change in the budget process only to find it is permanent feel violated.

A good rule of thumb: The longer the impact of a change, the slower the change should be paced. One of my predecessors changed the deacons from being an administrative board (making decisions for the church) to a ministry group (concerned with meeting people's needs). This change removed the deacons from the budget process and permitted women to serve as deacons.

Such a fundamental change, however, didn't happen overnight. This wise pastor led the church to this position over a number of years, and the pace was slow. Now eighteen years later, this deacon ministry is alive and well.

● *Listen for underlying issues.* Budget battles may not be about money but about someone's personal crisis. The opposition may not result as much from differing priorities as from a hurt or misunderstanding. Often conflicts over a change in budgeting provide opportunities to find the real issue.

A person in a church I once served was highly vocal about a change the budget committee was proposing. This man had used his Sunday-morning Bible-study class as a platform to oppose the new budget.

When I heard one Sunday afternoon of his abuse of his role as teacher, I was angry and ready to confront him, but his wife called me before I had the chance. She suggested I go by and see him at work. "He really needs his pastor right now," she said.

When I went by his office on the following Monday, he told me of the discouragement he felt about his work and how a remark I had made in the pulpit appeared to be insensitive to people in his situation. At the conclusion of the visit, he told me he owed me an apology for what he had done in the previous day's Bible-study hour.

Later one of our older, wiser church leaders explained to me, "Pastor, it's not socially acceptable to stand in a Bible class and oppose your pastor for his insensitivity, but it is acceptable to oppose the programs your pastor supports."

● *Maintain your character even if you have to modify your vision.* Vision and mission are changeable. Character is a nonnegotiable. Leading a church to redirect its resources will be an ongoing process requiring compromise and a change in direction from time to time. But rarely does one lose his or her ministry in a congregation over a disagreement regarding funding.

Sometimes, however, in an uncompromising passion to sell our vision to the congregation, we modify our character. The results are usually disastrous. A highly respected pastor in one community I served wanted his church to have its own retreat center. He was a visionary leader who could inspire people to follow him. But in the process of selling this idea, he exaggerated the benefits offered by one of the proposed sites, and he publicly lost his temper with one family who questioned him in the process.

The church voted to buy the retreat center, but from then on, the church discussed his visionary ideas less and his character more. He eventually left the church, bitter and angry, even though for several years he had been highly effective. Our vision can be modified more easily than our character repaired and restored.

—Gary Fenton

Resources

Callahan, K. 1992. Effective church finances. San Francisco: HarperSanFrancisco.

Callahan, K. 1992. Giving & stewardship in an effective church. San Francisco: HarperSanFrancisco.

Schaller, L. 1992. Seven-day-a-week church. Nashville: Abingdon.

How to Budget

People give to the church so good things can happen in the kingdom of God. If a church presents a well-planned, nonwasteful spending program, donors will increase their giving. They also will reap the benefit of seeing their prayers answered through effective ministry programs. The key is to budget intentionally and wisely.

Setting Up a Committee

The first step in preparing a budget is to set up a budget committee. This committee should not be the finance committee, which is usually made up of skillful business people. Rather, the budget committee should include a much broader representation from among the church members. In essence, the budget committee will be setting the ministry priorities of the church for the coming year. Therefore, the more people who see that the budget is fair and advances the church's ministries, the easier it is to raise the money to cover the budget.

People will buy into things they have had a part in planning. If money is tight and programs are being cut, it is better for many people to see that the cuts are being handled fairly. Thus, representatives from a broad spectrum of church ministries should help develop the budget.

The budget committee members decide how they want to budget. Do they want to estimate income first and budget expenses within that estimate? Or do they want to budget expenses first and then try to raise the income to cover the budgeted expenses? The conservative approach is to make the budget fit the estimated income. This is the better method for churches with serious money problems.

Budgeting Expenses

The key word for budgeting expenses is *participation*. The budget committee must establish a process that gathers information on spending needs from every program in the church. One way to do this is to use "bottom-up budgeting." In bottom-up budgeting, the lowest units gather all the costs of running their units. They also prepare proposals for new programs. Then they pass this information up through the organization. For example, the teen Sunday school class meets and decides what activities they would like to do next year, estimating what they will cost. They prepare a budget request that asks for $300 for lesson materials, $200 for refreshments for monthly fellowship meetings, and $500 for an annual retreat, for a total of $1,000.

The Sunday school department would collect this type of estimate from all the classes and then make its recommendation to the budget committee. Each unit in the church would do this, with every ministry contributing to the budget. Because they took part in planning ministry, people would feel a greater sense of ownership for their programs and be more likely to support them with their time and money.

Estimating Income

The budget committee might have budgeted expenses before it estimated income. In this case it must figure out how to cover the expenses. One approach is to publish the preliminary budget and ask for pledges from the members, based on the proposed programs. This encourages people to commit their pledges to the programs, be-cause they know how the money will be used when it is given. If the committee calls for pledges without a preliminary budget, people make their decisions based on their personal finances alone.

After gathering pledges, the budget committee combines them with information about past giving trends in order to develop a realistic income estimate for the coming year. Then the committee must adjust the budgeted expenses to stay within the amount of pledged funds and other expected income.

—Mack Tennyson

Zero-Based Budgeting

Many churches produce their annual budgets like this: review last year's budget, change it slightly, and announce this year's budget. Churches that do this usually view their budget process as a necessary evil, a yearly, unavoidable hassle to dispatch quickly before moving on to more important "spiritual" concerns. Yet budgeting this way often separates a church's financial workings from its true ministry goals. The budget becomes full of sacred cows, items that exist only because of tradition or particular members' pet projects.

Another Way to Budget

There is another, more positive, way to budget. A budget should be an important planning tool that is developed by members who are prayerfully setting their ministry priorities and goals. For example, if the church is beginning to focus on youth evangelism, it must eventually boil all the sermons and board resolutions and speeches down to more money for that purpose. One way to implement that type of process is to use zero-based budgeting (ZBB)

With ZBB, the budgeting process starts off with zero in every budget category. The church must challenge and approve every planned expense that goes into the budget. Church leaders test all potential projects against the church's overall mission and goals, keeping only those that best advance those goals. Projects that miss that mark are discarded. Though this approach requires the finance committee to make difficult, unpopular decisions, no longer will things be done a certain way merely because "that's the way we've always done it before."

Zero-based budgeting requires every ministry of the church to identify each function it performs and estimate the cost of doing that function. The church must then decide which programs best meet the church's overall mission. Those programs are included in the budget, in order of priority, until the expected yearly income is all accounted for. Now the church has a clear description of the results it can expect for each dollar to be spent.

Zero-Based Benefits

The zero-based approach provides several benefits. First, it requires a thoughtful ministry-evaluation process. In-depth ministry planning—identifying purposes, goals, and objectives—must precede funding decisions. Second, it establishes direct accountability from each ministry group. Suppose the youth minister said he could run a youth retreat for $500. If this amount is included in the budget, the church is "buying" a youth retreat. The youth minister will be held accountable to deliver. Contrast this with the typical budget that gives a specific amount to the youth department in an open-ended allocation.

The third advantage of ZBB is that it offers participation by each ministry leader. This gives the leaders a sense of ownership and increases their confidence in the budget's fairness. If their projects are turned down, ministry leaders can quickly recognize why.

Jimmy Carter popularized ZBB; he was going to use it to balance the United States budget. He quickly became discouraged when he discovered the law protected most items so firmly that they were out of his control. There was no way to go back to a zero base.

We may well encounter a similar problem in the church. We can start out with a zero base, but after adding in the mortgage and salaries, we may be surprised at how little discretionary money is left. Such tight budgets, however, demand careful planning, too. We'll want to allocate wisely whatever leftover funds we do have. ZBB can help us.

—*Mack Tennyson*

Financial Audits

Like other not-for-profit organizations, churches have a fiduciary responsibility to ensure that their financial records are accurate and meet legal requirements. Often bylaws require the services of an outside professional accountant to verify the accuracy of the church books. There are three levels of service offered by accountants: compilations, reviews, and audits.

Basic Compilations

Considered by many the minimum in bookkeeping services, a *compilation* of financial statements can provide the basic structure for a church's accounting system. Literally, a compilation means that the accountant has compiled—pulled together—financial statements using information provided by the church, without audit or other verification.

In a compilation, an accounting service will see that financial statements are prepared on a regular basis. A good accountant usually will either do for the client or prompt the client to do the basic tasks necessary for good bookkeeping, such as reconciling bank accounts or recording all transactions in a general ledger.

A compilation involves an external third party, which can serve churches as an objective source for the veracity of the accounting procedures. For smaller churches, a compilation is often the only accounting performed, so it offers at least minimal assurances that the books are in order.

More Rigorous Reviews

In a *review*, the accountant spends more time analyzing financial data and questioning people about specific transactions. As a result, the accountant accepts a higher level of responsibility, and the church has greater assurance that its financial statements are in order.

However, reviews can cost nearly as much as an audit and are not commonly used by nonprofit organizations. Also, the reviewed financial statements generally are not accepted by organizations that require an audit.

Audits for Assurance

An audit of financial statements is the ultimate in outside, independent accounting services. A financial-statement audit for nonprofit organizations is usually prepared

on a cash or an accrual basis. Auditors selectively test transactions, such as cash receipts and disbursements, and often request written confirmations from banks, lenders, donors, and others, as needed. A small audit typically takes a minimum of a few weeks; a more complicated audit requires several months.

At the beginning the auditor should document in writing the expectations for the audit in an engagement letter. The process is concluded with an opinion on the financial statements, which may range from "unqualified" (meaning the auditors believe the financial statements present the organization's financial position fairly) to "adverse" (some serious deficiency needs to be corrected in the financial statements). The auditor must be independent of the church, both in fact and appearance.

The Appropriate Service

In deciding on the appropriate level of accounting, churches should consider their needs and budget. For example, an audit will be needed if the church intends to apply for a bank loan that requires periodic audited financial statements from borrowers. Audits may also be necessary if a church receives federal funds for activities, such as a day-care center.

Organizations often authorize an audit when there is a change in financial officers, such as an incoming board, pastor, or treasurer. In addition, factors inherent in the organization may make a periodic external examination of the records prudent. Examples include when one person has a lot of control without much oversight, when there is high turnover of personnel, or when finances or operating expenses differ significantly from budget or expectation.

The accounting profession is generally efficient in providing services. Nonprofit organizations may discover that compilation services compare favorably with the cost of a full-time, in-house accountant and often provide additional professional competence difficult to obtain in-house.

—Diccy P. Thurman

Internal Audits

Churches need to have their financial records audited for reasons of stewardship, reputation, protection of assets, and record updating. For churches that find the cost of a professional outside financial audit prohibitive, an alternative is the internal audit. While it cannot provide all the assurances of an outside audit, it is better than no audit at all.

The audit committee examines four main areas: income, expenses, record keeping, and reporting. In each area, the audit committee performs a number of tasks.

Watching Income

An audit establishes that all monies received are properly handled.

● To determine if the cash-receipts process is documented, complete, and adequate, the auditors review the counting procedures for clarity and completeness, review the forms used to record the count and determine if all cash can be properly accounted and classified, inquire whether any funds are received that do not go through the counting process, and review the list of counting personnel and compare it to the group of record-keeping people to ensure separation of duties.

● To determine if all cash items are properly accounted for, recorded, deposited, and safeguarded, the committee reviews deposit dates and amounts on bank deposits and compares them to reported dates and amounts.

Examining Expenses

There are four areas in the church's expenses that concern the auditors.

● To determine whether there is proper authorization for expenditures, the auditors review the invoice-authorization process for adequacy, inquire how bills are distributed to responsible parties for approval, and determine the adequacy of the approval process.

● To determine whether approved bills are paid and all expenditures are authorized, the auditors trace a sample of approved invoices to the ledger and to canceled checks showing payment, making sure the amount, date, check number, and payee correspond; and trace a sample of canceled checks to the ledger and to approved invoices, again seeing that the amounts, dates, check number, and payee agree.

● To determine if assets are properly safeguarded, the auditors obtain a copy of the signature-authorization cards for all bank accounts and review the list, inquire whether these are the proper people to be listed, determine whether blank checks are kept in a secure place, verify proper substantiation for payments to any board member, and review the list of the church's physical assets.

● To verify that salaries, wages, and related payroll taxes are disbursed properly, the auditors add figures in payroll worksheets across the lines and down the columns to find any errors, and then compare the sums to canceled payroll checks; and recompute salaries and taxes, and compare the results to the amounts on the payroll checks.

Checking Record Keeping

The auditors next follow a number of procedures to satisfy themselves that the records are properly maintained.

● To determine if bank statements are properly reconciled, the auditors inspect bank reconciliations, identify outstanding checks, and investigate reconciling items. They also recalculate a sample of bank reconciliations.

● To review cutoff procedures for adequacy, the auditors review check-number sequences at year-end, checking dates to determine the month expenses were paid.

● To determine if all necessary documents are on file and safe-guarded, the auditors inspect all legal documents on file, including employment contracts, board minutes, mortgages, treasurer reports, and tax information returns (W-2, 1099); review documents in the safe-deposit box and inspect signature cards; and inspect mortgage payments for reasonableness.

● To determine if all necessary income tax forms were properly filed, the auditors inspect the dates tax returns were filed and compare them to the dates legally required.

● To review the invoice-filing system, the auditors inspect the filing system for orderliness and completeness.

● To determine if income and expenses are properly recorded, the auditors inspect the general ledger, recalculate a sample of items, and investigate any checks made payable to "cash"; compare totals to the treasurer's report; and trace interest and dividend income from statements to the ledger.

● To determine if salaries and wages were paid in accordance with contracts, the auditors compare compensation per employees' contracts to actual payments, and compare wages authorized by the board to actual payments to the employees.

Watching Reporting

This part of the audit checks the accuracy of treasurer's reports and budgets and looks for ways to improve them.

● To determine the accuracy and adequacy of treasurer's reports, the auditors recalculate a sample of the treasurer's reports; determine the reason for significant variances of spending over the budgeted amount for line items; verify that balances tie to bank statements; and consider information that may be helpful that is not currently included in the reports.

● To review the budgeting process for adequacy, the auditors inquire how the budget is compiled and present suggestions for appropriate member participation in the process.

● To determine if sensitive computer records are adequately safeguarded, the auditors determine if important records on the church computer are backed up regularly and if the church offices and computers are locked when not in use.

Presenting the Report

When the internal audit is completed, the auditors submit a report to the proper body—often the congregation at the annual meeting—and file a copy for future reference. The report includes a review of the auditing process, the findings of the auditors, documentation backing the findings, and written recommendations for any changes.

—Todd Zastrow

Trusts and Endowments

Endowments or trust gifts make it possible for a church to fund projects that might otherwise be delayed or left undone. But while special gifts provide a tremendous financial lift to any church, they are a blessing that requires thought and time, since they add administrative responsibilities for the church and they sometimes reduce members' giving to special projects.

Charitable Trust Options

Handled properly, charitable trusts are a win-win proposition for a church. The trust is responsible for making payments to the beneficiaries, and the church is not liable for any trust expenses, since it does not own those assets.

Common ways generous people use charitable trusts to give money to churches include:

● *Charitable remainder unitrusts.* Donors may use these to make a future gift to the church and receive a stream of current or future income. A donor places assets that will pass to the church at a future date (or upon the donor's death) in a trust, while retaining an income flow from the assets. The amount paid to the donor fluctuates, based on the trust balance.

Tax benefits to the donor include a charitable deduction for the present value of the future gift and, if the trust is funded with appreciated property, the donor avoids paying capital-gains tax.

A charitable remainder unitrust is irrevocable. The donor may change the beneficiary but cannot withdraw the contributions made to the trust.

● *Charitable remainder annuity trusts.* These are similar to the unitrust, except the donor receives a fixed dollar amount from the trust every year for life, whether or not the trust assets grow. Many donors find the guaranteed fixed stream of income comforting.

● *Revocable charitable trusts.* With a revocable trust, the church will receive the gift "some day," if the donor does not revoke it. When the donor dies, the gift is then irrevocable. Perhaps as many as 95 percent of all revocable gifts are never revoked or changed.

Management Considerations

Most trust funds must be invested and accounted for separately. There are also annual filings to be made with the Internal Revenue Service. Some churches hire an outside manager for the funds; others choose to handle the responsibilities internally, but charitable-trust programs and agreements should be set up only with professional counsel.

Other management considerations include:

● *Handling trust and endowment restrictions.* Donors should be encouraged to make their gifts without restrictions. This provides the ultimate flexibility for the church's governing body. Also, restrictions that are too specific may make it difficult to carry out the donor's wishes at some future date.

● *Minimizing the negative impact*

on congregational giving. When trust or endowment money is used for capital expenses, such as painting a building or renovating a room, members may feel they do not need to contribute. The best use of trust and endowment funds is to use them to challenge church members to give for a particular capital improvement or specific ministry.

For example, a congregation may need $100,000 to complete the renovation of church property. Interest income from a matured trust or endowment fund may be designated to pay for part of the total cost of the project. The trust or endowment funds may provide, for example, $25,000 of the project funding. The remainder must be raised by the congregation. This method recognizes the congregation's responsibility for giving.

● *Promoting trusts and endowments.* Trusts and endowments are ordinarily solicited through an information program within the church that promotes wills and trusts. User-friendly seminars and literature on the subject sensitize people to their needs for these planned-giving vehicles. A pastor's endorsement can also help generate trusts and endowments.

—Daniel D. Busby

Handling Church Investments

Most churches have funds to invest, perhaps from the sale of property, money restricted for a future building project, or endowment money for scholarships. But where should a church invest these funds?

There are basic investment prin-

ciples churches can follow when making decisions about their money:

● Invest short-term money for the short term and long-term money for the long term.

● Investment earnings should be

reinvested, unless needed to fund budgeted expenses.

- Make capital preservation the major rule of investing.
- Diversify the investments of large sums of money.
- Obtain counsel from one or more Christian investment professionals.
- Investment decisions should generally be made by a subcommittee of the church board, with the church treasurer sitting on that committee.

Thumbs-Up Investments

The kinds of funds available for investment determine the best kinds of investment to make. Fund types include:

- *Operational funds and other short-term monies.* Funds that will be needed within three to six months are usually kept in interest-bearing bank accounts (federally insured) or money-market accounts.
- *Funds held for the longer term (more than three to six months).* Long-term, unrestricted cash should usually be invested first in any church debt. Funds not invested in a church's own debt are generally placed in certificates of deposit (CDs), Treasury Bills, or other federal-agency issues. Government securities offer maximum safety and relative liquidity.

Another good investment option is a short-term, government-bond mutual fund. These funds have limited market volatility and may offer a rate of return higher than money-market rates.

But what if the church board wants a higher return on excess funds than is available through CDs and other government securities?

Should churches invest in growth mutual funds or purchase individual stocks or bonds? Prudent stewardship dictates that church funds (other than permanently restricted or term funds) should not be invested in vehicles other than interest-bearing checking accounts, CDs, money market funds, short-term government securities, or other similar investment vehicles.

- *Term or permanently restricted funds.* A church member may have donated money that can be used only after a term, for example, ten years. Or the principal of a gift may be restricted for perpetuity and the interest designated for specified purposes. To invest these types of funds on a short-term basis would be poor stewardship. For long-term investing, equities (the ownership interest of common and preferred stock in a corporation) have generally outperformed other types of investments. Therefore at least a portion of these funds should be invested in equities. Blue-chip growth and income mutual funds are a possibility. It is best to diversify between several funds and then practice patience.

Thumbs-Down Investments

There are some investment vehicles that a church should avoid:

- *Tax-free municipal bonds.* Church funds should never be invested in tax-free municipal bonds since these are attractive only to individuals and organizations that pay income taxes.
- *Investments with excessive risk.* A church should generally avoid the following investment vehicles:

—Investments with church members, their friends, or relatives.

—Oil and gas ventures, small businesses, limited partnerships, or real estate (unless it is property that will eventually be used by the church).

—Commodity futures, penny stocks, purchase of options, purchase of warrants, "selling short" or trading in securities on margin, investment derivatives, and hedge funds.

● *Too-good-to-be-true ventures.*

Investment scam artists often focus on churches. How can a scam be sniffed out? First, if it sounds too good to be true, it usually is. Other clues include promises of unreasonably high rates of return, clever but confusing descriptions of the product, sketchy or few written materials, and reluctance to give a list of "satisfied customers."

—Daniel D. Busby

37

Spending Church Money

Churches are often long on ministry potential but short on cash. While for-profit organizations are primarily concerned with making a profit, not-for-profit organizations, such as churches, are concerned with spending available resources wisely.

One important measure of a church's fiscal credibility is its ability to stick to an approved budget, especially in its spending. While there must be allowance for expense variations from the budget, a reasonable, consistent pattern of expenses reassures members their money is being used wisely. A lack of fiscal integrity, on the other hand, will breach donors' confidence and negatively impact giving.

Often the pastor is the interpreter of the church's financial condition to the church, providing information on both revenues and expenses through the bulletin and from the pulpit. But behind the pastor's role as spokesperson must stand a complete and valid system for collecting and spending money.

Building In Spending Controls

There are three key elements for controlling the disbursement of church funds: (1) The person who approves purchases should not prepare checks for payment; (2) the individual who prepares the checks

477

ideally should not be authorized to sign them; (3) the person authorized to sign checks should not be the person who approves purchases or payments.

In many small churches, one person performs all three of the above procedures. At a minimum, however, the people who count the weekly offerings should be different than those who pay the bills. But it is better to segregate the functions of purchase approval, check preparation, and check signing to improve control over the disbursement of funds.

In some situations, it may be wise to require two signatures on every check or on checks over a certain amount. The dollar level (for example, $500, $1,000, or $5,000) will vary according to the size of the church. The need for a policy of more than one signature should be determined by the level of control a church has over its fund expenditures. For example, if a larger church has a business administrator on staff who approves purchases, and all check requests require the approval of the church treasurer before checks are written, one signature may be sufficient for most checks. In most churches, one signature is adequate on checks of a modest amount. However, if a church does not have a budget and there are no written procedures for expending funds, two signatures on all checks can help offset other controls that are lacking.

Access to the church checking account should be limited generally to no more than two or three people. At the same time, having more than one person authorized to sign checks is useful when the treasurer is on vacation or otherwise unavailable. The authorized signatories, however, should not include the pastor or associate pastors. This would be a serious breach of good internal control.

Blank checks should never be signed. If small purchases are needed, the petty-cash fund should be used. When larger immediate expenditures are required, payment should be handled through open accounts with vendors or the church credit card. Otherwise, the expenditure should wait until an exact amount can be determined and documentation is available.

One bank account will be sufficient for a church if the accounting records distinguish the various types of funds (such as operating, building, and scholarship). However, if the church has trust or endowment funds, it is generally best to handle these funds through separate bank accounts.

How effective is a budget in controlling spending? The church budget provides a general guide for expenses, but it is not a straitjacket beyond which expenditures cannot be made. Unexpected expenses often cause certain budget lines to be overexpended. For example, if the plumbing malfunctions in a church rest room and the maintenance budget has been fully expended for the church year, it is doubtful that the repair should be postponed to the next fiscal year.

It may be possible to compensate for overspent budget line items by underspending other lines. However, in some cases, the unforeseen expenses are so great that the entire expense budget is over the projections. Some churches require that expenses over budget receive specific approval by the church governing board.

Defining a Spending Policy

There are a number of practices a church can consider adopting in its spending policies. Here are a few:

● *Treasurer term limitation.* Limiting the treasurer's term to three years is often a good idea. This gives incumbents a needed break and provides opportunities for other qualified people to serve. It also protects the church from traditionalizing practices that may not be in the church's best interest.

● *Bank signatories.* The board should annually adopt a resolution that authorizes the church's check signers for the year. Otherwise, there may be individuals authorized on the bank signature cards who are no longer church officers.

● *Benevolence fund.* It's good to establish criteria on who may receive monetary assistance through the church, and to adopt a policy detailing how the funds will be disbursed. A formal board-approved benevolence fund is an excellent method for handling gifts earmarked for needy individuals. (Contributions that qualify as a charitable deduction must be made to a church or other qualified charity. Contributions made directly by a donor to needy individuals are not deductible.)

● *Accountable-expense reimbursement plan.* A church can save income tax dollars for ministers and other staff members by reimbursing ministry-related expenses under an accountable expense-reimbursement plan. A formal plan should be adopted by the governing board that outlines the procedures for providing expense advances, repaying excess advances, and reimbursing expenses.

Any advances, allowances, and reimbursements that do not qualify under accountable-expense plan rules are considered additional income for ministers and other church staff members. They may not be deductible.

● *Travel expenses.* Churches need to develop basic travel policies for ministers and staff. These may include:

—Type of payment: Will actual travel expenses be reimbursed or will the church use a per diem method? Will the church reimburse the use of a personal vehicle, and, if so, at what rate per mile?

—Type of transportation: Will the church pay for air travel and under what circumstances?

—Family travel: Will expenses be reimbursed for spouses and children? If so, how will the expenses be allocated? How will reporting to the IRS be handled by the church?

Setting Up a Payment System

One of the most important principles of disbursing funds is to pay virtually all expenses by check. (The petty-cash fund is the exception.) Consistency is the key. It may be tempting, for example, to use cash from a Sunday offering to pay an honorarium for a speaker that spoke that day, but offerings should always be deposited to the bank intact—without any cash withdrawals.

A good rule of thumb is that all cash expenditures should be made through petty cash, and all major payments should be made by checks drawn on a bank account used only for church transactions.

While some churches still write checks manually, increasingly

---

Petty Cash

While church expenses generally should be paid by check, there are some small-dollar items that are better paid through a petty cash fund, which reduces the need to write numerous checks for small amounts. The following steps can be used to establish and administer a church petty cash fund:

● *Define the rules.* Which expenses can legitimately be reimbursed from petty cash and which cannot? A church secretary may have different needs for small expenditures than the pastoral staff. We should consider all the potential users before setting guidelines.

The rules should be as specific as possible. For example, should payroll advances be permitted from petty cash? Probably not. Items often paid from petty cash include postage stamps, small office supplies, and delivery charges.

One person should be the primary custodian of the fund. The use of part-time staff may require one or two alternate custodians. Another approach that fosters greater accountability is giving each person a personal cash box.

● *Communicate the rules.* The rules must be communicated effectively (and in writing) before we can expect people to toe the mark. It's good to spell out how the system works so that everyone understands who is entitled to what, and when. The written policy should be given to new staff members as part of new-employee orientation.

● *Allow no exceptions.* The rules for the fund must be uniformly applied, whether the fund is used by the senior pastor or the janitor.

Getting Started

A petty cash fund of $50 or $100 is often adequate for small churches. Larger churches may have multiple petty cash funds of differing

churches are using computer financial software. Either way, the checks should be preprinted in consecutive numbers. All spoiled checks should be marked "void" and kept on file for review during the annual audit. If the church uses a manual checkbook, it should be a large, desk-type checkbook with three checks to a page and large stubs on which to write a full description of each payment. As each check is written, the date, payee, amount, account number, and purpose of the payment should be entered on the stub. A running balance of the amount in the bank is maintained by subtracting the amount of each check from the existing balance shown on the check stub. If computer software is used for making payments, expense types are distinguished by account numbers, and checkbook balances are obtained by printing out a check register.

Some churches use voucher-type checks (manual or computerized). The voucher portion is used to describe payment and provide a

---

amounts in various departments. However, the number of petty cash funds and the balances in them should have practical limits to keep the funds from becoming simply an option for writing checks.

The size of the fund may be increased or decreased from time to time as needed, but it should be sufficient to cover payments for a short period—several weeks or a month. If the fund is kept in a locked desk or file drawer rather than a locked safe, the smaller the fund, the better.

To open a petty cash fund, the church treasurer writes a check to "Petty Cash" in the amount determined for the fund. The check is cashed by the custodian of the fund, and the currency and coins are placed in a box or drawer.

As funds are disbursed from the fund, a petty cash slip or voucher (including date of the reimbursement, the amount, the purpose of the payment, and the signature of the person receiving the funds) is completed and placed in the cash box. If an invoice or receipt is available, it should be attached to the slip for filing. The petty cash slips are kept with the petty cash. At all times, the total of the unspent petty cash and the petty cash slips should equal the fixed amount of the petty cash fund.

When the cash in the fund is getting low, the beginning balance of the fund is reconciled to the ending balance. If the cash and the vouchers in the fund do not equal the original amount of the fund, an adjustment for "cash long" or "cash short" is made. A check is then written, again payable to "Petty Cash," for an amount equal to the expense slips. The reimbursement brings the fund up to the fixed balance. Church expense accounts are then charged, based on the various petty cash expenses.

For good internal control, the church audit committee should make occasional surprise counts of the petty cash fund.

—Daniel D. Busby

detailed breakdown of the accounts to which the expenditure is charged. A duplicate of each check can then be retained in the church's accounting files.

Banks periodically return canceled checks (or photocopies of them) and a statement of the church's bank account. Reconciling this statement with the check register without fail is an important step in keeping accurate records.

How to Pay the Bills

Most bills can be paid once a month. Payments should be based on *original* copies of invoices and other supporting documentation; otherwise it is too easy to pay the same item twice. Payments should not

---

Payroll

"Call the workers and pay them their wages" (Matt. 20:8b). Today it's not that simple. Churches must not only pay their workers but also must comply with numerous federal payroll laws.

Common Payroll Pitfalls

Some churches fail to comply with federal payroll requirements, perhaps believing that churches are exempt from payroll laws. But the IRS does penalize churches for noncompliance. Penalties range from $50 for failure to issue a W-2 to 100 percent of the amount of taxes that should have been withheld from an employee but were not. Let's look at some common payroll problems and how to avoid them.

● *Failing to issue correct W-2 or 1099 forms.* Churches are required by law to issue W-2 or 1099 forms each year for everyone on their payroll. Employees, including most ministers, should get W-2 forms. Most ministers have dual tax sta-

tus. They are considered employees for income-tax purposes, but are always self-employed for social security taxes.

One problem is that churches issuing W-2s and 1099s often make mistakes on them. For example, a minister's housing allowance should not be reported on a W-2. However, love offerings, bonuses, and expenses paid from nonaccountable reimbursement plans should be reported as income on a W-2.

● *Not withholding income taxes from unordained employees.* Although the law does not require churches to withhold income taxes from ministers' pay, churches must withhold taxes from unordained employees, who should complete a W-4 form. Churches can obtain IRS Publication 15, which explains how to calculate withholding.

Ministers treated as employees for income-tax purposes can voluntarily complete a W-4, authorizing the church to withhold income

be made from month-end statements, since typically they do not show the detail of services or products provided.

When a check is written, the supporting document should be marked "Paid" and the date and check number recorded on it. If checks are prepared for the treasurer's signature by someone else, the treasurer should see the supporting document before signing the check. The supporting material should then be filed in a paid-bills file, in alphabetical order by payee. Checks should never be made payable to "Cash," since it is essential to know for what purpose funds are being used. However, issuing checks to "Petty Cash" is acceptable when replenishing the petty-cash fund.

To effectively manage cash flow, checks should be written only when there are funds available to cover them. Some churches write

---

taxes. While this is not legally required, it may help ministers budget better.

● *Confusing FICA and SECA.* Because most ministers have a dual tax status, churches must understand the difference between the two types of social security taxes. FICA (Federal Insurance Contributions Act) taxes are the employee's social security taxes; employers withhold FICA and make matching FICA contributions on behalf of employees. SECA (Self-Employment Contributions Act) taxes are self-employment taxes for self-employed individuals, such as most ministers, who pay their own contributions to the social security system. A church doesn't do the minister a favor by withholding and paying FICA as if the minister were an employee. In fact, this arrangement is illegal, because ministerial income is always subject to SECA, not FICA.

Churches can assist their ministers by providing a special pay supplement for paying SECA, but this supplement is taxable income and must be reported as such. Also, such a SECA supplement should never be reported as FICA payments on a minister's W-2, as this is incorrect and may result in miscalculated social security benefits.

● *Incorrectly identifying independent contractors.* Churches cannot avoid paying FICA for employees by calling them independent contractors. For the IRS, an employee is someone who performs regular duties for a church, does it at the direction of the church, and works on the church premises. For example, the IRS is unlikely to consider a full-time church secretary an independent contractor.

● *Not following federal reporting and deposit requirements.* Churches may have three different kinds of taxes to report and deposit: the employees' withheld share of FICA, the employer's share of FICA, and federal income taxes withheld from employees. Churches withholding income taxes or FICA must file an employer's quarterly tax return (Form 941). Churches opposed to social security that have filed Form 8274 should use Form 941E.

—*Julie L. Bloss*

checks when bills are due and then hold those checks for days, weeks, or even months until sufficient cash is available to release the checks for payment. This confusing practice makes balancing the checkbook and reconciling bank statements complicated and difficult.

Another entangling practice is to predate or postdate checks, which results in unreliable accounting records. For example, if a church year ends on June 30, a check prepared on June 20 and postdated to July 5 could be used to try to cover a year-end budget shortage in a cash-basis accounting system (this would not impact an accrual-accounting system). Conversely, a check issued on June 28 relating to a purchase that will occur after July 1 could be written in an effort to "use up" budget money in the current year. If expenses are not consistently recorded in the correct year, financial reports will be unreliable.

Other considerations in paying bills include:

● *Approval of expenditures.* How a church approves the spending of its money may depend on its size. In a small church, the treasurer may be authorized to approve expenses if funds are available in an approved budget. In a larger church, an elaborate system of expense approvals may be necessary to manage disbursements.

Although every church should have a budget, many don't. When there is no budget, the treasurer must use his or her judgment as to the appropriateness of an expense item and must also determine whether funds are generally available. This is an unfair position in which to place a treasurer.

It is good policy to have the church board provide authorization for all expenditures of funds. A standing authorization may be provided for certain routine items such as salaries, fringe benefits, utilities, and debt-amortization payments. But this standing authorization should be done through a resolution that specifies exactly what is authorized.

Many expenses relate to church departments (Sunday school, children, youth, seniors, maintenance). Good fiscal policies often require the approval of a department representative before an expense is paid.

● *Use of purchase orders.* Purchase orders authorize the expenditure of funds within dollar limits for specified items or services. They are based on purchase requests submitted by church staff and volunteers. Purchase orders are generally submitted to the treasurer, who issues them only after the purchase request is compared to the appropriate budget line item to determine if funds are available. In this way, they are a good system for keeping purchases within approved limits. Purchase orders also allow for directing purchases to specific vendors, thereby providing for the possibility of price discounts. Many larger churches find purchase orders helpful.

● *Documentation of expenses.* Every check should have some sort of written document to support it—an invoice, petty-cash voucher, travel-expense report, payroll time sheet, and so on. There are some instances when written documentation may not be required. For example, church policy may state that no documentation is needed for travel-related expenses for individual items of $25 or less (other than air fare or motels). This type of policy is a reasonable one and is within Internal Revenue Service guidelines.

There may be other good reasons why written documentation is not available. The treasurer must have the discretion to determine when the lack of documentation is acceptable. For example, it is usually sufficient when paying an honorarium to have only a written check request indicating the date of the speaking engagement. Or a pastor may have lost an invoice for a ministry expense he or she paid personally. If the amount requested is reasonable in relation to the expense, a written explanation of the item and the reason the documentation is missing should be adequate.

● *Keeping records.* All checks that are written should be recorded in a cash-disbursements journal. The journal may be prepared manually or by computer. Manually prepared cash-disbursement journals should have an adequate number of columns to distribute the major expense categories. It is helpful to use "total" and "detail" expense columns to create a double-entry posting and balancing system.

● *Expense reimbursements to church staff.* Expense reimbursements often create special concerns for churches. Although some staff members may think the mere listing of types of expenses provides sufficiently detailed documentation, more detailed information is necessary for adequate documentation. If ministry miles are being reimbursed, a daily log of ministry versus personal miles should be submitted to the church treasurer, with commuting miles between the church and the minister's residence categorized as personal.

Expenses for entertaining church-related people should reflect the date, ministry purpose, and names of those entertained—generally on the receipt itself (which states the place). Receipts may be inappropriate, however, for meals prepared for entertainment at the minister's residence, because food was purchased relating to personal meals as well as ministry-related entertaining. In such cases, a reasonable cost-per-meal amount should be set and used as a basis for reimbursement.

● *Paying workers.* When payments are made to people who work for the church, the status of the person as an employee or independent contractor must be determined. This applies to every pastor, secretary, janitor, musician, and day-care worker who receives remuneration.

A worker's status determines what federal, state, and local laws need to be followed in paying the worker. For example, employees receive a Form W-2 at year-end, while independent contractors receive a form 1099-MISC. Also, employees are often subject to state worker's compensation laws, but independent contractors are not. The differences are many and important—enough so, that it is a wise practice to seek competent tax counsel about any gray areas, to avoid legal problems.

Avoiding Misappropriation of Church Funds

It is sad that the subject of misappropriation of church funds even needs to be addressed. But church funds do occasionally disappear when proper financial controls are not followed. Those handling church funds are human and thus subject to temptation.

Misappropriation of church funds generally occurs between the time money is placed in the offering plate and when it is deposited in the bank. But it can also happen with cash disbursements. Any treasurer, if inclined, can find ways to manipulate the books to cover misappropriation. Checks can be written to fictitious payees and then cashed by the church treasurer. Or treasurers can write checks to themselves and charge them to an expense account or offset them against offering income.

Ineffective administration can make the church nearly as guilty as the one misusing funds. When church leaders fail to enact prudent fiscal controls, they may help cause someone to stumble. Churches can protect themselves and their treasurers against misappropriation if they develop a board-approved, written set of procedures for handling cash disbursements, and consistently determine that the procedures are being followed, typically as a part of the annual external or internal audit process.

—Daniel D. Busby

Resources

Holck, M. 1986. Complete handbook of church accounting. Englewood Cliffs, N.J.: Prentice-Hall.

Pollock, D. 1993. Business management in the local church. Chicago: Moody.

Vargo, R. 1989. Effective church accounting. New York: Harper & Row.

Wise Shopping

In a unique way, pastors and church leaders are stewards of the resources of God's kingdom. This demands of pastors their best efforts at making every dollar count. One way church leaders can spend ministry dollars with confidence is by adopting a carefully formulated purchasing strategy.

Needs or Wants?

Because ministry resources are often scarce, the first step in wise shopping is to determine whether the purchase meets a bona fide need or only a want. Buying "wants" is not wrong, but such purchases should come from excess (discretionary) funds. How can one know the difference between a wise and unwise purchase?

● *Never buy on impulse.* Any time someone says an opportunity must be taken now or missed forever, it's probably better to miss it. We mortals need time between a buying opportunity and a sale to consider whether the purchase is really necessary.

● *Establish an accountability process.* If part of a larger staff, church leaders can become accountable for purchases by making themselves accountable to a fellow staff member—one who will not be inclined to affirm a purchase unless it is truly wise. The same can be done with a friend, a church member, or an associate at another church.

Five Rules

● *Plan ahead.* By planning ahead, we can buy in large quantities, which saves money by reducing both the cost per item and the amount of time spent shopping. It also allows us to take advantage of seasonal pricing (such as purchasing paint, building supplies, and other spring and summer items in the winter when demand is low and prices can be negotiated) and to take our time; since we aren't pressured to make a fast purchase, we can spend more time researching to make sure we are getting the best product for the church.

● *Buy informed.* When buying something also used by professional tradesmen, we can ask members of that trade what they would look for if it were their purchase. For instance, a landscaper can say which lawnmower provides the most even

cut for the least amount of maintenance, and even where the best buys are.

● *Don't make church membership or faith the issue.* Some church leaders feel strongly about purchasing from church members or other Christians whenever possible. However, several arguments bear consideration: First, we need opportunities to build natural bridges with unbelievers. What better time to model integrity and earn the right to share the gospel than when dealing with vendors?

Second, if something goes wrong or a product is faulty, it may be easier to resolve the issue if the vendor is outside the church. This helps us avoid building up bitterness or ill feelings among our flock or staff.

Third, if the problem is not cooperatively redeemable, we are told in Scripture not to take our brother to court. But we are not given this restriction with unbelievers.

● *Get three bids.* Although this rule may feel like an exercise in futility, it enhances good stewardship. It also enables us to objectively negotiate a price that is reasonable for both parties. When negotiating, we shouldn't be afraid to ask for a lower price or for extras to be thrown in at the same price. It's surprising how often the seller agrees.

● *Don't pay unnecessary sales tax.* Some states exempt churches and other not-for-profit organizations from paying sales tax on purchases. This should be investigated with the state government. Organizations that have paid sales tax unnecessarily have been pleasantly surprised at their newfound savings.

—*Nick B. Nicholaou*

38

Tax and Law Considerations

Churches minister in an increasingly litigious and regulated society that makes awareness of legal obligations essential. For example, according to statistics released by the National Center for State Courts, more than 93 million new legal cases were filed in state courts in 1991. These included nearly 20 million civil lawsuits, and this number is expected to double by the year 2000.

As all levels of government become more regulatory, there will be more and more points of intersection between government regulation and the autonomy of the local church. Being uninformed about legal obligations can be costly, resulting in fines and penalties. While such costs in the past were borne by the church, there will be increasing focus in the years ahead on the personal liability of church leaders. So what are the most important legal and tax concerns for church leaders? Consider the following dozen issues.

Incorporation

Churches should incorporate for many reasons, but mainly to protect members from personal liability for the actions of fellow members. For example, members may be personally liable for the sexual molestation of children by another member in the course of a church-sponsored youth activity. This potential liability should be a concern to any member of an unincorporated church. While incorporation will not protect a member from liability for his or her own actions, it will protect other members who did not participate in the member's actions.

Unfortunately, many church leaders do not know if their church is incorporated. In some cases, churches have incorporated in the past but have lost their corporate status because they incorporated for a limited term instead of an indefinite (perpetual) term. For this reason, it is wise to check the church's articles of incorporation to see if the church was incorporated for a specific term.

In some states, churches can lose their corporate status by failing to submit an annual corporate report to the secretary of state. In these states, churches should contact the office of secretary of state in the state capital to ascertain the church's status.

Some church leaders are opposed to incorporation on theological grounds. However, theological opposition to incorporation will not be a defense against charges of personal liability of church members. Church leaders who block incorporation on theological grounds should share their position with the church membership. After all, it is entirely possible that church members will not hold the same theological position when they discover the potential consequences, and they should not be exposed to personal liability without their knowledge and consent.

Child Abuse

The problem of child abuse on church premises and during church activities continues to plague churches. Fortunately, more churches are beginning to take this risk seriously. Many incidents have been avoided through setting up systems of "preventive maintenance." Church leaders must resist complacency in this area, implementing a screening program at the very least. Such steps not only protect the church from a lawsuit and negative publicity, but, far more importantly, they also protect the children of the church.

Pastoral Counseling

Many churches have been sued as a result of the sexual misconduct of ministers during counseling sessions. Sadly, many such suits have proved the truth of sexual-misconduct charges. However, some charges prove false, though it is difficult for a minister to prove innocence, since most of the cases boil down to "my word against hers."

A church can significantly reduce the risk of such incidents—and of false allegations—in a number of ways. First, the church can adopt a rule forbidding any counseling with a member of the opposite sex unless a third person is present. The third person can be the pastor's spouse or another staff member. A second approach is to require that the pastor engage in opposite-sex counseling only by telephone. A third (and less effective) approach is to prohibit off-premises counseling without a third person present and to restrict counseling on church premises. Such restrictions could include a requirement that opposite-sex counseling occur only during office hours and be limited to not more than 45 minutes, with a maximum of four sessions with the same person. Of course, some exceptions would be in order for any of these approaches, for example, when the counselee is a relative or above a certain age.

Negligent Supervision

Churches can be sued if they failed to exercise due care in the supervision of their activities. The basic rule to follow is this: Always have a sufficient number of trained adults present during any activity. For example, it's best not to conduct a youth activity involving swimming or mountain climbing without a number of qualified adults supervising and leading the way.

Another common problem in many churches is the practice of releasing children from Sunday school or children's church prior to the end of the adult service. A church can be responsible for any injuries that occur to a child who is released before the return of the parent or guardian.

Child-Abuse Reporting

Pastors often learn of child abuse in the course of counseling or through reports from nursery staff or youth workers. Therefore, they should clearly understand their responsibilities under state law regarding the need to report known incidents of abuse. In many states, ministers are considered "mandatory reporters," meaning that they can be criminally liable for failing to report. A number of courts have rejected the defense made by some pastors that they failed to report abuse because they wanted to deal with the problem "within the congregation" as a matter of church discipline. A few states excuse ministers from reporting abuse if they learned of it in the course of a privileged communication. It's imperative to check the state law often, for this one area of law changes often.

Copyright

Few areas of law impact churches more pervasively than copyright law, yet it involves the application of special rules that are not clearly understood by church staff members, leaders, musicians, and even some publishers and attorneys. As a result, there is widespread misinformation and noncompliance with the law, which can result in enormous financial liabilities.

The most important point to remember is that churches are subject to copyright law. This means that a church cannot without permission: (1) make copies of copyrighted materials (including music, books, and magazines articles); (2) make a "derivative work" based on a copyrighted work (such as an arrangement of a copyrighted song, or a new edition or workbook based on a copyrighted book); or (3) publicly perform a copyrighted work. Violation of these rules constitutes copyright infringement.

There are a few ways to avoid copyright infringement. We can obtain permission from the copyright owner, obtain a license to use the material, or claim "fair use." Also, the performance of religious music at a church in the course of religious services is exempted from copyright infringement by law. Note that this exception applies only to *performing* religious music and not to *copying* the music.

Liability

The word *liability* refers to legal responsibility for personal injury or property damage. Ordinarily, legal responsibility is determined by the civil courts and measured in terms of monetary awards.

Churches are not immune from liability concerns. Quite to the contrary, their potential legal liability often is higher because of the nature and frequency of their activities. Churches with a preschool program or an active children's program face a significant risk of liability for a variety of personal injuries. This risk increases further if the church engages in overnight activities, has inadequate supervisory personnel, or fails to adequately screen those persons who work with children.

Liability falls into three major categories: bodily injury, personal injury not involving bodily injury, and property damage.

Bodily Injury

The risk of liability associated with bodily injury is the most significant liability risk for churches. Adults and children can be injured on church premises or in the course of church activities in numerous ways. A church can be liable for such injuries if it was negligent and its negligence was responsible for the injury.

Negligence refers to a failure to exercise reasonable care. To illustrate, assume a church uses an inexperienced driver with a poor driving record to transport children in a church vehicle. If the driver causes an accident that injures others, the argument could be made that the church was responsible for those injuries on the basis of its negligence in selecting the driver. That is, the church failed to exercise reasonable care in selecting the

Compliance with Organizational Documents

Church leaders should be familiar with their church charter, constitution, bylaws, or other organizational documents, since these documents ordinarily address many issues of internal administration. Church charters typically set forth the name, address, period of duration, and purposes of the corporation; the doctrinal tenets of the church; and the names and addresses of incorporators and directors. However, they rarely contain rules for the internal government of the corporation. For this reason, it is customary for churches to adopt rules for their internal operation. Such rules ordinarily are called bylaws, although occasionally they are referred to as a constitution or a constitution and bylaws.

Church bylaws ordinarily cover such matters as the qualifications,

---

driver, and its negligence was the cause of the injuries.

Bodily injury can occur in several other ways. Children can be molested or abused on church premises. Adults and children alike can slip on icy parking lots, wet floors, or darkened stairways. Children can be injured when released prior to being picked up by a parent or guardian, or while playing on playground equipment. Clergy and other counselors can have sexual contact with counselees.

Other Personal Injury

Churches can be liable for several kinds of personal injuries not involving bodily injury. Examples include defamation of character, invasion of privacy, wrongful dismissal of an employee, various kinds of discrimination, securities-law violations, copyright infringement, and breach of contract.

Property Damage

Churches also can be liable for property damage caused by the actions of their agents. Such damage ordinarily occurs in conjunction with the use of church vehicles. For example, a church employee negligently drives a church vehicle and collides with another vehicle, causing substantial damage. The church will be responsible for this damage if its employee was acting within the course of employment at the time of the accident.

Church Protection

A church can protect itself against liability in a number of ways. It can obtain insurance, avoid high-risk activities, institute a prevention or risk-management program that reduces the likelihood of various risks, and educate its leadership about the need to address issues of liability. Such actions not only will significantly reduce a church's risk of liability but also protect innocent victims, many of whom are members of the church family.

—Richard R. Hammar

selection, and expulsion of members; the time and place of annual business meetings; the calling of special business meetings; the required notice for annual and special meetings; quorums; voting rights; the selection, tenure, and removal of officers and directors; the filling of vacancies; the responsibilities of directors and officers; the method of amending bylaws; and the purchase and conveyance of property.

Other matters that should be a part of church bylaws (but often are not) include the adoption of a specific body of parliamentary procedure, a clause requiring disputes to be resolved through mediation or arbitration, a clause specifying how contracts and other legal documents are to be approved and signed, signature authority on checks, bonding of officers and employees who handle church funds, an annual audit by independent certified public accountants, an indem-

Nonprofit Status

Whether a church's annual budget is $20,000 or $2 million, the church is a nonprofit, tax-exempt entity. And no church wants to lose that privilege. To get the most of that tax-exempt status, church leaders need to know how tax laws governing churches work. Here's a rundown.

State and Local Advantages

Tax exemption normally doesn't occur as a result of special incorporation but rather from being nonprofit in nature. This status allows churches to benefit from state and local laws that exempt them from paying property taxes. Usually, churches pay no taxes on church property used for religious purposes. That may include the parsonage, if the church owns one.

A church cannot take advantage of its tax-exempt status to hold raw land or other real estate as investments. For example, some church-es that have acquired land for relocation have had to pay property taxes on the land until they built and occupied the new church on it.

In many states, a church should be exempt from state and local sales taxes on purchases for the church. Those making the purchases can call the church's tax-exempt status to the attention of a salesperson and present a copy of an exemption certificate or the church's state tax identification number to avoid sales taxes.

Federal Regulations

A religious organization qualifies for federal tax-exempt status under section 501(c)(3) of the Internal Revenue Code. Basically, this code exempts from federal taxation entities operated for religious, charitable, scientific, or educational purposes. Moreover, the law makes an important distinction between churches and other religious organ-

nification clause, specification of the church's fiscal year, and "staggered voting" of directors (a portion of the board is elected each year to ensure year-to-year continuity of leadership).

Personal Liability of Board Members

While a number of states have adopted statutes limiting the liability of uncompensated directors of nonprofit corporations for their ordinary negligence, church officers and directors may be personally liable for their actions in several situations, including:

● Personal tort liability for such actions as negligent operation of a church vehicle, negligent supervision of church workers and activities, copyright infringement, and wrongful termination of employees.

● Contract liability for executing a contract without authoriza-

---

izations, and churches are subject to rules even more lenient than those for other tax-exempt groups.

What is a church? The IRS considers all relevant facts and circumstances on a case-by-case basis. Characteristics they look for include a distinct legal existence, a recognized creed and form of worship, a definite ecclesiastical government, a formal code of doctrine and discipline, a distinct religious history, ordained ministers serving the congregation, a course of study required for ministers prior to ordination, an established place of worship, regular religious services, a consistent congregation, and schools for religious instruction of children. Churches don't have to satisfy all of these requirements, and the law is clear that congregational denominations can be treated the same as hierarchical ones.

Unlike other nonprofit organizations, churches don't have to apply to the IRS for tax-exempt status, and although other religious organizations have to file a Form 990 if their gross receipts exceed $25,000, churches don't. But churches do have to file a Form 990-T (Exempt Organization Business Income Tax Return) if they have $1,000 or more of unrelated income.

What is unrelated income? According to the IRS, it's income from any trade or business that is regularly carried on and not substantially related to the organization's exempt purpose or function. For example, if a church bookstore operates mainly as a retail outlet, making a substantial profit, its proceeds to the church likely would be considered unrelated income.

Another factor of note is that no part of a church's earnings, except for reasonable amounts for compensation, may go to the benefit of a private individual. So payment of excessive compensation to someone such as a pastor or board member would not be allowed by the IRS (the salary of Jim Bakker, for example, was considered excessive).

Other activities that jeopardize a church's tax-exempt status include significant lobbying efforts or any political campaigning for specific candidates.

—*Julie L. Bloss*

tion—or with authorization but without any indication of a representative capacity.

● Violating one of the "fiduciary duties" that every officer or director owes to a corporation, including the duties of due care and loyalty to the corporation.

● Violating or disregarding the terms of an express trust imposed by a donor on a contribution.

● Selling securities without registering as an agent (if required by state law), or engaging in fraudulent activities in the offer or sale of church securities.

● Willfully failing to withhold or pay federal payroll taxes.

Discrimination Laws

A bewildering number of antidiscrimination laws have been enacted by federal, state, and local governments. Many of these laws apply to the employment relationship, prohibiting covered employers from discriminating in employment decisions (including hiring, firing, and benefits) on the basis of race, color, national origin, gender, pregnancy, religion, age, and disability. At the federal level, coverage under these laws generally requires the church to have a minimum number of employees plus some impact on interstate commerce. Limited exemptions are available to religious organizations under some of these laws.

To illustrate, Title VII of the Civil Rights Act of 1964 makes it unlawful for an employer engaged in interstate commerce with 15 or more employees to discriminate in any employment decision on the basis of race, color, national origin, gender, pregnancy, or religion. However, the act exempts religious organizations, including churches, from the prohibition of religious-based discrimination in employment. It often is more likely that a church will be subject to state and local antidiscrimination laws.

Property Taxes

Every state property-tax law exempts places of religious worship. It is common for state law to exempt property "used exclusively" as a place of religious worship, but in many states the exemption is not automatic; an application for exemption must be filed and approved. The states vary widely with respect to the taxability of other church-owned property, but note the following:

● *Surrounding grounds.* Some state laws specify how much of the land surrounding the house of worship is exempt. Others do not. The courts interpret the exemption of a "house of worship" to include surrounding land reasonably necessary to accommodate worship.

● *Effect of rental income.* In some states, the generation of rental income negates any exemption. Many states recognize the partial-exemption principle, however, and exempt that portion of church-owned property that is not used for commercial or rental purposes.

● *Property under construction.* Generally, it does not qualify for exemption.

● *Parsonages.* A parsonage is a church-owned dwelling that is used as a residence by a minister. The parsonage is exempt in many states.

● *Vacant land.* The courts have split over the tax treatment of vacant land. The majority view seems to be that such land is taxable, even though it is acquired for future use as a church, unless it is used regularly for church activities (campouts, youth activities, recreational activities, sports, outdoor services, etc.).

● *Church-owned campgrounds.* The courts have split over the tax treatment of church-owned campgrounds. All states recognize a chapel and a reasonable amount of surrounding property to be exempt. The controversy concerns bunkhouses, residences, undeveloped land, and recreational facilities. Most courts have denied exemption to these portions of campgrounds.

Unrelated Business Income

The Internal Revenue Code imposes a tax (equivalent to the corporate income tax) on the unrelated business taxable income of an exempt organization. The income must be generated by an unrelated trade or business that is *regularly carried on.* A trade or business is any activity designed to generate income. Also, a trade or business does not become "related" merely because the earnings are used for exempt purposes, such as supporting the church ministry. The focus is on the nature of the activity, not the use of income from that activity. The line between a taxable commercial activity and an exempt one is often difficult to define. Unrelated business income does *not* include activities performed by volunteer workers; activities carried on for the convenience of the organization's members, students, or employees; or selling donated merchandise.

Rental income is given special treatment. Note the following rules: Rental income from property owned debt free is not unrelated business income. Rental income from indebted property (for example, subject to an "acquisition indebtedness") is unrelated business income in proportion to the amount of the debt, unless (1) at least 85 percent of the property (considering space, time of use, or both) is used for exempt purposes, or (2) the church plans to demolish the rental property within 15 years and use the land for exempt purposes (the church must notify the IRS of its plans after five years).

It is rare for a church to have unrelated business income. One example is the rental of a church parking lot to the patrons of neighboring businesses during the week.

Payroll Tax Reporting Requirements

An employer has legal obligations to withhold income taxes and FICA taxes from employees' wages and to pay them (along with the employer's share of FICA taxes) to the government. All churches are subject to at least some payroll-tax reporting requirements, because the courts have rejected the claim that imposing these obligations on churches violates the First Amendment.

The application of payroll tax reporting requirements to clergy involves two special rules that are often misunderstood: First, clergy are always self-employed for social security purposes, with respect to services performed in the exercise of ministry, and, second, clergy compensation is exempt from income tax withholding, whether a minister reports income taxes as an employee or as self-employed.

The following ten-step approach will help a church comply with reporting requirements:

Step 1: Obtain an employer identification number.

Step 2: Determine whether each worker is an employee or self-employed.

Step 3: Have each employee complete and return a W-4 (withholding allowance certificate).

Step 4: Compute the compensation of each worker.

Step 5: Determine how much income tax to withhold by using IRS Circular E (and wage and withholding allowance information).

Step 6: Withhold nonminister employees' shares of FICA taxes (unless the church filed Form 8274 and exempted itself from the employer's share of FICA taxes).

Step 7: Deposit payroll taxes.

Step 8: Complete and file quarterly employer's tax returns with the IRS (Form 941 or 941E).

Step 9: Issue a W-2 to each employee, and send a copy of each W-2 to the IRS, along with a W-3 transmittal form.

Step 10: Issue a 1099-MISC to each self-employed worker who was paid compensation of $600 or more, and send a copy of each 1099 to the Social Security Administration, along with a 1096 transmittal form.

Let's conclude with some good news: We do not have to passively wait to be sued and view litigation as inevitable. Through education and preventive maintenance, churches can significantly reduce their risk of a lawsuit.

—Richard R. Hammar

Resources

Bloss, J. 1993. The church guide to employment law. Matthews, N.C.: Christian Ministry Resources.

Cobble, J., R. Hammar, and S. Klipowicz. 1993. Child abuse prevention kit. Matthews, N.C.: Christian Ministry Resources.

Cobble, J., R. Hammar, and S. Klipowicz. 1994. The 1994 compensation handbook for church staff. Matthews, N.C.: Christian Ministry Resources.

Grange, G., R. Hammar, J. Cobble. 1994. Risk management for churches—a self-directed audit. Matthews, N.C.: Christian Ministry Resources.

Hammar, R. *Church law & tax report.* Matthews, N.C.: Christian Ministry Resources.

Hammar, R. *Church treasurer alert!* Matthews, N.C.: Christian Ministry Resources.

Hammar, R. 1990. The church guide to copyright law, 2nd ed. Matthews, N.C.: Christian Ministry Resources.

Hammar, R. 1991. Pastor, church & law, 2nd ed. Matthews, N.C.: Christian Ministry Resources.

Hammar, R. 1994. Church and clergy tax guide. Matthews, N.C.: Christian Ministry Resources.

Inurement

Tight Situations

Federal regulations state that no part of the net earnings of a church can *inure* to the benefit of an individual. Churches can, of course, pay clergy, but inurement occurs when churches pay their ministers too much or when ministers otherwise benefit excessively from money donated to the church.

Churches do not pay taxes, so special rules apply to them as tax-exempt organizations on how money can be used. Violating these IRS rules can lead to the revoking of a church's tax-exempt status.

From the IRS perspective, contributions are not deductible if they go to a church or any "charitable organization" set up to benefit specific *individuals*. Deductible donations are supposed to promote an organization's charitable purpose.

Most churches don't pay salaries outright that would raise IRS eyebrows, but there are more common trouble areas, such as:

● *Unfettered control over church funds.* A minister, treasurer, or any other single individual should not have unbridled discretion over church spending.

● *Payment of unsubstantiated "business expenses."* Churches should use accountable reimbursement plans (reimbursements are made only for approved and documented expenses) instead of paying credit card bills or reimbursing a minister's undocumented expenses.

● *Low- or no-interest loans.* Sometimes arranged to help pastors find housing in an expensive market, these loans pose an inurement problem and may constitute taxable income to ministers.

● *Large retirement gifts.* Giving a house or expensive car can backfire. The legal ramifications of a congregation's or an individual's generosity for a beloved pastor should first be checked with a tax attorney or CPA.

Case Studies

There are no black-and-white answers about what constitutes unreasonable compensation, but we do have some guidance from the courts and the IRS.

In one case, a federal court found that a yearly income of $115,680 paid by a church to its founder and his wife was not excessive. The same court concluded, however, that other church funds had inured to the benefit of the founder because the church paid him excessive royalties on church literature, and the founder had unfettered control over millions of the church's dollars.

This shows cash salary alone does not measure a minister's compensation. Bonuses, direct payment of personal expenses, and forgiveness of debts can add up to excessive income in the eyes of the IRS.

In the case of Jim Bakker and PTL, the court ruled that Bakker had failed to count as part of his taxable compensation items such as personal use of a corporate jet, enormous bonuses, cash "advances" he never repaid, and certain credit card bills. Concerning what Bakker could count as a reasonable salary, the court accepted a maximum of $177,156, noting that South Carolina's highest paid head of a state agency made less than $100,000 a year.

Safety in Salaries

A good guideline for avoiding inurement is to measure a minister's compensation against what local churches of comparable size are paying.

Three mistakes to avoid are:

● Comparing ministers' salaries with local business executives'. Executives are paid from corporate profits, but ministers are paid from funds given to promote religious and charitable objectives.

● Paying a minister a percentage of church revenue when that makes salary payments excessive. If the growth of church income pushes the salary amount to over a quarter of a million dollars, the IRS is likely to treat such compensation as unreasonable, and thus, inurement.

● Failing to include as income such compensation as personal use of an automobile, unaccounted-for cash advances, or substantial personal "gifts" given from tax-deductible donations to the church. All taxable compensation—not just cash salary—needs to be reported.

—Julie L. Bloss

Clergy Tax Matters

Each year an estimated 6,000 pastors are audited by the IRS. Any pastor who files his or her income-tax return with certain safe harbors in mind can freely hand over any records to an IRS auditor without worrying about the result.

Safe Harbors

What are a pastor's safe harbors? Here are five clergy-tax problem areas and their corresponding sanctuaries:

● *Reporting as self-employed.* Many ministers continue to report their primary ministerial compensation on Form 1040, Schedule C, as self-employed individuals. Yet the IRS classifies most local-church ministers as employees. Inappropriately filing as self-employed for income-tax purposes puts a pastor in a high-risk category for an audit, and audited pastors can be liable for underpaid back taxes and penalties.

Safe harbor: The vast majority of pastors generally should file as employees for income-tax purposes and receive a Form W-2 from the church. Use Schedule C for a pastor's church salary only when the pastor has an air-tight case for independent-contractor status.

● *Mixing salary and reimbursements.* Some churches, wanting to be flexible, begin to blur the distinction between salary and expense reimbursements. For example, a church decides it can afford a certain amount for the minister's salary and professional expenses—say, $36,000 annually. The minister receives $3,000 per month, tentatively allocated as $2,500 salary and $500 for professional expenses. At some point, often the end of the year, the minister realizes the professional expenses exceed the $500-a-month allocation. The church then adjusts the allocation so that, say, $2,400 a month is salary and $600 reimburses expenses. The IRS frowns on this practice, terming it "recharacterization of income" and imposing back taxes and penalties.

Safe harbor: Use a stated-salary approach. Set the gross salary at the beginning of the year and don't adjust it during the year based on the level of business and professional expenses reimbursed by the church.

● *Risky housing allowances.* Sometimes housing allowances aren't designated according to IRS regulations. The IRS disallows such practices as pastors setting their own housing allowance without an official action by the church or board, or establishing a housing-allowance figure retroactively after compensation is paid.

Safe harbor: Have the church make a written designation of the housing allowance in an official resolution before compensation is paid.

● *Fringe benefit fuzziness.* All fringe benefits are not necessarily tax-free. Tax law does, however, provide a tax-free safe harbor for benefits such as health insurance premiums paid by the church directly to the insurance carrier, group term life insurance up to $50,000 provided by the church, payments by the church to a denominational pension plan, and tax-sheltered annuities within certain annual limits. However, some so-called fringe benefits are taxable income, such as gifts from individuals that have been given through the church and group term life insurance in excess of $50,000.

Safe harbor: When figuring taxable income, include the value of all fringe benefits not specifically excluded by tax law.

● *Forgotten social security.* Ministers cannot opt out of social security merely because they consider it a poor investment. In fact, the only valid reason to opt out of social security is to be conscientiously opposed to the acceptance of *any* public insurance based on religious principles.

Safe harbor: Don't assume a pastor has opted out of social security just because he or she filed Form 4361. If an application is accepted, the IRS will send an approved copy of the form. Pastors should continue to pay social security taxes until they receive the form.

—*Daniel D. Busby*

Copyright Law and the Church

A copyright is a legal interest that the law confers upon certain literary and musical works (among others) for a limited time. Copyright owners have certain "exclusive rights" in their works, including the exclusive rights to copy, distribute, and publicly perform or display their works, and to make "derivative works" (such as editions, translations, and musical arrangements) that are based on the original work. No one else has the legal right to do any of these things without the copyright owner's consent.

The most common types of copyrighted materials include articles, books, music, recordings, and computer software. To be copyrightable, a work must be original and in a "tangible form." Some things cannot be copyrighted, such as titles, symbols, devices, discoveries, and ideas.

Common Misuses

What are practices among churches that may violate the copyright law? Two common infringements are:

● *Music.* A church's music program may violate the copyright law in a number of ways. Duplicating copyrighted choral music, making audio or video recordings of church services in which copyrighted music is performed, compiling "chorus booklets" or similar compilations of commonly sung music, making transparencies of copyrighted music for display during worship services, copying music for an accompanist, and making bulletin inserts containing the lyrics of copyrighted music—all of these violate the copyright owner's exclusive right to make copies of his or her work. In addition, making changes in copyrighted music may constitute a violation of the copyright owner's exclusive right to make derivative works.

● *Church publications.* These include church newsletters, bulletins, and literature that is duplicated for instructional purposes. Again, if such publications contain copyrighted materials—text or graphics—that are reproduced without consent, then they will constitute an infringement on the copyright owner's exclusive right to make copies.

What's Lawful

There are exceptions and ways to copy copyrighted materials legally.

● A church is free to copy a "public domain" work. Such works have lost their copyright protection (or they never were protected in the first place). Unfortunately, it is often difficult to determine whether a particular work is in the public domain.

● A church can always write the copyright owner (often, this will be the publisher) to obtain permission to make copies.

● A church can obtain a license authorizing it to make copies. By far the most comprehensive "blanket license" available today is offered by Christian Copyright Licensing, Inc., (CCLI) of Portland, Oregon (503/257-2230).

● The "fair use" of a copyrighted work is not an infringement of copyright. However, the concept of fair use is a narrow one that seldom

will justify the common church practices described above. One thing is clear: duplicating a work solely to avoid paying for it will seldom if ever be "fair use." Further, verbatim or nearly verbatim reproductions of an entire copyrighted work will almost never be deemed a fair use.

The Spirit of the Law

The importance of complying with copyright law is sometimes raised. After all, it is uncommon to hear of a church being sued for copyright violations. On deeper reflection, it is apparent that this question misses the mark. Especially for churches, the decision of whether or not to obey the law should not be based on the probability of "being caught."

The law itself takes copyright standards seriously. A church can be liable for $500 to $20,000 for a single infringement, and up to $100,000 if the infringement was intentional (as many are). A church that has committed several acts of infringement is potentially liable for enormous penalties.

It is proper for the church to support those of its people who write or compose sacred literature and music for the church, just as we often compensate clergy for the sacred services they provide on behalf of the church. Jesus said that the laborer is worthy of his hire. Observing copyright laws helps us to observe this rule.

—Richard R. Hammar

Index